Rick Steves®

LONDON

Rick Steves & Gene Openshaw

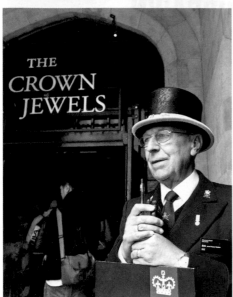

CONTENTS

Welcome to Rick Steves' Europe

Travel is intensified living—maximum thrills per minute and one of the last great sources of legal adventure. Travel is freedom. It's recess, and we need it.

I discovered a passion for European travel as a teen and have been sharing it ever since—through my bus tours, public television and radio shows, and travel guidebooks. Over the years, I've taught millions of travelers how to best enjoy Europe's blockbuster sights—and experience "Back Door" discoveries that most tourists miss.

Written with my talented co-author, Gene Openshaw, this book offers a balanced mix of London's blockbuster sights and underrated gems. It's selective: Rather than listing a lorry load of museums and galleries, we recommend only the best ones. And it's in-depth: Our self-guided museum tours and city walks provide insight into London's vibrant history and today's living, breathing culture.

We advocate traveling simply and smartly. Take advantage of our money- and time-saving tips on sightseeing, transportation, and more. Try local, characteristic alternatives to expensive hotels and restaurants. In many ways, spending more money only builds a thicker wall between you and what you traveled so far to see.

We visit London to experience it—to become temporary locals. Thoughtful travel engages us with the world, as we learn to appreciate other cultures and new ways to measure quality of life.

Judging by the positive feedback we receive from readers, this book will help you enjoy a fun, affordable, and rewarding vacation—whether it's your first trip or your tenth.

Happy travels!

Rick Steves

LONDON

London is the LA, DC, and NYC of Britain, all rolled into one of the grandest cities on the planet. It's quintessentially English, yet worldly. It's old and traditional, yet wildly new and modern—and with more world-class sights than anyone can see in a single visit.

Blow through the city on a double-decker bus, and take a pinch-me-I'm-in-London walk through the West End. Ogle the crown jewels at the Tower of London, gaze up at Big Ben, and see the Houses of Parliament in action. Cruise the Thames River, beachcomb its banks, and take a spin on the London Eye. Hobnob with the tombstones in Westminster Abbey; visit Leonardo, Botticelli, and Rembrandt in the National Gallery; and explore Harry Potter's magical realm at the film studio in Leavesden. Enjoy Shakespeare in a replica of the Globe Theatre and marvel at a glitzy, bombastic musical at a West End theater. Ascend the dome of St. Paul's Cathedral, then rummage through our civilization's attic at the British Museum.

London is more than its museums and landmarks. It's a living, breathing, thriving organism...a coral reef of humanity. You can enjoy some of Europe's best people-watching at Covent Garden, Victoria

Modern and traditional: street performer near Piccadilly Circus; Changing of the Guard on The Mall

Station, Piccadilly Circus, or any of the major stops on London's subway system, known affectionately as the Tube. Snap to at Buckingham Palace's Changing of the Guard, mingle with well-heeled shoppers at a posh department store, or haggle for bargains at a street market.

Wherever you go, enjoy the British accents and slang. Part of the fun of visiting this city is the illusion of hearing a foreign language and actually understanding it...most of the time.

London's had a long evolution into the multicultural trade center it is today. In AD 43, the Romans founded Londinium as a port on the Thames. Over the centuries, the city became the capital of England and overcame devastating plagues and fires.

In the 1700s, Britain explored (and exploited) the globe, establishing trading companies, collecting colonies, and building its empire, with London as its powerhouse command center. In 1805, Britannia ruled the waves, after defeating the French and Spanish armadas at the Battle of Trafalgar. At its peak (after World War I), the British Empire ruled nearly a quarter of the world's land and population. With colonies around the world, it was called "the empire on which the sun never sets."

In World War II, the British—inspired by Winston Churchill's stirring oratory and leadership—bravely withstood the

Tea Time

A spot of afternoon tea feels just right in London. Many fancy department stores, restaurants, and hotels offer this genteel tradition in elegant, pinkie-waving surroundings.

The cheapest "tea" on the menu is generally a "cream tea"; the most expensive is the "champagne tea." Cream tea is simply a pot of tea (loose, strained into your cup; the Brits always add milk), served with a homemade scone or two, jam, and thick, buttery clotted cream. For maximum elegant taste per calorie, I slice my scone thin like a miniature loaf of bread.

Afternoon tea—what many Americans would call "high tea"—is a pot of tea typically accompanied by a three-tiered tray of nibbles. The bottom tier holds dainty finger food (such as cucumber, egg and watercress, and smoked salmon crustless sandwiches cut into triangles); the middle tier holds scones; and the top tier has tiny cakes and pastries. Champagne tea includes all of the goodies, plus a glass of bubbly. High tea to the English generally means a more substantial late afternoon or early evening meal, often served with meat or eggs. Quantities can be enormous; most places allow you and a partner to share one cream tea and one afternoon tea.

Afternoon tea is universally leisurely, but the ambiance depends on the venue. Some of the fanciest have musical accompaniment, such as a piano or chamber orchestra, and require dressing up and reservations. Most tearooms welcome tourists in jeans and sneakers (and cost, on average, between £35 and £50). Some places serve tea all afternoon (12:00-18:30), some only from around 15:00 to 17:00.

For recommended tea spots, see the Eating in London chapter. ▮

Indulging in a leisurely tea is fun for young and old, whether a simple cream tea (top) or an afternoon tea with all the goodies.

Experience British pubs for traditional hearty grub or socializing over a pint of beer.

Nazis' relentless attacks in the Battle of Britain and the London Blitz. But during the turmoil of the war and its aftermath, Britain lost many of its colonies.

Though Great Britain's power has greatly diminished, London has grown in stature and size. The city is huge, with 9.4 million people, many of whom trace their roots to former colonies—giving London an international flair. With its recent exit from the European Union ("Brexit"), Britain is redefining itself yet again.

Foods from around the world add spice to London's restaurant scene—there's something for every taste bud. Along with a culturally diverse buffet of options, you'll find British standards like fish-and-chips, "bangers and mash" (sausages and mashed potatoes), and meat pies at characteristic pubs—a great place to experience London's extended living room and tip a pint in a pub with a chatty local. For an indulgent break, sip an afternoon tea with pinkie raised, and nibble on finger sandwiches and scones slathered with clotted cream.

London seems perpetually at your service, with an impressive slate of sights, entertainment, and eateries, all linked by a great transit system. Come prepared to celebrate the tradition and fanfare of yesterday while catching the cosmopolitan buzz of today. London truly is where the world comes together.

London by Neighborhood

Sprawling London becomes much more manageable when you think of it as a collection of neighborhoods.

The Thames River (pronounced "tems") runs roughly west to east through the city, with most sights on the North Bank. The tourist's London is roughly the area within the Tube's Circle Line—bordered by the Tower of London (to the east), Hyde Park (to the west), Regent's Park (north), and the South Bank (south). This four-mile-wide zone between the Tower and Hyde Park (about a 1.5-hour walk) holds most of the sights covered in this book.

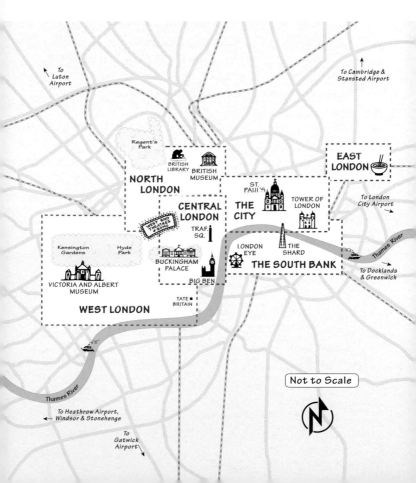

TOP NEIGHBORHOODS

Central London
This area contains Westminster and the West End. The Westminster district includes Big Ben, Parliament, Westminster Abbey, and Buckingham Palace—the grand government buildings from which Britain is ruled. Trafalgar Square, London's gathering place, has major museums, including the National Gallery. The West End is the center of London's cultural life, with bustling squares. Piccadilly Circus and Leicester Square host cinemas, tourist traps, and nighttime glitz. Soho and Covent Garden are thriving people zones with theaters, restaurants, pubs, and boutiques. And Regent and Oxford streets are the city's top shopping zones.

North London
Neighborhoods in this part of town—including Bloomsbury, Fitzrovia, and Marylebone—contain the exceptional British Museum and overhyped Madame Tussauds Waxworks. Nearby, along busy Euston Road, is the British Library, plus a trio of train stations (one of them, St. Pancras International, is linked to the Continent by the Eurostar "Chunnel" train).

The City
In London's modern financial district, called simply "The City," gleaming skyscrapers are interspersed with historical landmarks, such as St. Paul's Cathedral, legal sights (Old Bailey), and the Museum of London. The Tower of London and Tower Bridge lie at The City's eastern border.

Buckingham Palace (opposite); Houses of Parliament and Big Ben; Piccadilly Circus; Parthenon Galleries at the British Museum; Beefeaters at the Tower of London

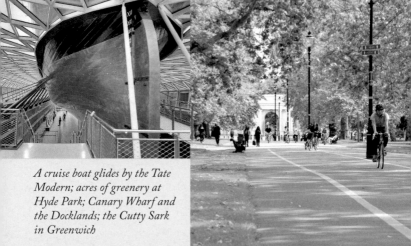

A cruise boat glides by the Tate Modern; acres of greenery at Hyde Park; Canary Wharf and the Docklands; the Cutty Sark in Greenwich

East London

Just east of The City is the East End, once the gritty haunt of Jack the Ripper, and now an increasingly gentrified neighborhood of hipsters, pop-up shops, busy markets, and stalls that dish up cuisine from around the world. It's a foodie destination, especially the Shoreditch neighborhood.

The South Bank

The South Bank of the Thames River offers major sights—the Tate Modern, Shakespeare's Globe, and London Eye—linked by a fun riverside promenade. Within this area, Southwark stretches from the Tate Modern to London Bridge. Pedestrian bridges connect the South Bank with The City and Trafalgar Square on the North Bank.

West London

This huge area contains upscale neighborhoods—Mayfair, Belgravia, Chelsea, South Kensington, and Notting Hill—plus excellent museums (Victoria & Albert Museum, Tate Britain, and more), my top hotel recommendations, enticing restaurants, trendy shops, bustling Victoria Station, and the vast green expanses of Hyde Park and Kensington Gardens.

Greater London

Historic Greenwich shows off its naval heritage and fine observatory, and the Docklands is London's skyscraping Manhattan.

Kew Gardens is a lush park with an elegant greenhouse, and Hampton Court Palace was home to royalty. The Warner Bros. Studio Tour thrills Harry Potter fans.

Day Trips

While there are a world of options, here are three of my favorite day trip destinations:

Windsor, set on the Thames, boasts the queen's castle and a vibrant town center (an hour away by train).

Cambridge, world renowned for its university, has stately colleges, beautiful chapels, and punt tours on the River Cam (50 minutes by train).

Stonehenge is the iconic prehistoric stone circle, 5,000 years old and a marvel to this day (2 hours by train-and-bus combo).

Planning and Budgeting

The best trips start with good planning. Here are ideas to help you decide when to go, design a smart itinerary, set a travel budget, and prepare for your trip. For my best general advice on sightseeing, accommodations, restaurants, and more, see the Practicalities chapter.

PLANNING YOUR TIME

As you read this book and learn your options...

Decide when to go.

July and August are peak season—my favorite time—with long days, the best weather, and the busiest schedule of tourist fun. Prices and crowds don't go up in summer as dramatically in Britain as they do in much of Europe, except for holidays and festivals (listed in the appendix). Still, travelers in spring and fall enjoy lower prices, smaller crowds, decent weather, and the full range of sights and tourist fun spots. London's sights are more crowded on three-day weekends, especially Bank Holidays on the first and last Mondays in May, and the last Monday in August. Easter week can also be very busy.

Winter travelers find fewer crowds and soft room prices, but shorter sightseeing hours. The weather can be cold and dreary, and nightfall draws the shades on sightseeing well before dinnertime. While England's rural charm falls with the leaves, London sightseeing is fine in the winter, and is especially popular during the Christmas season.

For specific temperatures, see the climate chart in the appendix.

Work out a day-by-day itinerary.

The following day plans offer suggestions for how to maximize your sightseeing, depending on how many days you have. You can adapt these itineraries to fit your own interests. To find out what days sights are open, check the "Daily Reminder" in the Orientation chapter. Note major sights where advance reservations are smart or a free Rick Steves audio tour is available.

London in One, Two, or Three Busy Days
Day 1

Use my self-guided Westminster Walk to link these sights:

9:00	Be in line at Westminster Abbey (opens at 9:30, closed Sun) to tour it with fewer crowds.
11:00	Visit the Churchill War Rooms.
13:00	Lunch at the museum's café, or finish Westminster Walk and lunch near Trafalgar Square.
15:00	Visit the National Gallery, and any sights nearby that interest you (National Portrait Gallery or St. Martin-in-the-Fields Church).
Evening	Dinner and a play in the West End.

Day 2

8:30	Take a double-decker hop-on, hop-off London sightseeing bus tour (from Victoria Station or Green Park).
10:00	Hop off at Trafalgar Square and walk briskly to Buckingham Palace to secure a spot to watch the...
11:00	Changing of the Guard (nearly daily—confirm online).
14:00	After lunch, tour the British Museum.
16:00	Tour the British Library.
Evening	Choose from a play, concert, or walking tour, or shopping at one of London's elegant department stores (Harrod's, Liberty, and Fortnum & Mason are often open late).

Day 3

9:00	Tower of London (opens Sun-Mon at 10:00).
12:00	Grab a picnic, catch a boat at Tower Pier, and have lunch while cruising to Blackfriars Pier.

13:00   Tour St. Paul's Cathedral and climb the dome (closed Sun except for worship).

15:00   Walk across the Millennium Bridge to the South Bank to visit the Tate Modern, Shakespeare's Globe, and other sights.

Evening   Catch a play at Shakespeare's Globe.

London in Seven Days
Day 1
9:00   Tower of London (opens Sun-Mon at 10:00).

13:00   Have a picnic lunch on a boat cruise from Tower Pier to Westminster Pier.

14:30   Tour Westminster Abbey, and consider their evensong service (usually at 17:00, at 15:00 on Sun, spoken on Wed).

17:00   Follow my Westminster Walk.

Evening   Choose from a play, concert, or a London Walks tour. See the Entertainment in London chapter for more ideas.

Day 2
8:30   Take a double-decker hop-on, hop-off bus tour (from Victoria Station or Green Park).

10:00   Get out at Trafalgar Square, walk to Buckingham Palace, and snare a spot to watch the...

11:00   Changing of the Guard (nearly daily—confirm online).

12:00   Walk through St. James's Park.

13:00   Have lunch, then tour the Churchill War Rooms.

15:30   Tour the National Gallery.

Day 3
9:00   Follow Part 2 of my self-guided walk through The City (from St. Clement Danes to St. Paul's), and take my St. Paul's Cathedral Tour.

12:00   Lunch at a historic pub or sandwich shop—or hold off until you reach Borough Market (across the river).

13:00   Carry on with Part 3 of The City Walk.

15:00   Cross London Bridge and follow my Bankside Walk. Tour the Tate Modern (or circle back in the

Take a hop-on, hop-off bus tour to get a city overview; browse the bounty of food stalls at Borough Market.

	evening if it's open late). Stroll the Jubilee Walkway from the Millennium Bridge to the London Eye.
Evening	Choose a South Bank sight that's open late: London Eye, a Shakespeare play at the Globe, or the Tate Modern (some Fri-Sat).

Day 4

10:00	Tour the British Museum, then have lunch.
14:00	Tube to Leicester Square to take my West End Walk to see Covent Garden and Soho, then browse along Regent Street on my Regent Street Shopping Walk.
16:30	Enjoy afternoon tea (Fortnum & Mason is nearby, or consider The Wolseley, Brown's Hotel, or The Capital Hotel).

Day 5

In the **morning**, explore a street market of your choice (go on a busy day, often best on weekends—check the Shopping in London chapter).

In the **afternoon**, visit any of these major sights: British Library, Tate Britain, Museum of London, Imperial War Museum, Hampton Court Palace, or Kew Gardens (consider cruising to Kew and returning by Tube).

Day 6
10:00	Cruise from Westminster Pier to Greenwich.
11:15	Tour the salty sights of Greenwich; return by Tube.
16:00	From Liverpool Street Station, take my East End Walk, followed by dinner at a Brick Lane curry house or a trendy Shoreditch eatery.

Day 7
10:00	Tour the Victoria & Albert Museum.

After lunch, fill your last day with more sightseeing, another London Walks tour, or shopping.

With More Time
Windsor, Cambridge, and Stonehenge each make a satisfying one-day visit. Any one of these is arguably more rewarding than Days 5, 6, or 7 in London.

Victoria & Albert Museum; punting on the River Cam in Cambridge; the royal family's official home, Windsor Castle

PLANNING YOUR BUDGET

Run a reality check on your dream trip. You'll have major transportation costs in addition to daily expenses.

Flight: A round-trip flight from the US to London costs about $900-1,500, depending on where you fly from and when.

Public Transportation: For a one-week visit, allow about $50 for the Tube and buses (for a 7-Day Travelcard transpor-

tation pass). Round-trip train rides to day-trip destinations cost about $28 for Windsor, $35 for Cambridge, and $54 for Salisbury, where you can catch a $20 bus to Stonehenge. You can save money by taking buses instead of trains. Add $60-100 if you plan to take a taxi between London's Heathrow Airport and your hotel (or save money by taking the Tube, train, bus, or airport shuttle).

Budget Tips: To cut your daily expenses, take advantage of the deals you'll find throughout London and mentioned in this book.

Save money on public transit (the Tube, buses, and light rail) by getting an Oyster card or 7-Day Travelcard.

Many of London's major museums and smaller churches are free (donations are requested, but optional). Sights that charge admission often sell tickets online in advance—which will save you a few pounds per person. For more ideas, see "Affording London's Sights" in the Sights chapter and tips for discounted theater tickets in the Entertainment in London chapter.

Some businesses—especially hotels and walking-tour companies—offer discounts to my readers (look for the RS% symbol in the listings in this book).

AVERAGE DAILY EXPENSES PER PERSON

★ **$225**

Lodging
Based on two people splitting the cost of a $180 double room (includes breakfast)
$90

Meals
$15 for lunch and $30 for dinner. $5 for coffee or tea
$50

Sights and Entertainment
This daily average works for most people.
$60

City Transit
Buses, Tube, or taxis/Uber
$25

Reserve your rooms directly with the hotel and book good-value rooms early. Some hotels offer a discount if you pay in cash and/or stay three or more nights (check online or ask). Rooms can cost less in spring and fall (May, June, Sept, and Oct) and more in peak-season summer. Even seniors can sleep cheaply in hostels (most have private rooms) for about $45 per person. Or check Airbnb-type sites for deals.

It's no hardship to eat inexpensively in London. Many restaurants have early-bird or pre-theater specials on weekdays. You can get tasty, affordable meals at pubs, street markets, fast-food joints, and good chain restaurants (many offer sandwiches to go). Cultivate the art of picnicking in atmospheric settings.

When you splurge, choose an experience you'll always remember, such as a West End show or a day trip to Stonehenge. Minimize souvenir shopping; focus instead on collecting wonderful memories.

BEFORE YOU GO

You'll have a smoother trip if you tackle a few things ahead of time. For more details on these topics, see the Practicalities chapter and RickSteves.com, which has helpful travel-tip articles and videos.

Make sure your travel documents are valid. If your passport is due to expire within six months of your ticketed date of return, you need to renew it. Allow six weeks or more to renew or get a passport (www.travel.state.gov). Check for current Covid entry requirements, such as proof of vaccination or a negative Covid-19 test result.

Arrange your transportation. Book your international flights. Overall, Kayak.com is the best place to start searching for flights. If you'll be traveling beyond London, figure out your transportation options: bus or train (and either a rail pass or individual train tickets), rental car, or a cheap flight. (You can wing it in Europe, but it may cost more.) If you'll be taking the Eurostar train to the Continent, it's smart to buy your ticket ahead.

Book rooms well in advance, especially if your trip falls during peak season or any major holidays or festivals.

Reserve ahead for key sights and tours. Virtually every major sight in and around London (including free ones) offers the chance to prebook in advance online. This is especially helpful for avoiding ticket lines. Among the sights which include this option are **Westminster Abbey, St. Paul's Cathedral, British Museum, London Eye, Warner Bros. Studio Tour** (for Harry Potter fans, in Leavesden), and **Stonehenge**.

Study the **London Walks** tour schedule. Although you don't need to book the tours ahead, it's easier (and fun) to choose a favorite or two in advance to splice into your itinerary rather than figuring it out in London.

For simplicity, I **book plays** while in London (but if you have your heart set on a hot show, buying tickets in advance is safer). For the current schedule, visit www.officiallondontheatre.co.uk.

Consider travel insurance. Compare the cost of insurance to the cost of your potential loss. Check whether your existing insurance (health, homeowners, or renters) covers you and your possessions overseas.

Call your bank. Alert your bank that you'll be using your debit and credit cards in Europe. Ask about transaction fees, and, if you don't already have one, get a "contactless" credit card (request your card PIN too). You don't need to bring pounds along; you can withdraw pounds from cash machines in Europe.

Use your smartphone smartly. Sign up for an international service plan to reduce your costs, or rely on Wi-Fi in Europe instead. Download any apps you'll want on the road, such as maps, transit schedules, and Rick Steves Audio Europe (see sidebar).

Pack light. You'll walk with your luggage more than you think. I travel for weeks with a single carry-on bag and a day pack. Use the packing checklist in the appendix as a guide.

Rick's Free Video Clips and Audio Tours

Travel smarter with these free, fun resources:

Rick Steves Classroom Europe, a powerful tool for teachers, is also useful for travelers. This video library contains about 500 short clips excerpted from my public television series. Enjoy these videos as you sort through options for your trip and to better understand what you'll see in Europe. Check it out at Classroom. RickSteves.com (just enter a topic to find everything I've filmed on a subject).

Rick Steves Audio Europe, a free app, makes it easy to download my audio tours and listen to them offline as you travel. For this book (look for the 🎧), these audio tours include my walks through West-

minster and Historic London: The City, and tours of the British Museum, British Library, and St. Paul's Cathedral. The app also offers interviews (organized by country) from my public radio show with experts from Europe and around the globe. Find it in your app store or at RickSteves.com/AudioEurope.

Travel Smart

If you have a positive attitude, equip yourself with good information (this book), and expect to travel smart, you will.

Read—and reread—this book. To have an "A" trip, be an "A" student. Note opening hours of sights, closed days, crowd-beating tips, and whether reservations are required or advisable. Check the latest at RickSteves.com/update.

Be your own tour guide. As you travel, get up-to-date info on sights, reserve tickets and tours, reconfirm hotels and travel arrangements, and check transit connections. Visit the local tourist information office (TI).

Outsmart thieves. Pickpockets abound in crowded places where tourists congregate. Treat commotions as smokescreens for theft. Keep your cash, credit cards, and passport secure in a money belt tucked under your clothes; carry only a day's spending money in your front pocket or wallet. Don't set valuable items down on counters or café tabletops, where they can be quickly stolen or easily forgotten.

Minimize potential loss. Keep expensive gear to a minimum. Bring copies or take photos of your important documents (passport and cards) to aid in replacement if they're lost or stolen. Back up photos and files frequently.

Guard your time and energy. Taking a taxi (or Uber) can be a good value if it spares you an exhausting walk or gets you to your hotel quickly after a late-night show. To avoid long lines, follow my crowd-beating tips, such as making advance reservations, or sightseeing early or late.

Be flexible. Even if you have a well-planned itinerary,

expect changes, strikes, closures, sore feet, bad weather, and so on. Your Plan B could turn out to be even better.

Connect with the culture. Interacting with locals carbonates your experience. Enjoy the friendliness of the British people. Ask questions; most locals are happy to point you in their idea of the right direction. Set up your own quest for the best silly sign, street food, or "Oh, wow!" moment. When an opportunity pops up, make it a habit to say "yes."

London...here you come!

ORIENTATION TO LONDON

London is more than 600 square miles of urban jungle—a world in itself and a barrage on all the senses. On my first visit, I felt extremely small. To grasp London more comfortably, see it as the old town in the city center without the modern, congested sprawl. (Even from that perspective, it's still huge.) The four-mile stretch between the Tower of London and Hyde Park (about a 1.5-hour walk) looks like a milk bottle on its side (see map on next page) and holds 80 percent of the sights mentioned in this book.

With a core focus and a good orientation, you'll get a sampling of London's top sights, history, and cultural entertainment, and a good look at its ever-changing human face.

This chapter offers helpful hints and details on London's tourist services, a rundown of your options for getting around, and recommendations for organized tours. For an overview of the city's neighborhoods and detailed day plans, see the previous chapter.

Overview

TOURIST INFORMATION

It's amazing how hard it can be to find unbiased sightseeing information and advice in London. You'll see "Tourist Information" offices advertised here and there, but most are private agencies that make a big profit selling tours and advance sightseeing and/or theater tickets; others are run by Transport for London (TFL) and are primarily focused on providing public-transit advice.

The City of London Information Centre, on the street just below St. Paul's Cathedral, is the only publicly funded—and impartial—"real" TI (Mon-Sat 9:30-17:30, Sun 10:00-16:00; Tube: St. Paul's, +44 20 7606 3030 or +44 20 7332 3456, www.visitthecity.co.uk, cic@cityoflondon.gov.uk, well run by Inma).

ORIENTATION

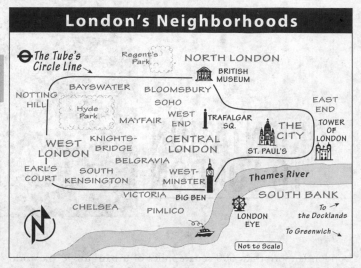

London's Neighborhoods

The Tube's Circle Line

Regent's Park

NORTH LONDON

BRITISH MUSEUM

NOTTING HILL

BAYSWATER

BLOOMSBURY

SOHO

EAST END

Hyde Park

MAYFAIR

WEST END

TRAFALGAR SQ.

THE CITY

TOWER OF LONDON

WEST LONDON

KNIGHTS-BRIDGE

CENTRAL LONDON

ST. PAUL'S

BELGRAVIA

EARL'S COURT

SOUTH KENSINGTON

WEST-MINSTER

Thames River

VICTORIA

BIG BEN

SOUTH BANK

CHELSEA

PIMLICO

LONDON EYE

To the Docklands

To Greenwich

Not to Scale

While officially a service of The City (London's financial district), this office also provides information about the rest of London. It sells Oyster cards and London Passes (see page 578) and stocks various free publications: the *Welcome to London* brochure (with basic orientation info and good Tube and bus map), *London Planner* (a monthly that lists sights, events, and hours), the biweekly *Official London Theatre Guide*, a free Tube map, schedules for Thames River boat services, and brochures describing self-guided themed walks in The City (including Dickens, modern architecture, Shakespeare, film locations, and walks for kids). They also have a free sightseeing app that includes small discounts at various points around The City.

The TI gives out a free map of The City and sells several citywide maps (look for the good £1 map, which covers what you'll want to see and includes a miniscule Tube map and a handy map of key bus routes). Skip their theater box office; you're better off booking direct.

Visit London, which serves the greater London area, doesn't have an office you can visit in person—but does have an information-packed website (www.visitlondon.com).

ARRIVAL IN LONDON

For more information on getting to or from London, see the London Connections chapter.

By Train: London has nine major train stations, all connected by the Tube (subway). All have ATMs, and many of the larger stations also have shops, fast food, exchange offices, and luggage storage. From any station, you can ride the Tube or taxi to your hotel.

By Bus: The main intercity bus station is Victoria Coach Station, one block southwest of Victoria train/Tube station.

By Plane: London has six airports. Most tourists arrive at Heathrow or Gatwick airport, although flights from elsewhere in Europe may land at Stansted, Luton, Southend, or London City airport. For hotels near Heathrow and Gatwick, see the Sleeping in London chapter.

HELPFUL HINTS

Theft Alert: Wear a money belt and keep your wallet in your front pocket. The Artful Dodger is alive and well in London. Be on guard, particularly on public transportation and in places crowded with tourists, who, considered naive and rich, are targeted. The Changing of the Guard scene is a favorite for thieves. More than 7,500 purses are stolen annually at Covent Garden alone.

Pedestrian Safety: Cars drive on the left side of the road—which can be as confusing for foreign pedestrians as for foreign drivers. Before crossing a street, I always look right, look left, then look right again just to be sure.

Londoners are champion jaywalkers. If you're tempted to join them, keep in mind that jaywalking is treacherous when you're jet-lagged and disoriented about which direction traffic is coming from.

Medical Problems: Local hospitals have good-quality 24-hour emergency care centers, where any tourist who needs help can be seen by a doctor. Your hotel has details. St. Thomas' Hospital, immediately across the river from Big Ben, has a fine reputation.

Getting Your Bearings: London is well signed, with thoughtfully designed, pedestrian-focused maps all over town. These are especially handy when exiting Tube stations. In this sprawling city—where predictable grid-planned streets are relatively rare, and stepping out of a Tube station into a buzzing neighborhood can be disorienting—it's also smart to use a good map.

Useful Apps: Google Maps is a wonderful navigation tool. In addition to walking directions, it figures out which public-transit connection (by Tube or bus) best suits your journey (make sure you've downloaded maps "offline" in advance, or you have a good data plan). If you're online, it constantly updates—so you'll know how long you'll wait for the next bus, or if there's

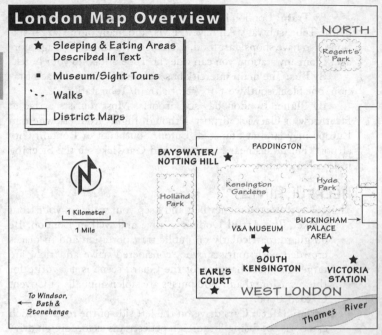

London Map Overview

★ Sleeping & Eating Areas Described In Text

■ Museum/Sight Tours

‵·· Walks

☐ District Maps

NORTH

Regent's Park

PADDINGTON

BAYSWATER/ NOTTING HILL ★

Kensington Gardens

Hyde Park

Holland Park

1 Kilometer

1 Mile

V&A MUSEUM ■

BUCKINGHAM PALACE AREA

SOUTH KENSINGTON ★

EARL'S COURT ★

VICTORIA STATION ★

WEST LONDON

To Windsor, Bath & Stonehenge ←

Thames River

a delay on the Tube. Other good route-planning apps include Mapway's free **Tube Map London Underground** and **Bus Times London** apps (www.mapway.com), as well as the **City-mapper** app.

🎧 For free audio versions of some of the self-guided walks and tours in this book (Westminster Walk, Historic London: The City Walk, and tours of the British Museum, British Library, and St. Paul's Cathedral), get the **Rick Steves Audio Europe** app (see page 22).

Many London museums (especially smaller ones) have done away with handheld audioguides. The free **Bloomberg Connects** app replaces these, providing in-depth audio commentary on several good museums, including the Churchill War Rooms, Sir John Soane Museum, Courtauld Gallery, Wallace Collection, and more. Outside of London, it also covers the Imperial War Museum in Duxford (near Cambridge). This lineup nicely complements the major sights covered by my Rick Steves Audio Europe app. At most museums you can connect to free Wi-Fi to stream the tour.

Bookstores: Located between Covent Garden and Leicester Square, the very good **Stanfords Travel Bookstore** stocks a huge selection of guidebooks (including current editions of my titles), travel-related novels, maps, and gear (Mon-Wed 9:00-18:00, Thu-Sat until 19:00, Sun 12:00-18:00, 7 Mercer Walk,

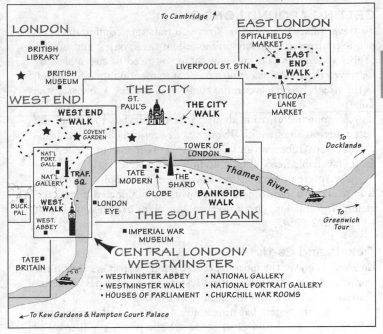

Tube: Leicester Square, +44 20 7836 1321, www.stanfords. co.uk).

Two impressive **Waterstones** bookstores have the biggest collection of travel guides in town: on Piccadilly (Mon-Sat 9:00-20:00, Sun 12:00-18:00, café, great views from top-floor bar—see sidebar on page 94, 203 Piccadilly, +44 20 7851 2400) and on Trafalgar Square (same hours, café, +44 20 7839 4411).

Daunts Books, in a church-like Edwardian building, is a North London staple known for arranging books by geography, regardless of subject or author; it's the kind of bookstore you'll enjoy getting lost in (Mon-Sat 9:00-20:00, Sun 11:00-18:00, 83 Marylebone High Street, Tube: Baker Street, +44 20 7724 2295, www.dauntbooks.co.uk).

Foyles' flagship store is a world of books (and literary events), between Soho and Covent Garden (Mon-Sat 9:00-19:00, Sun 11:30-18:00, café, 107 Charing Cross Road, +44 20 7437 5660, www.foyles.co.uk).

Baggage Storage: Train stations have left-luggage counters, where each bag is scanned (just like at the airport); expect a wait (£12.50/24 hours per item, most stations open daily 8:00-21:00). You can also store bags at the airports (similar rates and hours). Book online in advance at www.left-baggage. co.uk.

GETTING AROUND LONDON

To travel smart in a city this size, you must get comfortable with public transportation. London's excellent taxis, buses, and subway (Tube) system can take you anywhere you need to go—a blessing for travelers' precious vacation time, not to mention their feet. And, as the streets become ever more congested, the key is to master the Tube.

For more information about public transit (bus and Tube), the best source is the helpful *Welcome to London* brochure, which includes both a Tube map and a handy schematic map of the best bus routes (available free at TIs, museums, and hotels).

For specific directions on how to get from point A to point B on London's transit, detailed transit maps, updated prices, and general information, check www.tfl.gov.uk or call the info line at +44 343 222 1234.

Tickets and Cards

London's is one of the most expensive public transit systems in the world, so for most tourists, the Oyster card transit pass is better than individual tickets. Here's the lowdown.

The transit system has nine zones, but almost all tourist sights are within Zones 1 and 2, so those are the prices I've listed. For more information, visit www.tfl.gov.uk/tickets.

Individual Tickets: Paper tickets for the Tube are ridiculously expensive (£6.30/Tube ride). At every Tube station, tickets are sold at easy-to-use self-service machines (hit "Adult Single" and enter your destination). Tickets are valid only on the day of purchase. But unless you're literally taking only one Tube ride your entire visit, you'll save money (and time) with an Oyster card.

Oyster Card: A pay-as-you-go Oyster card allows you to ride the Tube, buses, Docklands Light Railway (DLR), and Overground (suburban trains) for a little over half the cost of individual tickets. To use the card, simply touch it against the yellow card reader at the turnstile or entrance. It flashes green and the fare is automatically deducted. (You must tap your card again to "touch out" as you exit the Tube, but not buses.)

Buy the card at any Tube station ticket machine, or look for nearby shops displaying the Oyster logo, where you can purchase a card or add credit without the wait. You'll pay £5 up front for the card, then load it with credit.

One ride between Zones 1 and 2 during peak time costs £3 (£2.50 during off-peak). An automatic price cap guarantees you'll never pay more than £7.70 in one day for rides within Zones 1 and 2. If you think you'll take more than two rides in a day, £8 of credit will cover you, but it's smart to add a little more if you expect to

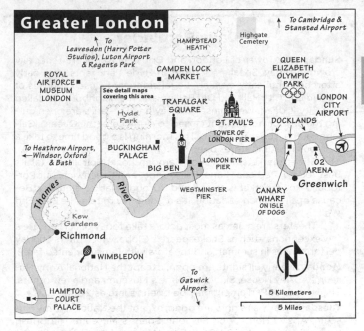

Greater London

To Cambridge & Stansted Airport

HAMPSTEAD HEATH

Highgate Cemetery

To Leavesden (Harry Potter Studios), Luton Airport & Regents Park

CAMDEN LOCK MARKET

QUEEN ELIZABETH OLYMPIC PARK

ROYAL AIR FORCE MUSEUM LONDON

See detail maps covering this area

Hyde Park

TRAFALGAR SQUARE

ST. PAUL'S

DOCKLANDS

LONDON CITY AIRPORT

TOWER OF LONDON PIER

To Heathrow Airport, Windsor, Oxford & Bath

BUCKINGHAM PALACE

BIG BEN

LONDON EYE PIER

O2 ARENA

CANARY WHARF ON ISLE OF DOGS

Greenwich

WESTMINSTER PIER

Thames

River

Kew Gardens

Richmond

WIMBLEDON

To Gatwick Airport

5 Kilometers

5 Miles

HAMPTON COURT PALACE

travel outside the city center. If you're staying six or more days, consider adding a 7-Day Travelcard to your Oyster card (details below).

Oyster cards are not shareable among companions for the same ride; all travelers need their own. If your balance gets low, simply add credit—or "top up"—at a ticket machine, shop, or with the Transport for London (TFL) Oyster app. You can always see how much credit remains on your card, either on the app or by touching your card to the pad at any ticket machine. After your last ride, you can get a refund for your unused balance up to £10; visit any ticket machine that gives change and select "Pay as you go refund." For balances of more than £10, you can claim a refund online. Or save the credit for a future trip; it never expires.

Contactless: As an alternative to a physical Oyster card, you can use a tap-enabled credit card, or link a credit card to your phone or smartwatch, to pay for rides at the same low Oyster rates. For details, visit www.tfl.gov.uk and search "contactless."

Passes and Discounts

7-Day Travelcard: Various Tube passes and deals are available, but the only option of note is the 7-Day Travelcard. This is the best choice if you're staying six or more days and plan to use public transit a lot (£38.40 for Zones 1-2; £70.30 for Zones 1-6). For most travelers, the Zone 1-2 pass works best. Heathrow Airport is in Zone 6, but there's no need to buy the Zones 1-6 version if that's

Daily Reminder

Sunday: The Tower of London and British Museum are especially crowded today. Speakers' Corner in Hyde Park rants from early afternoon until early evening. Legal sights are closed (Houses of Parliament, City Hall, and Old Bailey) and the neighborhood called The City is dead. Westminster Abbey and St. Paul's are open during the day for worship but closed to sightseers (the Queen's Galleries at the Abbey is closed). This morning is a good time to take a bus tour. Most big stores open late (11:30) and close early (18:00).

Street markets flourish at Camden Lock, Spitalfields (at its best today), Petticoat Lane, Brick Lane, and Greenwich, but Portobello Road market is closed and Borough Market is quieter. Because of all the market action, it's a good day to take the East End Walk.

Theaters are quiet, as most actors take today off. (There are a few exceptions, such as Shakespeare's Globe, which offers Sunday performances in summer, and theaters with family-oriented fare.)

Monday: Nearly all sights are open, except the National Army Museum, Apsley House, Sir John Soane's Museum, and a few others. The Houses of Parliament may be open as late as 22:30.

Tuesday: Nearly all sights are open, except the National Army Museum, Apsley House, and Sir John Soane's Museum. The British Library is open until 20:00, and the Houses of Parliament may be open as late as 22:00.

Wednesday: Nearly all sights are open. The British Library is open until 20:00, and the Houses of Parliament may be open as late as 22:00.

the only ride outside the city center you plan to take—instead you can pay a small supplement to cover the difference. You can add the 7-Day Travelcard to your Oyster card or purchase the paper version at any National Rail train station.

Families: A paying adult can take up to four kids (ages 10 and under) for free on the Tube, Docklands Light Railway (DLR), Overground, and buses. Kids ages 11-15 get a discount. Explore other child and student discounts at www.tfl.gov.uk/tickets—or ask a Tube station employee.

River Cruises: A Travelcard gives you a 33 percent discount on most Thames cruises (described later under "Tours in London: By Boat"). The Oyster card gives you roughly a 10 percent discount on Thames Clippers (including the Tate Boat museum ferry).

By Tube

London's subway system is called the Tube or Underground (but never "subway," which, in Britain, refers to a pedestrian underpass). The Tube is one of this planet's great people-movers and usually

Thursday: Nearly all sights are open. The British Library is open until 20:00.

Friday: All sights are open, except the Houses of Parliament. Sights open late include the British Museum (selected galleries until 20:30), National Gallery (until 21:00), National Portrait Gallery (until 21:00), Victoria and Albert Museum (possibly some Fri until 22:00), and possibly Tate Modern.

Saturday: Most sights are open, except legal ones (Old Bailey, City Hall; skip The City). The Houses of Parliament are open only with a tour. The Tate Modern may be open late. The Tower of London is especially crowded today. Today's the day to hit the Portobello Road market; the Camden Lock and Greenwich markets are also good.

Notes: St. Martin-in-the-Fields church offers concerts on select weekday afternoons and evenings (several nights a week at 19:30, jazz Wed at 20:00).

Evensong occurs nearly daily at St. Paul's (Sun at 15:15 and Tue-Sat at 17:00), Westminster Abbey (Sun at 15:00, Mon-Tue and Thu-Sat at 17:00), and Southwark Cathedral (Sun at 15:00, Tue-Fri 17:30, some Sat at 16:00).

Big Bus London runs night tours starting from the London Eye. See London by Night buses leave Green Park each evening starting at 19:30.

The London Eye spins nightly (last ascent 20:30 or later in summer).

the fastest long-distance transport in town (runs Mon-Sat about 5:00-24:00, Sun about 7:00-23:00; Central, Jubilee, Northern, Piccadilly, and Victoria lines also run Fri-Sat 24 hours). Two other commuter rail lines are tied into the network and  use the same tickets: the Docklands Light Railway (called DLR) and the Overground. The new Crossrail system is being built through central London connecting Heathrow with Paddington, Bond, and Liverpool Street Tube stations on the Elizabeth line before continuing to the city's outlying eastern neighborhoods.

Get your bearings by studying a map of the system. At the back of this book, you'll find a Tube map of the city center, with color-coded lines and names. You can also pick up a free, more

ORIENTATION

extensive Tube map at any station, or download a transit app (described earlier).

Each line has a name (such as Circle, Northern, or Bakerloo) and two directions (indicated by the end-of-the-line stops). Find the line that will take you to your destination, and figure out roughly which direction (north, south, east, or west) you'll need to go to get there.

At the Tube station, to pass through the turnstile with an Oyster card, touch it flat against the turnstile's yellow card reader, both when you enter and exit the station. If you're using contactless pay, hold your credit card, smartphone, or smartwatch above the reader. With a paper ticket or paper Travelcard, feed it into the turnstile, reclaim it, and hang on to it—you'll need it later.

Find your train by following signs to your line and the (general) direction it's headed (such as Central Line: Eastbound).

Since some tracks are shared by several lines, double-check before boarding: Make sure your destination is one of the stops listed on the sign at the platform. Also, check the electronic signboards that announce which train is next, and make sure the destination (the end-of-the-line stop) is the direction you want. Some trains—particularly on the Circle and District lines—split off for other directions, but each train has its final destination marked above its windshield and on the side of the cars.

Trains run about every 3-10 minutes. (The Victoria line brags that it's the most frequent anywhere, with trains coming every 100 seconds at peak time.) A general rule of thumb is that it takes 30 minutes to travel six Tube stops (including walking time within stations), or roughly 5 minutes per stop.

When you leave the system, "touch out" with your Oyster card (or a contactless method) at the electronic reader on the turnstile, or feed your paper ticket into the turnstile (it will eat your now-expired ticket). With a paper Travelcard, it will spit out your still-valid card. Check maps and signs for the most convenient exit.

The system can be fraught with construction delays, breakdowns, and strikes. Pay attention to signs and announcements explaining necessary detours. Rush hours (8:00-10:00 and 16:00-19:00) can be packed and sweaty. If one train is stuffed—and another is coming in three minutes—it may be worth a wait to avoid the sardine routine. Also, the cars closer to the middle of the train are generally more crowded, so if you anticipate crowds, stand closer to the ends of the platform. I've often scored a seat on an otherwise packed train using this simple strategy. (But note that at a few shorter stations, the doors of the cars at the very start and end of the train can't open—listen for announcements and move closer to the middle of the train if necessary.)

For help, check out the "Plan a Journey" feature at www.tfl.gov.uk.

Tube Etiquette and Tips

- When your train arrives, stand off to the side and let riders exit before you board.
- When the car is jam-packed, avoid using the hinged seats near the doors of some trains—they take up valuable standing space.
- If you're blocking the door when the train stops, step out of the car and off to the side, let others off, then get back on.
- Talk softly in the cars. Listen to how quietly Londoners communicate and follow their lead.
- On escalators, stand on the right and pass on the left. But note that in some passageways or stairways, you might be directed to walk on the left (the direction Brits go when behind the wheel).
- Discreet eating and drinking are fine; drinking alcohol and smoking are banned.
- Be zipped up to thwart thieves.
- Carefully check exit options before surfacing to street level. Signs point clearly to nearby sights—you'll save lots of walking by choosing the right exit.

By Bus

If you figure out the bus system, you'll swing like Tarzan through the urban jungle of London (see sidebar for a list of handy routes). Get in the habit of hopping buses for quick little straight shots, even just to get to a Tube stop. However, during bump-and-grind rush hours (8:00-10:00 and 16:00-19:00), you'll usually go faster by Tube.

You can't buy single-trip tickets for buses, and you can't use cash to pay when boarding. Instead, you must have an Oyster card, a paper Travelcard, or a one-day Bus & Tram Pass (£5.20, can buy on day of travel only—not beforehand, from ticket machine in any Tube station). If you're using your Oyster card, any bus ride in downtown London costs £1.65 (capped at £4.95/day).

Handy Bus Routes

The best views are upstairs on a double-decker. Check the bus stop closest to your hotel—it might be convenient to your sightseeing plans. For a color version of this map, see the fold-out map at the back of this book. Here are some of the most useful routes:

Route #9: High Street Kensington to Knightsbridge (Harrods) to Hyde Park Corner to Trafalgar Square to Aldwych (Somerset House).

Route #11: Victoria Station to Westminster Abbey to Trafalgar Square to St. Paul's and Liverpool Street Station and the East End.

Route #15: Trafalgar Square to St. Paul's to Tower of London.

Route #23: Paddington Station to Marble Arch, Hyde Park Corner, Knightsbridge, Albert Hall, High Street Kensington, and on to Hammersmith.

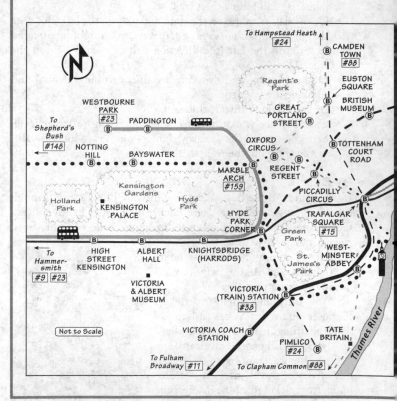

Route #24: Pimlico to Victoria Station to Westminster Abbey to Trafalgar Square to Euston Square, then all the way north to Camden Town (Camden Lock Market) and Hampstead Heath.

Route #38: Victoria Station to Hyde Park Corner to Piccadilly Circus to British Museum.

Route #88: Tate Britain to Westminster Abbey to Trafalgar Square to Piccadilly Circus to Oxford Circus to Great Portland Street Station (Regent's Park), then north to Camden Town.

Route #148: Westminster Abbey to Victoria Station to Notting Hill and Bayswater (by way of the east end of Hyde Park and Marble Arch).

Routes #159: Marble Arch to Oxford Circus to Piccadilly Circus to Trafalgar Square to Westminster and the Imperial War Museum. In addition, bus #139 also makes the corridor run between Marble Arch, Oxford Circus, Piccadilly Circus, and Trafalgar Square.

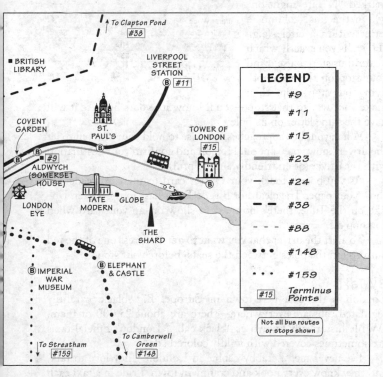

The first step in mastering London's bus system is learning how to decipher the bus-stop signs. The accompanying photo shows a typical sign listing the buses (the N91, N68, etc.) that come by here and their destinations (Oakwood, Old Coulsdon, etc.). In the first column, find your destination on the list—e.g., to Paddington (Tube and rail station). In the next column, find a bus that goes there—the #23 (routes marked "N" are night-only). In the final column, a letter within a circle (e.g., "H") tells you exactly which nearby bus stop to use. Find your stop on the accompanying bus-stop map, then

O			
Oakwood ⬦	N91		Ⓞ Ⓧ
Old Coulsdon	N68	Aldwych	
Old Ford	N8	Oxford Circus	
Old Kent Road Canal Bridge	53, N381		Ⓠ
	453		Ⓞ Ⓡ
	N21		Ⓖ
Old Street ⬦ ≋	243	Aldwych	
Orpington ≋	N47		Ⓖ
Oxford Circus ⬦	Any bus		Ⓣ
	N18		Ⓖ

P			
Paddington ⬦ ≋	23, N15		Ⓗ Ⓞ Ⓣ
Palmers Green ≋	N29		
Park Langley	N3		Ⓐ Ⓞ
Peckham	12		Ⓐ Ⓟ
	N89, N343		Ⓖ
	N136		Ⓐ Ⓝ
	N381		Ⓞ
Penge Pawleyne Arms	176		Ⓖ
	N3		Ⓐ Ⓞ
Petts Wood ≋	N47		Ⓖ
Pimlico Grosvenor Road	24		Ⓑ Ⓝ
Plaistow Greengate	N15		Ⓑ Ⓔ
Plumstead ≋	53		Ⓞ
Plumstead Common	53		Ⓞ
Ponders End	N279		Ⓖ

make your way to that stop—you'll know it's yours because it will have the same letter on its pole.

When your bus approaches, it's wise to hold your arm out to let the driver know you want on. Hop on and confirm your destination with the driver (often friendly and helpful).

As you board, touch your Oyster card to the card reader, or show your paper Travelcard or Bus & Tram Pass to the driver. Unlike on the Tube, there's no need to show or tap your card when you hop off.

To alert the driver that you want to get off, press one of the red buttons (on the poles between the seats) before your stop.

By Taxi

London is the best taxi town in Europe. Big, black, carefully regulated cabs are everywhere—there are about 25,000 of them. (While historically known as "black cabs," London's official taxis are sometimes covered with wildly colored ads.)

I've never met a crabby cabbie in London. They love to talk, and they know every nook and cranny in town. I ride in a taxi each day just to get my London questions answered. Drivers must pass a rigorous test on "The Knowledge" of London geography to earn their license.

If a cab's top light is on, just wave it down. Drivers flash their lights when they see you wave. They have a tight turning radius, so you can hail cabs going in either direction. If waving doesn't work, ask someone where you can find a taxi stand. Telephoning a cab will get you one in a few minutes but costs a little more (+44 871 871 8710).

Rides start at £3.20. The regular tariff #1 covers most of the day (Mon-Fri 5:00-20:00), tariff #2 is during "unsociable hours" (Mon-Fri 20:00-22:00 and Sat-Sun 5:00-22:00), and tariff #3 is for nighttime (22:00-5:00) and holidays. Rates go up about 20 percent with each higher tariff. Extra charges are explained in writing on the cab wall. All cabs accept credit and debit cards, including American cards. Tip a cabbie by rounding up (maximum 10 percent).

Connecting downtown sights is quick and easy and will cost you about £10-12 (for example, St. Paul's to the Tower of London, or between the two Tate museums). For a short ride, three adults in a cab generally travel at close to Tube prices—and groups of four or five adults should taxi everywhere. All cabs can carry five passengers, and some take six, for the same cost as a single traveler.

Don't worry about meter cheating. Licensed British cab meters come with a sealed computer chip and clock that ensures you'll get the correct tariff. The only way a cabbie can cheat you is by taking a needlessly long route. One serious pitfall, however, is taking a cab when traffic is bad to a destination efficiently served by the Tube. On one trip to London, I hopped in a taxi at South Kensington for Waterloo Station and hit bad traffic. Rather than spending 20 minutes and £2 on the Tube, I spent 40 minutes and £16 in a taxi.

If you overdrink and ride in a taxi, be warned: Taxis charge up to £60 for "soiling" (a.k.a., pub puke).

By Uber

Uber can be cheaper than a taxi, and can be a handy alternative if there's a long line for a taxi or if no cabs are available. On the other hand, you won't get the experience of being in a classic black cab, and Uber drivers generally don't know the city as well as regular cabbies (and don't have the access to some fast lanes that taxis do). Still, if you like using Uber, it can work great here.

By Car

If you have a car, stow it—you don't want to drive in London. A minimum £15 **congestion charge** is levied on any private car that enters the city center daily 7:00-22:00 (excluding Dec 25). The system has cut down traffic jams, bolstered London's public transit, and made buses cheaper and more user-friendly. Today, most vehicles in the city center are buses, taxis, and service trucks. If you do need to drive, it's quick and easy to register your vehicle (including rental cars) using the Transport for London website, where payment options are outlined (www.cclondon.com, +44 343 222 2222; you'll need the vehicle registration number and country of registration). Penalties are painfully stiff for late payments.

By Boat

It's easy to connect downtown London sights between Westminster and the Tower of London by boat (see later).

By Bike

London operates a citywide bike-rental program similar to ones in other major European cities, and new bike lanes are still cropping up around town. Still, London isn't (yet) ideal for biking. Its network of designated bike lanes is far from complete, and the city's many one-way streets (not to mention the need to bike on the "wrong" side) can make biking here a bit more challenging than it sounds. If you're accustomed to urban biking, it can be a good option for connecting your sightseeing stops, but if you're just up for a joyride, stick to London's large parks.

Santander Cycles, intended for quick point-to-point trips, are fairly easy to rent and a giddy joy to use. These cruisers have big, cushy seats, a bag rack with elastic straps, and three gears. Approximately 750 bike-rental stations are scattered throughout the city. To rent a bike, you'll pay an access fee (£2/day). The first 30 minutes are free; if you keep the bike for longer, you'll be charged £2 for every additional 30-minute period. Maps

showing docking stations are available at major Tube stations, at www.tfl.gov.uk, and via the Santander Cycles app.

Helmets are not provided, so ride carefully. Stay to the far-left side of the road and watch closely at intersections for *left*-turning cars. Be aware that in most parks (including Hyde Park/Kensington Gardens) only certain paths are designated for bike use—you can't ride just anywhere. Maps posted at park entrances identify bike paths, and non-bike paths are generally clearly marked.

Some bike tour companies also rent bikes (for details, see their listings later in this chapter).

Tours in London

🎧 To sightsee on your own, download my free Rick Steves Audio Europe app with **audio tours** that illuminate some of London's top sights and neighborhoods, including my Westminster Walk, Historic London: The City Walk, and tours of the British Museum, British Library, and St. Paul's Cathedral (see the sidebar on page 22 for details).

▲▲BY HOP-ON, HOP-OFF DOUBLE-DECKER BUS

London is full of hop-on, hop-off bus companies competing for your tourist pound. These once-over-lightly bus tours drive by all the famous sights, providing a stress-free way to get your bearings and see the biggies: Piccadilly Circus, Trafalgar Square, Big Ben, St. Paul's, the Tower of London, Marble Arch, Victoria Station, and beyond. With a good guide, decent traffic, and nice weather, I'd sit back and enjoy the entire tour. (If traffic is bad or you don't like your guide, you can hop off and try the next departure.) Routes can vary; some have live (English-only) guides, while others have recorded, dial-a-language narration. Pick up a map from any flier rack (or check online) and study the color-coded system.

Buses run daily about every 10-15 minutes in summer and every 10-20 minutes in winter, starting at about 8:30. The last full loop usually leaves Victoria Station at around 20:00 in summer, and 17:00 in winter. Sunday morning—when traffic is light and many museums are closed—is a fine time for a tour. Traffic is at its peak around lunch and during the evening rush hour (around 17:00).

Big Bus is the most established bus company and the one I'd probably go with (www.bigbustours.com). You'll also see **Tootbus** (www.tootbus.com) and **Golden Tours** (www.goldentours.com).

As an example of pricing, the basic, one-day Big Bus ticket costs £39 (substantial discounts if you book online). This gives you access to two basic overview tours: Red buses offer a live guide and a 2.5-hour tour with the main sights, while the blue route provides recorded narration and a 1.5-hour tour around Hyde Park and the museum district (includes the Thames River boat trip by City Cruises between Westminster and the Tower of London; pricier "Premium" and "Deluxe" multiday tickets include walking tours and other extras). To sort through your options and to book, see www.bigbustours.com. You can also buy (full-price) tickets from drivers, or from staff at street kiosks.

Smart Sightseeing: Prepurchase Tickets Online

Most big London sights sell tickets in advance online, saving you time by not having to wait in ticket-buying lines (though you may still have to wait in a security line). And at some sights, you'll get a slightly discounted price for prebooking online, too.

Major sights that offer advance tickets include Westminster Abbey, the Houses of Parliament, the Churchill War Rooms, St. Paul's Cathedral, the Tower of London, the London Eye, Windsor Castle, and Stonehenge (book well in advance for access to the inner stones). If heading to the Harry Potter Warner Bros. Studio tour in Leavesden, book as far ahead as possible (tickets *may* be an option closer to your visit—but why risk it?).

Even some free sights—such as the British Museum, National Gallery, National Portrait Gallery, Victoria and Albert Museum, Tate Britain, Tate Modern, Natural History Museum, and Science Museum—set up reservation systems as a social-distancing measure during the Covid-19 pandemic. These may still be in place when you visit; if you have a major sight on your list (basically, any sight with a tour chapter in this book), check the website to see if prebooking is an option.

Booking Process: Some sights allow you to book the day before, or even the same day; a few require you to book a few days ahead—check each sight's website for details. Upon booking, you should immediately receive an email, usually with a QR code, that acts as your digital ticket. (If you don't get it, check your junk folder.) When you arrive at the sight, look for a line marked "ticket holders," find the ticket on your phone, let the attendant scan it, and walk right in. It's not necessary to print your ticket (provided you can easily find it on your phone).

BY BUS OR CAR

London by Night Sightseeing Tour

Various bus tour companies offer a 1- to 2-hour circuit after hours, with no extras (e.g., walks, river cruises), at a lower price. While the narration can be lame, the views at twilight are grand—though note that it stays light until late on summer nights, and London just doesn't do floodlighting as well as, say, Paris. Options include **Big Bus** (£29, cheaper online, departs from London Eye, www.bigbustours.com); **Golden Tours** (£24, departs from Belvedere Road next to London Eye, +44 20 7233 7030; www.goldentours.com); and **See London By Night** (£24, live guides, departs from Green Park next to the Ritz Hotel, +44 20 7183 4744, www.seelondonbynight.com). For a memorable and economical evening,

ORIENTATION

munch a scenic picnic dinner on the top deck. (There are plenty of takeaway options near the various stops.)

Driver-Guide

If you'd like a private driver—whether for in-city trips or for day-tripping outside of London—consider **David Stubbs** (£395 for 1-3 people, £415 for 4-6 people, £450 for 7-8, also does tours to the Cotswolds, Stonehenge, Stratford, Windsor Castle, and Bath; mobile +44 7775 888 534, www.londoncountrytours.co.uk, info@londoncountrytours.co.uk).

▲▲ON FOOT

Top-notch local guides lead (sometimes big) groups on walking tours through specific slices of London's past. Each company's website lists their options. For most walking tours, simply show up at the announced location and pay the guide. Then enjoy two chatty hours of Dickens, Harry Potter, the Plague, Shakespeare, street art, the Beatles, or whatever is on the agenda. I'd skip the "free" tours you may see advertised (which aren't actually free—your guide gets paid only if you tip); the professional companies described below are reasonably priced and high-quality.

London Walks

Just perusing this leading company's fascinating lineup opens me up to dimensions of London I never considered, and inspires me to stay longer. Their two-hour walks are led by top-quality professional guides ranging from archaeologists to actors (£15, exact cash or contactless card, walks offered year-round, private tours available, +44 20 7624 3978, www.walks.com).

London Walks also offers good-value day trips into the countryside, a handy option for those with limited time (reserve ahead; £25 plus £25-75 for transportation and admission costs: Stonehenge/Salisbury, Oxford/Cotswolds, Cambridge, Windsor, and so on).

Beatles Walks

Fans of the still-Fab Four can take one of three Beatles walks (London Walks has two that run 5 days/week; for more on Beatles sights, see page 79).

Jack the Ripper Walks

Each walking tour company seems to make most of its money with "haunted" and Jack the Ripper tours. Many guides are historians and would rather not lead these lightweight tours—but, in tourism as in journalism, "if it bleeds, it leads" (which is why the juvenile London Dungeon is one of the city's busiest sights). While almost no hint of the dark and scary London of Jack the Ripper's time survives, guides do a good job of spinning the story. Think of this

Combining a London Bus Tour and the Changing of the Guard

For a grand and efficient intro to London, consider catching an 8:30 departure of a hop-on, hop-off overview bus tour, riding most of the loop (which takes just over 1.5 hours, depending on traffic). Hop off just before 10:00 at Trafalgar Square (Cockspur Street, stop "S") and walk briskly to Buckingham Palace to find a spot to watch the Changing of the Guard ceremony at 11:00.

mile-long walk, starting at the Tower of London, as a cheap night out with a few laughs. It's still light out in summer, so the scare factor is limited to the tales of the victims' miserable lot in life and the gory way in which they were killed.

Two reliably good two-hour tours start every night at the Tower Hill Tube station exit. **London Walks** leaves nightly at 19:30, plus summer Saturdays at 15:00 (£15, reservations required, +44 20 7624 3978, www.jacktheripperwalk.com). **Ripping Yarns,** which leaves nightly at 18:30, is guided by off-duty Yeoman Warders—the Tower of London "Beefeaters" (£10, confirm availability online, mobile +44 7858 470 171 or +44 7813 559 301, www.jack-the-ripper-tours.com). After taking both, I found the London Walks tour more entertaining, informative, and with a better route (along quieter lanes, with less traffic), starting at Tower Hill and ending at Liverpool Street Station.

Private Walks with Local Guides

Standard rates for London's registered Blue Badge guides are about £180-200 for four hours and £295 or more for nine hours (+44 20 7611 2545, www.guidelondon.org.uk or www.britainsbestguides.org). I know and like these fine local guides: **Sean Kelleher,** an engaging storyteller who knows his history (+44 20 8673 1624, mobile +44 7764 612 770, sean@seanlondonguide.com); **Britt Lonsdale,** who's great with families (£265/half-day, £365/day, +44 20 7386 9907, mobile +44 7813 278 077, brittl@btinternet.com); **Joel Reid,** an imaginative guide who breathes life into the major sights but also loves sharing off-the-beaten-track London (mobile +44 7887 955 720, joelyreid@gmail.com); **Mike Dickson** (£300/half-day, £450/day; mobile +44 7769 905 811, michael.dickson5@btinternet.com); and two others who work in London when they're not on the road leading my Britain tours: **Tom Hooper** (mobile +44 7986 048 047, tomh1@btinternet.com) and **Gillian Chadwick** (£300/day, mobile +44 7889 976 598, gillychad21@gmail.com). If you have a particular interest, London Walks (see earlier) has a huge selection of guides and can book one for your exact focus (£230/half-day; privatewalks@walks.com).

BY BIKE

Many of London's best sights can be laced together with a pleasant pedal through its parks.

London Bicycle Tour Company

Three tours leave from their base next to the Imperial War Museum, south of the Thames. Sunday is the best, as there is less car traffic; optional helmets are included. The following tour times are for peak season (April-Oct); times are different off-season. Always book ahead (**Classic Tour**—daily at 10:30, 8 miles, £34, 3 hours, includes Westminster, Covent Garden, and St. Paul's; **Love London Tour**—daily at 14:30, 8 miles, £39, 3 hours, includes Westminster, Buckingham Palace, Hyde Park, Soho, and Covent Garden; **Original Bike Tour**—daily at 14:00, 9 miles, 3.5 hours, includes south side of the river to Tower Bridge, the East End, The City, and St. Paul's). They also rent bikes (£4/hour, £24/day; credit or debit card required, office open daily 9:30-19:00, shorter hours Nov-March, 74 Kennington Road, +44 20 7928 6838, www.londonbicycle.com).

Fat Tire Bike Tours

These bike tours cover the highlights of downtown London on two different itineraries (RS%—£2 discount with this book): **Royal London** (£28, daily at 10:15 in peak season, may also run at 15:30 in summer, 7 miles, 4 hours, meet at Queensway Tube station; includes Parliament, Buckingham Palace, Hyde Park, and Trafalgar Square) and **River Thames** (£32, 3/week in summer at 10:15, 4.5 hours, meet just outside Southwark Tube Station; includes London Eye, St. Paul's, Tower of London, and Borough Market). Their guiding style is light, mixing history with humor (must reserve ahead, helmets and kids' bikes available, off-season tours also available, mobile +44 7882 338 779 or +1 866 614 6218, www.fattiretours.com/london). They also offer a range of walking tours that include an East End market tour, a beer-tasting pub tour, and a VIP tour of the Tower of London.

▲▲BY CRUISE BOAT

London offers many made-for-tourist cruises, most on slow-moving, open-top boats accompanied by entertaining commentary. Several companies offer essentially the same trip. Generally speaking, you can either do a **short city-center cruise** by riding a boat 30 minutes from Westminster Pier to Tower Pier (particularly handy if you're interested in visiting the Tower of London anyway) or take a **longer cruise** that includes a peek at the East End, riding from

Westminster all the way to Greenwich (save time by taking the Tube back).

Each company runs cruises daily, about twice hourly, from morning until dark; many reduce frequency off-season. Boats come and go from various docks in the city center. The most popular places to embark are Westminster Pier (at the base of Westminster Bridge across the street from Big Ben) and London Eye Pier (also known as Waterloo Pier, across the river).

A one-way trip within the city center costs about £12; going all the way to Greenwich costs about £3 more. Most companies charge around £5 more for a round-trip ticket. Others sell hop-on, hop-off day tickets (around £24). But I'd rather savor a one-way cruise, then zip home by Tube.

You can buy tickets at kiosks on the docks; always ask about discounts (they vary by company). With a Travelcard, you get a 33 percent discount off most cruises; the Oyster card can often be used as payment but nets you a discount only on Thames Clippers. You can purchase drinks and overpriced snacks on board. Budget travelers can pack a picnic for the cruise.

The three dominant companies are **City Cruises** (handy 45-minute cruise from Westminster Pier to Tower Pier; www.cityexperiences.com), **Thames River Services** (fewer stops, classic boats, friendlier and more old-fashioned feel; www.thamesriverservices.com), and **Circular Cruise** (full cruise takes about an hour, operated by Crown River Services, www.circularcruise.london). I'd skip the **London Eye**'s River Cruise from London Eye Pier, as it's more expensive and shorter. The speedy **Thames Clippers** (described later) are designed more for no-nonsense transport than lazy sightseeing.

To compare your options in one spot, head to Westminster Pier, which has a row of kiosks for all the big outfits.

Cruising Downstream, to Greenwich: Both **City Cruises** and **Thames River Services** head from Westminster Pier to Greenwich. The cruises are usually narrated by the captain, with most commentary given on the way to Greenwich. The companies' prices are about the same, though their itineraries are slightly different (Thames River Services makes only one stop en route and takes an hour, while City Cruises makes two stops and adds about 15 minutes). The **Thames Clippers** boats, described below, are cheaper and faster (about 20-55 minutes to Greenwich), but have no commentary and no up-top seating.

Thames Boat Piers

Thames boats (both tour and commuter boats) stop at these piers in the town center and beyond. While Westminster Pier is the most popular, it's not the only dock in town. Consider all the options (listed from west to east, as the Thames flows—see the color maps in the front of this book).

Millbank Pier (North Bank): At the Tate Britain museum, used primarily by the Tate Boat ferry service (express connection to Tate Modern at Bankside Pier).

Westminster Pier (North Bank): Near the base of Big Ben, offers round-trip sightseeing cruises and lots of departures in both directions (though the Thames Clippers boats don't stop here). Nearby sights include Parliament and Westminster Abbey.

London Eye Pier (a.k.a. **Waterloo Pier,** South Bank): At the base of the London Eye; good, less-crowded alternative to Westminster, with many of the same cruise options (Waterloo Station is nearby).

Embankment Pier (North Bank): Near Covent Garden, Trafalgar Square, and Cleopatra's Needle (the obelisk on the Thames). This pier is used mostly for special boat trips, such as some RIB (rigid inflatable boats) and lunch and dinner cruises.

Festival Pier (South Bank): Next to the Royal Festival Hall, just downstream from the London Eye.

Blackfriars Pier (North Bank): In The City, not far from St. Paul's.

Bankside Pier (South Bank): Directly in front of the Tate Modern and Shakespeare's Globe.

London Bridge Pier (a.k.a. **London Bridge City Pier,** South Bank): Near the HMS *Belfast* and the start of my Bankside Walk.

Tower Pier (North Bank): At the Tower of London, at the east edge of The City and near the East End.

St. Katharine's Pier (North Bank): Just downstream from the Tower of London.

Canary Wharf Pier (North Bank): At the Docklands, London's new "downtown."

Greenwich, Kew Gardens, and **Hampton Court Piers:** These outer London piers may also come in handy.

Cruising Upstream, to Kew Gardens and Hampton Court Palace: Thames River Boats leave for Kew Gardens from Westminster Pier (£16 one-way, £23 round-trip, 2-4/day depending on season, 1.5 hours, boats sail April-Oct, about half the trip is narrated, www.thamesriverboats.co.uk). Most boats continue to Hampton Court Palace for an additional £4 (and another 1.5 hours).

ORIENTATION

Because of the river current, you can save 30 minutes cruising from Hampton Court back into town (depends on the tide—ask before you commit). Romantic as these rides sound, it can be a long trip... especially upstream.

Commuting by Clipper

The sleek, 220-seat catamarans used by **Thames Clippers** (branded as "Uber Boat by Thames Clippers") are designed for commuters rather than sightseers. Think of the boats as express buses on the river—they zip through London every 20-30 minutes, stopping at most of the major docks en route. They're fast: roughly 20-30 minutes from Embankment to Tower, 10 more minutes to Docklands/Canary Wharf, and 15 more minutes to Greenwich. The boats are less pleasant for joyriding than the cruises described earlier, with no commentary and no open deck up top (the only outside access is on a crowded deck at the exhaust-choked back of the boat, where you're jostling for space to take photos). Any one-way ride in Central London (roughly London Eye to Tower Pier) costs about £8; a one-way ride to East London (Canary Wharf and Greenwich) is about £10, and a River Roamer all-day ticket costs £19 (discounts online and with Travelcard and Oyster card, can also reserve and pay via Uber app, www.thamesclippers.com).

Thames Clippers also offers two express trips. The **Tate Boat** ferry service, which directly connects the Tate Britain (Millbank Pier) and the Tate Modern (Bankside Pier), is made for art lovers (£9 one-way, covered by River Roamer day ticket; buy ticket at kiosks or self-service machines before boarding—or use contactless payment, Oyster card, or Uber app; for frequency and times, see www.thamesclippers.com). The **O2 Express** runs only on nights when there are events at the O2 arena (departs from London Eye Pier, can sell out in advance).

Regent's Canal Cruises

Several companies offer cruises on historic Regent's Canal, through Regent's Park, Little Venice, and Camden Lock Market. Check out **London Waterbus Company** (www.londonwaterbus.com), **Jason's Trip** (www.jasons.co.uk), or the good ship *Jenny Wren*, which offers 1.5-hour guided canal boat cruises from Walker's Quay in Camden Town (April-Oct, weekends only in March, Walker's Quay, 250 Camden High Street, 3-minute walk from Tube: Camden Town; +44 20 7485 4433, www.walkersquay.com). While in Camden Town, stop by the popular, punky Camden Lock Market (described in the Shopping in London chapter).

SIGHTS IN
LONDON

London is packed with world-class museums and attractions. For efficient sightseeing, I've clustered sights by neighborhood. When you see a 📖 in a listing, it means the sight is covered in much more depth in a self-guided walk or tour chapter. A 🎧 means the walk or tour is available as a free audio tour (via my Rick Steves Audio Europe app—see page 22). Some walks and tours are available in both formats—take your pick.

Check RickSteves.com/update for any significant changes that have occurred since this book was published. For money-saving tips, see the "Affording London's Sights" sidebar in this chapter.

Free Museums and Donations: Many of London's great museums don't charge admission—though they do suggest a donation (typically £5). Confusingly, some paid sights (which are classified as charities) have two prices: the actual price, and a suggested, inflated price that includes an added donation. I've listed only the actual price.

Advance Tickets: You must book ahead for The Making of Harry Potter: Warner Bros. Studio Tour. For summer, weekends, and holiday periods, consider booking ahead (or risk wasting time in long lines) for the following London sights: Westminster Abbey, the Houses of Parliament, the Churchill War Rooms, St. Paul's Cathedral, the Tower of London, and the London Eye. Even some free sights allow you to book ahead online—which can be wise if you anticipate crowds—such as the British Museum, National Gallery, National Portrait Gallery, Victoria and Albert Museum, Tate Britain, Tate Modern, Natural History Museum, and Science Museum.

Central London

WESTMINSTER

These sights are listed in roughly geographical order from Westminster Abbey to Trafalgar Square, and are linked in the 📖 Westminster Walk chapter and my free 🎧 audio tour.

▲▲▲Westminster Abbey

The greatest church in the English-speaking world, Westminster Abbey is where England's kings and queens have been crowned and buried since 1066. Like a stony refugee camp huddled outside St. Peter's Pearly Gates, Westminster Abbey has many stories to tell. To experience the church more vividly, take a live tour, or attend evensong or an organ concert.

Cost and Hours: £24, £5 more for timed-entry ticket to worthwhile Queen's Diamond Jubilee Galleries, family ticket available, cheaper online, includes fine multimedia guide; Abbey—Mon-Fri 9:30-16:30, Wed until 19:00 (main church only), Sat 9:00-16:30 (Sept-April until 14:00), guided tours available; Queen's Galleries—Mon-Fri 10:00-16:00, Sat 9:30-15:30, stays open later on summer Wed; cloister—Mon-Sat 9:30-17:30; closed Sun to sightseers but open for services; last entry one hour before closing; Tube: Westminster or St. James's Park, +44 20 7222 5152, www.westminster-abbey.org.

Music: The church hosts evensong performances daily except Wednesday, when it's spoken instead of sung (Mon-Sat at 17:00, Sun at 15:00). A free 30-minute organ recital is usually held on Sunday at 17:00.

📖 See the Westminster Abbey Tour chapter.

▲▲Houses of Parliament (Palace of Westminster)

This Neo-Gothic icon of London, the site of the royal residence from 1042 to 1547, is now the meeting place of the legislative branch of government. Like the US Capitol in Washington, DC, the complex is open to visitors. While Parliament is in session, wait in line for free entrance to see a couple of the grandest halls and other rooms, and watch debates in one or both of the public galleries (either the bickering House of Commons or the sleepy House of Lords). Otherwise, you must visit via a tour (either guided or audioguide).

Whichever you choose, your visit will include the cavernous

and historic Westminster Hall, St. Stephen's Hall, and the Central Lobby (may be under renovation).

Cost and Hours: Free when Parliament is in session, otherwise must visit with a paid tour (see later); nonticketed entry generally Oct-late July; House of Commons—Mon 14:30-22:30, Tue-Wed 11:30-19:30, Thu 9:30-17:30; House of Lords—Mon-Tue 14:30-22:00, Wed 15:00-22:00, Thu 11:00-19:30; last entry depends on debates; exact day-by-day schedule at www.parliament.uk.

Tours: Audioguide-£22.50, guided tour-£29, tours available Sat year-round 9:00-16:30 and most weekdays during recess (late July-Sept), 1.5 hours. Confirm the tour schedule and book ahead at www.parliament.uk or by calling +44 20 7219 4114. The ticket office also sells tours, but there's no guarantee same-day spaces will be available (ticket office open Mon-Fri 10:00-16:00, Sat 9:00-16:30, closed Sun, in Portcullis House next to Westminster Tube Station, entrance on Victoria Embankment). For either a guided tour or an audioguide, arrive at the visitors entrance on Cromwell Green 20-30 minutes before your tour time to clear security.

Crowd-Beating Tips: For the public galleries, lines tend to be longest at the start of each session, particularly on Wednesdays; for the shortest wait, show up later in the afternoon (but don't push it, as things sometimes close down early).

□ See the Houses of Parliament Tour chapter.

Nearby: Across the street from the Parliament building's St. Stephen's Gate, the **Jewel Tower** is a rare remnant of the old Palace of Westminster, used by kings until Henry VIII. The crude stone tower (1365-1366) was a guard tower in the palace wall, overlooking a moat. It contains an exhibit on the medieval Westminster Palace and the tower (£6.50, April-Oct Wed-Sun 10:00-17:00, closed Mon-Tue, off-season Sat-Sun only until 16:00, +44 20 7222 2219). Next to the tower is a quiet courtyard with picnic-friendly benches.

Big Ben, the 315-foot-high clock tower at the north end of the Palace of Westminster, is named for its 13-ton bell, Ben. The light above the clock is lit when Parliament is in session. The face of the clock is huge—you can actually see the minute hand moving. For a good view of it, walk halfway over Westminster Bridge.

▲▲▲Churchill War Rooms

This excellent sight offers a fascinating walk through the underground headquarters of the British government's WWII fight against the Nazis in the darkest days of the Battle of Britain. It has two parts: the war rooms themselves, and a top-notch museum dedicated to the man who steered the war from here, Winston Churchill. For details on all the blood, sweat, toil, and tears, pick

SIGHTS

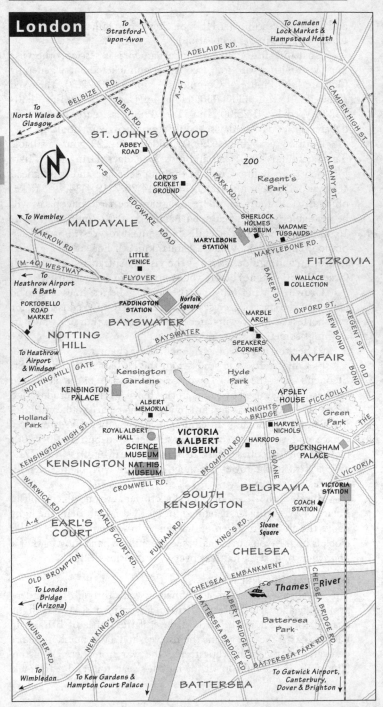

London

To Stratford-upon-Avon

To Camden Lock Market & Hampstead Heath

ADELAIDE RD.

BELSIZE RD.

ABBEY RD.

A-41

To North Wales & Glasgow

CAMDEN HIGH ST.

ST. JOHN'S WOOD

ABBEY ROAD

ZOO

Regent's Park

PARK RD.

ALBANY ST.

N

A-5

LORD'S CRICKET GROUND

EDGWARE ROAD

To Wembley

MAIDAVALE

HARROW RD.

SHERLOCK HOLMES MUSEUM

MADAME TUSSAUDS

MARYLEBONE STATION

MARYLEBONE RD.

FITZROVIA

(M-40) WESTWAY

LITTLE VENICE

BAKER ST.

WALLACE COLLECTION

To Heathrow Airport & Bath

FLYOVER

OXFORD ST.

NEW BOND ST.

REGENT ST.

PORTOBELLO ROAD MARKET

PADDINGTON STATION

Norfolk Square

MARBLE ARCH

BAYSWATER

NOTTING HILL

BAYSWATER

SPEAKERS' CORNER

MAYFAIR

OLD BOND

To Heathrow Airport & Windsor

NOTTING HILL GATE

Kensington Gardens

Hyde Park

APSLEY HOUSE

PICCADILLY

Green Park

THE

Holland Park

KENSINGTON PALACE

ALBERT MEMORIAL

KNIGHTS-BRIDGE

HARVEY NICHOLS

KENSINGTON HIGH ST.

ROYAL ALBERT HALL

VICTORIA & ALBERT MUSEUM

HARRODS

SLOANE

BUCKINGHAM PALACE

KENSINGTON

SCIENCE MUSEUM

NAT. HIS. MUSEUM

BROMPTON RD.

VICTORIA

WARWICK RD.

CROMWELL RD.

SOUTH KENSINGTON

BELGRAVIA

VICTORIA STATION

A-4

EARL'S COURT

EARLS COURT RD.

FULHAM RD.

KING'S RD.

Sloane Square

COACH STATION

OLD BROMPTON

CHELSEA

To London Bridge (Arizona)

NEW KING'S RD.

KING'S RD.

CHELSEA EMBANKMENT

Thames River

CHELSEA BRIDGE RD.

MUNSTER RD.

ALBERT BRIDGE RD.

BATTERSEA BRIDGE RD.

Battersea Park

To Wimbledon

To Kew Gardens & Hampton Court Palace

BATTERSEA

BATTERSEA PARK RD.

To Gatwick Airport, Canterbury, Dover & Brighton

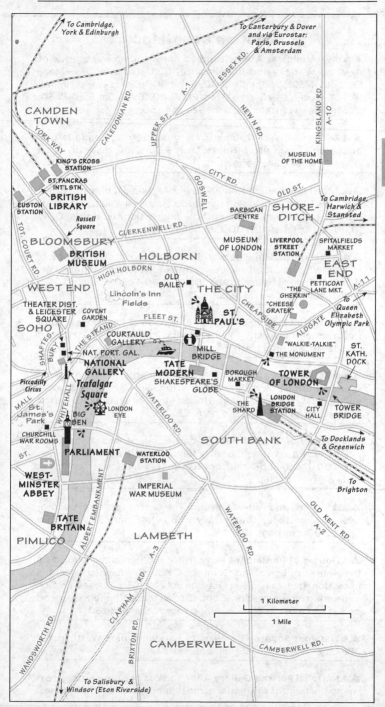

To Cambridge, York & Edinburgh

To Canterbury & Dover and via Eurostar: Paris, Brussels & Amsterdam

CAMDEN TOWN

YORK WAY

CALEDONIAN RD.

UPPER ST.

A-1

NEW N RD.

ESSEX RD.

KINGSLAND RD.

A-10

MUSEUM OF THE HOME

KING'S CROSS STATION

ST. PANCRAS INT'L STN.

EUSTON STATION

BRITISH LIBRARY

CITY RD.

GOSWELL

OLD ST.

SHORE-DITCH

To Cambridge, Harwich & Stansted

Russell Square

TOT. COURT RD.

BLOOMSBURY

CLERKENWELL RD.

BARBICAN CENTRE

BRITISH MUSEUM

HOLBORN

MUSEUM OF LONDON

LIVERPOOL STREET STATION

SPITALFIELDS MARKET

HIGH HOLBORN

OLD BAILEY

THE CITY

EAST END

WEST END

Lincoln's Inn Fields

ST. PAUL'S

CHEAPSIDE

PETTICOAT LANE MKT.

"THE GHERKIN"

ALDGATE

A-11

THEATER DIST. & LEICESTER SQUARE

COVENT GARDEN

FLEET ST.

"CHEESE GRATER"

To Queen Elizabeth Olympic Park

SOHO

SHAFTES-BURY

THE STRAND

COURTAULD GALLERY

NAT. PORT. GAL.

MILL. BRIDGE

"WALKIE-TALKIE"

THE MONUMENT

ST. KATH. DOCK

Piccadilly Circus

NATIONAL GALLERY

Trafalgar Square

TATE MODERN

SHAKESPEARE'S GLOBE

Borough Market

TOWER OF LONDON

St. James's Park

MALL

WHITEHALL

BIG BEN

LONDON EYE

THE SHARD

LONDON BRIDGE STATION

CITY HALL

TOWER BRIDGE

CHURCHILL WAR ROOMS

ST.

PARLIAMENT

WATERLOO RD.

SOUTH BANK

To Docklands & Greenwich

WEST-MINSTER ABBEY

ALBERT EMBANKMENT

WATERLOO STATION

IMPERIAL WAR MUSEUM

To Brighton

TATE BRITAIN

PIMLICO

LAMBETH

A-3

WATERLOO RD.

OLD KENT RD.

A-2

WANDSWORTH RD.

CLAPHAM RD.

BRIXTON RD.

CAMBERWELL

CAMBERWELL RD.

1 Kilometer

1 Mile

To Salisbury & Windsor (Eton Riverside)

SIGHTS

London at a Glance

▲▲▲**Westminster Abbey** Britain's finest church and the site of royal coronations and burials since 1066. **Hours:** Abbey—Mon-Fri 9:30-16:30, Wed until 19:00, Sat 9:00-16:30 (Sept-April until 14:00); Queen's Galleries—Mon-Fri 10:00-16:00, Sat 9:30-15:30; closed Sun except for worship. See page 50.

▲▲▲**Churchill War Rooms** Underground WWII headquarters of Churchill's war effort. **Hours:** Daily 9:30-18:00, may stay open later in summer. See page 51.

▲▲▲**National Gallery** Remarkable collection of European paintings (1250-1900), including Leonardo, Botticelli, Velázquez, Rembrandt, Turner, Van Gogh, and the Impressionists. **Hours:** Daily 10:00-18:00, Fri until 21:00. See page 61.

▲▲▲**British Museum** The world's greatest collection of artifacts of Western civilization, including the Rosetta Stone and the Parthenon's Elgin Marbles. **Hours:** Daily 10:00-17:30, Fri until 20:30 (select galleries only). See page 73.

▲▲▲**British Library** Fascinating collection of important literary treasures of the Western world. **Hours:** Mon-Thu 9:30-20:00, Fri until 18:00, Sat until 17:00, Sun 11:00-17:00. See page 75.

▲▲▲**St. Paul's Cathedral** The main cathedral of the Anglican Church, designed by Christopher Wren, with a climbable dome and daily evensong services. **Hours:** Mon-Sat 8:30-16:30, closed Sun except for worship. See page 82.

▲▲▲**Tower of London** Historic castle, palace, and prison housing the crown jewels and a witty band of Beefeaters. **Hours:** Tue-Sat 9:00-17:00, Sun-Mon from 10:00; Nov-Feb closes one hour earlier. See page 86.

▲▲▲**Victoria and Albert Museum** The best collection of decorative arts anywhere. **Hours:** Daily 10:00-17:45, may stay open Fri until 22:00. See page 107.

▲▲**Houses of Parliament** Famous for Big Ben and occupied by the Houses of Lords and Commons. **Hours:** When Parliament is in session, generally open Oct-late July Mon-Thu, closed Fri-Sun and during recess late July-Sept. Guided tours offered year-round on Sat and most weekdays during recess. See page 50.

▲▲**Trafalgar Square** The heart of London, where Westminster, The City, and the West End meet. See page 61.

▲▲**National Portrait Gallery** A *Who's Who* of British history, featuring portraits of this nation's most important historical figures.

Hours: May be closed for renovation; if open likely daily 10:00-18:00, Fri until 21:00. See page 62.

▲▲**Covent Garden** Vibrant people-watching zone with shops, cafés, street musicians, and an iron-and-glass arcade that once hosted a produce market. See page 63.

▲▲**Changing of the Guard at Buckingham Palace** Hour-long spectacle at Britain's royal residence. **Hours:** May-July daily at 11:00, Aug-April Sun-Mon, Wed, and Fri. See page 69.

▲▲**London Eye** Enormous observation wheel, dominating—and offering commanding views over—London's skyline. **Hours:** Daily 10:00-20:30 or later, Sept-May 11:00-18:00. See page 89.

▲▲**Imperial War Museum** Exhibits examining military conflicts from the early 20th century to today. **Hours:** Daily 10:00-18:00. See page 90.

▲▲**Tate Modern** Works by Monet, Matisse, Dalí, Picasso, and Warhol displayed in a converted powerhouse complex. **Hours:** Daily 10:00-18:00, may stay open later Fri-Sat. See page 95.

▲▲**Shakespeare's Globe** Timbered, thatched-roof reconstruction of the Bard's original "wooden O." **Hours:** Theater complex, museum, and actor-led tours generally daily until 12:30, sometimes later. Plays are also staged here. See page 96.

▲▲**Tate Britain** Collection of British painting from the 16th century through modern times, including works by Blake, the Pre-Raphaelites, and Turner. **Hours:** Daily 10:00-18:00. See page 101.

▲▲**Natural History Museum** A Darwinian delight, packed with stuffed creatures, engaging exhibits, and enthralled kids. **Hours:** Daily 10:00-18:00. See page 107.

▲▲**Greenwich** Seafaring borough just east of the city center, with *Cutty Sark* tea clipper, Royal Observatory, other maritime sights, and a pleasant market. **Hours:** Most sights open daily 10:00-17:00. See page 109.

▲▲**Kew Gardens** Greenhouses, an arboretum, and many gardens hosting diverse plants from around the world. **Hours:** Mon-Thu 10:00-19:00, Fri-Sun until 20:00, closes earlier Sept-March. See page 116.

▲▲**Hampton Court Palace** The opulent digs of Henry VIII. **Hours:** Daily 10:00-18:00, Nov-March until 16:30. See page 117.

SIGHTS

Winston Churchill (1874-1965)

As the 20th century dawned, 25-year-old Winston Churchill was making a name for himself in Britain. Working as a newspaper reporter embedded with British troops in South Africa, he was on a train attacked by Boers. Churchill was captured and held as a POW. Meanwhile, back home, the London papers were praising the young man's heroism for saving fellow train passengers. After two weeks, Churchill escaped from the Boer camp—he slipped through a bathroom window, scaled a wall, walked nonchalantly through an enemy town, hopped a freight train, and was smuggled out of the country. He emerged to find himself famous.

Churchill later entered politics. He first followed in his father's (Lord Randolph Churchill) Conservative Party footsteps, but his desire for social reform drove him to switch to the Liberal Party. (He would later flip back to Conservative.) For three decades, Churchill held numerous government posts, serving as Chancellor of This, Undersecretary of That, and Minister of The Other. He earned praise for prison reform and for developing new-fangled airplanes for warfare; he was criticized for the heavy-handed way he broke labor strikes and for bungling the pacification of Iraq. During World War I, he took a break from pol-

up the included audioguide at the entry, and dive in. Allow 1-2 hours for your visit.

Cost and Hours: £29 timed-entry ticket (buy online in advance), includes essential audioguide; daily 9:30-18:00, may stay open later in summer, last entry one hour before closing; on King Charles Street, 200 yards off Whitehall—follow signs, Tube: Westminster; +44 20 7930 6961, www.iwm.org.uk/churchill-war-rooms. The museum's gift shop is great for anyone nostalgic for the 1940s.

Advance Tickets Recommended: While you can buy a ticket on-site, ticket-buying lines can be long (1-2 hours), so it's smart to buy a timed-entry ticket online in advance. You still may have to wait up to 30 minutes in the security line.

Cabinet War Rooms: The 27-room, heavily fortified nerve

itics to personally command British troops on the Western Front.

In 1929, Churchill-the-career-bureaucrat retired from politics. He wrote books (*History of the English-Speaking Peoples*) and spoke out about the growing threat of fascist Germany. When World War II broke out, Prime Minister Chamberlain's appeasement policies were discredited, and—on the day that Germany invaded the Netherlands—the king appointed Churchill prime minister. Churchill guided the nation through its darkest hour (see sidebar on page 288). His greatest contribution may have been his stirring radio speeches that galvanized the will of the British people.

Despite the Allies' victory over the Nazis, Churchill lost the 1945 election. Though considered the ideal man to lead Britain during war, many believed that he and his Conservative Party colleagues were not the best choice to lead the country in peace and during rebuilding. Never one to be idle, he remained active in politics (especially in world affairs) as Leader of the Opposition. In 1946, he gave a speech at a Missouri college, which included the famous Cold War line, "From Stettin in the Baltic to Trieste in the Adriatic, an Iron Curtain has descended across the Continent." In 1951, Churchill was again elected prime minister and served for four years before he retired in 1955. When he died at age 90 in 1965, his state funeral in St. Paul's attracted leaders from around the world. Churchill, a legend in his own time, was buried in the family plot at Bladon, a mile from Blenheim Palace, the place of his birth.

center of the British war effort was used from 1939 to 1945. Churchill's room, the map room, and other rooms are just as they were in 1945. As you follow the one-way route, the audioguide explains each room and offers first-person accounts of wartime happenings here. Be patient—it's well worth it. While the rooms are spartan, you'll see how British gentility survived even as the city was bombarded—posted signs informed those working underground what the weather was like outside, and a cheery notice reminded them to turn off the lights to conserve electricity.

Churchill Museum: Don't bypass this museum, which occupies a large hall amid the war rooms. It dissects every aspect of the man behind the famous cigar, bowler hat, and V-for-victory sign. It's extremely well presented and engaging, using artifacts, quotes, political cartoons, clear explanations, and interactive exhibits to bring the colorful statesman to life. You'll get a taste of Winston's wit, irascibility, work ethic, passion for painting, American ties, writing talents, and drinking habits. The exhibit shows Winston's warts as well: It questions whether his party-switching was just

Affording London's Sights

London is one of Europe's most expensive cities, with the dubious distinction of having some of the world's steepest admission prices. But with its many free museums and affordable plays, this cosmopolitan, cultured city offers days of sightseeing thrills without requiring you to pinch your pennies (or your pounds).

Free Museums: Free sights include the British Museum, British Library, National Gallery, National Portrait Gallery, Tate Britain, Tate Modern, Wallace Collection, Imperial War Museum, Victoria and Albert Museum, Natural History Museum, Science Museum, National Army Museum, Sir John Soane's Museum, the Museum of London, Museum of the Home, the Guildhall, and on the outskirts of town, the Royal Air Force Museum London. Most of these museums request a donation of about £5, but whether you contribute is up to you. If you feel like supporting these museums, renting audioguides, using their café, and buying a few souvenirs all help. Note that you can reserve a time slot even at free museums—worth doing to avoid lines at busy times.

Free Churches: Smaller churches let worshippers (and tourists) in free, although they may ask for a donation. The big sightseeing churches—Westminster Abbey and St. Paul's—charge higher admission fees, but offer free evensong services nearly daily (though you can't stick around afterward to sightsee). Westminster Abbey also offers free organ recitals most Sundays.

Other Freebies: London has plenty of free performances, such as lunch concerts at St. Martin-in-the-Fields (see page 478) and summertime movies at The Scoop amphitheater near City Hall (see page 481). There's no charge to enjoy the pageantry of the Changing of the Guard, rants at Speakers' Corner in Hyde Park (on Sun afternoon), displays at Harrods, the people-watching scene at Covent Garden, and the colorful streets of the East End. It's free to view the legal action at the Old Bailey and the legislature at work in the Houses of Parliament. You can get into a bit of the Tower of London and Windsor Castle by attending Sunday services in each place's chapel (chapel access only). And, Greenwich is an inexpensive outing. Many of its sights are free, and the DLR journey is cheap.

Good-Value Tours: The London Walks tours with professional guides (£15) are one of the best deals going. (Note that the guides for the "free" walking tours are unpaid by their companies, and they expect tips—I'd pay up front for an expertly guided tour

political opportunism, examines the basis for his opposition to Indian self-rule, and reveals him to be an intense taskmaster who worked 18-hour days and was brutal to his staffers (who deeply respected him nevertheless).

A long touch-the-screen timeline lets you zero in on events in his life from birth (November 30, 1874) to his first appointment as

instead.) Hop-on, hop-off big-bus tours, while expensive (around £40), provide a great overview and include free boat tours as well as city walks. (Or, for the price of a transit ticket, you could get similar views from the top of a double-decker public bus.) A one-hour Thames ride to Greenwich costs about £15 one-way, but most boats come with entertaining commentary. A three-hour bicycle tour is about £34.

Buy Tickets Online: Tickets for many of London's most popular and expensive sights can be purchased online in advance, which will not only save you from standing in ticket-buying lines, but also will usually save you a few pounds per ticket.

Pricey...but Worth It? Big-ticket sights worth their hefty admission fees are the Tower of London, Kew Gardens, Shakespeare's Globe, and the Churchill War Rooms. The London Eye has become a London must-see—but you may feel differently when you see the price. St. Paul's Cathedral becomes more worthwhile if you climb the dome for the stunning view. Hampton Court Palace is well-presented and a reasonable value if you have an interest in royal history. The Queen charges royally for a peek inside Buckingham Palace and her fine art gallery and carriage museum. Madame Tussauds Waxworks is pricey but still hard for many to resist. Harry Potter fans gladly pay the Hagrid-sized fee to see the sets and props at the Warner Bros. Studio Tour.

Totally Pants (Brit-speak for Not Worth It): The London Dungeon is gimmicky, overpriced, and a terrible value...despite the long line. The cost of the wallet-bleeding ride to the top of The Shard is even more breathtaking than the view from Western Europe's tallest skyscraper.

Theater: Compared with Broadway's prices, London's theater can be a bargain. Seek out the freestanding TKTS booth at Leicester Square—or check their website—to get discounts from 25 to 50 percent on good seats (and full-price tickets to the hottest shows with no service charges). Buying directly at the theater box office can score you a great deal on same-day tickets, and even popular shows may have some seats under £20 (possibly with restricted views). A £5 "groundling" ticket for a play at Shakespeare's Globe is the best theater deal in town. Tickets to the Open Air Theatre at north London's Regent's Park start at £25. For more on these options, see the Entertainment in London chapter.

prime minister in 1940. Many of the items on display—such as a European map divvied up in permanent marker, which Churchill brought to England from the postwar Potsdam Conference—drive home the remarkable span of history this man influenced. Imagine: Churchill began his military career riding horses in the cavalry and ended it speaking out against nuclear proliferation. It's all the more amazing considering that, in the 1930s, the man I regard as the greatest statesman of the 20th century was seen as a washed-up loony ranting about the growing threat of fascism.

Eating: Rations are available at the **$$ museum café** or, better, get a pub lunch at the nearby **$$ Westminster Arms** (food served downstairs, on Storey's Gate, a couple of blocks south of the museum).

Horse Guards

Mounted sentries change at the top of every hour, courtyard guards change Monday-Saturday at 11:00 (Sun at 10:00), and a colorful dismounting ceremony takes place daily at 16:00. The rest of the day, they just stand there—making for boring video (at Horse Guards Parade on Whitehall, directly across from the Banqueting House, between Trafalgar Square and 10 Downing Street, Tube: Westminster, www.changing-guard.com). Buckingham Palace pageantry is canceled when it rains, but the Horse Guards change regardless of the weather.

The **Household Cavalry Museum** shows off 350 years of cavalry tradition, with uniforms, weapons, video clips, and a peek into the stables (£9.50, daily 10:00-18:00, Nov-March until 17:00, enter on back side of Horse Guards building). At five minutes after each hour you can see horses return from the changing of the mounted sentries who guard the entrance to Horse Guards Parade.

▲Banqueting House

England's first Renaissance building (1619-1622) is still standing. Designed by Inigo Jones, built by King James I, and decorated by his son Charles I, the Banqueting House came to symbolize the Stuart kings' "divine right" management style—the belief that God himself had anointed them to rule. The house is one of the few London landmarks spared by the 1698 fire and the only surviving part of the original Palace of Whitehall. Today it opens its doors to visitors, who enjoy a restful 10-minute audiovisual history, a 45-minute audioguide, and a look at the exquisite banqueting hall itself. As a tourist attraction, it's basically one big room, with sumptuous ceiling paintings by Peter Paul Rubens. At Charles I's request, these paintings drove home the doctrine of the legitimacy of the divine right of kings. Ironically, in 1649—divine right ignored—King Charles I was famously executed right here.

Cost and Hours: £7, includes audioguide, daily 10:00-17:00, may close for government functions—though it's always open at least until 13:00 (call ahead for recorded info), immediately across Whitehall from the Horse Guards, Tube: Westminster, +44 20 3166 6155, www.hrp.org.uk.

ON TRAFALGAR SQUARE
▲▲Trafalgar Square
London's central square, the climax of most marches and demonstrations, is a thrilling place to simply hang out. Lord Nelson stands atop his 185-foot-tall fluted granite column, gazing out toward Trafalgar, where he lost his life but defeated the French fleet. Part of this 1842 memorial is made from his victims' melted-down cannons. He's surrounded by spraying fountains,

giant lions, hordes of people, and—until recently—even more pigeons. A former London mayor decided that London's "flying rats" were a public nuisance and evicted Trafalgar Square's venerable seed salesmen (Tube: Charing Cross).

▲▲▲National Gallery
Displaying an unsurpassed collection of European paintings from 1250 to 1900—including works by Leonardo, Botticelli, Velázquez, Rembrandt, Turner, Van Gogh, and the Impressionists—this is one of Europe's great galleries. The collection is huge; following the route suggested in my self-guided tour will give you the best quick visit. For a more thorough tour, use one of the gallery's excellent audioguides. Or, if you're very tight on time, follow one of the gallery's recommended routes connecting just the highlights. Whatever time you spend here is worth it.

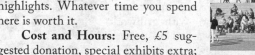

Cost and Hours: Free, £5 suggested donation, special exhibits extra; daily 10:00-18:00, Fri until 21:00, last entry to special exhibits one hour before closing; daily free guided tours available, floor plan-£2; on Trafalgar Square, Tube: Charing Cross or Leicester Square, +44 20 7747 2885, www.nationalgallery.org.uk.

📖 See the National Gallery Tour chapter.

▲▲National Portrait Gallery

Due to a lengthy renovation, this museum may be closed when you visit.

Put off by halls of 19th-century characters who meant nothing to me, I used to call this museum "as interesting as someone else's yearbook." But if it's open, a selective walk through this 500-year-long *Who's Who* of British history is quick and free, and puts faces on the story of England.

Some highlights: Henry VIII and wives; portraits of the "Virgin Queen" Elizabeth I, Sir Francis Drake, and Sir Walter Raleigh; the only real-life portrait of William Shakespeare; Oliver Cromwell and Charles I with his head on; portraits by Gainsborough and Reynolds; the Romantics (William Blake, Lord Byron, William Wordsworth, and company); Queen Victoria and her era; and the present royal family, including the late Princess Diana and the current Duchess of Cambridge—Kate.

The collection is well-described, not huge, and in historical sequence, from the 16th century on the second floor to today's royal family, usually housed on the ground floor.

Cost and Hours: Free, £5 suggested donation, special exhibits extra; when it reopens likely daily 10:00-18:00, Fri until 21:00; excellent audioguide-£3, floor plan-£2; entry 100 yards off Trafalgar Square (around the corner from National Gallery, opposite Church of St. Martin-in-the-Fields), Tube: Charing Cross or Leicester Square, +44 20 7306 0055, www.npg.org.uk.

☐ See the National Portrait Gallery Tour chapter.

▲St. Martin-in-the-Fields

The church, built in the 1720s with a Gothic spire atop a Greek-type temple, is an oasis of peace on wild and noisy Trafalgar Square.

St. Martin cared for the poor. "In the fields" was where the first church stood on this spot (in the 13th century), between Westminster and The City. Stepping inside, you still feel a compassion for the needs of the people in this neighborhood—the church serves the homeless and houses a Chinese community center. The modern east window—with grillwork bent into the shape of a warped cross—was installed in 2008 to replace one damaged in World War II.

A freestanding glass pavilion to the left of the church serves as the entrance to the church's underground areas. There you'll find the concert ticket office, a gift shop, brass-rubbing center, and the recommended support-the-church Café in the Crypt.

Cost and Hours: Free, donations welcome; Mon-Fri 8:30-18:00, Sat-Sun from 9:00, closed to visitors during services—listed at the entrance and on the website; Tube: Charing Cross, +44 20 7766 1100, www.stmartin-in-the-fields.org. The church is famous for its concerts, including a free lunchtime concert several days a week and evening concerts (for details, see page 478 of the Entertainment in London chapter, as well as the church's website).

THE WEST END AND NEARBY

The following areas are linked and covered in more detail in the 🕮 West End Walk chapter.

▲Piccadilly Circus

Although this square is slathered with neon billboards and tacky attractions (think of it as the Times Square of London), the sur-

rounding streets are packed with great shopping opportunities and swimming with youth on the rampage.

Nearby Shaftesbury Avenue and Leicester Square teem with fun-seekers, theaters, Chinese restaurants, and street singers. To the northeast is London's Chinatown and, beyond that, the funky Soho neighborhood. And curling to the northwest from Piccadilly Circus is genteel Regent Street, lined with exclusive shops.

▲Soho

North of Piccadilly, once-seedy Soho has become trendy—with many recommended restaurants—and is well worth a gawk. It's the epicenter of London's thriving, colorful youth scene, a fun and funky *Sesame Street* of urban diversity.

▲▲Covent Garden

The centerpiece of this boutique-ish shopping district is an iron-and-glass arcade. The "Actors' Church" of St. Paul, the Royal Opera House, and the London Transport Museum (described next) all border the square, and theaters are nearby. The area is a people-watcher's delight, with cigarette eaters, Punch-and-Judy acts, food that's not good for you (or your wallet), trendy crafts, and row after row of boutique

SIGHTS

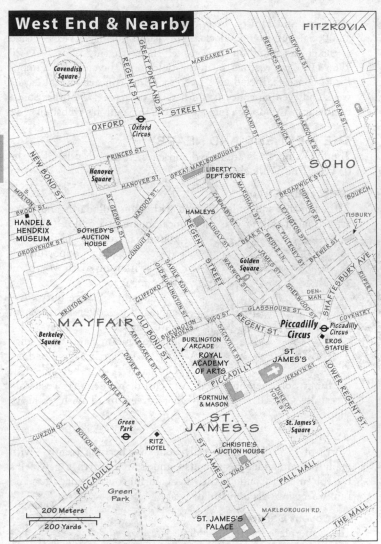

shops and market stalls. For more on this square, see page 205. Better Covent Garden lunch deals can be found by walking a block or two away from the eye of this touristic hurricane (check out the places north of the Tube station, along Endell and Neal Streets, and see my suggestions on page 428).

▲London Transport Museum

This modern, well-presented museum, located right at Covent Garden, is fun for kids and thought-provoking for adults (if a bit overpriced). Whether you're cursing or marveling at the double-

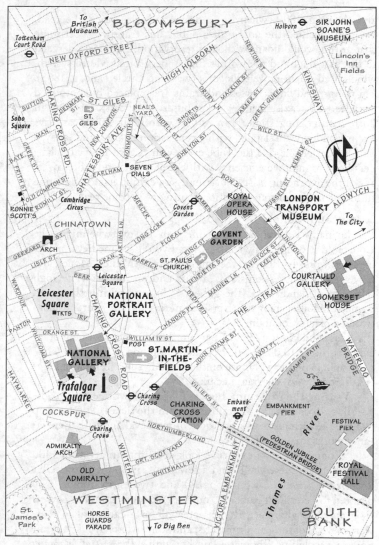

deckers and Tube, the growth of Europe's third-biggest city (after Istanbul and Moscow) has been made possible by its public transit system. Kids enjoy picking up the "stamp card," then punching it with old-fashioned ticket punchers at the different exhibits.

Cost and Hours: £18.50, kids under 18 free, daily 10:00-18:00, last entry 45 minutes before closing; pleasant upstairs café with Covent Garden view; in southeast corner of Covent Garden courtyard, Tube: Covent Garden, +44 20 7379 6344, www. ltmuseum.co.uk.

Visiting the Museum: Take the elevator up to the top floor...

and the year 1800, when horse-drawn vehicles ruled the road. London invented the notion of a public bus traveling a set route that anyone could board without a reservation. Next, you descend to the first floor and the world's first underground Metro system, which used steam-powered locomotives (the Circle Line, c. 1865). On the ground floor, horses and trains are replaced by motorized vehicles (cars, taxis, double-decker buses, streetcars), resulting in 20th-century congestion. How to deal with it? In 2003, car drivers in London were slapped with a congestion charge, and today, a half-billion people ride the Tube every year. Learn how city planners hope to improve efficiency with better tracks and more coverage of the expanding East End. Finally, an exhibit lets you imagine futuristic modes of transportation waiting to become real.

▲Courtauld Gallery

While many London art museums can be overwhelming, the Courtauld is delightfully concise. Here you'll see medieval paintings and works by Rubens, the Impressionists (Manet, Monet, and Degas), Post-Impressionists (Cézanne and an intense Van Gogh self-portrait), and more. The gallery is located within the grand Somerset House; enjoy the riverside eateries and the courtyard featuring a playful fountain.

Cost and Hours: £9, £11 Sat-Sun, can be more for temporary exhibits, daily 10:00-18:00, free audio tour on Bloomberg Connects app, in Somerset House on the Strand, Tube: Temple or Covent Garden, www.courtauld.ac.uk.

Visiting the Museum: The art is shown in three easy-to-digest floors, connected by a staircase. From the ticket desk, head up to **Floor 1,** with just one large room of medieval and early Renaissance works (mainly altarpieces).

Floor 2 is a more extensive look at European art from 1400 through 1800. Here you'll find a few gems, including Botticelli's *The Trinity with Saints* (in Room 4) and two entire rooms (6-7) devoted to Peter Paul Rubens. You'll see sketches from the *Descent from the Cross* altarpiece Rubens created for a cathedral in Antwerp; several of his gauzy portraits; and some works by his contemporaries, including Thomas Gainsborough's *Portrait of Margaret Gainsborough*.

Floor 3 is the museum's highlight: Impressionism and the 20th century. You'll begin in a room of early Impressionist works, from the likes of Monet (including a study for his famous *Luncheon in the Grass*), Pissarro, Boudin, Cézanne, Renoir, and Degas *(Two Dancers on a Stage)*. Duly impressed, continue into the Great Room, with one of the best single-room collections of Impressionist and Post-Impressionist works anywhere. It's an easy-to-appreciate sampling of the greats: Cézanne's *The Card Players;* Tahitian works by

Gauguin; tiny pointillist paintings by Seurat; Manet's *A Bar at the Foiles-Bergère*; portraits by Toulouse-Lautrec and Modigliani; and the gallery's pièce de résistance, a striking self-portrait of Vincent Van Gogh with a bandaged ear. Also on floor 3 is a gigantic, three-part ceiling painting, *The Myth of Prometheus*, which Austrian Secessionist Oskar Kokoschka (a contemporary of Klimt and Schiele) painted for the ceiling of a London bigwig's home; and—hiding down a little hall past the elevator—a room devoted to the Bloomsbury Group, the Virginia Woolf-led artistic movement from 1910s London.

SIGHTS

Handel & Hendrix in London

This quirky, fascinating museum will likely be closed for renovation when you visit. When open, you're able to tour the rooms of two well-known musicians from different eras—who coincidentally lived in these two neighboring flats. You'll see a few personal effects and period furniture, and learn about their different-yet-similar lives and music. Though the museum brings things to life, little of what's on display was actually owned by either Handel or Hendrix.

Cost and Hours: When open likely £10, Mon-Sat 11:00-18:00, closed Sun, 25 Brook St, Tube: Bond Street, +44 20 7495 1685, www.handelhendrix.org.

Visiting the Museum: In 1723, the 38-year-old German composer, George Frideric Handel, moved in and made this flat his home for the next 36 years. You'll see the room where he wrote "Messiah"—a 2.5-hour oratorio created in three weeks—and the kind of harpsichord he might have used. In the dressing room, Handel's servants would get him into his foppish clothes and long, white, and curly powdered wigs. Finally, there's the bedroom, decorated with a canopy bed. It was here that Handel entertained guests, indulged in rich food and drink, got fat, and ultimately died in 1759.

Two centuries later, another long-haired, foreign-born musician with a flair for outrageous fashions and unrestrained decadence, who'd first found fame in London, moved in. It was the summer of '68, and Jimi Hendrix, a rock guitarist from Seattle, unknowingly rented the flat next door to Handel's. He gigged at nearby clubs and afterward invited fellow musicians (George Harrison, Steppenwolf, the Bee Gees, and others) back to his pad. On display, you'll see Hendrix's record album collection, including some by Handel. Jimi's bedroom is meticulously reconstructed with period artifacts. Imagine Jimi in his trademark floppy hat, kicking back on the psychedelic bed, cushioned by surrealistic pillows, cradling his guitar, sipping wine, and penning the lyrics to "Voodoo Child."

BUCKINGHAM PALACE AREA

The working headquarters of the British monarchy, Buckingham Palace is where the Queen carries out her official duties as the head of state. She and other members of the royal family also maintain apartments here. The property hasn't always been this grand— James I (1603-1625) first brought the site under royal protection as a place for his mulberry plantation, for rearing silkworms. The wide boulevard called The Mall was built in 1911 as a ceremonial approach.

Combo-Tickets: A £55 "Royal Day Out" combo-ticket covers the three palace sights that charge admission: the State Rooms, the Queen's Gallery, and the Royal Mews. You can also pay for each of these sights separately (prices listed later). For more information or to book online, see www.royalcollection.org.uk. Many tourists are more interested in the Changing of the Guard, which costs nothing at all to view.

▲State Rooms at Buckingham Palace

This lavish home has been Britain's royal residence since 1837, when the newly ascended Queen Victoria moved in. When today's Queen is at home, the royal standard flies (a red, yellow, and blue flag); otherwise, the Union Jack flaps in the wind. The Queen opens her palace to the public—but only for a couple of months in summer, when she's out of town.

Cost and Hours: £30 for State Rooms and throne room, includes audioguide; July-Aug daily 9:30-19:30, Sept-Oct until 18:30, closed Nov-June, last entry 75 minutes before closing; limited to 8,000 visitors a day by timed entry—book ahead online or arrive early at the palace's Visitor Entrance (opens at 9:00); Tube: Victoria, +44 303 123 7300—but Her Majesty rarely answers.

Queen's Gallery at Buckingham Palace

A small sampling of Queen Elizabeth's personal collection of art is on display in five rooms in a wing adjoining the palace. Her 7,000 paintings, one of the largest private art collections in the world, are actually a series of collections built upon by each successive monarch since the 16th century. The Queen rotates the paintings, enjoying some privately in her many palatial residences while sharing others with her subjects in public galleries in Edinburgh and London. The exhibits change two or three times a year and are lovingly described by the included audioguide.

Because the gallery is small and security is tight (involving lines), visit this gallery only if you're a patient art lover interested in the current exhibit. Men shouldn't miss the mahogany-trimmed urinals.

Cost and Hours: Around £15 but can change depending on exhibit, daily 10:00-17:30, from 9:30 late July-Sept, last entry 75 minutes before closing, Tube: Victoria, +44 303 123 7301.

Royal Mews

A visit to the Queen's working stables is likely to be disappointing unless you follow the included audioguide or the hourly guided tour (April-Oct only, 45 minutes), in which case it's fairly entertaining—especially if you're interested in horses and/or royalty. You'll see only a few of the Queen's 30 horses (most active between 10:00 and 12:00), a fancy car, and a bunch of old carriages, finishing with the Gold State Coach (c. 1760, 4 tons, 4 mph). Queen Victoria said absolutely no cars. When she died, in 1901, the mews got its first Daimler. Today, along with the hay-eating transport, the stable is home to five Bentleys and Rolls-Royce Phantoms, with at least one on display.

Cost and Hours: £14; mid-May-Sept Thu-Mon 10:00-17:00, closed Tue-Wed, likely closed off-season but check online, last entry 45 minutes before closing; generally busiest immediately after Changing of the Guard, guided tours on the hour in summer; Buckingham Palace Road, Tube: Victoria, +44 303 123 7302.

▲▲Changing of the Guard at Buckingham Palace

This is the spectacle every London visitor must see at least once: stone-faced, bearskin-hatted guards changing posts with much fanfare, accompanied by a brass band. (This is also where you'll see nearly every tourist in London gathered in one place at the same time.)

The most famous part takes place right in front of Buckingham Palace at 11:00. But before and after that, over the course of about an hour, several guard-changing ceremonies and parades converge within a few hundred yards of Buckingham Palace in a perfect storm of red-coated pageantry, more or less simultaneously. Most tourists just show up near the palace gate and get lost in the crowds, but if you're savvy, you can catch a satisfying glimpse from less crowded locations with much less wait than if you station yourself at the palace gate (see the "Changing of the Guard Timeline" sidebar). Once it's all over, unwind with a stroll through nearby St. James's Park.

SIGHTS

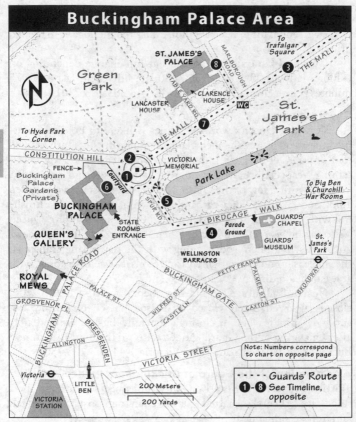

Buckingham Palace Area

Green Park

St. James's Park

St. JAMES'S PALACE

To Trafalgar Square

THE MALL

MARLBOROUGH ROAD

CLARENCE HOUSE

WC

LANCASTER HOUSE

STABLE YARD RD

THE MALL

To Hyde Park Corner

CONSTITUTION HILL

VICTORIA MEMORIAL

Park Lake

To Big Ben & Churchill War Rooms

FENCE

Buckingham Palace Gardens (Private)

Courtyard

SPUR RD

BIRDCAGE WALK

GUARDS' CHAPEL

BUCKINGHAM PALACE

STATE ROOMS ENTRANCE

Parade Ground

GUARDS' MUSEUM

St. James's Park

QUEEN'S GALLERY

WELLINGTON BARRACKS

ROYAL MEWS

PALACE ROAD

PALACE ST.

BUCKINGHAM GATE

PETTY FRANCE

PALMER ST.

BROADWAY

GROSVENOR PL.

WILFRED ST.

CASTLE LN.

CAXTON ST.

BUCKINGHAM PALACE ROAD

ALLINGTON

BRESSENDEN

VICTORIA STREET

Victoria

LITTLE BEN

200 Meters

200 Yards

VICTORIA STATION

Note: Numbers correspond to chart on opposite page

- - - - Guards' Route

1 - 8 See Timeline, opposite

Cost and Hours: Free; confirm hours online but most likely May-July daily at 11:00, Aug-April Sun-Mon, Wed, and Fri, no ceremony in very wet weather; exact schedule subject to change—for the day's plan, check www.householddivision.org.uk (search "Changing the Guard") or call +44 20 7766 7300; Buckingham Palace, Tube: Victoria, St. James's Park, or Green Park. Or hop into a big black taxi and say, "Buck House, please."

Tips: Download the official app for maps and background on the pageantry (www.rct.uk). The only public WC in the area is near St. James's Palace, just inside the gate to the park from Marlborough Road.

Viewing the Official Ceremony: The center of all this fanfare is the half-hour ceremony that takes place in the forecourt (between the palace and the fence) in front of Buckingham Palace. At 11:00 a batch of fresh guards meets the Old Guard in the courtyard, where the captain of the Old Guard hands over the keys. As the band plays, soldiers parade regimental flags (or "colours"), get

Changing of the Guard Timeline

When	What
10:00	Tourists gather by the ❶ fence outside Buckingham Palace and the ❷ Victoria Memorial.
10:45	Cavalry guards, headed up ❸ The Mall back from their Green Park barracks, pass Buckingham Palace en route to the Horse Guards (except on Sundays).
10:57	❹ The New Guard, led by a band, marches in a short procession from Wellington Barracks down ❺ Spur Road to Buckingham Palace.
11:00	Guards converge around the Victoria Memorial before entering the ❻ fenced courtyard of Buckingham Palace for the main Changing of the Guard ceremony. (Meanwhile, farther away along Whitehall, the Horse Guard changes guard—except on Sundays, when it's at 10:00.)
11:10	Relief guards leave from Buckingham Palace along The Mall to Clarence House, via ❼ Stable Yard Road.
11:25	The remaining Old Guard leaves St. James's Palace for Buckingham Palace.
11:37	Cavalry guards, headed down The Mall back to their Green Park barracks from Horse Guards, pass Buckingham Palace.
11:40	The entire Old Guard, led by a band, leaves Buckingham Palace and heads up Spur Road for Wellington Barracks, while a detachment of the New Guard leaves Buckingham Palace to march up The Mall to take over at ❽ St. James's Palace (arriving around 11:45).

SIGHTS

counted and inspected—all with a lot of shouting—and finally exchange compliments before the tired guards return to Wellington Barracks, and a subset of the New Guard heads off to take over at St. James's Palace.

By the Palace Fence: If the actual changing of the Buckingham Palace guards is a must-see for you, show up at least an hour early to get a place front and center, next to the fence (shorter travelers should aim for two hours ahead in high season).

Near the Victoria Memorial: If you can't get a spot right by the gates, try the high ground on the circular Victoria Memorial, which can give you good (if more distant) views of the palace as well as the arriving and departing processions along The Mall and Spur Road. If grabbing an early spot, think about whether you'll still have a view once the crowds fill in—balustrades and other raised spots go quickly.

Following the Procession: If the main ceremony doesn't seem worth all the waiting and jostling, you can still enjoy plenty of fun fanfare—and the thrill of participating in the action—by planting yourself on the route of a string of processions that happen before, during, and after the official guard changing at Buckingham Palace.

To catch as much as possible, here's what I'd do:

Show up at St. James's Palace by 10:30 to see its soon-to-be-off-duty guards mobilizing in the courtyard (grab a spot just across Marlborough Road from the courtyard; people grouped on the palace side of the street will be asked to move when the inspection begins).

Just before they prepare to leave (at 10:43), march ahead of them down Marlborough Road to The Mall and pause at the corner to watch them parade past, possibly with a band, on their way to Buckingham Palace.

Then cut through the park and head to the Wellington Barracks—where a fresh batch of guards is undergoing inspection before they leave (at 10:57) for Buckingham Palace.

March along with the New Guard and their full military band, from the barracks to Buckingham Palace.

If it's too packed to see any of the action behind the palace gates, snap a few photos of the passing guards—and the crowds—before making your way back up The Mall, to where it meets Stable Yard Road, in time to watch several more processions: relief guards coming from Buckingham Palace at 11:10 for a switch of sentries at Clarence House (Prince Charles' official home), then other guards heading down The Mall *toward* Buckingham Palace at 11:25, and, at 11:37, a procession of cavalry guards en route from the Horse Guards to their barracks in Green Park.

Finally, at about 11:45, plant yourself back at the corner of The Mall and Marlborough Road for a great photo op as one last procession, the bulk of St. James's Palace New Guard, makes its way from Buckingham Palace to start its shift.

Join a Tour: Local tour companies such as **Fun London Tours** more or less follow the route above but add in history and facts about the guards, bands, and royal family to their already entertaining march. These walks add color and good value to what can otherwise seem like a stressful mess of tourists (£18, £20 on Sun, Changing of the Guard tour starts at Piccadilly Circus at 9:40 Mon-Sat, 9:15 Sun, must book online in advance, www.funlondontours.com).

North London

BLOOMSBURY

The Bloomsbury neighborhood—just north of Soho—is dominated by the great British Museum, with smaller museums tagging along nearby.

▲▲▲British Museum

Simply put, this is the greatest chronicle of civilization...anywhere. A visit here is like taking a long hike through *Encyclopedia Bri-*

tannica National Park. The vast British Museum wraps around its Great Court (the huge entrance hall), with the most popular sections filling the ground floor: Egyptian, Assyrian, and ancient Greek, with the famous frieze sculptures from the Parthenon in Athens. The museum's stately Reading Room—famous as the place where Karl Marx hung out while formulating his ideas on communism and writing *Das Kapital*—sometimes hosts special exhibits.

Cost and Hours: Free, £5 suggested donation, some temporary exhibits extra (and with timed ticket); daily 10:00-17:30, Fri until 20:30 (select galleries only), least crowded late on weekday afternoons, especially Fri; free guided tours offered; Great Russell Street, Tube: Tottenham Court Road, ticket desk +44 20 7323 8181, www.britishmuseum.org.

See the ▢ British Museum Tour chapter or download my free ∩ audio tour.

▲Sir John Soane's Museum

Architects love this quirky place, as do fans of interior decor, eclectic knickknacks, and Back Door sights. Tour this furnished home on a bird-chirping square and see 19th-century chairs, lamps, wood-paneled nooks and crannies, sculptures, and stained-glass skylights just as they were when the owner lived here. As professor of architecture at the Royal Academy, Soane created his home to be a place of learning, cramming it floor to ceiling with ancient relics, curios, and famous paintings, including several excellent

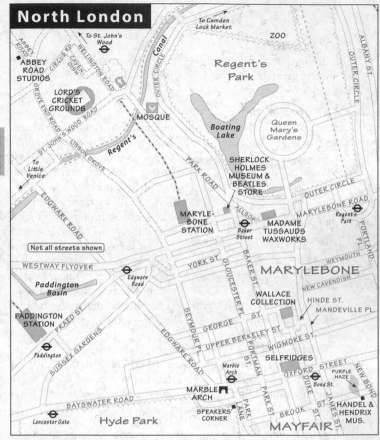

North London

To Camden Lock Market

To St. John's Wood

ZOO

Regent's Park

ABBEY ROAD STUDIOS

CIRCUS RD.

CAVEN DISH

WELLINGTON ROAD

GROVE END ROAD

ST. JOHN'S LISSON GROVE

ABBEY ROAD

LORD'S CRICKET GROUNDS

MOSQUE

Regent's

Boating Lake

Queen Mary's Gardens

To Little Venice

EDGWARE ROAD

PARK ROAD

SHERLOCK HOLMES MUSEUM & BEATLES STORE

ALLSOP

OUTER CIRCLE

MARYLEBONE ROAD

Regent's Park

ALBANY ST.

OUTER CIRCLE

PORTLAND PL.

MARYLE-BONE STATION

Baker Street

MADAME TUSSAUDS WAXWORKS

Not all streets shown

WESTWAY FLYOVER

Edgware Road

York St.

GLOUCESTER PL.

BAKER ST.

MARYLEBONE

WEYMOUTH

NEW CAVENDISH

Paddington Basin

PADDINGTON STATION

Paddington

PRAED ST.

SUSSEX GARDENS

EDGWARE ROAD

SEYMOUR PL.

GEORGE ST.

UPPER BERKELEY ST.

PORTMAN ST.

WALLACE COLLECTION

HINDE ST.

MANDEVILLE PL.

WIGMORE ST.

SELFRIDGES

OXFORD STREET

DUKE ST.

Bond St.

PURPLE HAZE

NEW BOND

Marble Arch

MARBLE ARCH

PARK LANE

PARK ST.

BROOK ST.

JAMES ST.

HANDEL & HENDRIX MUS.

BAYSWATER ROAD

Lancaster Gate

Hyde Park

SPEAKERS' CORNER

MAYFAIR

Canalettos and Hogarth's series on *The Rake's Progress* (which is hidden behind a panel in the Picture Room and opened randomly at the museum's discretion, usually twice an hour). Soane even purchased the Egyptian sarcophagus of King Seti I (Ramesses II's father, on display in the basement) after the British Museum turned it down—at the time, they couldn't afford the £2,000 sticker price.

In 1833, just before his death, Soane established his house as a museum, stipulating that it be kept as nearly as possible in the state he left it. If he visited today, he'd be entirely satisfied by the diligence with which the staff safeguards his treasures. You'll leave wishing you'd known the man.

Cost and Hours: Free, but donations much appreciated; Wed-Sun 10:00-17:00, closed Mon-Tue, can have long lines—especially Sat; advance reservations may be possible online; tours of private apartments are worth considering—get information and prebook online; free audio tour on Bloomberg Connects app; 13 Lincoln's

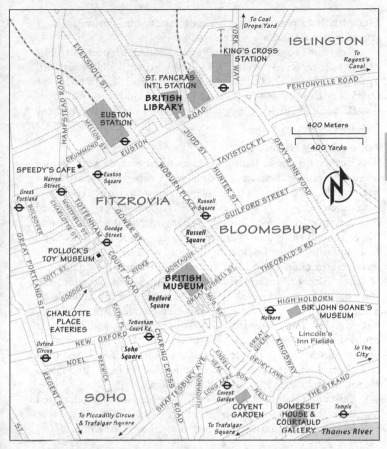

Inn Fields, quarter-mile southeast of British Museum, Tube: Holborn, +44 20 7405 2107, www.soane.org.

FITZROVIA

A bit farther north and west of Bloomsbury, Fitzrovia features a cluster of big train stations (Euston, St. Pancras, King's Cross)—and, tucked between them, the British Library.

▲▲▲British Library

Here, in just two rooms, are the literary treasures of Western civilization, from early Bibles to Shakespeare's *Hamlet* to Lewis Carroll's *Alice's Adventures in Wonderland* to the *Magna Carta*. You'll see the Lindisfarne Gospels transcribed on an illuminated manuscript, Beatles lyrics scrawled on the back of a greeting card, and Leonardo da Vinci's genius sketched into his notebooks. The British Empire built its greatest monuments out of paper; it's through literature that England made her most lasting and significant contribution to civilization and the arts.

Cost and Hours: Free, £5 suggested donation, special exhibits may have entry fee; Mon-Thu 9:30-20:00, Fri until 18:00, Sat until 17:00, Sun 11:00-17:00; 96 Euston Road, Tube: King's Cross St. Pancras or Euston, +44 33 0333 1144, www.bl.uk.

🕮 See the British Library Tour chapter or 🎧 download my free audio tour.

Pollock's Toy Museum

This rickety old house, with glass cases filled with toys and games lining its walls and halls, is a time-warp experience that brings back childhood memories to people who grew up without batteries or computer chips. It also gives a sense of the history of childhood itself, starting from when "childhood" as we know it now first came to be. Though the museum is small, you could spend a lot of time here, squinting at the fascinating toys and well-loved dolls that entertained the children of 19th- and early-20th-century England.

The included information is fascinating. For example, the story of Theodore Roosevelt refusing to shoot a bear cub while on a hunting trip was celebrated in 1902 cartoons, resulting in a new, huggable toy: the Teddy Bear. It was popular for good reason: It could be manufactured during World War I without rationed products; it coincided with the new belief that soft toys were good for a child's development; it was an acceptable "doll for boys"; and it was *the* toy children kept long after they'd grown up.

Cost and Hours: £9, kids-£4.50, Mon-Sat 10:00-17:00, closed Sun, 1 Scala Street, Tube: Goodge Street, +44 20 7636 3452, www.pollockstoymuseum.co.uk. A fun retro toy shop is attached.

MARYLEBONE

Farther west, Marylebone is an upscale residential area that draws travelers for its Madame Tussauds and Sherlock Holmes museums. Better than either of those, however, is the Wallace Collection. Marylebone High Street, connecting Regent's Park to Soho, is a lovely shopping street (see the Shopping in London chapter).

▲Wallace Collection

Sir Richard Wallace's fine collection of 17th-century Dutch Masters, 18th-century French Rococo, medieval armor, and assorted aristocratic fancies fills the sumptuously furnished Hertford House on Manchester Square. From the rough and intimate Dutch lifescapes of Jan Steen to the pink-cheeked Rococo fantasies of François Boucher, a wander through this little-visited mansion makes you nostalgic for the days of the empire. This collection would be a big deal in a midsize city, but here in London it gets pleasantly lost. It feels more like visiting a classic English manor estate than a museum. It's thoroughly enjoyable.

Cost and Hours: Free, £5 suggested donation, special exhibits may have additional charge, daily 10:00-17:00, free audio tour on Bloomberg Connects app, just north of Oxford Street on Manchester Square, Tube: Bond Street, +44 20 7563 9500, www.wallacecollection.org.

Tours: Free "highlights" tours Thu-Sat at 14:30. At 13:00, they often have more in-depth talks on specific works—call or check online to confirm times.

Eating: The museum's lovely, light-filled atrium contains a **$$$ restaurant** serving lunch as well as reasonably priced afternoon tea (tea served 14:30-16:30, open similar hours as museum, reservations smart); across the atrium is a simpler **$ café.**

Background: Sir Richard Wallace's biography is as peculiar as the collection. Born the recognized-but-illegitimate son of Richard Seymour-Conway, 4th Marquess of Hertford, Wallace was denied the ancestral title but inherited the family collection at his father's death, became a respected philanthropist, and was eventually knighted by Queen Victoria. Upon his own death

his widow bestowed the collection to the people of England under the clever condition that it retain the name Wallace, and not the name of his father.

Visiting the Museum: The manageable collection is displayed on three floors—not much in the basement; fine arts, medieval treasures, and armor on the ground floor; and an even finer painting collection on the top floor.

As you enter the ground floor, on the right you'll find plush drawing rooms filled with medieval relics, and to the left (through the gift shop) are the collections of Oriental and European armor—one of the finest such collections in Britain.

Head up the red-carpeted grand staircase to the upper floor, packed with paintings. At the top of the stairs, turn left to begin a clockwise spin around this floor. First, turn left, then left again into the Oval Drawing Room—busy with Boucher and Fragonard—pink, giddy, and Rococo. A highlight is the small but symbolism-packed Rococo masterpiece *The Swing* (1767), by Jean-Honoré Fragonard. The woman is being pulled on the swing by her husband. He's on the right, hidden in shadows, literally "in the dark"—unaware that his wife is having an affair with the man hiding in the bushes on the left. The rascal holds his arm erect as he peeps up this swinging lady's skirt and watches her shoe fly off, symbolizing sexual abandon.

From here, retrace your steps, then bear right to walk through the three-part East Gallery. This wing is interesting for its small-scale 17th-century Dutch paintings by Jan Steen and others who could paint quiet, intimate, and rowdy slices of life—usually conveying a folk moral rather than a religious lesson.

You'll pop out in the Great Gallery, at the far end of the building. This giant room contains paintings by the big names of the 17th century: Rembrandt, Rubens, Velázquez, Titian, Van Dyck, Murillo, and Hals. One of the museum's best-known paintings is *The Laughing Cavalier* (1624) by Frans Hals (see photo). With his hat perched at a jaunty angle, the man smirks enigmatically with unhappy eyes...more of a polite chuckle or a bemused snort.

Continue to the far end of the Great Gallery, then work your way back to the front of the building through the three-part West Gallery. The third room takes you on a trip to 18th-century Venice. It's filled with romantically staged scenes painted by Canaletto and Guardi—purchased as souvenirs by aristocrats on the Grand Tour before the age of postcards.

Looping back around, just before stepping back out to the landing, watch on the left for the easy-to-miss, dimly lit Boudoir Cabinet—a tiny room that glitters with exquisite bits of 18th-century French luxury, including jeweled snuff boxes, miniatures (a sign of friendship or political allegiance), and spanky pornography for the upper class.

Then head back down to the main floor. Before leaving, go out the door behind the staircase, into the building's pretty glassed-in atrium.

▲Madame Tussauds Waxworks

This waxtravaganza is gimmicky, crass, and crazy expensive, but dang fun...a hit with the kind of tourists who skip the British Museum. The original Madame Tussaud did wax casts of heads lopped off during the French Revolution (such as Marie-Antoinette's). She took

Beatles Sights

London's city center is surprisingly devoid of sights associated with the famous '60s rock band. To see much of anything, consider taking a guided walk (see page 43).

For a photo op, go to **Abbey Road** and walk the famous crosswalk pictured on the *Abbey Road* album cover (north-

west of Regent's Park, Tube: St. John's Wood, get information and buy Beatles memorabilia at the small "Beatles coffee shop" window in the station). From the Tube station, it's a five-minute walk west down Grove End Road to the intersection with Abbey Road. The Abbey Road Studios is the low-key white building to the right of Abbey House (it's still a working studio, so you can't go inside). Ponder the graffiti on the low wall outside, and...imagine. To re-create the famous cover photo, shoot the crosswalk from the roundabout as you face north up Abbey Road. Shoes are optional. Next door is the Abbey Road Store, with a classy variety of studio memorabilia, and a timeline out front tracing the building's musical history (daily 9:30-18:00).

Nearby is **Paul McCartney's current home** (7 Cavendish Avenue): Continue down Grove End Road, turn left on Circus Road, and then right on Cavendish. Please be discreet.

The famous **"Get Back" rooftop concert** on January 30, 1969—the Beatles' final performance—did not take place on Abbey Road, but at the band's Apple Corps headquarters (3 Saville Row, on the western edge of Soho).

The **Beatles Store** at 231 Baker Street sells T-shirts, mugs, pins, and old vinyl (open eight days a week, 10:30-18:00, Tube: Baker Street, +44 20 7935 4464, www.beatlesstorelondon. co.uk; another rock memorabilia store is across the street).

her show on the road and ended up in London in 1835. These days, they've dumped anything really historical (except for what they claim is the blade that beheaded Marie-Antoinette) because "there's no money in it and we're a business." Now it's all about hanging with the royals, singing with Lady Gaga, and partying with Benedict Cumberbatch, the Beckhams, and The Beatles. The gallery, which sprawls through several rooms of a huge building, is one giant photo-op—the whole point is jockeying for position to snap the best picture of your travel buddy with a famous "person." It's extremely crowded and chaotic, as everyone clamors to press the wax with their heroes, while dodging tourist-trinket kiosks and photographers standing by to overcharge you for a print. These wax sculptures are eerily realistic—count how many times you say "excuse me" after bumping into a dummy.

Cost and Hours: £34, kids-£30.50 (free for kids under 3), up to 25 percent cheaper online, extra cost for Marvel 4-D experience and Fast Track shorter-line access, combo-deals with the London Eye and other related attractions; hours vary (check online) but roughly July-Aug and school holidays daily 8:30-18:00, Sept-June Mon-Fri 10:00-16:00, Sat-Sun 9:00-17:00, these are last entry times—it stays open roughly two hours later; Marylebone Road, Tube: Baker Street, +44 871 894 3000 or +44 20 7487 0351, www.madametussauds.com.

Crowd-Beating Tips: This attraction (like the related London Eye) is always worth booking ahead—both to save money and to save time in ticket lines. Even if you simply buy tickets on your phone on the way to the exhibit, you'll be glad you did. It tends to be less crowded after about 15:00.

Visiting the Waxworks: First you'll join the paparazzi on the red carpet with A-list stars, then you'll head through several themed sections, featuring Hollywood stars new and old, popular movie characters, sports heroes (including some unfamiliar-to-Americans cricket players and footballers), the royal family (pose with the Queen, Will, and Kate...or settle for Charles and Camilla), scientists, artists, writers, musicians, and world leaders.

Downstairs are exhibits that sometimes have lines—pick and choose if it's worth the wait. A small exhibit explains the casting process and the history of Madame Tussaud and her waxy army. Then you'll board a Disney-type people-mover and cruise through a kid-pleasing "Spirit of London" once-over-very-light history of this city. You can choose to pay a few pounds extra for a nine-minute Marvel Super Heroes "4-D" show—a 3-D movie heightened by wind, "back ticklers," and other special effects. It's totally silly, requires yet another wait in line, and leaves the crowd buzzing with sensory overload—a fitting finale to the entire Waxworks experience.

Sherlock Holmes Museum

Around the corner from Madame Tussauds, this meticulous re-creation of the (fictional) apartment of the (fictional) detective sits at the (real) address of 221b Baker Street. The first-floor replica (so to speak) of Sherlock's study delights fans with the opportunity to play Holmes and Watson while sitting in authentic 18th-century chairs. The second and third floors offer fine exhibits on daily Victorian life, showing off furniture, clothes, pipes, paintings, and chamber pots; in other rooms, models are posed to enact key scenes from Sir Arthur Conan Doyle's famous books.

Cost and Hours: £15, Tue-Sun 10:00-17:00, closed Mon, consider prebooking online to avoid lines; large gift shop for Holmes connoisseurs, including souvenirs from the BBC-TV series; 221b Baker Street, Tube: Baker Street, +44 20 7224 3688, www.sherlock-holmes.co.uk.

Nearby: Next door to the Sherlock Holmes Museum is the **Beatles Store**—jammed with Fab Four memorabilia (see the "Beatles Sights" sidebar).

Fans of BBC-TV's *Sherlock* series—which this museum doesn't cover—can grab a bite or snap a photo at Speedy's Café, the filming location for the show's 221b exterior (a quick Tube ride away, near Euston Station at 187 North Gower Street, Tube: Euston Square).

REGENT'S CANAL

Slicing east-west across the middle of North London is Regent's Canal, a waterway built in the early 19th century. Today, some parts of the canal remain industrial, while others have become gentrified. Here are some highlights:

Camden Lock Market: This market is named for the Hampstead Road Locks—the first of 13 along the length of Regent's Canal, allowing a gradual change in water level. The market, which provides a good look at the canal, is worth exploration (for details, see page 460), as is the area surrounding the market, which wears its industrial shabbiness with pride.

Coal Drops Yard: Farther east, a five-minute walk behind St. Pancras and King's Cross train stations, is a glittering new development of shopping malls, high-end restaurants, and office blocks. This was where coal would arrive on train cars, to be dropped onto barges along the canal for distribution around London.

Little Venice: The most charming area along Regent's Canal is Little Venice, where it splits off from the Grand Union Canal (west of Marylebone and northwest of Paddington Station, Tube: Warwick Avenue). In this very local-feeling area, Amsterdam-style houseboats line the canal. From here, various companies offer lazy boat trips along the canal, including some that connect to Camden Lock Market (for details, see page 48). It's also possible to borrow a city bike from the Little Venice area and cycle along the canal 2.5 miles to the market, then leave your bike there. Be aware you can't follow the canal the entire way—you'll occasionally detour into busier neighborhood streets—but it's still a pleasant pedal along the canal and the back edge of Regent's Park.

The City

When Londoners say "The City," they mean the one-square-mile business center in East London that 2,000 years ago was Roman Londinium. The outline of the Roman city walls can still be seen in the arc of roads from Blackfriars Bridge to Tower Bridge. Within The City are 23 churches designed by Sir Christopher Wren, mostly just ornamentation around St. Paul's Cathedral. Today, while home to only 10,000 residents, The City thrives with around 400,000 office workers coming and going daily. It's a fascinating district to wander on weekdays, but since almost nobody actually lives there, it's dull in the evening and on Saturday and Sunday.

Many of the following sights are covered in more detail in 📖 the Historic London: The City Walk chapter and 🎧 my free audio tour.

ST. PAUL'S CATHEDRAL AND NEARBY
▲▲▲St. Paul's Cathedral

Wren's most famous church is the great St. Paul's, its elaborate interior capped by a 365-foot dome. Since World War II, St. Paul's

has been Britain's symbol of resilience. Despite 57 nights of bombing, the Nazis failed to destroy the cathedral, thanks to St. Paul's volunteer fire watchmen, who stayed on the dome. Today you can climb the dome for a great city view. The crypt is a world of historic bones and memorials, including Admiral Nelson's tomb and interesting cathedral models.

Cost and Hours: £21, £19 online; includes church entry, dome climb, crypt, tour, and audioguide; Mon-Sat 8:30-16:30 (dome opens at 9:30), closed Sun except for worship; book ahead online to skip the line (15-45 minutes in summer and on weekends), guided tours offered; Tube: St. Paul's, +44 20 7246 8350, www.stpauls.co.uk.

Music: Evensong services are free (Mon-Sat at 17:00, Sun at 15:15; Mon evensong usually spoken, not sung); nonpaying visitors are not allowed to linger afterward.

Cheap Trick: To get a free cityscape view nearly as good as the expensive view from St. Paul's dome, head for the rooftop terrace at One New Change shopping mall, just behind the church. To reach it, walk through the churchyard (to the left of the church as you face it), cross the busy street, turn right, and head toward One New Change. Behind the escalators, you'll find glass elevators where you can ride to the top floor for a fine view of St Paul's and of London.

☐ See the St. Paul's Cathedral Tour chapter or ☊ download my free audio tour.

▲Old Bailey

To view the British legal system in action—lawyers in little blond wigs speaking legalese with an upper-crust accent—spend a few minutes in the visitors' gallery at the Old Bailey courthouse, called the "Central Criminal Court." Don't enter under the dome; continue up the block about halfway to the modern part of the building—the entry is at Warwick Passage.

Cost and Hours: Free, generally Mon-Fri 10:00-13:00 & 14:00-17:00 depending on caseload, last entry at 12:40 and 15:40 but often closes an hour or so earlier, closed Sat-Sun, fewer cases in Aug; no kids under 14; no big bags—if you have a bag, they can tell you where to check it nearby; 2 blocks northwest of St. Paul's on Old Bailey Street (down a tunnel called Warwick Passage, follow signs to public entrance), Tube: St. Paul's, +44 20 7248 3277, www.cityoflondon.gov.uk.

The Guildhall

Hiding out in The City, the Guildhall offers visitors a grand medieval hall and a delightful painting gallery for free. This area has been a gathering place since ancient Roman times (on the square, note the circular outline of the Roman amphitheater that once stood here). The meeting spot for guilds in medieval times, it still hosts about 100 professional associations today.

The venerable **hall**, which survived both the Great Fire of 1666 and bombing in World War II, dates from the 15th century and is a rare bit of civil architecture surviving from the Middle Ages.

Adjoining the old hall is the **Guildhall Art Gallery,** giving insight into old London society with mostly Victorian paintings of numerous London scenes. One of the best Victorian collections in London, it's well-described and organized into themes (home, beauty, faith, leisure, work, love, and imagination), and includes dreamy Pre-Raphaelite works. In the basement is a well-presented exhibit on a Roman amphitheater discovered during a building project in 1988.

Cost and Hours: Free, Mon-Sat 10:00-17:00, Sun 12:00-16:00, 6 blocks northeast of St. Paul's on Gresham Street, Tube: St. Paul's or Bank, +44 20 7332 3404, www.guildhall.cityoflondon.gov.uk.

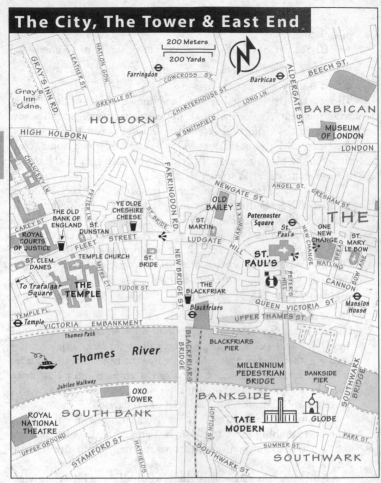

The City, The Tower & East End

200 Meters
200 Yards

N

Farringdon
COWCROSS ST.
Barbican
Barbican
BEECH ST.
ALDERGATE ST.

GRAY'S INN RD.
LEATHER LN.
HATTON GDN.
GREVILLE ST.
CHARTERHOUSE ST.
LONG LN.

Gray's Inn Gdns.
HOLBORN
W. SMITHFIELD
BARBICAN
MUSEUM OF LONDON

HIGH HOLBORN
LONDON

CHANCERY LN.
FETTER LN.
NEWGATE ST.
ANGEL ST.
GRESHAM ST.
THE

CAREY ST.
THE OLD BANK OF ENGLAND
YE OLDE CHESHIRE CHEESE
ST. DUNSTAN
OLD BAILEY
ST. MARTIN
WARWICK LN.
Paternoster Square
St. Paul's
ONE NEW CHANGE
ST. MARY LE BOW

ROYAL COURTS OF JUSTICE
FLEET STREET
LUDGATE HILL
ST. PAUL'S
BREAD ST.
BOW LANE
WATLING

ST. CLEM. DANES
TEMPLE CHURCH
ST. BRIDE
PETER'S HILL
CANNON

To Trafalgar Square
THE TEMPLE
MITRE CT.
TUDOR ST.
THE BLACKFRIAR
QUEEN VICTORIA ST.
Mansion House

TEMPLE PL.
Temple
VICTORIA EMBANKMENT
Thames Path
Blackfriars
UPPER THAMES ST.

BLACKFRIARS BRIDGE
BLACKFRIARS PIER

Thames River

Jubilee Walkway
OXO TOWER
MILLENNIUM PEDESTRIAN BRIDGE
BANKSIDE PIER
SOUTHWARK BRIDGE

ROYAL NATIONAL THEATRE
SOUTH BANK
BANKSIDE
TATE MODERN
GLOBE

UPPER GROUND
STAMFORD ST.
HATFIELDS
HOPTON ST.
SOUTHWARK ST.
SUMNER ST.
PARK ST.
SOUTHWARK

▲Museum of London

This regular stop for local school kids gives the best overview of London history in town. Scale models and costumes help you visualize everyday life in the city through history—from Neanderthals, to Romans, to Elizabethans, to Victorians, to Mods, to today. The displays are chronological, spacious, and

informative without being overwhelming, with enough whiz-bang multimedia displays (including the Plague and the Great Fire) to spice up otherwise humdrum artifacts.

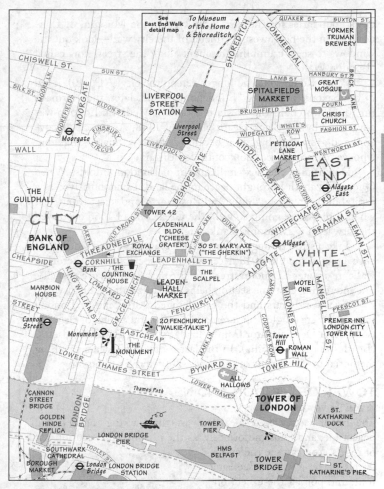

Cost and Hours: Free, daily 10:00-18:00, last entry one hour before closing, see the day's events board for special talks and tours, café, lockers, 150 London Wall at Aldersgate Street, Tube: Barbican or St. Paul's plus a 5-minute walk, +44 20 7001 9844, www. museumoflondon.org.uk.

Visiting the Museum: The first part of the tour zips quickly through a half-million years, when Britain morphed from peninsula to island, Neanderthals speared mammoths, and Stone Age humans huddled in crude huts on the South Bank of the Thames.

In 54 BC, Julius Caesar invaded, and the Romans built "Londinium" on the north bank. The settlement quickly became the hub of Britain and a river-trade town, complete with arenas, forums, baths, a bridge across the Thames, and a **city wall.** That wall—arcing from the present Tower of London to St. Paul's—defined the city's boundaries for the next 1,500 years. The Museum of London sits on the northwest perimeter of the city wall—look out the windows to see a crumbling remnant along the street, now called "London Wall."

When Rome could no longer defend the city (AD 410), it fell to the Saxons (becoming "Lundenburg") and, later, the Normans (in 1066), who built the Tower of London. Medieval London was devastated by the Black Death plague of 1348. As the city recovered and grew even bigger, it became clear to wannabe kings that whoever controlled London controlled Britain.

Downstairs, the next millennium of London unfolds. When Queen Elizabeth I brought peace to the land, London thrived as a capital of theaters (the Globe and Rose), arts, and ideas. Then, just when things were going so well, the Great Fire of 1666 destroyed the city, leaving London a blank slate.

Take a stroll through a Georgian **"pleasure garden"** to experience a day in the life of 18th-century high society. The **"Victorian walk"** re-creates a London street and life in the world's greatest city. The interesting costume section helps humanize all the history.

Two world wars and the car changed 20th-century London into a concrete jungle. But it remained a cultural capital of elegance (see an Art Deco elevator from Selfridge's) and a global trendsetter (Beatles-era memorabilia). In the last room, you'll see a touching memorial to the victims of the July 7, 2005 terrorist bombings.

TOWER OF LONDON AND NEARBY
▲▲▲Tower of London

The Tower has served as a castle in wartime, a king's residence in peacetime, and, most notoriously, as the prison and execution site of rebels. You can see the crown jewels, take a witty Beefeater tour, and ponder the executioner's block that dispensed with troublesome heirs to the throne and a couple of Henry VIII's wives.

Note that lines can be long; see page 293 for tips on getting in quicker. After your visit, consider taking the boat to Greenwich from here (see cruise info on page 46).

Cost and Hours: £28.90, £1 more at "peak" times (Fri-Sun), family ticket available; Tue-Sat 9:00-17:00, Sun-Mon from 10:00; Nov-Feb closes one hour earlier, last entry 1.5 hours before closing; free Beefeater tours available, skippable audioguide-£5, Tube: Tower Hill, +44 333 206 000, www.hrp.org.uk.

📖 See the Tower of London Tour chapter.

Tower Bridge

The iconic Tower Bridge (often mistakenly called London Bridge) was built in 1894 to accommodate the growing East End. While fully modern and hydraulically powered, the drawbridge was designed with a retro Neo-Gothic look.

The bridge is most interesting when the drawbridge lifts to let ships pass, as it does a thousand times a year (best viewed from the Tower side of the Thames). For the bridge-lifting schedule, check the website or call.

You can tour the bridge at the **Tower Bridge Exhibition,** with a history display and a peek at the Victorian-era engine room that lifts the span. Included in your entrance is the chance to cross the bridge—138 feet above the road along a partially see-through glass walkway. As an exhibit, it's overpriced, though the adrenaline rush and spectacular city views from the walkway may help justify the cost.

Cost and Hours: £10.60, daily 9:30-18:00, may stay open later in summer, enter at northwest tower, Tube: Tower Hill, +44 20 7403 3761, www.towerbridge.org.uk.

Nearby: The best remaining bit of London's **Roman Wall** is just north of the Tower (at the Tower Hill Tube station). The chic **St. Katharine Dock,** just east of Tower Bridge, has private yachts and mod shops. Across the bridge, on the South Bank, is the upscale Butlers Wharf area, as well as City Hall, museums, the Jubilee Walkway, and, towering overhead, the Shard.

East London

▲The East End

Immediately east of The City (and Liverpool Street Station), London's East End is a vibrant neighborhood with great eateries, lively markets, and interesting street art. It's also known as "Banglatown" for its Bangladeshi communities and curry houses along Brick Lane. Anchoring the area is Old Spitalfields Market, filled with merchants and creative food counters.

But like other East End districts, it's had a rough past. Every great city needs an "East End"—the downwind-from-industry, poor workers' quarter where rents are cheap, immigrants with different religions and customs can find comfort in numbers, and the everyday people who power the economic engine of that city find a humble home. In medieval times, this was the less desirable end, in part because it was downwind from the noxious hide-tanning district. London's east/west disparity was exacerbated in Victorian times, when the wind carried the pollution of a newly industrialized London. And it was during this time that Jack the Ripper terrorized this neighborhood.

This area has also long been the city's arrival point for new immigrants, from the French Protestant Huguenots (late 16th century), to Ashkenazi Jews (late 19th century), to Bangladeshi refugees (1970s). This mixing of cultures—along with a spirit of redevelopment—has given this area a wonderful energy that's well worth exploring.

☐ See the East End Walk chapter.

▲Museum of the Home

This low-key but well-organized museum is housed in an 18th-century almshouse north of Liverpool Street Station. Its 11 rooms

are each furnished as a living room from a different age, from 1600 to 2000, and each is very well described. The museum also has a café and terrace garden.

Cost and Hours: Free, £3 suggested donation, fee for some exhibits and events, Tue-Sun 10:00-17:00, closed Mon, last entry one hour before closing, garden open April-Oct, 136 Kingsland Road, +44 20 7739 9893, www.museumofthehome.org.uk.

Getting There: Take the Tube to Liverpool Street, then ride the bus 10 minutes north (bus #149 or #242—leave station through Bishopsgate exit and head left a few steps to find stop; hop off at the Pearson Street stop, just after passing the brick museum on the right). Or take the East London line on the Overground to the Hoxton stop, which is right next to the museum.

The South Bank

The South Bank of the Thames is a thriving arts and cultural center, tied together by the riverfront Jubilee Walkway. For fun lunch options in this area, consider one of the nearby street food markets (see the Eating in London chapter).

▲Jubilee Walkway

This riverside path is a popular pub-crawling pedestrian promenade that stretches all along the South Bank, offering grand views of the Houses of Parliament and St. Paul's. On a sunny day, this is the place to see Londoners out strolling. The Walkway hugs the river except just east of London Bridge, where it cuts inland for a couple of blocks. It has been expanded into a 60-mile "Greenway" circling the city, including the 2012 Olympics site.

▲▲London Eye

This giant Ferris wheel, towering above London opposite Big Ben, is one of the world's highest observational wheels and London's

answer to the Eiffel Tower. Riding it is a memorable experience, even though London doesn't have much of a skyline, and the price is borderline outrageous. Whether you ride or not, the wheel is a sight to behold.

Designed like a giant bicycle wheel, it's a pan-European undertaking: British steel and Dutch engineering, with Czech, German, French, and Italian mechanical parts. It's also very "green," running extremely efficiently and virtually silently. Twenty-eight people ride in each of its 32 air-conditioned capsules (representing the boroughs of London) for the 30-minute rotation (you go around only once). From the top of this 443-foot-high wheel—the second-highest public viewpoint in the city—even Big Ben looks small. Built to celebrate the new millennium, the Eye has become a permanent fixture on the London skyline and inspired countless other cities to build their own wheels.

Cost and Hours: £33.50, family ticket and combo-ticket with Madame Tussauds and other attractions available; daily 10:00-20:30 or later, Sept-May generally 11:00-18:00, check website for latest schedule, these are last-ascent times, Tube: Waterloo or Westminster. Thames boats come and go from London Eye Pier at the foot of the wheel.

Advance Tickets: The London Eye has gone all digital. Given that this is a very crowded and popular sight, your best bet is to pre-book a ticket at www.londoneye.com once you know when you'll be visiting. On-site, ticket sales are mainly at self-service kiosks (which you may have to wait to use). If you book online, simply head straight

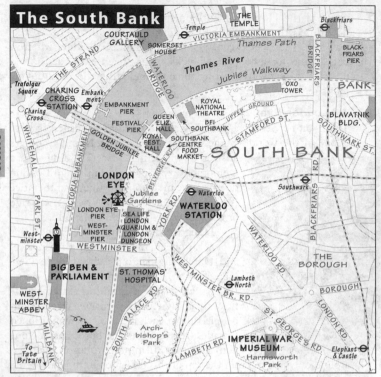

The South Bank

THE TEMPLE
Temple
Blackfriars
COURTAULD GALLERY
VICTORIA EMBANKMENT
Thames Path
SOMERSET HOUSE
BLACK-FRIARS BRIDGE
BLACK-FRIARS PIER
THE STRAND
WATERLOO BRIDGE
Thames River
Jubilee Walkway
OXO TOWER
BANK
Trafalgar Square
CHARING CROSS STATION
Embankment
EMBANKMENT PIER
ROYAL NATIONAL THEATRE
UPPER GROUND
BLAVATNIK BLDG.
Charing Cross
FESTIVAL PIER
QUEEN ELIZ. HALL
BFI SOUTHBANK
STAMFORD ST.
SOUTHWARK ST.
WHITEHALL
GOLDEN JUBILEE BRIDGE
ROYAL FEST. HALL
SOUTHBANK CENTRE FOOD MARKET
SOUTH BANK
VICTORIA EMBANKMENT
BELVEDERE RD.
LONDON EYE
Jubilee Gardens
Waterloo
Southwark
BLACKFRIARS RD.
LONDON EYE PIER
YORK RD.
WATERLOO STATION
PARL. ST.
WEST-MINSTER PIER
SEA LIFE LONDON AQUARIUM & LONDON DUNGEON
Westminster
WESTMINSTER
WATERLOO RD.
THE BOROUGH
BIG BEN & PARLIAMENT
ST. THOMAS' HOSPITAL
WESTMINSTER BR. RD.
Lambeth North
BOROUGH
LONDON RD.
WEST-MINSTER ABBEY
SOUTH PALACE RD.
Arch-bishop's Park
ST. GEORGES RD.
MILLBANK
LAMBETH RD.
IMPERIAL WAR MUSEUM
Harmsworth Park
Elephant & Castle
To Tate Britain

for the ticket-holders line, show the ticket on your phone, and line up to board.

Crowd-Beating Tips: The London Eye is busiest between 11:00 and 17:00, especially on weekends year-round and every day in July and August. If you have your heart set on riding, keep an eye on the website as the date approaches—if tickets are going fast, buy one (they can sell out). Even if you buy in advance, you may wait 30-45 minutes to board your capsule. The more expensive Fast Track ticket saves you a bit of time, but you may still have to wait so it's probably not worth the extra cost.

By the Eye: The area next to the London Eye has developed a cotton-candy collection of kitschy, kid-friendly attractions. There's a game arcade, the Sea Life London aquarium, the London Dungeon, and the Shrek's Adventure amusement ride.

▲▲Imperial War Museum

This impressive museum covers the wars and conflicts of the 20th and 21st centuries—from World War I, through World War II and the Holocaust, to the Cold War. It's overloaded with weapons, uniforms, vehicles, flags, posters, and other artifacts, all thoughtfully explained. But its real strength is the way it pauses to introduce real

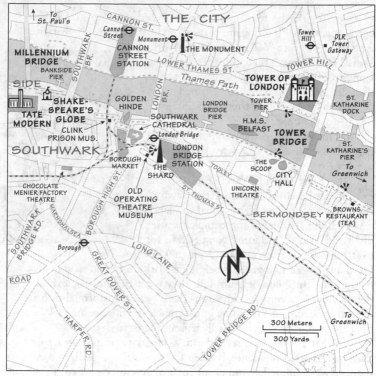

people whose lives were impacted by war (often women and people of color, whose stories are too often ignored in many "war museums"). Rather than glorify war, the museum explores the human toll and raises provocative questions about one of civilization's more uncivilized, persistent traits. Allow plenty of time, as this powerful museum can be engrossing.

Cost and Hours: Free, £5 suggested donation, daily 10:00-18:00, Tube: Lambeth North or Elephant & Castle; buses #3, #12, and #159 from Westminster area; +44 20 7416 5000, www.iwm.org.uk.

The Building: The museum is housed in what once was the Royal Bethlam Hospital. Also known as "the Bedlam asylum," the place was so wild that it gave the world a new word for chaos. Back in Victorian times—before reality shows and YouTube—locals paid admission to visit the asylum for entertainment.

Visiting the Museum: From the entrance, head downstairs

to Level 0—the bottom of the **atrium**—and gaze up at notable battle machines. The Spitfire plane flew in the Battle of Britain. And the towering V-2 rocket from World War II is a reminder that 3,000 of these were launched from Germany, screamed across the Channel at 3,000 mph, and rained down on British cities, killing thousands and leaving 30-foot craters.

From here, the displays unfold chronologically as you work your way up from floor to floor.

The First World War (Level 0): The exhibit, set in Great Britain at the dawn of the 20th century just as its global influence was peaking, considers the complex causes of World War I (including competition for overseas colonies from upstart Germany). As Germany began to invade its neighbors, Britain hoped to stay out of the fray. But once Belgium fell, they went to war. The exhibit details how war, once a "chivalrous duel," was transformed into a "dastardly slaughter": machine guns, trench warfare, cannons lobbing three-foot shells, and deadly chemical gas.

The battle lines soon settled into a stalemate stretching across Europe. At the five-month Battle of the Somme, a million men died or were injured, without an inch of territory gained. (You can view the same film about that battle that 20 million Brits watched in horror—seeing, for the first time, the brutality their boys were experiencing in Europe.) This was "total war"—involving all of society—and you'll learn how the home front was enlisted to support the troops. To simulate the wartime experience, you'll walk through a reconstructed trench, with a tank rearing overhead. When World War I finally ended, Europe was left ruined and shattered. A provocative final film asks whether it was all worth it.

The Second World War (Level 1): Just 20 years removed from the War to End War, the rise of nationalist leaders and economic crisis led to an even bigger war. You'll see how Hitler's annexation of Austria and Czechoslovakia was met with a failed appeasement effort by Britain. Even after Hitler invaded Poland in 1939, Britain and its allies did nothing. But when Hitler invaded Belgium, the Netherlands, and France in 1940, Britain finally came to their aid...only to be humiliated on the battlefield. You'll see the humble wooden fishing boat *Tamzine,* which evacuated troops stranded on the beach at Dunkirk (in northern France) across the Channel back to Britain. "The battle of France is over," Winston Churchill said, "but the battle of Britain is about to begin."

So it did. Exhibits capture "The Blitz"—aerial bombardment, night after night, by Nazi *Luftwaffe* planes, starting in summer 1940. Some 42,000 were killed, and three million people—mostly children—were evacuated to the countryside. You'll walk through a typical wartime home, and see an actual Enigma machine, which the Nazis used to send encoded messages (that code was eventually cracked by Alan Turing at Bletchley Park). In 1941, the war become global when Hitler invaded the Soviet Union in June, and Japan attacked Pearl Harbor in December. With the Russians and Americans on their side, Britain had a fighting chance. You'll learn about "The Big Three"—Churchill, FDR, and Stalin—who met in Tehran in November 1943 to coordinate the attack that came to be known as D-Day (June 6, 1944).

The exhibit pauses to consider the Pacific theater and the exploitation of people who were conscripted into the "British" war effort—and the fighting in Eastern Europe. And you'll see how the RAF (Royal Air Force) turned the tables on Hitler, bombing Germany (much as the Luftwaffe had bombed England) to sever supply lines and weaken the war machine.

Stirring newsreel footage shows the reaction to the war's end in various countries, both the victors and the defeated. The exhibit ends by pondering the overall cost of war—an estimated 60 million human lives snuffed out—and the painful legacy of total war.

Out on the terraces overlooking the atrium, you'll see a variety of so-called **"Witnesses of War,"** including a mangled X-7 submarine and part of a big, black Lancaster bomber.

Holocaust Galleries (Level 2): This exhibit methodically tells the story of the Holocaust, employing powerful profiles of individuals—mainly Jews—who were targeted by Hitler. You'll learn about the rise of fascism and hateful propaganda, and the "Race Laws" that caused growing isolation and danger for Germany's Jews. Hitler's "Final Solution" was to slaughter all Jews; grisly images tell the story of concentration camps liberated at the end of the war. In the final room, you can listen to testimonial footage from people who were involved in this horrible blemish on history, which ultimately murdered six million people.

Peace and Security, 1945-2014 (Level 2): In the galleries overlooking the atrium, you're greeted by a casing of the bomb that was dropped on Hiroshima—setting the tone for an eclectic assortment of artifacts that tries to capture the post-WWII years. Facing the atrium, first go around the right side. You'll watch newsreel footage that aimed to reteach British citizens how to live normal lives after the war. Then you'll see various items related to British military involvement in later decades, such as the Falklands War and "The Troubles" in Ireland. (For some much-needed comic relief, look for the caricatured puppet of Margaret Thatcher, used

SIGHTS

London's Best Views

Though London is a height-challenged city, you can get lofty perspectives on it from several high-flying places. For some viewpoints, you need to pay admission, and at the bars or restaurants, you'll need to buy a drink.

London Eye: Ride the giant Ferris wheel for stunning London views. See page 89.

St. Paul's Dome: You'll earn a striking, unobstructed view by climbing hundreds of steps to the cramped balcony of the church's cupola. 📖 See the St. Paul's Cathedral Tour chapter.

One New Change: Get fine, free views of St. Paul's Cathedral and surroundings—nearly as good as those from St. Paul's Dome—from the rooftop terrace of the One New Change shopping mall just behind and east of the church. See page 82.

Tate Modern: One of the best, easiest, and cheapest views (free) is to head to the Tate Modern's annex—the Blavatnik Building—and ride the elevator to floor 10, where you'll enjoy sweeping views of the skyline (plus the Tate's own tower in the foreground). You can also ride to floor 6 of the main building. 📖 See the Tate Modern Tour chapter.

20 Fenchurch (a.k.a. "The Walkie-Talkie"): Get 360-degree views of London from the mostly enclosed Sky Garden, complete with a thoughtfully planned urban garden, bar, restaurants, and lots of locals. It's free to access but you'll need to make reservations in

on the satirical 1980s TV show *Spitting Image*.) Circle back around past the big bomb and head along the other side of the atrium. Here you'll see an actual chunk of the Berlin Wall (there's another one in the park just outside the museum); a gigantic tile portrait of Saddam Hussein, removed by British soldiers in Iraq; twisted 9/11 wreckage from the Twin Towers; a UN armored peacekeeping vehicle; and the actual witness stand from the trial of two Libyan nationals accused of plotting the Lockerbie bombing, which killed 270 people on British soil.

The Rest of the Museum (Levels 3 and 4): These two floors generally have temporary exhibits shedding light on why humans fight. Crowning the museum on level 5, the **Lord Ashcroft Gallery** celebrates Britain's heroes who received the Victoria and George Crosses.

FROM TATE MODERN TO CITY HALL

These sights are in Southwark (SUTH-uck), the core of the tourist's South Bank. Southwark was for centuries the place Londoners would go to escape the rules and decency of the city and let their hair down. Bearbaiting, brothels, rollicking pubs, and theater—you

advance and bring photo ID (Mon-Fri 10:00-18:00, Sat-Sun 11:00-21:00, 20 Fenchurch Street, Tube: Monument, https://skygarden.london/sky-garden). If you can't get a reservation, try arriving before 10:00 (or 11:00 on weekends) and ask to go up. Once in, you can stay as long as you like.

National Portrait Gallery: A mod top-floor restaurant peers over Trafalgar Square and the Westminster neighborhood. ◻ See the National Portrait Gallery Tour chapter.

Waterstones Bookstore: Its hip, low-key, top-floor café/bar has reasonable prices and sweeping views of the London Eye, Big Ben, and the Houses of Parliament (see page 29, on Sun bar closes one hour before bookstore, www.5thview.co.uk).

The Shard: The observation decks that cap this 1,020-foot-tall skyscraper offer London's most commanding views, but at an outrageously high price. See page 99.

Primrose Hill: For dramatic 360-degree city views, head to the huge grassy expanse at the summit of Primrose Hill, just north of Regent's Park (off Prince Albert Road, Tube: Chalk Farm or Camden Town, www.royalparks.org.uk/parks/the-regents-park).

The Thames River: Various companies run boat trips on the Thames, offering a unique vantage point and unobstructed, ever-changing views of great landmarks (see page 45).

SIGHTS

name the dream, and it could be fulfilled just across the Thames. A run-down warehouse district through the 20th century, it's been gentrified with classy restaurants, office parks, pedestrian promenades, major sights (such as the Tate Modern and Shakespeare's Globe), and a colorful collection of lesser sights. The area is easy on foot and a scenic—though circuitous—way to connect the Tower of London with St. Paul's.

◻ Many of the following sights are covered in more detail in the Bankside Walk chapter.

▲▲Tate Modern

Dedicated in the spring of 2000, the striking museum fills a derelict old power station across the river from St. Paul's—it opened the new century with art from the previous one. Its powerhouse collection includes Dalí, Picasso, Warhol, and much more. Of equal interest are the many temporary exhibits featuring more current,

Crossing the Thames on Foot

You can cross the Thames on any of the bridges that carry car traffic over the river, but London's pedestrian bridges are more fun. **The Millennium Bridge** (see photo) connects the sedate St. Paul's Cathedral with the great Tate Modern. **The Golden Jubilee Bridge,** well-lit and with a sleek, futuristic look, links bustling Trafalgar Square on the North Bank with the London Eye and Waterloo Station on the South Bank.

cutting-edge art. A new annex—built on the site of the power station's switch house and connected to the main building by sky-bridge—shows off more of the Tate's collection and has beautiful views from its 10th-floor terrace. Each year, the main hall features a different monumental installation by a prominent artist.

Cost and Hours: Free, £5 suggested donation, fee for special exhibits; open daily 10:00-18:00, may stay open later Fri-Sat, last entry 45 minutes before closing, especially crowded on weekends (crowds thin out Fri and Sat evenings—when open); free guided tours available, view restaurant on top floor; across the Millennium Bridge from St. Paul's; Tube: Southwark, London Bridge, St. Paul's, Mansion House, or Blackfriars plus a 10-15-minute walk; or connect by Tate Boat museum ferry from Tate Britain—see page 48; +44 20 7887 8888, www.tate.org.uk.

📖 See the Tate Modern Tour chapter.

▲Millennium Bridge

The pedestrian bridge links St. Paul's Cathedral and the Tate Modern across the Thames. This is London's first new bridge in a century. When it opened, the $25 million bridge wiggled when people walked on it, so it promptly closed for repairs; 20 months and $8 million later, it reopened. Nicknamed the "blade of light" for its sleek minimalist design (370 yards long, four yards wide, stainless steel with teak planks), its clever aerodynamic handrails deflect wind over the heads of pedestrians.

▲▲Shakespeare's Globe

This replica of the original Globe Theatre was built, half-timbered and thatched, as it was in Shakespeare's time. (This is the first thatched roof constructed in London since they were outlawed after the Great Fire of 1666.) It serves as a working theater by night and offers tours by day. The original Globe opened in 1599, debuting Shakespeare's play *Julius Caesar*. The Globe originally accommodated 2,200 seated and another 1,000 standing. Today, slightly smaller and leaving space for reasonable

aisles, the theater holds 800 seated and 600 groundlings.

Its promoters brag that the theater melds "the three A's"—actors, audience, and architecture—with each contributing to the play. The working theater hosts authentic performances of Shakespeare's plays with actors in period costumes, modern interpretations of his works, and some works by other playwrights.

The complex's smaller Sam Wanamaker Playhouse—an indoor, horseshoe-shaped Jacobean theater—allows the show to go on in the winter, when it's too cold for performances in the outdoor Globe. Seating fewer than 350, the playhouse is more intimate and sometimes uses authentic candle lighting for period performances. While the Globe mainly presents Shakespeare's works, the

playhouse tends to focus on the works of his contemporaries (Jonson, Marlow, Fletcher) and some new plays, though there's some crossover.

For details on attending a performance in either space, drop by the box office (details on page 476). While the play's the thing, a tour is worthwhile, too—and a nice way to see the impressively reconstructed space if you don't have the time or attention span to devote to a full-length performance.

Touring the Globe: Tours depart from the box office every half hour and last about 50 minutes (£17, £10 for kids 5-15; schedule can change—check online; during outdoor theater season—April-mid-Oct—last tours generally depart Mon at 17:00, Tue-Sat at 12:30, Sun at 11:30; off-season last tours Mon-Sat at 12:30, Sun at 16:00; Tube: Mansion House or London Bridge plus a 10-minute walk, or a short walk across the Millennium Bridge from St. Paul's Cathedral; +44 20 7902 1400, www.shakespearesglobe.com). During outdoor theater season, they sometimes run a £13.50 alternative "Shakespeare Walking Tour" of the outdoor areas nearby, as well as

SIGHTS

the archaeological site of the Rose Theatre, a contemporary of the original Globe.

On the main Globe tour, energetic, theatrical, and knowledgeable guides bring the Elizabethan period to life. You'll see the stage and the various seating areas for the different classes of people, and learn how the new Globe is similar to the old Globe (open-air performances, standing-room by the stage, no curtain) and how it's different (female actors today, lights for night performances, concrete floor). The tour does not show dressing rooms, costume shops, or rehearsals.

Eating: The **$$$ Swan at the Globe** café offers a sit-down restaurant (for lunch and dinner, reservations recommended, +44 20 7928 9444), a drinks-and-plates bar, and a sandwich-and-coffee cart (Mon-Fri 8:00-closing, depends on performance times, Sat-Sun from 10:00).

The Clink Prison Museum

Proudly the "original clink," this was, until 1780, where law-abiding citizens threw Southwark troublemakers. Today, it's a low-tech torture museum filling grotty old rooms with papier-mâché gore. There are storyboards about those unfortunate enough to be thrown in the Clink, but little that seriously deals with the fascinating problem of law and order in Southwark, where 18th-century Londoners went for a good time.

Cost and Hours: Overpriced at £8, Mon-Fri 10:00-18:00, Sat-Sun until 19:30, open later in summer; 1 Clink Street, Tube: London Bridge, +44 20 7403 0900, www.clink.co.uk.

Golden Hinde Replica

This is a full-size replica of the 16th-century warship in which Sir Francis Drake circumnavigated the globe from 1577 to 1580. Commanding the original ship (now long gone), Drake earned his reputation as history's most successful pirate. This replica, however, has logged more than 100,000 miles, including a voyage around the world. A puppet show and "pirate school" entertain the kids (each happens twice a day). While the ship is fun to see, its interior is not worth touring.

Cost and Hours: £5, daily 10:00-18:00, off-season until 17:00, Tube: London Bridge, +44 20 7403 0123, www.goldenhinde.co.uk.

▲Southwark Cathedral

While made a cathedral only in 1905, this has been the neighborhood church since the 13th century, and comes with some interesting history. The enthusiastic docents give impromptu tours if you ask.

Cost and Hours: Free, £2 map serves as photo permit, daily

8:00-18:00, Tube: London Bridge, +44 20 7367 6700, www. cathedral.southwark.anglican.org.

Music: The cathedral hosts evensong Sun at 15:00, Tue-Fri at 17:30, and some Sat at 16:00; organ recitals are Mon at 13:15 and music recitals Tue at 15:15 (call or check website to confirm times).

▲Old Operating Theatre Museum and Herb Garret

Climb a tight and creaky wooden spiral staircase to a church attic where you'll find a garret used to dry medicinal herbs, a fascinating exhibit on Victorian surgery, cases of well-described 19th-century medical paraphernalia, and a special look at "anesthesia, the defeat of pain." Then you stumble upon Britain's oldest operating theater, where limbs were sawed off way back in 1821. (See page 315 for a full description.)

Cost and Hours: £7.50, Thu-Sun 10:30-17:00, closed Mon-Wed, 9a St. Thomas Street, Tube: London Bridge, +44 20 7188 2679, oldoperatingtheatre.com.

The Shard

Rocketing dramatically 1,020 feet above the south end of the London Bridge, this addition to London's skyline is by far the tallest building in Western Europe...for now. Designed by Renzo Piano (best known as the co-architect of Paris' Pompidou Center), the glass-clad pyramid shimmers in the sun and its prickly top glows like the city's nightlight after dark. Its uppermost floors are set aside as public viewing galleries, but the ticket price is as outrageously high as the building itself, especially given that it's a bit far from London's most exciting landmarks. (For a list of cheaper view opportunities in London, see the sidebar on page 94.)

Cost and Hours: £28 in advance, £32 same-day (in person or online), best to book online in advance both to save money and time in line, advance ticket includes free return ticket in case of bad weather, family ticket available; least crowded on weekday mornings, but perhaps better photo opportunities in the early evening (less haze); hours vary, check online—typically April-July and Sept-Oct Sun and Wed-Fri 11:00-19:00, Sat 13:00-21:00, closed Mon-Tue; Aug daily 13:00-21:00; shorter hours Nov-March; Tube: London Bridge—use London Bridge exit and follow signs, +44 844 499 7111, www.theviewfromtheshard.com.

Visiting the Shard: From the entrance on Joiner Street (just off St. Thomas Street) you'll take a two-part elevator ride up to the 68th floor, then climb up one story to the main observation platform. It's equipped with cool telescopes that label major landmarks and even let you see how the view from here would appear at other times of the day. From here you've got great views of

SIGHTS

St. Paul's, the Tower of London, Southwark Cathedral (straight down), and, in the distance, the 2012 Olympic stadium in one direction, and the Houses of Parliament in the other (find Buckingham Palace, just left of the Eye). On the clearest days, you can see 40 miles out, and a few people say they've been able to make out ships on the North Sea. Even in bad weather it's mesmerizing to watch the constant movement of the city's transit system, which looks like a model-train set from this height. Ascending to the 72nd floor gets you to the open-air deck, where the wind roars over the glass enclosure.

Alternate Plan: The **Aqua Shard bar** on the 31st floor offers views from half the height for the price of a fancy drink (free to ride up, but if they're at capacity they can turn you away, bar open 12:00-24:00; "smart casual" dress code—no sportswear, shorts, or flip-flops; access the bar from separate entrance on St. Thomas Street, www.aquashard.co.uk).

HMS *Belfast*

This former Royal Navy warship, a veteran of World War II that took part in the D-Day invasion, clogs the Thames just upstream from the Tower Bridge. The huge vessel—now manned with wax sailors—thrills kids who always dreamed of sitting in a turret shooting off their imaginary guns. If you're into WWII warships, this is the ultimate. Otherwise, it's just an expensive opportunity to get lots of exercise with a nice view of Tower Bridge.

Cost and Hours: £22.70, kids 5-15-£11.35, kids under 5-free, family ticket available, includes audioguide; daily 10:00-18:00, Nov-Feb until 17:00, last entry one hour before closing; Tube: London Bridge, +44 20 7940 6300, www.iwm.org.uk/visits/hms-belfast.

City Hall

The glassy, egg-shaped building near the south end of Tower Bridge is London's City Hall, designed by Sir Norman Foster, the architect who worked on London's Millennium Bridge and Berlin's Reichstag. Nicknamed "the Armadillo," City Hall houses the office of London's mayor—it's here that the mayor consults with the Assembly representatives of the city's 25 districts. An interior spiral ramp allows visitors to watch and hear the action below in the Assembly Chamber. On the lower ground floor is a large aerial photograph of London. Next to

City Hall is the outdoor amphitheater called The Scoop (see page 481 for info on performances).

West London

▲▲Tate Britain

One of Europe's great art houses, Tate Britain specializes in British painting from the 16th century through modern times. The museum has a good representation of William Blake's religious sketches, the Pre-Raphaelites' naturalistic and detailed art, Gainsborough's aristocratic ladies, and the best collection anywhere of J. M. W. Turner's swirling works.

Cost and Hours: Free, £5 suggested donation, fee for special exhibits; daily 10:00-18:00, last entry 45 minutes before closing; free tours generally daily; on the Thames River, south of Big Ben and north of Vauxhall Bridge, Tube: Pimlico, Tate Boat museum ferry goes directly to the museum from Tate Modern—see page 48; +44 20 7887 8888, www.tate.org.uk.

📖 See the Tate Britain Tour chapter.

Victoria Station

From underneath this station's iron-and-glass canopy, trains depart for the south of England and Gatwick Airport. While Victoria Station is famous and a major Tube stop, few tourists actually take trains from here—most just come to take in the exciting bustle. It's a fun place to be a "rock in a river" teeming with commuters and services. The station is surrounded by big red buses and taxis, travel agencies, and lousy eateries. It's next to the main intercity bus station (Victoria Coach Station) and some moderately priced lodgings.

Westminster Cathedral

This cathedral, the largest Catholic church in England and just a block from Victoria Station, is strikingly Neo-Byzantine, but not very historic or important to visit. Opened in 1903, the church has an unfinished interior, with a spooky, blackened ceiling waiting for the mosaics that are supposed to be placed there. While it's definitely not Westminster Abbey, half the tourists wandering around inside seem to think it is. Take the lift to the top of

SIGHTS

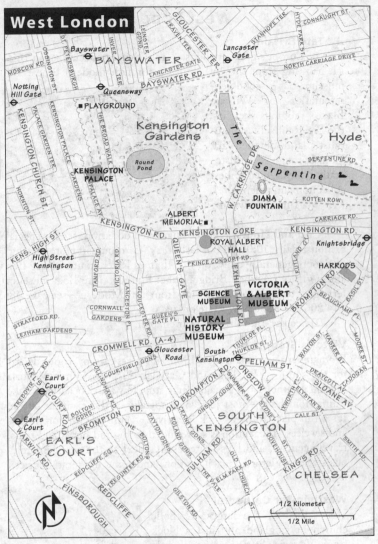

West London

BAYSWATER

Bayswater

Notting Hill Gate

Queensway

PLAYGROUND

Kensington Gardens

Round Pond

KENSINGTON PALACE

KENSINGTON CHURCH ST.

Lancaster Gate

NORTH CARRIAGE DRIVE

Hyde

The Serpentine

SERPENTINE RD.

DIANA FOUNTAIN

ROTTEN ROW

ALBERT MEMORIAL

KENSINGTON RD.

KENSINGTON GORE

CARRIAGE RD.

KENSINGTON RD.

Knightsbridge

KENS. HIGH ST.

High Street Kensington

ROYAL ALBERT HALL

PRINCE CONSORT RD.

HARRODS

SCIENCE MUSEUM

VICTORIA & ALBERT MUSEUM

BROMPTON RD.

NATURAL HISTORY MUSEUM

CROMWELL RD. (A-4)

Gloucester Road

South Kensington

PELHAM ST.

THURLOE ST.

CORNWALL GARDENS

LEXHAM GARDENS

STRATFORD RD.

OLD BROMPTON RD.

ONSLOW SQ.

SLOANE AV.

CALE ST.

Earl's Court

EARL'S COURT

BROMPTON RD.

SOUTH KENSINGTON

KING'S RD.

CHELSEA

FINSBOROUGH

REDCLIFFE

FULHAM RD.

1/2 Kilometer

1/2 Mile

the 273-foot bell tower for a view of the glassy office blocks of Victoria Station.

Cost and Hours: Free entry, £6 for the lift; church—daily 7:00-19:00; tower—daily 9:30-17:00, Sat-Sun until 18:00; 5-minute walk from bus terminus in front of Victoria Station, just off Victoria Street at 42 Francis Street, Tube: Victoria, www.westminstercathedral.org.uk.

SIGHTS

▲National Army Museum

This museum tells the story of the British army from 1415 through the Bosnian conflict and Iraq, and how it influences today's society. The five well-signed galleries are neatly arranged by theme—"Army," "Battle," "Soldier," "Society," and "Insight"—with plenty of interactive exhibits for kids. History buffs appreciate the carefully displayed artifacts, from 17th-century uniforms to Wellington's battle cloak. Other highlights of the collection include the skeleton of Napoleon's horse, Lawrence of Arabia's silk robe, and Burberry's signature trench coat (originally designed for WWI soldiers).

Cost and Hours: Free, £5 suggested donation; Wed-Sun 10:00-17:30, closed Mon-Tue; Royal Hospital Road, Chelsea, Tube: 10-minute walk from Sloane Square, exit the station and head south on Lower Sloane Street, turn right on Royal Hospital Road, the museum is two long blocks ahead on the left, +44 20 7730 0717, www.nam.ac.uk.

HYDE PARK AND NEARBY

A number of worthwhile sights border this grand park, from Apsley House on the east to Kensington Palace on the west.

▲Apsley House (Wellington Museum)

Having beaten Napoleon at Waterloo, Arthur Wellesley, the First Duke of Wellington, was once the most famous man in Europe.

He was given a huge fortune, with which he purchased London's ultimate address, Number One London. His refurbished mansion offers a nice interior, a handful of world-class paintings, and a glimpse at the life of the great soldier and two-time prime minister. Those who know something about Wellington ahead of time will appreciate the place much more than those who don't, as there's scarce biographical background. The place is well described by the included audioguide, which has sound bites from the current Duke of Wellington (who still lives at Apsley).

Cost and Hours: £12.50, Wed-Sun 11:00-17:00, closed Mon-Tue, shorter hours Nov-March, open only Sat-Sun in Jan-March, 20 yards from Hyde Park Corner Tube station, +44 20 7499 5676 or +44 370 333 1181, www.english-heritage.org.uk.

Visiting the House: An 11-foot-tall marble statue of Napoleon, clad only in a fig leaf, greets you. Napoleon commissioned the sculptor Canova to make it for him but didn't like it, and after Napoleon's defeat, Wellington acquired it as a war trophy. It's one of several images of his former foe that Wellington acquired for his home. The two great men were polar opposites—Napoleon the daring general and champion of revolution, Wellington the play-it-safe strategist and conservative politician—but they're forever linked in history.

The core of the collection is a dozen first-floor rooms decorated with fancy wallpaper, chandeliers, a few pieces of furniture, and wall-to-wall paintings from Wellington's collection. You'll see fancy dinnerware and precious objects given to the Irish-born general by the crowned heads of Europe, who were eternally grateful to him for saving their necks from the guillotine. The highlight is the large ballroom, the Waterloo Gallery, decorated with Anthony van Dyck's *Charles I on Horseback* (over the main fireplace), Diego Velázquez's earthy *Water-Seller of Seville* (to the left of Van Dyck), and Jan Steen's playful *Dissolute Household* (to the right). Just outside the door, in the Portico Room, is a large portrait of the Duke of Wellington by Francisco Goya—the original subject is said to have been Napoleon's brother, but when Wellington prevailed Goya deftly adjusted the face.

Downstairs is a small gallery of Wellington memorabilia, including a pair of Wellington boots, which the duke popularized—Brits today still call rubber boots "wellies."

Nearby: Hyde Park's pleasant rose garden is picnic-friendly. **Wellington Arch,** which stands just across the street, is open to the public but not worth the charge (lousy views and boring exhibits).

▲Hyde Park and Speakers' Corner

London's "Central Park," originally Henry VIII's hunting grounds, has more than 600 acres of lush greenery, Santander Cycles rental stations, the huge man-made Serpentine Lake (with rental boats and a lakeside swimming pool), the royal Kensington Palace (described next), and the ornate Neo-Gothic Albert Memorial across from the Royal Albert Hall (for more about the

park, see www.royalparks.org.uk/parks/hyde-park). The western half of the park is known as Kensington Gardens. The park is huge—study a Tube map to choose the stop nearest to your destination.

On Sundays, from just after noon until early evening, **Speakers' Corner** offers soapbox oratory at its best (northeast corner of the park, Tube: Marble Arch). Characters climb their stepladders, wave their flags, pound emphatically on their sandwich boards, and share what they are convinced is their wisdom. Regulars have resident hecklers who know their lines and are always ready with a verbal jab or barb. "The grass roots of democracy" is actually a holdover from when the gallows stood here and the criminal was allowed to say just about anything he wanted to before he swung. I dare you to raise your voice and gather a crowd—it's easy to do.

The **Princess Diana Memorial Fountain** honors the "People's Princess," who once lived in nearby Kensington Palace. The low-key circular stream, great for cooling off your feet on a hot day, is in the south-central part of the park, near the Albert Memorial and Serpentine Gallery (Tube: Knightsbridge). A similarly named but different sight, the **Diana, Princess of Wales Memorial Playground,** in the park's northwest corner, is loads of fun for kids (Tube: Queensway).

Kensington Palace

For nearly 150 years (1689-1837), Kensington—sitting primly on its pleasant parkside grounds—was the royal residence. Queen Vic-

toria, who was born and grew up here, moved to Buckingham Palace when she took the crown at age 18, and that's where monarchs have lived ever since. But lesser royals continued to bunk at Kensington: Princess Diana lived here both during and after her marriage to Prince Charles (1981-1997). More recently,

Will and Kate moved in. However—as many disappointed visitors discover—none of these more recent apartments are open to the public. Instead, a visit here includes some historic state rooms (including the ones where Victoria spent her childhood), as well as changing temporary exhibits—some better than others. While there's lots of history here, it's not very well told, and this sight is best appreciated by royalists and completists; London has other palaces that are far more interesting.

Cost and Hours: £16, daily 10:00-18:00, Nov-Feb until 16:00, last entry one hour before closing, a long 10-minute stroll through Kensington Gardens from either High Street Kensington or Queensway Tube stations, +44 844 482 7788, www.hrp.org.uk.

Visiting the Palace: Entering through the ground floor, you'll proceed upstairs into the **Victoria: A Royal Childhood** exhibit. This begins by showing off some sparkling, diamond-encrusted tiaras (plus an emerald-encrusted one, designed by Prince Albert; and one that could be "reversed" to be worn as a necklace), then proceeds through the beautifully decorated rooms where Victoria spent her childhood—including the very place she was born. You'll see some of her playthings, pages from her diary, letters between royals, loads of portraits, and so on. While this is all mildly charming, it's a pity to think that—in this city that was so shaped by Victoria—London's first and only museum that's truly *about* Victoria covers only the first 18 years of her life, and none of her many achievements. (For more on Victoria's complete life and times, see the sidebar in the Britain: Past & Present chapter.)

Circle back downstairs, then continue up to the **King's State Apartments** (from the time of George II), followed by the **Queen's State Apartments** (from Queen Mary II and Queen Anne)—each reflecting the era and personality of the monarch who lived there.

Outside: Garden enthusiasts enjoy popping into the secluded Sunken Garden, 50 yards from the exit. A statue of Princess Diana was unveiled here in 2021, on what would have been her 60th birthday. If it's open, consider afternoon tea at the nearby Orangery (see page 444), built as a greenhouse for Queen Anne in 1704.

▲▲▲Victoria and Albert Museum

The world's top collection of decorative arts encompasses 2,000 years of art and design (ceramics, stained glass, fine furniture, clothing, jewelry, carpets, and more), displaying a surprisingly interesting and diverse assortment of crafts from the West, as well as Asian and Islamic cultures. There's much to see, including Raphael's tapestry cartoons, Leonardo da Vinci's notebooks, the huge Islamic Ardabil Carpet (4,914 knots in every 10 square centimeters), a cast of Trajan's Column that depicts the emperor's conquests, and pop culture memorabilia, including the jumpsuit Mick Jagger wore for the Rolling Stones' 1972 world tour.

Cost and Hours: Free, £5 donation requested, fee for some special exhibits, consider prebooking online to save time in line, daily 10:00-17:45, may stay open Fri until 22:00, free tours daily, on Cromwell Road in South Kensington, Tube: South Kensington, from the Tube station a long tunnel leads directly to museum, +44 20 7942 2000, www.vam.ac.uk.

📖 See the Victoria and Albert Museum Tour chapter.

▲▲Natural History Museum

Across the street from the Victoria and Albert, this mammoth museum is housed in a giant and wonderful Victorian, Neo-Romanesque building. It was built in the 1870s specifically for the huge collection (50 million specimens). Exhibits are wonderfully explained, with lots of creative, interactive displays. It covers everything from life ("creepy crawlies," human biology, our place in evolution, and awe-inspiring dinosaurs) to earth science (meteors, volcanoes, and earthquakes).

Cost and Hours: Free, £5 donation requested, fee for special exhibits, consider prebooking online to save time in line, daily 10:00-18:00, last entry one hour before closing, helpful £1 map, long tunnel leads directly from South Kensington Tube station to museum (follow signs), +44 20 7942 5000, exhibit info and reservations +44 20 7942 5011, www.nhm.ac.uk. Free visitor app available via the "Visit" section of the website.

Visiting the Museum: Enter by the main Cromwell Road entrance (in the middle of the long building), which is easiest for getting oriented. You step into Hintze Hall, with a big *Diplodocus* skeleton; midway up the far staircase, Charles Darwin sits as if upon a throne overseeing it all. Review the "What's on Today" board for special events and tours, and note which sections are closed. For more information, ask one of the many helpful guards scattered throughout the museum.

The building is organized into several color-coded "zones." The Blue Zone (to the left) has the biggest animals and biggest crowds: dinosaurs, a life-size blue whale model, and other stuffed-and-mounted mammals.

Straight ahead, up the stairs behind Darwin, is the Cadogan Gallery Treasures, housing a rotating display of the museum's greatest hits, including a dodo skeleton, moon rock, stuffed specimen of the extinct great auk, fossil of the earliest known bird *(Archaeopteryx)*, and the *Iguanodon* tooth that kicked off human awareness of dinosaurs.

To the right are the Red and Green zones, with a dramatic escalator ride up to experience an earthquake, and rooms tracing the evolution of the earth and its creatures. Don't miss a room called "The Vault" that contains rare and precious stones, including a meteorite from Mars, the Aurora Pyramid of Hope—displaying 296 diamonds showing their full range of natural colors—and this description of some microscopic cosmic diamonds: "These are the oldest things you will ever see."

Keep exploring. The Orange Zone (far left) lets you see today's scientists at work in their labs.

Even with limited time to spend here, pop in, if only for the dinosaur collection—including a realistic animatronic *T. rex*—and to hear English children exclaim, "Oh, my goodness!"

▲Science Museum

Next door to the Natural History Museum, this sprawling wonderland for curious minds is kid-perfect, with themes such as measuring time, exploring space, climate change, the evolution of modern medicine, and the Information Age. It offers hands-on fun, with trendy technology exhibits, a state-of-the-art IMAX theater (shows—£12, £10 for kids, family ticket available), the Garden—a cool play area for children up to age seven, plus several other pay-to-enter attractions, including Wonderlab kids area (£11, £9 for kids). Look for the family "What's On" brochure and ask about tours and demonstrations at the info desk.

Cost and Hours: Free, £5 donation requested, consider pre-booking online to save time in line, daily 10:00-18:00, may close Mon-Tue in winter, last entry 45 minutes before closing, Exhibition Road, Tube: South Kensington, +44 333 241 4000, www.sciencemuseum.org.uk.

Greater London

EAST OF LONDON
▲▲Greenwich

This borough of London is an easy, affordable boat trip or DLR (Docklands Light Railway) journey from downtown. Along with majestic, picnic-perfect parks are the stately trappings of Britain's proud nautical heritage (the restored *Cutty Sark* clipper, the over-the-top-ornate retirement home for sailors at the **Old Royal Naval College,** and the comprehensive **National Maritime Museum**). It's also home to the **Royal Observatory Greenwich,** with a fine museum on how Greenwich Mean Time came to be and a chance to straddle the Eastern and Western hemispheres at the prime meridian. Boasting several top-notch museums (including some free ones), Greenwich is worth considering and easy to combine with a look at the Docklands (described on page 112).

📖 See the Greenwich Tour chapter.

Queen Elizabeth Olympic Park

London refashioned this park—the biggest new park to open in the city in a century—from the site of the 2012 Olympic Games. You'll find miles of parkland trails and waterways, kids' play areas, an array of sporting venues (London Aquatics Centre, Lee Valley VeloPark, Copper Box Arena), quirky sculpture, and places to eat. The park is huge—bigger than Hyde Park/Kensington Gardens. It's also quite beautiful, laced with canals and tributaries of the Lea River.

Cost and Hours: Free and always open, +44 800 0722 110, www.queenelizabetholympicpark.co.uk.

SIGHTS

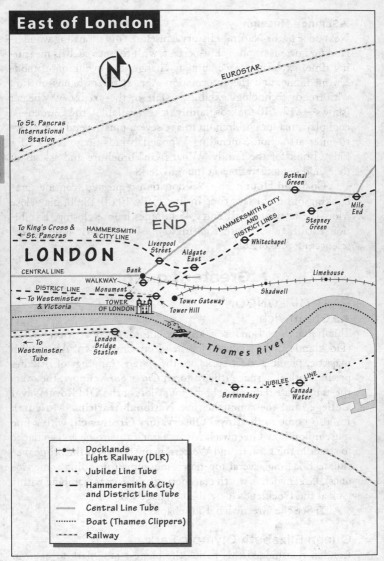

East of London

EUROSTAR

To St. Pancras International Station

To King's Cross & St. Pancras

HAMMERSMITH & CITY LINE

LONDON

CENTRAL LINE

DISTRICT LINE

To Westminster & Victoria

WALKWAY

Monument

Bank

EAST END

Liverpool Street

Aldgate East

Tower Gateway

Tower Hill

TOWER OF LONDON

To Westminster Tube

London Bridge Station

Thames River

HAMMERSMITH AND DISTRICT LINES

Bethnal Green

Stepney Green

Mile End

Whitechapel

Shadwell

Limehouse

Bermondsey

Canada Water

JUBILEE LINE

Docklands Light Railway (DLR)

Jubilee Line Tube

Hammersmith & City and District Line Tube

Central Line Tube

Boat (Thames Clippers)

Railway

Getting There: From central London by Tube, it's a 30-minute ride to the Stratford station. Follow exits toward Queen Elizabeth Olympic Park and Westfield Stratford City. Outside the Tube exit, take another escalator up to "The Street" (which is actually the outdoor part of the Westfield shopping center), bear left at the digital fountain past the line of restaurants, cross the street at The Cow pub, and the park is directly ahead of you, across the road.

Visiting the Park: The best overview of the park is along a 500-yard-long berm called the **Greenway,** which sits at the park's

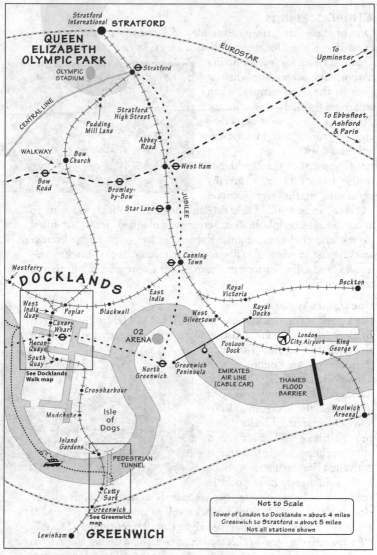

Not to Scale
Tower of London to Docklands = about 4 miles
Greenwich to Stratford = about 5 miles
Not all stations shown

southern perimeter, or at the **Knight's Bridge** (toward the park's northern edge), looking south back over the buildings. The easiest landmark to head for is the **View Tube**, just outside the park—a covered shelter with a free lookout tower, café, WC, and maps. There's also the hard-to-miss red, 350-foot viewing tower called the **Orbit**, which was designed as an Eiffel-Tower-like landmark and has been compared to a giant hookah. The Orbit also hosts the world's longest, tallest, and transparent tunnel slide (£17 includes Orbit entrance, plus one ride).

▲The Docklands

One of the most striking examples of London's recent eastward expansion is the Docklands. Nestled around a hairpin bend in the Thames, this area was London's harbor and warehouse district back in the 19th century, when Britannia ruled the waves. Today, glittering new skyscrapers rise from those historic canals and docks.

The heart of the Docklands is the Isle of Dogs, a marshy peninsula in the river's curve. But don't expect Jolly Olde England here. The Docklands is more about businesspeople in suits, creatively planned parks, art-filled plazas, and chain restaurants. Even so, traces of its rugged dock-worker past survive. You'll see canals, former docks, brick warehouses, and a fine history museum. Most impressive of all, there's not a tourist in sight.

Docklands Walk

For a peek at the Docklands, ride the DLR to Heron Quays (from Bank Station in downtown London or from Greenwich); you can also ride the Jubilee Tube line from downtown London to Canary Wharf. This 30-minute walk ends at the only real sight in the area, the Museum of London Docklands. Ideally, time your visit here for late afternoon on a weekday, when the area is enlivened by business workers headed for happy hour (to fit in

the museum before closing, begin the walk a couple of hours before closing time). The Docklands works well as an add-on at the end of a day in Greenwich—you'll pass right through on the way home.

• *Exit the Heron Quays DLR station, turn right, then angle left across the street to the plaza in front of the arched Canary Wharf Tube station.*

❶ **Canada Square:** You're surrounded by soaring skyscrapers, glitzy shopping malls, lively cafés, and hurried businesspeople. The tallest building—immediately to your left—is Canary Wharf Tower, with its pyramid-shaped cap peaking at 800 feet. This was briefly the tallest building in Europe, though now it just seems quaint compared to the newer and taller London skyscrapers.

Flash back 200 years to this area's heyday as a shipping harbor. This eastern edge of the city was notorious for its smelly industries

Docklands Walk

To Central London

MUSEUM OF LONDON DOCKLANDS

WALK ENDS **5**

MARRIOTT

Poplar

To Stratford (Olympic Park) & London City Airport

BILLINGSGATE FISH MARKET

West India Quay

4 WEST INDIA DOCKS

CANARY WHARF TOWER

Westferry Circus

WEST INDIA AVE.

Cabot Square

Canary Wharf DLR

THAMES CLIPPERS BOAT DOCK

To London

STAIRS

To Greenwich

FOOTBRIDGE

MIDDLE DOCK

3

Canary Wharf Tube (Jubilee Line)

1

2 Jubilee Place Park

WALK BEGINS

Heron Quays

Thames River

WESTFERRY RD.

MARSH WALL

SOUTH DOCK

HILTON

South Quay Plaza

South Quay

To Greenwich

100 Meters

100 Yards

1 Canada Square
2 Jubilee Place Park
3 Mackenzie Walk
4 West India Quay
5 Museum of London Docklands

Docklands Light Railway (DLR)

SIGHTS

(bone boiling, gluemaking, chemical works)—conveniently downwind from the rest of London. But by the late 1700s, 13,000 ships a year were loaded and unloaded in central London, congesting the Thames. So in 1802, the world's largest-of-its-kind harbor was built in the Docklands, organizing shipping for the capital of the empire upon which the sun never set. "Canary Wharf"—the name for the whole neighborhood—is a reminder of London's trading connection with distant ports such as the Canary Islands, off the western coast of Africa.

Where sailors once drank grog while stevedores unloaded cargo, today thousands of office workers (the stevedores of the Information Age) populate a forest of skyscrapers.

Take the little path to the right of the Tube entrance and go for a quick stroll in **2 Jubilee Place Park:** Opened in 2002 on the 50th anniversary (Golden Jubilee) of Queen Elizabeth's rule, this delightful little park was designed with a futuristic people-friendliness: plenty of green spaces, waterways, public art, and good public-transit service. The entire ensemble sits upon one of three underground shopping malls.

• *Back on Canada Square, walk a few steps toward Canary Wharf Tower, then turn left along the canalside promenade called...*

❸ **Mackenzie Walk:** Stroll along the canal (called Middle Dock), a surviving remnant of the many artificial harbors and canals from the Docklands' 19th-century shipping heyday. The land here on the Isle of Dogs was marshy, flooded by the Thames, and unsuitable for farming or habitation. But it was perfect for accommodating large seagoing vessels. Beginning around 1800, industrious Londoners channeled the water into canals and lined them with docks. Picture the lively scene: burly men offloading goods from anchored ships, while an army of poor laborers bustled between storage warehouses, dry docks for ship repair, and various shipbuilding enterprises. Each dock specialized in a particular product—spices, coal, and, apparently, Mackenzies.

• *Keep going along the canalside promenade, passing under the DLR bridge. When you reach the arched footbridge, turn right and hike up Cubitt Steps, cut through the middle of Cabot Square (with a classic view of Docklands skyscrapers, plus some cool modern sculptures), and continue straight out the other side. Steps lead down to a footbridge that crosses another canal to the...*

❹ **West India Quay:** This row of 19th-century brown-brick warehouses typifies today's Docklands. Standing side by side are elements of the old Docklands (the warehouses, the canal, a few barges) and the new (the esplanade of umbrella-shaded restaurants, the modern Marriott). Back in the 19th century, the water lapped up right against those buildings. You can still see the rustic gates to the lofts. Imagine heavily laden cargo boats off-loading there.

The big gray cranes-on-tracks are a reminder of the one-two punch that spelled the end of the Docklands: During World War II, Hitler's Blitz targeted this major industrial asset with more than 2,000 bombs. The Docklands struggled for several decades and never regained its status as a port. With the advent of container shipping in the 1960s, London's shipping industry moved farther east, to deep-water docks. The old Docklands became a derelict and dangerous wasteland. Until a generation ago, local surveys ranked it as one of the least desirable places to call home. It was said that for every Tube stop you lived east of central London, your life expectancy dropped one year.

But all this misfortune paid off in the 1980s, when investors realized that the Docklands was ripe for redevelopment...the perfect place to host a new and vibrant economic center. Over the past few decades, Britain's new Information Age industries—banking, finance, publishing, and media—have set up shop here.

For more of the story of the Docklands, visit the ❺ **Museum of London Docklands,** in the left part of the row of warehouses (described below).

Returning to Central London: Retrace your steps to the Canary Wharf **Tube** station for the Jubilee line, or head to the other end of the West India Quay to catch the **DLR** (stop: West India Quay) toward Bank, where you can transfer to the Tube's Central line or (via underground tunnels) to the Monument stop on the Circle and District lines. To catch a **boat** (slower but very scenic), return to Cabot Square, turn right, and walk five minutes along West India Avenue to the round Westferry Circus park; the Thames Clippers dock is just beyond (£8.70 one-way, boats leave every 20-30 minutes, 10- to 30-minute trip to major London docks). Or, if you fancy a peek at **Queen Elizabeth Olympic Park** or want to continue to **Greenwich,** DLR trains go in each direction from West India Quay.

Museum of London Docklands

This modern and interesting museum, which fills an old sugar warehouse, gives the Docklands historic context. In telling the story of the world's leading 19th-century port, it also conveys the story of London. It has a nice café, a hip bar, and a great kids' play area. Ride the elevator up to the third floor, then work your way down, going on a 300-year walk through the story of commerce on the Thames.

Cost and Hours: Free, £5 suggested donation, daily 10:00-17:00, +44 20 7001 9844, www.museumoflondon.org.uk/docklands.

Visiting the Museum: Start on the **third floor,** with "No. 1 Warehouse"—a space that shows off the original purpose of this building. In old London, back when London's port was at London Bridge, the Docklands was a barely inhabited swamp far to the east. Exhibits show how the Docklands rapidly developed in the 1800s, including a history of the building itself, the tools and techniques used for weighing and storing goods, and even a mummified Tom and Jerry. Next, a thought-provoking section traces the ramifications of transatlantic trade, sugar, and slavery.

The **second floor** explores London's growth after 1800—its population was more than one million by 1810. Kids enjoy strolling through a gritty reconstruction of "Sailortown," listening to the salty voices of those who lived and worked in quarters like this. A painted *Stevedores* banner from the 1889 dock strike is a reminder that while the Industrial Revolution first exploited workers, it later empowered them to rise up. During World War II, the Docklands was a prime target for Nazi bombers bent on crippling British shipping. Find the claustrophobic, dome-shaped "consul shelter," where dockworkers could take cover in case of attack. There's also a re-creation of the top-secret fuel pipeline that was laid under the English Channel after D-Day to supply the Allies on the Continent. The final section, "New Port, New City," traces the Docklands' post-WWII rebuilding.

When you're finished, step out into today's Docklands and take in this combination of old and new.

WEST OF LONDON
▲▲Kew Gardens

For a fine riverside park and a palatial greenhouse jungle to swing through, take the Tube or the boat to every botanist's favorite escape, Kew Gardens. While to most visi-tors the Royal Botanic Gardens of Kew are simply a delightful opportunity to wander among 50,000 different types of plants, to the hardworking organization that runs them, the gardens are a way to promote the understanding and preservation of the botanical diversity of our planet.

Cost and Hours: £19.50, kids 4-15-£5, kids under 4—free; Mon-Thu 10:00-19:00, Fri-Sun until 20:00, closes earlier Sept-March—check schedule online, glasshouses close at 17:30 in high season—earlier off-season; free one-hour orientation tours daily at 11:00 and 13:30, plus seasonal tours at 12:30; +44 20 8332 5655, www.kew.org.

Getting There: Take the Tube to Kew Gardens. From the station, pass through the tunnel under the tracks, which deposits you in a little community of plant-and-herb shops, a two-block walk straight ahead to Victoria Gate (the main garden entrance). Boats also run to Kew Gardens from Westminster Pier (April-Oct; see page 47).

Visiting the Gardens: Pick up a map brochure and check at the gate for a monthly listing of the best blooms. Garden lovers could spend days exploring Kew's 300 acres. To get your bearings, you could hop on the **tourist tram,** which departs from the Victoria Gate for a guided

40-minute loop around the grounds (adults-£6.50, kids-£2.50); while billed as "hop-on, hop-off," the tram is often crowded and the frequency is sparse (hourly, maybe more at peak times), so it works best to stay on for the full ride.

For a quick visit, skip the tram and spend a fragrant hour wandering through three buildings in the eastern part of the gardens, near the Victoria Gate: The **Palm House** is a hot and humid Victorian world of iron, glass, and tropical plants that was built in 1844. As you enter, look right for the spiral staircase that leads up to a walkway around the top of the space, offering views over the palm fronds. Just beyond is a **Waterlily House** that Monet would swim for (closed in winter). Nearby is the **Princess of Wales Conservatory,** a meandering modern greenhouse with many different climate zones growing countless cacti, bug-munching carnivorous plants, and more—look for the jagged, modern roofline (this sometimes houses temporary exhibits requiring a separate ticket). Also in this zone, kids enjoy the **Children's Garden.**

With more time, meander to the western end of the complex. The **Temperate House** is home to deciduous plants—less exotic for London than the Palm House, but still pleasant. Here too is the **Treetop Walkway,** a 200-yard-long scenic steel walkway that puts you high in the canopy 60 feet above the ground. And nearby—close to the Lion Gate—is the **Great Pagoda,** rising high above the treetops (closed in winter).

Eating: Kew Gardens has two large self-service cafeterias onsite. Near the Palm House in the eastern part of the park is the fine **$$ Orangery,** with lots of seating both inside and out. Farther west, near the Temperate House, is the **$$ Pavilion,** a modern, boxy building with a Costa Rican menu.

Nearby: To complete your Kew Gardens outing, hop on bus #65 (stops just outside the Victoria and Lion Gates) just a few minutes to the adjacent town of **Richmond.** This pleasant, fun-to-explore bedroom community has an enormous village green at its center (and it's the end station for the District line—making for an easy return to central London). Richmond will especially appeal to fans of the Apple TV+ series *Ted Lasso*: You can see the narrow street where Ted lives (called Paved Court in real life) and the exterior of his "local," The Crown and Anchor (The Princes Head in real life; the interiors are filmed in a studio).

▲▲Hampton Court Palace

Fifteen miles up the Thames from downtown, the 500-year-old palace of Henry VIII, William and Mary, and other royals is worth ▲▲▲ for palace aficionados. If the Tower of London is about England's royal origins, and Buckingham Palace and Windsor are about the modern royals, then Hampton Court Palace is about

Combining Hampton Court Palace with Kew Gardens or Windsor

Because Hampton Court Palace, Kew Gardens, and Windsor Palace are in the same general direction, it can be efficient to pair a Hampton Court Palace visit with the other sights. For details on visiting Windsor, see the Day Trips chapter.

Windsor/Hampton: Take a morning train to Windsor, spring for a taxi to Hampton Court Palace (£30-40, 30-45 minutes), then take the train back to London. (In summer, there may be a shuttle bus connecting the two palaces for about £10—ask at the Windsor TI.)

Hampton/Kew Gardens: Take the train from London Waterloo to Hampton Court Palace, then taxi to Kew Gardens (£20, about 30 minutes). If you're on a tight budget, the transit connection between Hampton Court and Kew is long but doable: Take bus #R68 from Hampton Court Station to the West Park Road stop (about one hour), then walk about a half-mile to the Kew Gardens gate (walk up West Park Road to, then through, the Kew Gardens train station).

Windsor/Hampton/Kew Gardens: This requires smart time management, serious stamina, and a willingness to invest in taxis. Get to Windsor when the castle opens, taxi to Hampton Court Palace, then taxi again to Kew Gardens for a late-after-noon stroll (best on weekends, when Kew is open later).

those who came in the middle. The stately brick-and-stone palace stands overlooking the Thames and includes some fine Tudor halls and Georgian-era rooms, all made engaging by a sharp, well-produced, included audioguide. The sculpted gardens out back are the cherry on top. As it's more time-consuming to visit than sights within London proper, you'd be forgiven for skipping the trip. But anyone with a healthy interest in the history of English royalty won't regret coming here.

Cost and Hours: £25, may be cheaper online, family ticket available, daily 10:00-18:00, Nov-March until 16:30, last entry one hour before closing—but you'll need 2-3 hours to see the place; café, +44 20 3166 6000, www.hrp.org.uk.

Getting There: From London's Waterloo Station, take a South West train. The train will drop you on the far side of the river from the palace—just walk across the bridge (2/hour, 35 minutes). Consider arriving at or departing from the palace by boat (connections with London's Westminster Pier, see page 47); it's a relaxing and scenic three- to four-hour cruise past two locks and a fun new/old riverside mix.

Background: Hampton Court was originally the palace of Henry VIII's minister and right-hand-man, Cardinal Thomas

Wolsey. When Wolsey realized Henry VIII was experiencing a little palace envy, he gave the mansion to his king...clever guy. The Tudor palace was also home to Elizabeth I and Charles I. Later, when William and Mary moved in, they renovated about one-third of the palace (with help from Christopher Wren).

Visiting the Palace: From the ticket office, take the long walkway to the palace entrance. The hedge maze, "Magic Garden" children's area, and the big **$$ Tiltyard Café** are down a side path to the left just before the main gate.

Get oriented at the **Base Court.** The heart of the Tudor palace, this courtyard is prickly with chimneys (a major status symbol indicating many fireplaces). The fountain is a replica of one that Henry VIII—famous for his decadent parties—built to flow with wine. The clock tower straight ahead is a helpful landmark.

Pick up your audioguide just to the left of the clock tower. Use the free map to find your way to the audioguide tour routes. Most of the audioguide routes begin either from this court, from the adjoining **Clock Court** (to find it, go under the clock tower), or from the grassy **Fountain Court,** at the far end of the complex. You'll find yourself spinning your way around the palace, always winding up back in one of the three main courtyards. Red-vested docents throughout the complex are happy to answer questions.

Of the many choices, I'd consider these, in roughly this order of priority:

Henry VIII's Apartments: Begin with a bang by entering under the clock tower, to the left. Step into the breathtaking Great Hall, with its marvelous hammerbeam ceiling. Henry VIII was famous for (among other things) his rollicking and debauched parties, which filled this hall with unfathomable revelry. (At least, I can't fathom it.) The ceiling was once inlaid

with gold, and you can see six of the ten precious Abraham tapestries that kept this huge room warm and cozy. From here, you'll proceed through more royal rooms en route to Henry VIII's privy chamber. In the green hallway, find the portrait of Henry VIII's family. The adjacent doorway leads to his private balcony, looking down into the stunning Chapel Royal (and displaying a replica of his crown).

Henry VIII's Kitchens: This 16th-century food-production machine could keep 600 schmoozing courtiers well fed. The tour (which begins in the bottom-left corner of the Base Court) walks you through the entire operation, engaging all of your senses—introducing you to characters who worked here, inviting you to pick up and heft kitchen utensils, and embellishing the experience with sound effects and smells. Stepping into the

gargantuan three-room kitchen itself, imagine the place buzzing and smoking with hundreds of food preparers.

At the end of the kitchens, dip into the **Chapel Royal**—which you saw earlier from Henry's balcony—for a closer look at the wood-carved decor and the starry-sky-and-gold-beam ceiling.

Young Henry VIII's Story: This exhibit (enter on the right side of Base Court) challenges your perceptions about the bloated, depraved, brutal old Henry VIII by introducing you to the dashing, athletic, young Henry VIII. The story is told through the eyes of three key figures: Henry himself; his first wife, Catherine of Aragon; and his right-hand man, Thomas Wolsey. The intimate wood-paneled rooms here are less impressive than other parts of the palace, but the historic paintings are cleverly narrated by the audioguide.

William III's Apartments: At the end of the Young Henry VIII section, stairs lead up to these apartments, from about 150 years after Henry's time. William and Mary renovated this part of the palace (partly with the help of Christopher Wren) in the Baroque style of the age: vast halls clad in handsome wood paneling, high domed white ceilings, and magnificent views out to the carefully manicured privy garden they built for

themselves. While grand, these rooms are less intimate and colorful. After all, William and Mary were no Henry VIII. Downstairs, the private apartments are more personal, and include the orangery where William stored his orange and bay trees in the winter.

Rest of the Palace: If you have time or interest, check out the

"**Georgian Story**" apartments (decorated in the post-William-and-Mary age of the Hanoverian kings); the **Cumberland Art Gallery** (with lesser-known works by Rembrandt, Caravaggio, Van Dyck, Gainsborough, Warhol, and others); the **Mantegna Gallery** (nine massive "Triumphs of Caesar" paintings by Italian Renaissance pioneer Andrea Mantegna); and the **Baroque Story** (a 13-minute film about that artistic style).

Before leaving, stroll in the **gardens** (door at far end of grassy Fountain Court). Meticulously pruned hedges line up on geographical axes and fountains gurgle. As you step out into the gardens, don't miss the easy-to-overlook entrance (immediately on the right) to William and Mary's walled privy garden, like a mini-Versailles.

NORTH OF LONDON
Royal Air Force Museum London
This huge aerodrome and airfield contain planes from World War II's Battle of Britain up through the Gulf War. You can climb inside some of the planes, try your luck in a cockpit, and fly with the Red Arrows in a flight simulator.

Cost and Hours: Free, £5 suggested donation, flight simulators—£3-6, daily 10:00-18:00, Nov-Feb until 17:00, café, shop, Grahame Park Way, 30-minute ride from downtown London plus another 15 minutes by foot, Tube: Colindale—top of Northern Line Edgware branch, +44 20 8205 2266, www.rafmuseum.org.uk.

Hampstead Heath
This surprisingly vast expanse of greenery sprawls over a square mile and a quarter at the northern edge of downtown London. It features rolling, scrubby pastures ("heath") as well as tranquil wooded areas. Its most popular viewpoint, Parliament Hill, offers distant views of London's fast-growing skyline. At the northeast corner of the park is a chunk of land owned by English Heri-tage, where a stately palace called Kenwood House overlooks a pasture, pond, and gentle wood; inside is a fine art collection, plus an inviting café (and WCs). Maps posted at each entrance to the park help get you oriented. On a sunny day, the park is crammed with Londoners communing with nature—relieved to escape from their bustling burg. The adjoining village of Hampstead is quaint and cute; a stroll through here is almost as pleasant as the park itself.

Harry Potter's London

Harry Potter's story is set in a magical Britain, and the places mentioned in the books, except London, are fictional, but you can visit many real film locations (note that some are an unmagical disappointment in person). For diehards, here's a sampling.

Harry's story begins in suburban London, in the fictional town of Little Whinging. In *The Sorcerer's Stone* (2001), the gentle giant Hagrid touches down on his flying motorcycle at #4 Privet Drive, where baby Harry is raised by his antimagic aunt and uncle. The scene was shot in **Bracknell** (pop. 50,000, 10 miles west of Heathrow) on a street of generic brick rowhouses called Picket Close.

Later, 10-year-old Harry first realizes his wizard powers when talking with a boa constrictor, filmed at the **London Zoo's Reptile House** in Regent's Park (Tube: Great Portland Street).

Big Ben and **Parliament,** along the Thames, welcome Harry to the modern city inhabited by Muggles (nonmagic folk). London bustles along oblivious to the parallel universe of wizards. Hagrid takes Harry shopping: They enter the glass-roofed **Leadenhall Market** (Tube: Bank) and approach the **storefront** at 42 Bull's Head Passage—the entrance to The Leaky Cauldron pub. The pub's back wall parts, opening onto the magical Diagon Alley, where Harry shops for wands, cauldrons, and wizard textbooks. He pays for them with gold Galleons from goblin-run Gringotts Wizarding Bank, filmed in the marble-floored **Australia House** (Tube: Temple), home of the Australian Embassy.

Harry catches the train to Hogwarts at **King's Cross Station.** (The fanciful exterior shown in the 2002 *Chamber of Secrets* was shot in nearby **St. Pancras International Station.**) Inside the glass-roofed train station, on a **pedestrian sky bridge** over the tracks, Harry heads to platform 9¾, where he and his new buddy Ron magically push their luggage carts through a brick pillar be-

Getting There: Hampstead Heath is just a 20-minute Tube ride from downtown London. The handiest Tube stop is the one called Hampstead (on the convenient Northern line/Edgware branch, which runs north-to-south through London's city center). This stop is in the middle of the charming village of Hampstead, from which it's about a 10-minute walk to the park (turn left out of the station to head one block down Hampstead High Street, then turn left on Flask Walk and follow it until it becomes Well Walk and eventually runs into East Heath Road; the park is in front of

tween the platforms. (For a fun photo-op, head to King's Cross Station's track 9 to find the *Platform 9¾ sign*, the luggage cart that looks like it's disappearing into the wall, and a Harry Potter gift shop.)

A red steam train—the Hogwarts Express—speeds the boys through the (Scottish) countryside to Hogwarts, where Harry will spend the next seven years. The steam engine used in filming is on display at a Platform 9¾ exhibit at the **Harry Potter Warner Bros. Studio Tour.**

In *The Prisoner of Azkaban* (2004), Harry careens through London's lamp-lit streets on a purple three-decker bus (also on display at the Harry Potter Warner Bros. Studio Tour) that dumps him at The Leaky Cauldron pub. In this film, the pub's exterior was shot on rough-looking Stoney Street at the southeast edge of **Borough Market,** by The Market Porter pub, with trains rumbling overhead (Tube: London Bridge).

In *The Order of the Phoenix* (2007), the Order takes to the night sky on broomsticks, zooming down the Thames and over London, passing over plenty of identifiable landmarks, including **Tower Bridge,** the **London Eye, Big Ben,** and **Buckingham Palace.** They arrive at Sirius Black's home at "Twelve Grimmauld Place," filmed at a parklike square called Lincoln's Inn Fields, near Sir John Soane's Museum (Tube: Holborn).

The **Millennium Bridge** is attacked by Death Eaters and collapses into the Thames in the dramatic finale to *The Half-Blood Prince* (2009). For *Order of the Phoenix* and *Deathly Hallows: Part 1* (2010), the real government offices of **Whitehall** serve as exteriors for the Ministry of Magic. Also for *Deathly Hallows,* Harry, Ron, and Hermione fight off disguised Death Eaters in a Muggle café, filmed in the West End's bustling **Piccadilly Circus.** Other London settings, like Diagon Alley, only exist at Warner Bros. Studio in Leavesden (20 miles north of London), where most of the films' interiors were shot.

For a different experience, check out the live production of *Harry Potter and the Cursed Child, Parts One and Two* (see page 472 for details).

you, with Parliament Hill still a ways in and to the right). The station called Hampstead Heath, directly at the southern tip of the park and closer to Parliament Hill, is on the less convenient Overground line; however, bus #24 easily (though slowly) connects Victoria Station and downtown London (including Trafalgar Square) with the Hampstead Heath stop.

Hampstead Heath combines well with a visit to the fun and funky Camden Lock Market (see page 460), which is on both the Northern Tube line and the bus #24 route.

SIGHTS

Highgate Cemetery

Located in the tea-cozy-cute village of Highgate, north of the city, this Victorian cemetery represents a fascinating, offbeat piece of London history. Built as a private cemetery, this was the fashionable place to bury the wealthy dead in the late 1800s. It has themed mausoleums, professional mourners, and several high-profile residents in its East Cemetery, including Karl Marx, George Eliot, and Douglas Adams. The tomb of "Godfather

of Punk" Malcolm McLaren (former manager of the Sex Pistols) is often covered with rotten veggies. The West Cemetery is the final home of such luminaries as George Michael, Bob Hoskins, John Galsworthy, and Lucian Freud. Highgate runs along the eastern edge of Hampstead Heath—making it possible to combine these two in a single day.

Cost and Hours: It's smart to reserve tickets for both East and West Cemeteries online in advance; East Cemetery—£4.50, £8.50 with 75-minute guided tour; older, creepier West Cemetery—£10, £14 with 75-minute tour; all West Cemetery tickets include entrance to East Cemetery; both open daily March-Oct 10:00-17:00, Nov-Feb until 16:00; Tube: Archway on the Northern Line/High Barnet branch, then a 15-minute walk; +44 20 8340 1834, www.highgatecemetery.org.

The Making of Harry Potter: Warner Bros. Studio Tour London

While you can visit several real-life locations in Britain where the Harry Potter movies were filmed (see sidebar on page 122), there's

only one way to see imaginary places like Hogwarts' Great Hall, Diagon Alley, Dumbledore's office, and #4 Privet Drive: Visit the Warner Bros. Studio in Leavesden, where Daniel Radcliffe and company brought the tale of the boy wizard to life.

Attractions include the actual sets used for the films (Hogwarts bridge, Hagrid's hut), several familiar costumes and props (such as the Nimbus 2000, the Sorting Hat, the Sword of Gryffindor, Hagrid's motorcycle, and a Hogwarts Express attraction), video interviews with the actors and filmmakers, and exhibits about how the films' special effects were created.

Your visit starts with an intro film and brief overview by a live guide. Then you're free to wander through large halls with the sets, props, and costumes. You may be impressed by the level of detail the super-enthusiastic designers put into even the simplest of props. The visit culminates with a stroll down Diagon Alley and a room-sized 1:24-scale model of Hogwarts.

Plan Ahead: It's essential to buy a ticket far in advance (entry possible only with reserved time slot). Allow about three hours at the studio, plus nearly three hours to get there and back. This experience will eat up the better part of a day.

Cost and Hours: £50, purchase timed-entry ticket online in advance, kids ages 5 to 15-£40, family ticket available; opening hours flex with season—first tour at 9:00 or 10:00, last tour as early as 14:30 or as late as 18:30, audio/videoguide-£5, café, +44 345 084 0900, www.wbstudiotour.co.uk.

Getting There: Leavesden is about 20 miles northwest of London. Reaching the studio is easy, requiring a **train and shuttle bus** connection. Give yourself at least 90 minutes to get from your central London hotel to the studio for your appointed time. First, take the frequent train from London Euston to Watford Junction (£13-20 round-trip, about 5/hour, 20 minutes). At Watford Junction, exit the station and look left to find the bus stop. Catch the Mullany's Coaches shuttle bus (instantly recognizable by its bright paint job) to the studio tour (2-4/hour, 15 minutes, fare included with studio ticket). Detailed **driving** directions are available on the website.

More direct (and more expensive), Golden Tours runs multiple daily **buses** between three London locations (Victoria Station, Baker Street, or King's Cross) and the studio (price includes round-trip bus and studio entrance: adults-£90, kids-£85, £40 for round-trip bus only; generally leaves London as early as 7:30, then throughout the day until around 16:00, studio tour begins 1.5-2 hours after bus departs, reserve ahead at www.goldentours.com).

WESTMINSTER WALK

From Big Ben to Trafalgar Square

Just about every visitor to London strolls along historic Whitehall from Big Ben to Trafalgar Square. This easy nine-stop walk gives meaning to that touristy ramble. Under London's modern traffic and big-city bustle lie 2,000 fascinating years of history. You'll get a whirlwind tour as well as a practical orientation to London.

Orientation

Length of This Walk: Allow one hour for a leisurely walk, and add more time if you tour the Churchill War Rooms (1-2 hours) and the Banqueting House (30-60 minutes). Other nearby sights include the Houses of Parliament, Westminster Abbey, National Gallery, National Portrait Gallery, and St. Martin-in-the-Fields.

Getting There: Take the Tube to Westminster, then take the Westminster Pier exit. The walk ends at Trafalgar Square (nearest Tube stop: Charing Cross).

Churchill War Rooms: £29, buy ticket in advance online; daily 9:30-18:00, may stay open later in summer, last entry one hour before closing.

Banqueting House: £7, includes audioguide, daily 10:00-17:00, may close for government functions—though it's always open at least until 13:00.

Horse Guards: It's free to watch the Horse Guards change at Horse Guards Parade on Whitehall (mounted sentries change at the top of every hour, courtyard guards change Mon-Sat at 11:00, Sun at 10:00, dismounting ceremony daily at 16:00, get the latest at www.changing-guard.com).

Tours: ∩ Download my free Westminster Walk audio tour.

Services: WCs along this walk are at Westminster Pier (pay), in

Supreme Court (free), at the intersection of Bridge Street and Whitehall (underground, pay), and at Trafalgar Square (free, in square, at National Gallery, and downstairs at St. Martin-in-the-Fields).

Eateries: See page 428 for recommendations near Trafalgar Square, and page 145 for places near Westminster Abbey.

The Walk Begins

• *Start halfway across Westminster Bridge.*

❶ Westminster Bridge
Views of Big Ben and Parliament

• *First look upstream, toward the Parliament.*

Ding dong ding dong. Dong ding ding dong. Yes, indeed, you are in London. **Big Ben** is ac-tually "not the clock, not the tower, but the bell that tolls the hour." However, since the 13-ton bell is not visible, everyone just calls the whole works Big Ben. Named for a fat bureaucrat, Ben is scarcely older than my great-grandmother, but it has quickly become the city's symbol. The tower—officially named the "Elizabeth Tower" in honor of Queen Elizabeth II's Diamond Jubilee—is 315 feet high. The clockfaces are 23 feet across, and the 13-foot-long minute hand sweeps the length of your body every five minutes. For fun, call home from near Big Ben at about three minutes before the hour to let your loved one hear the bell ring. Or, if you're a real enthusiast, ask about tours that climb up inside the tower to see the clockworks and view (see page 159).

Big Ben hangs out in the north tower of the Houses of Parliament (still known to Brits as the "Palace of Westminster"), which stretches along the Thames. Britain is ruled from this long building, which for five centuries was the home of kings and queens. Then, as democracy was foisted on tyrants, a parliament of nobles was allowed to meet in some of the rooms. Soon, commoners were elected to office, the neighborhood was shot, and the royalty moved to Buckingham Palace. While most of the current building looks medieval with its prickly flamboyant spires, it was actually reconstructed in the "Neo-Gothic" style after an 1834 fire destroyed the palace (which itself had been rebuilt following a fire in 1512).

Today, the House of Commons meets in one end of the building. The House of Lords debates and advises in the other end of this 1,000-room complex, providing a tempering effect on extreme governmental changes. The two houses are very much separate: Notice the riverside tea terraces with the color-coded awnings—royal red for Lords, common green for commoners. Alluding to the traditional leanings of the two chambers, locals say, "Green for go...red for stop" (for tips on visiting the Houses of Parliament, see page 157). The modern Portcullis Building (with the black tube-like chimneys), across Bridge Street from Big Ben, holds offices for many of the 650 members of the House of Commons. They commute to the Houses of Parliament by way of an underground passage.

Looking south, in the distance beyond the Houses of Parliament, you'll see the huge Vauxhall district—redeveloped and thriving today after being a WWII bomb-site wasteland until about 1990. It's also home to the headquarters of MI6 (the local CIA) where James Bond would check in when in London. Across the river from the Houses of Parliament is St. Thomas Hospital. Three of its five brown-and-cream buildings survived World War II. The two bombed sections were replaced with the hospital's towering new wing.

• *Now look north (downstream).*

Views of the London Eye, The City, and the Thames

Built in 2000 to celebrate the millennium, the London Eye—originally nicknamed "the London Eyesore," but now generally appreciated by locals—is a giant Ferris wheel standing 443 feet tall. It slowly spins 32 capsules, each filled with a maximum of 28 visitors, up to London's best viewpoint (with up to 40 miles' visibility on a rare clear day). Aside from Big Ben, Parliament, St. Paul's Cathedral (not visible from here), and the wheel itself, central London's skyline is not overwhelming; it's a city that wows from within.

Next to the wheel sprawls the huge former County Hall building, now a hotel and tourist complex (with the Shrek's Adventure ride and the London Dungeon). The London Eye marks the start of the Jubilee Walkway, a pleasant one-hour riverside promenade along the South Bank of the Thames, through London's vibrant, gentrified arts-and-cultural zone. Along the way, you have views across the river of St. Paul's stately dome and the financial district, called The City.

London's history is tied to the **Thames,** the 210-mile river

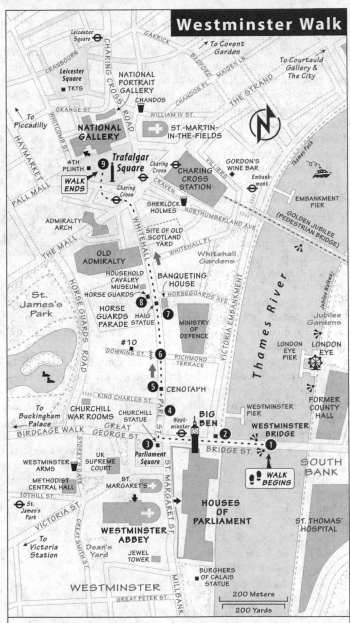

Westminster Walk

Leicester Square

To Covent Garden

To Courtauld Gallery & The City

CRANBOURN

GARRICK

BEDFORD

MAIDEN LN.

Leicester Square

■ TKTS

CHARING CROSS ROAD

NATIONAL PORTRAIT GALLERY

CHANDOS

CHANDOS PL.

THE STRAND

WHITCOMB ST.

ORANGE ST.

WILLIAM IV ST.

To Piccadilly

NATIONAL GALLERY

ST.-MARTIN-IN-THE-FIELDS

VILLIERS

GORDON'S WINE BAR

Thames Path

HAYMARKET

4TH PLINTH

Trafalgar Square

Charing Cross

CHARING CROSS STATION

Embankment

9

WALK ENDS

CRAVEN

EMBANKMENT PIER

PALL MALL

Charing Cross

NORTHUMBERLAND AVE.

GOLDEN JUBILEE (PEDESTRIAN BRIDGE)

SHERLOCK HOLMES

ADMIRALTY ARCH

THE MALL

WHITEHALL

SITE OF OLD SCOTLAND YARD

WHITEHALL PL.

Whitehall Gardens

OLD ADMIRALTY

HOUSEHOLD CAVALRY MUSEUM

Horse Guards

BANQUETING HOUSE

HORSEGUARDS AVE.

Jubilee Walkway

St. James's Park

HORSE GUARDS ROAD

8

HORSE GUARDS PARADE

HAIG STATUE

7

MINISTRY OF DEFENCE

Jubilee Gardens

Thames River

#10

DOWNING ST.

6

RICHMOND TERRACE

VICTORIA EMBANKMENT

LONDON EYE PIER

LONDON EYE

KING CHARLES ST.

To Buckingham Palace

CHURCHILL WAR ROOMS

PARL ST.

5

CENOTAPH

WESTMINSTER PIER

FORMER COUNTY HALL

CHURCHILL STATUE

BIRDCAGE WALK

GREAT GEORGE ST.

4

Westminster

BIG BEN

2

WESTMINSTER BRIDGE

STOREY'S GATE

UK SUPREME COURT

3

Parliament Square

BRIDGE ST.

1

SOUTH BANK

WESTMINSTER ARMS

ST. MARGARET'S

ST. MARGARET ST.

WALK BEGINS

METHODIST CENTRAL HALL

TOTHILL ST.

St. James's Park

VICTORIA ST.

GREAT SMITH ST.

HOUSES OF PARLIAMENT

ST. THOMAS' HOSPITAL

To Victoria Station

WESTMINSTER ABBEY

Dean's Yard

JEWEL TOWER

MILLBANK

BURGHERS OF CALAIS STATUE

WESTMINSTER

GREAT PETER ST.

200 Meters

200 Yards

WESTMINSTER

1 Westminster Bridge

2 Statue of Boadicea

3 Parliament Square

4 Walking along Whitehall

5 Cenotaph

6 #10 Downing Street & Ministry of Defence

7 Banqueting House

8 Horse Guards

9 Trafalgar Square

linking the interior of England with the North Sea. The city got its start in Roman times as a trade center along this watery highway. As recently as a century ago, large ships made their way upstream to the city center to unload. Today, the major port is 25 miles downstream, and tourist cruise boats ply the waters.

Look for the **boat piers** on either bank of the Thames. Several tour-boat companies offer regular cruises from Westminster Pier (on the left) or London Eye Pier (on the right). This is an efficient, scenic way to get from here to the Tower of London or Greenwich (downstream) or Kew Gardens (upstream). For details, see page 45.

Lining the embankment, beneath the lampposts, are little green copper **lions' heads** (just about 2 feet tall) with rings for tying up boats. Before the construction of the Thames Barrier in 1982 (the world's second-largest movable flood barrier, downstream near Greenwich), high tides from the nearby North Sea made floods a recurring London problem. The police kept an eye on these lions: "When the lions drink, the city's at risk."

Notice how pedestrians are protected from bridge traffic. In 2017, a terrorist used a vehicle as a weapon to kill four pedestrians on this bridge. A few months later, after another, similar attack on London Bridge, the government installed security barriers on eight Thames bridges. Londoners appreciate this pragmatic approach to keeping people safe—they know that when politicians and media overreact to a terrorist attack it only rewards and encourages the evil.

Until 1750, only London Bridge crossed the Thames. Then a bridge was built here. Early in the morning of September 3, 1802, William Wordsworth stood where you're standing and described what he saw:

> *This City now doth, like a garment, wear*
> *The beauty of the morning; silent, bare,*
> *Ships, towers, domes, theatres, and temples lie*
> *Open unto the fields, and to the sky;*
> *All bright and glittering in the smokeless air.*

• Near Westminster Pier is a big statue of a lady on a chariot.

❷ Statue of Boadicea, Queen of the Iceni

Riding in her two-horse chariot, daughters by her side, this Celtic Wonder Woman leads her people against Roman invaders. Julius Caesar was the first Roman general to cross the Channel, but even

he was weirded out by the island's strange inhabitants, who worshipped trees, sacrificed virgins, and went to war painted blue. Later, Romans would subdue and civilize them, naming this spot on the Thames "Londinium" and building roads that turned it into a major urban center.

WESTMINSTER

But Boadicea refused to be Romanized. In AD 60, after Roman soldiers raped her daughters, she rallied her people and "liberated" London, massacring its 60,000 Romanized citizens. However, the brief revolt was snuffed out, and she and her family took poison to avoid surrender.

• There's a civilized public WC down the stairs behind Boadicea. Cross the street to just under Big Ben and continue one block inland to the busy intersection of Parliament Square. It's worth waiting patiently at the crosswalks to cross over into the parklike Parliament Square to take in the surrounding sights.

❸ Parliament Square

Admire the vast length of the sandstone-hued **Houses of Parliament.** If Parliament is in session, the visitors entrance (midway down the building) is likely lined with tourists, enlivened by political demonstrations, and staked out by camera crews interviewing Members of Parliament (MPs) for the evening news. Only the core part, Westminster Hall, survives from the circa-1090s original. While the Houses of Parliament are commonly described as Neo-Gothic (even in this book), this uniquely English style is more specifically called Neo-Perpendicular Gothic. For a peek at genuine Perpendicular Gothic (the fanciest and final stage of that style), simply look across the street at the section of Westminster Abbey closest to the Houses of Parliament—it dates from 1484.

Across the square, the two white towers of **Westminster Abbey** rise above the trees. The broad boulevard of Whitehall (here

called Parliament Street) stretches away from the square up to Trafalgar Square.

Parliament Square is the heart of what was once a suburb of London—the medieval City of Westminster. In Roman and medieval times, the city was centered farther east, around St. Paul's Cathedral. But in the 11th century, King Edward the Confessor moved his court here, and the center of political power shifted to this area. Edward built a palace and a church (minster) here in the west, creating the city of "West Minster." Like Buda and Pest (later Budapest), London is two cities that grew into one. Over time, the palace evolved from a palace of the monarch into a meeting place for debating public policy—a parliament. Today's Houses of Parliament sit atop the remains of Edward's original palace.

Across from Parliament, the cute little church with the blue sundials, snuggling under the Abbey "like a baby lamb under a ewe," is **St. Margaret's Church.** Since 1480, this has been *the* place for politicians' weddings, including Winston and Clementine Churchill's.

The expanse of green between Westminster Abbey and Big Ben is filled with statues that honor famous statesmen for their contributions to Britain and to mankind. The statue of **Winston Churchill,** the man who saved Britain from Hitler, shows him in the military overcoat he was fond of wearing. According to tour guides, the statue has a current of electricity running through it to honor Churchill's wish that if a statue were made of him, his head wouldn't be soiled by pigeons. Most of the other statues are of prime ministers and military men long forgotten, but you may

recognize recent heroes such as **Nelson Mandela,** who battled South African apartheid, and the robed statue of **Mahatma Gandhi,** who helped liberate India from the British. And behind them (across the street) stands the man who liberated America's slaves, **Abraham Lincoln** (erected in 1920, patterned

after a similar statue in Chicago's Lincoln Park).

The white building (flying the Union Jack) at the far end of the square houses Britain's **Supreme Court.** On weekdays, you can wander the building after going through security, see a small exhibit on this recently sanctioned legal body, and observe any courts currently in session (it also has a café and WCs).

Parliament Square is the site of many political demonstrations—people waving signs and chanting slogans, sometimes about issues foreign to most Americans, and others very familiar.

In 1868, the world's first traffic light was installed on the corner where Whitehall now spills double-decker buses into the square. Another reminder of a bygone era is the little yellow "Taxi" lantern atop the fence on the street corner closest to Parliament. In pre-mobile phone days, when an MP needed a taxi, this lit up to hail one. And here's one more ancient artifact: Along the north side of Parliament Square are some nearly obsolete remnants of 20th-century technology—red phone booths, mainly used today by tourists wanting a photo-op with Big Ben.

• *Consider touring Westminster Abbey (*□ *see the Westminster Abbey Tour chapter). Otherwise, patiently go back across the street, walk away from the Houses of Parliament and the Abbey, and continue (north) up the right side of Parliament Street, which becomes Whitehall.*

❹ Walking Along Whitehall

Today, Whitehall is choked with traffic, but imagine the effect this broad street must have had on out-of-towners a little more than a century ago. In your horse-drawn carriage, you'd clop along a tree-lined boulevard past well-dressed lords and ladies, dodging street urchins. You'd try to take it all in, your eyes dazzled by the bone-white walls of this man-made marble canyon.

Whitehall is now the most important street in Britain, lined with the ministries of finance, treasury, revenue and customs (the first on the left), and so on. You may see limos and camera crews as important dignitaries enter or exit. Notice the security measures. Iron grates seal off the concrete ditches alongside the buildings for protection against explosives. And concrete balustrades and black bollards protect key government departments and pedestrians alike.

The black ornamental arrowheads topping the iron fences were once colorfully painted. But in 1861, Queen Victoria ordered them all painted black when her beloved Prince Albert ("the only one who called her Vickie") died. Possibly the world's most determined mourner, Victoria wore black for the standard two years of mourning—and then tacked on 38 more.

• *Continue up Whitehall. On your right, the* **Red Lion** *pub is so popular with Members of Parliament that they have a bell that gives an eight-minute warning, calling MPs back for votes. Across the street, a long one-block detour down King Charles Street leads to the* **Churchill War Rooms,** *the underground bunker of 27 rooms that was the nerve center of Britain's campaign against Hitler (see Sights in London for details). Farther along, you reach a tall, square stone monument in the middle of the boulevard.*

Whitehall of the Victorian Era

It was in the mid-1800s that Westminster and its main street, Whitehall, really came into their own.

Queen Victoria's 64-year reign was a time of unparalleled progress, peace, and expansion—both of the British Empire and the British middle class. One-fifth of the globe fell under British colonial rule. The Industrial Revolution was booming, churning out new products in textile factories, moving people and goods on steam trains, and lighting the streets with gas lamps. By the end of the century, electricity and telephones joined the world's first subway.

Whitehall ruled that empire. The Royal Navy was headquartered in the Old Admiralty Complex, and the army was by the Horse Guards (before later moving across the street to the new Ministry of Defence).

The police headquarters was at Scotland Yard. It got its name from a former Scottish palace that once stood there. Then in 1829, London's newly formed Metropolitan Police force moved in. Because they were directed by Sir Robert "Bob" Peel, the police came to be known as "bobbies." Originally, these police only arrested criminals actually caught in the act. But during Victoria's reign, Scotland Yard also opened a detective wing. They used forensics and intellectual know-how to investigate past crimes. (CSI: Whitehall?) That work inspired Arthur Conan Doyle's stories of the fictional private detective Sherlock Holmes, who used logic and science to solve crimes that baffled even Scotland Yard. These days, London's police force—popularly known as  "The Met"—is headquartered at "New" Scotland Yard. It's located not far from here, a few blocks west of Westminster Abbey.

Scotland Yard's most famous case was trying to find Jack the Ripper—a serial killer of the 1880s. He brutally murdered several prostitutes in East London, east of St. Paul's Cathedral. The case came to symbolize the tale of two cities that London had become by the Victorian Era. Here in Westminster, the police were headquartered in a clean neighborhood of shiny new marble buildings. Meanwhile, across town, the old city was in decay—a dirty den of criminals and Oliver Twist-type street urchins. Wealthy ladies and gentlemen were fleeing west. Westminster boomed while The City crumbled. For the next century, the western half turned its face away from its former city center.

Oh, and Jack the Ripper was never caught by Scotland Yard. Not even Sherlock Holmes could crack that case.

❺ Cenotaph

This monument honors those who died in World Wars I and II. The monumental devastation of these wars led to the drastic decline of the British Empire.

The actual cenotaph is the slab that sits atop the pillar—an empty tomb. You'll notice no religious symbols on this memorial. The dead honored here came from many creeds and all corners of Britain's empire. It looks lost in a sea of noisy cars, but on each Remembrance Sunday (closest to November 11), Whitehall is closed to traffic, the royal family fills the balcony overhead in the foreign ministry, and a memorial service is held around the cenotaph.

It was built to remember what Brits call "the Great War"—World War I. It's hard for an American to understand the war's long-term impact on Europe. On a single day (at the Battle of the Somme, 1916), the British suffered roughly as many casualties as the US did in the entire Vietnam War—nearly 60,000. It's said that if the roughly one million WWI dead from the British Empire were to march four abreast past the cenotaph, the sad parade would last for seven days.

• *Just past the cenotaph is a crosswalk. Cross to the other (west) side of Whitehall, to the black iron security gate guarding the entrance to Downing Street.*

❻ #10 Downing Street and the Ministry of Defence

Britain's version of the White House is where the prime minister and family live, at #10. It's the black-brick building 100 yards down the blocked-off street, on the right; there's a lantern and usually a security guard.

Like the White House's Rose Garden, the black door marked *10* is a highly symbolic point of power, popular for photo ops to mark big occasions. This is where suffragettes protested in the early 20th century, where Neville Chamberlain showed off his regrettable peace treaty with Hitler, and where Winston Churchill made famous the V-for-Victory sign. It's where President Barack Obama discussed global economic issues with Gordon Brown, and where David Cameron suffered his stunning Brexit defeat. His successor, Theresa May, was tasked with the unenviable challenge of implementing Brexit; not surprisingly, her tenure was brief, and in 2019, former London mayor Boris Johnson took over at #10. By the time you're standing here, this famous address may have yet another occupant.

It looks modest, but #10's entryway does open up into fairly impressive digs—the prime minister's offices (downstairs), residence (upstairs), and two large formal dining rooms. The PM's staff has offices here. Many on the staff are permanent bureaucrats, staying on to serve as prime ministers come and go. The cabinet meets at #10 on Tuesday mornings. This is where foreign dignitaries come for official government dinners, where the prime minister receives honored schoolkids and victorious soccer teams, and monthly addresses to the nation are given. Next door, at #11, the chancellor of the exchequer (finance minister) and family live, and #12 houses the PM's press office.

This has been the traditional home of the prime minister since the position was created in the early 18th century. But even before that, the neighborhood (if not the building itself) was a center of power, where Edward the Confessor and Henry VIII had palaces. The facade is, frankly, quite cheap, having been built as part of a middle-class cul-de-sac of homes by American-born George Downing in the 1680s. When the first PM moved in, the humble interior was combined with a mansion in back. During a major upgrade in the 1950s, they discovered that the facade's black bricks were actually yellow—but had been stained by centuries of Industrial Age soot. To keep with tradition, they now paint the bricks black.

The guarded metal gates were installed in 1989 to protect against Irish terrorists. Even so, #10 was hit and partly damaged in 1991 by an Irish Republican Army mortar launched from a van. These days, there's typically not much to see unless a VIP happens to drive up. Then the bobbies snap to and check credentials, the gates open, the car is inspected for bombs, the traffic barrier midway down the street drops into its bat cave, the car drives in, and… the bobbies go back to mugging for the tourists.

The huge Lego-like building across Whitehall from Downing Street is the **Ministry of Defence** (MOD), the "British Pentagon." This bleak place looks like a Ministry of Defence should. In front are statues of illustrious defenders of Britain. At the far right (in the beret, hands behind his back) stands "Monty"—**Field Marshal Bernard Law Montgomery** of World War II—who beat the Nazis in North Africa (defeating Erwin "The Desert Fox" Rommel at El Alamein), which gave the Allies a jumping-off point to retake Europe. Along with Churchill, Monty breathed confidence back into a demoralized British army, persuading them they could ultimately beat Hitler. A **memorial** honoring the women who fought and died in World War II stands in the middle of the street. Its empty uniforms evoke the often-overlooked sacrifices of Britain's female war heroes.

You may be enjoying the shade of London's **plane trees.** They do well in congested London: roots that thrive in clay, waxy leaves that self-clean in the rain, and bark that sheds and regenerates so pollution doesn't enter the trees' vascular systems.

Farther up Whitehall, flanked by the Welsh and Scottish government offices and (I hope) eternally pondering the cenotaph, is an equestrian statue. **Field Marshal Douglas Haig** (marked with his honorary title, *Earl Haig*) was commander in chief of the British army from 1916 to 1918. He was responsible for ordering so many brave and not-so-brave British boys out of the trenches and onto the killing fields of World War I.

• *At the corner (same side as the Ministry of Defence), you'll find the...*

❼ Banqueting House

This two-story building is just about all that remains of what was once the biggest palace in Europe—Whitehall Palace, which once

stretched from Trafalgar Square to Big Ben. Henry VIII started building it when he moved out of the Palace of Westminster (now the Parliament) and into the residence of the archbishop of York. Queen Elizabeth I and other monarchs added on as England's worldwide prestige grew.

Today, the exterior of Greek-style columns and pediments looks rather ho-hum, much like every other white marble building in London. But in 1620 it was a one-of-a-kind wonder—a big white temple rising above small half-timbered huts. Built by architect Inigo Jones, it sparked London's interest in the classical style. Within a century, London was awash in Georgian-style architecture, the English version of Neoclassical.

Facing the Banqueting House, look at the first-floor windows

The Banqueting House Through History

Imagine the many events this place has hosted over the centuries. Originally built as the royal dining hall for the sprawling Whitehall Palace, the Banqueting House also served as its de facto throne room. Picture ambassadors arriving here and walking the length of this hall lined with courtiers to pay homage to the king on his canopied throne. Loyal subjects knelt here to be made knights and nobles.

In the 1600s, the hall was famous throughout Europe as an occasional theater. Plays called "masques" were performed by torchlight and featured mask-wearing actors, singers and dancers, and elaborate costumes, sets, and special effects.

Picture the scene in 1622, when the brand-new Banqueting House was inaugurated with a performance of *The Masque of Augurs,* by Shakespeare protégé Ben Jonson (with set design by the hall's architect, Inigo Jones). King James and his courtiers crowded the balcony and tiered seats, and watched in awe as a parade of goofy commoners in masks entered the hall, singing and reveling, accompanied by two dancing bears. The comic chaos was suddenly interrupted by Greek gods who descended magically from the ceiling, eventually bringing harmony to the realm—just as a wise king does. And behind one of the masks, one of the actors was none other than 21-year-old Prince "I just can't wait to be king" Charles.

In 1649, the Banqueting House served a much more serious purpose—as an execution site for the public beheading of Charles I. Oliver Cromwell subsequently used this symbolic spot to legitimize his own leadership as Lord Protector. When Charles' son, Charles II, restored the monarchy in 1660, it was here that they celebrated.

In 1698, a massive fire destroyed Whitehall Palace, leaving only the name and the Banqueting House. The monarchs moved their residence elsewhere, eventually to Buckingham Palace. The Banqueting House became the Royal Chapel, complete with organ and pews.

Today, besides being a museum, the Banqueting House still functions much as it did in its heyday—hosting government receptions for foreign dignitaries or for Parliament. World-renowned classical musicians perform for the paying public. And it's a rent-a-hall for parties and dinners: You could rent the venue for a wedding for as little as $25,000.

(with the balustrade)—the site of one of the pivotal events of English history. On January 30, 1649, a man dressed in black appeared at one of the windows and looked out at a huge crowd that surrounded the building. He stepped out the window and onto a wooden platform. It was King Charles I. He gave a short speech to the crowd, framed by the magnificent backdrop of the Banqueting House. His final word was "Remember." Then he knelt and laid his neck on a block as another man in black approached. It was the executioner—who cut off the king's head.

Plop—the concept of divine monarchy in Britain was decapitated. But there would still be kings after Oliver Cromwell, the Protestant antimonarchist who brought about Charles I's death and then became England's leader. Soon after Cromwell's death, royalty was restored, and Charles' son, Charles II, got his revenge here in the Banqueting Hall...by living well. But, from then on, every king knew that he ruled by the grace of Parliament.

• *You can pop into the Banqueting House, following the self-guided tour below. Otherwise, skip to "Horse Guards."*

Banqueting House Interior

Start with the 10-minute video on the history of the House, which shows the place in banqueting action. History buffs might consider the included 45-minute audioguide. The low-ceilinged ground floor, a.k.a. the Undercroft, was King James I's personal wine cellar and tasting room. Climb to the first floor to find a portrait of the doomed king.

The main hall is impressive—two stories high, white with gold trim, full of light, and topped with colorful paintings in a gold-coffered ceiling. At 55 feet wide, 55 feet high, and 110 feet long, it's a perfect double cube. The chandeliers can be raised and lowered to accommodate any event. The throne is a modern reconstruction, but it gives an idea of the king's canopied throne that once stood here.

Ceiling Paintings: Charles I, who inherited the Banqueting House from his father, commissioned the famed Peter Paul Rubens to complete the decor. The paintings glorify Charles' dad, James I, the man who built the Banqueting House and who once told Parliament: "Kings are called gods...even by God himself."

To view the large oval painting in the center, *The Apotheosis of James I*, approach from the entrance, like a visiting ambassador, and watch the scene

WESTMINSTER

unfold. King James I (in red robe, with gray beard) rests his foot on a globe, as king of the whole world. Lady Faith (with a torch) and Miss Justice (with scales) lead him up into heaven, where baby angels blow trumpets and the goddess Minerva crowns him with the laurel wreath of wisdom. Minerva sticks her foot in our face, a triumph of illusion three centuries before 3-D glasses.

The painting above the throne, *The Peaceful Reign of King James*, shows wise King James seated on his throne, flanked by corkscrew columns from the temple of wise King Solomon. To the left, Peace embraces Plenty. Two angels swoop down at dramatic angles to adorn James with laurels, while a cherub holds his royal crown. Below, the Roman gods—Mercury, Mars, Minerva—arrive to help James subdue the serpents of rebellion.

In the painting above the entrance, *The Union of the Crowns,* James points his scepter at two ladies—England and Scotland—

warning them to get along. James united the two bickering countries, having been crowned both King of Scots (in 1567) and King of England (1603). Smoke clouds of peace rise in the background as Cupid (bottom left corner) torches the weapons of war. The ladies place a crown on a baby's head and lead him to the throne. It's James' son, the future Charles I. When Charles grew up, he had this painting hung so that he could see it (right-side up) while seated on the Banqueting House throne.

• *When you're finished ogling the paintings, head back outside. Cross to the other (west) side of Whitehall, where you'll see (and smell) the building known as Horse Guards, guarded by traditionally dressed soldiers—who are also called Horse Guards.*

❽ Horse Guards

For 200 years, soldiers in cavalry uniforms have guarded this arched entrance along Whitehall that leads to Buckingham Palace and one of its predecessors as royal residence, St. James's Palace.

Two different squads alternate, so depending on the day you visit, you'll see soldiers in either red coats with white plumes in their helmets (the Life Guards), or blue coats with red plumes

(the Blues and Royals). Together, they constitute the Queen's personal bodyguard. Besides their ceremonial duties here in old-time uniforms, these elite troops have fought in Iraq and Afghanistan. Both Prince William and Prince Harry have served in the Blues and Royals.

Stroll between the two guards, into the courtyard. The Horse Guards building was the headquarters of the British army from the time of the American Revolution until the Ministry of Defence was created in World War II. Back when this archway was the only access point to The Mall (the street leading to Buckingham Palace), it was a security checkpoint. Anyone on horseback had to dismount before passing through. Today, by tradition, you must dismount your bicycle, Vespa, or Segway and walk it through.

The Household Cavalry Museum (through the arch and to the right) offers a glimpse at the stables and a collection of uniforms and weapons (for details, see page 60).

• *Continue up Whitehall, passing the Old Admiralty (#26, on left), headquarters of the British navy that once ruled the waves. Across the street, behind the old Clarence Pub, stood the original Scotland Yard, headquarters of London's crack police force in the days of Sherlock Holmes. Finally, Whitehall opens up into the grand, noisy, traffic-filled Trafalgar Square.*

To reach the center of the square, cross a few streets at the crosswalks.

❾ Trafalgar Square

London's central meeting point bustles around the world's biggest Corinthian column, where **Admiral Horatio Nelson** stands 170 feet off the ground, looking over London in the direction of one of the greatest naval battles in history. Nelson saved England at a time as dark as World War II. In 1805, Napoleon was poised on the other side of the Channel, threatening to invade. Meanwhile, more than 900 miles away, the one-armed, one-eyed, and one-minded Lord Nelson attacked the French fleet off the coast of Spain at Trafalgar. The French were routed, Britannia ruled the waves, and the once-invincible French army was slowly worn down, then defeated at Waterloo. Nelson,

WESTMINSTER

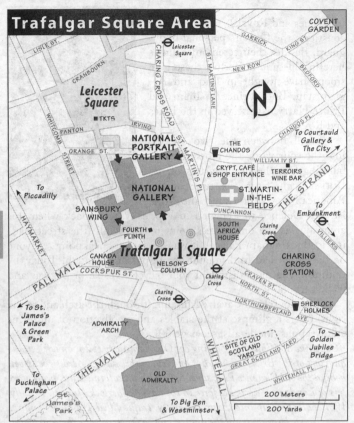

Trafalgar Square Area

while victorious, was shot by a sniper in the battle. He epitomized British pluck when he died, gasping, "Thank God, I have done my duty."

At the top of Trafalgar Square (north) sits the domed **National Gallery** with its grand staircase, and, to the right, the steeple of **St. Martin-in-the-Fields,** built in 1722, inspiring the steeple-over-the-entrance style of many town churches in New England (free lunch concerts—see page 478).

At the base of Nelson's column are bronze reliefs cast from melted-down enemy cannons, and four huggable lions dying to have their photo taken with you. The nearby fountains, lit by colored lights, can shoot water 80 feet in the air. There are numerous (somewhat boring) statues that dot the square. But focus on the pedestal on the northwest corner (the "fourth plinth," on the left), which is periodically topped with contemporary art.

Make your way to the top of the square and take in your surroundings. Trafalgar Square is the center of modern London, connecting Westminster, The City, and the West End. Spin clockwise 360 degrees and survey the city:

To the south (down Whitehall) is the center of government, Westminster. Panning right and looking southwest, through the Admiralty Arch and down the broad boulevard called The Mall, you can see Buckingham Palace in the distance. (Down Pall Mall is St. James's Palace and Clarence House, where Prince Charles lives when in London.) A few blocks northwest of Trafalgar Square is Piccadilly Circus. Directly north (a block behind the National Gallery) sits Leicester Square, the jumping-off point for Soho, Covent Garden, and the West End theater district (◫ see the West End Walk chapter).

The boulevard called the Strand takes you past Charing Cross Station, then eastward to The City, the original walled town of London and today's financial center. In medieval times, when people from The City met with the Westminster government, it was here. And finally, Northumberland Street leads southeast to the Golden Jubilee pedestrian bridge over the Thames. Along the way, you'll pass the Sherlock Holmes Pub (just off Northumberland Street, on Craven Passage), housed in Sir Arthur Conan Doyle's favorite watering hole, with an upstairs replica of 221b Baker Street.

Soak it in. You're smack-dab in the center of London, a thriving city atop two millennia of history.

WESTMINSTER ABBEY TOUR

Westminster Abbey is more than just an "abbey"—it's the most famous English church in Christendom, where royalty have been wedded, crowned, and buried since the 11th century. Indeed, the histories of Westminster Abbey and England are almost the same. A thousand years of English history—3,000 tombs, the remains of 30 kings and queens, and hundreds of memorials to poets, politicians, scientists, and warriors—lie within its stained-glass splendor and under its stone slabs.

Orientation

Cost: £24, £5 more for timed-entry ticket to Queen's Diamond Jubilee Galleries, family ticket available, cheaper online, includes fine multimedia guide. Praying is free, thank God.

Hours: Abbey—Mon-Fri 9:30-16:30, Wed until 19:00 (main church only), Sat 9:00-16:30 (Sept-April until 14:00); Queen's Galleries—Mon-Fri 10:00-16:00, Sat 9:30-15:30, stays open later on summer Wed; cloister—Mon-Sat 9:30-17:30; closed Sun to sightseers but open for services; last entry one hour before closing. Because special events and services can curtail opening hours, check ahead to confirm the Abbey's schedule.

Information: +44 20 7222 5152, www.westminster-abbey.org.

Timed-Entry Tickets: Avoid long ticket-buying lines (especially in summer) by buying a timed-entry ticket on the Abbey's website (don't buy tickets from copycat websites; use the official ".org" site). If you choose to add the Queen's Galleries, book that entry about an hour after you'll start your Abbey visit.

When to Go: It's most crowded every day at midmorning and all day Saturdays and Mondays. Visit early, during lunch, or late to avoid tourist hordes. Weekdays after 14:30 are less congested; come late and stay for the 17:00 evensong. On summer Wednesdays, the church stays open later for visitors; on these days, ask about live music and a bar that may be set up in the cloister garth (the grassy area in the middle of the cloister).

Dress Code: None, even for services.

Getting There: Near Big Ben and the Houses of Parliament (Tube: Westminster or St. James's Park; bus #24 whisks you right there from the Victoria Station neighborhood). Enter through the north door, which faces Parliament Square. One line is for ticket buyers; another (shorter) line is for those who bought tickets online.

Visitor Information: There's surprisingly little posted information on the Abbey's sights, so you must rely on the included multimedia guide, the vergers (docents dressed in red or black), or this book.

Church Services and Music: Mon-Fri at 7:30 (prayer), 8:00 and 12:30 (communion), 17:00 evensong (on Wed it's spoken, not sung); **Sat** at 17:00 (evensong); **Sun** services generally come with more music: at 8:00 (communion), 11:15 (sung Eucharist), and 15:00 (evensong). Services are free to anyone, though visitors who haven't paid church admission aren't allowed to linger afterward. Free **organ recitals** are usually held Sun at 17:00 (30 minutes). Things can change, so get the latest info for your particular day from posted signs or the Abbey's website. Additional services take place at **St. Margaret's**, the smaller church next door.

Tours: The included **multimedia guide** is excellent. Vergers (docents) give informative 90-minute **guided tours** (£10, schedule posted outside and inside entry, up to 5/day April-Sept, 2-4/day Oct-March).

Length of This Tour: Allow 1.5 hours. Add a half-hour for the (optional) Queen's Galleries.

Visitor Services: WCs are near the end of the visitors' route, in the cloister.

Eating: The Abbey's cloister has a **$$ Cellarium Café** with table service and simple fare (salads and sandwiches, £21 afternoon tea). Other options nearby: **$ Wesley's Café** at Methodist Central Hall across the street serves cheap breakfast and lunch ("street café" for takeout open Mon-Fri 8:00-15:00, Sat-Sun 9:00-16:00; sit-down basement café open Tue-Thu 9:00-15:00, closed Fri-Mon, longer hours possible in high season, good free WC); **$$ The Westminster Arms,** just past the Methodist Central Hall on Storey's Gate, serves pub grub (daily 12:00-20:00, eat downstairs). Picnickers can find benches at the nearby Jewel Tower, a half-block south of the Abbey.

Starring: Edwards, Elizabeths, Henrys, Annes, Marys, scientists, and poets.

The Tour Begins

You'll have no choice but to follow the steady flow of tourists through the church, along the route laid out for the audioguide. It's all one-way, and most days the crowds are a real crush. Here are the Abbey's top stops.

• *Walk straight in, entering the north transept. Pick up the map flyer that locates the most illustrious tombs and pick up your audioguide. Follow the crowd flow to the right, passing by a number of...*

❶ Memorials (the First of Many)

Westminster Abbey has become a place where the nation comes to remember its own. You'll pass by statues on tombs, stained glass on walls, and plaques in the floor, all honoring illustrious Brits, both famous and not so famous.

Passing through the blue gates, keep an eye out for **Scientists' Corner,** a cluster of memorials. There's one for Charles Darwin (plaque on the floor), star-watcher William Herschel (also on floor), Isaac Newton (statue on corner of the choir), and pioneer in electricity Michael Faraday (on the floor beneath Newton). In 2018, a famous contemporary physicist was laid to rest near Newton: "Here lies what was mortal of Stephen Hawking." His plaque on the floor depicts a black hole, along with his breakthrough equation that calculates the temperature *(T)* of a black hole's subtle radiation.

Continuing on, you'll pass by stained-glass portraits of illustrious kings and bishops and names of significant "civil engineers." In display cases are books of remembrance with names of soldiers who gave their lives. At the end of the aisle is **Prime Ministers' Corner,** with graves of Clement Attlee, Harold MacMillan, and Harold Wilson. (You'll get a better look at these later, at the end of the tour.)

• *Now enter the spacious nave and take it all in.*

❷ Nave

Look down the long and narrow center aisle of the church. Lined with the praying hands of the Gothic arches, glowing with light from the stained glass, this is more than a museum. With saints in stained glass, heroes in carved stone, and the bodies of England's

Westminster Abbey Tour

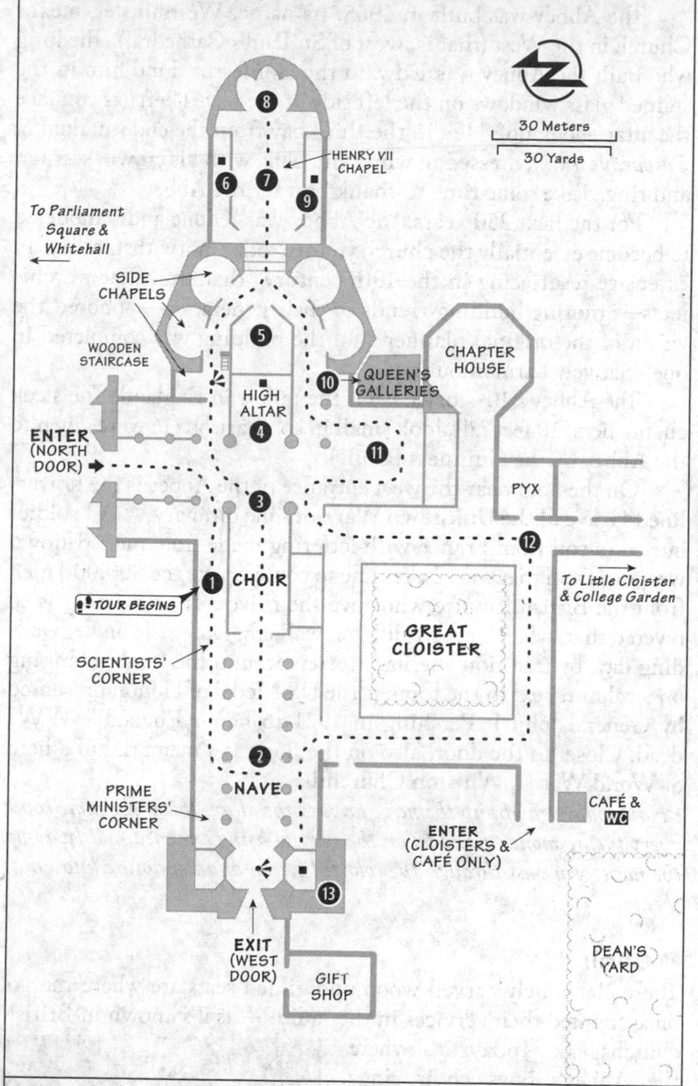

30 Meters

30 Yards

To Parliament
Square &
Whitehall

HENRY VII
CHAPEL

SIDE
CHAPELS

WOODEN
STAIRCASE

CHAPTER
HOUSE

QUEEN'S
GALLERIES

HIGH
ALTAR

ENTER
(NORTH
DOOR)

PYX

CHOIR

TOUR BEGINS

SCIENTISTS'
CORNER

GREAT
CLOISTER

To Little Cloister
& College Garden

PRIME
MINISTERS'
CORNER

NAVE

ENTER
(CLOISTERS &
CAFÉ ONLY)

CAFÉ &
WC

DEAN'S
YARD

EXIT
(WEST
DOOR)

GIFT
SHOP

WESTMINSTER ABBEY

1 Memorials
2 Nave
3 Choir
4 Coronation Spot
5 Shrine of Edward the Confessor
6 Tomb of Elizabeth I & Mary I
7 Chapel of King Henry VII

8 Royal Air Force Chapel
9 Tomb of Mary, Queen of Scots
10 Queen's Diamond Jubilee Galleries
11 Poets' Corner
12 Great Cloister
13 Coronation Chair

greatest citizens under the floor stones, Westminster Abbey is the religious heart of England.

The Abbey was built in 1065. Its name, Westminster, means Church in the West (that is, west of St. Paul's Cathedral). The king who built the Abbey was Edward the Confessor. Find him in the stained glass windows on the left side of the nave ("left" as you face the altar—look up). He's in the third bay from the end (marked *S. Edwardus rex...*), dressed in white and blue, with his crown, scepter, and ring. Take some time to thank him for the Abbey.

For the next 250 years, the Abbey was redone and remodeled to become essentially the church you see today, notwithstanding an extensive resurfacing in the 19th century. Thankfully, later architects—ignoring building trends of their generation—honored the vision of the original planner, and the building was completed in one relatively harmonious style.

The Abbey's 10-story nave is the tallest in England. The sleek chandeliers, 10 feet tall, look small in comparison (16 were given to the Abbey by the Guinness family).

On the floor near the west entrance of the Abbey is the flower-lined **Grave of the Unknown Warrior,** one ordinary WWI soldier buried in soil from France with lettering made from melted-down weapons from that war. Take time to contemplate the 800,000 men from the British Empire who gave their lives. Their memory is so revered that, when Kate Middleton walked up the aisle on her wedding day, by tradition she had to step around the tomb. Hanging on a column next to the tomb is the US Medal of Honor, presented by General John J. Pershing in 1921 to honor England's WWI dead. Closer to the door, also on the floor, is a memorial to a hero of World War II, Winston Churchill.

· *Now walk straight up the nave toward the altar. This is the same route every future monarch walks on the way to being crowned. Midway up the nave, you pass through the colorful screen of an enclosure known as the...*

❸ Choir

These elaborately carved wood and gilded seats are where monks once chanted their services in the "quire"—as it's known in British churchspeak. Today, it's where the Abbey's boys choir sings the evensong. The choir creates an intimate space for worship in this otherwise vast church.

Keep going. You're approaching the center of this cross-shaped church. Up ahead, the **"high" (main) altar**—which usually has a cross and candlesticks atop it—sits on the platform up the five stairs.

• *It's on this platform that the monarch is crowned.*

❹ Coronation Spot

The area immediately before the high altar is where every English coronation since 1066 has taken place. Imagine the day when Prince William becomes king.

The nobles in robes and powdered wigs look on from the carved wooden stalls of the choir. The Archbishop of Canterbury stands at the high altar. The coronation chair (which we'll see later) is placed before the altar on the round, brown pavement stone representing the earth. Surrounding the whole area are temporary bleachers for 8,000 VIPs, going halfway up the rose windows of each transept, creating a "theater."

Long silver trumpets hung with banners sound a fanfare as the monarch-to-be enters the church. The congregation sings, "I will go into the house of the Lord," as William parades slowly down the nave and up the steps to the altar. After a church service, he sits in the chair, facing the altar, where the crown jewels are placed. William is anointed with holy oil, then receives a ceremonial sword, ring, and cup. The royal scepter is placed in his hands, and—dut dutta dah—the archbishop lowers the Crown of St. Edward the Confessor onto his royal head. Finally, King William V stands up, descends the steps, and is presented to the people. As cannons roar throughout the city, the people cry, "God save the king!"

Royalty are also given funerals here. Princess Diana's coffin was carried to this spot for her funeral service in 1997. The "Queen Mum" (mother of Elizabeth II) had her funeral here in 2002. This is also where most of the last century's royal weddings have taken place, including the unions of Queen Elizabeth II and Prince Philip (1947), her parents (1923), her sister Princess Margaret (1960), and her son Prince Andrew (to Sarah Ferguson, 1986). In April 2011, Prince William and Kate Middleton strolled up the nave, passed through the choir, climbed the five steps to the high altar, and became husband and wife—and the future king and queen of the United Kingdom and its Commonwealth. Though royal marriages and funerals can happen anywhere, only one church can hold a coronation—the Abbey.

• *Now veer left and follow the crowd. Detour as you wish into the **side chapels**—the Chapel of St. Michael and Chapel of St. John the Baptist. In this land of dead kings and queens, you'll see effigies of the dead lying atop their tombs of polished stone. They lie on their backs or recline on their sides. Dressed in ruffed collars, they relax on pillows, clasping their hands in prayer, many buried side by side with their spouses.*

WESTMINSTER ABBEY

After exploring the chapels, pause at the freestanding wooden staircase on your right. This is the royal tomb that started it all.

❺ Shrine of Edward the Confessor

The holiest part of the church is the raised area behind the altar (where the wooden staircase leads—sorry, no tourist access except with verger tour). Step back and peek over the dark coffin of Edward I to see the tippy-top of the green-and-gold wedding-cake tomb of King Edward the Confessor—the man who built Westminster Abbey. It was finished just in time to bury Edward and to crown his foreign successor, William the Conqueror, in 1066. After Edward's death, people prayed at his tomb, and after they got good results, Edward was made a saint. His personal renown began the tradition of burying royalty in this church. Edward's tall, central tomb (which unfortunately lost some of its luster when Henry VIII melted down the gold coffin case) is surrounded by the tombs of eight other kings and queens.

• *Continue on. Now we enter the tangled world of a later royal family—the Tudors. At the back end of the church, climb the wide stone staircase and veer left into the private burial chapel holding the...*

❻ Tomb of Queens Elizabeth I and Mary I

Although only one effigy is on the tomb (Elizabeth's), there are actually two queens buried beneath it, both daughters of Henry VIII (by different mothers). Bloody Mary—meek, pious, sickly, and Catholic—enforced Catholicism during her short reign (1553-1558) by burning "heretics" at the stake.

Elizabeth—strong, clever, and Protestant—steered England on an Anglican course. She holds a royal orb symbolizing that she's queen of the whole globe. When 26-year-old Elizabeth was crowned in the Abbey, her right to rule was questioned (especially by her Catholic subjects) because she was considered the bastard seed of Henry VIII's unsanctioned marriage to Anne Boleyn. But Elizabeth's long reign (1559-1603) was one of the greatest in English history, a time when England ruled the seas and Shakespeare explored human emotions. When she died, thousands turned out for her funeral in the Abbey. Elizabeth's face on the tomb, modeled after her death mask, is considered a very accurate take on this hook-nosed, imperious "Virgin Queen" (she never married).

The two half-sisters disliked each other in life—Mary even had Elizabeth locked up in the Tower of London for a short time. Now they lie side by side for eternity. The Latin inscription ends, "Here we lie, two sisters in hope of one resurrection."

• *Now let's go meet the sisters' grandpa and grandma. Continue into the ornate, flag-draped room up three more stairs (directly behind the main altar).*

❼ Chapel of King Henry VII (the Lady Chapel)

The light from the stained-glass windows; the colorful banners overhead; and the elaborate tracery in stone, wood, and glass give this room the festive air of a medieval tournament. The prestigious Knights of the Bath meet here, under the magnificent ceiling studded with gold pendants. The ceiling—of carved stone, not plaster (1519)—is the finest English Perpendicular Gothic  and fan vaulting you'll see (unless you're going to King's College Chapel in Cambridge). The ceiling was sculpted on the floor in pieces, then jigsaw-puzzled into place. It capped the Gothic period and signaled the vitality of the coming Renaissance.

When convened here, the knights sit in their personal wooden stall with their coats of arms on the back, churches on their heads, their banner flying above, and the graves of dozens of kings beneath their feet. When the Queen worships here, she sits in the corner chair—the one topped with the lion crown (immediately to the right as you enter).

Behind the chapel's small altar is an iron cage housing tombs of the old warrior Henry VII of Lancaster and his wife, Elizabeth of York. Their love and marriage finally settled the Wars of the Roses between the two clans. The combined red-and-white rose symbol decorates the top band of the ironwork. Henry VII, the first Tudor king, was the father of Henry VIII and the grandfather of Elizabeth I. This exuberant chapel heralds a new optimistic postwar era as England prepares to step onto the world stage.

• *Go to the far end of the chapel and stand at the banister in front of the modern set of stained-glass windows.*

❽ Royal Air Force Chapel

Saints in robes and halos mingle with pilots in parachutes and bomber jackets. This tribute to WWII flyers is for those who earned their angel wings in the Battle of Britain (July-Oct 1940). Hitler's air force ruled the skies in the early days of the war, bombing at will, and threatening to snuff Britain out without a fight. But while determined Londoners hunkered down underground, British pilots in their Spitfires and Hurricanes took advantage of newly invented radar to get the jump on the more powerful Luftwaffe. These were the pilots about whom Churchill said, "Never...was so much owed by so many to so few."

The Abbey survived the Battle and the Blitz, but this window did not. As a memorial, a bit of bomb damage has been pre-served—the little glassed-over hole in the wall below the windows in the lower left-hand corner. The book of remembrances lists the 1,497 airmen (including one American) who died in the Battle of Britain.

You're also standing on the grave of **Oliver Cromwell,** leader of the rebel forces in England's Civil War. Or, rather, what had been his grave, when Cromwell was buried here from 1658 to 1661. Then his corpse was exhumed, hanged, drawn, quartered, and de-capitated, and the head displayed on a stake as a warning to anar-chists.

• *Exit the Chapel of Henry VII. Turn left into a side chapel with the tomb (the central one of three in the chapel).*

❾ Tomb of Mary, Queen of Scots

Historians get dewy-eyed over the fate of Mary, Queen of Scots (1542-1587). The beautiful, French-educated queen was held

under house arrest for 19 years by Queen Elizabeth I, who con-sidered her a threat to her sov-ereignty. Elizabeth got wind of an assassination plot, suspected Mary was behind it, and had her first cousin (once removed) beheaded. When Elizabeth died childless, Mary's son—James VI, King of Scots—also became King James I of England and Ireland. James buried his mum here (with her head sewn back on) in the Abbey's most sumptuous tomb.

• *Exit Mary's chapel and head back down the big stone stairs. Ahead of you, again, is the tomb of the church's founder, Edward the Confessor. Continue on, until you emerge in the south transept. Look for the door-way that leads to a stairway and elevator to the...*

❿ Queen's Diamond Jubilee Galleries

In 2018, the Abbey opened a space that had been closed off for 700 years—an internal gallery 70 feet above the main floor known as the triforium. This balcony—with stunning views over the nave—now houses a small museum of interesting objects related to the Abbey's construction, the monarchs who worshipped here, royal coronations, and more from its 1,000-year history. (Because of lim-ited space, a timed-entry ticket is required.)

Among the highlights you may see are small-scale versions of the statues of the 20th-century Christian martyrs that stand above the Abbey's main (west) door, including Martin Luther King, Jr. Some of the Abbey's oldest stones are the 900-year-old column capitals on display, curiously carved with faces and scenes. Do not miss the best view of the nave, straight down the axis to the front door. Nearby, among the collection of ritual objects (a big altarpiece, bishops' staffs, etc.), are decent views out the windows to Big Ben. You'll see numerous funeral effigies of monarchs, from the first crude wooden statue (of Edward III) to psychologically probing portraits (like Henry VII and his wife Elizabeth of York) to elaborately dressed, Madame Tussaud-quality wax figures.

In the coronation section, you'll see the wooden coronation chair of Queen Mary II—a specially built companion piece to the traditional chair (which we'll see later), because Mary was crowned alongside her husband, William. There are high-quality replicas of the priceless coronation regalia (the crown jewels), plus a few oddities like Prince William and Kate's marriage license.

Doubling back toward the entrance, don't miss the section of old books, which includes a teeny-tiny history of the Abbey and a medieval-era copy of the Magna Carta.

• *After touring the Queen's Galleries, return to the main floor. You're in...*

⓫ Poets' Corner

England's greatest artistic contributions are in the written word. Here the masters of arguably the world's most complex and expres-

sive language are remembered. (Many writers are honored with plaques and monuments; relatively few are actually buried here.)

• *Start with Chaucer, buried in the wall under the blue windows, marked with a white plaque reading* Qui Fuit Anglorum...

Geoffrey Chaucer (c. 1343-1400) is often considered the father of English literature. Chaucer's *Canterbury Tales* told of earthy people speaking everyday English, not French or Latin. He was the first great writer buried in the Abbey (thanks to his job as a Westminster clerk). Later, it became a tradition to bury other writers here, and Poets' Corner was built around his tomb. The blue windows have blank panels awaiting the names of future poets.

• *The plaques on the floor before Chaucer are gravestones and memorials to other literary greats.*

Lord Byron, the great lover of women and adventure: "Though the night was made for loving, / And the day returns too soon, / Yet we'll go no more a-roving / By the light of the moon."

Dylan Thomas, alcoholic master of modernism, with a Romantic's heart: "Oh as I was young and easy in the mercy of his means, / Time held me green and dying / Though I sang in my chains like the sea."

W. H. Auden, Brit-turned-American modernist on love, politics, and religion: "He was my North, my South, my East and West / My working week and Sunday rest / My noon, my midnight, my talk, my song / I thought that love would last forever: I was wrong."

Lewis Carroll, creator of *Alice's Adventures in Wonderland* and *Through the Looking-Glass:* "'Twas brillig, and the slithy toves / Did gyre and gimble in the wabe..."

T. S. Eliot, American-turned-British author of the influential *Waste Land:* "April is the cruellest month, breeding / Lilacs out of the dead land, mixing / Memory and desire, stirring / Dull roots with spring rain."

Alfred, Lord Tennyson, conscience of the Victorian era: "'Tis better to have loved and lost / Than never to have loved at all."

Robert Browning: "Oh, to be in England / Now that April's there."

• *Farther out in the south transept, look left to find a statue of...*

William Shakespeare: Although he's not buried here, this greatest of English writers is honored by a fine statue that looks over the others: "Life's but a walking shadow, a poor player that struts and frets his hour upon the stage and then is heard no more."

George Frideric Handel: High on the wall opposite Shakespeare is the German immigrant famous for composing the *Messiah* oratorio: "Hallelujah, hallelujah, hallelujah." The statue's features are modeled on Handel's death mask. Musicians can read the vocal score in his hands for "I Know That My Redeemer Liveth." His actual tomb is on the floor, next to...

Charles Dickens, whose serialized novels brought literature to the masses: "It was the best of times, it was the worst of times."

On the floor near Shakespeare, you'll also find the tombs of **Samuel Johnson** (who wrote the first English dictionary) and the great English actor **Laurence Olivier.** (Olivier disdained the "Method" style of acting—experiencing intense emotions in order to portray them. When co-star Dustin Hoffman stayed up all night in order to appear haggard for a scene, Olivier said, "My dear boy, why don't you simply try acting?")

And finally, near the center of the transept, find the small, white floor plaque of **Thomas Parr** (marked *THO: PARR*). Check the dates of his life (1483-1635) and do the math. In his (reputed) 152 years, he served 10 sovereigns and was a contemporary of Columbus, Henry VIII, Elizabeth I, Shakespeare, and Galileo. Famous simply for supposedly being an "Old, Old, Very Old Man," as poet John Taylor dubbed him in 1635, Parr is mentioned in works by celebrated writers such as Charles Dickens, Henry David Thoreau, Bram Stoker, Robert Graves, and James Joyce.

• *At this point (where they generally collect your audioguide), you exit the church (temporarily) at the south door, which leads to the...*

⓬ Great Cloister

You're entering the inner sanctum of the Abbey's monastery. The buildings that adjoin the church housed the monks. (The church is known as the "abbey" because it was the headquar-
ters of the Benedictine Order until Henry VIII kicked them out in 1540.) Cloistered courtyards like this gave them a place to stroll in peace while medi-
tating on God's creations.

• *Walk straight ahead down the cloister's first corridor. On the left, look for the entrance to the Chapter House.*

The **Chapter House** is a bright, airy, and impressive space where the monks had daily meetings. It features fine architecture and stained glass, some faded but well-described medieval paintings and floor tiles, and—in the corridor—Britain's oldest door.

A few steps farther down the corridor is the **Pyx Chamber.** This old, thick-walled room was a vault that once safeguarded the coins used to set the silver standard of the realm (a pyx is a small box that held gold and silver coins).

As you continue circling the clois-
ter, look back through the courtyard to the church exterior, and meditate on the **flying buttresses.** These stone bridges that push in on the church walls allowed Gothic architects to build so high.

If you need a bite or drink, or the WC, head for the Abbey café.

• *Continue all the way around the cloister and go back into the church for the last stop. Near the front door is a chapel, containing an object that makes this church so special among all of Britain's great churches. Peek through the grate to see the...*

⓭ Coronation Chair

A gold-painted oak chair waits here under a regal canopy for the next coronation. For every English coronation since 1308 (except two), it's been moved to its spot before the high altar to receive the royal buttocks. The chair's legs rest on lions, England's symbol.

The space below the chair originally held a big sandstone rock from Scotland called the Stone of Scone (pronounced "skoon"), symbolizing Scotland's unity with England's monarch. But in the 1990s, Britain gave Scotland more sovereignty, its own Parliament, and the Stone, which Scotland has agreed to loan to Britain for future coronations (the rest of the time, it's on display in Edinburgh Castle).

Next to the chapel with the chair hangs a 600-year-old **portrait of King Richard II**. The boy is only 10 years old, but with the sudden death of his father, greatness has been thrust upon him. He receives the royal orb and scepter, dons the crown, and takes his seat upon this very chair—ready to assume the mantle of kingship.

Finally, take one last look down the nave. Listen to and ponder this place, filled with the remains of the people who made Britain a world power—saints, royalty, poets, musicians, scientists, soldiers, politicians. Now step back outside into a city filled with the modern-day poets, saints, and heroes who continue to make Britain great.

HOUSES OF PARLIAMENT TOUR

With an epic history, the Houses of Parliament (home to the House of Commons and the House of Lords) remain the site of fierce verbal tussles among members of the UK's Conservative, Labour, and smaller parties. "Westminster" (as Brits call the place) appears almost nightly on TV, as the impressive backdrop to the latest political news. A visit here is a chance to see the British government in action.

The Houses are open and free to the public when Parliament is in session. You can stroll through the building's majestic rooms and watch Parliament give speeches and debate policy. When Parliament is recessed—in summer and on Saturdays year-round—you can still visit by paying for a guided tour or audioguide. In fact, recess is the best time for touring the lavish palace itself, as you have more freedom to roam and view additional rooms. My self-guided tour covers the main rooms you'll see with either option.

Orientation

Cost: Free when Parliament is in session; otherwise you must visit with a guided tour (£29) or audioguide (£22.50).

Hours: Open for nonticketed entry when Parliament is in session, generally from October to late July, Monday through Thursday (House of Commons—Mon 14:30-22:30, Tue-Wed 11:30-19:30, Thu 9:30-17:30; House of Lords—Mon-Tue 14:30-22:00, Wed 15:00-22:00, Thu 11:00-19:30; last entry depends on debates; day-by-day schedule at www.parliament.uk). When Parliament is not in session, you can visit only by booking a tour or renting an audioguide (described later).

Information: +44 20 7219 3000, www.parliament.uk.

When to Go: Expect lines—it may take 20-30 minutes to get through security, then another 20-60 minutes to be admitted to the House chambers.

You'll have the best chance of viewing both chambers if you arrive around 14:00. Lines are longest at the start of each day's session, but that's when the most fiery debates often occur (and it's almost impossible to enter on Wednesdays, when the prime minister normally attends). The later in the day you enter, the less crowded (and less exciting) it is. Avoid going at 16:00, when parliamentary functions make things extra busy.

Visiting weekdays after 18:00 can be efficient, since there are typically almost no lines or crowds, and it allows you to stretch your sightseeing day beyond when most sights close. However, it's also much quieter (only a few politicians participating in low-level debates), and you risk not getting in, as sessions can end well before their official closing time. But if you're in the vicinity, consider swinging by to see if you can go in.

Getting There: This gigantic riverside Neo-Gothic temple of government is London's most recognized symbol. The visitors entrance is around the back side (away from the river) on Cromwell Green, facing the buttresses of Westminster Abbey. Tube: Westminster.

Choosing a House: As you line up to enter the building, the guard may ask if you want to visit the House of Commons or the House of Lords. The House of Lords is less important politically, but they meet in a more ornate room, and the wait time is shorter (likely less than 30 minutes). The House of Commons is where major policy is made, but the room is sparse, and wait times are longer (30-60 minutes or more).

I choose "Lords" (because the line is shorter), but it really doesn't matter. Once inside the building, you'll be able to sightsee the public spaces described in this tour as you make your way to either chamber.

Visitor Information: To see what it's like when Parliament is in session, visit www.parliamentlive.tv. To preview a debate from home, tune in to "Prime Minister's Questions"; in the US, the broadcast airs live Wed mornings on C-SPAN2 and repeats Sun evenings on regular C-SPAN (www.c-span.org).

Tours: On Saturdays and whenever Parliament is in recess (such as late July-Sept), you can only enter by paying for a **guided tour** or an **audioguide,** which lets you sightsee on your own.

There are advantages to visiting during a recess: It may be less crowded, you have access to additional palatial rooms, and you can see the interior of both chambers without a wait—all while learning about the history of Britain's political system (audioguide tour-£22, guided tour-£28, 1.5 hours, both tours depart every 15-20 minutes on a timed-entry system, Sat 9:00-16:30 and most weekdays during recess—days and times vary, confirm schedule on website).

Book ahead online or by calling +44 20 7219 4114 to secure a time slot, or try booking on the spot at Portcullis House, near Westminster Bridge and Big Ben (ticket office open Mon-Fri 10:00-16:00, Sat 9:00-16:30, closed Sun, enter from Victoria Embankment). For either a guided tour or an audioguide, arrive at the visitors entrance on Cromwell Green 20-30 minutes before your tour time to clear security.

Big Ben Climb: Check the website for a planned new tour of Big Ben. On this fully guided visit, you'll hike up the 320 or so steps to the top of the clock tower to see the clockworks from the inside, plus sweeping views over London. The visit should coincide with the clock chiming at the top of the hour.

Length of This Tour: Once you clear the security rigmarole, it takes less than an hour to tour the interior and drop in—briefly—on a parliamentary session.

Starring: A grand building and a gaggle of chattering parliamentarians.

BACKGROUND

The Palace of Westminster has been the center of political power in England for nearly a thousand years. Around 1050, King Edward the Confessor moved here to be next to his newly constructed "minster" (church) in the "west"—Westminster Abbey. The Palace became the monarch's official residence, the meeting place of his noble advisors, and the supreme court of the land. In the 1500s, Henry VIII moved down the block to Whitehall Palace (now destroyed, see page 137), and later monarchs chose to live at Kensington and Buckingham Palaces. But Westminster Palace remained home to the increasingly powerful advisors, or Parliament.

In 1834, a horrendous fire gutted the Palace. It was rebuilt in a retro Neo-Gothic style that recalled England's medieval Christian roots— pointed arches, stained-glass windows, spires, and saint-like statues. At the same time, Britain was also retooling its government. Democracy was on the rise, the queen became a constitutional monarch, and Parliament emerged as the nation's ruling body. The Palace of Westminster became a symbol—a kind of cathedral—of democracy.

The Tour Begins

• *Enter midway along the west side of the building (across the street from Westminster Abbey), where a tourist ramp leads to the...*

❶ Visitors Entrance

Line up for the airport-style security check. You'll be given a visitor badge. If you have questions, the attendants are helpful.

• *Once past security, you pass through an open-air courtyard in the shadow of Big Ben, and enter Westminster Hall. Here (through the door to the right), you'll find the WCs, gift shop, and the Jubilee Café (which has live video feeds of Parliament in session). Now take in the cavernous...*

❷ Westminster Hall

This vast hall—covering 16,000 square feet—survived the 1834 fire, and is one of the oldest and most important buildings in England. In some ways, this hall is where modern democracy was born.

Begun in 1097, the hall first served as the heart of the monarch's residence, the Palace of Westminster. It was the glorious throne room. The king would preside from the far (south) end, atop a raised platform—dispensing justice, welcoming ambassadors, hosting his coronation banquet, toasting revelers. By the late-1200s, the hall had also become the place where nobles would occasionally gather with the king to address their concerns and simply talk (or *"parler"*)—the first Parliament.

The hall was extensively remodeled around 1390 by Richard II, who made it the grandest space in Europe. His self-supporting oak-timber roof (1397) wowed everyone. Unlike earlier roofs that spanned the hall with long beams, this "hammer-beam" roof uses short beams that jut horizontally out from the walls. They're part of a complex system of curved braces and arches that distribute the weight of the roof outward to the walls, not downward to the floor, so there's no need for supporting pillars. The 26 carved angels also do their part to hold up the 650-ton roof and tirelessly support the chandeliers with their necks.

Stroll the room to read various information displays and plaques (in the pavement) about the hall's history. In the 1300s, the hall began hosting not only assemblies of nobles (or "Lords") but gatherings of knights, mayors, and businessmen from towns and shires across England—what would become the "Commons."

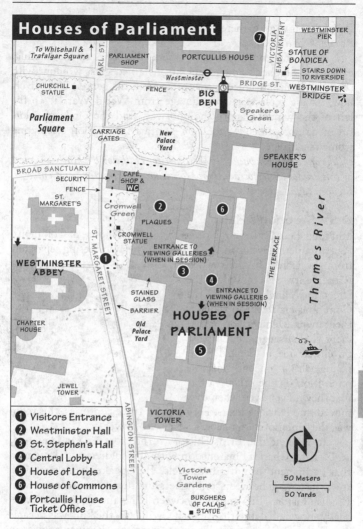

Houses of Parliament

To Whitehall & Trafalgar Square
PARL. ST.
PARLIAMENT SHOP
PORTCULLIS HOUSE
VICTORIA EMBANKMENT
WESTMINSTER PIER
STATUE OF BOADICEA
STAIRS DOWN TO RIVERSIDE

CHURCHILL STATUE
FENCE
Westminster
BRIDGE ST.
WESTMINSTER BRIDGE

Parliament Square
BIG BEN
Speaker's Green

CARRIAGE GATES
New Palace Yard

BROAD SANCTUARY
SPEAKER'S HOUSE

SECURITY FENCE
ST. MARGARET'S
CAFÉ, SHOP & WC

Cromwell Green
②
⑥

PLAQUES
CROMWELL STATUE

WESTMINSTER ABBEY
①
ENTRANCE TO VIEWING GALLERIES (WHEN IN SESSION)
③

Thames River

THE TERRACE

CHAPTER HOUSE
STAINED GLASS
④
ENTRANCE TO VIEWING GALLERIES (WHEN IN SESSION)

BARRIER
Old Palace Yard
HOUSES OF PARLIAMENT

⑤

JEWEL TOWER
VICTORIA TOWER

ABINGDON STREET

① Visitors Entrance
② Westminster Hall
③ St. Stephen's Hall
④ Central Lobby
⑤ House of Lords
⑥ House of Commons
⑦ Portcullis House Ticket Office

Victoria Tower Gardens
BURGHERS OF CALAIS STATUE

N
50 Meters
50 Yards

HOUSES OF PARLIAMENT

England's vaunted legal system was invented in this hall, as this was the major court of the land for 700 years. In 1305, the Scottish patriot William ("Braveheart") Wallace was tried here. In 1483, Richard ("Now is the winter of our discontent") III had his coronation after-party here. King Charles I was tried and sentenced to death here. Guy Fawkes was condemned for plotting to blow up the Halls of Parliament in 1605. (He's best remembered today for the sly-smiling "Guy Fawkes mask"—now the symbol of 21st-century anarchists.)

In more recent times, this hall has hosted the lying-in-state of Winston Churchill, George VI, and the Queen Mother. In 2011,

Britain's bigwigs gathered here for a speech by then-President Barack Obama.

At the far end of the hall, ascend the stairs to the landing, called "St. Stephen's Porch." The huge stained-glass window (with the UK's lion-and-unicorn coat of arms in the center) is relatively new, having replaced bomb damage from World War II. To the left of the window, above the doorway, find the circle of colorful medallions titled *New Dawn*—an art installation celebrating women's suffrage.

• *Take one more look back over Westminster Hall, with a king's-eye view of this cradle of democracy. Now continue up the stairs, and enter St. Stephen's Hall.*

❸ St. Stephen's Hall

This long, beautifully lit room was the original House of Commons. As Parliament developed, the Commons began meeting separately from the Lords. In 1530, when King Henry VIII moved up the street to Whitehall Palace, the Commons claimed this room as their own. Members of Parliament (MPs) sat in church pews on either side of the hall—the ruling faction on one side, the opposition on the other—a format they'd keep even when they moved into new chambers. For the next three centuries, this room was the center of Parliament, as it rose to power.

It was here that British history turned forever. On January 4, 1642, King Charles I marched in with 400 soldiers and demanded that Parliament turn over five rebels. The Speaker bluntly refused. It was a standoff between commoners and royalty unprecedented in English history. This impasse between King and Parliament eventually snowballed into the English Civil War, the king was decapitated, and Parliament finally emerged as the dominant power in English politics.

When the 1834 fire destroyed St. Stephen's Hall, the House of Commons moved to another room, where it remains today. For the rebuild, Parliament held a competition, and architect Charles Barry won with a stunning Neo-Gothic design. Take in the hall's exquisite decoration. It's a textbook example of the style known as Perpendicular Gothic. The stained-glass windows form a tall, rectangular grid that leads the eye up to the ceiling, which fans out into elaborately interconnected arches. This room sets the tone for the Perpendicular style we'll see throughout the palace.

The room's decorations emphasize the proud spirit that helped create modern democracy. The mosaic over the entrance depicts King Edward III, who ratified the House of Commons in the 1300s. The windows feature England's towns and boroughs, which gained a voice through the Commons. The statues that line the room honor distinguished parliamentarians, including Robert Walpole (England's first prime minister), as well as Edmund Burke and William Pitt, both of whom supported the democratic ideals of the American Revolution.

The room's murals depict major events in English history. It starts (on the left wall) in the year 877 with the English people rallying to drive off the Danes to preserve their independence. Next up is the almost-legendary 12th-century king, Richard the Lionheart. Then it's 1215, and the nobles force the tyrant King John to sign the Magna Carta—a charter that limited absolute monarchy and started the whole concept of a parliament. Next, English people read the Wycliffe Bible, which put the word of God in the hands of ordinary citizens. The mural on the opposite wall shows the courageous Speaker of the House Thomas More, standing up to a cardinal representing King Henry VIII, even though it would eventually cost More his life.

• *Now, put your camera away, and continue into the next room, the...*

❹ Central Lobby

This ornate, octagonal, high-vaulted room is often called the "heart of British government," because it sits in the geographical center of the Palace, midway between the House of Commons (to the left) and the House of Lords (right). Clerks bustle about. Constituents come to this lobby to petition, or "lobby," their MPs (from which the term may derive). Television newscasters interview MPs here for the evening news, with this magnificent Neo-Gothic backdrop. Video monitors list the schedule of meetings and events going on in this 1,100-room governmental hive.

This is the best place to admire the Palace's interior decoration—carved wood, chandeliers, statues, and floor tiles. Long, slender columns rise from the floor and fan out into a dazzling gilded ceiling studded with bosses, where Gothic ribs create a kaleidoscope effect. Architect Barry and his partner, Augustus Pugin, designed every detail inside and out, from the symbolism of the statues to the color of the upholstery.

The room's decor trumpets the enlightenment of the British governing system. The colorful mosaics over the four doors represent the countries of the United Kingdom. There's England's St. George and the dragon (to the right), Scotland's St. Andrew, Wales' St. David, and Ireland's St. Patrick. The room's many statues—of kings, queens, and 19th-century politicians—symbolize how the Crown and Parliament both have their place in British history.

• *This lobby marks the end of the public space where you can wander freely. From here, you'll visit the House of Lords or the House of Commons. If either house is in session, you'll go through a series of narrow halls and staircases to reach the upper viewing galleries. Once there, you'll need to check large belongings and refrain from taking photos.*

When Parliament is not in session—that is, if you're using the audioguide—you can still see the houses described next. You may also have access to additional rooms: The Divisions Corridor (used for counting MPs' votes), the vast Royal Gallery (where visiting heads of state are feted), the sumptuous Robing Room (where monarchs are dressed for special occasions), and more.

❺ House of Lords

When you're called, you'll walk to the Lords Chamber by way of the long **Peers Corridor.** Paintings on the corridor walls depict the antiauthoritarian spirit brewing under the reign of Charles I: You'll see Parliament rebuffing Charles' demands for the five MPs, and the freedom-seeking Pilgrims (third panel on left) leaving England for America on the Mayflower.

Passing through the mahogany-ceilinged **Peers Lobby,** you reach the **House of Lords Chamber,** where you'll watch the proceedings from the upper-level visitors gallery. Each day opens with a 30-minute session where four questions are posed to the government, usually followed by legislation and then debate.

The House of Lords consists of around 800 members, called "Peers." They are not elected by popular vote. Some are nobles who've inherited the position, or bishops whose seat comes with the job. Others are appointed by the Queen. These days, their role is largely advisory. They can propose, revise, and filibuster laws, but they have no real power to pass laws on their own. On any typical day, only a handful of the Lords actually shows up to debate. But despite (or because of) their lack of real power, the Lords are often considered less partisan and more objective, so people really do pay attention.

The Lords Chamber is church-like and impressive, with stained glass and intricately carved walls that suggest cathedral choir stalls. The benches where the Lords sit are always upholstered red (the ones in the House of Commons are green). At the far end is the Queen's huge gilded throne, with three seats—originally for Queen Victoria, Prince Albert, and their son. Today's Queen is the only one who may sit there, and only once a year, when she gives a speech to open Parliament. Above the throne, the mural depicts a scene appropriate to this traditional chamber: the first Christian king of England kneeling before a bishop to be baptized.

In front of the throne sits the woolsack—a cushion stuffed with wool. Here the Lord Speaker presides, with a ceremonial mace behind the backrest. To the Lord Speaker's right (our left) are the members of the ruling party (a.k.a. "government"). The first two rows in the seats closest to the woolsack are filled with bishops. To the Lord Speaker's left (our right) are the members of the opposition (the Labour Party, currently the largest opposition party in both houses). Unaffiliated Crossbenchers sit in between. All around the chamber, there are dangling microphones, high-def cameras, and video monitors, to amplify the Lords' messages to the world.

⑥ House of Commons

The **corridor** leading to the House of Commons is lined with murals celebrating Parliament's final triumph over monarchy in the 1600s. Heroic citizens hide patriots and defy the tyrannical King James II. Eventually, Parliament would emerge supreme, empowered with choosing the monarchs who would govern the country—the "Glorious Revolution" of 1688.

Pass through the relatively modest **Members Lobby,** with its statues of prime ministers who have strolled these corridors: Goateed Disraeli (Queen Victoria's favorite), Winston Churchill, and the "Iron Lady" Margaret Thatcher. You may see office boxes where MPs can get their messages, though these are becoming obsolete in a paperless world.

The **Commons Chamber**—with its green carpet and cushions—may be much less grandiose than the Lords', but this is where the sausage gets made. The House of Commons is as powerful as the Lords, prime minister, and Queen combined.

This seat of power is surprisingly small—barely 3,000 square feet. The chamber was destroyed in the Blitz, and Churchill rebuilt it with the same cube-shaped floor plan. Of today's 650-plus MPs, only 450 can sit—the rest have to stand at the ends. On any given day, most MPs are in their offices, located elsewhere in the complex or in nearby modern buildings.

As in the House of Lords, the ruling party sits on the right of the Speaker (our left), opposition on the left (our right). Television screens on the wall show the topic and who is speaking; the press box is to the left, above the government MPs. Members stand when they want to speak, waiting patiently to be called on by the Speaker.

Keep an eye out for two red lines on the floor, which must not be crossed when debating the other side. (They're supposedly two sword-lengths apart, to prevent a literal clashing of swords.) Between the benches is the canopied Speaker's Chair, for the chairman who keeps order and chooses who can speak next. A green bag on the back of the chair holds petitions from the public. The clerks sit at a central table that holds the ceremonial mace, a symbol of the power given Parliament by the monarch. Also on the table are the two "dispatch boxes"—old wooden chests that serve as lecterns, one for each side.

The Queen is not allowed in the Commons Chamber. The last monarch to enter a Commons Chamber was Charles I, and you know what happened to him. When the prime minister visits, he or she speaks from one of the boxes. Their ministers (or cabinet) join on the front bench, while lesser MPs (the "backbenchers") sit behind. It's often a fiery spectacle, as the prime minister defends their policies, while the opposition grumbles and harrumphs in displeasure. It's not unheard of for MPs to get out of line and be escorted out by the Serjeant at Arms and his Parliamentary bouncers. One furious MP even grabbed the Serjeant's hallowed mace and threw it to the ground. His career was over.

• *And so is our tour. Heading back out of the sprawling complex, be sure to get a good look at—if you haven't already—the Houses of Parliament's best-known symbol, its giant clock tower. Big Ben—or what tourists call "Big Ben"—is described in my* 📖 *Westminster Walk or* 🎧 *Westminster Walk audio tour.*

NATIONAL GALLERY TOUR

The National Gallery lets you tour Europe's art without ever crossing the Channel. With so many exciting artists and styles, it's a fine overture to art if you're just starting a European trip, and a pleasant reprise if you're just finishing. The "National Gal"—with Britain's greatest collection of paintings—is always a welcome interlude from the bustle of London sightseeing.

This tour gives you a quick chronological sweep through art history: medieval holiness, Renaissance realism, Dutch detail, Baroque excess, British restraint, and the colorful French Impressionism that leads to the modern world.

Cruise like an eagle with wide eyes for the big picture, seeing how each style progresses into the next. As with all museums, expect changes. Most likely, 80 percent of the paintings will be where I say they are, 10 percent will be found nearby, and 10 percent will be out on loan or in restoration. Enjoy the biggies quickly, leaving yourself enough time to circle back and browse.

Orientation

Cost: Free, £5 suggested donation; special exhibits extra.
Hours: Daily 10:00-18:00, Fri until 21:00, last entry to special exhibits one hour before closing.
Information: +44 20 7747 2885, www.nationalgallery.org.uk.
Getting There: It's as central as can be, overlooking Trafalgar

Square, a 15-minute walk from Big Ben and 10 minutes from Piccadilly. The closest Tube stop is Charing Cross or Leicester Square. Handy buses #9, #11, #15, and #24 (among others) pass by.

Visitor Information: The information desk in the lobby has a £2 floor plan (similar to this book's map, but with a few masterpieces highlighted). If you can't find a particular piece, ask the attendants stationed throughout the galleries.

Tours: Free one-hour **overview tours** leave from the Sainsbury Wing info desk (most likely Mon-Fri at 14:00). Ask the info desk about 10-minute talks on individual paintings (possibly Mon-Fri at 16:00). Download the free **Smartify app** for more about any painting in the galleries.

The museum is surprisingly family-friendly (especially on Sunday mornings). Check their website for a variety of **kids' activities.**

Length of This Tour: Allow 1.5 hours. If you have less time, focus on a few representative masterpieces: Van Eyck's *Arnolfini Portrait*, Leonardo's *Virgin and Child*, Rembrandt's self-portraits, Velázquez's *Rokeby Venus*, the Impressionists, and Van Gogh's *Sunflowers.*

Services: Cloakrooms are at each entrance (£2/item). You can take a small bag into the museum.

Cuisine Art: There are three eateries in the National Gallery. The **$$$ Ochre Restaurant,** on the first floor of the Sainsbury Wing; **$$ Muriel's Kitchen Café,** located near the Getty Entrance; and the **$ Espresso Bar,** near the Portico and Getty entrances, with sandwiches and pastries. Outside the Gallery, several options are on or near Trafalgar Square (see page 428).

Starring: You name it—Leonardo, Raphael, Rembrandt, Monet, and Van Gogh.

The Tour Begins

• *Enter through the Sainsbury Entrance (facing Trafalgar Square), in the modern annex to the left of the classical building. For the most up-to-date information on the current location of many paintings, buy a map.*

To start the tour, climb the stairs. At the top, turn left, entering Room 51. This is the first room of the Sainsbury Wing, which contains paintings showing the evolution of Renaissance art, starting in the medieval age.

MEDIEVAL (1200s-Early 1400s)

In Room 51 (and nearby rooms), shiny gold paintings of saints, angels, Madonnas, and crucifixions float in an ethereal gold never-never land. One thing is very clear: Medieval heaven was different from medieval earth. The holy wore gold plates on their heads. Faces were serene and generic. People posed stiffly, facing either directly out or to the side, never in between. Saints are recognized by the symbols they carry (a key, a sword, a book), rather than by their human features. Art in the Middle Ages was religious, dominated by the Church. The illiterate faithful could meditate on an altarpiece and visualize heaven. It's as though they couldn't imagine saints and angels inhabiting the dreary world of rocks, trees, and sky they lived in.

• *One of the finest medieval devotional paintings is in a small glass case all its own, in the middle of Room 51.*

❶ Anonymous, *The Wilton Diptych,* c. 1395-1399

Two saint/kings and St. John the Baptist present King Richard II (left panel) to the Virgin Mary and her rosy-cheeked baby (right

panel), who are surrounded by angels with flame-like wings. Despite the gold-leaf background, a glimmer of human realism peeks through. The kings have distinct, down-to-earth faces. And the outside shows not a saint, not a god, but a real-life deer lying down in the grass of this earth.

But the anonymous artist is struggling with reality. John the Baptist is holding a "lamb of God" that looks more like a Chihuahua. Nice try. Mary's exquisite fingers hold an anatomically impossible little foot. The figures are flat, scrawny, and sinless, with cartoon features—far from flesh-and-blood human beings. Still, Richard II himself (king of England from 1377 to 1399) knelt before this portable altarpiece to inspire his personal devotions to the Virgin.

• *Do an about-face, and from Room 51, pass through the adjoining Room 52 and into Room 53, entering the world of the...*

EARLY ITALIAN RENAISSANCE (1400s)

The Renaissance—or "rebirth" of the culture of ancient Greece and Rome—was a cultural boom that changed people's thinking about every aspect of life. In politics, it meant democracy. In religion, it meant a move away from Church dominance and toward the assertion of man (humanism) and a more personal faith. Science and secular learning were revived after centuries of superstition and ignorance. In architecture, it was a return to the balanced columns and domes of Greece and Rome. In painting, the Renaissance meant realism. Artists rediscovered the beauty of nature and the human body.

NATIONAL GALLERY

MEDIEVAL
① ANONYMOUS – The Wilton Diptych

EARLY ITALIAN RENAISSANCE
② UCCELLO – Battle of San Romano
③ CRIVELLI – The Annunciation, with Saint Emidius
④ BOTTICELLI – Venus and Mars
⑤ LEONARDO – The Virgin of the Rocks
⑥ LEONARDO – Virgin and Child with St. Anne and St. John the Baptist
⑦ VAN EYCK – The Arnolfini Portrait

HIGH RENAISSANCE
⑧ MICHELANGELO – The Entombment
⑨ RAPHAEL – Pope Julius II

MANNERISM
⑩ BRONZINO – An Allegory with Venus and Cupid
⑪ TINTORETTO – The Origin of the Milky Way

NORTHERN PROTESTANT ART
⑫ VERMEER – A Young Woman Standing at a Virginal

BAROQUE
⑬ REMBRANDT – Belshazzar's Feast
⑭ REMBRANDT – Self-Portrait at the Age of 63
⑮ RUBENS – The Judgment of Paris
⑯ VAN DYCK – Equestrian Portrait of Charles I
⑰ VELÁZQUEZ – The Rokeby Venus
⑱ CARAVAGGIO – The Supper at Emmaus

FRENCH ROCOCO
⑲ BOUCHER – Pan and Syrinx

BRITISH ROMANTIC ART
⑳ CONSTABLE – The Hay Wain
㉑ TURNER – The Fighting Téméraire

To Leicester Square ⊖ ↑ (5 min. walk)

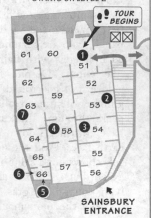

SAINSBURY WING

ENTRANCE ON LEVEL 0

SELF-GUIDED TOUR STARTS ON LEVEL 2

TOUR BEGINS

SAINSBURY ENTRANCE

NATIONAL GALLERY

With pictures of beautiful people in harmonious 3-D surroundings, they expressed the optimism and confidence of this new age.
• *In Room 53, find...*

② Uccello, *Battle of San Romano*, c. 1438-1440
This colorful battle scene shows the victory of Florence over Siena in 1432—and the battle for literal realism on the canvas. It's an early Renaissance attempt at a realistic, nonreligious, three-dimensional scene.

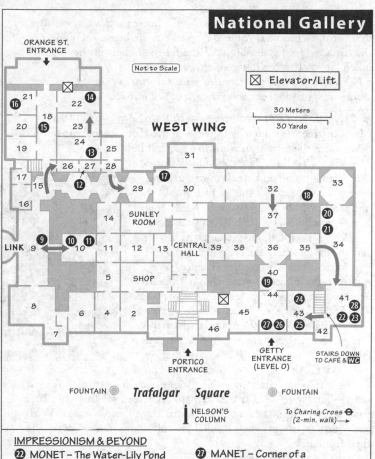

National Gallery

ORANGE ST.
ENTRANCE

Not to Scale

⊠ Elevator/Lift

WEST WING

30 Meters
30 Yards

LINK

SUNLEY
ROOM

CENTRAL
HALL

SHOP

PORTICO
ENTRANCE

GETTY
ENTRANCE
(LEVEL O)

STAIRS DOWN
TO CAFÉ & WC

FOUNTAIN ◉ *Trafalgar Square* ◉ FOUNTAIN

NELSON'S
COLUMN

To Charing Cross ⊖
(2-min. walk)——▶

NATIONAL GALLERY

<u>IMPRESSIONISM & BEYOND</u>

㉒ MONET – *The Water-Lily Pond*

㉓ RENOIR – *The Skiff*

㉔ SEURAT – *Bathers at Asnières*

㉕ VAN GOGH – *Sunflowers*

㉖ MONET – *Gare St. Lazare*

㉗ MANET – *Corner of a Café-Concert*

㉘ CÉZANNE – *Bathers*

Uccello challenges his ability by posing the horses and soldiers at every conceivable angle. The background of farmyards, receding hedges, and tiny soldiers creates an illusion of distance. The artist constructs a grid of fallen

lances in the foreground, then places the horses and warriors within it. Still, Uccello hasn't quite worked out the bugs: The figures in the distance are far too big, and the fallen soldier on the left isn't much larger than the fallen shield on the right.

• *For another artist who wrestled with painting a three-dimensional world on a two-dimensional surface, continue into Room 54.*

❸ Crivelli, *The Annunciation, with Saint Emidius,* 1486

Mary, in green, is visited by the dove of the Holy Spirit, who beams down from the distant heavens in a shaft of light.

Like Uccello's *Battle of San Romano,* there's a lot going on here. Notice the hanging rug, the peacock, the architectural minutiae that lead you way, way back, then *bam!*—you have a giant pickle in your face.

Crivelli combines meticulous detail with Italian spaciousness. The floor tiles and building bricks recede into the distance. We're sucked right in, accelerating through the alleyway, under the arch, and off into space. The Holy Spirit spans the entire distance, connecting heavenly background with earthly foreground. Crivelli creates an Escheresque labyrinth of rooms and walkways that we want to walk through, around, and into.

Renaissance Italians were interested in—even obsessed with—portraying 3-D space. Perhaps they focused their spiritual passion away from heaven and toward the physical world. With such restless energy, they needed lots of elbow room. Space, the final frontier.

• *Continue into Room 58, where the classical age is being "reborn."*

❹ Botticelli, *Venus and Mars,* c. 1485

Mars takes a break from war, succumbing to the delights of love (Venus), while impish satyrs play innocently with the discarded tools of death. In the early spring of the Renaissance, there was an optimistic mood in the air—the feeling that enlightened Man could solve all problems, narrowing the gap between mortals and the Greek gods. Artists felt free to use the pagan Greek gods as symbols of human traits, virtues, and vices. Venus has sapped man's medieval stiffness; the Renaissance has arrived.

• *Find your way to the dimly lit Room 66, with works by the genius who put the budding Renaissance techniques together.*

❺ Leonardo, *The Virgin of the Rocks,* c. 1491-1508

In this painting, Mary, the mother of Jesus, plays with her son and little Johnny the Baptist (with cross, at left) while an androgynous angel looks on. Leonardo brings this

holy scene right down to earth by setting it among rocks, stalactites, water, and flowering plants. But looking closer, we see that Leonardo has deliberately posed his people into a pyramid shape, with Mary's head at the peak, creating an oasis of maternal stability and serenity amid the hard rock of the earth. Leonardo, who was born illegitimate, may have sought in his art the young mother he never knew. Freud thought so.

• *Nearby is a drawing of a similar-looking scene of a harmonious family.*

❻ Leonardo, *Virgin and Child with St. Anne and St. John the Baptist,* c. 1499-1500

At first glance, this chalk cartoon (a full-size preparatory drawing for a painting) looks like a simple snapshot of two loving moms and two playful kids. The two children play—oblivious to the violent deaths they'll both suffer—beneath

their mothers' Mona Lisa smiles.

But follow the eyes: Shadowy-eyed Anne turns toward Mary, who looks tenderly down to Jesus, who blesses John, who gazes back dreamily. As your eyes follow theirs, you're led back to the literal and psychological center of the composition—Jesus—the Alpha and Omega. Without resorting to heavy-handed medieval symbolism, Leonardo drives home a theological concept in a natural, human way. Leonardo the perfectionist rarely finished paintings. This sketch—pieced together from two separate papers (see the line down the middle)—gives us an inside peek at his genius.

• *The Italian Renaissance spread north, influencing the art of the prosperous lands of (today's) Netherlands and Belgium. Stroll through Rooms 65 and 64, seeing how northern artists took Italian-style realism and applied it to portraits of everyday people and ordinary scenes. In Room 63, find...*

❼ Van Eyck, *The Arnolfini Portrait,* 1434

Called by some "The Shotgun Wedding," this painting was once thought to depict a wedding ceremony forced by the lady's swelling belly. Today it's understood as a portrait of a solemn, well-dressed, well-heeled couple, the Arnolfinis of Bruges, Belgium. It is a masterpiece of down-to-earth details.

Van Eyck has built a medieval dollhouse, inviting us to linger over the furnishings. Feel the texture of the fabrics, count the terrier's hairs, trace the shadows generated by the window. Each object is painted at an ideal angle, with the details you'd see if you were standing directly in front of it. So the strings of beads hanging on the back wall are as crystal clear as the bracelets on the woman.

To top it off, look into the round mirror on the far wall—the whole scene is reflected backward in miniature, showing the loving couple and a pair of mysterious visitors. Is one of them Van Eyck himself at his easel? Or has the artist painted you, the home viewer, into the scene?

The surface detail is extraordinary, but the painting lacks true Renaissance depth. The tiny room looks unnaturally narrow, cramped, and claustrophobic.

In medieval times (this was painted only a generation after *The Wilton Diptych*), everyone could read the hidden meaning of certain symbols—the chandelier with its one lit candle (love), the fruit on the windowsill (fertility), the dangling whisk broom (the woman's domestic responsibilities), and the terrier (Fido—fidelity).

By the way, the woman likely is not pregnant. The fashion of the day was to gather up the folds of one's extremely full-skirted dress. At least, that's what they told her parents.

• *Continue into Room 61. The great Florentine artist Michelangelo took the Italian Renaissance style to another level, ushering in the...*

NATIONAL GALLERY

Painting: From Tempera to Tubes

The technology of painting has evolved over the centuries.

1400s: Artists used tempera (pigments dissolved in egg yolk) on wood.

1500s: Still painting on wood, artists mainly used oil (pigments dissolved in vegetable oil, such as linseed, walnut, or poppy).

1600s: Artists applied oil paints to canvases stretched across wooden frames.

1850: Paints in convenient, collapsible tubes are invented, making open-air painting feasible.

The Frames: Although some frames are original, having been chosen by the artist, most are selected by museum curators. Some are old frames from other paintings, others are Victorian-era reproductions in wood, and still others are recent reproductions made of a composite substance to look like gilded wood.

HIGH RENAISSANCE (1490s-Early 1500s)

The Renaissance was born in Florence, but it flowered in Venice and Rome, before spreading north to the rest of Europe. The "Big Three" of the High Renaissance—Leonardo (whom we saw earlier), Michelangelo, and Raphael—were all Florence-trained. Like Renaissance architects (which they also were), they carefully composed their figures on canvas, "building" them into geometrical patterns that reflected the balance and order they saw in nature.

In Venice—a city grown wealthy by trading with the luxurious and exotic East—artists forged a happy-go-lucky art style that shows a taste for the finer things in life. Madonnas and saints were replaced by smooth-skinned, sexy, golden centerfolds. Venetian artists revived the classical world in all its pagan glory, creating beautiful scenes of sensuous Nature.

❽ Michelangelo, *The Entombment*, c. 1500-1501

Michelangelo, the greatest sculptor ever, proves it here in this "painted sculpture" of the crucified Jesus being carried to the tomb. Florentine artists like Michelangelo were inspired by ancient statues of balanced, anatomically perfect, nude Greek gods. Like a chiseled Greek god, this musclehead in red ripples beneath his clothes. Christ's naked body, shocking to the medieval

Church, was completely acceptable in the Renaissance world, where classical nudes were admired as an expression of the divine.

Renaissance balance and symmetry reign. Christ is the center of the composition, flanked by two people leaning equally, who support his body with strips of cloth. They, in turn, are flanked by two others.

The painting is not damaged, but it is unfinished. Michelangelo, 25 years old at the time, moved on to other projects before he got around to adding crucial details, even leaving a blank space in the lower right where Mary would have been.

Regardless of the lack of detail, Michelangelo lets the bodies do the talking. The two supporters strain to hold up Christ's body, and in their tension we, too, feel the great weight and tragedy of their dead god. Michelangelo expresses the divine through the human form.

• *To see how the Renaissance evolved even further, return to Room 51 (where we started), and cross to the main building (the West Wing) and the large Room 9. Here you'll find a work by the man some consider to epitomize the Renaissance, the great...*

❾ Raphael, *Pope Julius II*, 1511

The new worldliness of the Renaissance even reached the Church. Pope Julius II, who was more a swaggering conquistador than a pious pope, set out to rebuild Rome in Renaissance style, hiring Michelangelo to paint the ceiling of the Vatican's Sistine Chapel.

Raphael gives a behind-the-scenes look at this complex leader. On the one hand, the pope is an imposing pyramid of power, with a velvet shawl, silk shirt, and fancy rings boasting of wealth and success. But at the same time, he's a bent and broken man, his throne backed into a corner, with an expression that seems to say, "Is this all there is?"

• *And now for something completely different... continue into Room 10.*

MANNERISM (1520s-1600)

Mannerism, developed in reaction to the High Renaissance, subverts the balanced, harmonious ideal of the previous era with exaggerated proportions, asymmetrical compositions, and decorative color.

• *On the left wall, look for...*

❿ Bronzino, *An Allegory with Venus and Cupid*, c. 1545

You may not recognize this painting, but you might recognize a foot. Look closely at the figure of boy Cupid, on the left. His right foot became famous on TV in the 1970s and 1980s in the comedy show *Monty Python's Flying Circus*. As the show opened and circus music played, the credits would come to an end on the last note, with Cupid's giant foot coming down from above to squash the scene with a flatulent *ffft!* The Flying Circus used collage-style graphics like this to end sketches abruptly (rather than fumble for a punch line), thus making a seamless (if surreal) transition to the next bit.

• *Speaking of transitions, let's move on. To the right is a Titian painting best known as a 1990s album cover. And to the right of that is a naked woman and man spinning in midair.*

⑪ Tintoretto, *The Origin of the Milky Way,* c. 1575

In this scene from a classical myth, the god Jupiter places his illegitimate son, baby Hercules, at his wife's breast. Juno says, "Wait a minute. That's not my baby!" Her milk spurts upward, becoming the Milky Way.

Tintoretto places us right up in the clouds, among the gods, who swirl around at every angle. Jupiter appears to be flying almost right at us. An X composition unites it all— Juno slants one way while Jupiter tilts the other.

• *Now return to Room 9, turn right, pass through Room 15, and turn right again, into Room 26. Pause here to consider the sociopolitical changes that produced this art.*

NORTHERN PROTESTANT ART (1600s)

In the 1500s, Europe split into two camps—Catholic countries to the south, Protestant to the north—with each region adopting its own style of art.

So we switch from CinemaScope to a laptop screen—smaller canvases, subdued colors, everyday scenes, and scarcely a bare shoulder.

Money shapes art. While Italy had wealthy aristocrats and the powerful Catholic Church to purchase art, the North's patrons were middle-class, hardworking, Protestant merchants. They wanted simple, cheap, no-nonsense pictures to decorate their homes and offices. Greek gods and Virgin Marys were out, hometown folks and hometown places were in—portraits, landscapes, still lifes, and slice-of-life scenes. Painted with great attention to detail, this is art meant not to wow or preach at you, but to be enjoyed and lingered over. Sightsee through the next few rooms, featuring the art of rising mercantile nations like Holland and Belgium.

• *In Room 27, don't miss a quintessential Dutch scene...*

⑫ Vermeer, *A Young Woman Standing at a Virginal,* c. 1670

Inside a simple but wealthy Dutch home, a prim virgin plays an early piano called a "virginal." We've surprised her, and she pauses to look up at us.

By framing off such a small world to look at—from the blue chair in the foreground to the wall in back—Vermeer forces us to appreciate the tiniest details, the beauty of everyday things. We can meditate on the tiles lining the floor, the subtle shades of the white wall, and the pale, diffused light that seeps in from the window. Amid straight lines and rectangles, the woman's billowing dress adds a soft touch. The painting of a nude cupid on the back wall only strengthens this virgin's purity.

• *Continue into Room 28, turn left into Room 25, then left again into Room 24. Here you'll find larger, more ambitious works, including one by the greatest Dutch artist...*

⑬ Rembrandt, *Belshazzar's Feast,* c. 1635

Belshazzar, the wicked king of Babylon, has been feasting with God's sacred dinnerware when the meal is interrupted. The king turns to see the hand of God, burning an ominous message into the wall that Belshazzar's number is up. As he turns, he knocks over a goblet of wine. We see the jewels and riches of his decadent life.

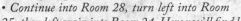

Rembrandt captures the scene at the most ironic moment. Belshazzar is about to be ruined. We know it, his guests know it, and, judging by the look on his face, he's coming to the same conclusion.

Rembrandt's flair for the dramatic is accentuated by the strong contrast between light and dark. Most of his canvases are a rich, dark brown, with a few crucial details highlighted by a bright light.

• *Do an about-face to pass through Room 23—full of portraits of middle-class Dutch men and women—and into Room 22, where you'll come face-to-face with one of the most probing portraits of all.*

⑭ Rembrandt, *Self-Portrait at the Age of 63,* 1669

Rembrandt throws the light of truth on...himself. He made this craggy self-portrait in the year he would die, at age 63. The greatest Dutch painter, he started out as the successful, wealthy young genius of the art world. But he refused to crank out commercial works. Rembrandt painted things that he believed in but no one would invest in—family members, down-to-earth Bible scenes, and self-portraits like this one.

Here, Rembrandt surveys the wreckage of his independent life. He was bankrupt, his mistress had just died, and he had also buried several of his children. We see a disillusioned, well-worn, but proud old genius.

• *While northern artists painted smallish everyday scenes, the Catholic south went a different direction. Go to the end of this hall and step into the long gallery of Room 18—full of big, colorful canvases—and take in the world of...*

BAROQUE (1600s)

The style popular with Catholic popes and aristocrats is called Baroque. This room holds big, colorful, emotional works by Peter Paul Rubens and others from Catholic Flanders (Belgium). Baroque art took the flashy Mannerist style and made it flashier; what had been dramatic now became downright shocking.

• *Here in Room 18, a good example of the glory of Baroque is...*

⓯ Rubens, *The Judgment of Paris,* c. 1636-1639

Rubens painted anything that would raise your pulse—battles, miracles, hunts, and, especially, fleshy women with dimples on all four cheeks. For instance, *The Judgment of Paris* is little more than an excuse for a study of the female nude, showing front, back, and profile all on one canvas.

• *One of Rubens' biggest fans was the Catholic king of England. Find his portrait, painted by a student of Rubens, around the corner in the adjoining Room 21.*

⓰ Van Dyck, *Equestrian Portrait of Charles I,* c. 1637-1638

King Charles sits on a huge horse, accentuating his power. The horse's small head makes sure that little Charles isn't dwarfed. Charles was a soft-on-Catholics king in a hardcore Protestant country until England's Civil War

NATIONAL GALLERY

(1648), when his genteel head was separated from his refined body by Cromwell and company.

Kings and bishops used the grandiose Baroque style to impress the masses with their power. Van Dyck's portrait style set the tone for all the stuffy, boring portraits of British aristocrats who wished to be portrayed as sophisticated gentlemen—whether they were or not.

• *Let's see more Baroque art from Catholic Europe. Use your map to retrace your steps through the Northern Protestant rooms, go through the green-wallpapered Room 29, and enter Room 30 (with red wallpaper). On the left-hand wall, you'll find...*

⑰ Velázquez, *The Rokeby Venus,* c. 1647-1651

Like a sensuous centerfold, Venus lounges diagonally across the canvas, admiring herself, with flaring red, white, and gray fabrics

to highlight her rosy white skin and inflame our passion. Horny Spanish kings loved Italian-style nudes despite Spain's strict Inquisition, the Church tribunal that rooted out bad behavior. This work by the king's personal court painter is a rare Spanish nude from that ultra-Catholic country. The sole concession to Spanish modesty is the false reflection in the mirror—if it really showed what the angle should show, Velázquez would have needed two mirrors...and a new job.

In 1914, the painting was slashed seven times by a knife-wielding vandal. She claimed she'd attacked "the most beautiful woman in mythological history" to protest the arrest of "the most beautiful character in modern history"—a fellow suffragette.

• *Exit out the far end of Room 30 into Room 32. On the right wall, find...*

⑱ Caravaggio, *The Supper at Emmaus,* 1601

After Jesus was crucified, he rose from the dead and appeared without warning to some of his followers. Jesus just wants a quiet meal,

but the man in green, suddenly realizing who he's eating with, is about to jump out of his chair in shock. To the right, a man spreads his hands in amazement, bridging the distance between Christ and us by sticking his hand in our faces.

In the spirit of Baroque,

Caravaggio took reality and exaggerated it. But whereas most artists amplified prettiness, Caravaggio exaggerated grittiness, using real, ugly, unhaloed people in Bible scenes. Caravaggio's paintings look like how a wet dog smells. Reality.

We've come a long way since the first medieval altarpieces that wrapped holy people in gold foil. From the torn shirts to the five o'clock shadows, from the blemished apples to the uneven part in Jesus' hair, we are witnessing a very human miracle.

• *Leave Room 32 at its midpoint, passing through a few galleries on your way to Room 40.*

FRENCH ROCOCO (1700s)

As Europe's political and economic center shifted from Italy to France, Louis XIV's court at Versailles became its cultural hub. Every curly-wigged aristocrat spoke French, dressed French, and bought French paintings. The Rococo art of Louis' successors was as frilly, sensual, and suggestive as the decadent French court. We see their rosy-cheeked portraits and their fantasies: lords and ladies at play in classical gardens, where mortals and gods cavort together.

• *One of the finest examples is the tiny...*

⑲ Boucher, *Pan and Syrinx,* 1759

Curious Pan seeks a threesome, but to elude him, Syrinx eventually changes into reeds, leaving him all wet.

Rococo art is like a Rubens that got shrunk in the wash—smaller, lighter pastel colors, frillier, and more delicate than the Baroque style. Same dimples, though.

• *Backtrack into the round hall, turn right, and head for the horse you see in the distance. Once you reach Room 34, the most eye-catching painting is of* **Whistlejacket,** *the famous racehorse of an 18th-century prime minister, captured on a blank background by George Stubbs. Mentally hop on and prance around the room, taking in the English country-garden ambience.*

BRITISH ROMANTIC ART (Early 1800s)

• *In Room 34, look for...*

❷⓿ Constable, *The Hay Wain,* 1821

The reserved British were more comfortable cavorting with nature than with the lofty gods. Come-as-you-are poets like Wordsworth found the same ecstasy just in being outside.

John Constable set up his easel out-of-doors, making quick sketches to capture the simple majesty of billowing clouds, spreading trees, and everyday rural life. Even British portraits (by Thomas Gainsborough and others) placed refined lords and ladies amid idealized greenery.

This simple style—believe it or not—was considered shocking in its day. The rough, thick, earth-toned paint and crude country settings scandalized art lovers used to the highfalutin, prettified sheen of Baroque and Rococo.

• *Nearby you'll see...*

❷❶ Turner, *The Fighting Téméraire,* 1839

Constable's landscape was about to be paved over by the Industrial Revolution. Soon, machines began to replace humans, factories belched smoke over Constable's hay cart, and cloud-gazers had to punch the clock. Romantics tried to resist it, lauding the forces of nature and natural human emotions in the face of technological "progress." But alas, here a modern steamboat symbolically drags a famous but obsolete sailing battleship off into the sunset to be destroyed.

Turner's messy, colorful style gives us our first glimpse into the modern art world—he influenced the Impressionists. Turner takes an ordinary scene (like Constable), captures the play of light with messy paints (like Impressionists), and charges it with mystery (like, wow).

• *To view more Constables, Stubbs horses, an enormous collection of Turners, and other British art, visit London's Tate Britain (📖 see the Tate Britain Tour). For now, let's head to the future of art. Exit out the far end of this gallery, into Room 41.*

IMPRESSIONISM AND BEYOND (1850-1910)

For 500 years, a great artist was someone who could paint the real world with perfect accuracy. Then along came the camera, and, click, the artist was replaced by a machine. But unemployed artists refused to go the way of *The Fighting Téméraire.*

They couldn't match the camera for painstaking detail, but they could match it—even beat it—in capturing color, the fleeting moment, the candid pose, the play of light and shadow, the quick impression. A new breed of artists burst out of the stuffy confines of the studio. They donned scarves and berets and set up their canvases in farmers' fields or carried their notebooks into crowded cafés, dashing off quick sketches in order to catch a momentary... impression.

• *The Impressionist paintings are dappled throughout Rooms 41-44, scattered here and there by the curators in an ever-changing array. Browse around to find your favorites. Here are a few of mine, starting (in Room 41) with the artist most associated with the Impressionist style.*

㉒ Monet, *The Water-Lily Pond,* 1899

In his Giverny home, near Paris, Monet planned an artificial garden, rechanneled a stream, built a bridge, and planted water lilies. Various paintings in the National Gallery collection show scenes from Monet's garden—a living work of art, an oasis of order and calm in a hectic world.

• *Another example of the Impressionist technique is the smaller canvas nearby...*

㉓ Renoir, *The Skiff,* 1875

It's a nice scene of boats on sun-dappled water. Now move in close. The "scene" breaks up into almost random patches of bright colors. The "blue" water is separate brushstrokes of blue, green, pink, purple, gray, and white. The rower's hat is a blob of green, white, and blue. Up close, it looks like a mess, but when you back up to a proper distance, *voilà!* It shimmers. This kind of rough, coarse brushwork (where you can actually see the brushstrokes) is one of the telltale signs of Impressionism. Renoir was not trying to paint the water itself, but the reflection of sky, shore, and boats off its surface.

• *Move into Room 43. Great works hang at either end of this gallery. Start with the big one to your right...*

㉔ Seurat, *Bathers at Asnières,* 1884

Viewed from about 15 feet away, this is a bright, sunny scene of people lounging on a riverbank. Up close it's a mess of dots, showing the Impressionist color technique taken to its logical extreme. The "green" grass is a shag rug of green, yellow, red, brown, purple, and white brushstrokes. The boy's "red" cap is a collage of red, yellow, and blue.

Seurat has "built" the scene dot by dot, like a newspaper photo, using small points of different bright colors. Only at a distance do the individual brushstrokes blend. Impressionism is all about color. Even people's shadows are not dingy black, but warm blues, greens, and purples.

• *Don't miss one of the don't-miss paintings in this museum, which is usually here in Room 43, directly opposite the Seurat.*

㉕ Van Gogh, *Sunflowers,* 1888

In military terms, Van Gogh was the point man of his culture. He went ahead of his cohorts, explored the unknown, and caught a bullet young. He added emotion to Impressionism, infusing life even into inanimate objects. These sunflowers, painted with characteristic swirling brushstrokes, shimmer and writhe in either agony or ecstasy—depending on your own mood.

Van Gogh painted these during his stay in southern France, a time of frenzied creativity, when he hovered between despair and delight, bliss and madness. A year later, he shot himself.

In his day, Van Gogh was a penniless nobody, selling only one painting in his whole career. In 1987, a different *Sunflowers* painting (he did a half-dozen versions) sold for $40 million (a salary of about $2,500 a day for 45 years), and could probably fetch five times that today.

• *Now continue along to Room 44. Look for works by...*

㉖ Monet, *Gare St. Lazare,* 1877

Claude Monet, the father of Impressionism, was more interested in the play of light off his subject than the subject itself. He uses smudges of white and gray paint to capture how sun filters through the glass roof of the train station and is refiltered through the clouds of steam.

㉗ Manet, *Corner of a Café-Concert,* 1878-1880

Imagine just how mundane (and therefore shocking) Manet's quick "impression" of this café must have been to a public that was raised on Greek gods, luscious nudes, and glowing Madonnas.

• *Finally, backtrack to Room 41, where we started the Impressionists section. This is a good place to end your National Gallery visit, with one of its most modern works...*

㉘ Cézanne, *Bathers,* c. 1894-1905

We've traveled from medieval spirituality to Renaissance realism to Baroque elegance and Impressionist colors. Before you spill out

into the 21st-century hub-bub of London, relax for a second with this gaggle of bathing nudes. These bathers are arranged in strict triangles à la Leonardo—the five nudes on the left form one triangle, the seated nude on the right forms another, and even the background trees and clouds are triangular patterns of paint.

Cézanne uses the Impressionist technique of building a figure with dabs of paint (though his "dabs" are often larger-sized "cube" shapes) to make solid, 3-D geometrical figures in the style of the Renaissance. In the process, his cube shapes helped inspire a radical new style—Cubism—bringing art into the 20th century.

• *Our tour is over, and the 21st century beckons. Exiting Room 45, you find yourself in the stairwell of the Gallery's main entrance (under the dome) on Trafalgar Square. Another set of stairs nearby (look for signs) can lead you elsewhere in the building. Otherwise, step back outside into Trafalgar Square. You're in the heart of London, surrounded by a lifetime of sights yet to enjoy.*

NATIONAL PORTRAIT GALLERY TOUR

Rockstar groupies, book lovers, movie fans, gossipmongers, and even historians all can find at least one favorite celebrity here. From Elizabeth I to Elizabeth II, Byron to Bowie, Keats to Kate, the National Portrait Gallery puts a face on 500 years, making "history" the simple story of flesh-and-blood people. Consider that, for the most part, these portraits were painted in the presence of their subjects—providing us with a tangible link to the real person in the painting. The Gallery is a great rainy-day museum for serious students, or a quick (and free) peek at the eccentric inhabitants of the British Isles. Due to a lengthy renovation, the museum may be closed when you visit. If it is open, expect changes to this tour.

Orientation

Cost: Free, £5 suggested donation; special exhibits extra.

Hours: May be closed for renovation when you visit. When open, likely daily 10:00-18:00, Fri until 21:00—often with music and drinks offered in the evening.

Information: +44 20 7306 0055, www.npg.org.uk.

Getting There: It's at St. Martin's Place, 100 yards off Trafalgar Square (around the corner from the National Gallery and opposite the Church of St. Martin-in-the-Fields). The closest Tube stops are Charing Cross and Leicester Square.

Visitor Information: A floor plan costs £2 (though this tour makes that map less necessary). The first-floor mezzanine level (just up the stairs from the main lobby) houses a bookshop and computer kiosks.

Tours: The £3 audioguide—highly recommended—offers several theme tours, or you can dial up any of 300 individual works. Look for "Portrait Explorer" computers that give info on virtually any portrait or artist in the extensive collection.

Length of This Tour: Allow 1.5 hours. If you're in a rush, focus on your favorite Brits through history.

Services: WCs are in the basement and on the third floor. Pay lockers and coat check (£2 donation) are both in the basement.

Cuisine Art: The elegant **$$$ Portrait Restaurant** on the top floor is pricey for lunch or dinner but offers afternoon tea, and has a fine view over the rooftops of Westminster (reservations wise, +44 20 7312 2490); you can also enjoy a drink at the bar with the same view. The **$$ Portrait Café** in the basement offers sandwiches, salads, and pastries. For more eateries near Trafalgar Square, see page 428.

Starring: Royalty (Henry VIII, Elizabeth I, Victoria), writers (Shakespeare, the Brontës), scientists (Newton, Darwin), politicians (Churchill), and musicians (Handel, McCartney).

OVERVIEW

The Gallery covers 500 years of history from top to bottom—literally. Start on the second floor and work chronologically down to modern times on the ground floor. Historians should linger at the upper floor; celebrity hunters will lose elevation quickly and head to the contemporary section. The portraits include many, many famous people from all walks of life, so use this chapter as an overview, then follow your interests, either with an audioguide or by reading the museum's informative labels.

The Tour Begins

• *From the lobby, ride the long escalator up to the second floor and start in Room 1, marked* The Tudors.

Second Floor

1500s: DEBUT

The small, isolated island of Britain (pop. four million) enters the world stage. The Tudor kings—having already settled family feuds (the Wars of the Roses), balanced religious factions, and built England's navy—bring wealth from abroad.

• *Find the large black-and-white sketch (cartoon) of Henry VIII with his hands on his hips.*

❶ Henry VIII (1491-1547), The Whitehall Mural Cartoon

Young, athletic, intense, and charismatic, with jeweled hands, gold dagger, and bulging codpiece (the very image of kingly power),

Henry VIII carried England on his broad shoulders from political isolation to international power.

In middle age, he divorced his older, dull-eyed, post-childbearing queen, **Catherine of Aragon** (see her portrait on the nearby wall), for the younger, shrewd, sparkling-eyed **Anne Boleyn** (near Catherine; see photo at right), in search of love, sex, and a

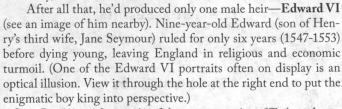

male heir. Nine months later, the future Elizabeth I was born, and the pope excommunicated adulterous Henry. Defiant, Henry started the (Protestant) Church of England, sparking a century-plus of religious strife between the country's Protestants and Catholics.

By the time Henry died—400 pounds of stinking, pus-ridden paranoia—he had wed six wives (see the sixth, sweet young **Katherine Parr,** opposite her predecessors), executed several of them (including Anne Boleyn), killed trusted advisors, and pursued costly wars (for more on Henry, see the sidebar).

After all that, he'd produced only one male heir—**Edward VI** (see an image of him nearby). Nine-year-old Edward (son of Henry's third wife, Jane Seymour) ruled for only six years (1547-1553) before dying young, leaving England in religious and economic turmoil. (One of the Edward VI portraits often on display is an optical illusion. View it through the hole at the right end to put the enigmatic boy king into perspective.)

• Go to Room 2, with portraits of the next generation of Tudors. Among them, you'll always find at least one image of...

❷ Elizabeth I (1533-1603)

Elizabeth I was pale, stern-looking, red-haired (like her father, Henry VIII), and wore big-shouldered power dresses. During her reign, she kept Protestant/Catholic animosity under control and made England a naval power and cultural capital.

Three different portraits (the displays change) depict the span of her life. The one with the most elaborate frame (with a crown on

National Portrait Gallery— Second Floor

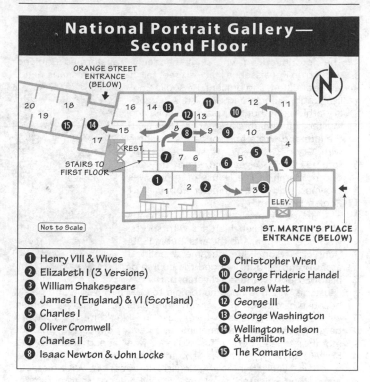

ORANGE STREET ENTRANCE (BELOW)

STAIRS TO FIRST FLOOR

Not to Scale

ST. MARTIN'S PLACE ENTRANCE (BELOW)

1 Henry VIII & Wives
2 Elizabeth I (3 Versions)
3 William Shakespeare
4 James I (England) & VI (Scotland)
5 Charles I
6 Oliver Cromwell
7 Charles II
8 Isaac Newton & John Locke
9 Christopher Wren
10 George Frideric Handel
11 James Watt
12 George III
13 George Washington
14 Wellington, Nelson & Hamilton
15 The Romantics

the top) shows her coronation at age 26, with the crown, scepter, and orb. At age 42 (see photo), she exudes a regal bearing. The largest painting *(The Ditchley Portrait)* captures her standing on a map of England, age 60. She looks ageless, always aware of her public image, resorting to makeup, dye, wigs, showy dresses, and pearls to dazzle courtiers.

The "Virgin Queen" was married only to her country, but she flirtatiously wooed opponents to her side. ("I know I have the body of a weak and feeble woman," she'd coo, "but I have the heart and stomach of a king.") When England's navy sank 72 ships of the Spanish Armada in a single power-shifting battle (1588), Britannia ruled the waves, feasting on New World spoils. Elizabeth surrounded herself with intellectuals, explorers, and poets.

• *Enter Room 3, with a portrait of...*

Henry VIII (1491-1547)

The notorious king who single-handedly transformed England was a true Renaissance Man—six feet tall, handsome, charismatic, well-educated, and brilliant. He spoke English, Latin, French, and Spanish. A legendary athlete, he hunted, played tennis, and jousted with knights and kings. He played the lute and wrote folk songs; his "Pastime with Good Company" is still being performed. When 17-year-old Henry, the second monarch of the House of Tudor, was crowned king in Westminster Abbey, all of England rejoiced.

Henry left affairs of state in the hands of others, and filled his days with sports, war, dice, women, and the arts. But in 1529, Henry's personal life became a political atom bomb, and it changed the course of history. Henry wanted a divorce, partly because his wife had become too old to bear him a son, and partly because he'd fallen in love with Anne Boleyn, a younger woman who stubbornly refused to be just the king's mistress. Henry begged the pope for an annulment, but—for political reasons, not moral ones—the pope refused. Henry went ahead and divorced his wife anyway, and he was excommunicated.

The event sparked the English Reformation. With his defiance, Henry rejected papal authority in England. He forced monasteries to close, sold off some church land, and confiscated everything else for himself and the Crown. Within a decade, monastic institutions that had operated for centuries were left empty and gutted (many ruined sites can be visited today, including the abbeys of Glastonbury, St. Mary's at York, Rievaulx, and Lindisfarne). Meanwhile, the Catholic Church was reorganized into the (Anglican) Church of England, with Henry as its head. Though Henry himself basically adhered to Catholic doctrine, he discouraged the veneration of saints and relics, and commissioned an English translation of the Bible. Hard-core Catholics had to assume a low profile. Many English welcomed this break from Italian religious influence, but others rebelled. For the next few generations, England would suffer through bitter Catholic-Protestant differences.

Henry famously had six wives. The issue was not his love life (which could have been satisfied by his numerous mistresses), but the politics of royal succession. To guarantee the Tudor family's dominance, he needed a male heir born by a recognized queen.

Henry's first marriage, to Catherine of Aragon, had been arranged to cement an alliance with her parents, Ferdinand and Isabel of Spain. Catherine bore Henry a daughter, but no sons. Next came Anne Boleyn, who also gave birth to a daughter. After a turbulent few years with Anne and several miscarriages, a frustrated

Henry had her beheaded at the Tower of London. His next wife, Jane Seymour, finally had a son (but Jane died soon after giving birth). A blind marriage with Anne of Cleves ended quickly when

she proved to be both politically useless and ugly—the "Flanders Mare." Next, teen bride Catherine Howard ended up cheating on Henry, so she was executed. Henry finally found comfort—but no children—in his later years with his final wife, Catherine Parr.

In 1536 Henry suffered a serious accident while jousting. His health would never be the same. Increasingly, he suffered from festering boils and violent mood swings, and he became morbidly obese, tipping the scales at 400 pounds with a 54-inch waist.

Henry's last years were marked by paranoia, sudden rages, and despotism. He gave his perceived enemies the pink slip in his signature way—charged with treason and beheaded. (Ironically, Henry's own heraldic motto was "Coeur Loyal"—true heart.) Once-wealthy England was becoming depleted, thanks to Henry's expensive habits, which included making war on France, building and acquiring palaces (he had 50), and collecting fine tapestries and archery bows.

Henry forged a large legacy. He expanded the power of the monarchy, making himself the focus of a rising, modern nation-state. Simultaneously, he strengthened Parliament—largely because it agreed with his policies. He annexed Wales, and imposed English rule on Ireland (provoking centuries of resentment). He expanded the navy, paving the way for Britannia to soon rule the waves. And—thanks to Henry's marital woes—England would forever be a Protestant nation.

When Henry died at age 55, he was succeeded by his nine-year-old son by Jane Seymour, Edward VI. Weak and sickly, Edward died six years later. Next to rule was Mary, Henry's daughter from his first marriage. A staunch Catholic, she tried to brutally reverse England's Protestant Reformation, earning the nickname "Bloody Mary." Finally came Henry's daughter with Anne Boleyn—Queen Elizabeth I, who ruled a prosperous, expanding England, seeing her father's seeds blossom into the English Renaissance.

London abounds with "Henry" sights. He was born in Greenwich (at today's Old Royal Naval College) and was crowned in Westminster Abbey. He built a palace along Whitehall and enjoyed another at Hampton Court. At the National Portrait Gallery, you can see portraits of some of Henry's wives, and at the Tower you can see where he executed them. Henry is buried alongside his third wife, Jane Seymour, at Windsor Castle.

❸ William Shakespeare (1564-1616)

Though Shakespeare was famous in his day, his long hair, beard, earring, untied collar, and red-rimmed eyes make him look less the celebrity and more the bohemian barfly he likely was (for more on Shakespeare's life and influence, see the sidebar on page 246). This unassuming portrait captures 45-year-old Shakespeare just before he retired from his career as actor, poet, and world's greatest playwright. The shiny, domed forehead is a beacon of intelligence. (I suspect Shakespeare liked this plain-spoken portrait.)

The museum attributes this portrait to a Shakespeare contemporary, John Taylor, and claims it's the only one that could have been painted during the Bard's lifetime. But other scholars insist it was done long after the writer's death. Compare this version with the one you can see in the British Library (see page 248.) One recently discovered portrait (not in the museum) depicts a 46-year-old Shakespeare looking like a matinee idol, with a full head of hair. The search goes on for the "real" Will.

• *Exit Room 3 (into the stairwell), turn right into Room 4, and find the portrait of James I on his throne that marks the end of the Elizabethan Age and the beginning of the…*

1600s: RELIGIOUS AND CIVIL WARS

Catholic kings bickered with an increasingly vocal Protestant Parliament until the English Civil War erupted (1642-1651), killing thousands, decapitating the king, and eventually establishing Parliament as the main power.

❹ James I of England and VI of Scotland (1566-1625)

When the "Virgin Queen" died childless, her cousin—an arrogant Scotsman—moved to genteel London and donned the royal robes. Deeply religious, he launched the "King James" translation of the Bible, but he alienated Anglicans (Church of England), harder-line Protestants (Puritans), and democrats everywhere by insisting that he ruled by divine right, directly from God. He passed on this attitude to his son, Charles.

• *Turn left and enter Room 5, with portraits of Civil War veterans.*

➎ Charles I (1600-1649)

Picture Charles' sensitive face (with scholar's eyes and artist's long hair and beard) severed from his elegant body (in horse-riding finery), and you've arrived quickly at the heart of the Civil War.

The short, shy, stuttering Charles angered Protestants and democrats by dissolving Parliament, raising taxes, and marrying a Catholic. Parliament formed an army, fought the king's supporters, arrested and tried Charles, and—outside the Banqueting House on Whitehall—beheaded him.

• *The man responsible was...*

➏ Oliver Cromwell (1599-1658)

Cromwell, with armor, sword, command baton, and a determined

look, was the Protestant champion and military leader. The Civil War pitted Parliamentarians (Parliament, Protestant Puritans, industry, and urban areas) against Royalists (King, Catholics, nobles, traditionalists, and rural areas). After Charles' execution, Cromwell led kingless England as "Lord Protector."

Stern Cromwell hated luxury and ordered a warts-and-all portrait (see wart on his left temple and scar between his eyebrows). He has a simple, bowl-cut hairstyle adorning his 82-ounce brain (49 is average). Speaking of heads, three years after Cromwell's death, vengeful Royalists exhumed his body, cut off the head, stuck it on a stick, and placed it outside Westminster Abbey, where it rotted publicly for 24 years.

• *Pass through Room 6 and into Room 7. Facing you is...*

➐ Charles II (1630-1685)

After two decades of wars, Cromwell's harsh rule, and Puritanical excesses (no dancing, theater, or political incorrectness), Parliament welcomed the monarchy back (with tight restrictions) under Charles II. England was ready to party.

Looking completely ridiculous,

with splayed legs, puffy face, big-hair wig, garters, and ribbons on his shoes, Charles II became a king with nothing to do, and he did it with grace and a sense of humor. Charles' picture is sandwiched between portraits of his devoted wife, Catherine of Braganza, and one of his well-known mistresses, the actress Nell Gwyn.

• *Make a U-turn right, entering Room 8. In the right corner are the bewigged and unamused...*

❽ Isaac Newton (1642-1727) and John Locke (1632-1704)

The 1600s, the Age of Enlightenment, saw scientific discoveries suggesting that the world operates in an orderly, rational way. Isaac Newton explained the universe's motion with the simplest of formulas ($f=ma$, etc.), and John Locke used human reason to plan a democratic utopia, coining phrases like "life, liberty..." that would inspire America's revolutionaries.

• *Walk straight ahead (through Room 9) to Room 10. Along the right wall, find...*

❾ Christopher Wren (1632-1723)

Christopher Wren—leaning on blueprints with a compass in hand—designed St. Paul's Cathedral, a glorious demonstration of mathematics in stone.

• *In Room 11, make a U-turn left, entering Room 12, with painters, writers, actors, and musicians of the 1700s.*

1700s: DOMESTIC STABILITY, WARS WITH FRANCE

Blossoming agriculture, the first factories, overseas colonization, and political stability from German-born kings (George I, II, III) allowed the arts to flourish. Overseas, England financed wars against Europe's No. 1 power, France.

❿ George Frideric Handel (1685-1759)

In London, an old form of art became something new—modern theater. Handel, a German who wrote Italian operas in England, had several smash hits in London (especially with the oratorio *Messiah*, on his desk), making musical theater popular with ordinary folk. Hallelujah.

• *Walk on to Room 13 for the portrait of...*

⓫ James Watt (1736-1819)

Deep-thinking Watt pores over plans to turn brainpower into work power. His steam engines (with a separate condenser to capture formerly wasted heat energy) soon powered gleaming machines, changing the focus of England's economy from grain and ships to iron and coal.

NATIONAL PORTRAIT GALLERY

• *Head to Room 14, where you'll find George III over your left shoulder and George Washington along the right wall.*

⑫ George III (1738-1820) and
⑬ George Washington (1732-1799)

Just crowned at 23, King George III gives little hint in this portrait that he will lead England into the drawn-out, humiliating "American War" (Revolutionary War) against a col-

ony demanding independence. George III, perhaps a victim of an undiagnosed disease, closed out the stuffy "Georgian" era (in Percy Shelley's words) "an old, mad, blind, despised, dying king."

Perhaps it was the war that drove him mad, or perhaps it was that his enemy, George Washington (portrait nearby), had the same hairdo. Washington was born in British-ruled Virginia and fought for Britain in the French and Indian War, but sided with the colonies in what the British called the "American War." This famous portrait of Washington is one of several versions of a 1796 portrait by Gilbert Stuart.

1800s: COLONIAL AND INDUSTRIAL GIANT

Britain defeated France (Napoleon) and emerged as the world's top power. With natural resources from overseas colonies (Australia, Canada, India, West Indies, China), good communications, and a growing population of seven million, Britain became the first industrial powerhouse, dotted with smoke-belching factories and laced with railroads.

• *Exit Room 14 into Room 8 and turn right, ending up in the bright aqua Room 17, featuring a red-jacketed man—the Duke of Wellington—flanked by portraits of other brave Brits who battled Napoleon.*

⑭ The Duke of Wellington (1769-1852), Admiral Horatio Nelson (1758-1805), and Emma, Lady Hamilton (1761-1815)

While the Duke of Wellington fought Napoleon on land (the final victory at Waterloo, near Brussels, 1815), Admiral Nelson battled France at sea (Battle of Trafalgar, off Spain, 1805).

Often displayed near Nelson is a portrait of Emma, Lady Hamilton, dressed in white, with her famously beautiful face turned coyly. She first met dashing Nelson on his way to fight the French in Egypt. She used the influence of her husband, Lord Hamilton, to restock Nelson's ships. Nelson's daring victory at the Battle of the Nile made him an instant celebrity, though the battle cost him an arm and an eye. The hero—a married man—returned home to woo, bed, and impregnate Lady H., with sophisticated Lord Hamilton's patriotic tolerance.

• *Step into Room 18.*

⑮ The Romantics

Not everyone worshipped industrial progress. Romantics questioned the clinical detachment of science, industrial pollution, and the personal restrictions of modern life. They reveled in strong emotions, non-Western cultures, personal freedom, opium, and the beauties of nature.

• *Scattered around the room, you may see...*

John Keats (1795-1821) broods over his just-written "Ode to a Nightingale." ("My heart aches, and a drowsy numbness pains / My sense, as though of hemlock I had drunk.")

Samuel Taylor Coleridge (1772-1834), at 23, is open-eyed, open-mouthed, and eager. ("And all should cry, Beware! Beware! / His flashing eyes, his floating hair! / ...For he on honey-dew hath fed, / And drunk the milk of Paradise." —"Kubla Khan")

Mary Wollstonecraft Shelley (1797-1851), in telling ghost stories with husband Percy Shelley and friend Lord Byron, conceived a tale of science run amok—*Frankenstein*—imitated by many. ("Ahhhhhhh, sweet mystery of life, at last I've found you!")

William Wordsworth (1770-1850): "The world is too much with us... / Little we see in Nature that is ours; / We have given our hearts away, a sordid boon!"

Percy Bysshe Shelley (1792-1822), political radical, sexual explorer (involving Mary and Claire Clairmont), traveler, and poet. ("O wild West Wind, thou breath of Autumn's being,... / If Winter comes, can Spring be far behind?")

George Gordon, **Lord Byron** (1788-1824), was athletic, exotic, and passionate about women and freedom. Famous and scandalous in his day, he became a Kerouacian symbol of the Romantic movement. ("She walks in beauty, like the night / Of cloudless climes and starry skies...")

Jane Austen (1775-1817) wrote of the landed-gentry class that surrounded her—its manners, love lives, and lifestyle. ("The person, be it gentleman or lady, who has not pleasure in a good novel, must be intolerably stupid.")

• *Backtrack to Room 15 and head downstairs one flight to the **first floor**. Turn right at the bottom of the stairs, pass through the long hall lined with busts (Room 22), and enter Room 21.*

First Floor

1837-1901: THE VICTORIANS

As the wealthiest nation on earth with a global colonial empire, Britain during Queen Victoria's long reign embraced modern technology, contributing to the development of power looms, railroads, telephones, motorcars, and electric lights. It was a Golden Age of science, literature, and middle-class morality, though pockets of extreme poverty and vice lurked in the heart of London itself.

• *Find a statue of a happy couple, titled* Queen Victoria and Prince Albert in Anglo-Saxon Dress. *Flanking the statue are more paintings of these popular monarchs.*

⑯ Queen Victoria (1819-1901) and Prince Albert (1819-1861)

Crowned at 18, the short (4'11"), plump, bug-eyed, quiet girl inherited a world empire. The next year, she proposed marriage (the custom) to the German Prince Albert.

They were a perfect match—lovers, friends, and partners—a model for middle-class couples. The white statue depicts the pair as genteel knight and adoring lady. Albert co-ruled, especially when "Vickie" was pregnant with their nine kids. "Bertie" promoted education, science, public works, and the Great Exhibition of 1851 in Hyde Park. When Albert died at 42, a heartbroken Victoria moped for 40 years. (For more on Victoria, see the sidebar on page 554.)

• *Double back through the long hall lined with stuffy busts of starched shirts (Room 22), browsing around the rooms branching off, which are filled with many prominent Victorians. Start with Room 23 and...*

⑰ Florence Nightingale (1820-1910)

Known as "the Lady with the Lamp" for her nightly nursing visits (though in this detail from a larger painting, she's standing lampless, in the center, with a piece of paper), Nightingale traveled to Turkey in 1854 to tend to Crimean War victims. In fact, her forte

National Portrait Gallery— First Floor

31 20

30

26 24 18

22

27 25 23 17

19

21

ROOM
32

TOUR
CONTINUES

16

21

TOUR ENDS

ELEV.

STAIRS FROM
SECOND FLOOR

STAIRS TO
MEZZANINE
& GROUND FLOOR

St. Martin's Place
Entrance (Below)

Not to Scale

16 Queen Victoria & Prince Albert
17 Florence Nightingale
18 Writers

19 Science & Technology
20 20th-Century Luminaries
21 Britain 1960-2000

was not hands-on nursing but efficient hospital administration (sanitation, keeping supplies stocked, transporting wounded), which ended up saving lives and raising public awareness about health issues. To learn more about her, you can visit the Florence Nightingale Museum, just across the Thames from Big Ben (in Gassiot House at 2 Lambeth Palace Road, Tube: Westminster, Waterloo, or Lambeth North).

• *Across the hall, in Room 24, you'll find several...*

18 Writers

Anne, Emily, and Charlotte Brontë (left to right, youngest to oldest, painted by brother Branwell), three teenage country girls, grew up to write novels such as *Wuthering Heights* (Emily, 1818-1848) and *Jane Eyre* (Charlotte, 1816-1855), about the complex family and love lives of England's rural gentry.

NATIONAL PORTRAIT GALLERY

To the left of the Brontës is a youthful **Charles Dickens** (1812-1870). He was only 12 years old when his dad was sent to a debtor's prison, forcing young Charles to work in a factory. The experience gave him a working-class perspective on British society. He became phenomenally successful writing popular novels *(Oliver Twist, A Tale of Two Cities, A Christmas Carol)* for Britain's educated middle-class.

In the adjoining Room 26 is **Alfred, Lord Tennyson** (1809-1892), the poet laureate of Victorian earnestness. ("Theirs not to reason why, / Theirs but to do and die; / Into the Valley of Death / Rode the six hundred.")
• *Head to Room 27.*

⑲ Science and Technology
Charles Darwin (1809-1882), with basset-hound eyes and long white beard, looks tired after a lifetime of reluctantly defending his controversial theory of evolution, which shocked an entire generation.

Michael Faraday (1791-1867), across from Darwin, shocked himself from time to time, harnessing electricity as the work force of the next century.
• *The long hall (Room 22) leads into Rooms 30 and 31.*

1900s: WORLD WARS
Two devastating world wars and an emerging US superpower shrank Britain from global empire to island nation. But the country remained a cultural giant, producing writers, actors, composers, painters, and Beatles.
• *These final rooms contain portraits of writers, politicians, generals, and socialites. The displays change frequently, so be prepared to put the book aside and browse.*

NATIONAL PORTRAIT GALLERY

⑳ 20th-Century Luminaries

In the **big group portrait** titled *Some Statesmen of the Great War*, find a bored-looking Winston Churchill. You may see a portrait of **George Bernard Shaw** (1856-1950)—playwright, critic, and political thinker—who brought socialist ideas into popular discussion. **Virginia Woolf** (1882-1941) wrote feminist essays ("A woman must have money and a room of her own if she is to write fiction.") and experimental novels (*Mrs. Dalloway* jumps back and forth in time) before filling her pockets with stones and drowning herself in a river to silence the voices in her head.

The **Duchess of Windsor** (see photo) caught the eye of **Edward, Duke of Windsor.** The Duchess' smug smile tells us she got her man. Edward VIII (1894-1972), great-grandson of Queen Victoria, became king in 1936 as a bachelor dating a common-born (gasp), twice-divorced (double gasp) American (oh no!) named Wallis Simpson (1896-1986). Rather than create a constitutional stink, Edward quietly abdicated, married Wallis, and moved to the Continent with her, living happily ever after. They hosted cocktail parties, played golf, and listened to servants call them "Your Majesty"—though they were now just plain Duke and Duchess of Windsor. (His brother "Bertie" took over as King George VI, and George VI's daughter became Queen Elizabeth II. Elizabeth—and all the other royals—essentially snubbed their disgraced aunt and uncle for the rest of their lives.)

In the darkest days at the beginning of World War II, with Nazi bombs raining on a wounded London, **Sir Winston Churchill** (1874-1965) rallied his people with stirring speeches from the Houses of Parliament. ("We shall fight on the beaches...We shall never surrender!") Britain's military chief, Field Marshall **Bernard Montgomery, 1st Viscount** (1887-1976, known as "Monty") points out the D-Day beaches of the decisive Allied assault.

Sir Laurence Olivier (1907-1989), movie and stage actor, played everything from romantic leads and Shakespeare heavies to character parts with funny accents. **Sir Noel Coward** (1899-1973) continued the British tradition of writing witty, sophisticated comedies about the idle rich. **Henry Moore** (1898-1986), the most famous 20th-century sculptor, combined the grandeur of Michelangelo, the raw stone of primitive carvings, and the simplified style of abstract art. **Dylan Thomas** (1914-1953) wrote abstract imagery with a Romantic's heart ("Do not go gentle into that good night..."). American-born poet **T. S. Eliot** (1888-1965) captured the quiet banality of modern life: "This is the way the world ends / Not with a bang but a whimper."

• *Backtrack to the staircase. Before going downstairs, continue past the stairwell into the long Room 32, filled with an exhibit on...*

NATIONAL PORTRAIT GALLERY

㉑ Britain 1960-2000

This ever-changing collection highlights the relationship between por-
traitist and subject. Often included
in this section are contemporary royals (including Queen Elizabeth II,
Prince Charles, and the late Princess
Di), politicians (Margaret Thatcher),
and fixtures of British popular culture
(Sir Paul McCartney and Mick Jagger,
among others).

• *Occasionally, there are still more contem-*
porary portraits on display. They may be
*downstairs on the **ground floor**. Just past*
the ticket desk are rooms set aside for tem-
porary exhibits. At other times they display portraits covering...

2000 TO THE PRESENT

London since the Swinging '60s has been a major exporter of pop
culture. The contemporary collection, located in Rooms 32-42,
changes often depending on who's hot, but you may find royal
youngsters (William and Harry, plus a famously creepy-looking
Kate), politicians (Tony Blair), entrepreneurs (Sir Richard Branson), classic-rock geezers (Sir Elton John, the late David Bowie),
and actors (Sir Michael Caine, Dame Judi Dench), as well as those
in lower-profile professions—writers (Sir Salman Rushdie, Doris
Lessing, Germaine Greer), scientists (Stephen Hawking), composers, painters, and intellectuals.

We've gone from battles to Beatles, seeing Britain's history in
the faces of its major players.

WEST END WALK

From Leicester Square to Piccadilly Circus

The West End, the area just west of the original walled City of London, is London's liveliest neighborhood. It's easy to get caught up in fantasies of jolly olde England, but the West End is where you'll feel the pulse of the living, breathing London of today. Theaters, pubs, restaurants, bookstores, global food, markets, and boutiques attract rock stars, punks, tourists, and ladies and gentlemen stepping from black cabs for a night on the town.

Most of this book's walks and tours focus on history, art, and museums. But this walk is about appreciating the London lifestyle: the entertainment energy at Leicester Square; the thriving popular hum of Covent Garden; the rock-and-roll history of Denmark Street; the bohemian, creative, hedonistic groove of Soho; and the bustling neon hub of Piccadilly Circus. Use the walk to get the lay of the land, then go explore—especially in the evening, when the neon glitters and London sparkles.

Orientation

Length of This Walk: Allow two hours to lace together these highlights.

When to Go: Take your pick—sightseeing by day, or nightlife after dark. Early evenings are ideal, since most pubs and squares are carbonated with locals enjoying a post-work pint or pre-theater bite. After that, join the bustle of people who should probably be grabbing a cab home.

Getting There: Take the Tube to the Leicester Square stop, which is a block from the square itself.

Finding Your Way: A more detailed map than the one provided here may help you find your way more quickly through the maze of irregular streets.

The Walk Begins

• *Start at Leicester Square. Stand at the top of the square and take in the scene.*

❶ Leicester Square

Leicester (LESS-ter) Square is a small park surrounded by glitzy cinema houses. It sits smack in the middle of the theater district—ground zero for London's enticing offerings of flashy musicals, intimate plays starring big-name actors, and much more (for details, see the Entertainment in London chapter). Here, at the entertainment center of London, a statue of Shakespeare looks out, as if pondering the quote chiseled into his pedestal: "There is no darkness but ignorance."

The square's **movie theaters**—the Odeon (Britain's largest cinema), Empire, and Vue—are famous for hosting red-carpet movie premieres. When Bradley Cooper, Benedict Cumberbatch, Keira Knightley, or Jennifer Lawrence needs a publicity splash, it'll likely be here. (Search online for "London film premieres" to find upcoming events.) On any given night, this area is a mosh-pit of clubs and partying teens in town from the suburbs.

Leicester Square is the central clearinghouse for daytime theater ticket sales. Check out the **TKTS booth** (see page 471) and ignore all the other establishments that bill themselves as "half-price" (they're just normal booking agencies). It's often cheaper still to buy tickets directly from one of the theaters we'll pass on this walk.

Global Studios, former home of **Capital Radio London** (next to the Odeon), played a role in rock and-roll history. Back in the 1960s, the British Invasion was in full swing—Beatles, Rolling Stones, The Who—but Brits couldn't hear much of it. The BBC was the only radio station in town, and it was mostly talk and Bach, with only a smattering of pop. Rock fans had to resort to "pirate" radio stations, beamed from Luxembourg or from ships at sea. Capital Radio was one of the first commercial stations allowed to play rock and roll—and that was in 1973! Ironically, within a few years, Capital had itself become mainstream. (The Clash struck back with their song "Capital Radio," which starts, "Yes, it's time for the Dr. Goebbels Show...") Today, Capital is owned by Global

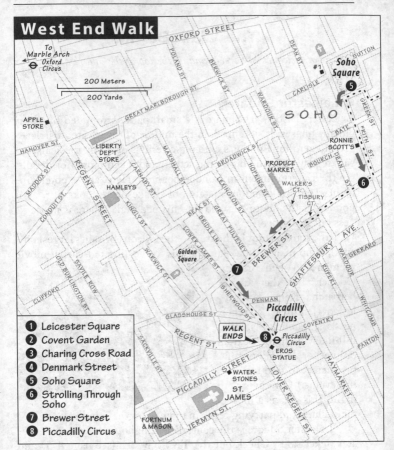

West End Walk

OXFORD STREET

To Marble Arch Oxford Circus

SOHO

Soho Square

#1

200 Meters
200 Yards

APPLE STORE

LIBERTY DEP'T STORE

HAMLEYS

RONNIE SCOTT'S

PRODUCE MARKET

WALKER'S CT.

TISBURY CT.

Golden Square

BREWER ST.

SHAFTESBURY AVE.

DENMAN

Piccadilly Circus

GLASSHOUSE ST.

WALK ENDS

Piccadilly Circus

EROS STATUE

REGENT ST.

WATERSTONES

ST. JAMES

FORTNUM & MASON

PICCADILLY STREET

JERMYN ST.

1 Leicester Square
2 Covent Garden
3 Charing Cross Road
4 Denmark Street
5 Soho Square
6 Strolling Through Soho
7 Brewer Street
8 Piccadilly Circus

(a British radio conglomerate) and FM 95.8 carries on as a major top-40 broadcasting power.

• *Exit Leicester Square from its top corner, heading east (past the Vue cinema) on Cranbourn Street. Cross Charing Cross Road and continue along Cranbourn to the **six-way intersection**.*

Pause here to notice two things: traffic and chain outlets. London's "Congestion Zone" pricing fights downtown traffic by charging regular vehicles big bucks to enter the center. Sure there's still lots of traffic, but it is limited to residents, taxis, service vehicles, city buses...and those willing to pay the fee to drive here. The eateries you see are typical of today's London. They look like one-offs, but are actually just chain outlets dressed up to look like one-offs. London's globalized, corporate food scene (like its hotel scene) is brutal on the mom-and-pop shop. While Londoners value supporting local merchants, chains can be a better economic value.

• *Now, angle right onto Garrick Street. Shortly afterward, turn left onto calm, brick-lined Floral Street. Soon, on the right, the tiny lane called*

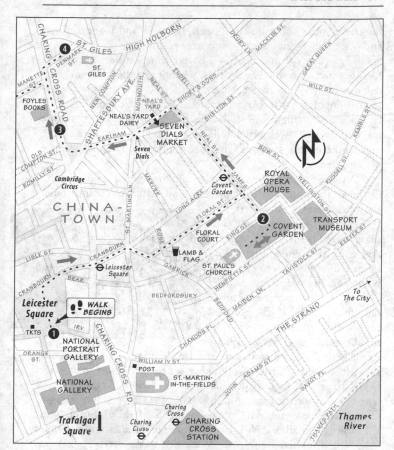

*Lazenby Court leads to the convivial non-corporate, Dickens-era **Lamb & Flag pub.** Farther along Floral Street, find the little passage (on the right) that leads into **Floral Court,** a recently spiffed-up courtyard with boutiques, elegant eateries, and generous greenery. There are many such passages and courtyards in this part of central London.*

Carry on along Floral Street until it opens onto traffic-free James Street. Turn right and head for...

❷ Covent Garden

Covent Garden (only tourists pluralize the name) is a large square teeming with people and street performers—jugglers, sword swallowers, magicians, beatboxers, and guitar players. London's buskers (includ-

ing those in the Tube) are auditioned, licensed, and assigned times and places where they are allowed to perform.

The square's centerpiece is a covered marketplace. A market has been here since medieval times, when it was the "convent" garden owned by Westminster Abbey. In the 1600s, it became a housing development with this courtyard as its center, done in the Palladian style by Inigo Jones. Today's fine iron-and-glass structure was built in 1830 (when such buildings were all the Industrial Age rage) to house the stalls of what became London's chief produce market.

A tourist market thrives here today (for details, see page 463). Go inside the market hall and poke around. After you enter through

the brick passage, look left for the diagram of shops. Inside the market, you'll hit the so-called Apple Market zone. Picture it in full Dickensian color, lined with fruit and vegetable stalls. Covent Garden remained a produce market until 1973 (look for photos from these days in the middle side aisles). After 1973, its venerable arcades were converted to boutiques, cafés, and antique shops. For a drink overlooking all the action on the square below, the Punch & Judy pub has a view terrace on the rooftop.

From inside the market hall, exit out the west end (to the right from where you entered). You're facing **St. Paul's Church** (not the famous cathedral), with its Greek temple-like facade and blue clockface (irregular hours, pay WCs just to the left). Known as the Actors' Church, it's long been a favorite of nervous performers praying for success. To go inside, pass through one of the gates on either side of the facade, and find the entrance around back. These gates also lead to a tranquil churchyard—a nice escape from the busker bustle on Covent Garden. Inside the church, the walls are lined with memorials to theater folk, some of whom (Chaplin, Karloff) you might recognize.

At the bottom (southeast) corner of Covent Garden is the **London Transport Museum,** which gives a well-presented look at the evolution of this city's famously well-planned mass transit system (see page 64).

Tucked into the top (northeast) corner of the square is the **Royal Opera House,** which showcases top-notch opera and ballet.

❸ From Covent Garden to Charing Cross Road

From Covent Garden, backtrack up James Street and continue

straight up narrow Neal Street, browsing your way northwest along the lively and colorful streets.

Two blocks up Neal Street, you'll pass through an up-and-coming shopping zone. Turn left on Short's Gardens. On the left, notice the entrance to **Seven Dials Market,** a thriving food court with a wide variety of street vendors assembled under a glass-covered courtyard. Just beyond, on the right (at #7), **Neal's Yard Dairy** sells a wide variety of cheeses from the British Isles. This is the original shop of what is now a thriving chain. Everything is well described, and they'll slice off a sample if you ask nicely.

Continue along Short's Gardens to the next intersection—called **Seven Dials**—where seven  sundials atop a pole mark the meeting of seven small streets. Built in 1694, this once served the timekeeping needs of this busy merchants' quarter. Continue straight ahead onto Earlham Street.

Continuing straight on Earlham Street, you'll spill out into **Cambridge Circus**— the busy intersection of Shaftesbury Avenue and Charing Cross Road—with its fine red-brick Victorian architecture and classic theaters. **Charing Cross Road** is the traditional home of London's bookstores. Cross Shaftesbury Avenue and carry on straight two blocks along Charing Cross to reach one of the biggest, **Foyles Books,** which puts on free events several nights a week—from book signings to jazz in their gallery (usually around 18:00 or 19:00, bookstore is on left at 107 Charing Cross Road, café and WCs, www.foyles.co.uk).

• *A few steps up from Foyles, turn right onto...*

❹ Denmark Street

This seemingly nondescript little street is a musician's mecca. In the 1920s, it was known as "Britain's Tin Pan Alley"—the center of the UK's music-publishing  industry, when songwriters here cranked out popular tunes printed as sheet music.

Later, in the 1960s, Denmark Street was the epicenter for rock and roll's British Invasion, which brought so much great pop music to the US. **Regent Sound Studio** (at #4, half a block down on the right, now a guitar store with a similar name) was a low-budget recording studio. It was here in 1964 that the Rolling Stones recorded the song that raised them from obscurity, "Not Fade Away." Other acts that recorded on Denmark Street include the Who ("Happy Jack"), the Kinks (who wrote a song called "Denmark Street"), the Beatles ("Fixing a Hole"), David Bowie, and Black Sabbath (who made their first two

records here—including the track "Iron Man"). Today, Regent is a music store, and the former studio's walls are lined with a wonderland of guitars.

While many of the original locations have closed, the legends live on. The storefront at **#20** (across the street and closer to Charing Cross Road) was formerly a music publishing house that employed a lowly office boy named Reginald Dwight. In 1969, on the building's rooftop, he wrote "Your Song" and went on to become famous as Sir Elton John. In the 1970s, the Sex Pistols lived in apartments above #6. The now-closed **12 Bar Café,** once at #25 on the left, helped launch the careers of more recent acts: Damien Rice, KT Tunstall, Jeff Buckley, and Keane.

Today, while it's gentrifying and has lost a bit of its "music row" character, Denmark Street still offers one-stop shopping for the modern musician: You could buy a vintage Rickenbacker guitar, get your sax repaired, take piano lessons, lay down a bass track, have a few beers, or tattoo your name across your knuckles like Ozzy Osbourne.

• *Backtrack up Denmark Street, cross Charing Cross Road, and head down Manette Street. Continue under the "Pillars of Hercules" passage, then turn right up Greek Street to...*

❺ Soho Square

The Soho neighborhood is London's version of New York City's Greenwich Village. It's a ritzy, raffish, edgy, and colorful area. Because of its eccentric 1970s landlord, porn publisher Paul Raymond, the Soho district escaped late-20th-century development. So, rather than soulless office towers, it retains its characteristic charm. And because the square has no real through-roads, it's almost traffic-free—strangely quiet and residential-feeling for being in the center of such a huge city.

Soho Square Gardens is a favorite place for a nap or picnic on a sunny afternoon (pick up picnic goodies from nearby shops).

The little house in the middle of the square is the gardener's hut. History plaques at each entrance tell the area's story, which dates back to 1731. Originally a "key garden," this was once a yard shared by the wealthy people who lived on this square. And

speaking of wealthy people, at #1, on the west (left) side of the square, the MPL building (McCartney Publishing Limited) houses offices of one of Britain's richest musicians, Sir Paul McCartney.

• *At the bottom of the square, exit down Frith Street. Stroll two blocks, enjoying the atmosphere as you make your way to the intersection with Old Compton Street.*

❻ Strolling Through Soho

The restaurants and boutiques here and on adjoining streets (such as Greek, Dean, and Wardour streets) are trendy and creative, the kind that attract high society when they feel like slumming it. Bars with burly, well-dressed bouncers abound. Private clubs cater to the late-night rock crowd.

Ronnie Scott's Jazz Club: This club, at 47 Frith Street, has featured big-name acts for more than 50 years. In 1970, Jimi Hendrix jammed here with Eric Burdon and War; it was the last performance before his death in a London apartment a few days later. Even today Ronnie Scott's is *the* place to go for jazz in London. Shows regularly sell out in advance—check at the box office when you pass by or reserve in advance (see page 480 for details).

• *Turn right on Old Compton Street and go one block to the intersection of Old Compton and Dean streets.*

Old Compton Street: You're at the center of the neighborhood. Take in the eclectic variety of people going by. You're surrounded by the buzz of Soho.

The many **rainbow flags** you see here recall a time when these streets were a center of London's LGBTQ scene. Homosexuality was illegal in the UK until 1967, when it was officially decriminalized. (A famous victim of this policy was Alan Turing, the mathematician who helped break the Nazis' secret code in World War II. He was subjected to chemical castration and ultimately died of cyanide poisoning—possibly self-inflicted.) When being gay was illegal, members of the clandestine community here in Soho adopted a secret slang called Polari. Some words—such as togs (clothes) or naff (tacky)—eventually migrated into the English mainstream.

Chinatown: At the corner of Dean and Old Compton, look

left for the pagoda-style arch down the street. South of here, on the other side of Shaftesbury Avenue, is London's underwhelming Chinatown. With Gerrard Street as its spine, it occupies what was once just more of Soho, with the same Soho artsy vibe. In the 1960s, the Chinese community gathered here, eventually dominated this zone, and non-Asian businesses moved out. The Chinese population swelled when the former British colony of Hong Kong was returned to China in 1997, but the neighborhood's identity is now threatened by developers eyeing this high-rent real estate.

• *Continue along Old Compton Street to where it hits Wardour Street (with a string of enticing restaurants just to the right). Crossing Wardour, Old Compton squeezes down into a narrow alley (Tisbury Court). Penetrate this sleazy passage of sex shows and blue-video shops, tolerate the barkers' raunchy come-ons, then jog a half-block right and turn left on Brewer Street.*

❼ Brewer Street: Sleaze and Porn Shops

Soho was a bordello zone in the 19th century. A smidge of that survives today in this area. Sex shops and video arcades mingle with upscale restaurants here in west Soho. While it's illegal in Britain to sell sex on the street, well-advertised "models" entertain (profitably) in their tiny apartments. And these days massage parlors that promise memorable endings are harder for the police to bust.

One block north of Brewer Street—up Walker's Court—Berwick Street hosts a produce market (closed Sun).

• *Our walk is nearly finished. Continue a few short blocks along Brewer Street, observing the fascinating metamorphosis of a neighborhood from sleaze to gentrification. When you reach The Crown tavern, at the intersection of Brewer Street and Sherwood Street (also called Lower James Street), turn left onto Sherwood Street and follow it one long, twisty block down, emerging into the bustling intersection known as...*

❽ Piccadilly Circus

London's most touristy square got its name from the fancy ruffled shirts—*picadils*—made in the neighborhood long ago. In the late 20th century, the square veered toward the gimmicky and tacky.

The square's center features a statue-on-a-pillar of a tipsy-but-perfectly balanced Eros. (Scholars say it's Anteros, the love god's brother, but Londoners call it Eros.) Until just a couple of years ago, Piccadilly was a famously busy traffic circle, with cars and big red buses spinning around the statue. Now—though still busy with cars—it's also a packed people zone. At night it's as bright as day—with neon lights pulsing and the 20-foot-high video ads painting the classic Georgian facades in a rainbow of colors. Black cabs honk, tourists crowd the attractions, and Piccadilly shows off big-city London at its glitziest.

• *Our walk is done. If you're up for more sightseeing, it's easy to connect from here to my "Regent Street Shopping Walk" (page 464). Several recommended restaurants are nearby (see map on page 424). If you're ready to move on, the Piccadilly Tube stop is here, and handy buses #38 and #159 stop near here (see page 36). It's all ready for you—you're at the center of London.*

BRITISH MUSEUM TOUR

In the 19th century, the British flag flew over one-fourth of the world. London was the empire's capital, where women in saris walked the streets with men in top hats. And England collected (read: stole) art as fast as it collected colonies.

Many criticize the British Museum's collection for having been built on plunder, at the expense of subjugated, faraway lands. And yet, as a sightseer who's mindful of this questionable legacy, the collection can still be appreciated for what it is: *the* chronicle of Western civilization.

History is a modern invention. Three hundred years ago, people didn't care about crumbling statues and dusty columns. Nowadays, we value a look at past civilizations, knowing that "those who don't learn from history are condemned to repeat it."

The British Museum is the only place I can think of where you can follow the rise and fall of three great civilizations—Egypt, Assyria (ancient Iraq), and Greece—in a few hours, with a coffee break in the middle. And while the sun never set on the British Empire, it will on you, so on this tour we'll see just the most exciting two hours.

Orientation

Cost: Free, £5 suggested donation (unload your spare change). Some temporary exhibits require a separate admission (and a timed ticket).

Hours: Daily 10:00-17:30, Fri until 20:30 (some galleries may close Fri night, but most of this tour should be open).

Information: Ticket desk +44 20 7323 8181, www.britishmuseum. org.

When to Go: Rainy days, Sundays, and school holidays are the

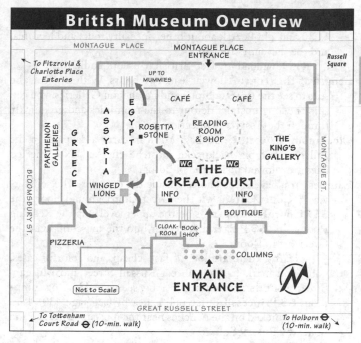

British Museum Overview

MONTAGUE PLACE

MONTAGUE PLACE ENTRANCE

Russell Square

To Fitzrovia & Charlotte Place Eateries

UP TO MUMMIES

EGYPT

ASSYRIA

GREECE

PARTHENON GALLERIES

ROSETTA STONE

CAFÉ   CAFÉ

READING ROOM & SHOP

THE KING'S GALLERY

MONTAGUE ST.

BLOOMSBURY ST.

WC   **THE GREAT COURT**   WC

WINGED LIONS

INFO   INFO

BOUTIQUE

PIZZERIA

CLOAK-ROOM   BOOK-SHOP

COLUMNS

Not to Scale

MAIN ENTRANCE

GREAT RUSSELL STREET

To Tottenham Court Road ⊖ (10-min. walk)

To Holborn ⊖ (10-min. walk)

most crowded times. The museum is least crowded late on weekday afternoons, especially on Fridays.

Getting There: The main entrance is on Great Russell Street. From the Tottenham Court Road Tube stop, take exit #2, walk straight ahead, and take the first right on Great Russell Street. The Holborn and Russell Square Tube stops are also nearby. Buses #38 and #24 are among the many that stop here (see page 36).

Getting In: There can be a long security line at the main entrance. It moves quickly, but if you hate waiting, circle around to the Montague Place entrance at the back (north side) of the building.

Visitor Information: Just inside the Great Court, you can pick up the basic map (£2 donation), but it's not essential for this tour. Don't bother with the pricey *Visitor's Guide* (skimpy text).

Tours: Free 30- to 40-minute **EyeOpener tours** by volunteers focus on select rooms (daily 11:00-15:45, generally every 15 minutes).

More in-depth 1.5-hour tours (£14) are offered Fri-Sun at 11:30 and 14:00. Ask about other specialty tours and lectures, and the museum's free **app.**

🎧 Download my free British Museum **audio tour.**

Length of This Tour: Allow at least two hours. With less time, be sure to see the Rosetta Stone and Parthenon Galleries; you can skip the long upstairs detour to the mummies and go quickly through the Assyrian collection.

Cloakroom: £2/coat, £2.50/bag. You can carry a daypack in the galleries, but big backpacks must be checked. No wheeled bags are allowed inside the building.

Eateries: You have three choices inside the complex. The self-service **$ Court Café** is on the Great Court ground floor. The **$$$ Court Restaurant** is on the upper level atop the Reading Room. The **$$ Pizzeria** is deeper into the museum, near the Greek art in Room 12.

Nearby, there are lots of fast, cheap, and colorful cafés, pubs, and markets along Great Russell Street and Museum Street. For other recommendations, see page 436. The sumptuous **$$ Princess Louise** pub is nearby (see page 430). Karl Marx picnicked on the benches near the museum entrance and in nearby Russell Square.

Starring: Rosetta Stone, Egyptian mummies, Assyrian lions, and the Parthenon sculptures.

The Tour Begins

The main entrance on Great Russell Street spills you into the Great Court, a glass-domed space with the round Reading Room in the center. From the Great Court, doorways lead to all wings. To the left are the exhibits on Egypt, Assyria, and Greece—our tour. We'll try to hit the highlights as we work chronologically.

The Great Court, Europe's largest covered square, is bigger than a football field. This people-friendly court—delightfully spared from the London rain—was for 150 years one of London's great lost spaces...closed off and gathering dust. Since the year 2000, it's been the 140-foot-wide hub of a two-acre cultural complex.

The stately round Reading Room (generally closed except for special exhibitions) was once a study hall for Oscar Wilde, Arthur Conan Doyle, Rudyard Kipling, T. S. Eliot, Virginia Woolf,

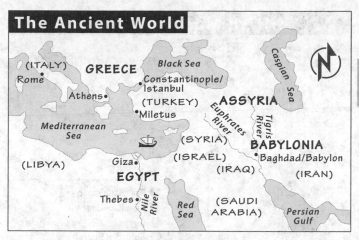

The Ancient World

(ITALY)
Rome
GREECE
Black Sea
Constantinople/
Istanbul
Athens•
(TURKEY)
•Miletus
Caspian Sea
ASSYRIA
Euphrates River
Tigris River
Mediterranean Sea
(SYRIA)
BABYLONIA
•Baghdad/Babylon
(LIBYA)
Giza•
(ISRAEL)
(IRAQ)
(IRAN)
EGYPT
Thebes•
Nile River
Red Sea
(SAUDI ARABIA)
Persian Gulf

W. B. Yeats, Mark Twain, and V. I. Lenin. Karl Marx formulated his ideas on communism and wrote *Das Kapital* here.

• *Start with ancient Egypt. The Egyptian Gallery is in the West Wing, to the left of the Reading Room. Enter the Egyptian Gallery. The Rosetta Stone is directly in front of you.*

ANCIENT EGYPT

Egypt was one of the world's first "civilizations"—a group of people with a government, religion, art, free time, and a written language. The Egypt we think of—pyramids, mummies, pharaohs, and guys who walk funny—lasted from 3000 to 1000 BC with hardly any change in the government, religion, or arts. Imagine two millennia of Nixon.

❶ Rosetta Stone

When this rock was unearthed in the Egyptian desert in 1799, it was a sensation in Europe. This black slab, dating from 196 BC,

caused a quantum leap in the study of ancient history. Finally, Egyptian writing could be decoded.

The hieroglyphic writing in the upper part of the stone was indecipherable for a thousand years. Did a picture of a bird mean "bird"? Or

was it a sound, forming part of a larger word, like "burden"? As it turned out, hieroglyphics are a complex combination of the two, surprisingly more phonetic than symbolic. (For example, the hieroglyph that looks like a mouth or an eye is the letter "R.")

British Museum—Egypt

Not to Scale

⊠ ELEVATOR

To 5, 6 & 7

GREAT COURT & READING ROOM

❶ Rosetta Stone
❷ King Ramesses II
❸ Egyptian Gods as Animals
❹ Colossal Scarab
❺ Up to Nebamun Hunting in the Marshes
❻ Up to Egyptian Funeral Objects
❼ Up to Gebelein Man
❽ Head & Arm of Amenhotep III
❾ Four Figures of Sekhmet
❿ Beard Piece of Great Sphinx
⓫ False Door & Architrave of Ptahshepses
⓬ Statue of Nenkheftka

ASSYRIA

WINGED LIONS

CLOAKROOM

The Rosetta Stone allowed linguists to break the code. It contains a single inscription repeated in three languages. The bottom third is plain old Greek (find your favorite frat or sorority), while the middle is medieval Egyptian. By comparing the two known languages with the one they didn't know, translators figured out the hieroglyphics.

The breakthrough came when they discovered that the large ovals (such as in the sixth line from the top) represented the name of the ruler, Ptolemy. Simple.

• *In the gallery to the right of the Stone, find the huge head of Ramesses.*

❷ King Ramesses II

When Moses told the king of Egypt, "Let my people go!" this was the stony-faced look he got. Ramesses II ruled for 66 years (c. 1290-1223 BC) and may have been in power when Moses cursed Egypt with plagues, freed the Israeli slaves, and led them out of Egypt to their homeland in Israel (according to the Bible, but not exactly corroborated by Egyptian chronicles).

This seven-ton statue (c. 1250 BC), made from two different colors of granite, is a fragment from a temple in Thebes. It shows

Ramesses with the traditional features of a pharaoh—goatee, cloth headdress, and cobra diadem on his forehead. Ramesses was a great builder of temples, palaces, tombs, and statues of himself. There are probably more statues of him in the world than there are cheesy fake *David*s. He was so concerned about achieving immortality that he even chiseled his own name on other people's statues. Very cheeky.

Picture what the archaeologists saw when they came upon this: a colossal head and torso separated from the enormous legs and toppled into the sand—all that remained of the works of a once-great pharaoh. Kings, megalomaniacs, and workaholics, take note.

• *Say, "Ooh, heavy," and climb the ramp behind Ramesses, looking for a variety of animals.*

❸ Egyptian Gods as Animals

Before technology made humans the alpha animal on earth, it was easier to appreciate our fellow creatures. Animals were stronger, swifter, and fiercer than feeble *Homo sapiens*. The Egyptians worshipped animals as incarnations of the gods.

Though the displays here change, you may see the powerful ram—the god Amun (king of the gods)—protecting a puny pharaoh under his powerful chin. The falcon is Horus, the god of the living. The speckled, standing hippo (with lion head) is Taweret, protectress of childbirth. Her stylized breasts and pregnant belly are supported by ankhs, symbols of life. (Is Taweret grinning or grimacing in labor?) Finally, the cat (with ear- and nose-rings) served Bastet, the popular goddess of stress relief.

Farther along the gallery, you'll see huge stone boxes. The famous mummies of ancient Egypt were wrapped in linen and then encased in finely decorated wooden coffins, which were then placed in these massive stone outer coffins.

• *At the end of the Egyptian Gallery is a big stone beetle.*

❹ Colossal Scarab

This species of beetle would burrow into the ground, then reappear—it's a symbol of resurrection, like the sun rising and setting, or death and rebirth. Scarab amulets were placed on mummies' chests to protect the spirit's heart from acting impulsively. Pharaohs wore the symbol of the beetle, and tombs and temples were decorated with them (this one, from c. 332 BC, probably once sat in a temple). The hieroglyph for scarab meant "to come into being."

Like the scarab, Egyptian culture was buried—first by Greece, then by Rome. Knowledge of the ancient writing died, condemning the culture to obscurity. But since the discovery of the Rosetta Stone, Egyptology has boomed, and Egypt has come back to life.

• *You can't call Egypt a wrap until you visit the mummies upstairs. Continue to the end of the gallery and up the West Stairs (four flights or elevator) to floor 3. At the top, enter Room 61 (a.k.a. the Michael Cohen Gallery), with objects and wall paintings from the tomb of Nebamun. As you enter the room, veer slightly left and head to the far wall to find a...*

❺ Painting of Nebamun Hunting in the Marshes

Nebamun stands in a reed boat, gliding through the marshes. He raises his arm, ready to bean a bird with a snakelike hunting stick. On the right, his wife looks on, while his daughter crouches between his legs, a symbol of fatherly protection.

This nobleman walks like Egyptian statues look—stiff and flat, like he was just run over by a pyramid. We see the torso from the front and everything else— arms, legs, face—in profile, creating the funny walk that has become an Egyptian cliché. (As if an early version of Cubism, we see various perspectives at once.)

But the stiffness is softened by a human touch. It's a family snapshot of loved ones from a happy time. The birds, fish, and plants are painted realistically, like encyclopedia entries. (The first "paper" came from papyrus plants like the bush on the left.) The only unrealistic element is the house cat (thigh-high, in front of the man) acting as a retriever—possibly the only cat in history that ever did anything useful.

When Nebamun passed into the afterlife, his awakening soul could look at this painting (c. 1350 BC) on the tomb wall and think of his wife and daughter—doing what they loved for all eternity.

• *Browse through Rooms 62–63, filled with displays in glass cases. There are several corpses on display. Find yourself a mummy. In other glass cases you'll find coffins, tomb paintings, canopic jars, statuettes, even animal mummies. These objects all have something to do with the...*

❻ Egyptian Funeral

Mummifying a body is much like following a recipe. First, disembowel it (but leave the heart inside), then pack the cavities with pitch, and dry it with natron, a natural form of sodium carbonate (and, I believe, the active ingredient in Twinkies). Then carefully bandage it head to toe with hundreds of yards of linen strips. Let it sit 2,000 years, and...*voilà!* Or just dump the corpse in the desert and let the hot, dry, bacteria-killing Egyptian sand do the work—you'll get the same results.

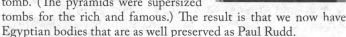

The mummy was placed in a wooden coffin, which was put in a stone coffin, which was placed in a tomb. (The pyramids were supersized tombs for the rich and famous.) The result is that we now have Egyptian bodies that are as well preserved as Paul Rudd.

The internal organs were preserved alongside the mummy in canopic jars, and small-scale statuettes of the deceased *(shabtis)* were

scattered around. Written in hieroglyphs on the coffins and the tomb walls were burial rites from the Book of the Dead. These were magical spells to protect the body and crib notes for the waking soul, who needed to know these passwords to get past the guardians of eternity.

Many of the mummies here are from the time of the Roman occupation, when fine memorial portraits painted in wax became popular. X-ray photos in the display cases tell us more about these people.

Don't miss the animal mummies. Cats (near the entrance to Room 62) were popular pets. They were also considered incarnations of the cat-headed goddess Bastet. Worshipped in life as the sun god's allies, preserved in death, and memorialized with statues, cats were given the adulation they've come to expect ever since.

• *Linger in Rooms 62 and 63, but remember that eternity is about the*

BRITISH MUSEUM

amount of time it takes to see this entire museum. In Room 64, in a glass case, you'll find what's left of a visitor who tried to see it all...

❼ Gebelein Man, Known as "Ginger"

This man died 5,400 years ago, a thousand years before the pyramids. His people buried him in the fetal position, where he could "sleep" for eternity. The hot sand naturally dehydrated and protected the body. With him are a few of his possessions: bowls, beads, and the flint blade next to his arm. His grave was covered with stones. Named "Ginger" by scientists for his wisps of red hair, this man from a distant time somehow seems so relatably human.

• *We'll continue with Egypt by going back downstairs. Backtrack to Room 61 and head back down the stairs to the Egyptian Gallery and the Rosetta Stone. Just past the Rosetta Stone, find a huge head (facing away from you) with a hat like a bowling pin.*

❽ Head and Arm of a Statue of Amenhotep III

Art served as propaganda for the pharaohs, kings who called themselves gods on earth. Put this red-granite head (c. 1370 BC) on top of an enormous body (which still stands in Egypt), and you have the intimidating image of an omnipotent ruler who demands servile obedience. Next to the head is, appropriately, the pharaoh's powerful fist—the long arm of the law.

Amenhotep's crown is actually two crowns in one. The pointed upper half is the royal cap of Upper Egypt. This rests on the flat, fez-like crown symbolizing Lower Egypt. A pharaoh wearing both crowns together is bragging that he rules a combined Egypt. As both "Lord of the Two Lands" and "High Priest of Every Temple," the pharaoh united church and state.

• *Along the wall to the left of the red-granite head (as you're facing it) are four black lion-headed statues.*

❾ Four Figures of the Goddess Sekhmet

The lion-headed goddess Sekhmet looks pretty sedate here (in these sculptures dating to c. 1360 BC), but she could spring into a fierce crouch when crossed. She was the pharaoh's personal bodyguard, who could burn his enemies to a crisp with flaming arrows.

The gods ruled the Egyptian cosmos like dictators in a big banana republic (or the US Congress). Egyptians bribed their gods for favors, offering food, animals, or money, or erecting statues like these.

Sekhmet holds an ankh. This key-shaped cross was the hieroglyph meaning "life" and was a symbol of eternal life. Later, it was adopted as a Christian symbol because of its cross shape and religious overtones.

• *A few paces directly in front of Amenhotep III, find a glass case containing a...*

❿ Beard Piece of the Great Sphinx

The Great Sphinx—a statue of a pharaoh-headed lion—crouches in the shadow of the Great Pyramids in Cairo. Time shaved off the sphinx's soft, goatee-like limestone beard, and a piece is now preserved here in a glass case. This hunk of stone is only a whisker—about three percent of the massive beard—giving an idea of the scale of the six-story-tall, 250-foot-long statue.

The Sphinx is as old as the pyramids (c. 2500 BC), built during the time known to historians as the Old Kingdom (2686-2181 BC), but this beard may have been added later, during a restoration (c. 1420 BC, or perhaps even later under Ramesses II).

• *Ten steps past the Sphinx's soul patch, on the left, is a 10-foot-tall, red-tinted "building" covered in hieroglyphics.*

⓫ False Door and Architrave of Ptahshepses

This limestone "false door" (c. 2400 BC) was a ceremonial entrance (never meant to open) for a sealed building, called a *mastaba*, that marked the grave of a man named Ptahshepses. The hieroglyphs of eyes, birds, and rabbits serve as

his epitaph, telling his life story, how he went to school with the pharaoh's kids, became an honored vizier, and married the pharaoh's daughter.

The deceased was mummified, placed in a wooden coffin that was encased in a stone coffin, then in a stone sarcophagus (like the **red-granite sarcophagus** in front of Ptahshepses' door), and buried 50 feet beneath the *mastaba* in an underground chamber.

Mastabas like Ptahshepses' were decorated inside and out with statues, steles, and frescoes like those displayed nearby. These pictured things that the soul would find useful in the next life—magical spells, lists of the deceased's accomplishments, snapshots of the deceased and his family while alive, and secret passwords from the Egyptian Book of the Dead. False doors like this allowed the soul (but not grave robbers) to come and go.

• *Just past Ptahshepses' false door is a glass case with a red-tinted statue.*

⑰ Statue of Nenkheftka

Painted statues such as this one (c. 2400 BC) represented the soul of the deceased. Meant to keep alive the memory and personality of the departed, this image would have greeted Nenkheftka's loved ones when they brought food offerings to place at his feet to nourish his soul. (In the mummification rites, the mouth was ritually opened, to prepare it to eat soul food.)

In ancient Egypt, you *could* take it with you. The Egyptians believed that after death, your soul lived on, enjoying its earthly possessions—sometimes including servants, who might be walled up alive with their dead master. (Remember that even the great pyramids were just big tombs for Egypt's most powerful.)

Statues functioned as a refuge for the soul on its journey after death. The rich scattered statues of themselves everywhere, just in case. Statues needed to be simple and easy to recognize, mug shots for eternity: stiff, arms down, chin up, nothing fancy. This one has all the essential features, like the simplified human figures on international traffic signs. To a soul caught in the fast lane of astral travel, this symbolic statue would be easier to spot than a more detailed one.

With their fervent hope for life after death, Egyptians created calm, dignified art that seems built for eternity.

• *Relax. One civilization down, two to go. Near the end of the gallery, on the right, are two huge, winged Assyrian lions (with bearded human heads) standing guard over the Assyrian exhibit halls.*

ANCIENT ASSYRIA

Long before Saddam Hussein, Iraq was home to other palace-building, iron-fisted rulers—the Assyrians.

Assyria was the lion, the king of beasts of early Middle Eastern civilizations. These Semitic people from the agriculturally challenged hills of northern Iraq became traders and conquerors, not farmers. They conquered their southern neighbors and dominated the Middle East for 300 years (c. 900-600 BC).

Their strength came from a superb army (chariots, mounted cavalry, and siege engines), a policy of terrorism against enemies ("I tied their heads to tree trunks all around the city," reads a royal inscription), ethnic cleansing and mass deportations of the vanquished, and efficient administration (roads and express postal service). They have been called the "Romans of the East."

The British Museum's valuable collection of Assyrian artifacts has become even more priceless since the recent destruction of ancient sites in the Middle East by ISIS terrorists.

⑬ Two Human-Headed Winged Lions

These stone lions guarded an Assyrian palace (11th-8th century BC). With the strength of a lion, the wings of an eagle, the brain of a man, and the beard of an ancient hipster, they protected the king from evil spirits and scared the heck out of foreign ambassadors and left-wing newspaper reporters. (What has five legs and flies? Take a close look. These winged quintupeds, which appear complete from both the front and the side, could guard both directions at once.)

Carved into the stone between the bearded lions' loins, you can see one of civilization's most im-

pressive achievements—writing. This wedge-shaped **(cuneiform)** script is the world's first written language, invented 5,000 years ago by the Sumerians (of southern Iraq) and passed down to their less-civilized descendants, the Assyrians.

• *Walk between the lions, glance at the large reconstructed wooden gates from an Assyrian palace, and turn right into the long, narrow red gallery (Room 7) lined with stone relief panels.*

BRITISH MUSEUM

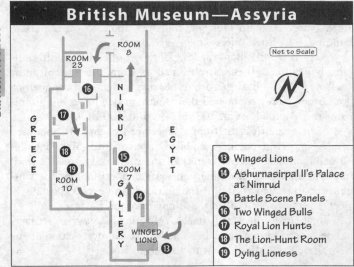

British Museum—Assyria

Not to Scale

ROOM 23
ROOM 8
NIMRUD
GREECE
EGYPT
ROOM 10
ROOM 7
GALLERY
WINGED LIONS

⑯ ⑰ ⑱ ⑲ ⑮ ⑭ ⑬

⑬ Winged Lions
⑭ Ashurnasirpal II's Palace at Nimrud
⑮ Battle Scene Panels
⑯ Two Winged Bulls
⑰ Royal Lion Hunts
⑱ The Lion-Hunt Room
⑲ Dying Lioness

⑭ Ashurnasirpal II's Palace at Nimrud

This gallery is a mini version of the throne room and royal apartments of King Ashurnasirpal II's Northwest Palace at Nimrud (9th century BC). The 30,000-square-foot palace was built atop a 50-acre artificial mound. The new palace was inaugurated with a 10-day banquet (according to an inscription), where the king picked up the tab for 69,574 of his closest friends. Entering, you would have seen the king on his throne at the far end, surrounded by these pleasant, sand-colored, gypsum relief panels (which were, however, originally painted and varnished).

That's Ashurnasirpal himself in the **first panel on your right**, with braided beard, earring, and fez-like crown, flanked by his supernatural hawk-headed henchmen, who sprinkle incense on him with pinecones.

The bulging forearms tell us that Ashurnasirpal II (r. 883-859 BC) was a conqueror's conqueror who enjoyed his reputation as a merciless warrior, using torture and humiliation as part of his distinctive management style. The room's panels chronicle his bloody career.

Under Ashurnasirpal's reign, the Assyrians dominated the Mideast from their capital at Nineveh (near modern Mosul). Ashurnasirpal II proved his power by building a brand-new palace in nearby Nimrud (called "Calah" in the Bible).

The cuneiform inscription running through the center of the panel is Ashurnasirpal's résumé: "The king who has enslaved all mankind, the mighty warrior who steps on the necks of his enemies, tramples all foes and shatters the enemy; the weapon of the gods, the mighty king, the King of Assyria, the king of the world, B.A., M.B.A., Ph.D., etc...."

• *A dozen paces farther down, on the left wall, are several relief panels (among many in this room that are worth focusing on).*

⓯ Panels with Battle Scenes

These relief panels show Assyria at war. Find the panel in which the Assyrians lay siege with a crude "tank" that shields them as they advance to the city walls to smash down the gate with a battering ram. The king stands a safe distance away behind the juggernaut and bravely shoots arrows.

Below the tank (in another panel called *Review of Prisoners*), prisoners are paraded before the Assyrian king, who is shaded by a

parasol. Ashurnasirpal II sneers and tells the captured chief, "Drop and give me 50." Above the prisoners' heads, we see the rich spoils of war—elephant tusks, metal pots, and so on.

In another panel nearby (called *Crossing a River*), enemy soldiers flee the slings and arrows of outrageous Assyrians by swimming across the Euphrates, using inflated animal bladders as life preservers. Their friends (way downstream in the castle) applaud their ingenuity.

The Assyrians, whose economy depended on booty, depopulated conquered lands with slavery and ethnic cleansing, then moved in Assyrian settlers. Despite their ruthless reputation, the Assyrians left a legacy as builders, rather than destroyers.

• *Exit the gallery at the far end, then hang a U-turn left. Pause at the entrance of Room 10c to see the impressive...*

⓰ Two Winged Bulls from the Palace of Sargon

These marble bulls (c. 710-705 BC) guarded the entrance to the city of Dur-Sharrukin ("Sargonsburg"), a new capital (near Nineveh/Mosul) with vast palaces built by Sargon II (r. 721-705 BC). The

30-ton bulls were cut from a single block, tipped on their sides, then dragged to their place by POWs. (In modern times, when the British transported them here, they had to cut them in half; you can see the horizontal cracks through the bulls' chests.)

Sargon II gained his reputation as a general by subduing the Israelites after a three-year siege of Jerusalem (2 Kings 17:1-6). He solidified his conquest by ethnically cleansing the area and deporting many Israelites (inspiring legends of the "Lost" Ten Tribes).

In 710 BC, while these bulls were being carved for his palace, Sargon II marched victoriously through the streets of Babylon (near present-day Baghdad), having put down a revolt there against him. His descendants would also have to deal with the troublesome Babylonians.

• *Sneak between these bulls and veer right (into Room 10), where horses are being readied for the big hunt.*

⓱ Royal Lion Hunts from the North Palace of Ashurbanipal

Lion hunting was Assyria's sport of kings. On the right wall are horses; on the left are the hunting dogs. And next to them, lions, resting peacefully in a garden, unaware that they will shortly be rousted, stampeded, and slaughtered.

Lions lived in Mesopotamia up until modern times, and it was the king's duty to keep the lion population down to protect farmers and herdsmen. This duty soon became sport, with staged hunts and zoo-bred lions, as the kings of men proved their power by taking on the king of beasts.

• *Continue ahead into the larger lion-hunt room. Reading the panels like a comic strip, start on the right and gallop counterclockwise.*

⓲ The Lion-Hunt Room

In these panels (c. 650 BC), the king's men release lions from their cages, then riders on horseback herd them into an enclosed arena. The king has them cornered. Let the slaughter begin. The chariot carries King Ashurbanipal, the great-grandson of Sargon II (not to be confused with Ashurnasirpal II, who ruled 200 years earlier, mentioned previously).

The last of Assyria's great kings, Ashurbanipal has reigned

now for 50 years. Having left a half-dozen corpses in his wake, he moves on, while spearmen hold off lions attacking from the rear.

• *At about the middle of the long wall...*

The fleeing lions, cornered by hounds, shot through with arrows, and weighed down by fatigue, begin to fall. The lead lion carries on even while vomiting blood.

This low point of Assyrian cruelty is, perhaps, the high point of their artistic achievement. It's a curious coincidence that civilizations often produce their greatest art in their declining years. Hmm.

• *On the wall opposite the vomiting lion is the...*

⑲ Dying Lioness

A lion roars in pain and frustration. She tries to run, but her body is too heavy. Her muscular hind legs, once a source of power, are now paralyzed.

Like these brave, fierce lions, Assyria's once-great warrior nation was slain. Shortly after Ashurbanipal's death, Assyria was conquered, and its capital at Nineveh was sacked and looted by an ascendant Babylon (612 BC). The mood of tragedy, dignity, and proud struggle in a hopeless cause makes this dying lioness one of the most beautiful of human creations.

• *Exit the lion-hunt room at the far end. Make your way back to the huge, winged lions who welcomed you to Assyria. Exit between them and make a U-turn to the right to head for the Greek section. Pass through Rooms 11–12 and turn right (if you're hungry, you can go straight to the Pizzeria) into Room 13, filled with Greek vases in glass cases.*

ANCIENT GREECE

In this room, you'll see lots of pottery—from the earliest, with geometric patterns (8th century BC), to painted black silhouettes on the natural orange clay, and then a few crudely done red human figures on black backgrounds. As you marvel at these beautiful creations, think of the people who made them.

The history of ancient Greece (600 BC–AD 1) could be subtitled "making order out of chaos." While Assyria was dominating the Middle East, "Greece"—a gaggle of warring tribes roaming the Greek peninsula—was floundering in darkness. But by about 700 BC, these tribes began settling down, experimenting with democracy, forming self-governing city-states, and making ties with other city-states. Scarcely two centuries later, they would be a relatively united community and the center of the civilized world.

During its Golden Age (500-430 BC), Greece set the tone for all of Western civilization to follow. Democracy, theater, literature, mathematics, philosophy, science, gyros, art, and architecture as we know them, were virtually all invented by a single generation of Greeks in a small town of maybe 80,000 citizens.

• In Room 13 is a Z-shaped glass case marked #8. It contains an item marked #231.

⑳ Black-Figured Amphora with Achilles Killing Penthesilea

Greeks poured wine from jars like this one, which is painted with a legend from the Trojan War. The Trojan War (c. 1200 BC)—part fact but mostly legend—symbolized Greece's long struggle to rise above war and chaos.

On the vessel (540-530 BC), Achilles of Greece faces off against the Queen of the Amazons, Penthesilea, who was fighting for Troy. (The Amazons were a legendary race of warrior women who cut off one breast to facilitate their archery skills.) Achilles bears down, plunging a spear through her neck, as blood spurts. In her dying moment, Penthesilea looks up, her gaze locking on Achilles. His eyes bulge wide, and he falls instantly in love with her. She dies, and Achilles is smitten.

Greek pottery was a popular export product for the sea-trading Greeks. On this jar, see the names of the two enemies/lovers ("AXILEV" and "PENOESIIEA") as well as the signature of the craftsman, Exekias.

• Continue to Room 15, then relax on a bench and read, surrounded by statues and vases in glass cases. On the entrance wall, find a...

㉑ Map of the Greek World, 520-430 BC

After Greece drove out Persian invaders in 480 BC, the city of Athens became the most powerful of the city-states and the center of the Greek world. Golden Age Greece was never really a full-fledged empire, but more a common feeling of unity among Greek-speaking people.

A century after the Golden Age, Greek culture was spread still farther by Alexander the Great, who conquered the Mediterranean

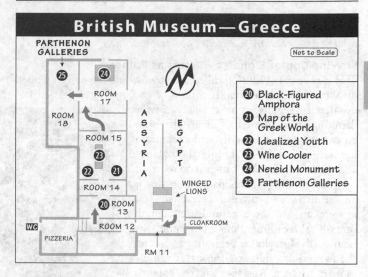

British Museum—Greece

PARTHENON
GALLERIES

Not to Scale

25

24

ROOM
17

ROOM
18

ROOM 15

23

22   21

ROOM 14

20 ROOM
13

WC

PIZZERIA

ROOM 12

RM 11

A S S Y R I A

E G Y P T

WINGED
LIONS

CLOAKROOM

20 Black-Figured
Amphora
21 Map of the
Greek World
22 Idealized Youth
23 Wine Cooler
24 Nereid Monument
25 Parthenon Galleries

world and beyond (including Persia). By 300 BC, the "Greek" world stretched from Italy and Egypt to India (including most of what used to be the Assyrian Empire). Two hundred years later, this Greek-speaking Hellenistic Empire was conquered by the Romans.
• *The evolution of Greek history is echoed in the evolution of their art. Start by finding a nude male statue (missing his arms and legs) on the left side of the room.*

22 Torso of an Idealized Youth (Kouros)

The Greeks saw their gods in human form...and human beings were godlike. They invented a statue type—the kouros (literally, "youth")—to showcase idealized bod-

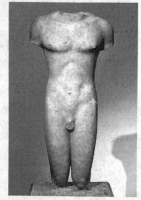

ies. In this example (c. 520-510 BC), the youth would have exemplified the divine orderliness of the universe with his once perfectly round head (it's now missing), symmetrical pecs, and navel in the center. The ideal man was geometrically perfect, a balance of opposites, the Golden Mean. In a statue, that meant finding the right balance between movement and stillness, between realistic human anatomy (with human flaws) and the perfection of a Greek god. Our youth is still a bit up-

tight, stiff as the rock from which he's carved. But—as we'll see—in just a few short decades, the Greeks would cut loose and create realistic statues that seemed to move like real humans.

• *Two-thirds of the way down Room 15 (on the left) is a glass case containing a vase painted with frisky figures, labeled...*

㉓ Wine Cooler Signed by Douris as Painter

This clay vessel (490 BC), called a *psykter,* would have been topped off with wine and floated in a bowl of cooling water. Its red-figure drawings show satyrs at a *symposium,* or

drinking party. These half-man/half-animal creatures (notice their tails) had a reputation for lewd behavior, reminding the balanced and moderate Greeks of their rude roots.

The reveling figures painted on this jar are realistic and three-dimensional; their movements are more naturalistic than the literally three-dimensional but quite stiff kouros. The Greeks are beginning to conquer the natural world in art. The art, like life, is more in balance. And speaking of "balance," if that's a Greek sobriety test, revel on.

• *Carry on into Room 17 and sit facing the Greek temple at the far end.*

㉔ Nereid Monument

Greek temples (like this reconstruction of a temple-shaped tomb from Xanthos, c. 390-380 BC) housed a statue of a god or goddess. Unlike Christian churches,

which serve as meeting places, Greek temples were the gods' homes. Worshippers gathered outside, so the most impressive part of the temple was its exterior. Temples were rectangular buildings surrounded by rows of columns and topped by slanted roofs.

The triangle-shaped space above the columns—the pediment—is filled with sculpture. Supporting the pediment are decorative relief panels, called metopes. Now look through the columns to the building itself. Above the doorway, another set of relief panels—the frieze—runs around the building (under the eaves).

The statues between the columns are Nereids—friendly sea nymphs with dramatic wavelike poses and windblown clothes; some appear to be borne aloft by sea animals. Notice the sculptor's delight in capturing the body in motion, and the way the wet clothes cling to the figures' anatomy.

Next, we'll see pediment, frieze, and metope decorations from Greece's greatest temple.

• *Head through the glass doors labeled* The Parthenon Galleries. *(The rooms branching off the entryway have helpful exhibits that reconstruct the Parthenon and its once-colorful sculptures.) Enter the vast hall lined with sculptures that once adorned the Parthenon.*

㉕ Parthenon Galleries

If you were to leave the British Museum, take the Tube to Heathrow, and fly to Athens, there, in the center of the old city, on top of the high, flat hill known as the Acropolis, you'd find the Parthenon—the temple dedicated to Athena, goddess of wisdom and the patroness of Athens. It was the crowning glory of an enormous urban-renewal plan during Greece's Golden Age. After Athens was ruined in a war with Persia, the city—under the bold leadership of Pericles—constructed the greatest building of its day (447-432 BC). The Parthenon was a model of balance, simplicity, and harmonious elegance, the symbol of the Golden Age. Phidias, the greatest Greek sculptor, decorated the exterior with statues and relief panels.

While the Parthenon building itself remains in Athens, many of the Parthenon's best sculptures are right here in the British Museum—the so-called Elgin Marbles, named for the shrewd British ambassador who had his men hammer, chisel, and saw them off the Parthenon in the early 1800s.

In 2009, in an attempt to bring the marbles back home, the Greek government built a state-of-the-art museum in Athens just to house the precious sculptures. Meanwhile, British authorities assert they rescued and preserved the marbles. This may have been true a century ago, but today this reason is unsatisfactory answer to many—especially now that Greece has built the marbles a proper home. This often-bitter controversy continues.

The marble panels you see lining the walls of this large hall are part of the frieze that originally ran around the exterior of the Parthenon, under the eaves. The statues at either end of the hall once filled the Parthenon's triangular-shaped pediments. Near the pediment sculptures, we'll also

British Museum—Parthenon Galleries

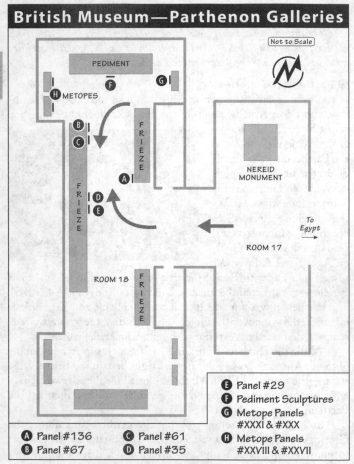

Not to Scale

PEDIMENT

F

G

H METOPES

B
C

FRIEZE

A

FRIEZE

D
E

NEREID MONUMENT

To Egypt →

ROOM 17

ROOM 18

FRIEZE

FRIEZE

E Panel #29
F Pediment Sculptures
G Metope Panels
#XXXI & #XXX
H Metope Panels
#XXVIII & #XXVII

A Panel #136   **C** Panel #61
B Panel #67   **D** Panel #35

find the relief panels known as metopes.

The Frieze: These 56 relief panels show Athens' "Fourth of July" parade, celebrating the birth of the city. On this day, citizens marched up the Acropolis to symbolically present a new robe to the 40-foot-tall, gold-and-ivory statue of Athena housed in the

Parthenon. The grand parade featured chariots, musicians, children, animals for sacrifice, and young maidens with offerings.

• *Start at the panels by the entrance* **A** *(#136) and work counterclockwise.*

Men on horseback lead the parade, all heading in the same direction—uphill. Prance on.

Notice the muscles and veins in the horses' legs and the intricate folds in the cloaks and dresses. Some panels have holes drilled in them, where gleaming bronze reins were fitted to heighten the festive look. All of these panels were originally painted in realistic colors. As you move along, notice that, despite the bustle of figures posed every which way, the frieze has one unifying

element—all the people's heads are at the same level, creating a single ribbon around the Parthenon.

• *Cross to the opposite wall.*

A two-horse chariot ❸ **(#67),** cut from only a few inches of marble, is more lifelike and three-dimensional than anything the Egyptians achieved in a freestanding statue.

Enter the girls (five yards to the left, ❻ **#61**), the heart of the procession. Dressed in pleated robes, they shuffle past the parade marshals, carrying incense burners and jugs of wine and bowls to pour out an offering to the thirsty gods.

The procession culminates on the far side of the door ❶ **(#35),**

in the presentation of the robe to Athena. A man and a child fold the robe for the goddess while the rest of the gods look on. Overseeing it all are Zeus and Hera ❺ **(#29),** the king and queen of the gods, seated, enjoying the fashion show and wondering what length hemlines will be this year.

• *Head for the set of pediment sculptures at the far right end of the hall.*

❻ **The Pediment Sculptures:** These statues were originally nestled nicely in the triangular pediment above the columns at the Parthenon's main (east) entrance. The missing statues at the peak of the triangle once showed the birth of Athena. Zeus had his head split open,

allowing Athena, the goddess of wisdom, to rise from his brain fully grown and fully armed, inaugurating the Golden Age of Athens.

The other gods at this Olympian banquet slowly become aware of the amazing event. The first to notice is the one closest to them, Hebe, the cupbearer of the gods (tallest surviving fragment). Frightened, she runs to tell the others, her dress whipping behind her. A startled Demeter (just left of Hebe) turns toward Hebe.

The only one who hasn't lost his head is laid-back Dionysus (the cool guy farther left). He just raises another glass of wine

to his lips. Over on the right, Aphrodite, goddess of love, leans back into her mother's lap, too busy admiring her own bare shoulder to even notice the hubbub. A chess-set horse's head screams, "These people are nuts—let me out of here!"

The scene had a message. Just as wise Athena rose above the lesser gods, who were scared, drunk, or vain, so would her city, Athens, rise above her lesser rivals.

This is amazing workmanship. Compare Dionysus, with his natural, relaxed, reclining pose, to all those stiff Egyptian statues standing eternally at attention.

Appreciate the folds of the clothes on the female figures (on the right half), especially Aphrodite's clinging, rumpled robe. Some sculptors would first build a nude model of their figure, put real clothes on it, and study how the cloth hung down before actually sculpting in marble. Others found inspiration at the *taverna* on wet T-shirt night.

Even without their heads, these statues, with their detailed anatomy and expressive poses, speak volumes.

Wander behind. The statues originally sat 40 feet above the ground. The backs of the statues, which were never intended to be seen, are almost as detailed as the fronts.

• *The metopes are the panels on the walls to either side. Start with the three South Metope panels on the right wall.*

Centaurs Slain Around the World

Dateline 500 BC—Greece, China, India: Man no longer considers himself an animal. Bold new ideas are exploding simultaneously around the world. Socrates, Confucius, Buddha, and others are independently discovering a nonmaterial, unseen order in nature and in man. They say man has a rational mind or soul. He's separate from nature and different from the other animals.

The Metopes: The metopes once decorated the gaps between the crossbeams above the Parthenon's columns. Here's the scene: The humans have invited some centaurs—barbarian half-man/half-horse creatures—to a wedding feast. All goes well until the brutish centaurs, the original party animals, get too drunk and try to carry off the women. A brawl breaks out.

In the central panel of the three 🄶 (#XXXI), a centaur grabs a man by the throat while the man pulls his hair. Meanwhile, the man tries fending off the centaur with his knee, while the centaur wraps his forelegs around the man's leg. The two stand eye to eye, and, at this point, the battle seems pretty evenly matched. But in #XXX (to the left), the centaur does the hair-pulling, and begins to drive

the man to his knees.

The story continues on the opposite wall. In the central panel 🄷 (#XXVIII), the centaurs take control of the party, as one rears back and prepares to trample the helpless man. The leopard skin draped over the centaur's arm roars a taunt. The humans lose face.

But the humans rally. To the left (#XXVII), the humans rise up and drive off the brutish centaurs. A centaur tries to run, but the man grabs him by the neck and raises his (missing) right hand to prepare to finish him off. Notice how graceful the man is, with his smooth skin offset by the rough folded cloak.

These metopes tell the story of the struggle between the forces of human civilization and animal-like barbarism. The Greeks had always prided themselves on creating order out of chaos. Within just a few generations, they went from nomadic barbarism to the pinnacle of early Western civilization. Now, the centaurs have been defeated. Civilization has triumphed over barbarism, order over chaos, and rational man over his half-animal alter ego.

Why are the Parthenon sculptures so treasured? The British of the 19th century saw themselves as the new "civilized" race, subduing "barbarians" in their far-flung empire. Maybe these carved stones made them stop and wonder—will our great civilization also turn to rubble?

REST OF THE MUSEUM

You've toured only the foundations of Western civilization on the ground floor of the West Wing. Upstairs you'll find still more artifacts from these ancient lands, plus Rome and the medieval civilization that sprang from it. Locate the rooms with themes you find interesting (Etruscan, Persian, Roman Britain, Dark Age Europe, and so on) and explore. Some highlights:

Lindow Man (a.k.a. the Bog Man): This victim of a druid human-sacrifice ritual, with wounds still visible, was preserved for 2,000 years in a peat bog (Room 50, upper floor, via East Stairs).

Sutton Hoo Ship-Burial: Finds from a seventh-century Anglo-Saxon burial site (Room 41, upper floor, via East Stairs).

Michelangelo's Drawings: The museum owns a complete cartoon (a full-scale preliminary drawing for another work of art) by Michelangelo—it's one of only two that survive (Room 90, level 4, accessed via the North Stairs or from the top of the Reading Room).

Enlightenment Gallery: Formerly known as the King's Library, this room held the British Library's treasures when it was founded in 1753. Today it displays objects that reveal the learning and wonder of the Age of Enlightenment (Room 1; long hall near the main entry, through the Grenville Shop).

And, of course, history doesn't begin and end in Europe. Look for remnants of the sophisticated, exotic cultures of Asia and the Americas (in North Wing, ground floor) and Africa (lower floor)—all part of the fabric of the human family.

BRITISH LIBRARY TOUR

The British Empire built its greatest monuments out of paper. It's through literature that England has made her lasting contribution to history and the arts. These national archives of Britain include more than 150 million items. A copy of every publication in the UK and Ireland is sent here. It's all housed on 380 miles of shelving in the deepest basement in London.

But everything that matters for your visit is in a single room dubbed "The Treasures." We'll concentrate on a handful of documents—literary and historical—that changed the course of history. Start with these top stops, then stray according to your interests.

Orientation

Cost: Free (£5 suggested donation); admission may be charged for some special exhibits.

Hours: Mon-Thu 9:30-20:00, Fri until 18:00, Sat until 17:00, Sun 11:00-17:00.

Information: +44 33 0333 1144, www.bl.uk.

Getting There: From the King's Cross St. Pancras Tube station, follow signs to British Library, exit onto (big, noisy) Euston Road, turn right, and go one long block to 96 Euston Road. Euston Tube station is also nearby. Buses #73, #204, and #390 (among others) also stop nearby.

Rotating Exhibits: Exhibits change often, and many of the museum's old, fragile manuscripts need to "rest" periodically in order to stay well preserved. Even some of the major items I describe here could be out of view.

Tours: Two £10 one-hour tours are offered daily—a Treasures Tour (generally in the morning) and a building tour (generally in the afternoon); book online or call +44 19 3754 6546. There are no audioguides for the permanent collection.

⌒ Download my free British Library audio tour.

Length of This Tour: Allow one hour.

Services: The library has a free coat check and lockers (no large bags).

Eating: The **$$$** upper-level restaurant has good hot meals. There's a **$$** café (sandwiches and drinks) on the upper level, next to the vast and fun pull-out stamp collection, and another **$$** café just inside the main entrance.

Starring: Bibles, Shakespeare, English Lit 101, Magna Carta, and—ladies and gentlemen—the Beatles.

The Tour Begins

Entering the library courtyard, you'll see a big statue of a naked Isaac Newton bending forward with a compass to measure the universe. The statue symbol-izes the library's purpose: to gather all knowledge and promote humanity's endless search for truth.

Stepping inside, you'll find the information desk and shop (the cloakroom and WC are down a short staircase to the right). Directly ahead, in the grand atrium that forms the middle of the building, you get glimpses of a 50-foot-tall wall of 65,000 books teasingly exposing its shelves. In 1823 the private "Library" of King George III was given to the people under the condition the books remain on display for all to see. The high-tech bookshelf—with moveable lifts to reach the highest titles—sits behind glass, inaccessible to commoners but ever-visible. Likewise, the reading rooms upstairs are not open to the public. The PACCAR Gallery houses temporary exhibits (requiring an admission charge).

Our tour is of the tiny but exciting area variously called "The Sir John Ritblat Gallery," "Treasures of the British Library," or just "The Treasures." This priceless literary and historical collection is held in one large, carefully designed, dimly lit room.

• *The entrance to the Treasures room is immediately to the left as you enter the building, next to the shop. From this small lobby, you may see a ticket desk and entrances to other (temporary) exhibits. But you want to climb the stairs up to the Treasures.*

Enter this darkened room and get oriented. Display cases are grouped according to theme: maps, sacred texts, music, and so on. The key to my self-guided tour is the title above the various cases. Focus on the big picture, and don't be too worried about locating every specific exhibit.

Start with the display case on the left as you enter, which is filled with...

❶ Maps and Views

These historic maps show how humans' perspective of the world has expanded over the centuries. These pieces of paper, encoded with information gleaned from travelers, could be passed along to future generations—each building upon the knowledge of the last.

The collection changes, but you'll likely see maps from different time periods, showing different perspectives. The earliest maps of, say, Britain or Europe featured only the small, local world that the mapmakers knew. These early maps put medieval people in an unusual position—looking down on their homeland from 50 miles in the air. Within a few centuries, maps of Europe were of such high quality they could still be used today to plan a trip. After Columbus' journey, the entire globe became fairly well mapped, except for the mysterious expanse of unknown land that lay beyond America's east coast—"Terra Incognita."

• *Move into the area dedicated to sacred texts from several cultures.*

❷ Sacred Texts (Including Early Bibles)

Here the cases contain sacred texts such as the Hebrew Torah, Muslim Quran, Buddhist sutras, and Hindu Upanishads. Browse the different versions of the sacred text of Christians, the Bible. (Some Bibles are displayed in the Sacred Texts area, while others might be in the Art of the Book display cases nearby.)

You'll likely see some old decaying fragments of parchment or papyrus. The writing is in ancient Latin, Greek, Egyptian, or other dead languages. Consider the fact that many of humankind's oldest writings were dedicated to spiritual aspirations. Often on display are some of the earliest versions of the Bible. These include some early bound books with pages, called a codex.

The **Codex Sinaiticus** (or the **Codex Alexandrinus** that may be on display instead) is one such bound book, from around AD 350. It's one of the oldest complete Bibles in existence—one of the first attempts

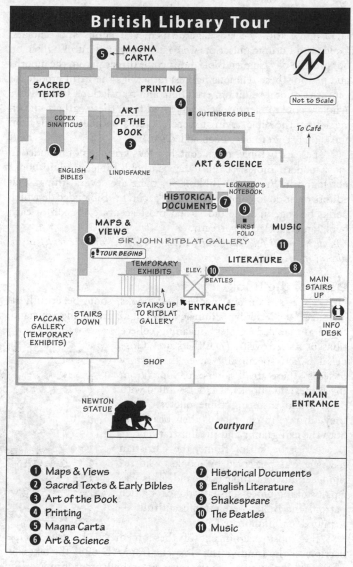

British Library Tour

MAGNA CARTA **5**

SACRED TEXTS

PRINTING

Not to Scale

To Café →

CODEX SINAITICUS

ART OF THE BOOK **3**

2

GUTENBERG BIBLE **4**

ENGLISH BIBLES

LINDISFARNE

ART & SCIENCE **6**

LEONARDO'S NOTEBOOK

HISTORICAL DOCUMENTS **7**

9

MAPS & VIEWS **1**

FIRST FOLIO

MUSIC

SIR JOHN RITBLAT GALLERY

11

TOUR BEGINS

LITERATURE

8

TEMPORARY EXHIBITS

ELEV. **10**

BEATLES

MAIN STAIRS UP

STAIRS DOWN

STAIRS UP TO RITBLAT GALLERY

↖ ENTRANCE

INFO DESK

PACCAR GALLERY (TEMPORARY EXHIBITS)

SHOP

MAIN ENTRANCE

NEWTON STATUE

Courtyard

BRITISH LIBRARY

1 Maps & Views
2 Sacred Texts & Early Bibles
3 Art of the Book
4 Printing
5 Magna Carta
6 Art & Science
7 Historical Documents
8 English Literature
9 Shakespeare
10 The Beatles
11 Music

to collect various books by different authors into one authoritative anthology. The Codex is in Greek, the language in which most of the New Testament was originally written. The Old Testament portions are Greek translations from the original Hebrew.

Jesus didn't speak English, of course—nor did Moses or Isaiah or Paul or any other Bible authors or characters. Jesus spoke Aramaic, a form of Hebrew. His words were written down in Greek, decades after his death. Various Greek manuscripts were compiled into anthologies like the Codex Sinaiticus. These were then translated into Latin, the language of medieval monks and scholars. Greek and Latin manuscripts were later translated into English. So our present-day English Bible didn't come directly from the mouths and pens of these religious figures; rather, it's the fitful product of centuries of oral tradition, evolution, and translation. Today, Bible scholars pore diligently over every word from these earliest known versions of the Bible, trying to separate Jesus' authentic words from those that seem to have been added later.

These early Bibles often contain a few writings not included in most modern Bibles. (Even today, Catholic Bibles contain books not found in Protestant Bibles.) So, there are several things that editors must do to compile the most "accurate" Bible: decide which books belong, find the oldest and most accurate version of each book, and translate it correctly.

• *Nearby, you'll find more early Bibles (along with other texts) in the display cases called...*

❸ Art of the Book

Here you'll see various medieval-era books, some beautifully illustrated. The lettering is immaculate, but all are penned by hand.

Some are labeled "Bibles," meaning collections of sacred writings. Others are "Gospels," which specifically cover the history of Jesus. There are "Psalters," or songs from the Bible, and "Books of Hours," filled with prayers and inspiring Bible quotes. What they all have in common is their beauty, in both the calligraphy and the illustrations.

After the fall of Rome, the Christian message was preserved by monks, who reproduced ancient Bibles by hand. This was a painstaking process, usually done for a rich patron. The Bibles were often beautifully illustrated, or "illuminated."

The most magnificent of these medieval British "monk-uscripts" is the **Lindisfarne Gospels,** from AD 698. The text is in Latin, the language of scholars ever since the Roman Empire. The illustrations—with elaborate tracery and interwoven decoration—mix Irish, classical, and even Byzantine forms. (You may be able to read an electronic copy of these manuscripts on a touch-screen computer, if those are up and running.)

These Gospels are a reminder that Christianity almost didn't make it in Europe. After the fall of Rome (which had established Christianity as the empire's official religion), much of Europe reverted to its pagan ways. People worshipped woodland spirits and terrible Teutonic gods. Lindisfarne was an obscure monastery of Irish monks on a remote island off the east coast of England. But during that chaotic time, it was one of the few beacons of light, tending the embers of civilization through the long night of the Dark Ages. It took 500 years before Christianity was fully re-established in Europe.

Elsewhere in the Art of the Book (or possibly in Sacred Texts), you'll likely see some **Early English Bibles**—the King James version, the Wycliffe Bible, or others. These date from the 15th, 16th, and 17th centuries. As recently as 1400, there was no English version of the Bible, though only a small percentage of the population understood Latin. A few brave reformers risked death to translate these sacred books into English and print them using Gutenberg's invention, the printing press. Within two centuries, English translations were both legal and popular. These Bibles were written in the same language you speak, but try reading them. The lettering is strange; the words are out-of-date and unintelligible. It clearly shows how quickly languages evolve.

The King James version (so-called because it was done during his reign) has been the most widely used English translation. Fifty scholars worked for four years, borrowing heavily from previous translations, to produce this Bible. Its impact on the English language was enormous, making Elizabethan English something of the standard, even after people stopped saying "thee" and "thou" and "verily verily."

Recent translations are more readable, using modern English speech patterns, and aim to be more accurate, based on better scholarship and translations of the earliest manuscripts. But there are still problems trying to translate old phrases to fit contemporary viewpoints. Case in point? Our generation's debate over the God of the Bible's preferred pronouns.

• *Move on to the wall of glass cases featuring early...*

❹ Printing

Printing was invented by the Chinese (what wasn't?). Centuries before the printing press in Europe, pictures of Buddha surrounded by prayers in Chinese characters were mass-produced. The faithful gained a blessing by saying the prayer, and so did the printer by reproducing it. The prints were made using wooden blocks carved with Chinese characters, dipped into paint or ink, and pressed by hand onto the page.

The **Gutenberg Bible**—though it may look like just another monk-made Latin manuscript—was so revolutionary because it was the first book printed in Europe using movable type (c. 1455).

Johann Gutenberg (c. 1397-1468), a German silversmith, devised a convenient way to reproduce written materials quickly, neatly, and cheaply—by printing with movable type. You scratch each letter onto a separate metal block, then arrange them into words, ink them up, and press them onto paper. When one job was done you could reuse the same letters for a new one.

This simple idea had immediate and revolutionary consequences. Suddenly, the Bible was available for anyone to read, fueling the Protestant Reformation. Knowledge became cheap and accessible to a wide audience, not just the rich. Books became the mass medium of Europe, linking people by a common set of ideas.
• *Through a doorway near the Sacred Texts and Art of the Book displays is a small room with the...*

❺ Magna Carta

How did Britain, a tiny island with a few million people, come to rule a quarter of the world? Not by force, but by law. The 1215 Magna Carta was the basis for England's constitutional system of government. Though historians talk about *the* Magna Carta, several different versions of the document exist, some of which are kept in this room.

The Articles of the Barons (labeled *King John*): In 1215, England's barons rose in revolt against the slimy King John. (The same King John appears as a villain in the legends of Robin Hood.) After losing London, John was forced to negotiate. The barons presented him with this list of demands. John, whose rule was worthless without the barons' support, had no choice but to acquiesce and affix his seal to it.

Magna Carta: A few days after John agreed to this original document, it was rewritten in legal form, and some 35 copies of the final version of the "Great Charter" were distributed around the kingdom.

This was a turning point in the history of government. Until then, kings had ruled by God-given authority, above the laws of men. Now, for the first time, there were limits—in writing—on how a king could treat his subjects. More generally, it established the idea of "due process"—the notion that a government can't infringe on citizens' freedom without a legitimate legal reason. This small step became the basis for all constitutional governments, including yours.

So what did this radical piece of paper actually say? Not much. (The entire text is written on the room's wall: "John, by the grace of God..." etc.) The specific demands were trivial by today's standards—the king's duties to widows and orphans, inheritance taxes, and so on. But the principle—that the king had to abide by them as law—was revolutionary.

• *If you'd like to actually read the document, turn around. Now return to the main room to find display cases featuring...*

❻ Art and Science

The printed word helped disseminate ideas across Europe, both religious and secular. During the Renaissance, people began turning their attention away from heaven and toward the nuts and bolts of the material world around them. Among the documents here, you might find some by trailblazing early scientists such as Galileo and Isaac Newton, and some by science-minded artists such as Albrecht Dürer and Michelangelo.

Pages from **Leonardo da Vinci's notebook** show his powerful curiosity, his genius for invention, and his famous backward and inside-out handwriting, which makes sense only if you know Italian and have a mirror. Leonardo's restless mind pondered diverse subjects, from how birds fly, to the flow of the Arno River, to military fortifications, to an early helicopter, to the "earthshine" reflecting onto the moon.

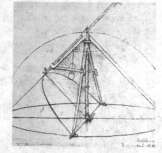

One person's research inspired another's, and books allowed knowledge to accumulate. Leonardo inspired Galileo, who championed the counter-commonsense notion that the earth spun around the sun. Galileo inspired Isaac Newton, who perfected the mathematics of those moving celestial bodies.

❼ Historical Documents

Nearby are many more historical documents. You may see letters by Henry VIII, Queen Elizabeth I, Darwin, Freud, Gandhi, and others. It's clear you could spend days in here browsing the collection. But for now, let's trace the evolution of...

❽ English Literature

As you peruse the various manuscripts, from many different time periods, think of how much the English language has changed. Four out of every five English words have been borrowed from other languages. The English language, like English culture (and London today), is a mix derived from foreign visitors and invaders. Some of the historic ingredients that make this cultural stew:

William Shakespeare (1564-1616)

William Shakespeare is the greatest author in any language, period. He expanded and helped define modern English. In one fell swoop, he made the language of everyday people as important as Latin. In the process, he gave us phrases like "one fell swoop," which we quote without knowing they're Shakespeare. (Without him, no one would ever "vanish into thin air," "play fast and loose," "have seen better days," do anything "without rhyme or reason," become a "laughingstock," or wish anything "good riddance.")

Shakespeare was born in Stratford-upon-Avon in 1564 to John Shakespeare and Mary Arden. Though his parents were probably illiterate, Shakespeare is thought to have attended Stratford's grammar school, finishing his education at 14. When he was 18, he married a 26-year-old local girl, Anne Hathaway, who was three months pregnant at the time with their daughter Susanna.

The next few years are a blank—following his marriage, Shakespeare disappeared from any historical record, not turning up again until seven years later. By this point, he was a budding poet and playwright in London. He soon hit the big time, writing and performing for royalty, founding (along with his troupe) the Globe Theatre (a replica of which now sits along the Thames' South Bank—see page 96), and raking in enough dough to buy New Place, a swanky mansion back in his hometown. Around 1611, the rich-and-famous playwright retired from the theater, moving back to Stratford, where he died at the age of 52.

With plots that entertained both the highest and the lowest minds, Shakespeare taught the theater-going public about human nature. His tool was an unrivaled mastery of the English language.

- First, there was the language of the original Celtic tribesmen from Bronze Age times.
- Next came the Latin-speaking Romans (AD 1-500), who conquered and colonized the isle of Britain.
- After the fall of Rome, Germanic tribes called Angles and Saxons moved in. English is a Germanic language, and the invaders named the island "Angle-land"—England.
- Next came the Vikings from Denmark (AD 800).
- Finally, there's the French-speaking Normans under William the Conqueror who arrived in the year 1066.
- *The English Literature exhibit is kept small and changes radically from*

Using borrowed plots, outrageous puns, and poetic language, Shakespeare wrote comedies (c. 1590—*Taming of the Shrew, As You Like It*), tragedies (c. 1600—*Hamlet, Othello, Macbeth, King Lear*), and fanciful combinations (c. 1610—*The Tempest*), exploring the full range of human emotions and reinventing the English language.

Perhaps as important was his insight into humanity. His father was a glovemaker and wool merchant, and his mother was the daughter of a landowner from a Catholic family. Some scholars speculate that Shakespeare's parents were closet Catholics, practicing their faith during the rise of Protestantism. It is this tug-of-war between two worlds, some think, that helped enlighten Shakespeare's humanism. Think of his stock of great characters and great lines: Hamlet ("To be or not to be, that is the question"), Othello and his jealousy ("It is the green-eyed monster"), ambitious Mark Antony ("Friends, Romans, countrymen, lend me your ears"), rowdy Falstaff ("The better part of valor is discretion"), and the star-crossed lovers Romeo and Juliet ("But soft, what light through yonder window breaks"). Shakespeare probed the psychology of human beings 300 years before Freud. Even today, his characters strike a familiar chord.

The scope of his brilliant work, his humble beginnings, and the fact that no original Shakespeare manuscripts survive raise a few scholarly eyebrows. Some have wondered if maybe Shakespeare had help on several of his plays. After all, they reasoned, how could a journeyman actor with little education have written so many masterpieces? And he was surrounded by other great writers, such as his friend and fellow poet, Ben Jonson. Most modern scholars, though, agree that Shakespeare did indeed write the plays and sonnets attributed to him.

His contemporaries had no doubts about Shakespeare—or his legacy. As Jonson wrote in the preface to the First Folio, "He was not of an age, but for all time!"

month to month. In other words, not every treasure described below is likely to be on display.

Beowulf is the first English literary masterpiece. The Anglo-Saxon epic poem, written in Old English (the earliest version of our language), almost makes the hieroglyphics on the Rosetta Stone look easy. The manuscript is from AD 1000, although the story itself dates to about 750. In this epic story, the young hero Beowulf defeats two half-human monsters threatening the kingdom. Beowulf symbolizes England's emergence from the chaos and barbarism of the Dark Ages.

Look for *The Canterbury Tales*. Six hundred years later, England was Christian, but it was hardly the pious, predictable, Sunday-school world we might imagine. Geoffrey Chaucer's bawdy collection of stories (c. 1410), told by pilgrims on their way to Canterbury, gives us the full range of life's experiences—happy, sad, silly, sexy, and devout. (Late in life, Chaucer wrote an apology for those works of his "that tend toward sin.")

While most serious literature of the time was written in scholarly Latin, the stories in *The Canterbury Tales* were written in Middle English, the language that developed after the French invasion of 1066 added a Norman twist to Old English.

This display is often a greatest-hits sampling of literature in English, from Brontë to Kipling to Woolf to Joyce to Dickens, whose novels were as popular in his time as blockbuster movies are today. Jane Austen's novels of upper-class young women seeking suitable husbands, though set in the 19th century, are enormously popular in the 21st. The original *Alice's Adventures in Wonderland* by Lewis Carroll created a fantasy world, where grown-up rules and logic were turned upside down. Also on display are superb works by contemporary writers, making it clear that Britain continues to be a powerful force in the world of ideas and imagination.

• *The most famous of England's writers generally gets his own display case.*

❾ Shakespeare

Shakespeare wrote his plays to be performed, not read. He published a few, but as his reputation grew, unauthorized "bootleg" versions began to circulate. Some of these were written by actors who were trying (with faulty memories) to re-create plays they had appeared in years before. Publishers also put out different versions of his plays.

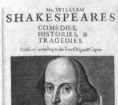

It wasn't until seven years after his death, in 1623, that a nearly complete collection of Shakespeare's plays was published, commonly known as the **First Folio.** Of the 750 printed, about 230 survive (most are in the US). Western literature owes much to this folio, which collects 36 of the 37 known Shakespeare plays (*Pericles* missed out). If the First Folio is not

out for viewing, the library should still have other Shakespeare items on display.

The engraving of Shakespeare on the title page is reportedly one of only two portraits done during his lifetime. Is this what he really looked like? No one knows. The best answer probably comes from Ben Jonson, in the introduction on the facing page. Jonson concludes, "Reader, look not on his picture, but his book."
• *Nearby are exhibits on music and...*

⑩ The Beatles

Bach, Beethoven, Brahms, Bizet...Beatles. Future generations will have to judge whether this musical quartet ranks with such artists, but no one can deny their historical significance. Look for photos of John Lennon, Paul McCartney, George Harrison, and Ringo Starr, who all hailed from Liverpool. The Beatles burst onto the scene in the early 1960s to unheard-of popularity. With their long hair and loud music, they brought counterculture and revolutionary ideas to the middle class, affecting the values of a whole generation. Touring the globe, they served as a link between young people everywhere.

Among the displays, you may find manuscripts of song lyrics written by Lennon and McCartney, the two guiding lights of the group. "I Want to Hold Your Hand" was the song that launched them to superstardom in America. "A Hard Day's Night" (see its lyrics, hand-scrawled on the back of a children's greeting card) and "Help" were title songs of two films capturing the excitement and chaos of the Beatles' hectic touring schedule. Some call "Ticket to Ride" the first heavy-metal song; others say it was "Helter Skelter." "Michelle," with a line in French, seemed oh-so-sophisticated. "Yesterday," by Paul, was recorded with guitar and voice backed by a string quartet—a touch of class from producer George Martin. Also, glance at the rambling, depressed, and cynical but humorous "untitled verse" by a young John Lennon. Is that a self-portrait at the bottom?

⑪ Music

Kind of an anticli-max after the Fab Four, I know, but there are manuscripts by Mozart, Beethoven, Chopin, and others. George Frideric Handel's famous oratorio, the *Messiah* (1741), is often on display. Handel, a German, became the

toast of London in the early 1700s, where musical theater was all the rage. Increasingly, he left Italian-language operas behind in favor of productions in English. The *Messiah* was written in a flash of inspiration—three hours of music in 24 days. When it got its London premiere in Covent Garden, King George II reportedly stood in respect during its most famous tune, the "Hallelujah" chorus. Here are the final bars. Hallelujah.

HISTORIC LONDON: THE CITY WALK

From Charing Cross Station to London Bridge

In Shakespeare's day, London consisted of a one-square-mile area surrounding St. Paul's. Well before then, back in Roman times, that square mile was a walled town called Londinium. Today, this neighborhood—known as both "The City" and "The Square Mile"—is the financial heart of London, densely packed with history and high-rises, and bustling with business.

This two-mile walk from Charing Cross Station to London Bridge parallels the Thames, on the same main road that's been used for centuries. Along the way, you'll see sights from The City's storied past, such as St. Paul's Cathedral, the steeples of other Wren churches, historic taverns, a Crusader church, and narrow alleyways with faint remnants of the London of Shakespeare and Dickens.

But you'll also catch The City in action today—especially if you visit on a weekday around lunchtime, when workers spill out onto the streets and The City is at its liveliest. See lawyers and judges in robes and wigs taking cigarette breaks, brokers in pin-striped power suits buying newspapers from Cockneys, and the last of a dying breed: elderly gentlemen with bowler hats and brollies (umbrellas) browsing for tailored shirts and Cuban cigars. Sip a pint in the same pub where Dickens did, and eavesdrop on a power lunch. Use this walk to help resurrect the London that was, then let The City of today surprise you with what is.

Orientation

Length of This Walk: The walk can be done at a sprint, and without entering any of the sights, in about two hours—but count on three or four hours, at least, to visit some of the sights described, plus another hour or two if you go inside St. Paul's

Cathedral, covered in the next chapter. The most important part of the walk—Part 2—can be done in a bit over an hour.

Be Selective: I've divided this walk into three parts. With limited time, skip Part 1 (about a mile's walk along the Strand) and start with Part 2, which takes you from St. Clement Danes to St. Paul's and is the most rewarding stretch.

At St. Paul's at the end of Part 2, you can either continue with Part 3 (to London Bridge), or call it quits. (From St. Paul's, it's easy to walk across the delightful Millennium Bridge to the Tate Modern, Shakespeare's Globe, and other Southwark sights.)

Along this walk, the sights most worth taking the time to go inside are St. Clement Danes, Temple Church, St. Bride's Church, and, of course, St. Paul's. The Royal Courts of Justice and Old Bailey are of interest only to legal eagles. Literary nuts will find it worthwhile to tour Dr. Johnson's House. The Guildhall is only worth visiting if you have ample time. And most visitors should skip the Monument climb.

Getting There: To do the full walk, begin near Trafalgar Square at Charing Cross Station (Tube: Charing Cross or Embankment). You'll head east on the Strand and end at London Bridge (where the Bankside Walk begins). Handy buses #15 and #11 (see page 36) travel along the Strand and Fleet Street from Trafalgar Square. To begin with Part 2, take the Tube directly to the Temple stop and pick up the walk at St. Clement Danes.

Tourist Information: The City of London TI is located next to St. Paul's; open Mon-Sat 9:30-17:30, Sun 10:00-16:00.

Courtauld Gallery: £9, £11 Sat-Sun, can be more for temporary exhibits, daily 10:00-18:00.

St. Clement Danes: Free, Mon-Fri 10:00-16:00, Sat-Sun until 15:00, closed to sightseers during worship (generally Sun at 11:00, Wed and Fri at 12:30), +44 20 7242 2382.

Temple Church: £5, irregular visiting hours, often Mon-Fri 10:00-16:00, usually closed Sat-Sun and can close at other times—confirm schedule at www.templechurch.com.

Dr. Johnson's House: £8, Mon-Sat 11:00-17:30, off-season until 17:00, closed Sun year-round, +44 20 7353 3745, www.drjohnsonshouse.org.

St. Bride's Church: Free, Mon-Fri 8:00-18:00, Sat generally 10:00-15:30, Sun 10:00-18:30; free lunch concerts usually Tue and Fri at 13:15; Sun choral Eucharist at 11:00 and evensong at 17:30; +44 20 7427 0133, www.stbrides.com.

St. Paul's Cathedral: £21, £19 online; open Mon-Sat 8:30-16:30, dome opens at 9:30, closed Sun except for worship.

St. Mary-le-Bow: Free, Mon-Fri 7:30-18:00, usually closed Sat-Sun.

The Guildhall: Free, Mon-Sat 10:00-17:00, Sun 12:00-16:00.

Bank Museum: Free, Mon-Fri 10:00-17:00, closed Sat-Sun, +44 20 7601 5545, www.bankofengland.co.uk/museum.

The Monument: £5.40 to climb the steps for the view, daily 9:30-18:00, +44 20 7626 2717, www.themonument.info.

Tours: ∩ Download my free Historic London: The City audio tour.

Eating: This walk passes a handful of historic and atmospheric pubs, which can be memorable for a meal (see page 430). If you're here on a weekday, you'll find plenty of places catering to local office workers with tasty, cheap, fast lunches. Two good options are the Italian deli/sandwich shop **$ Dilieto** (175 Fleet Street) and **$ Pílpel** falafel (down the alley across from Ye Olde Cheshire Cheese, near 146 Fleet Street). For top-quality coffee, try **Rosslyn** (exit south end of Bow Lane and turn left; 78 Queen Victoria Street).

THE CITY

OVERVIEW

The City stretches from Temple Church (near Blackfriars Bridge) to the Tower of London. This was the London of the ancient Romans, William the Conqueror, Henry VIII, Shakespeare, and Elizabeth I.

But The City has been stripped of its history by the Great Fire (1666), the WWII Blitz (1940-1941), and modern economic realities. Today, it's a neighborhood of modern bank buildings and retail stores. Only about 10,000 people live here, but The City is a hive of business activity on workdays—packed with almost half a million commuting bankers, legal assistants, and coffee-shop baristas.

The route is simple—a two-mile walk east along a single street that changes names as you go. The Strand becomes Fleet Street, which becomes Cannon Street.

The Walk Begins

• *Make your way to the front (Strand) entrance of Charing Cross Station (Tube: Charing Cross or Embankment; also just a short walk along the Strand from Trafalgar Square).*

If you're coming via the Embankment stop, consider first climbing up to the Golden Jubilee pedestrian bridge (follow signs for the

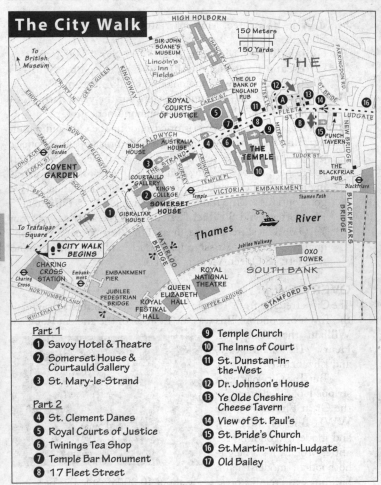

The City Walk

150 Meters
150 Yards

SIR JOHN SOANE'S MUSEUM

Lincoln's Inn Fields

THE OLD BANK OF ENGLAND PUB

ROYAL COURTS OF JUSTICE

THE

PUNCH TAVERN

THE BLACKFRIAR PUB

AUSTRALIA HOUSE

BUSH HOUSE

COVENT GARDEN

COURTAULD GALLERY

KING'S COLLEGE

SOMERSET HOUSE

GIBRALTAR HOUSE

THE TEMPLE

TUDOR ST.

CITY WALK BEGINS

CHARING CROSS STATION

Embankment

EMBANKMENT PIER

JUBILEE PEDESTRIAN BRIDGE

ROYAL FESTIVAL HALL

QUEEN ELIZABETH HALL

ROYAL NATIONAL THEATRE

Thames River

Thames Path

Jubilee Walkway

OXO TOWER

SOUTH BANK

STAMFORD ST.

To British Museum

To Trafalgar Square

Part 1
1 Savoy Hotel & Theatre
2 Somerset House & Courtauld Gallery
3 St. Mary-le-Strand

Part 2
4 St. Clement Danes
5 Royal Courts of Justice
6 Twinings Tea Shop
7 Temple Bar Monument
8 17 Fleet Street

9 Temple Church
10 The Inns of Court
11 St. Dunstan-in-the-West
12 Dr. Johnson's House
13 Ye Olde Cheshire Cheese Tavern
14 View of St. Paul's
15 St. Bride's Church
16 St. Martin-within-Ludgate
17 Old Bailey

Embankment Pier *exit) for good views of the London Eye and sky-scrapers before starting this walk. (If you miss this photo op, there's an-other good one early in the walk, on Waterloo Bridge.)*

PART 1: THE STRAND
(FROM CHARING CROSS TO THE CITY)

This busy boulevard, home to theaters and retail stores, was for-merly a high-class riverside promenade, back before the Thames was tamed with retaining walls in the 19th century.

The venerable **Charing Cross Station** still has a terminus hotel (a standard part of station design in the early days of rail trav-el) and remains a busy transportation hub.

The station is named for the **Charing Cross monument,** which stands quietly out of place amid all the commotion in front

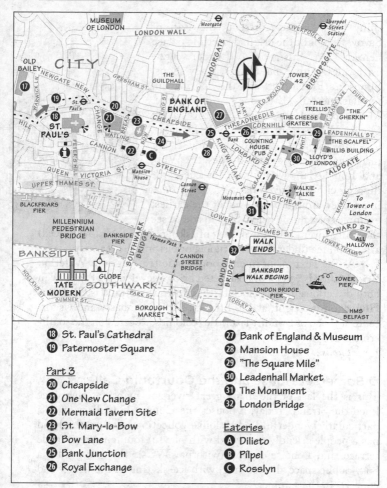

18 St. Paul's Cathedral
19 Paternoster Square

Part 3
20 Cheapside
21 One New Change
22 Mermaid Tavern Site
23 St. Mary-le-Bow
24 Bow Lane
25 Bank Junction
26 Royal Exchange

27 Bank of England & Museum
28 Mansion House
29 "The Square Mile"
30 Leadenhall Market
31 The Monument
32 London Bridge

Eateries
A Dilieto
B Pilpel
C Rosslyn

of the station. This monument is a Victorian Age replacement of the original, medieval "Eleanor Cross." When Queen Eleanor died in 1290, her body was carried from Nottingham to Westminster Abbey. King Edward I had a memorial "Eleanor Cross" built at each of the 12 places his wife's funeral procession spent the night during that long, sad trek. Charing Cross marks the final overnight stop.

• *Walk (with the monument and train station on your right) a few blocks up the Strand. On the left, you'll pass Southampton Street, which leads to* **Covent Garden** *(described in my West End Walk). Ahead on the right is the drive-up entrance to the...*

❶ Savoy Hotel and Savoy Theatre

The hotel sparkles after a three-year £250 million renovation. Its shiny gold knight represents the Earl of Savoy, who built the original riverside palace here in 1245. This is one of London's ritziest locales, with Rolls-Royces, fancy shops, Simpson's Restaurant, and the doorman in top hat and tails. Everyone has stayed here. Monet painted the Thames at the Savoy; Oscar Wilde romanced Lord Douglas; Chaplin, Sinatra, and Burton-and-Taylor made the scene; as did the Beatles, the Who, and Bob Dylan, who filmed his cue-card-flipping clip for *Subterranean Homesick Blues* in an alley around back—one of the earliest examples of a music video. Step inside to see

the spiffy foyer under the pretext of asking about their (overpriced) afternoon tea under the glass cupola or visiting the tea shop.

At the next major intersection, a side trip out onto **Waterloo Bridge** affords you an unobstructed bridge-level view of the city in both directions. A half-block farther down the Strand is **Gibraltar House** (on the right, at 150 Strand), a quasi-embassy and visitors center for one of Britain's last little "colonies," located on the southern tip of Spain.

• *Next up is...*

❷ Somerset House and the Courtauld Gallery

This is the last of the many great riverside mansions that once lined the Strand. Today, it houses the Courtauld Gallery (with a particularly wonderful Impressionist collection—see page 66) and has a people-friendly courtyard with playful fountains, a riverside terrace, and a choice of cafés (with pay WCs). The courtyard is a busy public space all year long, with ice-skating in the winter and concerts in the summer.

• *Continuing on, you'll encounter two different churches left Strand-ed in the middle of traffic when the road was widened around them. The first is...*

❸ St. Mary-le-Strand

With its clean, white interior lit by blue-and-green stained glass, this church is an oasis of quiet. Charles Dickens' parents were married here.

To the right of the church (in the ugly concrete building) is **King's College**, one of the world's top universities, with 20,000 current students and a distinguished list of former students that includes John Keats, Florence Nightingale, and Desmond Tutu.

Straight ahead and across the street is **Bush House,** former home of the BBC's World Service.

And just beyond (on the left) is **Australia House,** a kind of embassy for that member of the British Commonwealth. It's most famous for its role as the goblin-run Gringotts Wizarding Bank in the Harry Potter movies. Though it's not open to visiting Muggles, you can step into the lobby—enter at the far side—and gaze through glass doors at the chandeliered room they filmed in. The building sits on a multibranched intersection where the flow of traffic is a marvel to watch.

• *At the intersection in front of Australia House, behind the statue of William Gladstone—Queen Victoria's longest-serving prime minister—is a second traffic-island church. This is St. Clement Danes, and the start of Part 2 of this walk.*

PART 2: FLEET STREET, WREN CHURCHES, AND THE HEART OF THE CITY

❹ St. Clement Danes

Built by Christopher Wren (1682), the church was blitzed heavily in World War II. Today, it's a busy Royal Air Force chapel and a memorial to the 125,000 RAF servicemen who gave their lives in both world wars. Outside stand statues of brave airmen. Inside, hundreds of gray medallions in the stone floor are dedicated to various squadrons. Lining the walls are Books of Remembrance—10 thick volumes (with a page respectfully turned each day). This is the first of several Wren-built churches (steeple added later) we'll see on the walk. Of the 50-some he originally built, 23 Wren churches still dot London. Pick up the tourist guide at the entry for more information on the church.

• *Past St. Clement Danes, on the left side of the street, are the Gothic arches, pinnacles, and turrets of the...*

❺ Royal Courts of Justice

When movie stars sue tabloids for libel, when media mogul Rupert Murdoch is called to testify in a corruption inquiry, or when ex-Beatles pay out $50 million divorce settlements, the trial is likely to be held here, at Britain's highest civil court. (Criminal cases are heard down the street at the Old Bailey.) Paparazzi often litter the entrance, awaiting a celeb

or a lawyer (many of whom are celebrities themselves). The 76 courtrooms in this Neo-Gothic complex are open to the public on weekdays. At least step into the lobby to see the vast Gothic entry hall (submit to a security check to go farther in). This is just one of several legal buildings in the neighborhood.

• *Underground public WCs are in the median in front of the courts. Across the street is...*

❻ Twinings Tea Shop

When this slender store at #216 first opened its doors ("established 1706"), tea was an exotic concoction from newly explored lands.

(The Chinese statues at the entrance remind us that tea came first from China, then India.) This store has been in the Twining family for nearly 300 years. The Twinings shop is narrow, but explore its depths. In the back, there are a few display cases of historic tea-related knickknacks, and a tea bar where you can taste a sample and learn tea tips from a chatty host.

In the 1700s, London was in the grip of a coffee craze, and "coffee houses" were everywhere. These were rather seedy places, where "gentlemen" went for coffee, tobacco, and female companionship. Tea offered a refreshing change of pace, and the late-in-the-day "cuppa" (as well as "afternoon tea") soon became a national institution. These days—as you'll see on this walk—coffee has made a comeback in London in the form of modern Starbucks-style coffee shops.

• *Several doors down, the building at #229—which used to be a pub called The Wig and Pen—is a rare survivor of the Great Fire of 1666. Up ahead, in the middle of the street, is a small statue of a winged creature.*

❼ Temple Bar Monument

A statue of a griffin, a mythological beast with an eagle's wings and a lion's body, marks the official border between the City of Westminster and The City of London. The Queen, who presides over Westminster, does not pass this point without ceremonial permission of The City's Lord Mayor. The relief at its base shows Queen Victoria submitting to this ritual in 1837.

• *Cross the border, leaving Westminster and en-*

tering The City. Ahead on the left (194 Fleet Street) is The Old Bank of England pub—a former bank with a lavish late-Victorian interior that serves lunches to the 9-to-5 crowd. (To imagine a fancy 19th-century bank, pop inside.)

Up a few storefronts, on the right side of the street, look above the street-level shops to find an old building with black-framed, stained-glass bay windows.

❽ 17 Fleet Street

This half-timbered, three-story, Tudor-style building (1610) is one of the few to survive the Great Fire. In Shakespeare's day, the entire City was packed, rooftop to rooftop, with wood and plaster buildings like this. Many were five and six stories high, with narrow frontage. Little wonder that a small fire could spread so quickly and become the Great Fire of 1666.

The building may be flying the red-and-yellow flag of Spain's Catalan region, as it now houses the Catalan tourist board.

• *Pass underneath the house, through the passageway called Inner Temple Lane. This leads a half-block to the exotic...*

❾ Temple Church

The church's round shape and crenellated, castle-turret roofline mark this as a Crusader church (1185) from the days of King

Richard the Lionheart. In the courtyard on the far side of the church, a tiny statue of a Crusader knight on horseback stands atop a pillar. This church was the headquarters of the Knights Templar, a band of heavily armed, highly trained monks who dressed in long white robes (decorated with red crosses) beneath heavy armor. In their secret rituals, the knights were sworn to chastity and to the protection of pilgrims on their way to the Muslim-held Holy Land.

Visiting the Church: If the church is open (it has erratic hours), step inside and buy a ticket. On the left, walk under the rotunda of the circular "nave," patterned after the Church of the Holy Sepulchre in Jerusalem. Exhibits explain the connection between this church and the Magna Carta: The Knights Templar remained loyal to King John, making this his home base in London around the time the nobility compelled him to sign the Magna Carta. Some of those negotiations likely took place right here.

Notice the tombs of honored knights that lie face-up on the floor. A knight's crossed legs indicate that he probably died peacefully at home. Surrounding the serene knights are grotesque faces, perhaps the twisted expressions seen in distant wars. While faces like these were original, the entertaining ones you see today were redone during Victorian times—with a sense of humor, from the looks of it. But the message of the heads remains serious: the agonizing consequences for nonbelievers.

WILLIAM MARSHAL
second Earl of Pembroke (died 1231)

By 1300, the Knights Templars' mission of protecting pilgrims had become a corrupt "protection" racket, and they'd grown rich loaning money to kings and popes. Those same kings and popes condemned the monks as heretics and sodomites and confiscated their lands (1312). The Temple Church was rented to lawyers, who built the Inns of Court around it.

• *Abutting, surrounding, and extending from the Temple Church is a vast complex of buildings covering a full city block between the Strand/Fleet Street and the Thames, known collectively as...*

❿ The Inns of Court

This is an utterly delightful escape from the congested, narrow sidewalks of The City. Take a moment to wander through the peaceful maze of buildings, courtyards, narrow lanes, nooks, gardens, fountains, and century-old gas lamps, where lawyers take a break from the Royal Courts. The complex is a self-contained city of lawyers, with offices, lodgings, courtrooms, chapels, and dining halls. Law students must live here (and are even required to eat a number of meals on the premises) to complete their legal internship.

You'll see barristers in modern business suits and ties, plus a few in traditional wigs and robes, as they prepare to do legal battle. The wigs are a remnant of French manners of the 1700s, when every self-respecting European gentleman wore one.

• *Get lost. Don't worry—when you go uphill, you'll eventually spill back out onto the busy street. Return to 17 Fleet Street, which marks the spot where the Strand becomes...*

Fleet Street

"The Street" was the notorious haunt of a powerful combination—

lawyers and the media. In 1500, Wynkyn de Worde moved here with a newfangled invention, a printing press, making this area the center of an early Information Age. In 1702, the first daily newspaper appeared. Soon you had the *Tatler,* the *Spectator,* and many others pumping out both hard news and paparazzi gossip for the hungry masses. Just past St. Dunstan church (described next), you'll see a building decorated with mosaiced names of some bygone newspapers: the *Dundee Evening Telegraph,* the *People's Journal,* and so on.

London became the nerve center of a global, colonial empire, and Fleet Street was where every twitch found expression. Hard-drinking, ink-stained reporters gathered in taverns and coffeehouses, pumping lawyers for juicy pretrial information, scrambling for that choice bit of must-read gossip that would make their paper number one. They built an industry that still endures. Even in this digital age, Britain supports about a dozen national newspapers, selling more than 9 million papers a day.

Today, busy Fleet Street bustles with almost every business *except* newspapers. The industry made a mass exodus in the 1980s for offices elsewhere, replaced by financial institutions. As you walk along, you'll see the former offices of the *Daily Telegraph* (135 Fleet Street) and the *Daily Express* (#121—peek into the lobby to see its classic 1930s Art Deco interior). The last major institution to leave (in summer 2005) was the Reuters news agency (#85, opposite the *Daily Express*).

• *Heading 50 yards east past 17 Fleet Street, you'll find...*

⓫ St. Dunstan-in-the-West

This church stands where the Great Fire of September 1666 finally ended. The fire started near London Bridge. For three days it swept westward, fanned by hot and blustery weather, leveling everything in its path. As it approached St. Dunstan, 40 theology students battled the blaze, holding it off until the wind shifted, and the fire slowly burned itself out.

From this survivor to the end of our walk (1.5 miles), we'll be passing through the fire's path of destruction. It left London a Sodom-and-Gomorrah wasteland so hot it couldn't be walked on for weeks. (For more on the fire, see the end of the 📖 Bankside Walk chapter.)

Today, St. Dunstan is one of the few churches with a thriving congregation (of Orthodox Romanians) in this now depopulated and secularized district. (They also offer lunchtime concerts—see page 478.) An unbroken line of vicars dating back to 1237 is listed in the vestibule. The clock on the bell tower outside (1670) features London's first minute hand and has two slaves gonging two bells four times an hour.

Alongside the church is a rare contemporary statue of Queen Elizabeth I. This 1586 depiction of Elizabeth is the only surviving statue carved during her reign. The scepter and orb symbolize her religious and secular authority.

• *Continue east on Fleet Street. A half-block past Fetter Lane, turn left through a covered alleyway at #167. (Don't take the alleyway called Red Lion Court; you want the alleyway 20 paces farther, immediately across from #54.) Follow signs through the narrow lanes directing you to* Dr. Johnson's House.

Narrow Lanes: 1700s London

"Sir, if you wish to have a just notion of the magnitude of this city, you must...survey the innumerable little lanes and courts," said the writer Samuel Johnson in 1763 to his young friend and biographer, James Boswell. These twisting alleyways and cramped buildings that house urban hobbits give a faint glimpse of rebuilt 1700s London, a crowded city of half a million people. After the Great Fire, London was resurrected in brick and stone instead of wood, but they stuck to the same medieval street plan, resulting in narrow lanes of brick buildings like these.

• *The narrow lanes eventually spill out onto Gough Square, about a block north of Fleet Street, where you'll find...*

⑫ Dr. Johnson's House (17 Gough Square)

"When a man is tired of London, he is tired of life," wrote Samuel Johnson, "for there is in London all that life can afford." Johnson (1709-1784) loved to wander these twisting lanes, looking for pungent slices of London street life that he could pass along in his weekly columns called "The Rambler" and "The Idler."

At age 28, Johnson arrived in London with one of his former students, David Garrick, who went on to revolutionize London theater. Dr. Johnson prowled the pubs, brothels, coffeehouses, and illicit gaming pits where terriers battled cornered rats while men bet on the outcome. Johnson—described as "tall, stout," and "slovenly in his dress"—became a well-known ec-  centric and man-about-town, though he always seemed to live on the fringes of poverty. At the far end of Gough Square is a statue of Johnson's beloved black cat Hodge, who dined on oysters. The pedestal quotes Johnson himself: "Hodge—a very good cat indeed."

Johnson inhabited this house from 1748 to 1759. He prayed at St. Clement Danes, drank in Fleet Street pubs, and, in the attic of the house, produced his most famous work, *A Dictionary of the English Language*. Published in 1755, it was the first great English-language dictionary, starring Johnson's 42,773 favorite words culled from all the books he'd read. It took Johnson and six assistants more than six years to sift through all the alternate spellings and Cockney dialects of the world's most complex language. He standardized spelling and pronunciation, explained each word's etymology, and occasionally put his own droll spin on words. ("Oats: a grain, which is generally given to horses, but in Scotland supports the people.")

Visiting the House: While the exhibits are fascinating for hard-core Johnson fans (I met one once), the old house is interesting in itself, even for the casual visitor (as long as you don't mind paying the steep admission). You'll climb four stories through period furniture and sparse exhibits, passing a first edition of Johnson's dictionary and pictures of Johnson, Garrick (in the role of Richard III), and Boswell. Nothing is roped off or behind glass, and you can browse at will. See objects Johnson once owned: his walking stick, a chair, a letter carrier, and a brick from something that fascinated him—the Great Wall of China. Portraits bring to life his urbane circle of friends (which included actress Sarah Siddons, painter Sir Joshua Reynolds, and writer Oliver Goldsmith), many of whom socialized at the home of the sophisticated Elizabeth Montagu. Finally, you arrive in the top-floor garret where literary history was made—the birthplace of the dictionary that standardized our English language.

London's Great Plague of 1665

The Grim Reaper—in the form of the bacteria *Yersinia pestis* (bubonic plague)—rode through London on fleas atop a black rat. It killed one in six people, while leaving the buildings standing. (The next year, the Great Fire consumed the buildings.) It started in the spring as "the Poore's Plague," neglected until it spread to richer neighborhoods. During the especially hot summer, 5,000 died each week. By December, the congregation at St. Bride's (you'll see the church later) was 2,111 souls fewer.

Victims passed through several days of agony: headaches, vomiting, fever, shivering, swollen tongue, and swollen buboes (lumps) on the groin glands. After their skin turned blotchy black (the "Black Death"), they died. "Searchers of the Dead" carted bodies off to mass graves, including one near St. Bride's. Both the victims and their families were quarantined under house arrest, with a red cross painted on the door and a guard posted nearby, and denied access to food, water, or medical attention for 40 days—a virtual death sentence even for the uninfected.

The disease was blamed on dogs and cats, and paid dog-killers destroyed tens of thousands of pets—which brought even more rats. People who didn't die tried to leave. The Lord Mayor quarantined the whole city within the walls, so the only way out was to produce (or purchase) a "certificate of health."

By fall, London was a ghost town, and throughout England, people avoided Londoners like the Plague. It took the Great Fire of 1666 to fully cleanse London of the disease. Some scholars have suggested that a popular nursery rhyme refers to the dreaded disease (while others brush this off as bunk):

Ring around the rosie (flower garlands
 to keep the Plague away)
A pocket full of posies (buboes on the groin)
Ashes, ashes (your skin turns black)
We all fall down (dead).

• *At the other end of Gough Square, turn right at the statue of Hodge and head back toward Fleet Street, noticing the lists of barristers (trial lawyers) on the doorways (e.g., next to the door at 9 Gough Square). They work not as part of a firm, but as freelancers sharing offices and clerks. Stay to the left as you wind downhill through the alleys, and look near Fleet Street for the entrance of...*

⓭ Ye Olde Cheshire Cheese Tavern

Johnson often—and I do mean often—popped 'round here for a quick one, sometimes with David Garrick and his sleazy actor friends.

"The Cheese" dates from 1667, when it was rebuilt after the Great Fire, but it's been a tavern since 1538. It's a four-story warren of small, smoky, wood-lined rooms, each offering different menus, from pub grub to white-tablecloth meals. A traditional "chop house," it serves hearty portions of meats to power-lunching businessmen. Even if you don't go in, check out the menu posted outside, and the list of monarchs who have reigned during the Cheese's existence—right up to Queen Elizabeth II.

Inside, you can sit in Charles Dickens' favorite seat, next to a coal fireplace (in the "Chop Room," main floor) and order a steak-and-kidney pie and some spotted dick (sponge pudding with currants, served in winter). Sip a pint of Samuel Smith (the house beer of the current owners) and think of Samuel Johnson, who drank here pondering various spellings: "pint" or "pynte," "color" or "colour," "theater" or "theatre." Immerse yourself in a world largely unchanged for centuries—a world of reporters scribbling the news over lunch; of Alfred, Lord Tennyson inventing rhymes and Arthur Conan Doyle solving crimes; of W. B. Yeats, Teddy Roosevelt, and Mark Twain.

• *Back out on Fleet Street, you're met with a cracking...*

⓴ View of St. Paul's

If you were standing here on December 30, 1940, the morning after a German Luftwaffe firebomb raid, you'd see nothing but a flat, smoldering landscape of rubble, with St. Paul's rising above it almost miraculously intact. (For more on the Blitz, see the sidebar on page 288.)

Christopher Wren (1632-1723)

After London burned, King Charles II turned to his childhood friend Christopher Wren to rebuild it. The 33-year-old Wren was not an architect, but he'd proven his ability in every field he'd touched: astronomy (mapping the moon and building a model of Saturn), medicine (using opium as a general anesthetic, making successful blood transfusions between animals), mathematics (a treatise on spherical trigonometry), and physics (his study of the laws of motion influenced Newton's "discovery" of gravity). Wren also invented a language for the deaf, studied refraction and optics, and built weather-watching instruments.

Though domed St. Paul's is Wren's most famous church, the smaller churches around it better illustrate his distinctive style: a steeple over the west entrance; an uncluttered, well-lit interior; Neoclassical (Greek-style) columns; a curved or domed plaster ceiling; geometrical shapes (e.g., round rosettes inside square frames); and fine carved woodwork, often by his favorite whittler, Grinling Gibbons.

Standing here in September 1666, you'd see nothing but smoke and ruins. The Great Fire razed everything, including the original St. Paul's Cathedral. And standing here a year earlier, in September 1665, you'd hear "Bring out yer dead!" as they carted away 70,000 victims of the bubonic plague. After the double-whammy of plague and fire, the architect Christopher Wren was hired to rebuild St. Paul's and The City.

Even today, we see the view that Wren intended—a majestic dome hovering above the hazy rooftops, surrounded by the thin spires of his lesser churches. In the foreground below St. Paul's (between you and the dome) is the slender, lead-covered steeple of St. Martin-within-Ludgate, perfectly offsetting St. Paul's more massive dome. Wren's 23 surviving churches are more than plenty for today's secular ghost town of a city.

• From Ye Olde Cheshire Cheese, head about a block toward the dome of St. Paul's, cross the street, and walk a half-block down tiny St. Bride's Avenue to see the stacked-tier steeple of...

⓭ St. Bride's Church

The 226-foot steeple, Wren's tallest, is stacked in layers as it tapers to a point. It's said to have inspired the wedding cake. Supposedly, a Fleet Street baker named Mr. Rich gazed out his shop window at St. Bride's as he made the first multitiered cake. (By the way, the word "Bride" in St. Bride's is only coincidental. The church was dedicated to St. Brigid—or Bride—of Kildare long before the steeple or any wedding cakes.)

St. Bride's, built between 1671 and 1675, was one of the first of Wren's churches to open its doors after the Fire. St. Bride's is nicknamed both "The Cathedral of Fleet Street" and "The Printer's Church." Step inside. Notice that the pews bear the names of departed journalists. It has been home to newspaper reporters, scholars, and literati ever since 1500, when Wynkyn de Worde set up his printing press here on church property. De Worde's press first served the literate clergy of St. Bride's, but was soon adopted by secular scholars, bookmakers, and newspapers, as Fleet Street became a global center for printed information.

During World War II, St. Bride's suffered terribly in the Blitz. (Today's structure was largely rebuilt after the war.) But thanks to Hitler's bombs, St. Bride's was instantly excavated down to its sixth-century Saxon foundations. In the church's back-left corner, head down to the **crypt** to walk through the layers of history that were revealed from six previous churches that stood on this spot—including items such as Roman coins, medieval stained glass, and 17th-century tobacco pipes. Also in the crypt (in a glass case on the left as you enter) is a wedding dress—worn by the wife of the Fleet Street baker whose wedding cake was inspired by St. Bride's steeple.

Nearby: Just past St. Bride's Church on Fleet Street is **$$ The Punch Tavern,** draped with memories of the venerable London political magazine famous for its satirical cartoons. Peek in to see Punch and his twin wife Judy looking down on a perfectly Victorian scene. These characters from a popular puppet show came onto the London scene 350 years ago. The characters gave the magazine its name, and the pub became the magazine staff's hangout. In the back room hang huge, colorful Victorian-era pastels of Punch and Judy. Don't be shy—the tavern is proud of its history and welcomes curious visitors popping in for a quick look. It's also a friendly place to order a drink or a meal (respected for their gins and pies, 99 Fleet Street).

• *The valley between St. Bride's and St. Paul's is the...*

Fleet River and Ludgate

The Fleet River—now covered over by Farringdon Road—still flows southward, crossing underneath Fleet Street on its way to the Thames at Blackfriars Bridge. In medieval times, the river formed the western boundary of the walled city. As you cross the "river" and continue toward St. Paul's, you're hiking up Ludgate Hill. This was one of the three hills in the area, and was where some of London's first inhabitants built. The ancient Romans of Londinium may have built a temple to their goddess of hunting where St. Paul's stands today. You're getting closer and closer to the city's medieval origins—the city Shakespeare would have known.

Up ahead, you'll spy the lead-covered steeple that graces another of Wren's churches—⓰ **St. Martin-within-Ludgate.** The church stands on the site of what was once the city wall. In medieval and Elizabethan times, this was one of the gated entrances to the city, known as Ludgate.

• *Just before St.-Martin-within-Ludgate, pause and look left down Old Bailey Street to see a dome crowned by a golden statue of justice, which marks the...*

⓱ Old Bailey: Central Criminal Court

England's most infamous criminals—from the king-killers of the Civil War to the radically religious William Penn, from the "crimi-

nally homosexual" Oscar Wilde to the Yorkshire Ripper—were tried here, in Britain's highest criminal court. On top of the copper dome stands the famous golden Lady who weighs and executes Justice with scale and sword. The Old Bailey is built on the former site of Newgate Prison, with its notorious execution-by-hanging site. While seeing it from the outside is plenty for most, those interested in the legal system can visit courtrooms and watch justice doled out the old-fashioned way to modern-day offenders (see page 83).

Bewigged barristers argue before stern judges while the accused sit in the dock.

• *Continue up Ludgate Hill to...*

⓲ St. Paul's Cathedral

The greatest of Wren's creations is the rebuilt St. Paul's—England's national church and the heart of The City. Wren labored for more than 40 years on the church, both designing and overseeing construction of what was then the second-largest dome in the world. Unlike many church architects, Wren lived long enough to see his masterpiece completed. (For details on touring the church, 📖 see the St. Paul's Cathedral Tour chapter or 🎧 download my free audio tour.)

THE CITY

If you're not paying to enter the great church, you can pop into the basement (entry to left of front) for a café, fine WCs, a shop, and a peek at the memorials in the crypt. Belly up to the iron Churchill Gates. Standing on a plaque honoring Churchill, you can see the tomb of Admiral Lord Nelson directly below the dome.

• *Find the Temple Bar gate—a white stone archway—directly to the left of the church (straight ahead, as you exit the crypt). The gate was once the west entrance to the City of London. Relocated here, it now welcomes you to...*

⓳ Paternoster Square

Before stepping through the **gate,** take a moment to appreciate its details. This gate originally stood a half-mile west of here. It marked "Temple Bar," the boundary between the City of London and Westminster, where the griffin monument now stands (described earlier). The original Temple Bar gate was built of stone by St. Paul's architect, Christopher Wren, in 1672.

But given the increase in traffic and new construction around it, the gate didn't "fit" at Temple Bar anymore. It was disassembled in 1878 and carted off to ornament the rural estate of a brewery owner. Finally, in 2004, the 2,700 stones were brought back to The City and painstakingly rebuilt here in Paternoster Square.

Go through the arch into the fine **square** and enjoy a view of the dome from behind the church's red-brick Chapter House (a good example of Wren's Neoclassicism). This square was designed in the early 21st century to save views of the church, while allowing maximum modern development here in the city center. In warm weather, locals hang out here, relaxing in slingback chairs with a fine view of London's grandest dome.

• *You've seen the heart of The City. If time is tight, you can wrap up here. A bus stop is immediately below St. Paul's, and a Tube stop is around its back end. Or you can walk down to the Millennium Bridge, which cuts across the river to the Tate Modern and Shakespeare's Globe.*

With more time, however, it's worth continuing. We'll head through Shakespeare's London, then through the banking district to a modern world of skyscrapers, before ending on London Bridge.

PART 3: CHEAPSIDE, THE BANKING DISTRICT, AND "THE SQUARE MILE"

• *From where you entered Paternoster Square, angle right through the square, striding past the* Shepherd and Sheep *statue, and head up the pedestrian street called Paternoster Row, then cross the busy cross street. Bearing a bit to the right, you'll be walking along the street called...*

⑳ Cheapside: Shakespeare's London

This was the main east-west street of Shakespeare's London, which had a population of about 200,000 back then. The wide street hosted The City's marketplace ("cheap" meant market), seen today in the names of the streets that branch off from it: Bread, Milk, Honey. Rebuilt cheaply after the war, more recently it has been upgraded with glassy facades—leaving Cheapside anything but.

A half-block past New Change Street (at around 40 Cheapside, on the right) is the ㉑ **One New Change** shopping mall, with WCs and a (free) glass elevator that leads to a rooftop terrace and views of St. Paul's Cathedral and the London cityscape.

Continue along Cheapside Street. If you were to detour two blocks south on Bread Street, you would not see even a trace of the ㉒ **Mermaid Tavern,** Shakespeare's favorite haunt—but that's where it stood, near the modern junction with Cannon Street. In the early 1600s, "Sweet Will" would meet Ben Jonson, Sir Walter Raleigh, and John Donne at the Mermaid for food, ale, and literary conversation. Francis Beaumont, one of the group, wrote: "What things have we seen / Done at the Mermaid! heard words that have been / So nimble, and so full of subtle flame..."

• *Otherwise, head straight toward the pointy steeple just past One New Change on the right. This marks...*

㉓ St. Mary-le-Bow

From London's earliest Christian times, a church has stood here. The steeple of St. Mary-le-Bow, rebuilt after the Fire, is one of Wren's most impressive. He incorporated the ribbed-arch design of the former church (a "bow" is an arch) in the steeple's midsection. In the courtyard is a statue of a smiling figure from American history—Captain **John Smith.** In 1607, Smith established an English colony in Jamestown, Virginia, USA before retiring here near the church.

Inside the church, see not one but two pulpits, used today for point-counterpoint debates of moral issues. The church was rebuilt after being hit by WWII bombs. The crucifix hanging from the ceiling is a gift of atonement from the people of Bavaria.

This is the very center of old London, where, in medieval times, the church's bells rang each evening, calling Londoners safely back in to the walled town before the gates were locked. To be born "within the sound of Bow bells" long defined a true local, or "Cockney."

This is also the "Cockney" neighborhood of plucky streetwise urchins, where a distinctive Eliza Doolittle dialect is sometimes still spoken. Today's Cockney is the hard accent of rough-and-tumble, working-class Londoners. A famous example of Cockney today would be the GEICO gecko on American TV ads. There are no Hs. "Are you 'appy, 'arry?" "Where's your 'orse? ...'urry up now." (Another fun element of the Cockney dialect—its creative rhyming slang—is described in the sidebar, next page.) Nineteenth-century social climbers added extra H's in order not to sound Cockney. "I hunderstand you are hinterested in renting my hattic."

These days, few people actually live within the sound of Bow bells. The City's population, while over 400,000 during working hours, falls to about 10,000 at night.

• *Just around and behind St. Mary-le-Bow is...*

㉔ Bow Lane

Today, pedestrian-only Bow Lane features smart clothing shops, sandwich bars, and pubs. The entire City once had narrow lanes like Bow, Watling, and Bread streets. Explore this area between Cheapside and Cannon streets.

When Shakespeare bought his tights and pointy shoes in Bow Lane, the shops were wooden, the streets were dirt, and the toilet

Cockney Rhyming Slang

The East End (specifically, the area around the Church of St. Mary-le-Bow) is known as the traditional home of the Cockneys. This colorful, working-class group spoke in a quirky pastiche that was the opposite of the Queen's English...think Audrey Hepburn as Eliza Doolittle in *My Fair Lady,* Dick van Dyke as the chimneysweep in *Mary Poppins,* or Don Cheadle in *Ocean's Eleven.*

One colorful Cockney invention that survives from the mid-19th century is the neighborhood's unique rhyming slang. According to urban legend, the Cockneys devised this secret way of talking to confuse policemen who might be listening. Another theory suggests that it was used between market vendors in order to rip off customers. Either way, Cockney rhyming slang helped create a sort of neighborhood pride for this downtrodden community.

Here's how it works: Simply replace an everyday word with a nonsensical phrase that rhymes with it. Instead of stairs, it's "apples and pears"—often shortened to simply "apples," as in, "I'm walking up the apples." For teeth, it's "Hampstead Heath" (or just "hampstead": "The dentist took a bloody good whack at me hampsteads").

Some Cockney rhyming slang words have become integrated into everyday American speech. For example, "blow a raspberry" comes from the slang "raspberry tart" for fart. And did you ever notice that "getting down to brass tacks" rhymes with "facts"? Many others—including several on the list on the next page—remain widely used as slang throughout the UK (if not in the US).

The tradition has continued into the 21st century—though these days it's done as a fun bit of irony, rather than as an actual secret language. For curry, they might say "Ruby Murray"—also the name of an Irish pop singer from the 1950s. Someone might

was a ditch down the middle of the road. (The garbage brought rats, and rats brought plagues, like the one in 1665.) You bought your water in buckets carted up from the Thames. And at night, the bellman walked the streets, ringing the hour.

(For more Shakespearean ambience, it's a three-block walk south from St. Paul's to the river, where the Millennium Bridge crosses the Thames to Shakespeare's Globe, a reconstruction of the theater where many of Shakespeare's plays premiered. See page 96.)

• *From Bow Lane, return to busy Cheapside and continue east. After a block, King Street leads left to the fanciful facade of* **The Guildhall,** *a free art gallery and a fine medieval meeting hall (consider side-tripping there if you have ample time; for details see page 83).*

Keep going east on Cheapside a few blocks to the long, wide intersection where nine streets meet, called Bank Junction (Tube: Bank). In

suggest, "After work, let's head to the pub for some Britneys" (Britney Spears = beers), or "Go wash yer Chevy" (Chevy Chase = face). Cockney rhyming slang has even made it into the hallowed halls of Parliament: During a heated Brexit debate, one member said, "Nobody has a Scooby-Doo (clue) what's going on!"

Cockney Rhyming Slang	Translation
a la mode	code
Adam and Eve	believe
Barnet Fair (barnet)	hair (hairstyle)
bubble and squeak (bubble)	Greek
butcher's hook (butcher's)	look
china plate (china)	mate (friend)
deep sea diver	fiver (£5 note)
loaf of bread (loaf)	head
Mutt and Jeff (mutton)	deaf
plates of meat (plates)	feet
porkpies (porkies)	lies
rabbit and pork (rabbit)	talk
Scapa Flow (scarper)	go
septic tank (septic, seppo)	Yank (American)
tea leaf	thief
trouble and strife	wife
whistle and flute	suit

So the next time you find yourself 'avin' a rabbit with a Cockney, slip the bartender a deep sea diver to buy him a Britney and ask him about his trouble and strife's new barnet. Or take a butcher's at his fancy whistle and flute, and try out the local a la mode. Maybe he'll tap his loaf and say, "Not bad fer a seppo."

THE CITY

the middle of all the traffic is a tiny park with a Wellington-on-horseback statue. Walk there and find the pyramid-shaped metal info post showing "The Heart of the City." From here, survey...

❷❺ Bank Junction

You're entering financial London, which helped invent the capitalist economy centuries ago. The skyscrapers up ahead house the multinational companies that continue to make London one of the globe's financial capitals. "The Square Mile" hosts 500 foreign and British banks. London, centrally located amid the globe's time zones, can find someone around the world to trade with 24 hours a day. Bank Junction is also the place where crowds of angry demonstrators often gather to protest greedy bankers and governments that seem to enable them.

• *Look across the square at the eight-columned entrance to the...*

THE CITY

㉖ Royal Exchange: When London's original stock exchange opened, "stock" meant whatever could be loaded and unloaded onto a boat in the Thames. Remember, London got its start as a river-trading town. Soon, Londoners were gathering here, trading slips of paper and "futures" in place

of live goats and chickens. Traders needed money changers, who needed bankers...and London's financial district boomed. Today, you can step inside to a skylight-covered courtyard lined with traders of retail goods and cappuccinos.

• *To the left of the Royal Exchange is the city-block-sized Bank of England (main entrance just across Threadneedle Street from the Royal Exchange entrance).*

㉗ Bank of England: This 3.5-acre, two-story complex houses the country's national bank. In 1694, it loaned £1.2 million to King William III at 8 percent interest to finance a war with France; it's managed the national debt ever since. It's an investment bank (a banker's bank), loaning money to other financial institutions. Working in tandem with the government (nationalized 1946, independent 1997), "The Old Lady of Threadneedle Street" sets interest rates, prints pound notes, and serves as the country's Fort Knox, housing stacks of gold bars.

The complex has a good **Bank Museum** inside (enter from far side, on Bartholomew Lane). See banknotes from 1699, an old safe, and account books. Also see current pound notes—with a foil hologram and numbers visible under UV light (to stay one step ahead of counterfeiters). The museum's highlight is under the rotunda: a real gold bar that's worth more than $500,000 (check today's rates at the entrance) and weighs 28 pounds. Try lifting it.

• *Opposite the Royal Exchange is Mansion House, marked by its six (not eight) columns.*

㉘ Mansion House: This is the official residence of The City's Lord Mayor. The Lord Mayor governs not all of London but just this neighborhood. In the year 2000, a new post was created— "Mayor of London"—overseeing all of London. But the "Lord Mayor of the City" still carries out the old traditions, presiding from this palatial building. Once a year, he rides the streets in the Lord Mayor's Coach, a gilded carriage pulled by six white horses that looks like something out of *Cinderella*.

• *Walk a block down Cornhill, with the Royal Exchange on your left, and a monument to James Henry Greathead (the 19th-century engineer who made constructing the Tube possible by inventing the "traveling shield"). A couple of blocks farther, on the right at Cornhill #50, pop into* **The Counting House** *pub—built as a bank in 1893 (and my favorite lunch stop in this area).*

Cross Gracechurch Street and carry on straight up Leadenhall Street. At the first corner, look right at the ornate entry to the Leadenhall Market (with the giant "Walkie-Talkie" skyscraper towering above it). We'll return here after a quick side trip. Zip ahead to the next corner to see a towering modern forest of skyscrapers, the new face of The City. Stand at the corner of Leadenhall Street and Lime Street, just past the building wearing all its pipes on the outside.

㉙ The Square Mile's Skyscrapers

You're in the heart of "The Square Mile" (also called "One Square Mile"), the richest square mile on earth. When there's bad eco-nomic news, TV reporters declare, "The Square Mile won't like this."

This area was dam-aged during a bombing by the Irish Republican Army (IRA) in 1992, which partly set in mo-tion the drive to remake the neighborhood in a bold new style. And recently, these businesses have been investing heavily in towering skyscraper office blocks, in a dizzying game of architectural one-upmanship. Get oriented with this spin tour:

Begin by facing the hulking, tapering building on your left, where you have a great view of the sturdy, zigzag girders that sup-port the structure. This is the Leadenhall Building (738 feet tall, from 2014). It's also called **The Cheese Grater** (standard issue for any new building is a tongue-in-cheek nickname). Panning right, you may either see the shorter, dark **St. Helen's** tower (embarrass-ingly short at 378 feet, and an "old-timer" from 1969), or construc-tion for 1 Undershaft, a.k.a. **The Trellis,** which is slated to replace it. So named for its distinctive cross-hatched bracing, The Trellis is planned to soar to 966 feet, making it the tallest building in The City (and the second-tallest in London, after The Shard). Farther to the right, looming over a church, is **The Gherkin**—the Sir Nor-man Foster-designed icon of The City's dazzling new architectural age (officially called 30 St. Mary Axe, 591 feet tall, 2004).

Farther right, Leadenhall Street runs along a new forest of glassy skyscrapers, including **The Scalpel** (620 feet tall, 2018) and, to the right of that, the unimaginatively named **Willis Building** (410 feet tall, tucked back from Leadenhall Street, 2008). Final-ly, on the nearest corner is the distinctive Lloyd's Building, also

THE CITY

The Great Fire

The stones of St. Paul's flew from the building, the lead melting down the streets in a stream... God grant mine eyes may never behold the like... Above 10,000 homes all in one flame, the noise and crackling and thunder of the impetuous flames, the shrieking of women and children, the hurry of the people, the fall of the towers, houses, and churches was like a hideous storm.

—John Evelyn, eyewitness

known as **The Inside-Out Building** (312 feet tall, 1986). Like Paris' Pompidou Center, it wears its industrial works on the outside and was designed by the same team, Renzo Piano and Richard Rogers.

• *Now that you're oriented to The City's emerging skyline, backtrack half a block down Leadenhall Street, turn left on Whittington Avenue, and enter...*

➌⓪ Leadenhall Market

Initially the site of Londinium's Roman Forum, this spot has hosted 2,000 years of commerce. It was named for the new-fangled lead roof of the medieval market hall. Today's hall—a classic 19th-century Victorian structure, still sporting its evocative iron meat hooks—is a getaway for office workers. Given the value of land in this 21st-century environment of skyscrapers, this survives only because it's protected by the government. Exploring

here, you'll see taverns, shops, and even an old-fashioned shoeshine station. The creaky old market's juxtaposition against high-rises is thought to have inspired J. K. Rowling to create Diagon Alley; in the Harry Potter movies, the entrance to the Leaky Cauldron was filmed here (in Bull's Head Passage).

• *At the center of the market, turn right and head out to big and busy Gracechurch Street, then turn left and go three blocks to...*

❸❶ The Monument to the Great Fire of 1666

Called "The Monument," this recalls two themes that have dominated this walk—the Great Fire and Christopher Wren. This
202-foot column is Wren's tribute to
the Great Fire that gave him a blank
canvas upon which to create modern
London. At 2:00 in the morning of
September 2, 1666, a small fire broke
out in a baker's oven in nearby Pudding
Lane. Supposedly, if you tipped The
Monument over (to the east), its top
would fall on the exact spot. Fanned
by hot, blustery weather, the fire swept
westward, leaping from house to house
until The City was a square mile of
flame.

Wren's memorial is a classic—a
Doric column made of Portland stone that was quarried in Dorset in southwestern England and London's new favorite building
material. The column's bristly top is made of gilded bronze and
meant to depict a Greek urn sprouting flames, symbolizing the
1666 Fire. Inside the hollow column is a spiral staircase you can
pay to climb—but it's generally not worthwhile. After walking up
311 steps, you'll mostly get a view of the tall new buildings that
have been built all around it.

• *From here, go uphill a short block on Monument Street, then turn left
to hike out over the river on...*

❸❷ London Bridge

We'll end our walk at The City's beginning. (For the history of
London Bridge, see page 312.)

The City was born as a river-trading town. The Thames flows
west to east, from the interior of England to the open sea. It's a
tidal river from here to the sea, so ancient and medieval boats could
hitch rides on the tide in both directions. London Bridge, first built
by the ancient Romans, established a north-south axis through the
city. Soon, goods from every corner of the world were pouring into
this, one of the modern world's first great urban centers. Today, the
bridge is overshadowed by the mammoth skyscraper known as The
Shard, which rockets dramatically up over a thousand feet—a symbol of a still-growing city. With its worldwide financial network
and cultural heritage, The City—a proud survivor of plagues, fires,
blitzes, and economic changes (even great recessions)—is thriving.
Today's London still straddles the Thames as you look downstream
to the rest of the world.

• *From here, the Tower of London (□ see the Tower of London Tour chapter) is a 10-minute walk east, down the parklike riverside path. The Bankside Walk (□ see the Bankside Walk chapter) begins right here on London Bridge. The start of the East End Walk (□ see the East End Walk chapter) is a 20-minute walk (up Gracechurch/Bishopsgate) or one Tube stop to the north, at Liverpool Street Station. Or you can return to Charing Cross and Trafalgar Square on the Tube (Monument stop nearby) or bus #15 (from Cannon Street).*

ST. PAUL'S CATHEDRAL TOUR

No sooner was Sir Christopher Wren selected to refurbish Old St. Paul's Cathedral than the Great Fire of 1666 incinerated it. Within a week, Wren had a plan for a whole new building...and for the city around it, complete with some 50 new churches. For the next four decades he worked to achieve his vision—a spacious church, topped by a dome, surrounded by a flock of Wrens.

St. Paul's is England's national church. There's been a church on this spot since 604. It was the symbol of London's rise from the Great Fire of 1666 and of the city's survival of the Blitz of 1940. It's been the site of important weddings (Prince Charles and Lady Diana) and state funerals (Prime Ministers Churchill and Thatcher). It's the masterpiece of England's greatest Neoclassical architect. Today, it's the center of the Anglican faith. Military buffs will find memorials to many great wars and their war heroes. Dome climbers will be rewarded with expansive views over London's skyline.

Orientation

Cost: £21, £19 online. Admission includes church entry, dome climb, crypt, tour, and audioguide. Free on Sun but officially open only to worshippers, and only part of the church.

Hours: Mon-Sat 8:30-16:30 (dome opens at 9:30), closed Sun except for worship. Sometimes closed for special events—check online. The church is also open Mon-Sat 16:15-18:00 for evening worship (which begins at 17:00). It's always free to enter the church to worship, but your visit is restricted to the back of the nave.

Information: +44 20 7246 8350, www.stpauls.co.uk.

Avoiding Lines: Purchasing tickets online in advance saves a little time (and a little money); otherwise the wait can be 15-45 minutes in summer and on weekends. To avoid crowds in general, arrive first thing in the morning.

Getting There: Located in The City; Tube: St. Paul's (other nearby Tube stops include Mansion House, Cannon Street, and Blackfriars). You can take handy buses #15 and #11 (see page 36). Careful: Don't head for tiny St. Paul's Church near Covent Garden; your destination is St. Paul's Cathedral, in The City.

Music and Church Services: Worship times are available on the church's website. Communion is generally Mon-Sat at 8:00 and 12:30. On Sunday, services are held at 8:00, 10:15 (Matins), 11:30 (sung Eucharist), 15:15 (evensong), and 18:00. The rest of the week, evensong is at 17:00 (Mon evensong is usually spoken, not sung). If you come 20 minutes early for evensong worship (under the dome), you may be able to grab a big wooden stall in the choir, next to the singers. On some Sundays, there's a free organ recital at 16:45.

Tours: There are 1.5-hour **guided tours** Mon-Sat at 10:00, 11:00, 13:00, and 14:00 (call to confirm or ask at church). Free 30-minute, volunteer-led **"highlights" tours** are offered throughout the day. The **audioguide** (included with admission) contains video clips that show the church in action.

🎧 Download my free St. Paul's Cathedral **audio tour.**

Climbing the Dome ("Galleries"): It's 528 steps to the top (and, if it's open, a "mere" 257 to the Whispering Gallery partway up). (While there's an elevator for people with disabilities, it does not go up into the dome's galleries—only down to the crypt.) Allow an hour to go up and down. The tower has three levels, called galleries. The climb gets steeper, narrower, and more claustrophobic as you go higher. It's a one-way system, so you can't come back down until you reach the next level.

Length of This Tour: Allow one hour, two if you climb the dome. If you're in a rush, skip the crypt and the dome.

Eating: Nearby Paternoster Square has several places to get a quick bite.

Nearby: A helpful TI is located across the street from the church, toward the river. Just behind the church, to the east, is the One New Change modern shopping mall topped by a terrace with great views of the church—not a bad substitute for the dome climb (free elevator to top floor). Millennium Bridge is a five-minute walk south, leading to the South Bank (Tate Modern and Shakespeare's Globe).

Starring: Sir Christopher Wren, his dome, and World War II.

The Tour Begins

Even now, as skyscrapers encroach, the 365-foot-high dome of St. Paul's rises majestically above the rooftops of the neighborhood.

The tall dome is set on classical columns, capped with a lantern, topped by a six-foot ball, and iced with a cross. As the first Anglican cathedral built in London after the Reformation, it is Baroque: St. Peter's in Rome filtered through clear-eyed English reason.

Viewing St. Paul's facade from in front of the church, you can see the story of Paul's conversion told in the stone pediment (triangular piece up top). A blinding flash of light leaves Saul sightless on the road to Damascus (see cityscape, lower left). When his sight is restored he becomes Paul, the Christian. This was the pivotal mo-

ment in the life of the man who established Christianity as a world religion through his travels, writing, and evangelizing.

While Paul stands on the top, Peter (with the annoying cock that crowed three times, symbolizing his betrayal of Jesus) is to the left, and James is on the right. The four evangelists at the towers' bases each carry the gospel they wrote. As Queen Anne was on the throne when the church was finished in 1710, the statue in front portrays her.

• *Enter, buy your ticket, and stand at the far back of the nave, behind the font.*

❶ Nave

Look down the nave through the choir stalls to the stained glass at the far end. This big church feels big. At 515 feet long and 250 feet wide, it's Europe's fourth largest, after those in Rome (St. Peter's), Sevilla, and Milan. The spaciousness is accentuated by the rela-

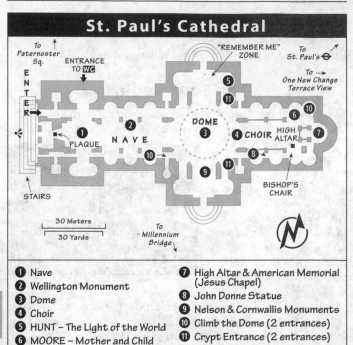

St. Paul's Cathedral

To Paternoster Sq.

ENTRANCE TO WC

ENTER

"REMEMBER ME" ZONE

To St. Paul's

To One New Change Terrace View

DOME ③

NAVE

① PLAQUE

② Wellington Monument

⑤

⑪

⑥ ⑩

④ CHOIR HIGH ALTAR ⑦

⑧

⑩

⑪

⑨

BISHOP'S CHAIR

STAIRS

30 Meters
30 Yards

To Millennium Bridge

① Nave
② Wellington Monument
③ Dome
④ Choir
⑤ HUNT – The Light of the World
⑥ MOORE – Mother and Child

⑦ High Altar & American Memorial (Jesus Chapel)
⑧ John Donne Statue
⑨ Nelson & Cornwallis Monuments
⑩ Climb the Dome (2 entrances)
⑪ Crypt Entrance (2 entrances)

ST. PAUL'S CATHEDRAL

tive lack of decoration. The simple, cream-colored ceiling and the clear glass in the windows light everything evenly. Wren wanted this: a simple, open church with nothing to hide. Unfortunately, only this entrance area keeps his original vision—the rest was en- crusted with 19th-century Vic- torian ornamentation.

Just inside the main door, a diamond-shaped **plaque** on the floor honors the guards ("Men and Women of St. Pauls Watch") who worked so valiantly from 1939 until 1945 to save the church from WWII destruction. On the wall immediately to the right of the door, a dirty panel of stone remains, reminding visitors how dark the entire church was before undergoing a huge cleaning in preparation for the 300th anniversary of the first service held here. Remarkably, this is the first great church completed in the lifetime of its architect (built 1675-1710).

• *Walk about 50 feet down the nave, then turn around and glance up. The organ trumpets seem to say, "Come to the evensong and hear us play."*

Ahead and on the left is the towering, black-and-white...

❷ Wellington Monument

It's so tall that even Wellington's horse has to duck to avoid bumping its head. Wren would have been appalled, but his church has become so central to England's soul that many national heroes are buried here (in the basement crypt). General Wellington, Napoleon's conqueror at Waterloo (1815) and the embodiment of British stiff-upper-lippedness, was honored here in a funeral packed with 13,000 fans. The church is littered with memorials. While all the monuments are upstairs, all the tombs are downstairs.

• *Stroll up the same nave Prince Charles and Lady Diana walked on their 1981 wedding day. Imagine how they felt making the hike to the altar with the world watching. Grab a chair underneath the impressive...*

❸ Dome

The dome you see from here, painted with scenes from the life of St. Paul, is only the innermost of three. From the painted interior

of the first dome, look up through the opening to see the light-filled lantern of the second dome. Finally, the whole thing is covered on the outside by the third and final dome, the shell of lead-covered wood that you see from the street. Wren's ingenious three-in-one design was psychological as well as functional—he wanted a low, shallow inner dome so worshippers wouldn't feel diminished.

Around the base of the dome, you'll see a circular walkway called the Whispering Gallery (which may be closed to visitors). The dome is constructed with such acoustic precision that secrets whispered from one side of it are heard on the opposite side, 170 feet away.

Christopher Wren (1632-1723) was the right man at the right time. Though the 31-year-old astronomy professor had never built a major building in his life when he got the commission for St. Paul's, his reputation for brilliance and his unique ability to work with others carried him through. The church has the clean lines and geometric simplicity of the age of Newton, when reason was holy and God set the planets spinning in perfect geometrical motion.

For more than 40 years, Wren worked on this site, overseeing every detail of St. Paul's and the 65,000-ton dome. It's estimated that the dome cost $850 million (in today's dollars). At age 75,

Wren got to look up and see his son place the cross on top of the dome, completing the masterpiece.

On the floor directly beneath the dome is a brass grate—part of a 19th-century attempt to heat the church. Encircling it is Christopher Wren's name and epitaph, written in Latin: *Lector, si monumentum requiris circumspice.* ("Reader, if you seek his monument, look around you.")

Now review the ceiling: Behind is Wren simplicity and ahead is Victorian ornateness.

• *The choir area blocks your way, but you can see the altar at the far end under a golden canopy.*

❹ Choir

English churches, unlike most in Europe, often have a central choir area (a.k.a. a "quire" or "chancel"), where church officials and the singers sit. (If you attend an evensong service, you can see St. Paul's well-known choir of 30 boys and 12 men in action, singing psalms.) St. Paul's—a cathedral since 604—is home to the local Anglican bishop. He presides in the chair at the far end, on the right, which may have a carved bishop's hat hanging overhead.

The ceiling above the choir is a riot of glass mosaics, representing God (above the altar) and his creation. The mosaics are very Victorian. In fact, Queen Victoria complained that the earlier ceiling was "dreary and undevotional." The Dean and chapter wisely took note and had it spiffed up with this brilliant mosaic work... textbook late Victorian. In separate spheres, eight "Angels of the Morning" hold up creatures of the earth, sea, and sky.

Beyond the choir, the high altar (the marble slab with crucifix and candlesticks—we'll go closer for a look later) sits under a huge canopy with corkscrew columns. The canopy looks ancient, but it dates from 1958, when it was rebuilt after being heavily damaged in October 1940 by the bombs of Hitler's Luftwaffe. For regular services, the priest stands beneath the dome on the low wooden platform.

• *In the north transept (to your left as you face the choir), find the big painting of Christ, in a golden wood altarpiece. Glare? Try walking side to side to find the best viewing angle.*

❺ *The Light of the World,* 1904

In the dark of night, Jesus—with a lantern, halo, jeweled cape, and crown of thorns—approaches an out-of-the-way home in the woods, knocks on the door, and listens for an invitation to come in. A Bible passage on the picture frame says: "Behold, I stand at the door and knock..." (Revelation 3:20).

In his early twenties, William Holman Hunt (1827-1910) was in the dark night of a spiritual crisis when he heard this verse

The Anglican Communion

St. Paul's Cathedral is the symbolic (but not official) nucleus of the earth's 70 million Anglicans. The Anglican Communion is a loose association of churches—including the Church of England and the Episcopal Church in the US—with common beliefs. The rallying point is *The Book of Common Prayer,* their handbook for worship services.

Forged in the fires of Europe's Reformation, Anglicans see themselves as a "middle way" between Catholics and Protestants. They retain much of the pomp and ceremony of traditional Catholic worship but with Protestant elements such as married priests (and, recently, female priests); attention to Scripture; and a less hierarchical, more consensus-oriented approach to decision making. Among Anglicans there are divisions, from Low Church congregations (more evangelical and "Protestant") to High Church (more traditional and "Catholic").

The Church of England, the largest single body, is still the official religion of the state, headed by the archbishop of Canterbury (who presides in Canterbury but lives in London). In 1982, Pope John Paul II and the then-archbishop of Canterbury met face-to-face. In 2010, Pope Benedict XVI visited London and joined the archbishop in prayer. Pope Francis has indicated that he wants to continue bridging the gap that has existed since the Reformation. These symbolic gestures signal a new ecumenical spirit.

knocking in his head. He opened his soul to Christ, his life changed forever, and he tried to capture the experience in paint. As one of the Pre-Raphaelites who adored medieval art (see page 362), he used symbolism, but only images the average Brit-on-the-street could understand. The door is the closed mind, the weeds the neglected soul, the darkness is malaise, while Christ carries the lantern of spiritual enlightenment.

In 1854, Hunt debuted *The Light of the World* (not this version, but a smaller one now at Oxford). The critics savaged it—"syrupy," "too Catholic," "simple"—but the masses lapped it up. It became the most famous painting in Victorian England—in fact, in the whole world. It was taken on tour through the vast British Empire, and was reproduced in countless engravings. It became a pop icon that inspired sermons, poems, hymns, and countless Christ-at-the-door paintings in churches and homes. Hunt's humble-hippie image of Christ was stamped forever on the minds of generations of schoolkids. It was so popular that late in life Hunt was asked to do this larger version specifically for St. Paul's. Nearly blind, he needed an assistant. (*The Guardian* newspaper once published a list of "Britain's Ten Worst Paintings." They honored *The Light of the World* as number seven, comparing it to a plastic crucifix.)

Near the painting, look for a new section called **"Remember Me,"** honoring the UK's Covid-19 victims, with a space designed for quiet contemplation of those who were lost.

• *Return to the area underneath the dome and walk along the left side of the choir, toward the altar. We're headed for a couple of sights that remember World War II, when London—and St. Paul's—were heavily bombed by the Germans. Londoners took refuge underground, in Tube stations called into use as ad-hoc bomb shelters. On the left at the far end of the aisle, pause at the modern statue—an egg-shaped mother cradling a blob-shaped baby.*

❻ *Mother and Child,* 1983

Britain's (and perhaps the world's?) greatest modern sculptor, Henry Moore, rendered a traditional subject in marble in an abstract, minimalist way. This Mary-and-Baby-Jesus was inspired by the sight of British moms nursing babies in WWII bomb shelters. Moore intended the viewer to touch and interact with the art. It's OK.

• *Continue up the four steps to the high altar at the far end of the church. Behind it is an area of special significance for visiting Americans.*

❼ High Altar and American Memorial Chapel (Jesus Chapel)

St. Paul's is a place of remembrance for many victims of Britain's wars. The church took on special significance in World War II.

The neighborhood around St. Paul's was largely destroyed during the Blitz and the Battle of Britain, but the church itself—thanks to good fortune and a heroic effort by Londoners—survived.

In 1940, however, one bomb did pierce the dome and obliterate the **high altar.** As you admire today's beautiful altar—the canopy with its corkscrew columns, the carved wood of the choir stalls, the mosaics overhead, the stained-glass windows—remember that this whole space had to be rebuilt.

There's no better place to appreciate the sacrifices of World War II than the area behind the main altar with three stained-glass windows, dubbed the **American Memorial Chapel**. This special spot in St. Paul's honors the Americans who sacrificed their lives to save Britain in World War II. An inscription on the floor reads: "To the American Dead of the Second World War, From the People of Britain."

Each of the three windows has a central core of religious scenes, but the brightly colored panes that arch around them have some unusual iconography: American. Spot the American eagle (center window, to the left of Christ), George Washington (right window, upper-right corner), and symbols of all 50 states (find your state seal). In the carved wood beneath the windows, you'll see birds and foliage native to the US. And at the very far right of the paneling, check out the tiny tree "trunk" (amid foliage, below the bird)—it's a US rocket ship circa 1958, shooting up to the stars.

Britain is very grateful to its WWII saviors, the Yanks, and remembers them religiously with the Roll of Honor (immediately behind the altar). This 500-page book under glass lists the names of 28,000 US servicemen and women based in Britain who gave their lives during the war.

• *Take a last look at the high altar and the view back to the entrance from here. Look up and enjoy the Victorian mosaic ceiling above the choir. Then continue around the altar and head back toward the entrance, using the other aisle. On the wall to your left, standing white in a black niche, is a statue of...*

❽ John Donne

John Donne (1573-1631), shown here wrapped in a burial shroud, was not only a great poet, but also a passionate preacher. He spent the last decade of his life working in old St. Paul's. Donne personally chose to be portrayed here in a shroud to capture the melancholy he felt after his wife's death. The statue is one of the few treasures to survive the Great Fire of 1666. You can still see the dark scorch marks on the urn beneath Donne's feet.

Imagine hearing Donne deliver a funeral sermon here, with the huge church bell tolling in the background: "No man is an island...Any man's

St. Paul's, the Blitz, and the Battle of Britain

Nazi planes mercilessly firebombed London in 1940. Even though The City around it burned to the ground, St. Paul's survived, giving hope to the citizens. The church took two direct hits, crum-

bling the altar and collapsing the north transept. On December 29, 1940, some 28 bombs fell on the church. The surrounding neighborhood was absolutely flattened, while the church rose above it, nearly intact. Some swear that many bombs bounced miraculously off Wren's dome, while others credit the heroic work of local firefighters. (There's a memorial chapel to the firefighters who kept watch over St. Paul's with hoses cocked.) Still, it's clear from the damage that St. Paul's was not fully Blitz-proof.

Often used synonymously, the Blitz and the Battle of Britain are actually two different phases of the Nazi air raids of 1940-1941. The Battle of Britain (June-Sept 1940) pitted Britain's Royal Air Force against German planes trying to soften up Britain for a land-and-sea invasion. The Blitz (Sept 1940-May 1941) was Hitler's punitive terror campaign against civilian London.

In the early days of World War II, the powerful, technologically superior Nazi army quickly overran Poland, Belgium, and France. The British army hightailed it out of France, crossing the English Channel from Dunkirk, and Britain hunkered down, waiting to be invaded. Hitler bombed R.A.F. airfields while his

death diminishes me, because I am involved in Mankind. Therefore, never wonder for whom the bell tolls—it tolls for thee."
• *And also for dozens of people who lie buried beneath your feet, in the crypt where you'll end your tour.*

But first, in the south transept, at the base of the pillar facing the altar, find the...

❾ Horatio Nelson Monument and Charles Cornwallis Monument

Admiral Horatio Nelson (1758-1805) leans on an anchor, his coat draped discreetly over the arm he lost in battle.

In October 1805, England trembled in fear as Napoleon—bent on world conquest—prepared to invade from across the Channel. Meanwhile, hundreds of miles away, off the coast of Spain, the daring Lord Nelson sailed the HMS *Victory* into battle against the

ground troops massed along the Channel. Britain was hopelessly outmatched, but Prime Minister Winston Churchill vowed, "We shall fight on the beaches...We shall fight in the fields and in the streets...We shall never surrender."

Britain fought back. Though greatly outgunned, they had a new and secret weapon—radar—that allowed them to get the jump on puzzled Nazi pilots. Speedy Spitfires flown by a new breed of young pilots shot down 1,700 German planes. By September 1940, the German land invasion was called off, Britain counterattacked with a daring raid on Berlin...and the Battle of Britain was won.

A frustrated Hitler retaliated with a series of punishing air raids on London itself, known as the Blitz. All through the fall, winter, and spring of 1940-1941, including 57 consecutive nights, Hermann Göring's Luftwaffe pummeled London, killing 20,000 and leveling half the city (mostly from St. Paul's eastward). Residents took refuge deep in the Tube stations. From his Whitehall bunker, Churchill made radio broadcasts exhorting his people to give their all, their "blood, toil, sweat, and tears."

Late in the war (1944-1945), Hitler ordered another round of terror-inducing attacks on London (sometimes called the "second Blitz") using car-sized V-1 and V-2 bombs, an early type of cruise missile. But Britain's resolve had returned, the United States had entered the fight, and the pendulum shifted. Churchill could say that even if the empire lasted a thousand years, Britons would look back and say, "This was their finest hour."

Churchill's state funeral was held in 1965 at St. Paul's in a bittersweet remembrance of Britain's victory.

French and Spanish navies. His motto: England expects that every man shall do his duty.

Nelson's fleet smashed the enemy at Trafalgar, and Napoleon's hopes for a naval invasion of Britain sank. Unfortunately, Nelson took a sniper's bullet in the spine and died. The lion at Nelson's feet groans sadly, and two little boys gaze up—one at Nelson, one at Wren's dome. You'll find Nelson's tomb directly beneath the dome, downstairs in the crypt.

Opposite Nelson is a monument to another military man, **Charles Cornwallis** (1738-1805), honored here for his service as governor general of Bengal (India). Yanks know him better as the general who lost the American Revolutionary War (or "American War," as it's known here) when George Washington—aided by French ships—forced his surrender at Yorktown in 1780.

• *There are several entrances to the dome and its galleries, but only one is open to the public at any given time—look for signboards or ask one of the church volunteers.*

❿ Climb the Dome

The 528-step climb is worthwhile, and each level (or gallery) offers something different.

Partway up, you may be able to walk around the **Whispering Gallery** (257 shallow steps, with views of the church interior)—

or it may be closed while they install safety measures. If you're able to access it, whisper sweet nothings into the wall, and your partner (and anyone else) standing far away can hear you. Exactly how it works is debated (some even question *if* it works). Most likely, the sound does not travel up and over the dome to the diametrically opposite side (as it would in a perfect sphere). Rather, it goes around the curved wall horizontally, so you don't have to stand in any particular spot. For the best effects, try whispering (not talking) with your mouth close to the wall, while your partner stands a few dozen yards away with an ear to the wall.

After another set of (steeper, narrower) stairs, you're at the **Stone Gallery,** with views of London. If you're exhausted, claustrophobic, or wary of heights, this middle level might be high enough. (The top level has very little standing room.)

Finally, a long, tight metal staircase takes you to the very top of the cupola, the **Golden Gallery.** (Just before the final dozen

stairs to the top, there's a tiny window at your feet that allows you to peek directly down—350 feet—to the church floor.) Once at the top, you emerge to stunning, unobstructed views of the city. Looking west, you'll see the London Eye, and you might be able to make out the towers of Westminster Abbey. To the

south, across the Thames, is the rectangular smokestack of the Tate Modern, with Shakespeare's Globe nestled nearby. To the east sprouts a glassy garden of skyscrapers, including the 600-foot-tall, black-topped Tower 42, the bullet-shaped 30 St. Mary Axe building (nicknamed "The Gherkin"), and two more buildings easily ID'd by their nicknames—"The Cheese Grater" and "The Walkie-Talkie." Farther in the distance, the cluster of skyscrapers marks Canary Wharf and the Docklands. Just north of that was the site of the 2012 Olympic Games, now a pleasant park. Demographers speculate that the rapidly growing East End and Docklands may eventually replace the West End and The City as the center of London. So as you look to the east, you're gazing into London's future.

• *Descend the dome to church level, then follow signs directing you downstairs to the...*

⓫ Crypt

Many famous people are buried here. Start by locating the central tomb of **Horatio Nelson,** who wore down Napoleon (follow signs to *Admiral Lord*
Nelson). It's a big coffin-on-a-pedestal in a round alcove at the center of the crypt, directly beneath the dome. Nearby (toward the altar) is the black granite tomb of the **Duke of Wellington** (who finished Napoleon off). The

flags near the tomb were carried at his funeral procession.

Continuing up the central axis of the crypt, you enter a chapel. At the chapel's altar, turn right to reach **Christopher Wren**'s tomb—a simple black slab elevated like a bench, with no statue. Just above it is a hunk of rough Portland stone quarried but unused by Wren while building St. Paul's; see his triangle brand on the left end. These few stones are not much of an honor for the man who built this great church. "If you seek his monument..." you'll be disappointed.

Use your visitor's map to find other **tombs and memorials:** of painters Turner and Reynolds (located near Wren); of Florence Nightingale (near Wellington); and a memorial to George Washington, who lies buried back in old Virginny.

Back near Nelson's tomb you'll find **temporary exhibits** (they change frequently) that chronicle important events in the church's long history, and models of previous churches that stood on this spot.

The crypt contains a fine gift shop and WCs. From the far end—beyond those services—you can exit directly outside, into the square behind St. Paul's. Walk straight ahead through the Temple Bar gate, into the modern space called Paternoster Square...and look back for one of the best views of Wren's great monument.

TOWER OF LONDON TOUR

This mighty tower and royal palace is soaked in history and blood. William I, still getting used to his new title of "Conqueror," built the stone White Tower (1077-1097) to keep defeated Londoners in line. The Tower also served as an effective lookout for detecting invaders coming up the Thames. William's successors enlarged the site to its present 18-acre size and added its defensive walls. Because of the security it provided, the Tower served over the centuries as a royal residence, the Royal Mint, the Royal Jewel House, and, most famously, as the prison and execution site of those who dared oppose the Crown.

The Tower's hard stone and glittering jewels represent the ultimate power of the monarch. So does the executioner's block. You'll find more bloody history per square inch in this original tower of power than anywhere else in Britain. Today, though its military purpose is history, it's still home to the Yeoman Warders, a.k.a. the "Beefeaters," who host three million visitors a year.

Your visit has four parts: the lively Beefeater tour (included in admission price, 1 hour), the White Tower (home of the royal armories, which are worth your time), the crown jewels (best in Europe, generally with a bit of a wait), and the grounds and walls (a simple and enjoyable stroll).

Orientation

Cost: £28.90, £1 more at "peak" times (Fri-Sun), family ticket available.

Hours: Tue-Sat 9:00-17:00, Sun-Mon from 10:00; Nov-Feb closes one hour earlier. Last entry 1.5 hours before closing.

Information: +44 333 206 000, www.hrp.org.uk.

Advance Tickets: To avoid long ticket-buying lines, buy tickets in advance for a specific day on the Tower website (you'll be emailed a PDF that you can print out or simply show on your mobile device).

Avoiding Crowds: It's most crowded in summer, on weekends (especially Sundays), and during school holidays. Any time of year, the line for the crown jewels can be just as long as the line for tickets. For fewer crowds, arrive before 10:00 and go straight for the jewels. Alternatively, arrive in the afternoon, tour the rest of the Tower first, and see the jewels an hour before closing time.

Getting There: The Tower is in East London (Tube: Tower Hill). For speed, take the Tube (about 10 minutes from central London); for romance, take the boat. Thames Clippers makes the trip between the Tower of London and Westminster Pier near Big Ben in 30-45 minutes; the boat continues to Greenwich from the Tower Pier. For details about these cruises, see page 45. Bus #15 makes the trip from Trafalgar Square (see map on page 36).

Visitor Information: Upon arrival, pick up the free map/guide and printed schedule of the day's events and demonstrations (such as knights in armor explaining medieval fighting techniques). Everything inside is well described—skip the audioguide and Tower guidebook.

Sunday Worship: On Sunday morning, visitors are welcome on the grounds for free to worship in the Chapel Royal of St. Peter ad Vincula. You can see only the chapel—no sightseeing (9:15 Communion or 11:00 service with fine choral music, meet at west gate 30 minutes early and tell the Beefeater you're there to worship, dress for church, may be closed for ceremonies—call ahead to phone number listed earlier).

Yeoman Warder (Beefeater) Tours: Free, worthwhile, one-hour Beefeater tours leave about twice hourly from just inside the entrance gate (last tour departs 1.5 hours before closing). The boisterous Beefeaters are great entertainers, whose historical talks include lots of bloody anecdotes and corny jokes. Check the clock inside the entrance gate. If you just miss the start of a tour, you can join it in progress (just catch up to the group a bit ahead).

Length of This Tour: Allow two hours (or three if you add a Beefeater tour). With less time, see the crown jewels, and try to squeeze in a Beefeater tour to get an overview. If time allows, also tour the White Tower Museum.

Eating: The **$$ New Armouries Café,** inside the Tower, is a big, efficient, inviting cafeteria. Outside the Tower, there's a row of chain eateries along the river and behind the Welcome Centre, and various takeout stands all around. Picnicking is allowed on Tower grounds but not inside the buildings.

Nearby: Adjacent to the Tower is **Tower Hill** (at the Tube stop of the same name), where kings of yore ordered high-profile public executions. In a small park there, you'll find a memorial to those put to death on this spot (including Sir Thomas More and Thomas Cromwell). Nearby are two more memorials (WWI and WWII) and part of the old **Roman Wall.**

Starring: The crown jewels, Beefeaters, William the Conqueror, and Henry VIII.

The Tour Begins

❶ Entrance Gate

Even an army the size of the security line couldn't storm this castle. After the drawbridge was pulled up and the iron portcul-

lis slammed down, you'd have to swim a 120-foot moat; cross an island prowled by wild animals; then toss a grappling hook onto a wall and climb up while the enemy poured boiling oil on you. If you made it this far, you'd only be halfway there. You'd still have to swim a second moat (now the grassy parade ground we see today), then, finally, scale a second, higher wall. In all, the central keep (tower) was surrounded by two concentric rings of complete defenses. Yes, it was difficult to get into the Tower (if you were a foreign enemy)...but it was almost as impossible to get out (if you were an enemy of the state).

The second moat was cleverly designed to naturally "flush" with the tidal movements of the Thames. For centuries, this natural system effectively removed much waste from around the fortress. But eventually the moat silted up, and some of the greenest (and best-fertilized) grass in London grew in.

• *Show your ticket, enter, consult the daily event schedule, and consider catching a one-hour Beefeater tour (departs just inside the first gateway). Continue through the inner gate, where a bookstore on the right hands out a free map.*

When you're all set, go 50 yards straight ahead to the...

❷ Traitors' Gate

This was the boat entrance to the Tower from the Thames. Princess Elizabeth, who was a prisoner here before she became Queen

Elizabeth I, was carried down the Thames and through this gate on a barge, thinking about her mom, Anne Boleyn, who had been decapitated inside just a few years earlier. Many English leaders who fell from grace entered through here—Elizabeth was one of the lucky few to walk out.

• *Continue straight and turn left to pass underneath the archway just before the cannons (opposite the exit), which leads into the inner courtyard. The big, white tower in the middle is the...*

❸ White Tower

This square, 90-foot-tall tower is the original structure that gave this castle complex its name. William the Conqueror built it more than 950 years ago to put 15 feet of stone between himself and those he conquered. Over the centuries, the other walls and towers were built around it.

The keep was a last line of defense. The original entry (on the south side) is above ground level so that its wooden approach could be removed, turning the tower into a safe refuge. Originally, there were even fewer windows—the lower windows were added during a Christopher Wren-ovation in 1660. In the 13th century, the tower was painted white (hence the name).

Standing high above the rest of old London, the White Tower provided a gleaming reminder of the monarchy's absolute power over its subjects. If you made the wrong move here, you could be feasting on roast boar in the Banqueting Hall one night and chained to the walls of the prison the next. Torture ranged from stretching on the rack to the full monty: hanging by the neck until nearly dead, then "drawing" (cut open to be gutted), and finally quartering, with your giblets displayed on the walls as a warning. (Guy Fawkes, who tried to blow up Parliament with 36 barrels of gunpowder, received this treatment here.) Any cries for help were muffled by the thick stone walls—15 feet at the base, a mere 11 feet at the top.

• *The White Tower's excellent museum is worth touring and described next. However, if you're here early in the day, to beat the crowds, skip the museum for now and head directly for the crown jewels, immediately*

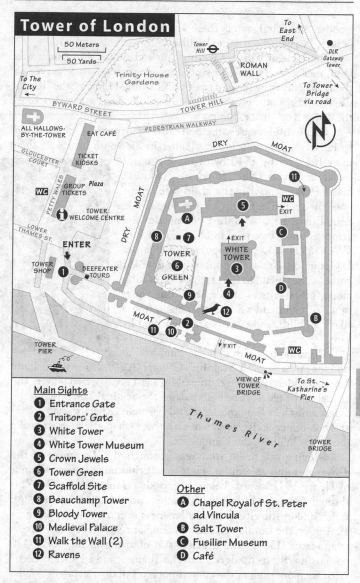

Tower of London

To East End

To The City

Trinity House Gardens

Tower Hill

ROMAN WALL

DLR Gateway Tower

To Tower Bridge via road

BYWARD STREET

TOWER HILL

PEDESTRIAN WALKWAY

ALL HALLOWS-BY-THE-TOWER

EAT CAFÉ

GLOUCESTER COURT

TICKET KIOSKS

DRY MOAT

DRY MOAT

WC

PETTY WALES

GROUP TICKETS

Plaza

TOWER WELCOME CENTRE

LOWER THAMES ST.

ENTER

TOWER SHOP

❶

BEEFEATER TOURS

❽

❼

Ⓐ

TOWER GREEN

❻

WHITE TOWER

❺

WC EXIT

Ⓒ

↑EXIT

❸

←EXIT

❹

❾

❷

❿ **❶**

MOAT

⓫

⓬

Ⓓ

Ⓑ

↓EXIT

WC

MOAT

TOWER PIER

VIEW OF TOWER BRIDGE

To St. Katharine's Pier

Thames River

TOWER BRIDGE

Main Sights
❶ Entrance Gate
❷ Traitors' Gate
❸ White Tower
❹ White Tower Museum
❺ Crown Jewels
❻ Tower Green
❼ Scaffold Site
❽ Beauchamp Tower
❾ Bloody Tower
❿ Medieval Palace
⓫ Walk the Wall (2)
⓬ Ravens

Other
Ⓐ Chapel Royal of St. Peter ad Vincula
Ⓑ Salt Tower
Ⓒ Fusilier Museum
Ⓓ Café

TOWER OF LONDON

behind the White Tower (circle around its right side—see map). Return to visit the museum, which is less crowded, after the Crown Jewels.

❹ White Tower Museum

Inside the White Tower, a one-way route winds through exhibits re-creating medieval life and the Tower's bloody history of torture and executions. You'll climb up, up, up, then back down again on wooden and spiral stairs. There are plenty of engaging exhibits to peruse; I've called out some highlights.

The **Line of Kings,** greeting you and spread throughout this level, includes an array of painted wooden horses, some carved in the 17th century by revered sculptor Grinling Gibbons, the "King's Carver." For centuries, these horses held the royal suits of armor in the Tower's original exhibits.

In the display cases, the first **suits of armor** you see belonged to Henry VIII—on a horse, slender in his youth (c. 1515), then more heavyset by 1540 (with his bigger-is-better codpiece). Next to Henry (and labeled *Prince Henry*) is the child-size armor once thought to be for his long-awaited male heir, Edward VI, who died young. But the armor actually belonged to Henry, Prince of Wales (1594-1612), the popular son of James I. Get up close to see the incredibly detailed battle scenes inlaid in the armor. Continuing along, other suits of armor, including those of a 6'8" giant and a 3'1" little person (more likely a child), and swords are identified by king.

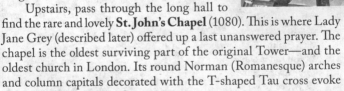

Upstairs, pass through the long hall to find the rare and lovely **St. John's Chapel** (1080). This is where Lady Jane Grey (described later) offered up a last unanswered prayer. The chapel is the oldest surviving part of the original Tower—and the oldest church in London. Its round Norman (Romanesque) arches and column capitals decorated with the T-shaped Tau cross evoke the age of William the Conqueror.

Moving on, make your way through the **Treasures of the Tower Armouries** exhibit. Here you'll find more personal armor of Henry VIII; swords belonging to kings, from George I (1714) through George VI (the Queen's father, who became king in 1936); lavish diplomatic gifts such as a Japanese samurai suit and an Indian dagger; the Lumley Horseman, England's oldest known equestrian statue (1580s); the heaviest suit of armor in the world (130 pounds!); artifacts dredged from the Thames; and artistically decorated weapons such as the contemporary Tiffany Revolver (1989).

Head to the next floor. Note, on your way up, that in the Tower's many tight **spiral staircases,** the central pillar is on your right. This was so attackers entering the tower couldn't freely swing their swords with their right arms—while defenders inside the tower could raise their swords easily.

On the top floor, ogle the giant dragon made from old weapons. In the case at the end of this hall, see the Tower's actual **execution ax** and chopping block. In 1747, this seven-pound ax sliced through the neck of Lord Lovat, a Scottish supporter of Bonnie Prince Charlie's claim to the throne. With his death, the ax was retired.

In the next room, kid-oriented, hands-on exhibits bring the history engagingly to life. I learned how hard it is to "nock" (pull back) an arrow.

On your way back down and out of the White Tower Museum, you'll be routed through the gift shop. It's easy to miss that the shop fills the **cellar**—the site of the notorious prison where many illustrious historical figures were held (and tortured).

• *Exiting the White Tower, straight ahead is the looooong line leading to the crown jewels. Get in line and pass the time reading ahead—inside, it will be too dark and crowded.*

❺ Crown Jewels

When you finally enter the building, you may be directed through a series of rooms with instructive warm-up videos. Any exhibits in here are designed to entertain the long line and play up the impressive list of kings and queens who have worn the crown jewels—from William I the Conqueror, to Henry VIII, to his daughter Elizabeth I, to Queen Elizabeth II (whose coronation took place in June 1953, though she had acceded to the throne the previous year—hence 2022's Platinum Jubilee). You may also see some of the ceremonial maces, swords, and trumpets that lead the actual coronation procession into Westminster Abbey.

The real exhibit begins in a room with the **royal regalia.** The monarch-to-be is anointed with holy oil poured from the eagle-beak flask (first case); handed the jeweled Sword of Offering (second case); and dressed in the 20-pound gold robe and other gear (third case). The 12th-century coronation spoon, last used in 1953 to anoint the head of Queen Elizabeth, is the most ancient object here (first case). Most of the medieval-era crown jewels were lost during Cromwell's 1648 revolution.

After being dressed and anointed, the new monarch prepares for the "crowning" moment.

• *Five glass cases display the various crowns, orbs, and scepters used in royal ceremonies. Ride the moving sidewalk that takes you past them. You're welcome to circle back and glide by again (I did, several times). Or, to get away from the crowds, hang out on the elevated viewing area with the guard. Chat with the guards—they're here to provide information (and to keep you from taking photos, which aren't allowed). The collection rotates, so as you glide by on the walkway, you may not see every crown described here.*

Scepter and Orb: After being crowned, the new monarch is handed these items. The **Sovereign's Scepter** is encrusted with the world's largest cut diamond—the 530-carat Star of Africa, beefy as a quarter-pounder. This was one of nine stones cut from the original 3,106-carat (1.37-pound) Cullinan diamond. The **orb** symbolizes how Christianity rules over the earth, a reminder that even a "divine monarch" is not above God's law. The coronation is a kind of marriage between the church and the state in Britain, since the king or queen is head of both, and the ceremony celebrates the monarch's power to do good for the whole of the nation.

St. Edward's Crown: On coronation day in Westminster Abbey, the archbishop places this crown upon the head of the new monarch. It's worn for 20 minutes, then locked away until the next coronation. The original crown, destroyed by Cromwell, was older than the Tower itself and dated back to 1061, the time of King Edward the Confessor, "the last English king" before William the Conqueror invaded from France (1066). This 1661 remake is said to contain some of the original's gold amid its 443 precious and semiprecious stones. Because the crown weighs nearly five pounds, weak or frail monarchs have opted not to wear it.

Other Crowns: Various other crowns illustrate a bit of regalia symbolism. The second case contains three Prince of Wales crowns (including the one belonging to Charles—the unusual one, in the middle). Notice these have only two arches, so they're technically "coronets." Kings and queens get four arches on their crowns, while emperors get eight arches (e.g., the Imperial Crown of India in the next case).

Crown of the Queen Mother: The final crown in this section, last worn by Elizabeth II's famous mum (who died in 2002), has the 106-carat Koh-I-Noor diamond glittering on the front (visible only from the right walkway). Because the Koh-I-Noor diamond is considered unlucky for male rulers, it adorns the crown of the king's wife. That means that, in the coming years (or decades), we'll likely see it on the head of Camilla, then Kate. This crown was remade in 1937 and given an innovative platinum frame.

• *Continuing on from the moving walkway, you'll pass cases of gilded platters and bowls used in the post-coronation banquet. Then bear left down the hall, where, in the first case on the left, you'll find...*

Queen Victoria Small Diamond Crown: It's tiny. Victoria had a normal-sized head, but this was designed to sit atop the wid-

The Beefeaters

The original duty of the Yeoman Warders (called "Beefeaters") was to guard the Tower, its prisoners, and the jewels. Their nickname may come from an original perk of the job—large rations of the king's beef. The Beefeaters dress in dark-blue knee-length coats with red trim and a top hat. The "ER" on the chest stands for the monarch they serve— Queen Elizabeth II (Elisabetha Regina in Latin). On special occasions, they wear red. All are retired noncommissioned officers from the armed forces with distinguished service records (and all were men until 2007).

These days, the 38 Yeoman Warders are no longer expected to protect the Tower. Instead, they've evolved into great entertainers, leading groups of tourists through the Tower. At night, they ritually lock up the Tower in the Ceremony of the Keys (possible to watch if you book upwards of four months in advance). They and their families make up the Beefeating community that live inside the Tower.

ow's veil she insisted on wearing for decades after the death of her husband, Prince Albert. This four-ounce job was made in 1870 for £50,000—personally paid for by the queen.

• *Moving on, you'll see more royal plates and bowls before you reach one final room, with one last crown.*

Imperial State Crown: This is what the Queen wears for official functions such as the State Opening of Parliament. When Victoria was queen, she insisted on wearing her small crown, but by law, this State Crown had to be carried next to her on a pillow, as it represents the sovereign. Among its 3,733 jewels are Queen Elizabeth I's former earrings (the hanging pearls, top center), a stunning 13th-century ruby look-alike in the center, and Edward the Confessor's ring (the blue sapphire on top, in the center of the Maltese cross of diamonds). When Edward's tomb was exhumed— a hundred years after he was buried—his body was "incorrupted." The ring on his saintly finger featured this sapphire and ended up on the crown of all future monarchs. This is the stylized crown you see representing the royalty on Britain's coins and stamps. It's depicted on the Beefeater uniforms and on the pavement at the end of the sliding walk.

• *The final room is the epilogue of the jewels collection, with videos show-*

ing attendants putting these precious items back into their cases after the last coronation—emphasizing that these are a vital part of an ongoing tradition.

Leave the jewels by exiting through the thick vault doors. You'll turn right and walk past the White Tower, proceeding straight ahead to the grassy field surrounded by buildings. This is…

❻ Tower Green

In medieval times, this spacious courtyard within the walls was the "town square" for those who lived in the castle. Knights exercised and jousted here, and it was the last place of refuge in troubled times. The Tower is still officially a royal residence, and the Queen's lodgings are on the south side of the green, in the white half-timbered buildings where a bearskin-hatted soldier stands guard.

The north side of the Green is bordered by the stone **Chapel Royal of St. Peter ad Vincula** ("in Chains"). Henry VIII built the current structure, and his most famous victims are buried here (among them his wives Anne Boleyn and Catherine Howard). The chapel's interior is open only on the Beefeater tour, except during the last hour of the day, when anyone can go inside. If you aren't on a tour, wait for one to come around, discreetly squeeze into the group while the Beefeater is talking outside the chapel, and go in with the group.

• Near the middle of Tower Green is a granite-paved square marked Site of Scaffold.

❼ Scaffold Site

The Tower's execution site looks pleasant enough today; the actual chopping block has been moved inside the White Tower, and a modern sculpture encourages visitors to ponder those who died.

It was here that enemies of the Crown would kneel before the king for the final time. With their hands tied behind their backs, they would say a final prayer, then lay their heads on a block, and—slit—the blade would slice through their necks, their heads tumbling to the ground. The headless corpses were buried in unmarked graves in Tower Green (to avoid becoming a shrine for their supporters) or

under the floor of the Chapel Royal of St. Peter ad Vincula. The heads were stuck on a stick and displayed at London Bridge. Passersby did not really see the heads—they saw grotesque spheres of insects and parasites.

Tower Green was the most prestigious execution site at the Tower. Common criminals were hanged outside the Tower. More prominent evil-doers were decapitated before jeering crowds atop Tower Hill (near today's Tube station). Execution inside the Tower walls was reserved for the most heinous traitors.

Henry VIII axed a couple of his ex-wives here (divorced readers can insert their own cynical joke). Anne Boleyn was the appealing young woman Henry had fallen so hard for that he broke with the Catholic Church in order to divorce his first wife and marry her. But when Anne failed to produce a male heir, the court turned against her. She was locked up in the Tower, tried in a kangaroo court, branded an adulteress and traitor, and decapitated.

Henry's fifth wife, teenage Catherine Howard, was beheaded and her body laid near Anne's in the church. Jane Boleyn (Anne's sister-in-law) was also executed here for arranging Catherine's adulterous affair behind Henry's back. Next.

Henry even beheaded his friend Thomas More (a Catholic) because he refused to recognize (Protestant) Henry as head of the Church of England. (Thomas died at the less-prestigious Tower Hill site near the Tube stop.)

The most tragic victim was 17-year-old Lady Jane Grey, who was manipulated into claiming the Crown for nine days during the scramble for power after Henry's death and the six-year reign and death of his sickly young son, Edward VI. When Bloody Mary (Mary I, Henry's daughter) took control, she forced her Protestant cousin Jane to kneel before the executioner. Young Jane bravely blindfolded herself, but then couldn't find the block. She crawled around the scaffolding pleading, "Where is it?!"

Years ago, a Beefeater, tired of what he called "Hollywood coverage" of the Tower, grabbed my manuscript, read it, and told me that in more than 900 years as a fortress, palace, and prison, the place held 8,500 prisoners. But only 120 were executed, and, of those, only 6 were executed inside it. Stressing the hospitality of the Tower, he added, "Torture was actually quite rare here."

• *Overlooking the scaffold site, on the left as you face the chapel, is the...*

❽ Beauchamp Tower

The Beauchamp Tower (pronounced "BEECH-um") was one of several places in the complex that housed Very Important Prisoners. If the humdrum ground-floor exhibit is crowded, skip it and climb upstairs to the building's highlight: an evocative room with walls covered in final messages—graffiti carved into the stone by bored and despondent inmates.

Picture Philip Howard, the Earl of Arundel (c. 1555-1595), warming himself by this fireplace and glancing out at the execution site during his 10-year incarcer-  ation. Having lived a devil-may-care life of pleasure in the court of Queen Elizabeth, the pro-Catholic Arundel was charged with treason by the Protestant government. He pleaded with the queen—his former friend— to at least let him see his wife and young children. She refused, unless he would renounce his faith. On June 22, 1587, he carved his family name "Arundell" into the chimney (graffiti #13) and wrote in Latin: *"Quanto plus afflictionis..."* ("The more we suffer for Christ in this world, the more glory with Christ in the next.") Arundel suffered faithfully another eight years here before he wasted away and died at age 40.

Graffiti #85 (knee level, near the window facing Tower Green) belongs to Lady Jane Grey's young husband, Lord Guilford Dudley. Locked in the Beauchamp Tower and executed the same day as his wife, Dudley vented his despair by scratching "IANE" into the stone. Cynics claim he was actually whining for his mommy, who was also named Jane.

Read other pitiful graffiti, like the musings of James Typping (#18). Imprisoned for three years "in great disgrace," he wonders what will happen to him: "I cannot tell but be death." Consider the stoic cry of Thomas Miagh (#29), an Irish rebel, who writes: "By torture straynge my truth was tried," having suffered some form of the rack. Thomas Clarke (#28), a Catholic priest who later converted to Protestantism, wrote pathetic poetry: "Unhappy is that man whose acts doth procure / the misery of this house in prison to endure." Many held on to their sense of identity by carving their family's coats of arms.

The last enemy of the state imprisoned in the Tower complex was one of its most infamous: the renegade Nazi Rudolf Hess. In 1941, Hitler's henchman secretly flew to Britain with a peace proposal (Hitler denied any such plan). He parachuted into a field, was arrested and held for four days in the Tower, and was later given a life sentence.

• *Back out on Tower Green, head down toward the river. At the bottom corner of the green is...*

❾ Bloody Tower

Climb the stairs to see the top of the spiky portcullis gate and its pulley mechanism. The adjacent room features a mellow presentation on Sir Walter Raleigh—poet, explorer, and political radical—who was imprisoned here for 13 years. In 1603, the English writer and adventurer was accused of plotting against King James and sentenced to death. The king commuted the sentence to life imprisonment in the Bloody Tower. While in prison, Raleigh wrote the first volume of his *History of the World*. Check out his rather cushy bedroom, study, and walkway (courtesy of the powerful tobacco lobby?). Raleigh promised the king a wealth of gold if he would release him to search for El Dorado. The expedition was a failure. Upon Raleigh's return, the displeased king had him beheaded in 1618.

Now head up the tight staircase for another sobering presentation about two of the Tower's most tragic victims. The 13-year-old King Edward V and his kid brother were kidnapped in 1483 during the Wars of the Roses by their uncle Richard III ("Now is the winter of our discontent...") and locked in the Bloody Tower, never to be seen again. End of story? Two centuries later, the skeletons of two unidentified children were found here. The 2013 discovery of the remains of Richard III (in Leicester, in central England) may allow modern DNA testing to solve this centuries-old mystery.

• *Follow the one-way route back down into Tower Green. Take the staircase on the right down to the main entrance ramp (back toward the river). Before passing under the Bloody Tower, notice the* **Torture in the Tower** *exhibit—a cellar filled with replica torture equipment.*

Walk under the Bloody Tower, cross the cobbled road, and bear right a few steps to find the stairs up onto the wall.

❿ Medieval Palace

The Tower was a royal residence as well as a fortress. These rooms were built around 1240 by Henry III, the king most responsible for the expansive Tower of London complex we see today. The well-described rooms are furnished as they might have been during the reign of his son, Edward I ("Longshanks"). You'll see his re-created bedroom, then—up a flight of stairs—his throne room, both with massive fireplaces to keep this cold stone palace cozy. After Cromwell temporarily deposed the monarchy (in the 17th century), the Tower ceased to be a royal residence except in name.

• *From the throne room, continue up the stairs to...*

⓫ Walk the Wall

The Tower was defended by state-of-the-art walls and fortifications in the 13th century. This walk offers a good look. From the walls, you also get a fine view of the famous bridge straddling the

Thames, with the twin towers and blue spans. It's not London Bridge (which is the nondescript bridge just upstream), but **Tower Bridge.** Although it looks somewhat medieval, this drawbridge was built in 1894, of steel and concrete. Sophisticated steam engines raise and lower the bridge, allowing tall-masted ships to squeeze through.

Gaze out at the bridge, the river, City Hall (the egg-shaped glass building across the river), the Shard (London's bold exclamation point), and life-filled London.

• *Before departing, let's say hello to the Tower's resident mascots. Find your way to the exit (toward the Thames), but before crossing that drawbridge, do an about-face and go back through the gate where you got your first glimpse of the White Tower. Immediately to your left, look for cages housing the...*

⑫ Ravens

According to goofy tradition, the Tower and the British throne are only safe as long as ravens are present here. These eight impressive birds—the traditionally required six, plus two spares—have clipped wings to keep them close. World War II bombing raids reduced the population to one. Some years ago, with their clipped wings, the birds had trouble mating, so a slide was built to help them get a bit of lift to facilitate the

process. Happily, that worked, and a baby raven was born. A children's TV show sponsored a nationwide contest to come up with a name. The winner: "Ronald Raven." Today, they mimic and answer tourists, and are as much a part of the Tower as the jewels.

Other Sights

Get out your Tower-issued map to check out other areas you can visit. The **Salt Tower** has graffiti scratched into its walls by prisoners, including by Henry Walpole, a staunch Catholic who was imprisoned here by Queen Elizabeth I, tortured on the rack, and had a finger torn off. At the **Fusilier Museum** you can see the uniforms, swords, and fusils (flintlock rifles) of the army of Redcoats who fought Napoleon, the American War of Independence, two World Wars ("Monty"—Field Marshal Bernard Montgomery of D-Day fame—was a Fusilier), and wars in the Persian Gulf.

Take one final look at the stern stone walls of the Tower. Be glad you can leave.

BANKSIDE WALK

Along the South Bank of the Thames

Bankside—the neighborhood between London Bridge and Black-friars Bridge—is the historic heart of the revitalized southern bank of the Thames. In ancient times "greater London" consisted of two Roman settlements straddling the easiest place to ford the river: One settlement was here, and the other was across the river—in the financial district known today as "The City."

From the Roman era until recently, the south side of the river was the "wrong side of the tracks." For centuries, it was London's red light district. In the 20th century, it became an industrial wasteland of empty warehouses and street crime. But today, the prostitutes and pickpockets are gone, replaced by a riverside promenade dotted with trendy pubs, cutesy shops, and historic tourist sights.

This half-mile Bankside Walk gives you plenty of history and sights to choose from—you can see it all, design your own plan, or just enjoy the view of London's skyline across the river.

Orientation

Length of This Walk: One hour (or up to a half-day if you tour Shakespeare's Globe and the Tate Modern).

Getting There: Take the Tube to the London Bridge stop. (The Monument stop, on the Circle Line, is also nearby.)

Old Operating Theatre Museum and Herb Garret: £7.50, Thu-Sun 10:30-17:00, closed Mon-Wed.

Southwark Cathedral: Free, £2 map serves as photo permit, daily 8:00-18:00 (but partially closed during frequent services—schedule posted out front).

Borough Market: Mon-Fri 10:00-17:00, Sat 8:00-17:00, Sun 10:00-15:00 and generally quieter.

Golden Hinde **Replica:** £5, daily 10:00-18:00, off-season until 17:00; fun to see from the outside but not worth entering.

The Clink Prison Museum: Overpriced at £8; Mon-Fri 10:00-18:00, Sat-Sun until 19:30, open later in summer.

Shakespeare's Globe: £17 for 50-minute guided tour; tours run every 30 minutes (see page 96 for info on tours or page 476 for tips on buying tickets to a performance).

Tate Modern: Free, £5 suggested donation, fee for special exhibits, daily 10:00-18:00, may stay open later Fri-Sat, last entry 45 minutes before closing, view restaurant.

Starring: Shakespeare's world, London Bridge, historic pubs, and views of the London skyline.

The Walk Begins

• *Start at the south end of London Bridge (across from where my Historic London: The City Walk ends). If arriving at the London Bridge Tube stop, take the "Borough High Street east" exit and turn right (north), pass the One London Bridge complex, and walk out on the bridge about 100 yards.*

❶ London Bridge

From here, you get an exhilarating overview of this sprawling home to more than 10 million souls. Most of this walk focuses on the London of Shakespeare's time, but the modern metropolis is something to behold, too. The City (across the river) is to the north, Tower Bridge is east, and the Thames flows from west to east (left to right). Looking to the east (downstream), you'll see the following:

Downstream

• Tower Bridge, the Neo-Gothic towered drawbridge that many Americans mistakenly call London Bridge.

• The HMS *Belfast* (in the foreground, docked on the southern bank), a WWII Royal Navy cruiser that's open to tourists.

• Canary Wharf Tower (the distant 800-foot skyscraper with pyramid top and blinking light), built in 1990 on the Isle of Dogs. In 2012 it lost its standing as the UK's tallest building to The Shard. This marks the Docklands, London's "new Manhattan" and a thriving business district. This was once the biggest

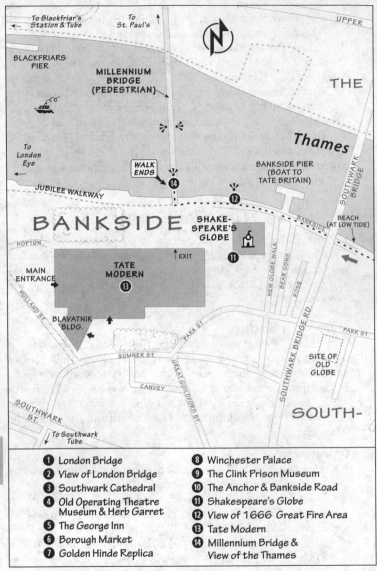

BANKSIDE

1 London Bridge
2 View of London Bridge
3 Southwark Cathedral
4 Old Operating Theatre Museum & Herb Garret
5 The George Inn
6 Borough Market
7 Golden Hinde Replica
8 Winchester Palace
9 The Clink Prison Museum
10 The Anchor & Bankside Road
11 Shakespeare's Globe
12 View of 1666 Great Fire Area
13 Tate Modern
14 Millennium Bridge & View of the Thames

port in the world, serving the empire upon which "the sun never set," but today the wharves have moved farther out to accommodate bigger ships.

- The "Pool of London." This is the stretch of river between Tower Bridge (a drawbridge) and London Bridge, which marks the farthest point seagoing vessels can sail inland. In the 18th century, this was the busiest port in the world.

• *Now spin left to continue our counterclockwise tour.*

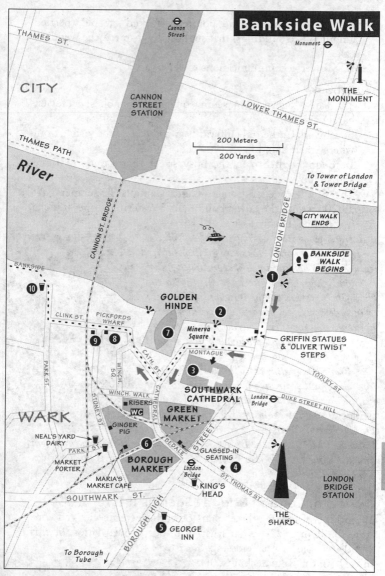

North Bank

- The Tower of London (four domed spires and a flag rising above the trees).
- The "Square Mile" of brand-new skyscrapers, including 20 Fenchurch Street (a.k.a. "The Walkie-Talkie") and, behind it, the Leadenhall Building (a.k.a. "The Cheese Grater").
- St. Paul's Cathedral (to the northwest, with a dome like a state capitol and twin spires).

- St. Bride's Church, the pointed, stacked steeple (nestled among office buildings) that supposedly inspired the wedding cake.
- BT Tower, a communications tower.

South Bank
- The Tate Modern art museum (square brick smokestack tower, barely visible).
- Southwark Cathedral (100 yards away, may not be visible from where you're standing).
- Borough High Street, the busy street that London Bridge spills onto.
- The Shard, one of London's most famous skyscrapers. At 1,020 feet, it's the tallest building in Western Europe. It looks unfinished, but that's art.

• *Retrace your steps to the south end of the bridge. Watch for one of the small **griffin statues** (winged lions holding shields) at the south end of London Bridge, which guard the entrance to The City. They marked the jurisdiction of The City to include both sides of the all-important river. For centuries, they said, "Neener neener" to late-night partiers who got locked out of town when the gates shut tight at curfew.*

From the griffin, cross the busy street and find the small staircase next to the southwest griffin, by the building marked Two London Bridge. *These stairs will impress fans of Charles Dickens'* Oliver Twist—*they're the setting of the infamous "Meeting on the Bridge." At the bottom of the stairs, turn right and walk one long block to where Minerva Square opens up. Here you can head to the river for a...*

❷ View of London Bridge (Such as It Is)

The bridge of today—three spans of boring, traffic-clogged concrete, built in 1972—is (at least) the fourth incarnation of this 2,000-year-old river crossing.
In AD 50, the Romans built the first wooden footbridge to Londinium (rebuilt many times), which was pulled down by boatmen in 1014 to retake London from Danish invaders. (They celebrated with a song passed down to us as "London Bridge is falling down, my fair lady.")

The most famous version—crossed by everyone from Richard the Lionheart, to Henry VIII, to Shakespeare, to Newton, to Darwin—was built around 1200 and stood for more than six centuries, the only crossing point into this major city. Built of stone on many thick pilings, stacked with houses and shops that arched over the roadway and bulged out over the river, with its own chapel and a fortified gate at each end, it was a neighborhood unto itself (pop. 300). Picture Mel Gibson's head boiled in tar and stuck on a spike along the bridge (like the Scots rebel William Wallace in 1305, depicted in *Braveheart*), and you'll capture the local color of that time.

In 1823, the famous bridge was replaced with a more modern (but less impressive) brick one. In 1967, that brick bridge was sold to an American, dismantled, shipped to Arizona, and reassembled (all 10,000 bricks) in Lake Havasu City. (Humor today's Brits, who'd like to believe the Yank thought he was buying Tower Bridge.) It was only then that today's bridge was built.

• *Turn your back to the Thames and face the cathedral. The main entrance is most likely straight ahead, through the courtyard (or you may be directed to circle around to the right side of the church).*

❸ Southwark Cathedral

This neighborhood parish church is where Shakespeare prayed while his brother Edmund rang the bells. The Southwark (SUTH-uck) church dates back to 1207, though the site has had a church for at least a thousand years, and inhabitants for 2,000. The church is simply filled with history. (And it also has a handy, free WC.)

Visiting the Church: Step inside and stand at the back of the nave. Consider the £2 information-packed flier, which also gives you permission to take photos.

❹ **View down the Nave:** Clean and sparse, with warm golden stone, the church is a symbol of the urban renewal of the whole Bankside/Southwark area. Its WWII damage has been repaired, with replacement windows of unstained glass on the right side. The nave bends slightly to the left (the chandelier, ceiling arches, and altar don't line up until you take two baby steps left) as a medieval tribute to Christ's bent body on the cross.

• *From here, we'll do a counterclockwise loop around the church. To start, head up the right aisle, pausing just before the transept.*

❺ **Shakespeare Monument:** William reclines in front of a backdrop of the 16th-century Bankside skyline (view looking

BANKSIDE

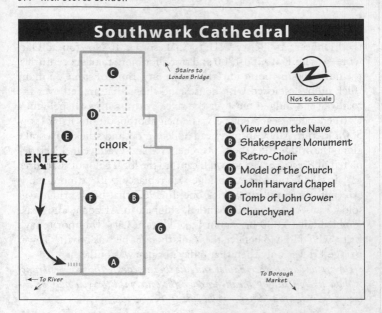

Southwark Cathedral

Stairs to London Bridge

Not to Scale

CHOIR

ENTER

Ⓐ View down the Nave
Ⓑ Shakespeare Monument
Ⓒ Retro-Choir
Ⓓ Model of the Church
Ⓔ John Harvard Chapel
Ⓕ Tomb of John Gower
Ⓖ Churchyard

← To River

To Borough Market

BANKSIDE

north). Find (left to right) the original Globe Theatre, Winchester Palace, Southwark Cathedral, and the old London Bridge with its arched gate—complete with heads on pikes. Shakespeare seems to be dreaming about the many characters of his plays, depicted in the stained-glass window above (see Hamlet addressing a skull, right window). To the right is a plaque to the

American actor Sam Wanamaker, who spearheaded the building of a replica of Shakespeare's Globe Theatre (explained later in this chapter). Shakespeare's brother Edmund is buried in the church, possibly under a marked slab on the floor of the choir area, near the very center of the church. (The Bard lies buried in his hometown of Stratford-upon-Avon.)

• *Continue along the right aisle straight through the transept, all the way up to the area behind the main altar.*

Ⓒ **Retro-Choir:** The 800-year-old crisscross arches and stone tracery in the windows are some of the oldest parts of this historic church. Located in the heart of the industrial district, the church was heavily bombed during World War II and then rebuilt.

• *Now loop back toward the entrance, along the opposite aisle. Partway up, next to a gate leading into the altar/choir area, look for a...*

Ⓓ **Model of the Church:** This model (marked *Church and*

Priory of St. Mary Overy) shows both the church and old Winchester Palace complex—a sprawling waterfront estate that housed bishops from the 12th through 17th centuries. Across the river from The City, the bishops essentially ran their own little city-state from this cathedral and palace complex. Remember this model: We'll see the very scant ruins of the Winchester Palace farther along on this walk.

• *Step into the choir area for a peek at the altar, the impressive carved-stone screen behind it (from 1520), and the carved wooden seats of the choir. Then continue up the aisle toward the entrance. Just before the transept, on the right, is the entrance to...*

❺ John Harvard Chapel: The Southwark-born son of an inn-keeper (see the record of baptism at the bottom of the window) inherited money from the sale of The Queen's Head tavern, got married, and sailed to Boston (1637), where he soon died. The money and his 400-book library funded the start of Harvard University.

• *Just beyond the transept, on the right, watch for the colorful...*

❻ Tomb of John Gower: The poet and friend of Chaucer (c. 1400) rests his head on his three books, one written in Middle English, one in French, and one in Latin—the three languages from which modern English soon emerged.

• *Across from where you came in, notice a door that leads out into the...*

❼ Churchyard: This space, tranquil aside from the occasional passing train, feels like a respite from the congested city. Enjoy the statue of Shakespeare composing his works under a cherry tree, take a deep breath, then head back through the church to continue our walk.

• *From here, this walk is a pick-and-choose collection of sights. Face the cathedral, with the Thames at your back. If you'd like to visit the* **Old Operating Theatre Museum** *and* **The George Inn,** *turn left, retrace your steps up the "Oliver Twist" stairs, and turn right along busy Borough High Street (use the map to locate these sights). To head straight to* **Borough Market,** *simply curl around the right side of the cathedral, skip ahead to #6 on this walk, and you'll be in the market action.*

❹ Old Operating Theatre Museum and Herb Garret

Back when the common cold was treated with a refreshing blood-letting, the Old Operating Theatre—a surgical operating room from the 1800s—was a shining example of "modern" medicine. Today a museum, this is a quirky, sometimes gross look at that painful transition from folk remedy to clinical health care. Originally part of a larger hospital complex, the Old Operating Theatre was boarded up when the hospital relocated, lying untouched for 100 years until its chance discovery in 1956. The location alone—in a long-forgotten attic above a church, reached by a steep spiral staircase—makes this odd place worth a visit.

Visiting the Museum: After buying your ticket, enter a big room under heavy timbers—the **Herb Garret,** which was used to dry herbs for the former hospital. Today, it displays healing plants used for millennia—different ones for each of the traditional four ailments (melancholic, choleric, sanguine, phlegmatic), supposedly caused by an imbalance in the body's traditional four substances, or "humours" (black bile, yellow bile, blood, and phlegm), corresponding to the earth's traditional four elements (earth, wind, fire, and Ringo). You'll also see some very antiquated, primitive, painful medical tools (ouch!). Florence Nightingale, the nurse famed for saving so many Crimean War soldiers wounded in Russia, worked here to improve sanitation and to turn nurses from low-paid domestics into trained doctors' assistants.

The small hallway leading to the theater displays crude anesthetics (ether, chloroform, three pints of ale), surgical instruments by Black & Decker (knives, saws, drills), and a glaring lack of antiseptics—that is, until young Dr. Joseph Lister discovered carbolic acid, which reduced the high rates of mortality (and halitosis).

Up the stairs, the **Old Operating Theatre** is the highlight—a semicircular room surrounded by railings for 150 spectators (truly a "theater"), where doctors operated on patients while med students observed.

The patients were often poor women, blindfolded for their own modesty. The doctors donated their time to help, practice, and teach (see the motto *Miseratione non Mercede:* "Out of compassion, not for profit"). The surgeries, usually amputations, were performed under very crude working conditions—under the skylight or by gaslight, with no sink, and only sawdust to sop up blood. (A false floor held another layer of sawdust to stop the blood before it dripped through to the ceiling of the church below.) The wood still bears bloodstains. Nearly one in three patients died. There was a fine line between Victorian-era surgeons and Jack the Ripper.

• *Notice that The Shard—London's tallest skyscraper—is just down the street beyond the Old Operating Theatre. Return to Borough High Street where, farther along (past the King's Head, on the left-hand side) you'll find a long, wide courtyard with not a right angle in sight. This is…*

❺ The George Inn

The George is the last of many "coaching inns" that once lined the main highway from London to all points south. Like Greyhound bus stations, each inn was a terminal for far-flung journeys, since coaches were forbidden inside The City. They offered food, drink, beds, and entertainment for travelers—Shakespeare, as a young actor, likely performed in The George's courtyard. On a sunny day, the courtyard is a fine place for a break from the Borough High Street bustle (food served all day long, several ales on tap—including their own brew).

• *Directly across Borough High Street from here you'll see various entrances to...*

❻ Borough Market

London's oldest vegetable market and public gathering spot is also simply the biggest and best of London's many wonderful food

markets—a great place to browse, shop, and eat. For food lovers, it's worth ▲▲▲.

The market first started a thousand years ago on London Bridge, where country farmers brought fresh goods to the city gates. It now sits under a Victorian arcade with a railroad rumbling overhead, knifing right through dingy apartment houses.

If you enjoy variety, there are few better places in London to find lunch. A few Borough Market tips: Don't choose a place to eat until you've done some surveying to understand your (many) options. The market is sprawling and confusing, but don't worry about getting lost; in fact, enjoy it.

Visiting the Market: For orientation purposes, here are a few landmarks: Cathedral/Bedale Street runs through the middle of the market, from Southwark Cathedral up to Borough High Street. This separates the heart of the market from the funkier **"Green Market"** zone (closer to the cathedral); there's a glassed-in section here, facing Borough High Street, with benches for sit-down munching.

The **main part of the market** is a fantastic maze of fruit vendors, cheesemongers, butchers, fishmongers, and prepared food stalls featuring cuisines from virtually everywhere on earth. To get your bearings, wander through until you pop out along Stoney Street, at the far (western) boundary of the market. Leading west from Stoney Street is Park Street, whose 19th-century ambience makes it a popular filming location. At this intersection, notice the colorful pub. Historically, the first trading started at 2:00 in the morning. Workers could knock off by sunrise for a pint here at the specially licensed Market Porter tavern.

Also at this intersection is the fragrant cheese shop at Neal's Yard Dairy. Across from Park Street, the Ginger Pig is *the* place for serious English sausage and bacon. Deeper in the heart of the market, look for the red stall of Maria's Market Café, a colorful eatery popular with market workers.

Finally, as you stand in the main part of the market facing Stoney Street, work your way to the right, through a maze of yet more amazing eateries, to find  loads more covered seating on risers (along the street called Winchester Walk; WCs below the risers). The people munching here look as if they're watching a performance...which, in a way, they are. (For more on eating at the market, see page 441.)

• *Walk to the river along Cathedral Street, veering left at the Y. (Alternatively, from the far end of the market, turn right down Stoney Street, then right again on Clink Street, and head for the colorful old ship.)*

❼ Golden Hinde Replica

As we all learned in school, "Sir Francis Drake circumcised the globe with a hundred-foot clipper." Or something like that...

Imagine a hundred men on a boat this size (yes, this replica is full-size) circling the globe on a three-year voyage, sleeping on the wave-swept decks, suffering bad food, floggings, doldrums, B.O., and attacks from foreigners. They explored unknown waters and were paid only from whatever riches they could find or steal along the way. (I took a bus tour like that once.)

The *Golden Hinde* (see the female deer, or hind, on the prow and stern) was Sir Francis Drake's flagship as he circumnavigated the globe (1577-1580). Drake, a farmer's son who followed the lure of the sea, hated Spaniards. So did Queen Elizabeth I, who hired him to plunder rich Spanish vessels and New World colonies in England's name.

With 164 men on five small ships (the *Hinde* was the largest, at 100 tons and 18 cannons), he sailed southwest, dipping around South America, raiding Spanish ships and towns in Chile, and inching up the coast perhaps as far as Canada. By the time it continued across the Pacific to Asia and beyond, the *Hinde* was

BANKSIDE

so full of booty that its crew replaced the rock ballast with gold ingots and silver coins. Three years later, Drake—with only one remaining ship and 56 men—sailed the *Hinde* up the Thames, unloading a fabulously valuable hoard of gold, silver, emeralds, diamonds, pearls, silks, cloves, and spices before the queen. A grateful Elizabeth knighted Drake on the main deck and kissed him on his *Golden Hinde*.

The *Hinde* was retired gloriously, but rotted away from neglect. Drake received a large share of the wealth, became enormously famous, and later gained more glory defeating the Spanish Armada (aided by "the winds of God") in the decisive battle in the English Channel, off Plymouth (1588), making England ruler of the waves.

The galleon replica is a working ship that has itself circled the globe. It is berthed at St. Mary Overie Dock ("St. Mary's over the river"), a public dock available for free to all Southwark residents. The Thames river trade thrived here for centuries until it fell victim to WWII bombing and container ships that require big berths and deep water. The docks are now concentrated far downstream, east of Tower Bridge. Only a few brick warehouses remain (just west of here), waiting to be leveled or yuppified. Although you can pay to enter the ship, it's not worth the cost of admission.

• *Now go up the street across from the Golden Hinde's gangplank (Pickfords Wharf) and head west. About 25 yards ahead on the left are the excavated ruins of...*

❽ Winchester Palace

All that remains today is a wall with a medieval rose window, but this was once a lavish 80-acre estate stretching along 200 feet of waterfront. It had a palace, gardens, fountains, stables, tennis courts, a working farm, and a fish-stocked lake. The wall marks the west end of the Great Hall (134 feet by 29 feet), the banquet room for receptions held by the palace's owner, the Bishop of Winchester.

Bishops from 1106 to 1626 lived here as wealthy, worldly rulers of the Bankside area, outside the jurisdiction of The City. They profited from activities that were illegal across the river, such as prostitution and gambling. They were a law unto themselves, with their own courts and prisons. One famous prison—the Clink—built by the bishops remained even after its creators were ousted by a Puritan Parliament.

• *Fifty yards farther west (along what is now called Clink Street) is...*

❾ The Clink Prison Museum

Now an overpriced and disappointing museum that feels like a Disney ride with a few historic artifacts tossed in, this prison gave us our expression "thrown in the Clink," from the sound of prisoners' chains. It burned down in 1780, but the underground cells remain, featuring historical information on wall plaques, many torture devices, and a generally creepy, claustrophobic atmosphere.

Originally part of Winchester Palace, it housed troublemakers who upset the smooth running of the bishop's 22 licensed brothels (called "the stews"), gambling dens, and taverns. Bouncers delivered drunks who were out of control, johns who couldn't pay, and prostitutes ("women living by their bodies") who tried to go freelance or cheated loyal customers. Offending prostitutes had their heads shaved and breasts bared, and were carted through the streets and whipped while people jeered. They might share cells side by side with "heretics"—namely, priests who'd crossed their bishops.

In 1352, debtors (who'd maxed out their MasterCards) became criminals, housed here among harder criminals in harsh conditions. Prisoners were not fed. They had to bribe guards to get food, to avoid torture, or even to gain their release. (The idea was that you'd brought this on yourself.) Prisoners relied on their families for money, prostituted themselves to guards and other inmates, or reached through the bars at street level, begging from passersby. Murderers, debtors, Protestants, priests, and many innocent people experienced this strange brand of justice...all part of the rough crowd that gave Bankside such a seedy reputation.

• *Carry on west and cross under the Cannon Street Bridge. Just ahead is...*

❿ The Anchor and Bankside Road

The Anchor is the last of the original 22 licensed "inns" (tavern/brothel/restaurant/nightclub/casino) of Bankside's red light district heyday in the 1600s. A tavern has stood here for 800 years. The big brick buildings behind the inn were once part of the mass-producing Anchor brewery, with the inn as its brewpub. (Even back in the 1300s, Chaucer wrote, "If the words get muddled in my tale / Just put it down to too much Southwark ale.")

In the cozy, mazelike interior are memories of greats who've drunk here (I have) or indulged in a new drug that hit London in the 1560s—tobacco. Shakespeare, who may have lived along Clink

Street, may have tippled here, especially because the original Globe Theatre was right behind The Anchor. Dr. Samuel Johnson also worked here while writing the famous dictionary that helped codify the English language and spelling (for more on Dr. Johnson, see page 262). Unfortunately, the pub is now part of a chain, which has adorned it with generic decor and standard-issue slot machines, as if completely oblivious to its history.

The Anchor marks the start of the once-notorious Bankside Road that runs along a river retaining wall. In Elizabethan times (16th century), the street was lined with "inns" offering one-stop shopping for addictive personalities. The streets were jammed with sword-carrying punks in tights looking for a fight, prostitutes, gaping tourists from the Borough High Street coaching inns, pickpockets, river pirates, highwaymen, navy recruiters kidnapping drunks, and many proper ladies and gentlemen who ferried across from The City for an evening's entertainment. And then there were the really seedy people—yes, actors.

• *If the tide is low, check out the beach below. This area is fun for beachcombing—old red roof tiles and little chunks of disposable clay tobacco pipes litter the rocks at low tide.*

Carry along the riverbank and cross under the green-and-yellow Southwark Bridge. While you're under there, notice the metal reliefs depicting London's "Frost Fair" of 1564. Because the old London Bridge was such a wall of stone, the swift-flowing Thames would back up and even freeze over during cold winters.

Emerging from under the bridge, head farther west on Bankside to...

⓫ Shakespeare's Globe

All the world's a stage,
And all the men and women merely players.
They have their exits and their entrances,
And one man, in his time, plays many parts.
    —As You Like It

By 1599, 35-year-old William Shakespeare was a well-known actor, playwright, and businessman in the booming theater trade. His acting company, the Lord Chamberlain's Men, built the 3,000-seat Globe Theatre, by far the largest of its day (200 yards from today's replica, where only a plaque stands now). The Globe premiered Shakespeare's greatest works—*Hamlet, Othello, King Lear,*

BANKSIDE

Macbeth—in open-air summer afternoon performances, though occasionally at night by the light of torches and buckets of tar-soaked ropes.

In 1612, it featured Shakespeare's *All Is True (Henry VIII)*. During Scene 4, a stage cannon boomed to announce the arrival of King Henry, who started flirting with Anne Boleyn. As the two actors generated sparks onstage, play-watchers smelled fire. Some stray cannon wadding had sparked a real fire offstage. Within an hour, the wood-and-thatch building had burned completely to the ground, but with only one injury: A man's pants caught fire and were quickly doused with a tankard of ale.

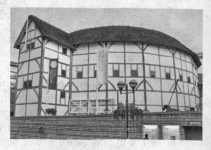

Built in 1997, the new Globe—round, half-timbered, thatched, with wooden pegs for nails—is a quite realistic replica, though slightly smaller (seating 1,500 spectators), located near the original site, and constructed with fire-repellent materials. Performances are staged almost nightly in summer—check at the box office (at the east end of the complex). For more on touring the Globe, see page 97.

Bankside's theater scene vanished in the 1640s, closed by a Parliament dominated by hardline Puritans. Drama seemed to portray and promote immoral behavior, and actors—men who also played women's roles—parodied and besmirched fair womanhood. Bearbaiting was also outlawed by the outraged moralists (to paraphrase the historian Thomas Macaulay)—not because it caused bears pain, but because it gave people pleasure.

• *From the Globe, belly up to the railing overlooking the Thames and imagine the view on September 2, 1666.*

⑫ View of 1666 Great Fire Area

On Sunday, September 2, 1666, stunned Londoners quietly sipped beers in Bankside pubs and watched The City across the river go up in flames. ("When we could endure no more upon the water," wrote Samuel Pepys in his diary, "we went to a little alehouse on the Bankside.") Started in a bakery shop near the Monument (north end of London Bridge) and fanned by strong winds, the fire swept westward, engulfing the mostly wooden city, devouring Old St. Paul's, and moving past what is now Blackfriars Bridge and St. Bride's to Temple Church (near the pointy, black, gold-tipped steeple of the Royal Courts of Justice).

In four days, 80 percent of The City was incinerated, including 13,000 houses and 89 churches. The good news? Incredibly, only nine people died, the fire cleansed a plague-infested city, and Christopher Wren was around to rebuild London's skyline.

The fire also marked the end of Bankside's era as London's naughty playground. Having recently been cleaned up by the Puritans, it now served as a temporary refugee camp for those displaced by the fire. And, with the coming Industrial Age, businessmen demolished the inns and replaced them with brick warehouses, docks, and factories to fuel the economy of a world power.

• *Continue on to the silvery pedestrian bridge. Hovering above you is a towering former power plant, now turned into a huge modern art museum.*

⓭ Tate Modern

London's large, impressive modern art collection is housed mostly in a former power station—typical of the move to renovate empty, ugly Industrial Age hulks on the South Bank. Even if you don't tour the collection, pop inside the Turbine Hall entrance (free) to view the spacious interior, decorated each year with a new industrial-sized installation by one of the world's top contemporary artists.

　📖 See the Tate Modern Tour chapter.

• *End this walk on the Millennium Bridge, enjoying a view of the Thames.*

⓮ Millennium Bridge and View of the Thames

This pedestrian bridge was built in 2000 to connect the Tate Modern with St. Paul's Cathedral and The City. For its first two glorious

days, Londoners made the pleasant seven-minute walk across... before the $25 million "bridge to the next millennium" started wobbling dangerously (insert your own ironic joke here) and was closed for rethinking. After much work, 20 months, and $8 million in retrofits, the bridge reopened. Nicknamed the "blade of light," it was designed (partly by Lord Norman Foster, who also did The Gherkin and City Hall downstream) to allow a wide-open view of St. Paul's. Now stabilized, it links two revital-ized sections of London.

From the Cotswolds to the North Sea, the Thames winds east-ward a total of 210 miles. London is close enough to the estuary to be affected by the North Sea's tides, so the river level does indeed rise and fall twice a day. In fact, one of the reasons Romans found this a practical location—even though it was about 40 miles in-land—was that their boats could hitch a free ride with the tides be-tween the sea and the town twice a day. But tides also mean floods. After centuries of periodic flooding (spring rains plus high tides), barriers to regulate the tides were built in 1982, east of Tower Bridge. The barriers also slow down the once fast-moving river.

The Thames is still a major commercial artery (east of Tower Bridge). In the previous two centuries, it ran brown with Industrial Revolution pollution. Today it's brown because of estuary silt—the Thames is now one of the cleanest rivers in the industrialized world.

• *Your walk is over. From here you can enjoy the Tate Modern or contin-ue strolling the South Bank (follow the Jubilee Walkway 20 minutes or so to the London Eye and Big Ben—particularly enjoyable in the evening). Or cross the Thames on the Millennium Bridge to a pedestrian mall that leads past the glassy Salvation Army headquarters (good café and small, free Salvation Army history display in daylight basement) to St. Paul's Cathedral and Tube station.*

TATE MODERN TOUR

Remember the 20th century? Accelerated by technology and fragmented by war, it was an exciting and chaotic time, with art as turbulent as the world that created it. The Tate Modern lets you walk through the explosive last century with a glimpse at its brave new art.

This Is Not a "Tour": The Tate Modern displays change constantly, making a painting-by-painting tour impossible. In addition, its collection is (controversially) organized by concept—"Artist and Society," for example—rather than by artist and chronology. Unlike the museum, this chapter is neatly chronological. It's not intended as a self-guided tour, but to give context to the various cultural periods that produced the art of the Tate Modern.

Read through this chapter for a general introduction and use it as a reference to focus on specific works. With this background in 20th-century art, you'll appreciate the Tate's even greater strength: art of the 21st century. After you see the Old Masters of Modernism (Matisse, Picasso, Kandinsky, and so on), push your mental envelope with works by Pollock, Miró, Bacon, Picabia, Beuys, Twombly, and beyond. Look past the painted canvases to appreciate the museum's many installations: entire rooms given over to a single artist to create a multimedia display.

When the Tate Modern opened in 2000, they anticipated two million visitors a year. More than twice that visited. In response, they've opened a new wing, doubling its exhibition space. The goal of the expansion—to foster interaction between art and community in the 21st century—is as modern as the collection itself.

Orientation

Cost: Free, £5 suggested donation; fee for special exhibits.

Hours: Daily 10:00-18:00, may stay open later Fri-Sat, last entry 45 minutes before closing.

Information: +44 20 7887 8888, www.tate.org.uk.

When to Go: This popular place is especially crowded on weekends. Crowds thin out on Friday and Saturday evenings (when open) and midday during the week.

Getting There: Located on the South Bank of the Thames, across from St. Paul's and near the Globe Theatre. You can take the **Tube** to Southwark, London Bridge, St. Paul's, Mansion House, or Blackfriars, then follow signs to the museum (10- to 15-minute walk); or catch Thames Clippers' **Tate Boat** ferry from the Tate Britain (Millbank Pier) for a 15-minute crossing (£9 one-way, departs every 30 minutes Mon-Fri 10:00-16:00, Sat-Sun 9:15-18:40, www.tate.org.uk/visit/tate-boat). But in good weather, the nicest approach is to **walk** across the Millennium Bridge from St. Paul's Cathedral.

Visitor Information: To navigate the current offerings, the Tate encourages you to download the official, free app (using their free Wi-Fi). They may not hand out printed maps. (Look for posted maps by elevators and escalators, and snap a photo with your phone.) You may find info desks, along with bookstores and ticket desks for the temporary exhibits, on the two lowest floors (levels  0 and 1). And helpful staff posted around the museum may be able to help you track down specific works.

Tours: Free 45-minute **guided tours** generally run at 12:00 and 13:00 (Natalie Bell Building) and 14:00 (Blavatnik Building); free 10-minute **gallery talks** take place on occasion (see info desk for details).

Length of This Tour: Allow at least an hour. Read this chapter ahead of time, then browse according to your tastes.

Services: You can check bags at the cloakroom on level 0 (free, £5 suggested donation). There are also lockers on level 0 of the Blavatnik Building. WCs are located near the escalator or elevator on most levels.

Cuisine Art: In the main Natalie Bell Building, coffee shops are on levels 1 and 3. On level 6, there's a **$$$ restaurant** and **casual bar** offering better views and lower prices (drinks and snacks). This perch provides stunning panoramas of St. Paul's and The City. In the Blavatnik Building, a **$$$$ restaurant** with views is on level 9 and a **$ bar** with limited food on level 1. Some trendy restaurants are several blocks southwest of the Tate, along the street named "the Cut" (near the Southwark Tube stop).

Starring: Picasso, Matisse, Dalí, and all the "classic" modern artists, plus the Tate Modern's specialty—British and American artists of the last half of the 20th century.

Know Your Tates: Don't confuse the Tate Modern with the Tate Britain (south of Big Ben), which features British art (📖 see the Tate Britain Tour chapter). But there is some crossover: Both Tates include some 20th- and 21st-century British artists.

Getting Started

The main entrance (called the Turbine Hall Entrance) is around the right side of the building (as you face it with the Thames at your back). Entering here, you'll descend the ramp into the vast Turbine Hall.

Log on to the free Wi-Fi, download the free app (or look for a posted map), and get orien-Tate-d. The museum has two buildings. You're on underground level 0 of the **Natalie Bell Building** (a.k.a. the Boiler House). It's connected by skybridges to the **Blavatnik Building** (a.k.a. the Switch House).

The art is displayed in both buildings. Works from the museum's permanent collection (that is, much of the art described in this chapter) is arranged into various themed exhibits that are identified on maps as **"Collection Displays."** Paintings by Picasso, for example, might be scattered in different rooms on different levels. Shuffled among these are **temporary exhibits,** some of which require paid tickets (popular ones sell out well in advance).

A good place to start is to ride the looong escalator from the Natalie Bell Building's level 0—near where you enter—up to level 2, which typically highlights a range of artworks from the permanent collection.

Beyond there, the app and posted maps show which floors of which building are featuring which exhibits; pick what sounds interesting, and use this chapter's overview of 20th-century art to augment your sightseeing.

Tate Modern

Overview of Modern Art

The following is a chronological overview of some of the modern artists and trends you will encounter at the Tate.

1900: VICTORIA'S LEGACY

Anno Domini 1900, a new century dawns. Europe is at peace, Britannia rules the world. Technology is about to usher in a Golden Age.

Claude Monet

Monet (1840-1926) captures the relaxed, civilized spirit of belle époque France and Victorian England with Impressionist snapshots of peaceful landscapes and middle-class family picnics. But the true subject is the shimmering effect of reflected light, rendered with rough brushstrokes and bright paints that look messy up close but blend at a distance. The newfangled camera made camera-eye realism obsolete. Artists began placing more importance on *how* something was painted rather than on *what* was painted.

1905: COLONIAL EUROPE

Europe ruled a global empire, tapping its dark-skinned colonies for raw materials, cheap labor, and bold new ways to look at the world. The cozy Victorian world was shattering. Nietzsche murdered God. Darwin stripped off Man's robe of culture and found a naked ape. Primitivism was modern. Ooga-booga.

Henri Matisse

Matisse (1869-1954) was one of the Fauves, or "wild beasts," who tried to inject a bit of the jungle into civilized European society. Inspired by "primitive" African and Oceanic masks and voodoo dolls, the Fauves made modern art that looked primitive: long, masklike faces with almond eyes; bright, clashing colors; simple figures; and "flat," two-dimensional scenes.

Matisse simplifies. A man is a few black lines and blocks of paint. A snail is a spiral of colored paper. A woman's back is an outline. Matisse's colors are unnaturally bright. The "distant" landscape is as crisp and clear as close objects, and the slanted lines meant to suggest depth are crudely done.

Traditionally, the canvas was like a window that you looked "through" to see a slice of the real world stretching off into the horizon. With Matisse, you look "at" the canvas like you do wallpaper—to appreciate the decorative pattern of colors and shapes.

Though his style is modern, Matisse builds on 19th-century art—the bright colors of Van Gogh, the primitive figures of Gauguin, the colorful designs of Japanese wood-block prints, and the Impressionist patches of paint that blend together only at a distance.

Paul Cézanne

Cézanne (1839-1906) brings Impressionism into the 20th century. Whereas Monet uses separate dabs of different-colored paint to "build" a figure, Cézanne "builds" a man with somewhat larger slabs of paint, giving him a kind of 3-D chunkiness. It's not hard to see the progression from Monet's dabs to Cézanne's slabs to Picasso's cubes—Cubism.

1910: THE MODERNS

The modern world was moving fast, with automobiles, factories, and mass communication. Motion

The Building as "Art"

Besides the art it houses, the Tate Modern's display space is a sight in and of itself. Here's a quick, round-trip route through the buildings that hits the highlights. You'll enjoy the modern architecture, get a sense of the wide variety of art on display, and be treated to a great view of London. As you go, linger wherever you'd like, seeing unexpected art that catches your eye.

Natalie Bell Building (Boiler House/Main Building)

The Turbine Hall (Level 0): Start at the main entrance, strolling majestically down the sloping ramp and into the massive empty space of this former electricity-generating powerhouse. The power station (with its 325-foot brick chimney) closed in 1981. It was refurbished with a glass roof, and reopened as a museum in the year 2000. Today, the Turbine Hall displays major art installations by contemporary artists—always one of the highlights of the art world. More exhibits are displayed in "The Tanks," to the right of the main hall.

• *Head upstairs (via the escalator near the ground-floor cloakroom) to level 2.*

Various Exhibits (Levels 2-4): These levels house a mix of themed exhibits pulled from the permanent collection (called "Collection Displays") and temporary exhibits (some free, some requiring

pictures captured the fast-moving world, while Einstein explored the fourth dimension: time.

Cubism and Pablo Picasso

Born in Spain, Picasso (1881-1973) moved to Paris as a young man. He worked with painter and sculptor Georges Braque in poverty so dire they often didn't know where their next bottle of wine was coming from.

Picasso's Cubist works show the old European world shattering to bits. He pieces the fragments back together in a whole new way, showing several perspectives at once (for example, looking up the left side of a woman's body and, at the same time, down at her right).

Whereas newfangled motion pictures capture several perspectives in succession, Picasso achieves it on a canvas with overlapping images. A single "cube" might contain an arm (in the foreground)

special admission).

• *Sightsee your way up through levels 2, 3, and 4. On level 4, walk across the "bridge" (with great views down into the Turbine Hall) and into the Blavatnik Building (Switch House).*

Blavatnik Building (Switch House/Annex)

Level 4: The twisted-pyramid, 10-story Blavatnik Building was constructed on the site of the power station's old switch house, and was designed by the same architectural firm that refurbished the Boiler House. It gave the Tate an extra quarter-million square feet of display space. Besides showing off more of the Tate's impressive collection, the space hosts changing themed exhibitions, performance art, experimental film, and interactive sculpture incorporating light and sound. Higher floors offer social and educational activities, including a children's gallery and several cafés. Some of this building's rooms are free to enter, while others require admission fees.

• *After exploring level 4, ride the (often-crowded) elevator up to the...*

Viewing Level (Level 10): This wraparound terrace (with a small café) offers stunning views of London (closes 30 minutes before the museum).

• *Take the elevator down to levels 3 and/or 2, which also have a mix of "Collection Displays" and special exhibits. Then make your way down (past more art and the misty fountain) to level 0. You're back at the Turbine Hall. Exit the way you came in, or head up to level 1 and use the exit that leads straight out toward the Thames.*

and the window behind (in the background), both painted the same color. The foreground and background are woven together so that the subject dissolves into a pattern.

Picasso, the most famous and—OK, I'll say it—the greatest artist of the 20th century, constantly explored and adapted his style to new trends. He made collages, tried his hand at "statues" of wood, wire, or whatever, and even made art out of everyday household objects. These multimedia works, so revolutionary at the time, have become stock-in-trade today. Scattered throughout the museum are works from the many periods of Picasso's life.

Futurism

The Machine Age is approaching, and the whole world gleams with promise in cylindrical shapes ("Tubism"), like an internal-combustion engine. Or is it the gleaming barrel of a cannon?

1914: WORLD WAR I

A soldier—shivering in a trench, ankle-deep in mud, waiting to be ordered "over the top," to run through barbed wire, over fallen comrades, and into a hail of machine-gun fire, only to capture a few hundred yards of meaningless territory that would be lost the next day. This soldier was not thinking about art.

World War I left nine million dead. (At times, the British Empire lost more men per month than America lost during the entire Vietnam War.) The war also killed the optimism and faith in humankind that had guided Europe since the Renaissance.

Expressionism

Cynicism and decadence settled over postwar Europe. Artists such as Grosz, Beckmann, and Kokoschka "expressed" their disgust by showing a distorted reality that emphasized the ugly. Using the lurid colors and simplified figures of the Fauves, they slapped paint on in thick brushstrokes, depicting a hypocritical, hard-edged, dog-eat-dog world—a civilization watching its Victorian moral foundations collapse.

Dada

When they could grieve no longer, artists turned to grief's giddy twin, laughter. The war made all old values a joke, including artistic ones. The Dada movement, choosing a purposely childish name, made art that was intentionally outrageous: a moustache on the *Mona Lisa*, a shovel hung on the wall, or a modern version of a Renaissance "fountain"—a urinal (by Marcel Duchamp...or was it I. P. Freeley?).

Dada was a dig at all the pompous prewar artistic theories based on the noble intellect of Rational Women and Men. While the experts ranted on, Dadaists sat in the back of the class and made cultural fart noises.

Hey, I love this stuff. My mind says it's sophomoric, but my heart belongs to Dada.

1920s: ANYTHING GOES

In the Jazz Age, the world turned upside down. Genteel ladies smoked cigarettes. Gangsters laid down the law. You could make a fortune in the stock market one day and lose it the next. You could dance the Charleston with the opposite sex, and even say the word "sex" while talking about Freud over cocktails. It was almost...surreal.

Surrealism

Artists caught the jumble of images on a canvas. A telephone made from a lobster, an elephant with a heating-duct trunk, Venus sleepwalking among skeletons. Take one mixed bag of reality, jumble it in a blender, and serve on a canvas—Surrealism.

The artist scatters seemingly un-related—yet easily recognizable—objects on the canvas, leaving us to trace the connections in a kind of connect-the-dots without numbers.

Further complicating the modern world was Freud's discovery of the "unconscious" mind, which thinks dirty thoughts while we sleep. Surrealists let the id speak. The canvas is an uncensored, stream-of-consciousness "landscape" of these deep urges, revealed in the bizarre images of dreams. Salvador Dalí, the most famous Surrealist, combined an extraordinarily realistic technique with an extraordinarily twisted mind. He painted "unreal" scenes with photographic realism, making us believe they could really happen. Dalí's images—crucifixes, political and religious figures, and naked bodies—pack an emotional punch.

1930s: DEPRESSION

As capitalism failed around the world, governments propped up their economies with vast building projects. The architecture style was modern, stripped-down (i.e., cheap), and functional. Propagandist campaigns championed noble workers in the heroic Social Realist style.

Piet Mondrian

Like blueprints for modernism, Mondrian's T-square style boils painting down to its basic building blocks: a white canvas, black lines, and the three primary colors—red, yellow, and blue—arranged in orderly patterns. (When you come right down to it, that's all painting ever has been. A schematic drawing of, say, the *Mona Lisa* shows that it's less about a woman than about the triangles and rectangles she's composed of.)

Mondrian (1872-1944) started out painting realistic landscapes of the orderly fields in his native homeland of Holland. Increasingly, he simplified his style into horizontal and vertical patterns. For Mondrian, who was heavily into Eastern mysticism, "up versus down" and "left versus right" were the perfect metaphors for life's dualities: good versus evil, body versus spirit, fascism versus communism, man versus woman. The canvas is a bird's-eye view of Mondrian's personal landscape.

TATE MODERN

Abstract Art

Abstract art simplifies. A man becomes a stick figure. A squiggle is a wave. A streak of red expresses anger. Arches make you want a cheeseburger. These are universal symbols that everyone from a caveman to a banker understands. Abstract artists capture the essence of reality in a few lines and colors, boldly capturing objects and ideas that even a camera can't—emotions, abstract concepts, musical rhythms, and spiritual states of mind.

With abstract art, you don't look "through" the canvas to see the visual world, but "at" it to read the symbolism of lines, shapes, and colors. Most 20th-century paintings are a mix of the real world (representation) and colorful patterns (abstraction).

1940s: WORLD WAR II

World War II was a global war (involving Europe, the Americas, Australia, Africa, and Asia) and a total war (saturation bombing of civilians and ethnic cleansing). It left Europe in ruins.

Alberto Giacometti's skinny statues have the emaciated, haunted, and faceless look of concentration-camp survivors. In the sweep of world war and overpowering technology, man is frail and fragile. All he can do is stand at attention and take it like a man.

Meanwhile, Francis Bacon's caged creatures speak for all of war-torn Europe when they scream, "Enough!" (For more on Bacon, see page 366.)

1950s: AMERICA, THE GLOBAL SUPERPOWER

As converted war factories turned swords into kitchen appliances, America helped rebuild Europe while pumping out consumer goods for its own booming population. Prosperity, a stable government, national television broadcasts, and a common fear of Soviet communism threatened to turn America into a completely homogeneous society.

Some artists, centered in New York, rebelled against conformity and superficial consumerism. (They'd served under Eisenhower in war and now had to in peace, as well.) They created art that was the very opposite of the functional, mass-produced goods of the American marketplace.

Art was a way of asserting your individuality by creating a completely original and personal vision. The trend was toward bigger canvases, abstract designs, and experimentation with new materials and techniques. It was called "Abstract Expressionism"—expressing emotions and ideas using color and form alone.

TATE MODERN

Jackson Pollock

"Jack the Dripper" attacks convention with a can of paint, dripping and splashing a dense web onto the canvas. Picture Pollock (1912-1956) in his studio, jiving to the hi-fi, bouncing off the walls, throwing paint in a moment of enlightenment. Of course, the artist loses some control this way—over the paint flying in midair and over himself in an ecstatic trance. Painting becomes a whole-body activity, a "dance" between the artist and his materials.

The intuitive act of creating is what's important, not the final product. The canvas is only a record of that moment of ecstasy.

Big, Empty Canvases

With all the postwar prosperity, artists could afford bigger canvases. But what reality are they trying to show?

In the modern world, we find ourselves insignificant specks in a vast and indifferent universe. Every morning, each of us must confront that big, blank, existential canvas, and decide how we're going to make our mark on it.

Another influence was the simplicity of Japanese landscape painting. A Zen master studies and meditates for years to achieve the state of mind in which he can draw one pure line. These canvases, again, are only a record of that state of enlightenment. (What is the sound of one brush painting?)

On more familiar ground, postwar painters were following in the footsteps of artists such as Mondrian. The geometrical forms here reflect the same search for order, but these artists painted to the musical 5/4 asymmetry of the Dave Brubeck Quartet's jazzy *Take Five*.

Patterns and Textures

Enjoy the lines and colors, but also a new element: texture. Some works have very thick paint piled on, where you can see the brushstrokes clearly. Some have substances besides paint applied to the canvas, or the canvas is punctured so the fabric itself (and the hole) becomes the subject. Artists show their skill by mastering new materials. The canvas is a tray, serving up a delightful buffet of different substances with interesting colors, patterns, shapes, and textures.

Mark Rothko

Rothko (1903-1970) made two-toned rectangles, laid on their sides, that seem to float in a big, vertical canvas. The edges are blurred, so if you get close enough to let the canvas fill your field of vision (as Rothko intended), the rectangles appear to rise and sink from the cloudy depths like answers in a Magic 8 Ball.

Serious students appreciate the subtle differences in color between the rectangles. Rothko experimented with different bases

20th-Century British Artists

Since 1960, London has rivaled New York as a center for the visual arts. You'll find British artists displayed in both the Tate Modern and the Tate Britain. Check out the Tate Britain Tour chapter for more on the following artists: David Hockney, Jacob Epstein, Gilbert and George, Henry Moore, Francis Bacon, and Barbara Hepworth.

for the same color and used a single undercoat (a "wash") to unify them. His early works are warmer, with brighter reds, yellows, and oranges; his later works are maroon and brown, approaching black.

Still, these are not intended to be formal studies in color and form. Rothko was trying to express the most basic human emotions in a pure language. (A "realistic" painting of a person is inherently fake because it's only an illusion of the person.) Staring into these windows onto the soul, you can laugh, cry, or ponder, just as Rothko did when he painted them.

Rothko, the previous century's "last serious artist," believed in the power of art to express the human spirit. When he found out that his nine large Seagram canvases were to be hung in a corporate restaurant, he refused to sell them, and they ended up in the Tate.

In his last years, Rothko's canvases—always rectangles—got bigger, simpler, and darker. When Rothko finally slashed his wrists in his studio, one nasty critic joked that what killed him was the repetition. Minimalism was painting itself into a blank corner.

1960s: POP AND POLITICS

The decade began united in idealism—young John F. Kennedy pledged to put a man on the moon, newly launched satellites signaled a united world, The Beatles sang exuberantly, peaceful race demonstrations championed equality, and the Vatican II Council preached liberation. By decade's end, there were race riots, assassinations, student protests, and America's floundering war in distant Vietnam. In households around the world, parents screamed, "Turn that down...and get a haircut!"

Culturally, every postwar value was questioned by a rising, wealthy, and populous baby-boom generation. London—producer of rock-and-roll music, film actors, mod fashions, and Austin Powers joie de vivre—once again became a world cultural center.

Though government-sponsored public art was dominated by big, abstract canvases and sculptures, other artists pooh-poohed the highbrow seriousness of abstract art. Instead, they mocked lowbrow popular culture by embracing it in a tongue-in-cheek way

(Pop Art), or they attacked authority with absurd performances to make a political statement (conceptual art).

Pop Art

America's postwar wealth made the consumer king. Pop Art is created from the popular objects of that throwaway society—soup cans, car fenders, tacky plastic statues, movie icons. Take a Sears product, hang it in a museum, and you have to ask: Is this art? Are mass-produced objects beautiful, or crap? Why do we work so hard to acquire them? Pop Art, like Dadaism before it, questions our society's values.

Andy Warhol (who coined "15 minutes of fame") concentrated on another mass-produced phenomenon: celebrities. He took publicity photos of famous people and reproduced them. The repetition—like the constant bombardment we get from recurring images on TV—cheapens even the most beautiful things.

Roy Lichtenstein took a comic strip, blew it up, hung it on a wall, and charged a million bucks—*wham*, Pop Art. Lichtenstein supposedly was inspired by his young son, who challenged him to do something as good as Mickey Mouse. The huge newsprint dots never let us forget that the painting—like all commercial art—is an illusionistic fake. The work's humor comes from portraying a lowbrow subject (comics and ads) on the epic scale of a masterpiece.

Op Art

Optical illusions play tricks with your eyes, the way a spiral starts to spin when you stare at it. These obscure scientific experiments in color, line, and optics suddenly became trendy in the psychedelic '60s.

1970s: THE "ME DECADE"

All forms of authority—"The Establishment"—seemed bankrupt. America's president resigned in the Watergate scandal, corporations were polluting the earth, and capitalism nearly ground to a halt when Arabs withheld oil.

Artists attacked authority and institutions, trying to free individuals to discover their full human potential. Even the concept of "modernism"—that art wasn't good unless it was totally original and progressive—was questioned. No single style could dictate in this postmodern period.

TATE MODERN

Earth Art

Fearing for the health of the earth's ecology, artists rediscovered the beauty of rocks, dirt, trees, even the sound of the wind, using them to create natural art. A rock placed in a museum or urban square is certainly a strange sight.

Performance Art

The Tate Modern's collection of "sculptures" by Joseph Beuys—assemblages of steel, junk, wood, and, especially, felt and animal fat—only hint at his greatest artwork: Beuys himself.

Imagine Beuys walking through the museum, carrying a dead rabbit, while he explains the paintings to it. Or taking off his clothes, shaving his head, and smearing his body with fat.

This charismatic, ex-Luftwaffe art shaman did ridiculous things to inspire others to break with convention and be free. He choreographed "Happenings"—spectacles where people did absurd things while others watched—and pioneered performance art, in which the artist presents himself as the work of art. Beuys inspired a whole generation of artists to walk on stage, cluck like a chicken, and stick a yam up themselves. Beuys will be Beuys.

New Media

Minimalist painting and abstract sculpture were old hat, and there was an explosion of new art forms. Performance art was the most controversial, combining music, theater, dance, poetry, and the visual arts. New technologies brought video, assemblages, installations, artists' books (paintings in book form), and even (gasp!) realistic painting.

Conceptual Art

Increasingly, artists are not creating an original work (painting a canvas or sculpting a stone) but assembling one from premade objects. The *concept* of which object to pair with another to produce maximum effect ("Let's stick a crucifix in a jar of urine," to cite one notorious example) is the key.

1980s: MATERIAL GIRL

Ronald Reagan in America, Margaret Thatcher in Britain, and corporate executives around the world ruled over a conservative and materialistic society. On the other side were starving Ethiopians, gay men with the new disease AIDS, people of color, and women—all demanding power. Intelligent, peaceful, straight white males assumed a low profile.

The art world became big business, with a Van Gogh painting fetching $54 million. Corporations paid big bucks for large, colorful, semiabstract canvases. Marketing became an art form. Gender and sexual orientation were popular themes. Many women picked up paintbrushes, creating bright-colored abstract forms hinting at vulva and penis shapes. Visual art fused with popular music, bringing us installations in dance clubs and fast-edit music videos. The crude style of graffiti art demanded to be included in corporate society.

1990s: MULTICULTURAL DIVERSITY

The communist-built Berlin Wall was torn down, ending four decades of a global Cold War between capitalism and communism. The new battleground was the "Culture Wars," the struggle to include all races, genders, and lifestyles within an increasingly corporate-dominated, global society.

Artists looked to Third World countries for inspiration and championed society's outsiders against government censorship and economic exclusion. A new medium, the internet, arose, allowing instantaneous multimedia communication around the world through electronic signals carried by satellites and fiber-optic cables.

2000—?

A new millennium dawned. Thanks to the internet, art has taken on a new sense of connectivity. A work of art can mean strangers meeting for intricate Flashmob street performances; graffiti artists like Banksy reaching the masses by tagging public spaces; and people everywhere sharing moments through social networking sites. Instagram selfies have become the modern Gainsborough portrait, presenting an idealized image to the world of how we wish to be seen. Technology has empowered everyone to make art.

VICTORIA & ALBERT MUSEUM TOUR

With one of the biggest, most eclectic collections of objects anywhere, the Victoria and Albert (V&A) has something for everyone. It bills itself as a museum for the decorative arts, and Martha Stewart types will be in hog heaven. You'll see furniture, glassware, clothing, jewelry, and carpets from every corner of the world. Throw in historical artifacts, and a few fine-arts masterpieces (painting and sculpture), and you have a museum built for browsing.

The V&A grew out of the Great Exhibition of 1851, that ultimate celebration of the Industrial Revolution. Now "art" could be brought to the masses through modern technology and mass production. The museum was founded on the idealistic Victorian notion that anyone can be continually improved by education and example. After much support from Queen Victoria and Prince Albert, the museum was renamed for the royal couple, and its present building was opened in 1909.

You could spend days in this place. The museum is large and gangly, with over 150 rooms and more than 12 miles of corridors. My quick tour gives you a sample of the V&A's range, covering fine art, historical objects, interior design, fashion, and beautiful objects from around the globe. Use this tour to get your bearings, then use the museum's map to wander at will.

Orientation

Cost: Free, £5 suggested donation; fee for some special exhibits.

Hours: Daily 10:00-17:45, may be open until 22:00 on some Fridays.

Information: +44 20 7942 2000, www.vam.ac.uk.

Getting There: The museum is in the South Kensington neighborhood (Tube: South Kensington). A pedestrian tunnel connects the Tube stop directly to the museum.

Visitor Information: Check the V&A's helpful website in advance for a list of current exhibits. Once at the museum, pick up the much-needed museum map (£1 suggested donation), or scan the QR code to view the map on your phone. Strategically located computers tell you more about the collection.

Tours: Free one-hour tours on various topics are offered daily from 10:30 to 15:30 (1-2/hour). Check the website for details on sporadic other tours and lectures.

Length of This Tour: Allow 1.5 hours (not counting the British Galleries). With limited time, don't miss the Cast Courts, the Fashion Galleries, and Raphael's Tapestry Cartoons.

Cloakroom: £2/item, mandatory for large bags.

Cuisine Art: The **$$ V&A Café** offers self-service lunch, as well as coffee, tea, and cakes; some of the seating is in the elegant Morris, Gamble, and Poynter Rooms— which formed the world's first museum restaurant. There are also **$ cafés** out in the Madejski Garden and another in the Sackler Courtyard. A lineup of fun eateries is two  blocks away, where Exhibition Road approaches the South Kensington Tube station (see page 433).

Starring: A little of everything—and all of it beautiful.

The Tour Begins

• *Start at the Grand Entrance lobby, on level 0. Depending on where you enter the museum, here's how to get to the start of our tour:*

*The easiest is to use the **Grand Entrance** directly from Cromwell Road.*

*If entering via the **pedestrian tunnel** from the South Kensington Tube stop, go up the stairs to level 0 and continue straight through a long sculpture gallery. After about 100 yards, turn right through the shop, which takes you to the Grand Entrance lobby.*

*If entering at the **Main Entrance** along Exhibition Road, turn right, then left, proceed 100 yards through the sculpture gallery, then turn right through the shop.*

Whichever route you take, once you reach the Grand Entrance lobby, look up into the rotunda.

❶ Dale Chihuly Chandelier

This modern chandelier/sculpture by the American glass artist epitomizes the spirit of the V&A's collection—beautiful manu-factured objects that demonstrate technical skill and innovation, wedding the old with the new, and blurring the line between arts and crafts.

Each blue-and-yellow strand of the chandelier is tied with a wire to a central spine. When the chandelier first went up in 2001, Chihuly said, "Too small," had it disassembled, and fired up still more glass bubbles.

Dale Chihuly (b. 1941)—face-famous for the eye patch he's worn since a car acci-dent—studied glassmaking in Venice, then set up his own studio/factory in Seattle, making art as the director of a creative team. He makes an old me-dium seem fresh and modern...and the V&A keeps his chandelier looking fresh with a long feather duster.

• *From the lobby, look up to the balcony (above the shop) and see the pointed arches of the...*

❷ Hereford Screen, 1862

In the 1800s, just as Britain was steaming into the future on the cutting edge of the Industrial Revolution, the public's taste went

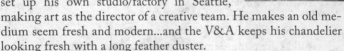

retro. This 35-by-35-foot, eight-ton rood screen (built for the Hereford Cathedral's sacred altar area) looks medieval, but it was created with the most modern materials the Industrial Revolution could produce. The metal parts were not hammered and hand-worked as in olden days, but are made of electro-formed copper. The parts were first cast in plaster, then bathed in molten copper with an electric current running through it, leaving a metal skin around the plaster. The entire project—which might have taken years in medieval times—was completed in five months.

George Gilbert Scott (1811-1878), who built the screen, re-designed much of London in the Neo-Gothic style, restoring old churches such as Westminster Abbey, renovating the Houses of Parliament, and building new structures like St. Pancras Station and the Albert Memorial—some 700 buildings in all.

The world turns, and a century later (1960s), the Gothic style was "out" again, modernism was in, and this screen was neglected and ridiculed. Considering that the V&A was originally called the Museum of Manufactures (1857), it's appropriate that the screen was brought here, where it shows off the technical advances of the Industrial Revolution.

• *To the right of the Grand Entrance lobby, look into a large hall of statues (Room 50a), including a spiraling statue of two battling men.*

❸ Giambologna, *Samson Slaying a Philistine,* c. 1562

Carved from a single block of marble, the statue shows the testy Israelite warrior rearing back, brandishing the jawbone of an ass, preparing to decapitate a man who'd insulted him. Samson pauses to make sure the Philistine looks him in the eye so he can see what's coming. Circle the statue and watch it spiral around its axis. Giambologna was clearly influenced by Michelangelo, who pioneered both the theme of the fallen enemy and the spiral-shaped pose that many artists imitated. Originally destined for a fountain in Florence, *Samson* instead found its way to London—the only major work of Giambologna's to leave Italy—in 1623. The V&A has (argu-ably) the best collection of Italian Renaissance sculpture outside Italy. We'll see more fine examples later.

• *Back at the Grand Entrance (near the revolving glass doors), find the entrance to the rooms labeled* Medieval & Renaissance, 300-1600. *It's down a few steps, on level -1 (Rooms 8-10).*

❹ Medieval and Renaissance Galleries, AD 300-1600

Walk through 1,200 years of decorative arts, seeing how the mix of pagan-Roman and medieval-Christian elements created modern Europe.

It's AD 300, and Rome's Europe-wide empire is beginning to unravel. Within two centuries, its political dominance would be over, but Rome's culture lived on in the Christian faith. Rooms 8-10 show how traditional Roman media (mosaics, carved ivory, column-and-arch building techniques) were adapted to make Christian-themed art and churches.

• *About three-fourths of the way down the long Room 8 is a glass case displaying the shoebox-sized...*

To Kensington Gardens

WC

CAFÉ | WC

MORRIS, GAMBLE & POYNTER ROOMS

SHOP

CLOAK-ROOM

To Science Museum

CAFÉ

Sackler Courtyard

BLAVATNIK HALL

Pond

MAIN ENTRANCE ➤

GARDEN CAFÉ

Madejski Garden

SIR ASTON WEBB SCREEN

PEDESTRIAN TUNNEL ENTRANCE (on Level -1)

(Level 0)

SCULPTURE

To Natural History Museum

❸ 40 FASHION

❷ 41 SOUTH ASIA ❶

❷ 42 ISLAM ❾

SHOP

CHINA

INDIA ❿

❹ 48a

❷ ❸ 50a

❶ ℹ

BRITISH GALLERIES (Level 1) ❺ 57-58

WC

8 ❹

WC

📱 TOUR BEGINS

Level 0 GRAND ENTRANCE

EXHIBITION ROAD

To South Kensington ⊖

CROMWELL ROAD

❺ Becket Casket, c. 1180

The blue-and-gold box contains the mortal remains (or relics) of St. Thomas Becket, who was brutally murdered. Look at the scene depicted along the side (lower panel): The archbishop of Canterbury is about to grab a chalice from the altar, when knights tiptoe up, draw their swords, and slice off his head. Two shocked priests throw up their hands.

Becket's soul (upper right) is borne aloft on a sling by two angels. His body is laid to rest (upper left) and blessed by the new bishop. Mourners kneel at the tomb, just as the man behind Becket's murder—King Henry II—is said to have done, out of remorse.

V&A MUSEUM

Victoria & Albert Museum Tour

1. Dale Chihuly Chandelier
2. Hereford Screen (above lobby)
3. GIAMBOLOGNA – Samson Slaying a Philistine
4. Medieval & Renaissance Galleries
5. Becket Casket
6. Boar & Bear Hunt Tapestry
7. Stairs to Leonardo Notebook
8. The Cast Courts
9. Islamic Art
10. Shiva Nataraja Statue
11. Possessions of Emperor Shah Jahan
12. Tipu's Tiger
13. Fashion Galleries
14. RAPHAEL – Tapestry Cartoons
15. British Galleries
16. Stairs up to Jewelry, Theater & British Silver

TEMPORARY EXHIBITS

JAPAN

CAST COURT 46a TRAJAN'S COLUMN, HENRY II

ROOM 46

CAST COURT 46b MICHELANGELO

WC

To 16

KOREA

STAIRS TO CAST COURTS VIEW

5   10a   6

☒ ELEVATOR/LIFT

N

Not to Scale

To Harrods & Hyde Park Corner →

BRUMPTON ROAD

Henry II had handpicked his good friend Thomas Becket (1118-1170) for the job of archbishop, assuming he'd follow the king's orders. In two days, Thomas was made a priest, a bishop, then archbishop—the head of all England's Christians. But when Becket proved loyal to the Church and opposed Henry's policies, the king, in a rash fit of anger, said he wanted Becket dead. Remorseful after his knights murdered the archbishop, Henry had 80 monks whip him, and then he spent all night at the foot of the tomb.

Just three years after his death, Becket was made a saint. Pieces of Becket's DNA—valuable relics—were conserved in this enamel-and-metal work box, a specialty of Limoges, France.

• *Continue straight to the far end of this long set of rooms. In Room 10a, you'll run right into...*

❻ Boar and Bear Hunt Tapestry, c. 1425-1430

Though most medieval art depicted the Madonna and saints, this colorful wool tapestry—woven in Belgium—provides a secular slice of life.

"Read" it from right to left: The nobles want to go hunting, so they hire some professional guides. One pro (in red) enters with his dogs and hunting horn, leading two nobles. His colleague (above) rousts bear cubs from their den, so the mama and papa bears can be flushed out into the open. Men and dogs (in the center) surround a bear, while another is lanced by a nobleman on horseback. Below, well-dressed ladies look on.

Continuing to the left, the hunt turns to wild boar, as two dogs flush one out of hiding. Finally (far left, bottom corner), the boar has been caught, and they begin to skin him for dinner.

In the nearby Room 10c, you'll find a **world map** (c. 1300) showing Christ sitting at the center of the known universe: Jerusalem. Try a little **brass rubbing** at the hands-on station.

• *Backtrack 50 yards and find the staircase (or use the elevator). Head upstairs two floors to level 1 to see how the foundation of civilization laid in medieval times would launch the Renaissance. You'll spill out into Rooms 62-64b, labeled* Medieval & Renaissance, 300-1600. *Enter through Room 64b, where you'll find (hiding behind a partition on the left) the tiny, pocket-size...*

❼ Notebook by Leonardo da Vinci, *Codex Forster III,* 1490-1493

Leonardo da Vinci—painter, sculptor, engineer, musician, and scientist—epitomized the merging of art, knowledge, and science we

call the Renaissance. He recorded his observations and inventions in tiny notebooks like this. This particular codex (or bound manuscript) dates from years when he was living in Milan, shortly before undertaking his famous *Last Supper* fresco. He was always busy, but completed little from this time.

The book's contents are all over the map: meticulous sketches of the human head, diagrams illustrating nature's geometrical perfection, a horse's leg for a huge equestrian statue, and even drawings of the latest ballroom fashions. The adjacent computer lets you scroll through three of his notebooks and even flip his backwards handwriting to make it readable.

In Room 64a (off to the left), an exhibit shows works by the sculptor Donatello, who blazed the artistic path followed by his fellow Florentine Michelangelo. This all leads (in Room 63, at the opposite end of Room 64) to works showing the new wealth of Europe as it enters the modern age.

• *Return to the top of the stairs and look across at the* Korea *and* Cast Courts *signs opposite. To go there, descend to level 0. Cross the big sculpture hall (Room 50b), and find two huge courts, Rooms 46a and 46b, labeled...*

❽ The Cast Courts: Replicas of Famous Statues

These plaster-cast versions of famous statues allowed 19th-century art students who couldn't afford a rail pass to study the classics.

The statues were made by coating the original with a nonstick substance, then laying wet plaster strips over it that dried to form a mold, from which a plaster cast was made. They look solid but are very fragile. (For an overhead view of both galleries, go up the stairs at the Cast Courts entryway, and then come back down.)

• *Begin in Room 46a (on the left), with the gigantic column in two pieces.*

Trajan's Column: Rising 140 feet and decorated with a spiral relief of 2,500 figures trumpeting the exploits of the Roman Emperor Trajan (c. AD 100), this is a copy of the world's grandest column from antiquity. The original column still stands in Rome, but the V&A's version was cast from a copy in Paris. In fact, they had to cut it in half to fit it here.

The column's relief unfolds like a scroll, telling the story of Trajan's conquest of Dacia (modern-day Romania). It starts at the bottom (the half with the pedestal) with a trickle of water that becomes a river and soon picks up boats full of supplies. Then come the soldiers themselves, who spill out from the gates of the city. A river god surfaces to bless the journey. Along the way (second band), they build roads and forts to sustain the vast enterprise. Trajan himself (fourth band, in military skirt with toga over his arm) mounts a podium to fire up the troops. They hop into a Roman galley (fifth band) and head off to fight the valiant Dacians in the middle of a forest (eighth band). Finally, at the very top, the Romans hold a sacrifice to give thanks for the victory, while the captured armor is displayed on the pedestal.

Originally, the entire story was painted in bright colors. If you unwound the scroll, it would stretch the length of two football fields—it's far longer than the frieze around Athens' Parthenon.

Near Trajan's Column are several casts of knights and ladies on their backs, staring at the ceiling (in faded hues of red, gold, and blue). Some of these (near where you entered, top row, far end) are the **Tomb Effigies of Henry II and Family.** This was a remarkable and dysfunctional royal family. King Henry II (1133-1189)—Becket's murderer—lies alongside his wife and their children. Henry's wife, Eleanor of Aquitaine (the one reading a book while dead), was the ex-wife of the King of France and was renowned as Europe's most sophisticated lady. The wedding of Henry and Eleanor united their two families' large land holdings, creating an "England" that stretched as far down as southern France. It would eventually take the Hundred Years' War (1336-1453) to sort out the current border between England and France.

As king, Henry placed church courts under secular control, causing the rift that led to Becket's bloody murder. In Henry's old age, his children rebelled, taking arms against him for their slice of the royal pie. Henry's heir, Richard the Lionheart, famous as the good guy in the Robin Hood legend, was actually an absentee monarch—a French-speaking dandy allied with the King of France. Younger son John, the "evil" King John of the Robin Hood legend, became a tyrant, prompting English nobles to make him sign the document called the Magna Carta, which established the principle that even kings must follow the law. (The British Library has a copy of the Magna Carta—□ see the British Library Tour.)

• *Now cross over to Room 46b, where you'll see a very famous statue.*

Michelangelo's *David*: While *David* steals the show, he is surrounded by other great works from throughout Michelangelo's career—from youthful optimism *(David)*, to his never-finished masterpiece (statues from the tomb of Julius II, including *Moses* and two *Slaves*), to full-blown midlife crisis (while sculpting the brooding Medici Tomb statues of Lorenzo and Giuliano). Compare Michelangelo's monumental *David* with Donatello's girlish *David* (nearby), and see Ghiberti's bronze Baptistery doors, which inspired the Florentine Renaissance.

David was a gift from Tuscany to Queen Victoria, who immediately donated it to the museum. *David*'s giant clip-on fig leaf is usually hanging around somewhere nearby (look on the back side of the pedestal he's standing on). This is the actual fig leaf that was hung on him when modest aristocrats visited (it was "the Victorian Age," after all). On the wall above David's right shoulder, you might recognize a copy of Raphael's *School of Athens* painting, pairing the biggest players of the Renaissance with the stars of antiquity (the original is in Rome's Vatican Museums). With Michelangelo front and center, it hangs appropriately over his most famous statue.

• *From the Cast Courts entryway, turn right and head down the long hallway, past Asian art and the shop, then turn right into Room 42, which contains art of the Islamic Middle East.*

❾ Islamic Art

While owing much to Islam as a religion, Islamic art also reflected a sophisticated secular culture. Many Islamic artists expressed themselves with beautiful but functional objects.

In the center of the room is the 630-square-foot Ardabil Carpet (1539-1540). Its silk-thread underpinnings are topped by a dense wool pile made of 304 knots per square inch. (Carpet connoisseurs will nod approvingly at this impressively high KPI number.) Woven on a huge standing loom, it likely took a dozen workers years to make. In the center of the design is a yellow medallion ringed with ovals, supporting two hanging lamps. If you sat on the carpet near the smaller of the two lamps, you'd have the illusion of a symmetrical pattern. The carpet is illuminated on the hour and half-hour.

Also in the room are more carpets, ceramics (mostly blue-and-white or red-and-white), and glazed tile—all covered top to bottom in similarly complex patterns. The intricate interweaving, repetition, and unending lines suggest the complex, infinite nature of God (Allah).

You'll likely see only a few pictures of humans or animals—the Islamic religion reserves the creation of living beings to God alone. However, secular art for homes and palaces was not bound by this, and you may see realistic depictions of men and women enjoying a garden paradise, a symbol of the Muslim heaven.

Notice floral patterns (twining vines, flowers, arabesques) and geometric designs (stars, diamonds). But the most common pattern is calligraphy—elaborate lettering of an inscription in Arabic, the language of the Quran (and the lettering used even in non-Arabic languages). A quote from the Quran on a vase or lamp combines the power of the message with the beauty of the calligraphy.

• Return to the hall and continue on. In the hallway (technically "Room" 47b) is a glass case with a statue of...

❿ Shiva Nataraja, 12th Century

The Hindu god Shiva—one of the hundreds, if not thousands, of godlike incarnations of Hinduism's eternal being, Brahma—steps lively and creates the world by dancing. His four arms are busy creating, and he treads on the sleepy dwarf of ignorance.

This bronze statue, one of Hinduism's most popular, is loaded with symbolism, summing up where humans came from and where we're going. Surrounded by a ring of fire, Shiva crosses a leg in time to the music. Smiling serenely, he blesses with one hand, while another beats out the rhythm of life with a hand drum. The cobra draped over his arm symbolizes the *Kundalini Sakti*, the cosmic energy inside each of us that can, with the right training, uncoil and bring us to enlightenment.

As long as Shiva keeps dancing, the universe will continue. But Shiva also holds a flame, a reminder that, at the end of time, he will transform into his female alter ego, Kali, and destroy the world by fire, clearing the slate for another round of existence.

• Head through the doorway into the adjoining Room 41, labeled South Asia. *You'll run right into a glass case in the center of the room containing small items that were the...*

⓫ Possessions of Emperor Shah Jahan, r. 1628-1658

Look at the wine cup (made of white nephrite jade, 1657) and—around back—the cameo portrait and thumb ring that belonged to one of the world's most powerful men.

Shah Jahan—or "King of the World"—ruled the largest empire of the day, covering northern India, Pakistan, and Afghanistan. His Mughal Empire was descended from Genghis Khan and the Mongol horde, who conquered and then settled in central Asia and converted to Islam. Shah Jahan was known for his building projects, especially the Taj Mahal (see a picture of it

The British in India

December 31, 1600: The British East India Company—a multi-national trading company owned by stockholders—is founded with a charter from Queen Elizabeth I. They're given a virtual monopoly on trade with India.

1600s: The British trade peacefully with Indian locals on the coast, competing with France, Holland, and Portugal for access to spices, cotton, tea, indigo, and jute (for ropemaking).

1700s: As the Mughal (Islamic) Empire breaks down, Britain and France vie for trade ports and inland territory. By the 1750s, Britain is winning. Britain establishes itself in Bombay, Madras, and Calcutta. First they rule through puppet Mughal leaders, then dump local leaders altogether.

1800s: By midcentury, two-thirds of the subcontinent is under British rule, exporting opium and tea (transplanted from its native China) and importing British-made cloth. Britain tries to reform Indian social customs (such as outlawing widow suicides) with little long-lasting effect. They build railways, roads, and irrigation systems.

1857-1858: The "Indian Mutiny"—sparked by high taxes, British monopoly of trade, and a chafing against foreign rule—is the first of many uprisings that slowly erode British power.

1900s: Two world wars drain and distract Britain while Indians lobby for self-rule.

August 15, 1947: After a decade of peaceful protests led by Mahatma Gandhi, India gains its independence.

nearby), built as a mausoleum for his favorite wife, Mumtaz, who bore him 14 children before dying in childbirth.

His unsuccessful attempts to expand the empire drained the treasury. In his old age, his sons quarreled over the inheritance. Imprisoned by his sons in the Agra fort, Shah Jahan died gazing across the river at the Taj Mahal, where he, too, would be buried. India's glory days were ending. And then came the British.

• *At the far end of Room 41 (in a case facing the rear door) is the huge wood-carved...*

⑫ Tipu's Tiger, 1790s

This life-size robotic toy, once owned by an oppressed Indian sultan (see Tipu's portrait and belongings nearby), is perhaps better called "India's revenge." The Bengal tiger has a British redcoat down, sinking its teeth into his neck. When you turned the crank, the Brit's left arm would flail, and both he and the tiger would roar through organ pipes. (The mechanism still works.)

Tipu, the Sultan of Mysore (1750-1799), called himself the

"Tiger of Mysore." He was well educated in several languages and collected a library of 2,000 books. An enlightened ruler, he built roads and dams and promoted new technology. Tipu could see that India was being swallowed up by the all-powerful British East India Company. He allied himself with France and fought several successful wars against the British, but he was eventually defeated and forced to give up half his kingdom to them. Tipu was later killed by the Brits in battle (1799), his palace ransacked, and his possessions—including this toy—were taken, like much of India, by the British East India Company.

• *Backtrack out of Room 41 and turn right, then right again into Room 40. Here you'll find the...*

⓭ Fashion Galleries

Centuries of English fashion are corseted chronologically into 40 display cases along a runway. You'll see the evolution of fashion from ladies' underwear, hoop skirts, and rain gear to high-society evening wear, men's suits, and more. The mantua dress, on the far right, is an example of court couture from the mid-18th century. Temporary exhibits here usually enliven the displays. Circle the room and reminisce about old trends—and how some are becoming new again. For more on English fashion, visit the British Galleries (described later).

• *Directly across the hall from Room 40 is the cavernous Room 48a, filled with...*

⓮ Raphael's Tapestry Cartoons

For Christmas in 1519, Pope Leo X unveiled 10 new tapestries in the Sistine Chapel, designed by the famous artist Raphael. The project was one of the largest ever undertaken by a painter—it cost far more than Michelangelo's Sistine ceiling—and when it was done, the tapestries were a hit, inspiring princes across Europe to decorate their palaces in masterpieces of cloth.

The V&A owns seven of the full-size designs by Raphael that were used to produce the tapestries (approximately 13 by 17 feet, done in tempera on paper, now mounted on canvas). The cartoons were sent to factories in Brussels, cut into strips (see the lines), and

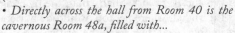

V&A MUSEUM

placed on the looms. The scenes are the reverse of the final product—lots of left-handed saints.

Raphael (1483-1520) chose scenes from the Acts of the Apostles—particularly of Peter and Paul, the two early saints most associated with Rome, the seat of the popes. Knowing where the tapestries were to be hung, Raphael was determined to top Michelangelo's famous Sistine ceiling, with its huge, dramatic figures and subtle color effects. He matched Michelangelo's

bodybuilder muscles (for example, the fishermen in *The Miraculous Draught of Fishes*), dramatic gestures, and reaction shots (as in the busy crowd scenes in *St. Paul Preaching in Athens*), and he exceeded Michelangelo in the subtleties of color.

Unfortunately, it was difficult to reproduce Raphael's painted nuances in the tapestry workshop. Traditional tapestries were simple, depicting either set patterns or block figures on a neutral background. Raphael challenged the Flemish weavers. Each brushstroke had to be reproduced by a colored thread woven horizontally. The finished tapestries (which are mostly still in the Vatican) were glorious, but these cartoons capture Raphael's original vision. If you'd like to compare them, notice that one cartoon *(The Miraculous Draught of Fishes)* is hanging opposite its tapestry; while impressive, the tapestry loses some of the subtlety of color and composition in the original.

• *From the Raphael room (48a), go up the staircase. At the top of the stairs (on level 1), turn left into Room 57. This is the heart of the British Galleries, featuring the Great Bed of Ware and Elizabethan miniatures.*

⑮ British Galleries

Room 57 covers the era of Queen Elizabeth I. Find rare miniature portraits—a popular item of the day—including Hilliard's oft-reproduced *Young Man Among Roses* miniature, capturing the romance of a Shakespeare sonnet. Also in the room are musical instruments and suits of armor—a love-and-war combination appropriate to the Elizabethan Age. Finally, there's the Great Bed of Ware. Built as a tourist-attracting gimmick by an English inn around

1600, this four-poster bed still wows. Look closely to see where couples notched their initials into the headboard and bedposts. You and six of your favorite friends could bed down here, taking a well-earned rest after this eclectic tour.

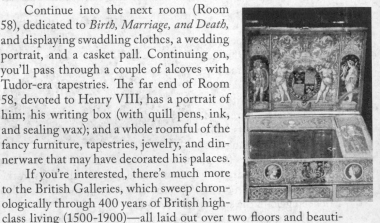

Continue into the next room (Room 58), dedicated to *Birth, Marriage, and Death,* and displaying swaddling clothes, a wedding portrait, and a casket pall. Continuing on, you'll pass through a couple of alcoves with Tudor-era tapestries. The far end of Room 58, devoted to Henry VIII, has a portrait of him; his writing box (with quill pens, ink, and sealing wax); and a whole roomful of the fancy furniture, tapestries, jewelry, and dinnerware that may have decorated his palaces.

If you're interested, there's much more to the British Galleries, which sweep chronologically through 400 years of British high-class living (1500-1900)—all laid out over two floors and beautifully described.

• *For now, pop out the doorway of Room 58. You'll notice we've come full circle: You're overlooking the Grand Entrance lobby. This tour is officially over. But if you'd like more suggestions, there's great stuff upstairs.*

⑯ Jewelry, Theater, Silver, and More

• *From the Grand Entrance lobby, pass through the shop, turn right into Room 24, and climb the staircase to level 2.*

Jewelry (Rooms 91-93): This collection is understandably popular. In one long, glittering gallery, you can trace the evolution of jewelry from ancient Egyptian, Greek, and Roman to the 20th century. The Art Nouveau style of Parisian jeweler Rene Lalique is hard not to love.

• *Exit the jewelry rooms at the far end and turn right down the corridor labeled* Leighton; *partway down on the left, you'll enter...*

Theater and Performance (Rooms 103-106): With artifacts

from ballet shoes to rock-and-roll tour posters, this exhibit records the history of live performance in the UK. Kids will enjoy the costumes from *The Lion King* and the dress-up costume box. Gen Xers will appreciate the Star Wars stormtrooper.

• *Exit the collection where you entered, turn right (into "Prints & Drawings"), then left to find...*

British Silver (Rooms 65-69): The displays in these galleries are bursting with flamboyant silver treasures dating from the 1600s to modern times, including teething rattles, gambling counters, punch bowls, and pitchers.

• *I'll leave you here (find exit stairs at the far end of Room 74), but there's plenty left to see. If you have stamina, use your V&A map to plot the rest of your Grand Tour of this museum.*

TATE BRITAIN TOUR

The National Gallery of British Art, otherwise known as the Tate Britain, features the world's best collection of British art—sweeping you from 1500 until today. This is people's art, with realistic paintings of Britons, their countryside, and scenes from their daily lives. What you won't see here are the fleshy goddesses, naked baby angels, and Madonna and Child altarpieces so popular elsewhere in Europe. The largely Protestant English abhorred the "graven images" of the wealthy Catholic world; many such images were even destroyed during the 16th-century Reformation. Protestants preferred portraits of flesh-and-blood English folk.

The Tate shows off Hogarth's stage sets, Gainsborough's ladies, Blake's angels, Constable's clouds, Turner's tempests, the naturalistic realism of the Pre-Raphaelites, and the camera-eye portraits of Hockney and Freud. Even if some of these names are new to you, don't worry. You'll likely see a few "famous" works you didn't know were British and exit the Tate Britain with at least one new favorite artist.

Be aware that this collection is characterized by constant churn—which pieces are on display, and where, changes all the time. This chapter isn't strictly a "tour" of the collection as it is a primer on British art—so that whatever state the Tate is in, you'll appreciate it.

Orientation

Cost: Free, £5 suggested donation; fee for special exhibits.
Hours: Daily 10:00-18:00, last entry 45 minutes before closing.
Information: +44 20 7887 8888, www.tate.org.uk.
Getting There: It's on the Thames River—on foot, it's just 15 minutes south of Big Ben. By **Tube,** ride to Pimlico station

and walk 10 minutes. The Thames Clippers' **Tate Boat** crosses from the Tate Modern (Bankside Pier) to the Tate Britain in 15 minutes (£9 one-way, departs every 30 minutes Mon-Fri 10:15-15:45, Sat-Sun 9:40-18:15). Or ride the **bus:** #87 leaves from the National Gallery and drops off in front of the Tate; #88 leaves from Oxford Circus, passes through Trafalgar Square and Whitehall, and drops off behind the museum; and #C10 conveniently connects this area to the Victoria Station hotel neighborhood.

Getting In: Enter on the west side of the building, at the Manton Entrance; here you'll find the coat check, information desk, and tickets for temporary exhibitions. Then make your way upstairs to tour the collection.

Visitor Information: Considering that exhibits are always changing, it's worth downloading the museum's helpful app (using the free Wi-Fi) for a current room-by-room guide. Paper maps may not be handed out; in a pinch, take a photo of the posted map with your phone.

Tours: Free **guided tours** are generally offered a few times daily; check the website for details.

Length of This Tour: Allow one hour.

Services: Bag and coat check are free.

Cuisine Art: The **$ Djanogly Café,** on the lower level on the way from the Manton Entrance to the main collection, has a cafeteria line with creative, well-priced meals.

Starring: Hogarth, Gainsborough, Reynolds, Blake, Constable, Pre-Raphaelites, and Turner.

Know Your Tates: Don't confuse the Tate Britain (British art) with the Tate Modern (on the South Bank of the Thames across from St. Paul's Cathedral).

ORIEN-TATE: GALLERY IN MOTION

This tour covers, in roughly chronological order, British paintings from 1500 to today. Remember: The Tate constantly rotates its vast collection of paintings, so it's difficult to predict exactly which works will be on display. Consider reading this chapter ahead of time as an overview of British art, then let the Tate surprise you with its current array of masterpieces.

The Tour Begins

Start upstairs, at the foyer of the Millbank entrance (the one that faces the Thames). Stand under the bright-white, glassed-in rotunda and look down the long central hall, usually adorned with sculpture or temporary installations.

Works from the early centuries are located in the west half of

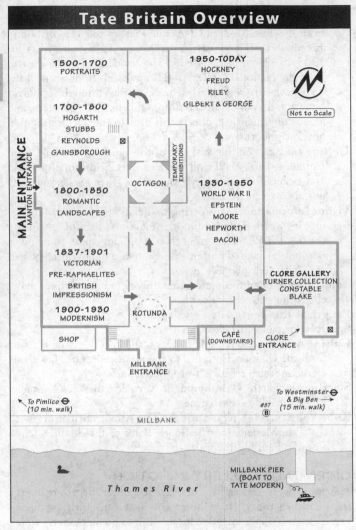

Tate Britain Overview

1500-1700
PORTRAITS

1700-1800
HOGARTH
STUBBS
REYNOLDS
GAINSBOROUGH

MAIN ENTRANCE
MANTON ENTRANCE

1800-1850
ROMANTIC
LANDSCAPES

OCTAGON

1837-1901
VICTORIAN
PRE-RAPHAELITES
BRITISH
IMPRESSIONISM

1900-1930
MODERNISM

ROTUNDA

SHOP

1950-TODAY
HOCKNEY
FREUD
RILEY
GILBERT & GEORGE

Not to Scale

TEMPORARY
EXHIBITIONS

1930-1950
WORLD WAR II
EPSTEIN
MOORE
HEPWORTH
BACON

CLORE GALLERY
TURNER COLLECTION
CONSTABLE
BLAKE

CAFÉ
(DOWNSTAIRS)

CLORE
ENTRANCE

MILLBANK
ENTRANCE

To Pimlico ⊖
(10 min. walk)

To Westminster ⊖
& Big Ben →
(15 min. walk)

#87
Ⓑ

MILLBANK

Thames River

MILLBANK PIER
(BOAT TO
TATE MODERN)

the building (to your left), and 20th-century art is in the east half. Also to the east, in the adjacent Clore Gallery, are the works of J. M. W. Turner, and often art by John Constable and William Blake.

• *Let's start our tour with Britain's earliest paintings. Head down the long central hall to the far-left end. Near the "Meeting Point," you'll find the doorway leading into the first room. As you enter, you'll see the date 1540-1650 on the floor. (The Tate organizes its rooms by date.) Step into the beginnings of British painting.*

1500-1700: PORTRAITS OF LORD AND LADY WHOEVERTHEYARE

In the first room (with art from the mid-16th century), you'll likely see lots of portraits. Stuffy portraits of a beef-fed society try to turn crude country nobles into refined men and delicate women. Men in ruffled collars clutch symbols of power. Women in ruffled collars, puffy sleeves, and elaborately patterned dresses display their lily-white complexions, turning their pinkies out.

English country houses often had a long hall built specially to hang family portraits like these. You could stroll along and see your noble forebears looking down their noses at you. Britain's upper crust had little interest in art other than as a record of themselves along with their possessions—their wives, children, jewels, furs, ruffled collars, swords, and guns. (Pre-Facebook, what option did they have?)

Continue into the adjoining Room 1650-1730, where you'll see more portraits, but in a slightly different style. Whereas the portraits from the 1500s are stern and dignified, the 1600s room exudes a more relaxed elegance, with leafy backdrops, bigger hair, and more décolletage.

• *In the next room (1730–1760), there's another step in the evolution.*

1700-1800: ART BLOSSOMS

With peace at home (under three King Georges), a strong overseas economy, and a growing urban center in London, England's artistic life began to bloom. As the English grew more sophisticated, so did their portraits. Painters branched out into other subjects, capturing slices of everyday life. The Royal Academy added a veneer of classical Greece to even the simplest subjects.

The era's most distinctive artist—William Hogarth—added a sober dose of realism to his canvases.

William Hogarth

In his self-portrait alongside his dog (*The Painter and his Pug*, 1745) Hogarth gazes directly out, observing the world and ready to put it on display, warts and all.

A born Londoner, Hogarth loved every gritty aspect of the big city. You'd find him in seedy pubs and brothels, at the half-price ticket booth in Leicester Square, at prizefights, cockfights, duels, and public executions—all with sketchbook in hand. An 18th-century

Charles Dickens, he exposed the hypocrisy of fat-bellied squires, vain ladies, and gluttonous priests. He also gave the upper classes a glimpse into the hidden poverty of "merry olde England"—poor soldiers with holes in their stockings, overworked servants, and unwed mothers.

And Hogarth loved the theater. "My picture is my stage," he said, "and my men and women my players." The curtain goes up, and we see one scene that tells a whole story, often satirizing English high society. The London theater scene came into its own during Hogarth's generation. He often painted series based on popular plays of the time.

Hogarth's portraits (and self-portraits) are unflinchingly honest, quite different from the powdered-wig fantasies of his contemporaries. Because Hogarth was an accomplished engraver, his works could be mass-produced and widely distributed, giving Londoners a sense of their city and themselves.

· *The following artists might be displayed in this room, or in either of the next two rooms (1760-1780 and 1780-1810). First, go on a scavenger hunt for a horse, which is probably by...*

George Stubbs

Stubbs was the Michelangelo of horse painters. He understood these creatures from the inside out, having dissected them in his studio. He even used machinery to prop the corpses up into lifelike poses. He painted the horses first on a blank canvas, then filled in the background landscape around them (notice the heavy outlines that make them stand out clearly from the countryside). The result is both incredibly natural—from the veins in their noses to their freshly brushed coats—and geometrically posed.

· *Not every British artist painted unvarnished reality. Also in this stretch of rooms, find paintings by two masters of the aristocratic style.*

Sir Joshua Reynolds and the Grand Manner

Real life wasn't worthy of a painting. So said Sir Joshua Reynolds, the pillar of Britain's Royal Academy. Instead, people, places, and things had to be gussied up with Greek columns, symbolism, and great historic moments, ideally from classical Greece.

In his portraits, he'd pose Lady Bagbody like the Medici Venus, or Lord Milquetoast like Apollo Belvedere. In landscapes you get Versailles-type settings of classical monuments amid perfectly manicured greenery. Inspired by Rembrandt, Reynolds sometimes used dense, clotted paint to capture the look of the Old Masters.

This art was meant to elevate the viewer, to appeal to his rational nature and fill him with noble sentiment. Sir Joshua Reynolds stood for all that was upright, tasteful, rational, brave, clean, reverent, and...zzzzzzz...

Thomas Gainsborough

Gainsborough showcased the elegant, educated women of his generation. He portrayed them as they wished to see themselves: a

feminine ideal, patterned after fashion magazines. The cheeks are rosy, the poses relaxed and S-shaped, the colors brighter and more pastel, showing the influence of the refined French culture of the court at Versailles. His ladies tiptoe gracefully toward us, with clear, Ivory-soap complexions that stand out from the swirling greenery of English gardens. (Though he painted portraits, he longed to do landscapes.) Gainsborough worked hard to prettify his subjects, but the results were always natural and never stuffy.

• *By the 1800s, British life was undergoing fundamental changes that would shape their preferences in art.*

1800-1850: THE INDUSTRIAL REVOLUTION

Newfangled inventions were everywhere. Railroads laced the land. You could fall asleep in Edinburgh and wake up in London, a trip that used to take days or weeks. But along with technology came factories coating towns with soot, urban poverty, regimentation, and clock-punching. Machines replaced honest laborers, and once-noble Man was viewed as a naked ape.

Strangely, you'll see little of the modern world in paintings of the time—except in reaction to it. Many artists rebelled against "progress" and the modern world. They escaped the dirty cities to commune with nature. Or they found a new spirituality in intense human emotions, expressed in dramatic paintings of episodes from history.

• *In rooms dedicated to the 1800s, you may see a number of big paintings devoted to the power of nature.*

"Romantic" Landscapes: Art and the Sublime

Artists of the Romantic style saw the most intense human emotions reflected in the drama and mystery of nature. Some Romantic artists produced huge, colorful landscapes depicting storms, burn-

ing sunsets, towering clouds, and crashing waves, all dwarfing puny humans and evoking awe mixed with terror.

History paintings reflected great moments from the past, from ancient Greece to medieval knights, and from Napoleon to Britain's battles abroad. These were seen as the classiest form of art, combining the high drama of heroic acts with refined technique.

Other artists made supernatural, religious fantasy-scapes. God is found within nature, and nature is charged with the grandeur and power of God.

• *You'll eventually spill into the large Room 1840-1890, plastered with paintings top to bottom. Here you'll often find some of the Tate Britain's best-known pieces, from when the British Empire was at its peak. Linger and find a favorite of your own.*

1837-1901: THE VICTORIAN ERA

In the world's wealthiest nation, the prosperous middle class dictated taste in art. They admired paintings that were realistic (showcasing the artist's talent and work ethic), depicting Norman Rockwell-style slices of everyday life.

We see families and ordinary people eating, working, and relaxing. Some paintings tug at the heartstrings, with scenes of parting couples, the grief of death, or the joy of families reuniting. Dramatic scenes from classical (Chaucer and Shakespeare) and popular literature get the heart beating. There's the occasional touching look at the plight of the honest poor, reminiscent of Dickens. Many paintings warn us to be good little boys and girls by showing the consequences of a life of sin. And then there are the puppy dogs with sad eyes.

The Pre-Raphaelites

You'll see medieval damsels in dresses and knights in tights, legendary lovers from poetry, and even a very human Virgin Mary as a delicate young woman. The women wear flowing dresses and have long, wavy hair and delicate, elongated, curving bodies. Beautiful.

Overdosed with the gushy sentimentality of their day, a band of 20-year-old artists—including Sir John Everett Millais, Dante Gabriel Rossetti, and William Holman Hunt—said "Enough!" and dedicated themselves to creating less saccharine art. Their Pre-Raphaelite Brotherhood (you may see the initials P.R.B. by the artist's signature) returned to a style "pre-Raphael"—that is, "medieval" in its simple style, in its melancholy mood, and often in its subject matter.

"Truth to Nature" was their slogan. Like the Impressionists who followed them, they donned their scarves, barged out of the stuffy studio, and set up outdoors, painting trees, streams, and people, like scientists on a field trip. Still, they often captured nature with such a close-up clarity that it's downright unnatural. And despite the Pre-Raphaelite claim to paint life just as it is, this is so beautiful it hurts.

This is art from the cult of femininity, worshipping Woman's haunting beauty, compassion, and depth of soul (proto-feminism or nouveau-chauvinism?). The artists' wives and lovers were their models and muses, and the art echoed their love lives. The people are surrounded by nature at its most beautiful, with every detail painted crystal clear. Even without the people, there is a mood of melancholy.

The Pre-Raphaelites hated overacting. Their subjects—even in the face of great tragedy, high passions, and moral dilemmas—bare-

ly raise an eyebrow. Outwardly, they're reflective, accepting their fate. But their sinuous postures speak volumes—with lovers swooning into each other, and parting lovers swooning apart. These volumes are footnoted by the small objects with symbolic importance placed around them: red flowers denoting passion, lilies for purity, pets for fidelity, and so on.

The colors—greens, blues, and reds—are bright and clear, with everything evenly lit, so that we see every detail. To get the luminous color, some painted a thin layer of bright paint over a pure white, still-wet undercoat, which subtly "shines" through. These canvases radiate a pure spirituality, like stained-glass windows.

In *The Lady of Shalott* (1888), John William Waterhouse depicts the dramatic climax of a legendary tale. The lady had spent her whole life shut up in a castle near King Arthur's Camelot, forbidden to look outside, upon pain of death. But one day, the handsome knight Lancelot rode by. She was so smitten that she couldn't help but look. Now she's boarded a boat, releasing the mooring chain, as she sets off into the unknown to find her beloved, whatever the cost.

The whole scene looks medieval, yet it was painted during an Industrial Age when Britain was leading the world in new technologies like electricity and trains.

Stand for a while and enjoy the exquisite realism and human emotions of these Victorian-era works...flesh-and-blood people painted realistically. Get your fill, because beloved Queen Victoria is about to check out, the modern world is coming, and, with it, new art to express modern attitudes.

• *In the next few rooms of this wing (1840-1890, 1890-1900, and 1900-1910) you may find hints of...*

British Impressionism

Realistic British art stood apart from the modernist trends in France, but some influences drifted across the Channel (Rooms 1890 and 1900). John Singer Sargent (American-born) studied with Parisian Impressionists, learning the thick, messy brushwork and play of light at twilight. James Tissot used Degas' snapshot technique to capture a crowded scene from an odd angle. And James McNeill Whistler (born in America, trained in Paris, lived in London) composed his paintings like music—see some of his paintings' titles. These collages of shapes and colors please the eye like a song tickles the ear. Whistler signed his paintings with his initials in the shape of a butterfly. You may also see sophisticated works by London's  own Bloomsbury Group, who put a British spin on French Post-Impressionism.

• *In the final room of this wing (1910-1930), you'll start to see some...*

1900-1930: BRITISH MODERNISM

World War I, in which Britain lost a million men, cast a long shadow over the land. Artists expressed the horror of war, particularly of dehumanizing battles pitting powerful machines against puny human pawns. At the same time, British art mirrored many of the trends and "-isms" pioneered in Paris. You'll see Cubism like Picasso's, abstract art like Mondrian's, and so on. But British artists also continued the British tradition of realistic paintings of people and landscapes. (Note: You'll find 20th-century artists' work both here in the Tate Britain and in the Tate Modern.)

• *Now cross over the central hall to the east wing. Here you'll find art that originates from well into the 20th century. The rooms are even less chronological than the west wing; use your museum app to find what's currently on display, and look for some of the following trends and artists.*

1930-1950: WORLD WAR II

As two world wars whittled down the powerful British Empire, it remained a major cultural force. And yet, the trauma of total war lingered.

• *If British painters were less than avant-garde, their sculptors were cutting edge. Be sure to seek out the distinctive statues of...*

Henry Moore

Moore carved the human body with the epic scale and restless poses of Michelangelo but with the crude rocks and simple lines of the primitives. Twice a week, as a young man, he went to the British Museum to sketch ancient statues, especially reclining ones (as in the Parthenon pediment). Later, in Paris, he came across plaster casts of the recumbent Mayan god, Chac Mool. Moore's statues—mostly female, mostly reclining—catch the primitive power of carved stone. Moore almost always carved with his own hands (unlike, say, Rodin, who modeled a small clay figure and let assistants chisel the real thing), capturing the human body in a few simple curves, with minimal changes to the rock itself.

The statues do look vaguely like what their titles say, but it's the stones themselves that are really interesting. Notice the texture and graininess of these mini Stonehenges; feel the weight, the space they take up, and how the rock forms intermingle.

During World War II, Moore passed time in the bomb shelters sketching mothers with babes in arms, a theme found in later works.

Barbara Hepworth

Hepworth's small-scale carvings in stone and wood—like "mini Moores"—make even holes look interesting. Though they're not exactly realistic, it isn't hard to imagine them being inspired by, say, a man embracing a woman (she called it "sex harmony"), or the shoreline encircling a bay near her Cornwall-coast home, or a cliff penetrated by a cave—that is, two forms intermingling.

Jacob Epstein

While his earlier works (which you may have seen in the opposite hall) are more traditionally figurative, his later works are gleaming, abstract statues that suggest mangled half-human/half-machine forms—reflecting the horrors of his time.

Francis Bacon

Bacon has become Britain's best-known 20th-century painter, exemplifying the angst of the early post-WWII years.

With a stiff upper lip, Britain survived the Blitz, World War II, and the loss of hundreds of thousands of men—but at war's end, the bottled-up horror came rushing out. Bacon's 1945 exhibition, opening just after Holocaust details began surfacing, stunned London with its unmitigated ugliness.

His deformed half-humans/half-animals—caged in a claustrophobic room, with twisted hunk-of-meat bodies and quadriplegic, smudged-mouth helplessness—can do nothing but scream in anguish and frustration. The scream becomes a blur, as though it goes on forever.

Bacon, largely self-taught, uses "traditional" figurativism, painting somewhat recognizable people and things. His subjects express the existential human predicament of being caught in a world not of your making, isolated and helpless to change it.

1950-2000: MODERN WORLD

No longer a world power, Britain in the Swinging '60s became a major exporter of pop culture. British art's traditional strengths—realism, portraits, landscapes, and slice-of-life scenes—were redone in the modern style (Room 1950 and on). Be aware that of all the Tate's changing displays, the modern collection changes the most. If these particular artists aren't on display, other equally deserving artists will be.

David Hockney

The "British Andy Warhol"—who is bleach-blond, horn-rimmed, gay, and famous—paints "pop"-ular culture with photographic realism. Large, airy canvases of L.A. swimming pools, double portraits of his friends in their stylish homes, or mundane scenes from the artist's own life capture the superficial materialism of the 1970s and 1980s. (Is he satirizing or glorifying it by painting it on a monumental scale with colorful detail?)

Hockney saturates the canvas with bright (acrylic) paint, eliminating any haze, making distant objects as clear and bright as close ones. This technique, combined with his slightly simplified "cut-out" figures, gives his paintings the flat look of a billboard.

Lucian Freud

Sigmund's grandson (who emigrated from Nazi Germany as a boy) puts every detail on the couch for analysis, then reassembles them all into surprisingly realistic works. His subjects, slightly on edge, look you right in the eye. Even the plants create an ominous mood. Everything is in sharp focus (unlike in real life, where you concentrate on one thing while your peripheral vision is blurred). His thick brushwork is especially good at capturing the pallor of British flesh.

In the great tradition of British portrait painting, Freud completed an unflinching (and controversial) portrait of Queen Elizabeth in 2001.

Bridget Riley
The pioneer of Op Art paints patterns of lines and alternating colors that make the eye vibrate (the way a spiral will "spin") when you stare at them. These obscure, scientific experiments in human optics suddenly became trendy in the psychedelic, cannabis-fueled 1960s. Like, wow.

Gilbert and George
The Siegfried and Roy of art satirize the "Me Generation" and its shameless self-marketing by portraying their nerdy, three-piece-suited selves on the monumental scale normally dedicated to kings, popes, and saints.

• *When you've finished browsing through the 20th-century art, make your way back to Room 1940-1950, which you passed through earlier. This is the entrance to the Clore Gallery, where you'll find art by Turner, as well as—usually—Constable and Blake.*

CLORE GALLERY
The Turner Collection
The Tate Britain has the world's best collection of works by J. M. W. Turner (1775-1851). Walking through his life's work, you can trace his progression from a painter of realistic historical scenes, through his wandering years, to Impressionist paintings of color-and-light patterns.

As you explore the collection, you'll watch Turner's style evolve from clear-eyed realism to hazy proto-Impressionism. You'll also see how Turner dabbled in different subjects: landscapes, seascapes, Roman ruins, snapshots of Venice, and so on. (While some of the specific paintings I refer to may not be on display, similar ones will be in their place.)

• *A good starting point for Turner is his...*

Self-Portrait as a Young Man: The son of a Covent Garden barber now dresses like a gentleman. His clear, realistic painting style caught the public's fancy. The full-frontal pose and intense gaze of this portrait show a young man ready to take on the world.

Royal Academy Years: Trained in the Reynolds school of grandiose epics, Turner painted the obligatory big canvases of great moments in history—*The Destruction of Sodom, Hannibal and His Army Crossing the Alps, The Lost ATM Card, Jason and the Argonauts,* and various shipwrecks. Not content to crank them out in the traditional staid manner, he sets them in expansive landscapes. Nature's stormy mood mirrors the human events, but is so grandiose it dwarfs them.

This is a theme we'll see throughout his works: The forces of nature—the burning sun, swirling clouds, churning waves, gathering storms, and the weathering of time—overwhelm men and wear down the civilizations they build.

Travels with Turner: Turner's true love was nature—he was a born hobo. Oblivious to the wealth and fame that his early paintings gave him, he set out traveling—mostly on foot—throughout England and the Continent, with a rucksack full of sketch pads and painting gear. He sketched the English countryside—not green, leafy, and placid as so many others had done, but churning in motion, hazed over by a burning sunset.

He found the "sublime" not in the studio or in church, but in the overwhelming power of nature. The landscapes throb with life and motion. He sets Constable's clouds on fire.

Italy's Landscape and Ruins: With a Rick Steves guidebook in hand, Turner visited the great museums of Italy, drawing inspiration from the Renaissance masters. He painted the classical monuments and Renaissance architecture. He copied masterpieces, admired the works of the French classicist Claude Lorrain, and fused a great variety of styles—a true pan-European vision. Turner's Roman ruins are not grand; they're dwarfed by the landscape around them and eroded by swirling, misty, luminous clouds.

Stand close to a big canvas of Roman ruins, close enough so that it fills your whole field of vision. Notice how the buildings seem to wrap around you. Turner was a master of using multiple perspectives to draw the viewer in. On the one hand, you're right in the thick of things, looking "up" at the tall buildings. Then again, you're looking "down" on the distant horizon, as though standing on a mountaintop.

Venice: I know what color the palazzo is. But what color is it at sunset? Or through the filter of the watery haze that hangs over Venice? Can I paint the glowing haze itself? Maybe if I combine two different colors and smudge the paint on...

Venice stoked Turner's lust for reflected, golden sunlight. You'll see both finished works and unfinished sketches...uh, which is which?

Seascapes: The ever-changing sea was his specialty, with waves, clouds, mist, and sky churning and mixing together, all driven by the same forces.

Turner used oils like many painters use watercolors. First, he'd lay down a background (a "wash") of large patches of color, then he'd add a few dabs of paint to suggest a figure. (Some artists might use pencil lines to sketch out their figures, but Turner avoided that.) The final product lacked photographic clarity but showed the power and constant change in the forces of nature. He was perhaps the most prolific painter ever, with some 2,000 finished paintings and 20,000 sketches and watercolors.

Late Works: The older Turner got, the messier both he and his paintings became. He was wealthy, but he died in a run-down dive, where he'd set up house with a prostitute. Yet the colors are brighter and the subjects less pessimistic than in the dark and brooding early canvases. His last works—whether landscape, religious, or classical scenes—are a blur and swirl of colors in

motion, lit by the sun or a lamp burning through the mist. Even Turner's own creations were finally dissolved by the swirling forces of nature.

These paintings are "modern" in that the subject is less important than the style. You'll have to read the title to "get" it. You could argue that an Englishman helped invent Impressionism a generation before Monet and his ilk boxed the artistic ears of Paris in the 1880s. Turner's messy use of paint to portray reflected light "Chunneled" its way to France to inspire the Impressionists.

• *Usually one room of the Clore Gallery is dedicated to Turner's great rival and contemporary...*

John Constable

Constable (1776-1837) brought painting back into the real world. Although the Royal Academy thought Nature needed makeup, Constable thought she was just fine. He painted the English landscape as it was—realistically, without idealizing it. With simple earth tones he caught leafy green trees, gathering gray skies, brown country lanes, and rivers with the color of the clouds reflected in them. Many details came from actual landscapes and villages from his childhood roots in Suffolk.

Clouds are Constable's trademark. Appreciate the effort involved in sketching ever-changing cloud patterns for hours on end—the mix of dark clouds and white clouds, cumulus and stratus, the colors of sunset. A generation before the Impressionists, he actually set up his easel outdoors and painted on the spot, a painstaking process before the invention of ready-made paints-in-a-tube (about 1850).

It's rare to find a Constable (or any British) landscape that doesn't have the mark of man in it—a cottage, hay cart, field hand, or a country road running through the scene. For him, the English countryside and its people were one.

In his later years, Constable's canvases became bigger, the style more "Impressionistic" (messier brushwork), and he worked more from memory than observation.

Constable's commitment to unvarnished nature wasn't fully recognized in his lifetime, and he was forced to paint portraits for his keep. The neglect caused him to ask a friend, "Can it therefore be wondered at that I paint continual storms?"

• *The final artist on our tour is also usually displayed either in or near the Turner section—look (or ask) around to find the otherworldly domain of...*

William Blake

At the age of four, Blake (1757-1827) saw the face of God. A few years later, he ran across a flock of angels swinging in a tree. Twenty years later, he was living in a run-down London flat with an illiterate wife, scratching out a thin existence as an engraver. But even in this squalor, ignored by all but a few fellow artists, he still had his heavenly visions, and he described them in poems, paintings, drawings, and prints.

One of the original space cowboys, Blake also was a unique artist, often classed with the Romantics because he painted in a fit of ecstatic inspiration rather than by studied technique. He painted angels, not the dull material world. While Britain was conquering the world with guns and nature with machines, and while his fellow Londoners were growing rich, fat, and self-important, Blake  turned his gaze inward, illustrating the glorious visions of the soul.

Blake's work hangs in a darkened room to protect his watercolors from deterioration. Enter his mysterious world and let your pupils dilate opium-wide.

His pen and watercolor sketches glow with an unearthly aura. In visions of the Christian heaven or Dante's hell, his figures have superhero musculature. The colors are almost translucent.

Blake saw the material world as bad, trapping the divine spark inside each of our bodies and keeping us from true communion with God. Blake's prints illustrate his views on the ultimate weakness of material, scientific man. Despite their Greek-god anatomy, his men look noble but tragically lost.

Blake's work was enormously influential on other artists and thinkers. He helped elevate British art from mundane portraits to the realm of the sublime.

A famous poet as well as painter, Blake summed up his distrust of the material world in a poem addressed to "The God of this World"—that is, Satan:

Tho' thou art Worship'd by the Names Divine
Of Jesus and Jehovah, thou art still
The Son of Morn in weary Night's decline,
The lost Traveller's Dream under the Hill.

REST OF THE MUSEUM

You've finished your walk through 500 years of British art. We've gone from Hogarth to Hockney, from Constable's placid landscapes to Turner's churning scenes, from Pre-Raphaelite fantasies to Blake's inner visions, from realistic portraits to...realistic portraits.

But the Tate's great strength is championing contemporary British art in special exhibitions; some are free and others charge admission. Explore the cutting-edge art from one of the world's thriving cultural capitals: London.

Or, enough Tate? Great. It's late.

EAST END WALK

From Spitalfields Market to Liverpool Street Station

London's East End is one of the city's most painfully hip post-Soho neighborhoods, pulsing with foodie hot spots and vibrant street art. But in centuries past, it was a different story. In 1888, this is where Jack the Ripper gruesomely slayed several young women, creating a sensation that still titillates travelers today. The neighborhood has also been the entry point for many immigrants to London—from French Protestants, to Ashkenazi Jews, to Bangladeshi refugees.

This walk through the heart of the East End basically traces a big rectangle—from Liverpool Street Station to Brick Lane and back. We'll dip into several colorful markets: Spitalfields, Truman, and Petticoat Lane. We'll pass by several Jack the Ripper sights (fascinating history, though frankly there's not much to see). And we'll stroll through the curry-scented streets of "Banglatown."

The East End is a neighborhood in transition—a battle zone between the 19th century and the 21st century. We'll see old brick buildings alongside glassy new offices, and trendy restaurants amid the clamor of new construction. The East End Preservation Society is working overtime to protect and preserve what it can of the old East End. It's fascinating to be an eyewitness to this complicated corner of the city just as it reinvents itself—again.

Orientation

Length of This Walk: About an hour. Allow more time on Sunday (when markets enliven and congest Brick Lane).

When to Go: I prefer to start around 16:00, to have time to see Old Spitalfields Market before vendors begin to close up shop, then hang around for dinner. Alternatively, start in the late morning if you want to hit all three markets and be done by lunch. The area is most vivid on Saturday and especially

Sunday, when the markets thrive (for more on the markets, see page 461).

Getting There: Ride the Tube to Liverpool Street.

Spitalfields Market: Sun-Fri 10:00-18:00—but vendors begin shutting down around 17:00, Sat from 11:00.

Christ Church: Generally Mon-Fri 10:00-16:00, Sun from 13:00, closed Sat for private events.

Truman and Brick Lane Markets: Busiest Sun 9:00-17:00, some activity Sat 11:00-18:00, no formal market Mon-Fri but still bustling with shops.

Petticoat Lane Market: Full market Sun 9:00-14:00, sometimes later; smaller markets on Wentworth Street Mon-Fri 9:00-14:00; no market Sat.

Eateries: Good eateries abound (for recommendations, see page 437).

Starring: Jack the Ripper history in London's old immigrant/industrial area; the curry houses of Banglatown; a variety of markets (glitzy Spitalfields and ragtag Petticoat Lane); and hipster foodie opportunities galore.

The Walk Begins

• *Arriving by Tube at the Liverpool Street stop, go upstairs to the train station, and follow signs to exit to* Bishopsgate (East). *You'll take a "subway" (Brit-speak for an underground passageway) beneath the street and pop out on Bishopsgate, facing the train station. Turn right (north) and walk two blocks to the glassy, modern NatWest building; just before it, turn right on Brushfield Street. Head toward the steeple of Christ Church, pausing after about a half-block at a towering statue of a goat on a pillar.*

❶ Spitalfields Market

You're approaching one of London's most thriving new/old market halls. A marketplace was first established here—just outside the walls of The City—in 1638; the market halls were modernized in the late 19th century, then renovated again in the early 21st century.

The statue is titled simply *I Goat* (by Kenny Hunter, 2010). According to the artist, the goat—resilient, yet the first to be sacrificed in hard times—is a poignant symbol for the many immigrants who have shaped the East End. For instance, the traditional big market day here is Sunday, thanks to Jewish immigrants, who needed the market to reopen after the Sabbath (Saturday) closure.

From the goat, angle left into the modern, glassy part of the market. It's a world of colorful restaurants, shops, and—on many days—market stalls selling upscale crafts, designer clothes,

EAST END

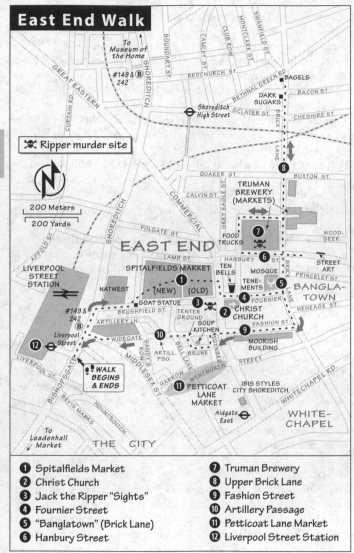

East End Walk

To Museum of the Home

#149 & 242

Shoreditch High Street

☠ Ripper murder site

N

200 Meters
200 Yards

EAST END

LIVERPOOL STREET STATION

NATWEST

SPITALFIELDS MARKET

GOAT STATUE

#149 & 242

Liverpool Street

ARTILLERY LN.

WIDEGATE

WALK BEGINS & ENDS

To Leadenhall Market

THE CITY

BAGELS

DARK SUGARS

TRUMAN BREWERY (MARKETS)

FOOD TRUCKS

STREET ART

WOOD-SEER

TEN BELLS

TENE-MENTS

MOSQUE

BANGLA-TOWN

CHRIST CHURCH

TENTER GROUND

SOUP KITCHEN

FASHION ST.

MOORISH BUILDING

ARTILL. PSG.

BRUNE

Petticoat Lane Market

IBIS STYLES CITY SHOREDITCH

Aldgate East

WHITE-CHAPEL

❶ Spitalfields Market	❼ Truman Brewery
❷ Christ Church	❽ Upper Brick Lane
❸ Jack the Ripper "Sights"	❾ Fashion Street
❹ Fournier Street	❿ Artillery Passage
❺ "Banglatown" (Brick Lane)	⓫ Petticoat Lane Market
❻ Hanbury Street	⓬ Liverpool Street Station

collectables, and vintage curiosities. This first section of the market feels modern and a bit sterile, dominated by chains. Eventually, as you bear left past the vendors, you'll reach the yellow-brick Old Spitalfields Market, under the original glass-and-steel roof (from 1876). Here you'll find one-off arts and crafts and an array of food stands (for more on eating here, see page 437).

• *Exit the market at the east end, where you can't miss the pointy spire of...*

❷ Christ Church

This stony church, with its towering 225-foot steeple, has a mysterious heritage. Many find occult symbolism in its curious design (without a cross on top). The church interior dates to 1711. That's when Queen Anne decided to build a place for the "God-less thousands who had no place to worship"—meaning to give immigrants a proper Protestant place to worship. Its stripped-down design suited Protestant tastes: simple wood paneling and whitewashed walls and columns. Even the frilly Corinthian column capitals and ceiling decorations are uniformly whitewashed. (The fine 19th-century stained-glass windows above the altar were added during the

"Romantic Age.") Look up to find the coat of arms of the UK: the lion and unicorn and motto *Dieu et Mon Droit*—"God and my right." Downstairs in the crypt is a modern café (with clean WCs).

• *Christ Church was ground zero for London's most famous serial killer.*

❸ Jack the Ripper "Sights"

In the autumn of 1888, several gruesome murders were committed within a few blocks of Christ Church. Many witnesses pinpointed the time of the crimes by remembering the church bells' chimes.

This was the decade of Sherlock Holmes and Dr. Jekyll and Mr. Hyde, when London was still a Dickensian tale of two cities. In the wee hours, a murderer slit the throats and cut out the guts of his victims—all women who lived and worked here on the poor and wretched side of town. London newspapers dubbed the killer "Jack the Ripper" and made a fortune sensationalizing the weeks-long murder spree.

The Ten Bells pub (to the left of the church) was the hangout of several of Jack the Ripper's victims, and criminologists speculate that Jack himself likely came here. The pub, established in 1753, is still a classic public house, where humble working folk can get out of their cramped apartments and enjoy a beer in a fancy living room setting.

The most heinous of the Ripper's crimes was committed about 50 yards directly opposite

Christ Church (though no actual building exists today). It was here that Mary Jane Kelly—a young Irish woman said to love drinking and singing Irish songs—was murdered inside her tiny apartment. The Ripper had several hours alone with the victim, and her body was left in a horribly mutilated state.

• *Another Ripper murder occurred about 200 yards north of Christ Church. We'll pass by there later in the walk. For now, start walking east, between the Ten Bells pub and Christ Church, down...*

❹ Fournier Street

The street still looks much like it did in Jack's day: lined with old lantern-like lampposts and brick apartment buildings. These are classic "tenements." (Though the word "tenement" now carries a negative connotation, it originally described any urban apartment building.) In the 1700s these were home to many Huguenots—French-Protestant religious refugees who settled here as silk weavers.

"Fournier" is one of many street names here with French origins—keep an eye out for others. It's not hard to imagine how this gaslit street would have looked on a foggy night in Jack the Ripper's time. Back then, most of London resembled this street—built of brick. The city's bricks were manufactured in factories right here in this gritty neighborhood, near the street called...Brick Lane.

• *Follow this line of former weaving houses to the end of the street, marked by the modern metal minaret of a mosque. At the intersection with Brick Lane, you're suddenly immersed in...*

❺ "Banglatown" (Brick Lane)

The neighborhood around Brick Lane has been dubbed "Banglatown" for its high concentration of Bangladeshi residents. Many arrived here as refugees of Bangladesh's horrific War of Independence from Pakistan in 1971. Britain, which had once counted Bangladesh among its colonial possessions (1757-1947), took them in.

The neighborhood **mosque,** Jamme Masjid, is housed in a classic old brick building topped with a modern minaret. This building has a history as dynamic as London itself: It was built as a French Huguenot chapel, became a Methodist chapel, was used as a Jewish synagogue, and was converted into a mosque in 1976.

Turn left and wander north down Brick Lane. It's a world of Bangladeshi and Indian restaurants and pungent food markets catering to locals. This stretch of road has been called **"the curry capital of Europe."** Neon signs advertise cheap specials, and awards hang in the windows proclaiming "best," "master," and "champion." Out front, pitchmen jockey for your business. The slightest hesitation on your part will result in an offer of a 20 percent discount. This is a great place to sample "Ruby Murray"—Cockney rhyming slang for "curry." Just like the US has its mash-up of cuisines called "Tex-Mex," England has "Balti." This is "Indian" food adapted to suit English tastes. It's so popular here that chicken tikka masala has replaced fish-and-chips as the national dish.

It's not all curry houses—despite the foodie pilgrims (who are very confused about all those old-school Bangladeshi restaurants), Brick Lane is still the main drag of a thriving local community. Strolling a couple of blocks, peek into barbershops, textile warehouses, and spice shops. Price an apartment at the real-estate office. (It may be more than you'd think—East End property values have skyrocketed with gentrification.)

• *After two blocks of walking along Brick Lane, you'll reach the corner with Hanbury Street. Next we'll visit sights in each direction.*

❻ Hanbury Street

• *First, head east (right) down Hanbury Street for some colorful...*

Street Art: The East End has provided a canvas for artists—both local and international—who have enlivened its drab streets with eye-popping murals. There arc always interesting new murals to check out all along this ever-changing strip. Some of the best examples are on the wall above the shisha lounge, on the left. The finest work here—high up on the wall—is a black-and-white crane by renowned Belgian street artist ROA, who has decorated derelict buildings from Berlin to New York. Next to that is a breakdancer doing a handstand, wearing an upside-down bearskin hat, by Argentinian artist Martín Ron.

Start making your way back to Brick Lane, tuning in to the wide variety of businesses along the way. Hanbury Street marks the boundary between "Banglatown" and the hipster zone farther north—exemplifying the transition going on in today's East End.

You'll see traditional local businesses (travel agency, printer, tailor) mixed in with trendy boutiques (vintage clothing, secondhand books, shared workspaces, artisanal pickles).

• *Back at Brick Lane, continue straight across the street and walk a few doors down to find #29, on the right—the scene of another Ripper murder.*

29 Hanbury Street: Although the building that once stood here has been replaced by a brewery warehouse, the building directly across the street (at #28) dates from the 19th century—giving you a feel for those times.

This was where the murder took place that started Ripper-mania. On the night of September 8, 1888, a flower seller and sometime-prostitute named Annie Chapman was murdered behind the tenement that once stood here. Her throat was slit and her body mutilated. The MO seemed curiously similar to another murder a week before, committed a half-mile from here. London had a serial killer in its midst. Scotland Yard was called in to examine #29 and interview witnesses—ushering in the era of forensic science and analytical detective work. In all, Jack the Ripper would kill five (and maybe as many as 10) women in a span of three months, most within the sound of the Christ Church bells. Jack was never caught.

• *Back on Brick Lane, just beyond Hanbury Street, the complex of brick buildings on both sides is the former...*

❼ Truman Brewery

The brewery, established in 1666, now houses the Truman Markets (on weekends), as well as trendy shops and a creative and colorful food hall. There's no specific "market" location, so browse around—the action spreads across several buildings and streets. The Vintage Market (on the left, in the basement, near the start of the street) has more vintage vendors than anyplace else in London.

Just after the brick skybridge, turn left to walk through the open-air courtyard. Café 1001, a local institution, kicks off a row of shops catering to the East End's newest wave of (hipster) immigrants: a record store with live acts, a taproom, a skate shop, and a handful of pop-up stores. At the end, the courtyard opens up into a pod of funky food trucks surrounded by famous works of street art. Look up to find a giant pink monster who appears to be eating a digestive biscuit, and—high up on the roof near where you entered—a bronze fisherman.

A half-block farther north on Brick Lane, you'll find the original old brewery smokestack. This is the epicenter of a youthful scene with several lively pub/café/nightclubs. Explore.

• *If you've seen enough of this slice of the East End, you can head back on Brick Lane the way you came and skip this next stop. Or you can extend your stroll to...*

❽ Upper Brick Lane: More Street Art (and Bagels!)

Farther up Brick Lane, you'll hit Buxton Street—another good spot for street art. As you continue toward the overhead train tracks, you'll start to see the difference between street art and graffiti. Notice the eclectic mix of businesses along here: souvenirs, book shop, vintage, traditional tea shop.

Two blocks after the rail bridge, at Bacon Street, is **Dark Sugars Cocoa House** (on the left, at #141a). Nibble on a free sample and peruse the wares: big hunks of chocolate, delicate pralines, and decadent chocolate drinks. This shop exemplifies the melting-pot nature of the East End. The big mural shows the shop's founders, including the Ghanaian British owner (who started out with a small stand in Old Spitalfields Market)...and the Orthodox Jewish investor who provided funding.

On the next block, step into **Brick Lane Beigel Bake** (it's the second—not the first—bagel shop on the left, at #159). This place feels like a throwback to the 1950s—a photograph of the shop's founder hangs high on the wall, like a shrine. There's often a line, but it moves fast. Be ready to order, as the service is not exactly patient. A warm-out-of-the-oven bagel is heavenly. For something more filling, try a bagel with salt beef—carved off the pink hunk displayed in the front window, with or without mustard and pickles. For something sweet, drop into Crosstown Donuts next door—a popular London chain.

The bagel (or *beigel*) shop is a reminder of the East End's Jewish heritage. Many Jews fled here from Eastern Europe during the 19th century—and increasing with the pogroms of the 1880s. At one time these streets were filled with Yiddish-language theaters (and some of those Jews later migrated to the US, where they were instrumental in establishing Hollywood's studio system).

If it's Sunday morning and the weather's nice, consider walking the rest of the way up Brick Lane to the Columbia Road flower market (about a 10-minute walk north). Otherwise, head back the way you came.

• *Turn around and backtrack all the way up Brick Lane, passing Fournier Street (where we entered).*

A few doors past Fournier Street, on the right, is a dilapidated building covered in smaller-scale street art: clever posters and snapshot works, most offering commentary on recent politics. Go a few paces down the alley just before the house to explore a courtyard slathered with more colorful street art.

A block past Fournier Street, turn right (west) on Fashion Street.

❾ Fashion Street: More Industrial Age Ambience

Stroll down Fashion Street past a long century-old building with a fanciful Moorish (Islamic) design. It now houses a fashion-design school.

More street art abounds on Fashion Street. A few steps down, turn to look back and spot a pointillist-style portrait of a man and a young girl. And near the end of the block, on the left, look for one of many works by Ghanaian-British street artist Dreph, who specializes in murals of inspirational Black women—"ordinary women who do extraordinary things." Collectively, the murals constitute a work titled *You Are Enough.*

Cross busy Commercial Street (there are crosswalks nearby), go a few more steps, and turn left on Toynbee Street. You'll pass a hair salon called "Jack the Clipper." Take the next right on Brune Street, where you'll see old tenements (on the left) that are still used to house the down and out—their afternoon sun now blocked by a huge office block. On the right (at #9) is the former "Soup Kitchen for the Jewish Poor." Charities like  this one encouraged 19th-century Jewish immigrants to settle in this neighborhood.

Continue on, turning right onto Tenter Ground, the street where weavers once dried cloth "on tenterhooks," giving us the phrase that means "uneasy." Look up to see the iron racks still rigged to the building.

• *At the end of Tenter Ground, turn left and head toward the building with a* Women *sign. This was where poor women entered to start their shift at a Victorian-era workhouse. Continue straight ahead, entering the very narrow street called...*

⑩ Artillery Passage

Henry VIII (around the year 1500) used this as a practice zone for his artillery. By the 19th century, this narrow lane was typical of streets in this densely packed neighborhood of grimy-faced factory workers. Jack the Ripper films always use this characteristic street. These days, it's lined with trendy, atmospheric eateries. **Ottolenghi,** which dominates the first stretch of the lane, is an outpost of one of London's hottest celebrity chefs, Yotam Ottolenghi. Born in Jerusalem, Ottolenghi specializes in Eastern Mediterranean cuisine. (For more on this restaurant, see page 438.)

Squeeze one block straight down this passage, to the intersection with Sandy's Row. Notice the tall bollard—a big black metal stake in the pavement. This boundary marker alerts you that you are now officially leaving the East End and reentering the City of

London. Consider the juxtaposition: The City is the richest "One Square Mile" on earth. Its gleaming skyscrapers tower nearby, while far below, in the East End, people still scrummage for "pants, three for a tenner."

• *Our walk is over. From here, you could continue straight ahead to Liverpool Street Station. Or, if it's early in the day, consider a brief detour to visit...*

⓫ Petticoat Lane Market

To reach the market, turn left on Sandy's Row, then go three blocks (down Sandy's Row and then Middlesex Street) to Wentworth Street, which leads left into the market. (On some days, you may run into the first market stalls almost immediately.) One of the oldest markets in Britain, Petticoat Lane has been selling cheap stuff to poor working people for 400 years. It's packed on Sunday; enticing food stalls line Goulston Street.

• *Head back to Liverpool Street Station—from Petticoat Lane, just follow Middlesex Street.*

⓬ Liverpool Street Station

Before moving on, take a moment to recall the events of July 7, 2005. At 8:45, a Tube train had just pulled out of the station when it was rocked by a terrorist bomb—the first of four to hit London that day, killing 52 people. But the next day, Londoners were back on the Tube.

• *The Liverpool Street Tube station can zip you to anywhere you'd like in town.*

Or, to extend your East End excursion, you could head a half-mile north to the Shoreditch neighborhood—a great destination for lunch or dinner. Restaurants are concentrated near the intersection of Shoreditch High Street and Commercial Street/Great Eastern Street (for details, see page 440). To get there, you can hike up busy Shoreditch Street, or—better—hop on bus #149 or #242 from Liverpool Station (stop D—to the right, as you face the station). Ride three stops north, to the stop called "Shoreditch High Street/Bethnal Green Road" (after going under the arched bridge).

GREENWICH TOUR

Still well within the city limits of London, the Royal Borough of Greenwich (GREN-ich)—England's maritime capital—feels like a small town all its own. Visitors come here for all things salty. The area's premier attraction is the *Cutty Sark* clipper. Next on the list is the Royal Observatory Greenwich, where you can literally straddle the planet's prime meridian and learn how the invention of Greenwich Mean Time advanced the art of seafaring.

Beyond these, choose your favorites. The fine National Maritime Museum traces the days when Britannia ruled the waves. The former Naval College—a campus of stately Baroque buildings dotting sweeping lawns—features the glorious Sistine Chapel-like Painted Hall. Then there's the town of Greenwich itself, with its appealing markets, Georgian architecture, fleet of nautical shops, plentiful parks, historic taverns, and hordes of tourists.

Greenwich's sights appeal to both serious students of the maritime sciences as well as kids and families. It's an easy day trip by boat or the Docklands Light Railway (DLR). And where else can you set your watch with such accuracy?

GETTING TO GREENWICH

It's a joy by boat or a snap by the DLR. For maximum efficiency and sightseeing, I take the boat there for the scenery and commentary, and take the DLR back to avoid late-afternoon boat crowds (this plan also allows you to stop at the Docklands on the way home).

By Boat: From central London, various tour boats—with commentary and open-deck seating—leave for Greenwich from the piers at Westminster, the London Eye, and the Tower of London (2/hour, 20-75 minutes).

Thames Clippers offers faster trips, with no commentary and only a small deck at the stern (departs every 20-30 minutes from several piers in central London, 20-55 minutes). Thames Clippers also connects Greenwich to the Docklands' Canary Wharf Pier (2-3/hour, 15 minutes).

For cruising details, see page 45.

By Docklands Light Railway (DLR): From the Bank-Monument Station in central London, take the DLR to Cutty Sark Station in central Greenwich; it's one stop before the main—but less central—Greenwich Station (departs at least every 10 minutes, 20-minute ride, all in Zone 2). The DLR works like the Tube; be sure to touch your card to the reader on the platform before and after your journey, or risk being fined.

Many DLR trains terminate at Canary Wharf, so make sure you get on one that continues to Lewisham or Greenwich. (If you do end up at Canary Wharf, you can catch a train to Greenwich's Cutty Sark Station within a few minutes). Or get off the DLR at Island Gardens, where you can enjoy the unique experience of walking under the Thames into Greenwich: To reach the pedestrian tunnel, exit the station, cross the street, and follow signs to *Island Gardens* for a good photo op. Then enter the red-brick Greenwich Foot Tunnel (opened in 1902), descend 86 spiral stairs (or ride the lift), hold your breath, and re-emerge on dry land at the bow of the *Cutty Sark*.

By Bus: Catch bus #188 from Russell Square near the British Museum (about 45 minutes to Greenwich).

Orientation to Greenwich

When to Go: To allow enough time to see everything—and to fit in a Docklands visit on your way back—head to Greenwich in the morning. The sights can be crowded with families and school groups, especially in summer and on weekends. If visiting at a very busy time, you can avoid the ticket-buying line by reserving your

tickets for the popular sights—the *Cutty Sark* and the Royal Observatory—in advance (explained later).

Opening Times: Greenwich's main sights are open daily from 10:00 to 17:00.

Markets: Thanks to its markets, Greenwich throbs with browsing Londoners on weekends. **Greenwich Market** is an entertaining mini Covent Garden, located in the middle of the block between the Cutty Sark DLR station and the Old Royal Naval College—right on your way to the sights. There are always global food stalls; Mondays, Wednesday, and weekends specialize in arts and crafts; Tue and Thu are for antiques; and Fridays are the whole shebang (open daily 10:00-17:30, www.greenwichmarketlondon.com).

The **Clocktower Market** sells overpriced old odds and ends on Greenwich High Road, near the post office (most likely Sat-Sun and bank holidays 10:00-17:00).

Exploring Back Streets: Allow time to browse Greenwich. The town has two sides: prim and proper (east of Church Street) and lived-in local (west of Church Street). Wander beyond touristy Church Street and Greenwich High Road to where flower stands spill onto the side streets, antique shops sell brass nautical knickknacks, and salty pubs tempt passersby. King William Walk, College Approach, and Nelson Road (all in the vicinity of Greenwich Market) are worth a look.

Visitor Information: The TI is within the **Greenwich Visitors Center,** inside the Old Royal Naval College gates. They sell tickets for Greenwich's various sights, and offer a full assortment of London tourist brochures and maps (daily 10:00-17:00, Pepys House, 2 Cutty Sark Gardens, +44 208 305 5235, www.visitgreenwich.org.uk).

Tours: A guided **city walk** departs from the TI Fri-Sun at 12:15, offering an overview of the major sights and ending outside the Royal Observatory—which you'll then visit on your own (£12, 1.5 hours, www.greenwichtours.co.uk). Your ticket to the Painted Hall includes a walking tour of the **Old Royal Naval College Grounds** and, on weekends, a tour of **filming locations** (see listing, later).

Length of This Tour: Allow about two hours simply to stroll about and enjoy the parks. Add several hours more to enter the sights (figure about an hour for the *Cutty Sark,* 30 minutes each for the Royal Naval College and the Queen's House, and an hour or two apiece for the National Maritime Museum and the Royal Observatory).

Starring: The *Cutty Sark,* the Royal Observatory with its prime meridian, the National Maritime Museum, the Painted Chapel, and expansive great views.

BACKGROUND

Greenwich—with its safe, deep harbor not far from the mouth of the Thames—helped put Britain on the map as a seafaring nation. For a thousand years, oceangoing ships docked and embarked from here (and from the Docklands, directly across the river). England's kings built palaces here. In the 1500s, Henry VIII (who was born here) made Greenwich the principal residence of his early reign. Elizabeth I was born here, and later queens would make Greenwich their near-London getaway.

In the 1600s, various monarchs commissioned architects Inigo Jones and Christopher Wren to beautify the town and palace. A Royal Observatory was built atop the bluff for charting the heavens to aid in seafaring. Other grand structures were built nearby to house retired seamen, and as a college for training naval officers. In modern times, as Britain's maritime focus shifted elsewhere, Greenwich's buildings were transformed into a pincushion of sights that connect today's Brits with their illustrious maritime past.

The Tour Begins

I've linked Greenwich's major sights with handy walking directions. Each attraction is described in full and rated; you can pick and choose which ones to enter. If you're in a rush, make a beeline to the sights that interest you. We'll start with the must-see *Cutty Sark*, meander through various other sights, and finish atop the hill at the Royal Observatory.

• *Our first stop is the* Cutty Sark. *If you arrive in Greenwich by boat, it's right in front of you. If you come by DLR, get off at the Cutty Sark stop, exit the station to the left, pass under the brick archway, and turn left. The* Cutty Sark *is just ahead on the right.*

▲▲*Cutty Sark*

When first launched in 1869, the Scottish-built *Cutty Sark* was the last of the great China tea clippers and the queen of the seas.

She was among the fastest clippers ever built, the culmination of centuries of ship design. With 32,000 square feet of sail—and favorable winds—she could travel 300 miles in a day. But as a new century dawned, steamers began to outmatch sailing ships

for speed, and by the mid-1920s the *Cutty Sark* was the world's last operating clipper ship. After a stint as a training ship, she was retired and turned into a museum in the 1950s.

In 2012, the ship was restored and reopened with a spectacular new glass-walled display space (though one critic groused that the ship now "looks like it has run aground in a giant greenhouse"). Displays explore the *Cutty Sark*'s 140-year history and the cargo

GREENWICH

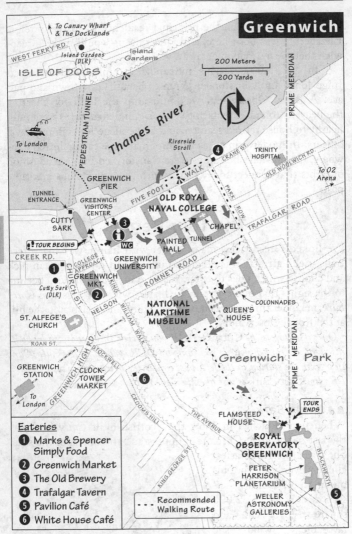

Greenwich

To Canary Wharf & The Docklands

WEST FERRY RD.

Island Gardens (DLR)

Island Gardens

ISLE OF DOGS

200 Meters

200 Yards

Thames River

To London

PEDESTRIAN TUNNEL

Riverside Stroll

FIVE FOOT WALK

CRANE ST.

PARK ROW

PRIME MERIDIAN

TRINITY HOSPITAL

OLD WOOLWICH RD.

To O2 Arena

GREENWICH PIER

TUNNEL ENTRANCE

GREENWICH VISITORS CENTER

CUTTY SARK

TOUR BEGINS

CREEK RD.

COLLEGE APPROACH

CHURCH ST.

KING WILLIAM WALK

OLD ROYAL NAVAL COLLEGE

PAINTED HALL

CHAPEL

TUNNEL

TRAFALGAR ROAD

ROMNEY ROAD

GREENWICH UNIVERSITY

GREENWICH MKT.

NELSON

NATIONAL MARITIME MUSEUM

QUEEN'S HOUSE

COLONNADES

ST. ALFEGE'S CHURCH

Cutty Sark (DLR)

ROAN ST.

GREENWICH STATION

To London

GREENWICH HIGH RD.

STOCKWELL

CLOCK-TOWER MARKET

Greenwich Park

PRIME MERIDIAN

GROOMS HILL

THE AVENUE

FLAMSTEED HOUSE

TOUR ENDS

KING GEORGE ST.

ROYAL OBSERVATORY GREENWICH

PETER HARRISON PLANETARIUM

WELLER ASTRONOMY GALLERIES

BLACKHEATH

Eateries

1 Marks & Spencer Simply Food

2 Greenwich Market

3 The Old Brewery

4 Trafalgar Tavern

5 Pavilion Café

6 White House Café

- - - Recommended Walking Route

she carried—everything from tea to wool to gunpowder—as she raced between London and ports all around the world.

Cost and Hours: £15, kids ages 4-15-£7.50, free for kids 3 and under, £25 combo-ticket with Royal Observatory; daily 10:00-17:00, last entry 45 minutes before closing; reservations +44 20 8312 6608, www.rmg.co.uk.

Crowd-Beating Tips: The ship can get busy on school holidays and on weekends. To skip the ticket-buying line, you can book a timed-entry ticket online in advance.

Visiting the *Cutty Sark*: You enter, and *bam*—there it is: the

Eating in Greenwich

Picnicking: Greenwich's parks are picnic-perfect. Gather picnic supplies before heading up the hill to the National Maritime Museum and Royal Observatory. **$ Marks & Spencer Simply Food** sells ready-made lunches (between the DLR station and the *Cutty Sark* at 55 Greenwich Church Street).

Greenwich Market: From Yorkshire pudding to paella to Thai cuisine, food stalls at the Greenwich Market offer an international variety of tasty options.

Pub Grub: Greenwich has almost 100 pubs, with some boasting that they're mere milliseconds from the prime meridian. **$$$ The Old Brewery,** in the Greenwich Visitors Center, is a gastropub decorated with all things beer. A brewery on this site once provided the daily ration of four pints of beer for pensioners at the hospital. Today it offers craft beers, wines, and cocktails along with classic British cuisine (+44 20 3327 1280). **$$ The Trafalgar Tavern,** with a casual pub and pricier, elegant dining room, is both bright and cozy—a historical place for an overpriced meal (Park Row, +44 20 8858 2909).

Tea, Coffee, and Light Food: A **$$** café is downstairs inside the ***Cutty Sark* museum,** directly underneath the suspended hull—a memorable setting. There are also two basic **$$** cafés in the **National Maritime Museum.** Up by the Royal Observatory, the elegant 1906 **$ Pavilion Café** offers tea, coffee, and counter-service food in a bright interior (it's in the park just beyond the planetarium, across the parking lot). At the bottom of Greenwich Park, near Croom's Hill, **$$ White House Café** offers an assortment of baked goodies and sandwiches. It has a small seating area inside and relaxing garden tables outside (Easter-Oct only, closed off-season). All work well for lunch or an afternoon snack, and close around the same time the sights do.

hull of a massive ship that could knife through the waves faster than any ship before it. Start your visit on the ship's **Lower Hold** (Deck 0). You can see the ship's guts—an iron rib cage, covered with wood and plated (outside) with gleaming copper. Watch the engaging three-minute video for a breezy introduction to the ship. The (fake) boxes of tea harken back to the ship's days in the Chinese tea trade...which didn't last long, as the Suez Canal soon opened, allowing steam-powered ships to reach China much faster than sailboats.

Next, head up to the low-ceilinged 'Tween Deck (Deck 1). The bales on display make it clear that the *Cutty Sark* turned to trading wool with Australia. She could make the 8,000-mile voyage from Aussie sheep farms to English textile factories in just over two and a half months. Besides China and Australia, the ship

GREENWICH

GREENWICH

called on ports all over the world. This deck is full of not-quite-gimmicky displays that succeed in making the ship's history come alive, even for adults. Find the fun video game that lets you attempt to beat Captain Woodget's record voyage sailing a wool-laden *Sark* from Sydney to London. Sit on the tilting benches for a seaborne feel, enjoy the oddly mesmerizing video at the stern, and get the figurehead's take on *Sark* history in the bow.

The open-air **Top Deck** is the highlight. Gaze up the three tall, stout masts, with their elaborate rigging of ropes and pulleys for raising the sails. The tallest mast reaches 150 feet, and could hold six square sails. Don't miss the video showing the rigger's view as he climbs high above the deck. Explore the cabins—the tiny sleeping berths, the galley, the heads—and ponder how little space was allotted to the crew of 30-35. Compare their accommodations with the "Master's Cabin" (up a few steps near the stern) for the captain and first mate. They had larger berths, their own WCs, and a wood-paneled "saloon" or common room. At the ship's stern,

you'll see the ship's steering wheel. The pilot spun the wheel, which turned a corkscrew that pivoted the rudder.

Exit the ship and head downstairs to the area where you're literally **Under the Ship.** Relax and enjoy the various exhibits while the 400,000-pound ship dangles overhead. Videos describe how the mighty vessel was designed and then preserved. Beneath the bow, note the compass rose that shows how many days at sea it'd take to reach major ports from here.

Finally, admire the colorful collection of **figurehead** statues that once adorned the prows of ships (most are from other ships).

In the center of the group is the *Cutty Sark*'s own figurehead: a white statue of a beautiful-but-fierce bare-breasted witch, holding the horse's tail she grabbed while chasing off a suitor. This mythological figure gave the ship its name, and the ship, in turn, inspired a famous whisky. The other figureheads range from the usual goddesses and maidens to Indian chiefs, Cleopatra, the goateed Prime Minister Benjamin Disraeli, and even Abraham Lincoln.

• *Leaving the museum, head left and find the visitors center—look for the door marked* Old Royal Naval College.

Greenwich Visitors Center

As well as having a helpful information desk, the visitors center contains a few exhibits introducing you to Greenwich over the centuries, as it served as a harbor, royal residence, seaman's hospital, scientific center, and nautical college. Models show how the various buildings evolved, and you'll see artifacts of the many people—kings, sailors, architects, and scientists—who left their mark on the town. Adjoining the Greenwich Visitors Center are the TI, free WCs, and, of course, a pub. This is also the departure point for tours of the Old Royal Naval College complex (described under "Painted Hall," later).

Cost and Hours: Free, daily 10:00-17:00, +44 20 8305 5235, www.ornc.org.

• *Leave through the far exit (away from the* Cutty Sark*) and turn right, then left, following signs for* Painted Hall. *Make your way between the buildings to the open quad, where dramatic identical-twin buildings make up the heart of the...*

Old Royal Naval College

Despite the name, these grand structures were built (1692) as a veterans' hospital to house disabled and retired sailors who'd served their country. King William III and Queen Mary II spared no expense. They donated land from the former royal palace and hired the great Christopher Wren to design the complex (though other architects completed it). Wren created a virtual temple to seamen. It was perfectly symmetrical, with classical double-columned arcades topped by soaring domes.

In 1873, the hospital was transformed into one of the world's most prestigious universities for training naval officers. Here they studied math, physics, and engineering for use at sea. During World War II, the college was a hive of activity, as Britain churned out officers to face the Nazis. In 1998, the Royal Navy moved out. Today, the buildings host university students, music students, business conventions, concerts, and film crews drawn to the awe-inspiring space.

Turn your back on the Thames to face the twin buildings: On the right is the Painted Hall, where the pensioners dined; and on the left is the Chapel of Sts. Peter and Paul, where they worshipped. Both are open to visitors and described later. Between the twin buildings is the Queen's House. Beyond that is the hill with the Royal Observatory.

• *The Painted Hall is sumptuous, but pricey to see; the chapel is less impressive, but still offers a good taste—and it's free.*

To check out the Painted Hall, find the entrance 50 paces back the way you came, on the left. To skip ahead to the chapel, walk across the lawn and enter under the dome.

▲Painted Hall

Originally intended as a dining hall for pensioners, this sumptuously painted room was deemed too glorious (and, in the winter, too cold) for that purpose. So almost as soon as it was completed, it became simply a showcase for visitors. Impressive as it is, the admission is quite steep to see gigantic paintings by an artist you've never heard of, featuring second-rate royals. But those who appreciate artistic spectacles and picking out lavish details will find it worthwhile.

Cost and Hours: £13.50, £1 cheaper online in advance, daily 10:00-17:00, sometimes closed for private events, www.ornc.org.

Tours: Your ticket includes an **audioguide;** a 45-minute guided tour of the Old Royal Naval College **grounds,** not including the Painted Hall (departs from the Greenwich Visitors Center at the top of each hour); and a 30-minute talk describing the **Painted Hall** (begins every 30 minutes). On weekends, it also includes a tour of **filming locations** (2/day Sat-Sun only, reserve ahead). I'd skip the various tours, but consider the hall talk if there's one starting soon. Otherwise, the description below covers the basics, and the audioguide provides more detail.

Visiting the Painted Hall: Buy your ticket in the undercroft (with a café and WCs), then head upstairs into the hall. Gape up at one of the largest painted ceilings in Europe—112 feet long. It's a big propaganda scene, glorifying the building's founders, William and Mary (William, as a Protestant monarch, had recently trounced the Catholic French King Louis XIV in a pivotal battle).

Look up and examine the scene. (You can crane your neck; lie down on the comfy padded benches, positioned just for this purpose; or use the clever wheeled mirrors.) In the center are William and Mary. Under his foot, William is crushing a shadowy figure with a broken sword...Louis XIV. William is handing a red cap (representing liberty) to the woman

GREENWICH

on the right, who holds the reins of a white horse (symbolizing Europe). On the left, a white-robed woman hands him an olive branch, a sign of peace. The message: William has granted Europe liberty by saving it from the tyranny of Louis XIV. Below the royal couple, the Spirit of Architecture shows them the plans for this very building (commemorating the sad fact that Mary died before its completion). Ringing the central image are the four seasons (represented by Zodiac signs), the four virtues, and—at the top and bottom—a captured Spanish galleon and a British man-of-war battleship.

Up the steps at the end of the room, along the wall of the upper hall, is a portrait of the family of King George I. On the right is the artist who spent 19 years of his life painting this hall, James Thornhill (he finally finished it in 1727). He's holding out his hand—reportedly, he didn't feel he was paid enough for this Sistine-sized undertaking.

Tunnel to the Chapel: If you paid for the Painted Hall, you can walk through a long tunnel under the lawn to get to the chapel (described next). Near the end of the tunnel on the right, don't miss the fun little **Skittle Alley**—a bowling-like game built to entertain the pensioners, using recycled nautical equipment. The lane is made of old ships; the pockmarked wooden balls were practice cannonballs; and the pins were once used to lash ropes on ships. You're welcome to try rolling a ball down the lane (with both hands, "granny"-style). As the equipment is far from precise, you're more likely to throw a gutterball than a strike.

• At the end of the tunnel, head up into the...

Chapel of Sts. Peter and Paul

Not surprisingly, you'll sense a nautical air in this fine chapel. Notice the rope motif in the floor tiles down the aisle. The enormous painting above the altar is by American Benjamin West. It depicts Paul (standing in red, near the luminous center) being bit by a poisonous viper. The crowd around him ripples in horror, but Paul casually drops the viper in the fire, miraculously without

being harmed. Soon after the chapel was completed, it was gutted by a fire and had to be redecorated all over again. The plans were too ambitious, so the designers cut corners. The six Ionic columns framing the entrance are expensive stone, but many others are painted wood. And the "sculptures" lining the nave high above are actually trompe l'oeil—3-D paintings meant to look real. But some items, such as the marble frame around the main door, are finely crafted from expensive materials.

Cost and Hours: Free, daily 10:00-17:00, service Sun at 11:00—all are welcome.

• *Leave the chapel and walk straight down to the water—enjoying the sweeping views across to the Docklands. When you hit the river, go through the gate and turn right for a quick...*

Riverside Stroll

Start by looking back toward the Old Royal Naval College for a great photo op. Notice how it's split into two parts; reportedly, Queen Mary, who lived in the Queen's House, didn't want her view blocked.

Looking directly across the river, you can see a round structure (brick base, glass dome)—that's the other end of the tunnel that runs under the Thames to near the *Cutty Sark*.

Turn right and wander east along the Thames on Five Foot Walk (named for the width of the path). The tallest of the Docklands skyscrapers is the 50-story, pyramid-shaped Canary Wharf Tower. (The nearby Landmark Pinnacle is just a few feet shorter.) The Docklands sits atop the Isle of Dogs, a formerly marshy patch in the Thames, where the river takes a hairpin turn. That slowed the river's flow, and made Green-wich a natural harbor from earliest times. From here you can also see the big, white, spiky **O2** dome a mile downstream. This stadium languished for nearly a decade after its controversial construction and brief life as the Millennium Dome. Intended to be a world's fair-type site and the  center of London's year 2000 celebration, it ended up as the topic of heated debates about cost overruns and its controversial looks. The site was finally bought by a developer a few years ago and rechristened "The O2" (a telecommunications company paid for the naming rights). Today it hosts sporting events and concerts. Next to the O2 are the towers of the Emirates Air Line cable car, which ferries passengers from the O2 across the Thames to, essentially, nowhere.

Continuing downstream, just outside the fenced college

grounds, you'll find the recommended **Trafalgar Tavern**—where a statue of Admiral Nelson stands out front. Dickens knew the pub well, and used it as the setting for the wedding breakfast in *Our Mutual Friend*. Built in 1837 in the Regency style to attract Londoners downriver, the upstairs Nelson Room is still used for weddings. Its formal moldings and elegant windows with balconies over the Thames are a step back in time and worth a peek.

GREENWICH

• *From the Trafalgar Tavern, turn with the river to your back and walk two long blocks up Park Row. After crossing busy Romney Road, turn right (through the gate near the corner) into the park. Walk past a row of huge anchors, toward the palatial buildings in the middle of the park. There's the Queen's House (the small building between two bigger ones), the National Maritime Museum (the big pink building just beyond), and the Royal Observatory on the hilltop. This trio, combined with the Cutty Sark, form the Royal Museums of Greenwich.*

Queen's House

This perfectly proportioned building is the best surviving reminder of the days when Greenwich was the palatial home to Britain's kings and queens. From earliest times, monarchs had a manor on these grounds, culminating in Henry VIII's grand Palace of Placentia. In 1616 the great architect Inigo Jones was hired by James I to build a house for his wife, Queen Anne of Denmark. James's act of devotion to his wife became a tradition, and the House was subsequently passed down from queen to queen, as a pleasant retreat.

Cost and Hours: Free, daily 10:00-17:00, +44 20 8858 4422, www.rmg.co.uk.

Exterior: Jones created a cubical building with geometric proportions and simple unadorned lines. It was surrounded by gardens, becoming the first Italian-style Palladian villa in Britain. Along with Jones's more-famous Banqueting House in London (described in the Westminster Walk chapter), the Queen's House helped set the tone for the Neoclassical architecture that has become London's signature "look."

GREENWICH

Interior: You'll enter through the cellar, then climb up to the **Great Hall**—a perfect 40-foot cube, ringed with a balcony. Here queens entertained their guests with grand views of the Thames between Wren's magnificent Old Royal Naval College.

From here, the genteel, spiral, blue-hued **Tulip Stairs** lead upstairs, where a balcony affords a different view down into the Great Hall. Take a spin through the many rooms on this level, with different quarters reserved for the queen, the king, and various servants. In the first large room—the **Queen's Presence Chamber**—examine the sumptuous *Armada Portrait* of Queen Elizabeth I (c. 1588). The imperious ginger-haired monarch—dressed in a big-shouldered gown studded with pearls and a huge lacy collar—celebrates England's stunning victory over the Spanish Armada. The windows behind her show the ships facing off for battle (left), and the storm at sea (right) that miraculously aided the Brits. Now Britannia rules the waves, and Elizabeth holds the scepter of power in one hand while the other rests across the globe, from England to America. The other rooms contain many paintings—most of them forgettable, and most of nautical themes: ships, famous sea battles, and portraits of admirals. You'll also see royal portraits and some fine landscapes. In the easy-to-miss **King's Writing Closet** is a *Wunderkammer* of curiosities, including a 2,000-year-old coin, a fossilized mammoth's tooth, and the serrated nose of a sawfish.

• *The National Maritime Museum is to the right, connected to the Queen's House by a colonnade. To reach the museum entrance, walk toward the hill, pass through the colonnade, and turn right to walk behind the building. You'll soon see a giant ship in a bottle, marking the entrance to the...*

▲National Maritime Museum

Great for anyone interested in the sea, this excellent, modern museum holds everything from a giant working paddlewheel to the uniform Admiral Horatio Nelson wore when he was killed at Trafalgar. A big glass roof tops three levels of slick, thoughtfully presented, kid-friendly exhibits about all things seafaring.

Cost and Hours: Free, daily 10:00-17:00, may close later in summer, +44 20 8858 4422, www.rmg.co.uk. The museum hosts frequent family-oriented events—singing, treasure hunts, and storytelling—particularly on weekends; ask at the desk. Listen for announcements alerting visitors to free tours on various topics. There's a café just inside the entrance, and another up by the Great Map on Floor 1.

Visiting the Museum: For a quick once-over, start on the top floor and work your way down.

Floor 2: In "Nelson, Navy, Nation," you'll see models of ships, uniforms, weapons, and whips used to keep sailors in line—all attesting to the vital importance of sea trade in making Britain great. Focus on the watershed Battle of Trafalgar (1805), when the Royal Navy defeated Napoleon's fleet, confirming that Britannia ruled the waves. See the Union Jack that flew from one of the 27 ships in Britain's convoy and the French cannonball that lodged itself into the bow of the British flagship, the HMS *Victory*. Finally, see holy relics of the great hero Admiral Horatio Nelson who led the British to victory. There's the uniform he was wearing on that fateful day. Notice how the jacket's right arm is pinned to the stomach—the way Nelson wore it after losing an arm in a previous battle. You can still make out traces of blood on the left sleeve. And in the left shoulder, you can see the bullet hole from a French musket. Just when victory was at hand, Nelson was mortally wounded, but he died knowing he'd secured Britain's future.

Also on Floor 2, you'll see "Forgotten Fighters" (WWI ships and weapons), the kid-friendly "All Hands" (where you can send a Morse code message), the "Ship Simulator" (where you can pilot a virtual ship down the Thames), and a "Polar Worlds" exhibit about the far-north and south reaches of our planet (with exhibits on indigenous peoples, polar exploration, and special equipment).

Floor 1: The floor's central courtyard is a big people-friendly space with a great map of the world on the floor, where kids play and adults sip lattes. In the "Traders" exhibit, you'll learn how this small island nation grew rich by trading all across the globe. Queen Elizabeth I sent forth explorers (1600s), and soon the East India Company (1700s) was importing silks, tea, and opium from China and India.

Meanwhile (in the "Atlantic Worlds" exhibit), Britain was colonizing the New World and fighting the Seven Years War (1756-63) with France for superiority over North America. The American colonies provided Britain with cotton, coffee, sugar, tobacco, fish, and metals. This productivity was largely thanks to slaves—and you'll see some chilling reminders of this. Continue downstairs (dipping into the peaceful stained glass of the Baltic Exchange, honoring the dead of WWI), to the...

Ground Floor: These large-scale exhibits are easy to enjoy. There are big ships, colorful figureheads, a long 1700s barge that once cruised the Thames, lighthouse technology, a detailed exhibit on the Battle of Trafalgar, the *Miss Britain III* that could travel at speeds up to 100 miles per hour, and many more salty odds and ends.

• *To reach the final sight in town—the Royal Observatory Greenwich—*

exit the Maritime Museum and follow signs and the crowds as you huff up the steep hill (allow 10-15 minutes).

Just below the observatory entrance, note the unassuming iron gate where cheapskates could see a free, more simplistic (and significantly less crowded) display of the prime meridian. A few steps farther uphill, pause at the display of public standards of length and see how your foot measures up to the official "foot."

Circle around behind the complex to buy your ticket and enter the courtyard of the...

▲▲Royal Observatory Greenwich

Located on the prime meridian (0° longitude), this observatory is famous as the point from which all time and distances on earth are measured. It was here that astronomers studied the heavens in order to help seafarers navigate. In the process, they used the constancy of the stars to establish standards of measurement for time and distance used by the whole world. The observatory's various sights walk you through these heady concepts. First, you can snap a selfie straddling the famous prime meridian line in the pavement. There's the original 1600s-era observatory and several early telescopes. You'll see the famous clocks from the 1700s that first set the standard of global time, as well as more recent timekeeping devices. Topping your visit off are great views over Greenwich and the distant London skyline. A visit here gives you a taste of the sciences of astronomy, timekeeping, and seafaring—and how they all meld together.

Cost and Hours: £16, £25 combo-ticket with *Cutty Sark,* advance timed-entry ticket recommended, daily 10:00-17:00, may close later in summer, +44 20 8858 4422, reservations +44 20 8312 6608, www.rmg.co.uk. For details on planetarium shows—sold at the same ticket office—see the end of this listing.

➋ Self-Guided Tour: After purchasing your ticket, enter the courtyard. (Note that some exhibits may be different after a recent renovation.)

Prime Meridian: Running through the middle of the small courtyard is "The Line"—the prime meridian. Visitors wait patiently to have their photographs taken as they straddle the line, with one foot in each hemisphere. This line divides the globe into 360 imaginary lines of longitude about 69 miles apart—180 lines to the east of here and 180 west. So, New York City (as the line markings say) is 73 degrees west of here. The prime meridian is set by lining it up with a huge telescope pointed at the constant heavens.

(You can glimpse today's telescope, located at the end of The Line, inside the low brick building.)

While watching all this fuss over a little line, consider that—unlike the equator—the placement of the prime meridian is totally arbitrary. It could just as well have been at my house, in Timbuktu, or even a few feet over—as, for a time, it was (the trough along the building's roofline shows where one astronomer had placed it).

The prime meridian established a fixed point from which to measure how fast the earth rotates on its axis, from 0° longitude back to 0° again. This allowed Greenwich's scientists to set a standard for time. This standard was soon adopted throughout the world as Greenwich Mean Time (GMT). Find the red Time Ball (on the tower atop the observatory's roof), which—since 1833—has dropped down the mast daily at exactly 13:00, helping all who see it to set their clocks.

• *Turn your attention to the cube-shaped building that holds the ball, the...*

Flamsteed House: This building was the original observatory—a simple tower atop a hill, away from city lights, where astronomers could set up telescopes to observe the heavens. It was built in 1675, a time when British ships were exploring and colonizing the globe. Astronomers here were tasked with finding more accurate navigating techniques than the old astrolabes and quadrants.

Inside, you first pass through the **apartments** of the head astronomer, now decorated with their portraits. You'll see John (first Astronomer Royal) Flamsteed, his successor Edmond (comet-discovering) Halley, and William Herschel, whose telescopes were so accurate that astronomers could set earth time according to the stars (not the sun).

Upstairs is the impressive, high-ceilinged **Octagon Room,** designed by Christopher Wren. The tall windows accommodated telescopes (as you can see from the replica on display). There's a portrait of (black-haired) Charles II, who started the observatory. Peruse the various Tompion-designed clocks that astronomers used here, and the 10-foot-tall grandfather clock powered by a swinging pendulum. These clocks were state-of-the-art in the 1600s, but so fragile and unwieldy that they could never be taken on board a ship to aid in navigation. For that part of the puzzle, head downstairs to the museum exhibits.

One level down you'll find a fascinating series of displays on the **"Longitude Problem"** and how it was solved (see the sidebar for an overview). First, see how the globe of the earth is divided into its 360-degree lines of longitude. Scientists knew it takes the earth 24 hours to spin all 360 degrees (or four minutes to spin one degree). Now, if you only had a clock accurate enough, you could figure out exactly what degree you were at anywhere on the earth.

GREENWICH

The Longitude Problem

Around 1700, as the ships of seafaring nations began to venture farther from their home bases, the alarming increase in the number of shipwrecks made it clear that navigational tools had to be improved. Determining latitude—the relative position between the equator and the North or South Pole—was straightforward; sailors needed only to measure the angle of the sun at noon. But figuring out longitude, or their east-west position, was not as easy without a fixed point (such as the equator) from which to measure.

In 1714, the British government offered the £20,000 Longitude Prize. Two successful solutions emerged, and both are tied to Greenwich.

The first approach was to observe the position of the moon, which moves in relation to the stars. Sailors would compare the night sky they saw with the sky over Greenwich by consulting a book of tables prepared by Greenwich astronomers. This told them how far they were from Greenwich—their longitude. Visitors to the Royal Observatory can still see the giant telescopes—under retractable roofs—that were used to carefully chart the heavens to create these meticulous tables.

The second approach was to create a clock that would remain completely accurate on voyages—no easy feat back then, when turbulence and changes in weather and humidity made timepieces notoriously unreliable at sea. John Harrison spent 45 years working on this problem, finally succeeding in 1760 with his fourth effort, the H4 (which won him the Longitude Prize). All four of his attempts are on display at the Royal Observatory.

So, how can a clock determine longitude? Every 15° of longitude equals an hour when comparing the difference in sunrise or sunset times between two places. For example, the time gap between Greenwich and New York City is five hours, which translates into a longitudinal difference of 75°. Equipped with an accurate timepiece set to Greenwich Mean Time, sailors could figure out their longitude by comparing sunset time at their current position with sunset time back in Greenwich.

Notice that both approaches use Greenwich as a baseline—either on an astral map or on a clock. That's why, to this day, the prime meridian and official world time are both centered in this unassuming London suburb.

If you're fascinated by the Longitude Problem, check out Dava Sobel's book on the topic, and the TV miniseries based on it—both entitled *Longitude*.

So, in the 1700s, Britain offered a £20,000 prize to anyone who could invent a clock that accurate.

The museum displays the **four original clocks** invented by one of the contestants, John Harrison. First up is so-called "H1." It took Harrison five years to build this clock. It was powered not by a pendulum but by two springs, which slowly uncoiled to constantly keep the cogwheels turning. (Springs would be much more reliable than a swinging pendulum aboard a rocking ship at sea.) Harrison had created the best clock ever—but not good enough to win the prize. So he spent the next five years building and testing H2, and another seventeen years working on H3. After six more years of work he'd produced the winning design—H4. It was not a huge sea clock but a small pocket watch. See the portrait at the end of the room of curly-haired Harrison holding the watch that won him 20,000 quid. On the scale of human achievement, this little timepiece is right up there with the printing press, the cotton gin, the telegraph, and the money belt.

One more floor down, you'll find a roomful of **time-keeping devices,** from ancient sundials to a church-tower clock to an incredibly accurate atomic clock that measures the ultra-stable rate of decay of cesium atoms. Today, the Greenwich time signal is linked with the BBC, which broadcasts the famous "pips" worldwide at the top of the hour, so listeners can set their clocks.

• *Back outside in the courtyard, take in the prime meridian once again, and consider that you're standing at what could be considered the nexus of space and time on Planet Earth.*

Then check out a few final sights around the courtyard. Save the observatory building for last, as you'll exit the complex through its gift shop.

Camera Obscura: Hiding in a corner of the courtyard is a thrillingly low-tech device. It's simply a dark room (or *camera obscura* in Latin) that lets in light through a pinhole-size prick in the roof. The light is reflected downward by a mirror and projected onto a flat disc. The effect is like watching a live feed of the scene outside. For thousands of years, humans have mastered this technology, for science and entertainment, done without electricity or machinery—Caveman TV.

View: Enjoy a great view of the symmetrical royal buildings, the Thames, and the Docklands and its busy cranes (including the prominent Canary Wharf Tower, with its pyramid cap). A chart helps you find various

Side margin: GREENWICH

landmarks: Canary Wharf, the huge O2 dome, and the towers of the Emirates Air Line cable car. To the left lies the square-mile City of London with its skyscrapers, the dome of St. Paul's Cathedral, and the Shard (farther to the left). At night (17:00-24:00), look for the green laser beam that the observatory projects into the sky. It extends along the prime meridian for 15 miles—a godsend for orbiting space aliens trying to get their bearings.

Meridian Observatory Building: This has a wide assortment of historical telescopes. The humongous one, designed by George Airy, is used today to define the prime meridian. (A video nearby shows the telescope in action.) The telescope, fixed firmly to the spinning earth, tracks the stars as they pass overhead, marking when they cross the start/finish line of the prime meridian. Glancing outside, notice that The Line is perfectly aligned with the shaft of the telescope.

You'll exit the observatory complex through the shop. To add one more detour, from within the shop find the steps up to the Great Equatorial Telescope from 1893, which fills the giant, green, bulb-shaped dome on top of the building. This was one of the largest telescopes in the world at the time, and helped solidify Greenwich's status as a scientific center.

• *Our tour through Greenwich is finished. If you have more time or interest, near the Royal Observatory are a couple of other sights.*

Nearby: The **Weller Astronomy Galleries** has interactive, kid-pleasing displays allowing you to guide a space mission and touch a 4.5-billion-year-old meteorite (free, daily 10:00-17:00).

The state-of-the-art, 120-seat **Peter Harrison Planetarium** offers entertaining and informative shows several times a day where they project a view of the heavens onto the interior of the dome (£10, shows about every 45 minutes during the observatory's opening times, no morning shows on school days, check schedule online). As these shows can sell out, consider getting tickets in advance online. Most shows are family-oriented, with early shows intended for young children.

• *To return to town, head back down the hill along The Avenue. The road becomes King William Walk and ends at the* Cutty Sark *and Greenwich Pier, where you can catch a boat or DLR train back to downtown London. If you have time and interest, you could hop off the DLR for a quick visit to the Docklands (see page 112).*

GREENWICH

SLEEPING IN LONDON

London is an expensive city for lodging. Focus on choosing the right neighborhood, which is as important as selecting the right hotel. I've picked a handful of my favorite neighborhoods (Victoria Station, South Kensington, Earl's Court, Bayswater, and North London) and recommend a range of options for each, from £20 bunks to deluxe £300-plus doubles with all the comforts. Because such comforts (and charm) come at a price, I've also listed big, modern, good-value chain hotels scattered throughout the city, along with hostels, dorms, and apartment rental information. For a few accommodations in Windsor and Cambridge, see the Day Trips chapter.

There's no getting around it: Cheap rooms in London are dumpy. (Midrange ones can be, too.) It's hard to find a room acceptable to most tastes for less than about £100. Hotels in the £120-130 range—where some of my recommendations fall—buy you a basic, reasonably cheery double with worn carpet and a private bath in a usually cramped, outdated, cracked-plaster building, or a soulless-but-comfortable room in a huge Motel 6-type place. Even accommodations that are quite nice can be in old buildings with crooked floors, ill-fitting doors, odd smells, and noisy plumbing. For a spacious, thoughtfully appointed splurge with modern

London's Hotel Neighborhoods

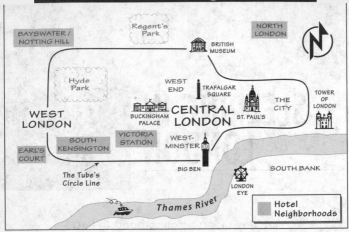

SLEEPING

amenities, expect to pay at least £200 for a double (and more often £300-400).

Most hotels offer an optional breakfast buffet for about £15-20 per person, though it's often not included in their quoted rates (you can choose whether to add breakfast when booking). Light eaters and budget travelers can opt out of the hotel breakfast and get coffee and a pastry at a neighborhood café for less.

I rank accommodations from $ budget to $$$$ splurge. For the best deal, contact small, family-run hotels directly by phone or email. When you book direct, the owner avoids a commission and may be able to offer a discount or perk such as a free breakfast. Book well in advance for peak season or if your trip coincides with a major holiday or festival (see the appendix). For details on reservations, short-term rentals, and more, see the "Sleeping" section in the Practicalities chapter.

BUDGET OPTIONS

If you're on a tight budget, consider the following alternatives to staying at an independently run hotel or guesthouse.

Chain Hotels: While lacking a personal touch, these at least come with some predictability. But not all chain hotels are created equal—narrow down your search by figuring out which chains suit your tastes (for a list of budget chains, see "Big, Good-Value, Modern Hotels," later), identify the neighborhoods you're interested in, then read reviews on hotel-booking websites (I like Booking.com).

Apartment Rentals: By booking a room or apartment (through Airbnb or similar site), you'll typically get more space and amenities while paying less than you would at a hotel. And you'll often get to stay in a more local-feeling building and neighborhood. While it's worth looking for places in the areas that appeal to you, keep an open mind. The farther from the city center you're willing to stay, the better the value. (I'd rather sleep in a palatial apartment a 20-minute Tube ride from downtown than pay the same for a grubby budget hotel a five-minute ride away.) See page 586 for tips on booking short-term rentals.

For more options for sleeping (relatively) cheap in London, browse these accommodation discount sites: www.londontown. com (an informative site with a discount booking service), athomeinlondon.co.uk and www.londonbb.com (both list central B&Bs), www.lastminute.com, www.visitlondon.com, and www. eurocheapo.com.

VICTORIA STATION NEIGHBORHOOD

The streets behind Victoria Station teem with accommodations. It's a safe, surprisingly tidy, and decent area without a hint of the

trashy, touristy glitz of the streets immediately surrounding the station. I've divided these accommodations into two broad categories: Belgravia, west of the station, feels particularly posh, with designer cupcake shops on every other corner. Pimlico, to  the east, feels more lived-in (though still quite nice) and is dotted with colorful eateries. All of my recommended hotels are within a five-minute walk of the Victoria Tube, bus, and train stations. Especially in summer, request a quiet back room; most of these B&Bs lack air-conditioning and may front busy streets.

Laundry: The nearest laundry option is **Pimlico Launderette,** about five blocks southwest of Warwick Square (self-service and same-day full service, open Mon-Sat 8:00-19:00, Sun until 17:00, last self-wash one hour before closing; 3 Westmoreland Terrace—go down Clarendon Street, turn right on Sutherland, and look for the launderette on the left at the end of the street; +44 20 7821 8692).

Parking: The 400-space Semley Place **NCP parking garage** is near the hotels on the west/Belgravia side (£40/day, just west of Victoria Coach Station at Buckingham Palace Road and Semley Place, +44 845 050 7080, www.ncp.co.uk). **Victoria Station car park** is cheaper but a quarter of the size; check here first, but don't hold your breath (£30/day, entrance on Eccleston Bridge between

SLEEPING

SLEEPING

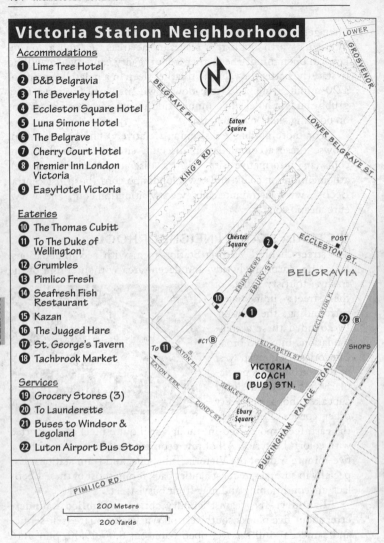

Victoria Station Neighborhood

Accommodations
1. Lime Tree Hotel
2. B&B Belgravia
3. The Beverley Hotel
4. Eccleston Square Hotel
5. Luna Simone Hotel
6. The Belgrave
7. Cherry Court Hotel
8. Premier Inn London Victoria
9. EasyHotel Victoria

Eateries
10. The Thomas Cubitt
11. To The Duke of Wellington
12. Grumbles
13. Pimlico Fresh
14. Seafresh Fish Restaurant
15. Kazan
16. The Jugged Hare
17. St. George's Tavern
18. Tachbrook Market

Services
19. Grocery Stores (3)
20. To Launderette
21. Buses to Windsor & Legoland
22. Luton Airport Bus Stop

200 Meters
200 Yards

Buckingham Palace Road and Bridge Place, +44 345 222 4224, www.apcoa.co.uk).

West of Victoria Station (Belgravia)

In Belgravia, the prices are a bit higher and your neighbors include some of the world's wealthiest people. These two places sit on tranquil Ebury Street, two blocks over from Victoria Station (or a slightly shorter walk from the Sloane Square Tube stop). You can cut the walk from Victoria Station to nearly nothing by taking a short ride on frequent bus #C1 (leaves from Buckingham Palace Road side of Victoria Station and drops you off on corner of Ebury

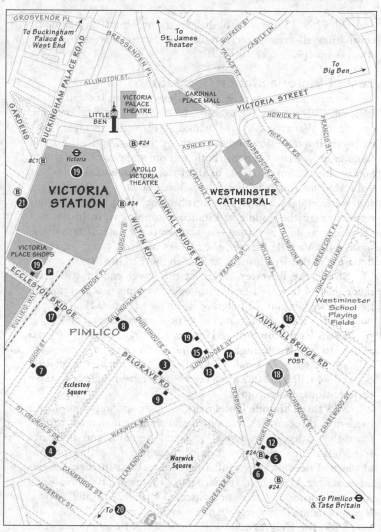

SLEEPING

and Elizabeth streets). Both places come with some street noise; light sleepers should request a room in the back.

$$$$ Lime Tree Hotel has 26 spacious, stylish, comfortable rooms; flowery, posh-feeling public spaces; the inviting Buttery restaurant, where breakfast is served; and a delightful garden in back (135 Ebury Street, +44 20 7730 8191, www.limetreehotel. co.uk, info@limetreehotel.co.uk, Charlotte).

$$$ B&B Belgravia comes with 17 bright, colorful rooms and high ceilings. It feels less than homey, but still offers good value for the location. Most of its rooms come with closets and larger-than-average space (family rooms, 66 Ebury Street,

+44 20 7259 8570, www.bb-belgravia.com, info@bb-belgravia.com). They also rent several studios and apartments on the same street (with check-in at the B&B).

East of Victoria Station (Pimlico)

This area feels a bit less genteel than Belgravia, but it's still plenty inviting, with eateries and grocery stores. Most of these hotels are on or near Warwick Way, the main drag through this area. Don't be overly impressed by higher prices; of these options, the Luna Simone and Cherry Court are both well run and two of my favorite good-value accommodations in all of London. Generally the best Tube stop for this neighborhood is Victoria (though the Pimlico stop works equally well for the Luna Simone). Handy bus #24 runs right through the middle of Pimlico—stopping right in front of the places on Belgrave Road—and connects the Tate Britain to the south with Victoria Station, the Houses of Parliament, Trafalgar Square, the British Museum, and much more to the north.

$$$$ The Beverley Hotel, at the lower end of this price range, has 14 tidy, well-equipped, modern rooms that feel upscale for the price (air-con, 13 Belgrave Road, +44 20 7630 1884, http://www.thebeverleylondon.com, info@thebeverleylondon.com).

$$$$ Eccleston Square Hotel is a splurge with professional polish. Its 39 stylish, high-tech rooms are located on a less-busy side street, facing a small park (air-con, elevator, 37 Eccleston Square, +44 20 3503 0694, www.ecclestonsquarehotel.com, stay@ecclestonsquarehotel.com).

$$$ Luna Simone Hotel rents 36 fresh, spacious rooms with modern bathrooms. It's traditional and smartly managed, run for more than 50 years by twins Peter and Bernard, and Bernard's son Mark. They still enjoy their work, and do it with a personal touch. Prices include a full English breakfast in their convivial cellar breakfast room (RS%, family rooms, 47 Belgrave Road near the corner of Charlwood Street, +44 20 7834 5897, www.lunasimonehotel.com, stay@lunasimonehotel.com).

$$$ The Belgrave has a big, stylish, glittery lobby and 72 chain-like rooms; while impersonal, it can be affordable considering the location and amenities (air-con, elevator, 80 Belgrave Road, +44 20 7828 8661, www.the-belgrave.com, info@the-belgrave.com).

$ Cherry Court Hotel, run by the friendly and industrious Patel family, rents 12 very small but bright and well-designed rooms with firm mattresses in a central location. Considering London's sky-high prices, this is an extraordinary budget choice (family rooms, fruit-basket breakfast in room, air-con, laundry, 23 Hugh Street, +44 20 7828 2840, www.cherrycourthotel.co.uk, info@

cherrycourthotel.co.uk, Neha answers emails and offers informed restaurant advice).

If considering chain hotels, the fine **$$$ Premier Inn London Victoria** is in this area (82 Eccleston Square, www.premierinn. com).

"SOUTH KENSINGTON," SHE SAID, LOOSENING HIS CUMMERBUND

To stay on a quiet street so classy it doesn't allow hotel signs, make "South Ken" your London home. This upscale area has plenty of colorful restaurants and easy access to the Victoria and Albert and Natural History museums; shoppers like being a short walk from Harrods and the designer shops of King's Road and Chelsea. When I splurge, I splurge here. The South Kensington Tube stop gives you access to both the handy Piccadilly and Circle/District lines, making it easy to get virtually anywhere in London; it's also easy to reach from Heathrow.

$$$$ Aster House, in a lovely Victorian town house, is run with care by kind Leonie, who's been welcoming my readers for years (I call it "my home in London"). It's a stately and sedate place, with 13 comfy rooms, a cheerful lobby, and a lounge. Enjoy breakfast or just kick back in the whisper-elegant Orangery, a glassy greenhouse (RS%, air-con, 3 Sumner Place, +44 20 7581 5888, www.asterhouse.com, asterhouse@gmail.com).

$$$$ Number Sixteen, for well-heeled travelers, packs over-the-top class into its 41 artfully imagined rooms, plush designer-chic lounges, and tranquil garden. It's in a labyrinthine building, with boldly modern decor—perfect for an urban honeymoon (air-con, elevator, 16 Sumner Place, +44 20 7589 5232, www. numbersixteenhotel.co.uk, sixteen@firmdale.com).

$$$$ The Pelham Hotel, a 52-room business-class hotel with crisp service and a pricey mix of pretense and style, is genteel, with low lighting and a pleasant drawing room and library among the many perks (air-con, elevator, fitness room, 15 Cromwell Place, +44 20 7589 8288, www.pelhamhotel.co.uk, reservations.thepelham@ starhotels.com).

NEAR EARL'S COURT

This neighborhood—a couple of Tube stops farther from South Kensington on the Piccadilly and Circle/District lines—is a nice compromise between local-feeling and accessible to travelers. It has a stately residential feel, and a high concentration of high-capacity, relatively expensive hotels. Solo travelers might consider one of the several quality chains here. The main drag that runs in front of the Tube station—Earl's Court Road—is lined with easy chain eateries.

SLEEPING

South Kensington Neighborhood

To Kensington Palace →

Kensington Gardens

ALBERT MEMORIAL

WEST CARRIAGE DRIVE

Hyde Park

SOUTH CARRIAGE DRIVE

To Knightsbridge →

KENSINGTON ROAD

ROYAL ALBERT HALL

ENNISMORE GARDENS

RUTLAND GATE

N

PRINCE CONSORT ROAD

PRINCE'S GARDENS

ALBERTOPOLIS

AYRTON ROAD

EXHIBITION ROAD

IMPERIAL COLLEGE ROAD

To Harrods →

BROMPTON ORATORY

BROMPTON RD.

SCIENCE MUSEUM

VICTORIA & ALBERT MUSEUM

NATURAL HISTORY MUSEUM

BROMPTON

CROMWELL ROAD

QUEENSBURY PL.

CROMWELL PLACE

THURLOE PLACE

Thurloe Square

BROMPTON ROAD

WALTON ST.

3

THURLOE STREET

4

5

QUEEN'S GATE

HARRINGTON ROAD

GLEN PL.

BUTE ST.

South Kensington

PELHAM STREET

SLOANE AVE.

REECE MEWS

6

9

2

ONSLOW SQUARE

SYDNEY PL.

PELHAM CRESCENT

LUCAN PLACE

7

1

Onslow Square

ROAD

ELYSTAN STREET

OLD BROMPTON ROAD

9

ONSLOW MEWS E.

ONSLOW GARDENS

SUMNER PLACE

H'WORTH PLACE

To Earl's Court →

ONSLOW

SOUTH KENSINGTON

SELWOOD GARDENS

8

FULHAM

CALE ST.

300 Meters

300 Yards

Accommodations
1 Aster House
2 Number Sixteen Hotel
3 The Pelham Hotel

Eateries & Other
4 Exhibition Road Food Circus

5 Daquise
6 Moti Mahal Indian Rest.
7 Old Brompton Road Eateries
8 The Anglesea Arms Pub
9 Groceries (2)

$$$$ The Resident Kensington is on a residential block a short walk from Earl's Court Tube station. It's professionally run and thoughtfully appointed; each of the 65 rooms has a small, efficient kitchenette (air-con, elevator, 25 Courtfield Gardens, +44 20 7244 2255, www.residenthotels.com/the-resident-kensington, kensington.reception@residenthotels.com).

$$$$ K+K Hotel George occupies a grand Georgian building on a quiet street just behind the Earl's Court Tube station. With spacious public areas, a wellness center, and 154 well-appointed rooms, it feels polished and professional (air-con, elevator, 1 Templeton Place, +44 20 7598 8700, www.kkhotels.com, hotel.george@kkhotels.com).

$$$$ NH London Kensington, part of a Spanish hotel chain, has 121 business-style rooms offering reliable comfort and class. Bonuses include a pleasant garden patio, a fitness center, and an extensive, tempting optional breakfast buffet (air-con, elevator, 202 Cromwell Road, +44 20 7244 1441, www.nh-hotels.com, nhkensington@nh-hotels.com).

$$$ Henley House Hotel is smaller and more warmly run than the others listed here, with 21 rooms in a modern, red-and-black color scheme. It fills a handsome brick town house overlooking a garden, a half-block from the Tube stop (discounts for longer stays, air-con, elevator, 30 Barkston Gardens, +44 20 7370 4111, www.henleyhousehotel.com, reservations@henleyhousehotel.com, Roberta).

BAYSWATER, NOTTING HILL, AND NEARBY

From the core of the tourist's London, vast Hyde Park spreads west, eventually becoming Kensington Gardens. Along the northern edge of the park sits Bayswater, with a cluster of good-value, reasonably priced accommodations in an area that's sleepy and very "homely" (Brit-speak for cozy). Your money will take you farther here than in most parts of central London—though the area can feel a bit sterile, and the hotels tend to be impersonal.

The Queensway Tube stop, while a couple of blocks from my recommendations, is handiest as it sits on the Central Line. I've also listed a few choices in the adjacent areas of Notting Hill (to the west), Paddington (to the east), and Holland Park (to the south)—each one just one or two Tube stops away.

Bayswater

Most of my Bayswater accommodations flank a peaceful, tidy park called Kensington Gardens Square (not to be confused with the much bigger Kensington Gardens adjacent to Hyde Park). One block east is the bustling street Queensway, a multicultural festival

SLEEPING

Earl's Court, Bayswater & Notting Hill

SLEEPING

Accommodations
1. The Resident Kensington
2. K+K Hotel George
3. NH London Kensington
4. Henley House Hotel
5. Vancouver Studios
6. Phoenix & Kensington Gardens Hotels
7. London House Hotel
8. Premier Inn Kensington
9. Garden Court Hotel
10. Portobello Hotel
11. Stylotel
12. Norwegian YWCA

Eateries
13. Cocotte
14. Farmacy
15. Hereford Road
16. Taqueria
17. The Prince Edward
18. Wagamama
19. Mazi
20. The Fish House of Notting Hill
21. Maggie Jones's
22. The Shed
23. The Churchill Arms Pub & Thai Kitchen
24. Café Diana
25. Groceries (5)
26. The Orangery (Afternoon Tea)

of commerce and eateries popular with young international travelers.

$$$ **Vancouver Studios** has 48 modern, tastefully furnished rooms that come with fully equipped kitchenettes (utensils, stove, microwave, and fridge), or you can pay for a continental breakfast. It's nestled between Kensington Gardens Square and Prince's Square and offers a more personal welcome than the others listed here. They have their own cozy coffee shop/bar and a tranquil garden patio out back (laundry, 30 Prince's Square, +44 7754 286 145, www.vancouverstudios.co.uk, info@vancouverstudios.co.uk).

$$$ **Phoenix Hotel** offers spacious, stately public spaces and 125 modern-feeling rooms with classy decor. While the rates can vary wildly, it's a good choice if you can get a deal (elevator, 1 Kensington Gardens Square, +44 20 7229 2494, www.phoenixhotel.co.uk, reservations@phoenixhotel.co.uk).

$$ **London House Hotel** has 103 modern, cookie-cutter rooms at reasonable prices (family rooms, air-con, elevator, 81 Kensington Gardens Square, +44 20 7243 1810, www.londonhousehotels.com, reservations@londonhousehotels.com).

$$ **Garden Court Hotel** is understated, with 40 simple, dated rooms (family rooms, air-con in most rooms, elevator, 30 Kensington Gardens Square, +44 20 7229 2553, www.gardencourthotel.co.uk, info@gardencourthotel.co.uk).

$$ **Kensington Gardens Hotel,** with the same owners as the Phoenix Hotel, laces 17 rooms together in a tall, skinny building (breakfast served at Phoenix Hotel, 9 Kensington Gardens Square, +44 20 7243 7600, www.kensingtongardenshotel.co.uk, info@kensingtongardenshotel.co.uk).

Notting Hill

Just west of Bayswater (Tube: Notting Hill Gate), spreading out from the northwest tip of Kensington Gardens, this area is famous for two things: It's the site of the colorful Portobello Road Market (see page 460), and was the setting of the 1999 Hugh Grant/Julia Roberts film of the same name.

The $$$$ **Portobello Hotel,** classy and personable, is on a quiet, upscale-feeling residential street in the heart of the neighborhood. Its 21 rooms and beautiful lobby/lounge are a tasteful mix of funky and elegant—both the style and location give it an urban-fresh feeling (air-con, elevator, 22 Stanley Gardens, +44 20 7727 2777, www.portobellohotel.com, stay@portobellohotel.com).

Paddington

The streets and squares around Paddington Station teem with "budget" (but still overpriced) hotels. While it lacks the stately character of my other recommended neighborhoods, it's handy to the Heathrow Express train and gives you access to several useful Tube lines.

The well-run **$$ Stylotel** feels like the stylish, super-modern, aluminum-clad big sister of the EasyHotel chain (see page 416). Their 42 rooms come with hard surfaces—hardwood floors, pre-fab plastic bathrooms, and metallic walls. While rooms can be cramped, the beds have space for luggage underneath. You may feel like an astronaut in a retro science-fiction film, but if you don't need ye olde doilies, this place works (RS%, family rooms, air-con, elevator, 160 Sussex Gardens, +44 20 7723 1026, www.stylotel. com, info@stylotel.com, Andreas). They have eight pricier suites across the street with kitchenettes and no breakfast.

NORTH LONDON

These hotels are north of Regent Street, a long walk or quick Tube or bus ride from the lively Soho area and Hyde Park. These are my closest hotels to the center of London, and some of my most expensive. The wide streets and grand homes (including Sherlock Holmes') give this area an elegant aura...which is only slightly compromised by the hordes of tourists flocking through to reach Madame Tussauds.

$$$$ The Sumner Hotel rents 19 good-sized but dated rooms in a 19th-century Georgian town house also sporting a lounge with fancy modern Italian furniture. While past its prime, this place is conveniently located north of Hyde Park and near the Oxford Street shopping zone (RS%, air-con, elevator, 54 Upper Berkeley Street, a block off Edgware Road, Tube: Marble Arch, +44 20 7723 2244, www.thesumner.com, hotel@thesumner.com).

$$$$ Charlotte Street Hotel, in the Fitzrovia neighborhood close to the British Museum, is higher-end than most of my listings. This plush place has inviting public spaces and 52 bright, elegant rooms (connecting family rooms, air-con, elevator, 15 Charlotte Street, Tube: Tottenham Court Road, +44 20 7806 2000, www. charlottestreethotel.com, reservations@charlottestreethotel.com).

$$$$ The Mandeville Hotel, at the center of the action just one block from Bond Street Tube station, has a genteel British vibe, with high ceilings, tasteful art, just-vibrant-enough colors, and 142 rooms. It's a worthy splurge for its amenities and location, especially if you score a good deal (air-con, elevator, Mandeville Place, +44 20 7935 5599, www.mandeville.co.uk, info@mandeville.co.uk).

Near Covent Garden

These two hotels—pricey for what you get, but oh so central—are a short walk from Covent Garden, in the heart of the action.

$$$ The Fielding Hotel is simple but offers a good location on a quiet lane. They rent 25 tight but tidy rooms (plus three

SLEEPING

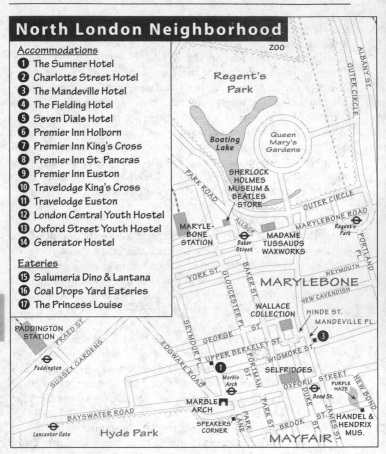

North London Neighborhood

Accommodations
1. The Sumner Hotel
2. Charlotte Street Hotel
3. The Mandeville Hotel
4. The Fielding Hotel
5. Seven Dials Hotel
6. Premier Inn Holborn
7. Premier Inn King's Cross
8. Premier Inn St. Pancras
9. Premier Inn Euston
10. Travelodge King's Cross
11. Travelodge Euston
12. London Central Youth Hostel
13. Oxford Street Youth Hostel
14. Generator Hostel

Eateries
15. Salumeria Dino & Lantana
16. Coal Drops Yard Eateries
17. The Princess Louise

apartments), serve no breakfast, and have almost no public spaces (family rooms, air-con, 4 Broad Court off Bow Street, Tube: Covent Garden, +44 20 7836 8305, www.thefieldinghotel.co.uk, reservations@thefieldinghotel.co.uk, well run by Sajaad).

$$ Seven Dials Hotel's 38 no-nonsense rooms are plain and fairly tight, but they're also clean and incredibly well located (some, but not all, have air-con). Since doubles here all cost the same, request a larger room when you book (family rooms, elevator, 7 Monmouth Street, Tube: Leicester Square or Covent Garden, +44 20 240 0823, www.sevendialshotel.co.uk, sevendialshotel@gmail.com, run by friendly and hardworking Hanna).

OTHER SLEEPING OPTIONS
Big, Good-Value, Modern Hotels

These chain hotels—popular with budget tour groups—offer all the modern comforts in a no-frills, practical package. If you can

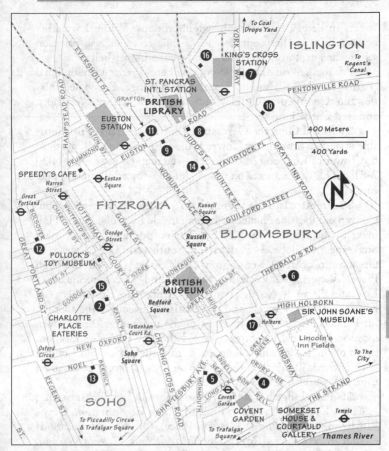

score a double for £100 (or less—often possible with promotional rates) and don't mind a modern, impersonal, American-style hotel, one of these can be a decent value in pricey London. This option is especially worth considering for families, as kids often stay for free.

While most of these hotels have 24-hour reception and elevators, breakfast generally costs extra (unless booked as part of a package), and the service lacks a personal touch (at some, you'll check in at a self-service kiosk).

Midweek prices are generally higher than weekend rates, and Sunday nights can be cheap. The best deals generally must be pre-paid a few weeks ahead and may not be refundable—read the fine print carefully.

I've listed a few of the dominant chains, along with a quick rundown on their more convenient London locations (see the map above to find chain hotels in North London). Quality can vary wildly, so check online reviews. Some of these branches sit on busy streets in dreary train-station neighborhoods. While I wouldn't necessarily rule these out, ask for a quieter room, use common sense when exploring after dark, and wear a money belt.

I've focused on affordable options here. Pricier London hotel chains include Millennium/Copthorne, Grange, Firmdale, Thistle, InterContinental/Holiday Inn, Radisson, Hilton, Marriott, and Red Carnation.

$$ Motel One, the German chain that specializes in affordable style, has a branch at Tower Hill, a 10-minute walk north of the Tower of London (24 Minories—see map on page 84, +44 20 7481 6420, www.motel-one.com, london-towerhill@motel-one.com).

$$ Premier Inn has more than 70 hotels in greater London. Convenient locations include a branch inside London County Hall (next to the London Eye), at Southwark/Borough Market (near Shakespeare's Globe, 34 Park Street), Southwark/Tate Modern (15 Great Suffolk Street), Kensington/Earl's Court (11 Knaresborough Place), Victoria (82 Eccleston Square), and Leicester Square (1 Leicester Place). In North London, three branches cluster between King's Cross St. Pancras and the British Museum: King's Cross, St. Pancras, and Euston. Just east of the museum is the Holborn location (27 Red Lion Street). Avoid the Tower Bridge location, south of the bridge and a long walk from the Tube—but London City Tower Hill, north of the bridge on Prescot Street (see map on page 84), works fine (www.premierinn.com).

$$ Travelodge has close to 70 locations in London, including at King's Cross (200 yards in front of King's Cross Station, Gray's Inn Road) and Euston (1 Grafton Place). Other handy locations include King's Cross Royal Scot, Marylebone, Covent Garden, Liverpool Street, Southwark, and Farringdon; www.travelodge.co.uk.

$$ Ibis, the budget branch of the AccorHotels group, has a few dozen options across the city, with a handful of locations convenient to London's center, including London Blackfriars (49 Blackfriars Road) and London City Shoreditch (5 Commercial Street). The more design-focused Ibis Styles has branches near Earl's Court (15 Hogarth Road) and Southwark, with a theater theme (43 Southwark Bridge Road; ibis.accorhotels.com).

$ EasyHotel, with several branches in good neighborhoods, has a unique business model inspired by its parent company, the easyJet budget airline. The generally tiny, super-efficient, no-frills rooms feel popped out of a plastic mold, down to the prefab ship's head-type "bathroom pod." Rates can be surprisingly low (with doubles as cheap as £30)—but you'll pay à la carte for expensive add-ons, such as TV use, Wi-Fi, luggage storage, fresh towels, and daily cleaning (breakfast, if available, comes from a vending machine). If you go with the base rate, it's like hosteling with privacy—a hard-to-beat value. But you get what you pay for (thin walls, flimsy construction, noisy fellow guests, and so on). They're only a good deal if you book far enough ahead to get a good price and skip the many extras. Locations include Victoria (34 Belgrave Road), South Kensington (14 Lexham Gardens), and Paddington (10 Norfolk Place); www.easyhotel.com.

$ Hub by Premier Inn—the budget chain's no-frills, pod-style division—offers extremely small rooms (just a little bigger than the bed) in convenient locations for low prices (as affordable as £69). They have a beautifully located branch right in the heart of Soho but tucked down a quieter back street (www.premierinn.com/gb/en/hub.html).

Hostels

Hostels can slash accommodation costs while meeting your basic needs. The following places are open 24 hours, have private rooms as well as dorms, and come with Wi-Fi.

¢ London Central Youth Hostel is the flagship of London's hostels, with all the latest in security and comfortable efficiency. Families and travelers of any age will feel welcome in this wonderful facility. You'll pay the same price for any bed—so try to grab one with a bathroom (families welcome to book an entire room, book long in advance; between Oxford Circus and Great Portland Street Tube stations at 104 Bolsover Street—see map on page 414, +44 345 371 9154, www.yha.org.uk, londoncentral@yha.org.uk).

¢ Oxford Street Youth Hostel is right in the shopping and clubbing zone in Soho (14 Noel Street—see map on page 414, Tube: Oxford Street, +44 345 371 9133, www.yha.org.uk, oxfordst@yha.org.uk).

¢ Generator Hostel is a brightly colored, hip hostel with a café and a DJ spinning the hits. It's in a renovated building tucked behind a busy street halfway between King's Cross and the British Museum (37 Tavistock Place—see map on page 414, Tube: Russell Square, +44 20 7388 7666, http://staygenerator.com, ask.london@generatorhostels.com).

¢ St. Christopher's Inn, a cluster of three hostels south of the Thames near London Bridge, has cheap dorm beds; one branch (the Oasis) is for women only. All have loud and friendly bars attached (must be over 18 years old, 161 Borough High Street, Tube: Borough or London Bridge, reservations +44 20 8600 7500, www.st-christophers.co.uk).

English is definitely a second language at **¢ Norwegian YWCA (Norsk K.F.U.K.)**—which is open to any Norwegian woman and to non-Norwegian women under 30. (Men must be under 30 with a Norwegian passport.) Located on a quiet street near Holland Park in the Kensington area, it offers a study, TV room, piano lounge, and an open-face Norwegian ambience (goat cheese on Sundays!). Those willing to share with strangers are most likely to get a bed (private rooms available, 52 Holland Park—see map on page 410, Tube: Holland Park, +44 20 7727 9346, www.kfukhjemmet.org.uk, kontor@kfukhjemmet.org.uk).

Dorms

These options—available during summer break (sometime in June through mid-Sept)—are all cheaper if you opt for a shared bathroom.

$ The University of Westminster makes some high-rise dorm rooms in central London available to travelers during summer break. They all come with access to well-equipped kitchens and big lounges (+44 20 7911 5181, www.westminster.ac.uk/summeraccommodation, summeraccommodation@westminster.ac.uk). Others include the **$ London School of Economics** (+44 20 7955 7676, www.lsevacations.co.uk, vacations@lse.ac.uk) and **$ University College London** (+44 20 7529 8975, www.ucl.ac.uk/residences, guest-bookings@ucl.ac.uk).

Apartment Rentals

Consider this option if you're traveling as a family, in a group, or staying several days. Websites such as Airbnb and VRBO let you correspond directly with property owners or managers, or consider one of the sites listed next. Some specialize in London, while others also cover areas outside of London. For more information on short-term rentals, see the Practicalities chapter.

OneFineStay.com focuses on finding stylish, contemporary flats (most of them part-time residences) in desirable London neighborhoods. While pricey, it can be a good choice if you're seeking a hip, nicely decorated home away from home.

SuperCityUk.com gives travelers a taste of what local London life is like, renting chic, comfortable aparthotels and serviced apartments in four buildings.

Other options include Cross-Pollinate.com, Coach House Rentals (www.chsrentals.com), VisitApartmentsLondon.co.uk, HomeFromHome.co.uk, and APlaceLikeHome.co.uk.

Near the Airports

It's so easy to get to Heathrow and Gatwick from central London, I see no reason to sleep at either one. But if you do, here are some options.

Heathrow: An **Aerotel** is inside the airport (Terminal 3), while **EasyHotel** and **Hotel Ibis London Heathrow** are a short bus or taxi ride away.

Gatwick: The South Terminal has a **Yotel,** while **Gatwick Airport Central Premier Inn** rents cheap rooms 350 yards away, and **Gatwick Airport Travelodge** has budget rooms about two miles from the airport.

SLEEPING

EATING IN LONDON

Far from the dated stereotypes of dreary British food, London is one of Europe's great food cities. Whether it's dining well with the upper crust, sharing hearty pub fare with mates, or venturing to a fringe neighborhood to try the latest hotspot or street food at a market, eating out is an essential part of the London experience. You could try a different cuisine for each meal and never eat "local" English food, even on a lengthy stay in London. The sheer variety of foods—from every corner of Britain's former empire and beyond—is astonishing.

My listings fall into two categories: neighborhood places handy to my recommended hotels, and destination dining areas (like Soho in Central London and Shoreditch in the East End). Considering how expensive London is, you might be tempted to eat cheaply here—and it's doable. On the other hand, if food is a priority, London is one of the most exciting cities for culinary exploration—and, if you choose carefully, well worth the investment.

EATING TIPS

I rank restaurants from **$** budget to **$$$$** splurge. For more advice on eating in London, including ordering, tipping, and British cuisine and beverages, see the "Eating" section of the Practicalities chapter.

Service: Virtually all London restaurants with table service automatically add a 12.5 percent service charge. No additional tip is necessary—locate this charge on your bill before paying to avoid double-tipping.

Finding Restaurants: London's food scene is constantly changing. For the latest, drop by a newsstand to get a weekly entertainment guide or an annual restaurant guide (both have extensive restaurant listings). Or visit www.squaremeal.co.uk, www.timeout.com, or the food section of www.theguardian.com for restaurant reviews and can't-miss meals.

Pubs: Many of London's 7,000 pubs serve traditional British classics at moderate prices (around £9-15). You can get beer almost any time of day (about 11:00-23:00, and later on Fridays and Saturdays). You can usually get food around 12:00-14:00 and 18:00-20:00. For more on pubs and pub grub, and for tips on ordering beer, see the Practicalities chapter. I list several historic pubs in London later in this chapter.

Chain Restaurants: Budget eating in London often means a modern, super-efficient chain restaurant—available in countless varieties, from burgers (Bleecker, Honest Burgers, and—gulp!—Five Guys and Shake Shack) and sushi (Yo!, Wasabi, and Itsu) to Indian (Masala Zone), Thai (Thai Square, Busaba), and more (Côte Brasserie, Ask, Pizza Express, Wagamama, and Loch Fyne)—offering essentially the same menu items at each location. For a description of some reliable chains, see page 593.

Street Markets: London thrives with street markets, many featuring the latest and trendiest food stalls. Markets are the perfect antidote to London's high prices and interchangeable chain restaurants. For more, see the "Food Markets" section in this chapter.

Picnicking: London has an array of carryout options, from Pret and Caffè Nero—selling fresh salads and sandwiches—to Marks & Spencer department stores (with a good deli) and their offshoot M&S Simply Food. I've listed several well-located supermarkets in this chapter.

CENTRAL LONDON

Central London is absolutely packed—with both locals and tourists—and restaurants are overflowing, even on a "quiet" night. On weekends and later in the evenings, sidewalks and even the streets become congested with people out barhopping and clubbing. If you're looking for peace and quiet and a calm meal, avoid Friday and Saturday evenings here and come early on other nights.

Many popular chain restaurants permeate this area. There's no need to clutter up my listings and maps with these—like Starbucks or McDonald's, you can count on seeing them wherever you go.

Heart of Soho

With its many theaters, reputation as a rollicking nightspot, and status as *the* place where budding restaurateurs stake their claim on London's culinary map, the Soho neighborhood is a magnet for diners. As it's close to London's must see's and do's, you could find yourself eating here a lot (convenient for dinner after a day of sightseeing, or before going to the theater). Even if Soho isn't otherwise on your radar, make a point to dine here at least once.

Locals are slightly put off by the high-rent, congested, glitzy Soho scene; they'd rather go to more up-and-coming neighborhoods (like Shoreditch in the East End). Still, Soho's super-convenient location makes it a perfect place for travelers to sample what's currently "in" in London (though you'll also find some reliable classics here).

$$$ Andrew Edmunds Restaurant is a tiny candlelit space where you'll want to hide your guidebook and not act like a tourist. This little place—with a loyal clientele—is the closest I've found to Parisian quality in a cozy restaurant in London. The extensive wine list, modern European cooking, and creative seasonal menu are worth the splurge (daily 12:30-15:30 & 17:30-22:45, these are last-order times, come early or call ahead, request ground floor rather than basement, 46 Lexington Street, +44 20 7437 5708, www.andrewedmunds.com).

$$ Mildreds, a vegetarian restaurant across from Andrew Edmunds, has a creative, fun menu and a tight, high-energy interior filled with happy herbivores (daily 12:00-23:00, vegan options, 45 Lexington Street, +44 20 7494 1634).

$$$ Bao Soho is a minimalist eatery selling top-quality Taiwanese cuisine, specializing in delicate and delectable steamed-bun sandwiches (portions are small so order more than one). This is a popular spot, often with a line across the street; try to arrive early or late (Mon-Sat 12:00-15:00 & 17:30-22:00, Sun 12:00-17:00, 53 Lexington Street).

$$$ Temper Soho pleases well-heeled carnivores. From the nondescript office-block entrance, you'll descend to a cozy, stylish cellar filled with rich smoke from meat grilling on open fires. The portions are small and pricey (order multiple courses), but meat lovers willing to pay leave satisfied (Mon-Sat 12:00-22:30, Sun until 21:00, 25 Broadwick Street, +44 20 3879 3834).

$$$ Kiln invigorates the taste buds with the explosive flavors of northern Thailand. Squeeze along the long, stainless-steel counter—peering into the wood-fired kilns where the frantic staff does all the cooking—or grab a table in the cramped cellar dining room.

The menu skews slightly to the adventurous (i.e., organ meat and strong sauces and curries), with delicious results (daily 12:00-15:00 & 17:00-23:00, 58 Brewer Street).

$$$ Bocca di Lupo, a stylish and popular option, serves half and full portions of classic regional Italian food. Dressy but with a fun energy, it's a place where you'll be glad you made a reservation. The counter seating, on cushy stools with a view into the lively open kitchen, is particularly memorable, or you can take a table in the snug, casual back end (daily 12:30-15:00 & 17:15-23:00, 12 Archer Street, +44 20 7734 2223, www.boccadilupo.com).

$$$ Kricket Soho serves upmarket "Indian-inspired cooking" a few steps from Piccadilly Circus. Opt for the tight, stylish, unpretentious main floor (with counter seating surrounding an open kitchen) or the dining room in the cellar. The small-plates menu is an education in Indian cuisine beyond the corner curry house, with *kulchas* (miniature naan breads with toppings), *kheer* (rice pudding), and KFC—Keralan fried chicken (Mon-Sat 12:00-14:30 & 17:15-22:30, closed Sun, 12 Denman Street, +44 20 7734 5612).

$$$$ NOPI is one of a handful of restaurants run by London celebrity chef Yotam Ottolenghi. The main floor seats diners at traditional tables; the cellar features communal tables looking into the busy kitchen. The cuisine is typical of Ottolenghi's masterful Eastern Mediterranean cooking, with an emphasis on seasonal produce. If you want to splurge in Soho, do it here (Mon-Sat 10:00-15:00 & 17:30-22:30, Sun until 16:00, 21 Warwick Street, +44 20 7494 9584, www.ottolenghi.co.uk).

$$ Hoppers is an easy entry into Sri Lankan cuisine- -reminiscent of Indian but with more tropical flourishes. You'll be glad the menu comes with a glossary of key terms—for example, *hopper* (a spongy yet firm rice-and-coconut pancake, shaped like a bowl), *kari* (Tamil for "curry"), and *roti* (flatbread). Be adventurous, and seek the waitstaff's advice (daily 12:00-14:30 & 17:30-22:30, 49 Frith Street, +44 20 3319 8110).

$$ Yalla Yalla is a bohemian-chic hole-in-the-wall serving up high-quality Lebanese street food—hummus, baba ghanoush, tabbouleh, and shawarmas. Eat in the cramped and cozy interior or at one of the few outdoor tables (daily 10:00-24:00, 1 Green's Court—just north of Brewer Street, +44 20 7287 7663).

Between Soho and Covent Garden: Cozy and convivial, **$$ Fernandez & Wells** is a delightfully simple wine, cheese, and ham bar. Grab a stool as you belly up to the big wooden bar. Share a plate of tapas, top-quality cheeses, and/or Spanish, Italian, or French hams with fine bread and oil, all while sipping a nice glass of wine. At lunch, they have quality sandwiches (Mon-Tue 8:00-21:00, Wed-Fri until 23:00; Sat 10:00-22:00, Sun until 17:00; 1 Denmark Street, +44 20 3302 9799).

Central London Restaurants

Heart of Soho
1. Andrew Edmunds Restaurant
2. Mildreds & Bao Soho
3. Temper Soho
4. Kiln
5. Bocca di Lupo
6. Kricket Soho
7. NOPI
8. Hoppers
9. Yalla Yalla

10. Fernandez & Wells
11. Gelupo Gelato

Near Carnaby Street
12. Kingly Court Eateries
13. Mother Mash & Dishoom

Chinatown
14. Four Seasons
15. Dumplings' Legend
16. Viet Food

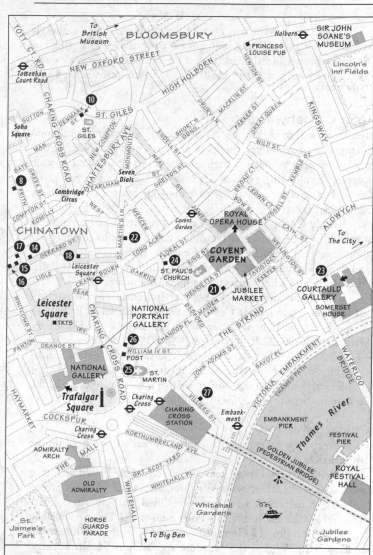

17 Rasa Sayang

18 Jen Café

<u>Swanky Splurges</u>

19 The Wolseley

20 Brasserie Zédel

21 Rules Restaurant

<u>Near Covent Garden</u>

22 Dishoom

23 Shapur Indian Restaurant

24 Lamb & Flag Pub

<u>Near Trafalgar Square</u>

25 St. Martin-in-the-Fields
Café in the Crypt

26 The Chandos Pub

27 Gordon's Wine Bar

<u>Afternoon Tea</u>

28 Fortnum & Mason

29 Brown's Hotel

Gelato: Across the street from Bocca di Lupo (listed earlier) is its sister *gelateria*, **Gelupo,** with a wide array of ever-changing but always creative and delicious dessert favorites. Take away or enjoy their homey interior (daily 11:00-23:00, 7 Archer Street, +44 20 7287 5555).

Near Carnaby Street

The area south of Oxford Circus between Regent Street and Soho Gardens entices hungry shoppers with attention-grabbing, gimmicky restaurants that fill the niche between chains and upscale eateries. Stroll along Ganton, Carnaby, Kingly, and Great Marlborough streets for something that fits your budget and appetite, or consider these.

Kingly Court, with three levels of international restaurants overlooking a convivial courtyard, is a handy place to comparison-shop for a meal. Favorites include **Le Bab,** serving elevated kebabs, and **Señor Ceviche,** with Peruvian raw fish fare (long hours daily, enter either at 9 Kingly Street or at 49 Carnaby Street).

$$$ Dishoom, the super-popular Indian restaurant (see full listing later, under "Near Covent Garden") also has a branch on Kingly Street, with the same top-notch fare and the same long lines (daily 8:00-23:00, 22 Kingly Street, +44 20 7420 9322).

$$ Mother Mash is a bangers-and-mash version of a fish-and-chips shop. Choose your mash, meat, and gravy and enjoy this simple, satisfying, and thoroughly British meal (daily 10:00-22:00, 26 Ganton Street, +44 20 7494 9644).

Chinatown

Chinatown is just next door to Soho. These listings straddle the two districts.

On the Main Drag, near the Archways: The intersecting main streets of Chinatown—Wardour Street and Gerrard Street, with the ornamental archways—are lined with touristy, interchangeable Chinese joints. **$$ Four Seasons** is a cheap, reliable, traditional standby (12 Gerrard Street, +44 20 7287 0900; second location at 23 Wardour). A bit more appealing is **$$ Dumplings' Legend.** The draw here is their dumplings—particularly *siu long bao* (soup dumplings), which you can see being made fresh through the glassed-in kitchen as you enter (no reservations; on pedestrian main drag, 15 Gerrard Street, +44 20 494 1200). Other options worth considering include **$$$ Viet Food,** featuring tapas-style Vietnamese small plates with a busy chef in the window (34 Wardour Street); and **$ Rasa Sayang,** a hole-in-the-wall serving Malaysian wok dishes (5 Macclesfield Street).

$ Jen Café, across the little square called Newport Place from the main Chinatown strip, is a humble Chinese corner eatery appreciated for its homemade dumplings. It's just stools and simple seating, with fast service, a fun and inexpensive menu, and a devoted following (Mon-Wed 11:00-20:30, Thu-Sun until 21:30, cash only, 4 Newport Place, +44 20 7287 9708).

Swanky Splurges in Central London

For elegant, traditional dining, try one of these classics.

$$$$ The Wolseley is the grand 1920s showroom of a long-defunct British car. The last Wolseley drove out with the Great Depression, but today this old-time bistro bustles with formal waiters serving traditional Austrian and French dishes in an elegant black-marble-and-chandeliers setting fit for  its location next to the Ritz. Although the food can be unexceptional, prices are reasonable considering the grand presentation and setting. Reservations are a must (cheaper soup, salad, and sandwich "café menu" available in all areas of restaurant, daily 11:30-23:00, 160 Piccadilly, +44 20 7499 6996, www.thewolseley.com). They're popular for their fancy cream tea or afternoon tea (details later, under "Taking Tea in London").

$$$ Brasserie Zédel is the former dining hall of the old Regent Palace Hotel, the biggest hotel in the world when built in 1915. Climbing down the stairs from street level, you're surprised by a gilded grand hall that feels like a circa 1920 cruise ship, filled with a boisterous crowd enjoying big, rich French food—old-fashioned brasserie dishes. With vested waiters, fast service, and paper tablecloths, it's great for a group of friends. After 21:30, the lights dim, the candles are lit, and it gets more romantic with live jazz (nightly inexpensive *plats du jour,* daily 11:30-24:00, 20 Sherwood Street, +44 20 7734 4888). Across the atrium is the hotel's original Bar Américain (which feels like the 1930s) and the Crazy Coqs venue—busy with "Live at Zédel" music, theater, comedy, and literary events (see www.brasseriezedel.com for schedule).

$$$$ Rules Restaurant, established in 1798, is as traditional as can be—extremely British, classy yet comfortable. It's a big, stuffy place, where you'll eat in a plush Edwardian atmosphere with formal service and plenty of game on the menu. (A warning reads, "Game birds may contain lead shot.") This is the place to dress up and splurge for classic English dishes (daily 12:00-23:00, between the Strand and Covent Garden at 34 Maiden Lane, +44 20 7836 5314, www.rules.co.uk).

Near Covent Garden

Covent Garden bustles with people and touristy eateries. The area feels overrun, but if you must eat around here, you have some good choices.

$$$ Dishoom, a small chain, is London's hotspot for up-scale Indian cuisine. The dishes seem familiar, but the flavors are a revelation. Confusingly, the Covent Garden location—one of the first—is billed as "New Dishoom" after a renovation (in keeping with the Indian tradition of "new"-ing refurbished movie houses). People line up early (starting around 17:00) for a seat, either on the bright, rollicking, brasserie-like ground floor or in the less-appealing basement. Reservations are possible only until 17:45. With its oversized reputation, long lines of tourists, and multiple locations, it's easy to think it's overrated. But the food is simply phenomenal (daily 8:00-23:00, 12 Upper St. Martin's Lane, +44 20 7420 9320, www.dishoom.com). Other locations include near King's Cross Station, Carnaby Street (listed earlier), Kensington (several blocks west of the Royal Albert Hall), and Shoreditch.

$$$ Shapur Indian Restaurant is a well-respected place serving classic Indian dishes from many regions, fine fish, and a tasty and filling *thali* combina-

tion platter (including a vegetarian version). It's small, low energy, and dressy, with good service (Mon-Fri 12:00-14:30 & 17:30-23:30, Sat 15:00-23:30, closed Sun, next to Somerset House at 149 Strand, +44 20 7836 3730, Syed Khan).

$$ Lamb and Flag Pub is a survivor—a spit-and-sawdust pub serving traditional grub (like meat pies) two blocks off Covent Garden, yet seemingly a world away. Here since 1772, this pub was a favorite of Charles Dickens and is now a hit with local workers. At lunch, it's all food. In the evening, the ground floor is for drinking and the food service is upstairs (long hours daily, 33 Rose Street, go up the narrow alley from Floral Street, +44 20 7497 9504).

Near Trafalgar Square

$$ St. Martin-in-the-Fields Café in the Crypt is just right for a tasty meal on a monk's budget—maybe even on a monk's tomb. You'll dine sitting on somebody's gravestone in an ancient crypt. Their enticing buffet line is kept stocked all day, serving breakfast, lunch, and dinner (hearty traditional desserts, free jugs of water). You'll find the café directly under St. Martin-in-the-Fields, facing Trafalgar Square—enter through the glass pavilion next to the church (generally daily 10:00-19:30, profits go to the church, Tube: Charing Cross, +44 20 7766 1158). On Wednesday evenings you can dine to the music of a live jazz band at 20:00 (food available until 21:00, band plays until 22:00; see page 478). While here, check out the concert schedule for the busy church upstairs (or visit www.stmartin-in-the-fields.org).

$$ The Chandos Pub's Opera Room floats amazingly apart from the tacky crush of tourism around Trafalgar Square. Look for it opposite the National Portrait Gallery (corner of William IV Street and St. Martin's Lane) and climb the stairs—to the left or right of the pub entrance—to the Opera Room. This is a fine Trafalgar rendezvous point and wonderfully local pub. They serve sandwiches and a better-than-average range of traditional pub meals for around £10-12—meat pies and fish-and-chips are their specialty. The ground-floor pub is stuffed with regulars and offers snugs (private booths) and more serious beer drinking. To eat on that level, you have to order upstairs and carry it down (kitchen open daily 11:30-21:00, Fri until 18:00, order and pay at the bar, 29 St. Martin's Lane, Tube: Leicester Square, +44 20 7836 1401).

$$ Gordon's Wine Bar is a candlelit 15th-century wine cellar filled with dusty old bottles, faded British memorabilia, and nine-to-fivers. At the bar, order food (cheese and meat platters and other cold dishes) and consider the many varieties of wine and port available by the glass (this place is passionate about port—even the house port is excellent). The low carbon-crusted vaulting deeper in the back seems to intensify the Hogarth-painting atmosphere. Although it's crowded—often downright packed with people sitting at shared tables—you can normally find a spot. When sunny, the crowd spills out onto the tight parkside patio, where they have table service (Mon-Sat 11:00-23:00, Sun 12:00-22:00, 2 blocks from Trafalgar Square, bottom of Villiers Street at #47—the door is locked but it's just around the corner to the right, Tube: Embankment, +44 20 7930 1408).

VICTORIA STATION NEIGHBORHOOD

These restaurants are within a few blocks of Victoria Station. As with the accommodations in this area, I've grouped them into east and west of the station (for locations, see the map on page 404).

Groceries: Inside Victoria Station you'll find an **M&S Simply Food** (near the front, by the bus terminus) and a **Sainsbury's Local** (at rear entrance, on Eccleston Street). A larger **Sainsbury's** is on Wilton Road near Warwick Way, a couple of blocks southeast of the station.

Pub Appreciation

The pub is the heart of the people's England, where all manner of folks have, for generations, found their respite from work and a home away from home. England's classic pubs are national treasures, with great cultural value and rich history, not to mention good beer and grub (you'll find details on beer and pub food in the Practicalities chapter). Their odd names can go back hundreds of years. Because so many medieval pub-goers were illiterate, pubs were simply named for the picture hung outside (e.g., The Crooked Stick, The Queen's Arms—meaning her coat of arms).

While pubs have been around for centuries, the pub scene really came alive in the late Victorian era (c. 1880-1905). During this period, pubs were independently owned and land prices were high enough to make it worthwhile to invest in fixing them up. The politics were pro-pub as well: Conservatives, backed by Big Beer, were in, and temperance-minded Liberals were out.

Especially in class-conscious Victorian times, traditional pubs were divided into sections by elaborate screens (now mostly gone), allowing the wealthy to drink in a more refined setting, while commoners congregated on the pub's rougher side. These were really "public houses," featuring nooks (snugs) for groups and clubs to meet, friends and lovers to rendezvous, and families to get out of the house at night. Each neighborhood has a "local" where everyone gathers.

Historic pubs still dot the London cityscape. The only place to see the very oldest-style tavern in the "domestic tradition" is at **$$$ Ye Olde Cheshire Cheese,** which was rebuilt in 1667 (after the Great Fire) from a 16th-century tavern (see description on page 264; pub grub, pricier meals in the **restaurant,** open daily, 145 Fleet Street, Tube: Blackfriars, +44 20 7353 6170). Imagine this mazelike place, with three separate bars, in the pre-Victorian era: With no bar, drinkers gathered around the fireplaces, while tap boys shuttled tankards up from the cellar. (This was long before barroom taps were connected to casks in the cellar. Oh, and don't say "keg"—that's a gassy modern thing.)

Late-Victorian pubs are more common, such as the lovingly restored **$$ Princess Louise,** dating from 1897 (open daily, Sun no food and closes at 17:00, 208 High Holborn, see map on page 414; Tube: Holborn, +44 20 7405 8816). These places are fancy, often with heavily embossed wallpaper ceilings, decorative tile work, fine-etched glass, ornate carved stillions (the big central hutch for storing bottles and glass), and even urinals equipped with a place to set your glass.

London's best Art Nouveau pub is **$$ The Blackfriar** (c. 1900-1915), with fine carved capitals, lamp holders, and quirky phrases worked into the decor. While now operated by a chain, it

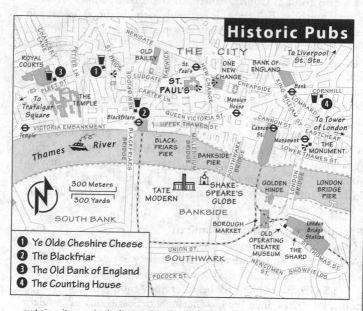

Historic Pubs

THE CITY

BANKSIDE

SOUTHWARK

1 Ye Olde Cheshire Cheese
2 The Blackfriar
3 The Old Bank of England
4 The Counting House

retains its period charm (open daily, outdoor seating, 174 Queen Victoria Street, Tube: Blackfriars, +44 20 7236 5474).

These days, former banks are being repurposed as trendy, lavish pubs, with elegant bars and freestanding stillions, which provide a fine center-piece.

Three such places are **$$ The Old Bank of England** (closed Sun, 194 Fleet Street, Tube: Temple, +44 20 7430 2255), **$$ The Jugged Hare** (open daily, 172 Vauxhall Bridge Road—see map on page 404, Tube: Victoria, +44 20 7614 0134, also see listing later in this chapter), and **$$ The Counting House,** with great sandwiches, homemade meat pies, fish, and fresh vegetables (open daily; gets really busy with the buttoned-down 9-to-5 crowd after 12:15, especially Thu-Fri; 50 Cornhill, Tube: Bank, +44 20 7283 7123).

At night, pubs are convivial watering holes. To experience the calmer side of pub tradition, drop by in late morning (from 11:00), when the pub is empty and filled with memories.

EATING

West of Victoria Station (Belgravia)

$$$ The Thomas Cubitt, named for the urban planner who designed much of Belgravia, is a trendy neighborhood gastropub packed with young professionals. It's pricey, a pinch pretentious, and popular for its modern English cooking. With a bright but slightly cramped interior and fine sidewalk seating, it's great for a drink or meal. Upstairs is a more refined and pricier restaurant with the same kitchen (food served daily 12:00-22:00, reservations recommended, 44 Elizabeth Street, +44 20 7730 6060, www.thethomascubitt.co.uk).

$$ Duke of Wellington pub is a classic neighborhood place with forgettable grub, sidewalk seating, and an inviting interior. A bit more lowbrow than my other Belgravia listings, this may be your best local glimpse of ye olde London (food served Mon-Sat 12:00-15:00 & 18:00-21:00, Sun lunch only, 63 Eaton Terrace, +44 20 7730 1782).

East of Victoria Station (Pimlico)

If you're looking for a good meal in this area, simply wander Wilton Road, which is lined with an enticing variety of eateries (including several of these choices). Best of all, chains are rare along here.

$$ Grumbles brags it's been serving "good food and wine at non-scary prices since 1964." Offering a delicious mix of "modern eclectic French and traditional English," this unpretentious little place with cozy booths inside (on two levels) and a few nice sidewalk tables is the best spot to eat well in this otherwise workaday neighborhood. Their traditional dishes are their forte (early-bird specials, open daily 12:00-14:30 & 18:00-23:00, reservations wise, half a block north of Belgrave Road at 35 Churton Street, +44 20 7834 0149, www.grumblesrestaurant.co.uk).

$ Pimlico Fresh's breakfasts and lunches feature fresh, organic ingredients, served up with good coffee and/or fresh-squeezed juices. This place is heaven if you need a break from your hotel's bacon-eggs-beans routine (takeout lunches, vegetarian options; Mon-Fri 7:30-18:00 or later, Sat-Sun from 9:00, breakfast served until 15:00, 86 Wilton Road, +44 20 7932 0030).

$$$ Seafresh Fish Restaurant is the neighborhood place for plaice—and classic and creative fish-and-chips cuisine. You can either step up to the cheaper **$ takeout counter,** or eat in—enjoying a white-fish ambience. Though Mario's father started this place in 1965, it feels like the chippy of the 21st century (daily 11:30-22:30, takeout from 11:00 and closed Sun, 80 Wilton Road, +44 20 7828 0747).

$$$ Kazan offers "Ottoman cuisine"—Turkish-style plates and mezes—in a modern and stylish atmosphere (daily 12:00-22:00, 93 Wilton Road, +44 20 7233 7100).

$$ The Jugged Hare, a 10-minute walk from Victoria Station, fills a lavish old bank building, with vaults replaced by kegs of beer and a kitchen. They have a traditional menu and a plush, vivid pub scene good for a meal or just a drink (food served Mon-Fri 11:00-21:00, Sat-Sun until 20:00, 172 Vauxhall Bridge Road, +44 20 7828 1543).

$$ St. George's Tavern, while part of a chain, is the neighborhood's most lively pub for an after-work drink or a full meal. They serve dinner from the same menu in three zones: on the sidewalk to catch the sun and enjoy some people-watching (mostly travelers with wheelie bags), in the ground-floor pub, and in a classier downstairs dining room with full table service (daily 12:00-22:00, corner of Hugh Street and Belgrave Road, +44 20 7630 1116).

$ Tachbrook Market, filling a short traffic-free block near several recommended hotels, is a delightful place to browse a variety of food stalls. Sit on a nearby curb with the locals for a quick lunch. There's also a row of produce, fish, and meat vendors, making this more local-feeling than most London street markets (Mon-Sat 8:00-18:00, closed Sun, on Tachbrook Street just off Warwick Way).

SOUTH KENSINGTON

These places are close to several recommended hotels and just a couple of blocks from the Victoria and Albert Museum and Natural History Museum (Tube: South Kensington; for locations see the map on page 408). The Anglesea Arms pub is a bit farther, but well worth the walk.

Exhibition Road Food Circus: This one-block-long pedestrian zone (on the Victoria and Albert Museum side of the South Kensington Tube station) is lined with enticing little eateries (all **$$** unless noted), including **Thai Square, Comptoir Libanais** (a Lebanese canteen), **Casa Brindisa** (tapas and shared Mediterranean-style dishes), and **$ Le Pain Quotidien** (hearty soups and sandwiches on homemade rustic bread). Facing down Exhibition Road is the best-regarded place in the area, **$$$ Daquise**—serving elevated Polish cuisine in a sophisticated but unstuffy atmosphere. With so many chain restaurants around, Daquise is a rare "destination" restaurant (daily 12:00-23:00, 20 Thurloe Street, +44 20 7589 6117).

Indian: $$ Moti Mahal, with minimalist-yet-upscale ambience and attentive service, serves delicious, mostly Bangladeshi cuisine. Consider chicken *jalfrezi* if you like spicy, and butter chicken if you don't (open for dinner Tue-Sun 17:30-23:30, also for lunch Sat-Sun 12:00-14:30, closed Mon, 3 Glendower Place, +44 20 7584 8428).

Old Brompton Road Eateries: This street, just one block from the South Kensington Tube station, is lined with a variety of good eateries. **$ Bosphorus Kebabs** is good for a quick bite of Turkish food (at #59); and **$$ Rocca,** at #73, is a bright and dressy Italian place with a heated terrace (daily 11:30-23:30, +44 20 7225 3413).

Classic London Pub: $$ The Anglesea Arms, with a great terrace buried in a classy South Kensington residential area, is a destination pub that feels like the classic neighborhood favorite. It's a thriving and happy place, with a woody ambience. While the food is the main draw, this is also a fine place to just have a beer. Don't let the crowds here put you off. Behind all the drinkers, in back, is an elegant, mellow step-down dining room a world away from any tourism (meals served daily 12:00-15:00 & 18:00-22:00; heading west from Old Brompton Road, turn left at Onslow Gardens and go down a few blocks to 15 Selwood Terrace; +44 20 7373 7960).

Supermarkets: Tesco Express (50 Old Brompton Road) and **Little Waitrose** (99 Old Brompton Road) are both open long hours daily.

BAYSWATER, NOTTING HILL, AND NEARBY

These are close to my recommended Bayswater and Notting Hill accommodations (for locations, see the map on page 410).

Near Bayswater Tube Station

While this neighborhood is a bit humdrum, it has more than its share of great eateries. Several of these might be worth a trip from elsewhere in London, just to dine.

$$ Cocotte is a "healthy rotisserie" restaurant specializing in delectable roast chicken, plus tempting sides and healthy salads (dine in or take away; daily 12:00-22:00, 95 Westbourne Grove, +44 20 3220 0076).

$$$ Farmacy is focused on organic vegan fare...with a side of pretense. The menu includes earth bowls, meatless burgers and tacos, and superfood smoothies. With an all-natural, woodgrain vibe, it feels like a top-end health food store (daily 9:00-16:00 & 18:00-22:00, 74 Westbourne Grove, +44 20 7221 0705).

$$$ Hereford Road is a cozy, mod eatery tucked away on Leinster Square, serving heavy, meaty English cuisine made with modern panache. Cozy two-person booths face the open kitchen up top; the main dining room is down below under skylights. There are also a few sidewalk tables (Tue-Sun 18:00-22:00, also open for lunch Fri-Sun 12:00-14:30, closed Mon, reservations smart, 3 Hereford Road, +44 20 7727 1144, www.herefordroad.org).

$$ Taqueria turns out delicious tacos, quesadillas, and other Mexican fare with big, bright, authentic flavors a short walk from my recommended Bayswater accommodations (daily 12:00-23:00,

141 Westbourne Grove, +44 20 7229 4734). Other tempting places line up along the same block.

$$ The Prince Edward serves good grub in a comfy, family-friendly, upscale-pub setting and at its sidewalk tables (daily 11:30-23:00, 2 blocks north of Bayswater Road at the corner of Dawson Place and Hereford Road, 73 Prince's Square, +44 20 7727 2221).

Supermarkets: Queensway is home to several supermarkets, including **Sainsbury's Local** and **Tesco Express** (both next to Bayswater Tube stop; a larger **Tesco** is near the post office farther along Queensway), and **Marks & Spencer** (inside Whiteleys Shopping Centre). All of these open early and close late (except on Sundays).

Notting Hill Gate

These are close to the Notting Hill Gate Tube stop.

$$$$ Mazi is a highly regarded Greek restaurant serving refined renditions of classic dishes, including Greek salad, grilled octopus, and *loukoumades* (doughnuts) in a contemporary, sophisticated setting. Since ordering several small plates can add up, the £19 two-course lunch is a good deal (daily 12:00-15:00 & 18:30-24:00, 12 Hillgate Street, +44 20 7229 3794).

$ The Fish House of Notting Hill is an old-fashioned and well-loved chippie, with takeaway on the ground floor and a more expensive **$$ table service** section upstairs (daily 12:00-21:00, 29 Pembridge Road, +44 20 7229 2626).

Supermarkets: Tesco Metro is a half-block from the Notting Hill Gate Tube stop (near intersection with Pembridge Road at 114 Notting Hill Gate).

Near Kensington Gardens

$$$$ Maggie Jones's has been feeding locals for over 50 years. Its countryside antique decor and candlelight make a visit a step back in time. It's a longer walk than most of my recommendations, but you'll get solid English cuisine. The portions are huge (especially the meat-and-fish pies, their specialty), and prices are a bargain at lunch. You're welcome to split your main course. The candlelit upstairs is the most romantic, while the basement is lively (daily 12:00-14:00 & 17:00-21:00, reservations recommended, 6 Old Court Place, east of Kensington Church Street, near High Street Kensington Tube stop, +44 20 7937 6462, www.maggie-jones.co.uk).

$$$$ The Shed offers farm-to-table dishes in a rustic-chic setting. Owned by three brothers—a farmer, a chef, and a restaurateur—The Shed serves locally sourced modern English dishes. The portions are hearty, with big, meaty flavors—a change of pace from London's delicate high-end dining scene. It's tucked a block off busy Notting Hill Gate (Mon-Sat 18:00-24:00, also open for lunch Tue-Sat 12:00-15:00, closed Sun, reservations smart, 122 Palace Gardens Terrace, +44 20 7229 4024, www.theshed-restaurant. com).

$$ The Churchill Arms Pub and Thai Kitchen is a combo establishment that's a hit in the neighborhood. It offers good beer and a thriving old-English ambience in front and hearty Thai dishes in an enclosed patio in the back. You can eat the Thai food in the tropical hideaway (table service) or in the atmospheric pub section (order at the counter). Bedecked with flowers on the exterior, it's festooned with Churchill memorabilia and chamber pots on the inside (including one with Hitler's mug on it—hanging from the ceiling farthest from Thai Kitchen—sure to cure the constipation of any Brit during World War II). Arrive by 18:00 or after 21:00 to avoid a line (food served daily 12:00-22:00, 119 Kensington Church Street, +44 20 7727 4242 for pub or +44 20 7792 1246 for restaurant).

$ Café Diana is a healthy little eatery serving sandwiches, salads, and Middle Eastern food. It's decorated—almost shrine-like—with photos of Princess Diana, who used to drop by for pita sandwiches (daily 8:00-23:00, cash only, 5 Wellington Terrace, on Bayswater Road, opposite Kensington Palace Garden gates, where Di once lived, +44 20 7792 9606, Abdul).

NORTH LONDON

To avoid the touristy crush right around the British Museum, head a few blocks west to the Fitzrovia area. Here, tiny Charlotte Place is lined with small eateries (including my first two listings); nearby, the much bigger Charlotte Street has several more good options (Tube: Goodge Street). The higher street signs you'll notice on Charlotte Street are a holdover from a time when they needed to be visible to carriage drivers. See the map on page 414 for locations.

$ Salumeria Dino serves up hearty £7 sandwiches, pasta, and Italian coffee. Dino, a native of Naples, has run his little shop for more than 30 years and has managed to create a classic-feeling Italian deli (also takeaway cappuccinos, Mon-Sat 8:00-17:00, closed Sun, 15 Charlotte Place, +44 20 7580 3938).

$$ Lantana, next door to Salumeria Dino, is an Australian coffee shop that sells modern soups, sandwiches, and salads in a sleek contemporary setting (Mon-Fri 8:00-18:00, Sat-Sun 9:00-16:00, 13 Charlotte Place, +44 20 7637 3347).

Coal Drops Yard Eateries: Farther north, in the Coal Drops Yard development just behind King's Cross Station (near the British Library), are branches of the renowned Indian restaurant **$$$ Dishoom;** the Chinese steamed-bun-filled-roll shop **$$$ Bao;** and the Sri Lankan place **$$ Hoppers** (see descriptions for each of these under "Central London," earlier in this chapter). In each case, the original sprouted in funky digs in Soho and is now expanding into glitzier, more spacious settings around the city—a common life cycle for trendy London restaurants. In addition to the enticing food options, Coal Drops Yard—a repurposed industrial site on Regent's Canal—is also simply a fun area to explore. Notice the corporate offices (including Google) in the super-modern office blocks nearby, and you'll understand why this seemingly out-of-the-way area is hopping after work.

EAST LONDON

Given its heritage of welcoming immigrants, it's no surprise that London's East End is its up-and-coming food mecca. Once known as *the* place to get authentic Indian and Bangladeshi food, it's now where lively restaurants, food trucks, and pop-ups come to get a toehold in an ever-evolving culinary scene. When in-the-know young locals eat out, they head for the East End—especially trendy Shoreditch. In many ways, this area is what Soho was 40 years ago (before tourism and gentrification): a vibrant, youthful, multicultural crucible of food, nightlife, and arts. I've focused on three areas: around Liverpool Street Station and Spitalfields Market; along Brick Lane; and near the Shoreditch High Street Tube station.

Spitalfields Market

Old Spitalfields Market Eateries: A few blocks east of Liverpool Street Station (and covered in my ▢ East End Walk), this cavernous hall is filled with a festival of eateries. The modern part of the market—to the west, closer to the train station—has big, brassy outposts of all the predictable London chains. It's much better to focus on the historic, Victorian-age Old Spitalfields Market section, where you'll find a more interesting array of small, one-off $-$$ eateries and pop-ups.

Under the steel-and-glass roof, make your way to "The Kitchens" section—nine different food counters surrounded by long, communal tables and even more food stalls. While the lineup is constantly changing, I've seen everything from Ethiopian fare to Peruvian street food. Nearby—toward Lamb Street—look for food trucks, including **Sud Italia**'s mobile oven (piping-hot, Naples-style pizzas) and **Crosstown Donuts** (gourmet sourdough doughnuts). Also around here is a wall of cheap eats: **Bleecker** (burgers), **Pilpel** (falafel), **Humble Crumble** (custard-drenched crumble dessert), and more. Whatever's trendy right now in London probably has an outpost here.

Hours vary, but most places open around 10:00 (11:00 on Sat) and start closing down around 17:00; after 18:00, it's mostly dead,

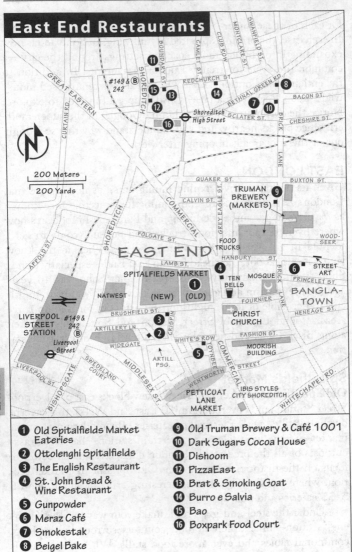

East End Restaurants

1. Old Spitalfields Market Eateries
2. Ottolenghi Spitalfields
3. The English Restaurant
4. St. John Bread & Wine Restaurant
5. Gunpowder
6. Meraz Café
7. Smokestak
8. Beigel Bake
9. Old Truman Brewery & Café 1001
10. Dark Sugars Cocoa House
11. Dishoom
12. PizzaEast
13. Brat & Smoking Goat
14. Burro e Salvia
15. Bao
16. Boxpark Food Court

so don't wait too late. On weekdays, some stay open until 20:00, but selection is limited (www.oldspitalfieldsmarket.com).

Near Spitalfields Market

These places are burrowed in the tight streets near Spitalfields, a couple of blocks east of Liverpool Street Station.

$$$$ Ottolenghi Spitalfields showcases the big flavors of celebrity chef Yotam Ottolenghi's modern Israeli/Eastern Mediterranean dishes. It's squeezed along tiny Artillery Lane, one of the East End's narrowest and most atmospheric streets. Its little shop in front displays its appetizers and desserts, and sells a few Ottolenghi products, such as preserves and cookbooks (Mon-Sat 8:00-22:30, Sun 9:00-18:00, reservations recommended, 50 Artillery Lane, +44 20 7247 1999, www.ottolenghi.co.uk).

$$$$ The English Restaurant, across from Spitalfields Market, started out as a Jewish bakery in the 17th century. It feels traditional for this trendy district, and is perhaps the best place to capture the ambience of the old East End. They serve up traditional British cuisine with a Belgian flair—like updated bread-and-butter pudding—in a snug dining room or a bistro-style bar area (Mon-Fri 8:00-23:00, Sat-Sun 9:30-18:00, 52 Brushfield Street, +44 20 7247 4110).

$$$ St. John Bread and Wine Restaurant, with a "nose to tail" philosophy, is especially popular at brunch—served until noon and featuring their award-winning bacon sandwich on thick bread with homemade ketchup (see if you can guess the special seasoning). They also have good lunches and dinners (daily 8:00-23:00, 94 Commercial Street, +44 20 7251 0848).

$$$ Gunpowder—a modern alternative to the traditional curry houses on nearby Brick Lane—offers a short and carefully crafted menu of updated Indian fare in a tight, noisy, cozy brick space (Mon-Sat 12:00-15:00 & 17:30-22:30, closed Sun, 11 White's Row).

On and near Brick Lane

Once synonymous with curry houses, historic Brick Lane now has many more options (though curry is still what many come here for).

$$ Brick Lane's Famous Curry Houses: This "Curry Row" comes with its own subculture—it's one of the only places in London where curbside hawkers pitch each eatery's "award-winning" pedigree and are eager to offer a discount. Ultimately, little distinguishes the options along here. Compare menus and deals, and take your pick. For something a notch above, head a half-block off Brick Lane to **Meraz Café,** offering a small, simple menu of Indian, Pakistani, and Bangladeshi dishes and homemade chutney (daily 11:00-23:00, 56 Hanbury Street, +44 20 7247 6999).

$$$ Smokestak feels like a classic East End eatery. The heavy-duty industrial interior is filled with tight tables and the rich smoke of an open fire—which grills meats to perfection. The owners started as a food truck, and this brick-and-mortar location carries on the meaty tradition. In addition to dry-aged beef and brisket, you'll find whole grilled fish and a few charred veggie options (Mon-Sat 12:00-15:00 & 17:30-23:00, Sun until 21:30,

EATING

reservations recommended, 35 Sclater Street, +44 20 3873 1733, www.smokestak.co.uk).

$ Beigel Bake, unpretentious and extremely old-school, is worth the short wait in line for fresh-baked bagels—served plain, smothered with cream cheese, or topped with salted beef, smoked salmon, salami, or chopped herring. Do your best to embrace the eccentrically grumpy service (open daily 24 hours, no seating—stand at the counter or take away, 159 Brick Lane, +44 171 729 0616).

Other Brick Lane Delights: The **Old Truman Brewery** hosts a fun courtyard of **$ food trucks** surrounded by prominent street art. Inside the brewery, **Café 1001** is a good place for coffee and cheap cafeteria fare.

At **Dark Sugars Cocoa House,** the sweet aroma of rich chocolate wafts through the open doors. Pop in for a taste—ask about their signature cardamom orange truffle or one of the fun pipettes. They also have decadent melted-chocolate drinks (daily 10:00-22:00, 141a Brick Lane, +44 7429 472 606).

Near Shoreditch High Street Tube Station

For upmarket, trendy, sit-down restaurants, head for the epicenter of East London's foodie scene: Shoreditch High Street. These choices are within a short walk of the area's Tube stop. Just north of here, Kingsland Road is nicknamed "Pho Mile" for its many Vietnamese eateries. You'll also find the original branch of London's famous upscale Indian restaurant, **Dishoom** (see description for Covent Garden branch, earlier; Shoreditch location at 7 Boundary Street—see the "East End Restaurants" map).

$$ PizzaEast delivers modern Italian pizzas and main dishes (crispy pork belly), all baked in their wood oven. Happy crowds perch on stools at communal tables. For dessert, their salted caramel tart is a favorite. It can get noisy at dinnertime and on Sundays with the market crowd; for a quieter ambience, come at lunch (Mon-Fri 12:00-24:00, Sat-Sun from 9:00, 56 Shoreditch High Street, +44 20 7729 1888).

$$$$ Brat, which has a Michelin star, is this area's upscale splurge. Sophisticated yet casual, with big windows, it fills the upstairs of an old warehouse (directly above Smoking Goat, listed next). The cuisine is uncomplicated modern English with Basque accents—top-quality fish, meats, and seasonal vegetables cooked on an open fire. Reserve ahead or show up right when they open for dinner to grab a first-come, first-served seat in the bar area (Mon-Sat 12:00-15:00 & 18:00-23:00, Sun 12:00-17:00, enter at 4 Redchurch Street—a few steps off Shoreditch High Street, www.bratrestaurant.com).

$$$ Smoking Goat is a Thai barbecue bar with dishes inspired by Bangkok canteens: chili-and-fish-sauce chicken wings, and smoked brisket and bone marrow *laab* (curry). The tight, convivial interior wraps around a big open kitchen and bar (Mon-Fri 12:00-15:00 & 17:30-23:00, Sat-Sun 10:00-23:00, 64 Shoreditch High Street).

$$$ Burro e Salvia has a pasta-making workshop up front and tables in the back for dining in. The menu is brief but delicious— a good place to get your homemade pasta fix. It's just a couple of short, street art-slathered blocks from Shoreditch High Street (daily 11:30-15:00, also open for dinner Thu-Sat 17:30-22:00, 52 Redchurch Street, +44 20 7739 4429).

Boxpark Food Court: Just outside the Shoreditch High Street Tube station, you'll find this (literally) elevated food court housed in repurposed train boxcars. Entrepreneurs rent time-limited "pop-up" space—an approach that allows them more stability than traveling to food markets, without the financial risk of opening a full restaurant. The ground floor mostly houses artists, but upstairs is a long string of food counters. Wander through and see what's available—usually a sampling of international cuisine with a modern twist (like Korean BBQ burritos, vegan burgers, and bubble waffles). There are several clusters of shared tables, and the long corridors between them are lined with benches. Their website lists the current lineup and each vendor's story (daily 11:00-23:00, 2 Bethnal Green, +44 20 7033 2899, www.boxpark.co.uk).

FOOD MARKETS

In this expensive city, one of the most cost-effective ways to sample local dishes is to graze through a food market. Many of these double as flea markets, so you'll find more details in the Shopping in London chapter—but don't overlook these for a memorable (or, at least, affordable) meal. You'll find English classics (meat pies, bangers and mash, grilled English cheddar cheese sandwiches) and cuisine from every corner of the globe. Most vendors accept credit cards. Keep track of which day of the week the various markets thrive, coordinate your sightseeing accordingly, and suddenly you're a temporary Londoner.

South London

Some of the best food markets in London are south of the Thames.

Borough Market: London's oldest fruit-and-vegetable market has been serving the Southwark community for more than 800 years.

Today, it's the granddaddy of all London food halls. Whether you're browsing for a gourmet picnic, a memorable meal, or just a quick between-sights bite—you'll find it here. There are as many people taking photos as buying fruit, cheese, and beautiful breads, but it's still a fun carnival atmosphere with fantastic food stalls. You'll see everything from diver-farmed oysters (bragging "from boat to Borough") and venison burgers to vividly colorful chutneys and delicacies from Croatia and Calabria...and more than a few cheesemongers (Mon-Fri 10:00-17:00, Sat from 8:00; Sun 10:00-15:00 and generally quieter; south of London Bridge, where Southwark Street meets Borough High Street; Tube: London Bridge, +44 20 7407 1002, www.boroughmarket.org.uk). To get fully oriented to the market—including places to sit, and a few specific eateries to look for—see page 317.

Southbank Centre Food Market: You'll find some of the city's most popular vendors in this weekends-only paradise of street food near the London Eye. Food vendors are wedged between ugly concrete buildings and elevated train tracks, but the selection is enticing and the location is handy (Fri-Sat 12:00-20:00, Sun until 18:00, closed Mon-Thu; immediately behind the Royal Festival Hall at Hayward Gallery—from the river, go around behind the buildings to find it; Tube: Waterloo, or Embankment and cross the Jubilee Bridge; +44 20 3879 9555, www.southbankcentre.co.uk). The market also hosts various festivals throughout the year (German Christmas, coffee, and chocolate are among the favorites).

Ropewalk (Maltby Street Market): This short-but-sweet, completely untouristy food bazaar bustles on weekends under a nondescript rail bridge in the shadow of The Shard. Two dozen vendors fill the narrow passage—about as long as a football field—with a festival of hipster/artisan carts selling a fun array of foods, such as decadent grilled cheese sandwiches, Venezuelan *arepas*, and a creative selection of Scotch eggs. Tucked among the carts are some good sit-down eateries, including The Walrus & The Carpenter for oysters and Spanish tapas bar Tozino (Sat 9:00-17:00, Sun 11:00-16:00, www.maltby.st). This area of South London—called Bermondsey—is a lowbrow but emerging neighborhood that's fun to explore for a slice of youthful, untrampled city. A short walk southeast of Tower Bridge, it has several rustic microbreweries tucked between auto-repair garages. You can also ride the Tube to Bermondsey, turn left out of the station, and catch bus #188 (toward Russell Square) just a few minutes to the Tanner Street stop; or you can catch bus #47 from the Monument Tube stop to the Boss Street stop.

Other London Markets

In West London, the **Portobello Road Market** in the Notting Hill neighborhood (see the Shopping in London chapter) is bursting with food stands. Near Victoria Station in Pimlico, drop by the very modest neighborhood market on **Tachbrook Street** (described on page 433).

In the East End, the **Old Spitalfields Market** (described on page 373) is one of London's best places to try a wide variety of food under one roof. Nearby, the axis formed by the **Truman Markets, Columbia Road Flower Market,** and (farther north) **Broadway Market** (described in the Shopping in London chapter) are also famous for their food; weekends are the ideal time to graze your way up and down this strip. Farther east, the **Greenwich Market** is a fun place for a meal if you're out for a day of nautical sightseeing (described on page 383).

North London's **Camden Lock Market** (see page 460) is bursting with creative eateries.

TAKING TEA IN LONDON

While visiting London, consider partaking in this most British of traditions. While some tearooms—such as the wallet-draining tea service at Claridges and the finicky Fortnum & Mason—still require a jacket and tie, most happily welcome tourists in jeans and sneakers (and cost, on average, £35-50). Most tearooms are usually open for lunch and close about 17:00. At all the places listed next, it's perfectly acceptable for two people to order one afternoon tea and one cream tea and share the afternoon tea's goodies. At many places, you can spring an extra £10 or so to upgrade to a boozy "champagne tea." For details on afternoon tea, see page 7.

Traditional Tea Experiences

$$$ The Wolseley serves a good afternoon tea between their meal service. Split one with your companion and enjoy two light meals at a great price in classic elegance (Mon-Fri 15:00-18:30, Sat-Sun from 15:30, see full listing on page 427).

$$$$ The Capital Hotel, a luxury hotel a half-block from Harrods, caters to weary shoppers with its intimate five-table, linen-tablecloth tearoom. It's where the ladies-who-lunch meet to decide whether to buy that Versace gown they've had their eye on. Even so, casual clothes, kids, and sharing plates are all OK (daily 12:00-17:30, book ahead—especially on weekends, 22 Basil Street—see the "West London" color map at the back of this book, Tube: Knightsbridge, +44 20 7591 1202, www.capitalhotel.co.uk).

$$$$ Fortnum & Mason department store offers tea at several restaurants within its walls. You can "Take Tea in the Parlour" for a reasonably priced experience (including ice cream and scones; Mon-Sat 10:00-18:00, Sun 12:00-17:30). The pièce de resistance is their Diamond Jubilee Tea Salon, named in honor of the Queen's 60th year on the throne (and, no doubt, to remind visitors of Her Majesty's visit for tea here in 2012 with Camilla and Kate). At royal prices, consider it dinner (daily 11:30-19:00, dress up a bit—no shorts, "children must be behaved," 181 Piccadilly—see the "West

EATING

London" color map at the end of this book, smart to reserve at least a week in advance, +44 20 7734 8040, www.fortnumandmason. com).

$$$$ Brown's Hotel in Mayfair serves a fancy afternoon tea in its English tearoom (you're welcome to ask for second helpings of your favorite scones and sandwiches). Said to be the inspiration for Agatha Christie's *At Bertram's Hotel*, the wood-paneled walls and inviting fire set a scene that's more contemporary-cozy than pinkie-raising classy (daily 12:00-17:30, reservations smart, no casual clothing, 33 Albemarle Street—see the "Central London Restaurants" map at the start of this chapter, Tube: Green Park, +44 20 7518 4155, www.roccofortehotels.com).

$$$$ The Orangery at Kensington Palace offers an elegant (and expensive) afternoon tea in its bright white hall near William and Kate's residence. The portions aren't huge, but who can argue with eating at a royal orangery or on the terrace? Check online to see if it's open after its lengthy renovation, and to find the latest cost and hours (a 10-minute walk through Kensington Gardens from either Queensway or High Street Kensington Tube stations to the orange brick building, about 100 yards from Kensington Palace—see map on page 410; +44 20 3166 6113, www.hrp.org.uk). If it's not yet open, I'd skip the "Pavilion"—a temporary tent set up to keep the tea business brewing while the project wraps up.

Other Places to Sip Tea

Taking tea is not just for tourists and the wealthy—it's a true English tradition. If you want the teatime experience but are put off by the price, consider these options, more in the £15-30 range.

$$$ Browns Restaurant at Butler's Wharf serves an affordable afternoon tea with brioche sandwiches, traditional scones, and sophisticated desserts (daily 15:00-17:00, 26 Shad Thames facing Tower Bridge—see the map on page 90, +44 20 7378 1700, www. browns-restaurants.co.uk).

At **$ Waterstones** bookstore you can put together a spread for around £10 in their fifth-floor view café (203 Piccadilly).

Museum Cafés: Many museum restaurants offer a fine inexpensive tea service. For example, the **$$$ Wallace Collection** serves reasonably priced afternoon tea and cream tea in its atrium (see page 77). Other museum cafés—including the one at the **$$ Victoria and Albert Museum**—may not offer a formal "afternoon tea," but you can assemble your own, à la carte tea and treats in elegant surroundings.

Shop Cafés: You'll find good-value teas at various cafés in shops and bookstores across London. Most department stores on Oxford Street (including those between Oxford Circus and Bond Street Tube stations) offer an afternoon tea.

LONDON WITH CHILDREN

London is a great city for kids. Big parks, colorful pageantry, engaging museums, and evocative historical sights make for happy little travelers. Add to that the buses, boats, trains, and Ferris wheels ready for riding, and your newly minted Londoners might never want to go home. The key to a successful family trip to this big city is making everyone happy, including the parents. My family-tested recommendations are designed to do just that.

Trip Tips

PLAN AHEAD

Involve your kids in trip planning. Have them read about the places that you may include in your itinerary (even the hotels you're considering), and let them help with your decisions.

Where to Stay
- Choose hotels in a kid-friendly area near a park. Bayswater and Notting Hill neighborhoods put you close to Kensington Gardens, with its imaginative playground (see Hyde Park listing later). Some of my recommended spots in North London are a stone's throw from Regent's Park.
- If you're staying more than a few days, think about renting an apartment (for more info on short-term rentals, see page 586).
- Consider hotels with restaurants, so older kids can go back to the room while you finish a leisurely dinner.
- London's big, budget chain hotels generally allow kids to sleep for free (see page 414).

What to Bring
- If traveling with infants, plan on bringing a light stroller for neighborhood walks and a child backpack for bus and Tube rides.
- Bring your own drawing supplies and books, as these supplies are pricey in Britain.
- For a touch of home at the hotel, bring some favorite movies.

EATING (AND DRINKING)

Try these tips to keep your kids content throughout the day.
- Eat dinner early (around 18:00) to miss the romantic crowd.
- Skip the famous places. Look instead for relaxed cafés, pubs (kids are welcome, though sometimes restricted to the restaurant section or courtyard area), or fast-food restaurants where kids can move around without bothering others.
- Quality chain restaurants pop up at many of the places you're likely to visit, providing some good go-to options that should please young palates. Look for Shake Shack, Wagamama Noodle Bar, and Pizza Express.
- Picnics work well; stop by a grab-and-go shop—such as Pret or Caffè Nero—or a supermarket with good takeout food, such as Sainsbury's Local or M&S Simply Food.
- Fun places to picnic are Hyde Park's rose garden, Kensington Gardens, the grounds of the Tower of London, Greenwich Park, or on the move—aboard a boat cruising the Thames or on an open-top sightseeing bus.
- Some of London's sights offer atmospheric eating options and good deals for families. St. Martin-in-the-Fields' Café in the Crypt, underneath the church, is more cozy than creepy. Aspiring royals will enjoy having afternoon tea at one of London's many tearooms.
- For older kids, be aware that the drinking age is 18 in Britain, but 16-year-olds can have beer, wine, and cider if accompanied by a meal and an adult. It's best to decide on a family policy beforehand.

SIGHTSEEING

The key to a successful London family vacation is to slow down. Tackle one or two key sights each day, mix in a healthy dose of pure fun at a park or square, and take extended breaks when needed.

Planning Your Time
- Involve your children in the trip. Let them help choose daily activities, pick lunch spots, and so on.
- Older kids and teens can help plan the details of a museum

visit, such as what to see, how to get there, and ticketing details.

- Follow this book's crowd-beating tips to a T to avoid long waits in line.
- Take advantage of Time Out London's frequently updated website, which includes handy kids' calendars listing activities, shows, and museum events, all searchable by date and location (www.timeout.com/london/kids).

Successful Sightseeing

- Deputize your child to lead you on my self-guided walks and museum tours. Turn your kid into your personal tour guide and navigator of the Tube system.
- Museum audioguides are great for older children. For younger children, hit the gift shop first so they can buy postcards and have a scavenger hunt to find the pictured artwork. When boredom sets in, try "I spy" games or have them count how many babies or dogs they can spot in all the paintings in the room. At each sight, ask about a kids' guide or flier.
- Most of the big museums—such as the Tate Modern, Tate Britain, and National Gallery—schedule children's activities on weekends. Some museums also offer "backpacks" with activities to make the visit more interesting. Ask at museum information desks.
- Many museums—such as the Science Museum, National Army Museum, and Museum of London Docklands—have play areas for children under age seven.
- Bring a sketchbook to a museum and encourage kids to select a painting or statue to draw. It's a great way for them to slow down and observe.
- For public WCs, try department stores, museums, and restaurants, particularly fast-food places.

Making or Finding Quality Souvenirs

- Buy your kids a trip journal, and encourage them to write down observations, thoughts, and favorite sights and memories. This journal could end up being their treasured souvenir.
- For a group project, keep a family journal. Pack a small diary and a glue stick. While relaxing over tea and scones, take turns writing or drawing about the day's events and include mementos such as museum ticket stubs and postcards.
- Teens might love shopping (or even window-shopping). See the Shopping in London chapter for fun areas.

MONEY AND SAFETY

Before your trip gets underway, talk to your kids about safety and money.

- Give your child a money belt and an expanded allowance; you are on vacation, after all. Let your children budget their funds by comparing and contrasting the dollar and pound.
- If you allow kids to explore a museum or neighborhood on their own, be sure to establish a clear meeting time and place.
- It's good to have a "what if" procedure in place in case something goes wrong. If your child has a mobile phone, enable the "Find My Phone" feature in case you get separated. Give your kids a business card from your hotel, along with your contact information and emergency taxi fare. Let them know to ask to use the phone at a hotel if they are lost.

STAYING CONNECTED

- If your kids have mobile phones, show them how to make calls in Britain (see "Staying Connected" in the Practicalities chapter).
- Most parents find it worth the peace of mind to buy supplemental messaging and data plans for the whole family. Adults can stay connected to teenagers while allowing them maximum independence, and teens can keep in touch with friends both old and new via apps such as FaceTime, WhatsApp, Facebook Messenger, Snapchat, Google Chat, or Skype.
- Readily available Wi-Fi (at hotels, some cafés, and all Starbucks and McDonald's) makes bringing a mobile device worthwhile.

Top Kids' Activities and Sights

CENTRAL LONDON

Covent Garden

This is a great area for people-watching and candy-licking. Kids like the **London Transport Museum,** with its interactive zone (see page 64).

Trafalgar Square and Nearby

This grand square, complete with huggable lion statues, is fun for kids (Tube: Charing Cross). At the **National Gallery** on Trafalgar Square, ask about their children's printed guides, audioguide programs, and events (Sunday mornings are especially kid-friendly).

📖 See the National Gallery Tour chapter.

CHILDREN

Also on Trafalgar Square is **St. Martin-in-the-Fields** church (see page 62). Next to the church is a glass pavilion, with a brass-rubbing center below that's fun for kids who'd like a souvenir to show for their efforts (for a small fee). For a meal, try the affordable Café in the Crypt, which has just the right spooky tables-on-gravestones ambience (see page 428).

Changing of the Guard and Horse Guards

Kids enjoy the bands and pageantry of the Buckingham Palace Changing of the Guard, but little ones get a better view at the inspection at St. James's Palace or Wellington Barracks (see page 69).

Most kids also like to watch the Horse Guards change daily (on Whitehall, between Trafalgar Square and #10 Downing Street, Tube: Westminster, see page 60).

Piccadilly Circus

This titillating district has lots of schlocky amusements; if you want to wander through an oversized M&M Store, this is the place. Be careful of fast-fingered riffraff. Hamleys toy store is just two blocks up Regent Street (listed below).

Shopping

If your teenager wants to bring home a few chic and cheap London fashions, **Oxford Street** (at the intersection of Regent Street) is a good place to start. Take the Tube to the Oxford Circus stop, and you'll be surrounded by lots of shops selling inexpensive, trendy clothes for teens. Stores include Topshop, Miss Selfridge, Zara, H&M, and Uniqlo. Sandwich shops and coffeehouses (including several Starbucks) offer easy rest stops. Also see the "Regent Street Shopping Walk" (on page 464).

Hamleys is the biggest toy store in Britain, with seven floors of toys (daily, 188 Regent Street, Tube: Oxford Circus, www.hamleys.com).

Harrods in Knightsbridge, with its over-the-top toy and food departments, can be fun for kids of all ages (see page 456).

Markets, particularly the Camden Lock Market, will hit the spot for finicky teenagers in need of loud music, cool clothes, and plenty of food choices (see page 460).

NORTH LONDON
Madame Tussauds Waxworks

Despite the lines outside and the crowds inside, the waxworks are popular with kids for gory stuff, pop and movie stars, everyone's favorite royals, and more (see page 78).

Books and Films for Kids

A Bear Called Paddington (Michael Bond, 1958). A bear winds up in a London train station, where he's found and adopted by a human family. The 2014 live-action remake, *Paddington,* and 2018 sequel follow the CGI bear's adventures in modern-day London.

The Chronicles of Narnia (C. S. Lewis, 1949-1954). Four siblings escape from WWII London into the magical world of Narnia (also a BBC miniseries and three feature-length films).

City Trails—London (Lonely Planet Kids, 2016). Follow Marco and Amelia as they find odd and wonderful secrets off the beaten path, giving quirky insights into contemporary and historic London.

Harry Potter books (J. K. Rowling, 1997-2007) and films (2001-2011). A young boy in England gets whisked off to a magical world of witchcraft and wizardry. There, he finds great friendships as well as grave evils.

A Little Princess (1939). In this film adaptation of the classic novel, Shirley Temple plays a girl whose fortunes fall and rise again in a Victorian London boarding school. The 1995 version, directed by Alfonso Cuarón, is also worth seeing.

The London Eye Mystery (Siobhan Dowd, 2007). Ted and Kat try to solve the mystery of their missing cousin, who disappeared after boarding the London Eye.

Kids' Travel Guide—London (Flying Kids, 2019). Explore London with a mix of interactive quizzes, tips, and coloring pages.

London Through Time (Angela McAllister, 2015). A boy and girl journey through time as they walk down one London street that folds out of this book to reveal the past.

Mary Poppins (1964). This beloved musical starring Julie Andrews and Dick Van Dyke is set in Edwardian London. The 2018 sequel, *Mary Poppins Returns,* takes place in 1930s London.

Mission London: A Scavenger Hunt Adventure (Catherine Aragon, 2014). Young explorers tackle spy-themed tasks while discovering the city.

This Is London (Miroslav Sasek, 1959, updated 2004). Vivid illustrations bring the English capital to life.

A Walk in London (Salvatore Rubbino, 2011). A mother and daughter experience the city—from the changing of the guard to St. Paul's Cathedral.

Wallace & Gromit TV series and films (1990-2012). Absent-minded inventor Wallace and his dog Gromit may live in northwest England, but these British characters are beloved by children around the country and the world.

Young Sherlock Holmes (1985). In this film, young Sherlock and his sidekick, Watson, work to solve the mystery of a series of nonsensical suicides (some scenes may be frightening for younger children).

CHILDREN

London Zoo and Regent's Park
This venerable animal habitat features more than 17,000 creatures and a fine petting zoo. Check online for feeding and event times (£22 for kids 3-15, free for kids 2 and under, £35 for adults, cheaper online, daily 10:00-18:00, shorter hours off-season, last entry one hour before closing; in Regent's Park; Tube: Baker Street, then bus #274; +44 344 225 1826, www.zsl.org). Regent's Park also has rental rowboats.

Pollock's Toy Museum
Kids will wonder how their grandparents ever survived without Xbox as they wander through this rickety old house filled with toys that predate batteries and microchips. Be aware, though, that you must exit through a neat toy shop (see page 76).

EAST LONDON
Tower of London
The crown jewels are awesome, and youngsters love the giant dragon constructed from old weapons and armor in the Arsenal. The Beefeater tour plays off kids in a memorable and fun way, and the welcome center offers quizzes, badges, and activities.

Avoid the long ticket lines by buying a voucher in advance. ⌂ See the Tower of London Tour chapter.

Museum of London
The museum has a very kid-friendly presentation that takes you from prehistoric times to the present. The events guide at the entrance details current kids' activities (see page 84).

THE SOUTH BANK
The Bankside Walk (see page 308) links several sights children might enjoy: The *Golden Hinde* ship, Shakespeare's Globe Theatre, Clink Prison Museum, and Old Operating Theatre.

London Eye and Nearby
The London Eye, a giant Ferris wheel, is a delight for the whole family (see page 89 for more information and crowd-avoidance tips). The same company runs the other two sights in the same complex (listed later), Madame Tussauds Waxworks, and the skippable London Dungeon—if you think you'll visit more than one of them, consider buying a combo-ticket to save some money. It's

CHILDREN

always cheaper to book these attractions in advance online—and you'll save time, as you can go straight to the ticket-holders line.

In the London Eye complex (Tube: Waterloo or Westminster), the small, pricey, but entertaining **Sea Life aquarium** resembles an overpriced theme park. Although there are far better aquariums elsewhere, this place packs in school groups and families looking for a break from museums (daily, www.visitsealife.com).

Next door, **Shrek's Adventure** is part walk, part 4-D ride. The crowded journey through Shrek's swamp re-creates scenes from the movie series (timed entry daily every 15 minutes, www.shreksadventure.com).

The fantastic and free **playground** in Jubilee Gardens, next to the London Eye complex, has an adventurous jungle gym of nets and logs for climbing and balancing.

HMS *Belfast*
Older kids might like scrambling across the decks of this WWII warship (see page 100).

WEST LONDON
Hyde Park
London's backyard is the perfect place for museum'd-out kids to play and run free. For older kids, the park has a tennis court, a putting green, and trails for running or biking. Young children will enjoy the Diana, Princess of Wales Memorial Playground in adjacent Kensington Gardens, with its Peter Pan-themed climbing equipment, including a huge wooden pirate ship (Tube: Queensway). Events such as music, plays, and clown acts are scheduled throughout the summer. The Serpentine Lake offers paddleboat rentals and a swimming area with a playground and a shallow kiddie pool (Easter-Oct daily 10:00-dusk, closed off-season; Tube: Knightsbridge, South Kensington, and more). The park is open daily from 5:00 in the morning until midnight (www.royalparks.org.uk).

Science Museums
The **Natural History Museum** features a wonderful world of dinosaurs, volcanoes, meteors, and creepy-crawlies, along with creative interactive displays (see page 107).

Next door to the Natural History Museum, the **Science Museum** offers lots of hands-on fun and IMAX movies (see page 109). The Garden play area on Floor B (basement level) entertains younger children (3-6) with water, textures, sounds, and climbing areas. This free museum also offers a variety of activities—like the Wonderlab—for a small fee.

Both the Natural History and Science museums are kid-friendly and can be clogged with school groups during the school year. Check for special events and exhibits (noted at each museum's entry and on their websites).

OUTSIDE THE CENTER

Cutty Sark

This beautifully restored sailing ship, now on dry land in Greenwich, is full of kid-friendly, hands-on displays (see page 385). Also in Greenwich, the **National Maritime Museum** has lots of kid-friendly exhibits for learning about life at sea (see page 394).

Queen Elizabeth Olympic Park

London's biggest park, complete with play areas, waterways, Olympic sights, and the world's longest, tallest tunnel slide, is a major draw for both kids and teens (see page 109).

The Making of Harry Potter: Warner Bros. Studio Tour

A nirvana for Potterphiles, this attraction (in Leavesden, a 20-minute train ride from London) lets fans young and old see the actual sets and props that were used to create the Harry Potter films. Shuttle buses run to the studio from the Watford Junction train station; for details, see page 124.

For a rundown of places in London where scenes from the movies were filmed, see the sidebar on page 122.

Kew Gardens

These famous 300-acre gardens include the Rhizotron and Treetop Walkway, which lets kids explore the canopy 60 feet above the ground on a 200-yard-long scenic steel walkway. Younger visitors will love the Children's Garden, with elements representing Earth, Air, Sun, and Water (see page 116).

London Museum of Water and Steam

This impressive collection of steam-powered pumping engines that once powered waterworks across the UK is mesmerizing for children. The engines operate only on weekends—search the website for "What's On" to make sure they're "in steam." The outdoor Splash Zone water-play area is fun in nice weather (free for kids under 18, £18 for adults, Sat-Sun 10:00-16:00, other days vary per local school holidays, Green Dragon Lane, Brentford, +44 20 8568 4757, www.waterandsteam.org.uk).

Day Trip to Windsor

If your kids are loopy over Legos, they'll love a visit to Legoland Windsor. The park is aimed at the 11-and-under crowd (see the Day Trips chapter for details).

Day Trip to Stonehenge

The mysterious, prehistoric stone circle at Stonehenge is a marvel for kids and adults alike. The sight's sleek visitor's center provides accessible explanations of what we know about Stonehenge—and what we don't (see the Day Trips chapter for details).

OTHER ACTIVITIES
Fun Transportation
A **Thames cruise** is a pleasant and easy way to see the city. Westminster Pier (near Big Ben) offers a lot of action, with round-trip cruises and boats to the Tower of London, Greenwich, and Kew Gardens. For details, see page 45.

Double-decker **hop-on, hop-off buses** drive by all the biggies in a two-hour loop and are fun for kids and stress-free for parents. You can stay on the bus the entire time, or hop on and hop off at any of the nearly 30 stops (see page 41).

Theater
The West End theaters have several shows that appeal to kids, including *Frozen, The Lion King, Matilda, Wicked,* and the two-part *Harry Potter and the Cursed Child* (see the Entertainment in London chapter). Or check out what's playing at the **Unicorn Theatre.** This modern complex presents professional theater for children on two stages (ask about family discounts, on the South Bank just behind City Hall, 147 Tooley Street, Tube: London Bridge; +44 20 7645 0560, www.unicorntheatre.com).

WHAT TO AVOID
The **London Dungeon**'s popularity with teenagers makes it one of London's most-visited sights. I enjoy gore and torture as much as the next boy, but this is lousy gore and torture, and I would not waste the time or money on it with my child. **The London Bridge Experience** (not to be confused with the Tower Bridge Exhibition) and **The London Tombs** are also to be avoided. They're copycat rip-offs of the London Dungeon.

CHILDREN

SHOPPING IN LONDON

London is great for shoppers—and, thanks to the high prices, even better for window-shoppers. This chapter will tell you where to get essentials, where to get souvenirs, where to browse through colorful street markets, and where to gawk at some high-end stores in this major fashion capital.

Most stores are open Monday through Saturday from roughly 9:00 or 10:00 until 17:00 or 18:00, with a late night on Wednesday or Thursday (usually until 19:00 or 20:00). Many close on Sundays. Large department stores stay open later during the week (until about 21:00 Mon-Sat) with shorter hours on Sundays.

Consider these tips for shopping in London:

- If all you need are souvenirs, a surgical strike at any souvenir shop will do.
- London's museums have extraordinarily good shops. The Transport Museum's is one of the best. Other sights with great shops include the British Museum, the National Gallery, the Victoria and Albert Museum, the Museum of London, the National Portrait Gallery, the Tate Modern, and the wacky selections at Pollock's Toy Museum and the Old Operating Theatre. (All of these museums are covered in the Sights in London or individual tour chapters.)
- Large department stores offer relatively painless one-stop shopping. Consider the down-to-earth Marks & Spencer (Mon-Sat 9:00-21:00, Sun 12:00-18:00, 173 Oxford Street, Tube: Oxford Circus; another at 458 Oxford Street, Tube: Bond Street or Marble Arch; see www.marksandspencer.com for more locations). Fancier department stores are listed later.
- For flea-market fun and bargains, try one of the many street markets.

- Gawkers as well as serious bidders can attend high-end auctions.

For information on **VAT refunds** and **customs regulations,** see page 575. Refuse any offers to charge your credit card in dollars. This is called **dynamic currency conversion** (DCC), and it's offered by some stores (including Harrods) as a "convenience." The very bad exchange rate they use is convenient only for increasing the store's profits. If asked which currency you want to pay in, always pay in the local currency rather than dollars.

Where to Shop

SHOPPING STREETS

London is famous for its shopping. The best and most convenient shopping streets are in the West End and West London (roughly between Soho and Hyde Park).

You'll find midrange shops along **Oxford Street** (running east from Tube: Marble Arch), and fancier shops along **Regent Street** (stretching south from Tube: Oxford Circus to Piccadilly Circus) and **Knightsbridge** (where you'll find Harrods and Harvey Nichols; Tube: Knightsbridge). Other streets are more specialized, such as **Jermyn Street** for old-fashioned men's clothing (just south of Piccadilly) and **Charing Cross Road** for books. **Floral Street,** connecting Leicester Square to Covent Garden, is lined with boutiques. My **"Regent Street Shopping Walk,"** at the end of this chapter, connects several shopping areas, including Oxford, Regent, Carnaby, and Jermyn streets.

Another fine street, which runs between Oxford Street and Marylebone Road, is **Marylebone High Street** (ending near Regent's Park and Madame Tussauds). It feels more quaint and less ritzy than some of the streets described above, and it's fun to browse for its combination of high-end chain stores, local one-off shops, art concept stores, clothing boutiques, and sleek home decor...all under handsome red-brick turreted townhouses. Along this street is the unique **Daunts Books,** filling an old townhouse with titles organized geographically (for details, see page 29).

FANCY DEPARTMENT STORES
Harrods

Harrods is London's most famous and touristy department store. With more than four acres of retail space covering seven floors,

it's a place where some shoppers could spend all day. (To me, it's still just a department store.) Big yet classy, Harrods has everything from elephants to toothbrushes (Mon-Sat 10:00-21:00, Sun 11:30-18:00, Brompton Road, Tube: Knightsbridge, +44 20 7730 1234, www.harrods.com).

Here's what I enjoy: On the ground floor, find the Food Halls, with their Edwardian tiled walls, creative and exuberant displays, and staff in period costumes—not quite like your local supermarket back home.

Ride the Egyptian Escalator—lined with pharaoh-headed sconces, papyrus-plant lamps, and hieroglyphic balconies—to the third floor, where you can find your way to the incredible toy department. Here you'll see an impressive Harry Potter section (wands go for upwards of £100) and such extravagances as child-size luxury pedal cars (£7,000)—the perfect gift for the child who has everything.

More than two dozen eateries are scattered throughout the store, including a sushi bar, deli, pizzeria, Ladurée *macaron* parlor, and burger bar.

Some people find Harrods overpriced and snooty. It's the only department store I've seen with its own gift shop—and Dale Chihuly chandelier (near the door 3 exit).

Harvey Nichols

Once Princess Diana's favorite and later Duchess Kate's, "Harvey Nick's" remains the department store *du jour* (Mon-Sat 10:00-20:00, Sun 11:30-18:00, near Harrods, 109 Knightsbridge, Tube: Knightsbridge, +44 20 7235 5000, www.harveynichols.com). Want to pick up a £20 scarf? You won't do it here, where they're more like £200 (and up). The store's fifth floor is a veritable food fest, with a gourmet grocery store, a fancy bar, an outdoor terrace, and a lively café. Consider a takeaway meal to eat on a bench in the Hyde Park rose garden two blocks away.

Fortnum & Mason

The official department store of the Queen, Fortnum & Mason embodies old-fashioned, British upper-class taste. While some feel it

SHOPPING

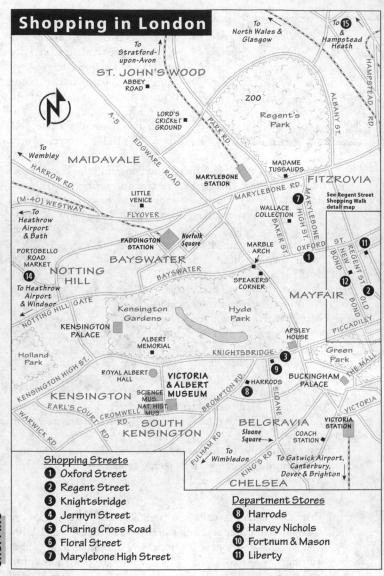

Shopping in London

To North Wales & Glasgow

To Hampstead Heath

To Stratford-upon-Avon

ST. JOHN'S WOOD

ABBEY ROAD

ZOO

Regent's Park

LORD'S CRICKET GROUND

PARK RD.

ALBANY ST.

HAMPSTEAD RD.

To Wembley

MAIDAVALE

EDGWARE ROAD

HARROW RD.

MADAME TUSSAUDS

FITZROVIA

MARYLEBONE STATION

MARYLEBONE RD.

See Regent Street Shopping Walk detail map

(M-40) WESTWAY

LITTLE VENICE

FLYOVER

WALLACE COLLECTION

BAKER ST.

HIGH ST.

OXFORD

ST.

NEW BOND

REGENT ST.

To Heathrow Airport & Bath

PADDINGTON STATION

Norfolk Square

BAYSWATER

MARBLE ARCH

MARYLEBONE

PORTOBELLO ROAD MARKET

NOTTING HILL

BAYSWATER

SPEAKERS' CORNER

MAYFAIR

OLD BOND

To Heathrow Airport & Windsor

NOTTING HILL GATE

Kensington Gardens

Hyde Park

PICCADILLY

Holland Park

KENSINGTON PALACE

ALBERT MEMORIAL

APSLEY HOUSE

Green Park

THE MALL

KENSINGTON HIGH ST.

ROYAL ALBERT HALL

VICTORIA & ALBERT MUSEUM

KNIGHTSBRIDGE

SLOANE ST.

BUCKINGHAM PALACE

KENSINGTON

EARL'S COURT RD.

CROMWELL RD.

SCIENCE MUS.

NAT. HIST. MUS.

HARRODS

BROMPTON RD.

VICTORIA

WARWICK RD.

SOUTH KENSINGTON

FULHAM RD.

BELGRAVIA

Sloane Square

VICTORIA STATION

COACH STATION

To Wimbledon

KING'S RD.

To Gatwick Airport, Canterbury, Dover & Brighton

CHELSEA

Shopping Streets

1. Oxford Street
2. Regent Street
3. Knightsbridge
4. Jermyn Street
5. Charing Cross Road
6. Floral Street
7. Marylebone High Street

Department Stores

8. Harrods
9. Harvey Nichols
10. Fortnum & Mason
11. Liberty

SHOPPING

is too stuffy, you won't find another store with the same storybook atmosphere. With rich displays and deep red carpet, Fortnum's feels classier and more relaxed than Harrods (Mon-Sat 10:00-21:00, Sun 11:30-18:00, elegant tea served in their Diamond Jubilee Tea Salon—see page 443, 181 Piccadilly, Tube: Green Park, +44 20 7734 8040, www.fortnumandmason.com; also see the "Regent Street Shopping Walk," later).

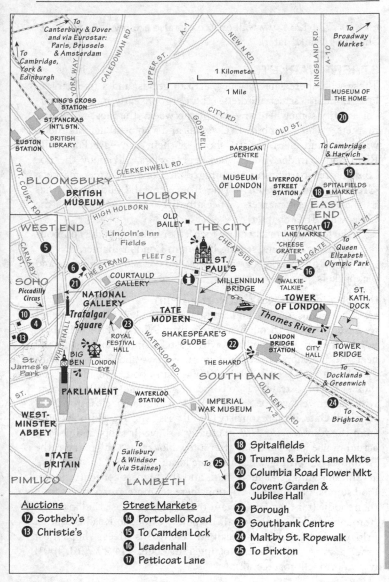

To Canterbury & Dover
and via Eurostar:
Paris, Brussels
& Amsterdam

To Cambridge,
York &
Edinburgh

1 Kilometer

1 Mile

To Broadway Market

KING'S CROSS STATION

ST. PANCRAS INT'L STN.

EUSTON STATION

BRITISH LIBRARY

MUSEUM OF THE HOME

20

To Cambridge & Harwich

BLOOMSBURY

HOLBORN

BARBICAN CENTRE

MUSEUM OF LONDON

LIVERPOOL STREET STATION

SPITALFIELDS MARKET

19

18

BRITISH MUSEUM

HIGH HOLBORN

OLD BAILEY

THE CITY

EAST END

WEST END

Lincoln's Inn Fields

CHEAPSIDE

PETTICOAT LANE MARKET

17

"CHEESE GRATER"

SOHO

Piccadilly Circus

5

6

21

COURTAULD GALLERY

FLEET ST.

ST. PAUL'S

MILLENNIUM BRIDGE

"WALKIE-TALKIE"

16

To Queen Elizabeth Olympic Park

ST. KATH. DOCK

NATIONAL GALLERY

Trafalgar Square

TATE MODERN

TOWER OF LONDON

10

4

13

23

SHAKESPEARE'S GLOBE

Thames River

TOWER BRIDGE

St. James's Park

BIG BEN

LONDON EYE

ROYAL FESTIVAL HALL

22

LONDON BRIDGE STATION

CITY HALL

To Docklands & Greenwich

PARLIAMENT

WATERLOO STATION

THE SHARD

SOUTH BANK

24

To Brighton

WEST-MINSTER ABBEY

IMPERIAL WAR MUSEUM

TATE BRITAIN

To Salisbury & Windsor (via Staines)

To **25**

PIMLICO

LAMBETH

Auctions	Street Markets	
12 Sotheby's	**14** Portobello Road	**18** Spitalfields
13 Christie's	**15** To Camden Lock	**19** Truman & Brick Lane Mkts
	16 Leadenhall	**20** Columbia Road Flower Mkt
	17 Petticoat Lane	**21** Covent Garden & Jubilee Hall
		22 Borough
		23 Southbank Centre
		24 Maltby St. Ropewalk
		25 To Brixton

SHOPPING

Liberty

Designed to make well-heeled shoppers feel at home, this half-timbered, mock-Tudor emporium is a 19th-century institution that thrives today. Known for its gorgeous "Liberty Print" floral fabrics, well-stocked crafts department, and castle-like interior, this iconic shop was a favorite of writer Oscar Wilde, who called it "the chosen resort of the artistic shopper" (Mon-Sat 10:00-20:00, Sun 12:00-18:00, Great Marlborough Street, Tube: Oxford Circus,

+44 20 7734 1234, www.liberty.co.uk, also see my "Regent Street Shopping Walk," later).

STREET MARKETS

Those who appreciate antiques, artisan goods, and a fine bargain love London's street markets. There's good early-morning market activity somewhere any day of the week. The most rewarding markets—which combine lively stalls and a colorful neighborhood with cute and characteristic shops of their own—are Portobello Road and Camden Lock Market. Hagglers will enjoy the no-holds-barred bargaining encouraged in London's street markets. **Greenwich** (a quick DLR ride from central London) also has its share of great markets, especially lively on weekends (see the Greenwich Tour chapter).

The following markets are focused on selling goods. For food-focused street markets, see the Eating in London chapter.

Warning: Markets attract two kinds of people—tourists and pickpockets.

Portobello Road Market (Notting Hill)

Classic, famous, quirky, and a bit dated, Portobello Road stretches for several blocks through the delightful Notting Hill neighborhood. Charming streets lined with pastel-painted houses and offbeat antique shops are enlivened on Fridays and Saturdays with 2,000 additional stalls (9:00-19:00), plus food, live music, and more. (The best strategy is to come on Friday; most stalls are open, with half the crowds of Saturday.) The first stretch, closest to Notting Hill Gate, is more touristy (you'll pass "The Travel Book Shop" from the film *Notting Hill*—actually a souvenir shop, and not the actual movie location). But after a few blocks, as you go under the A-40 overpass, things become more local; you'll see "The Canopy," an outdoor vintage fashion mall, and the highest concentration of food stands. Note that the options here are more greasy street food than foodie (for that, you'll want to head for the East End markets, Borough Market, or Ropewalk). While Portobello Road is best on Fridays and Saturdays, you can still enjoy this street's shops most other days as well (Tube: Notting Hill Gate, +44 20 7361 3001, www.portobelloroad.co.uk).

Camden Lock Market (Camden Town)

This huge, trendy arts-and-crafts market is divided into three areas, each with its own vibe (but all of them fresh and funky). The whole complex sprawls around an old-fashioned, still-functioning lock (used mostly for leisure boats) and its retro-chic, yellow-brick industrial buildings. The main market, set alongside the picturesque canal, features a mix of shops and stalls selling boutique crafts and artisanal foods. The market on the opposite side of Chalk Farm

Road is edgier, with cheap food stalls, lots of canalside seating, and punk crafts. The Stables, a sprawling, incense-scented complex, is decorated with fun statues of horses and squeezed into tunnels under the old rail bridge just behind the main market. It's a little lowbrow and wildly creative, with cheap clothes, junk jewelry, and loud music (daily 10:00-19:00, busiest on weekends, +44 20 3763 9999 or +44 20 7485 5511, www.camdenmarket.com).

Arriving by Tube, get off at the Chalk Farm stop, which allows you to avoid the tacky, crowded area between the market and the Camden Town Tube station (which bills itself as "The Camden Market," but lacks the real one's canalside charm). Bus #24 heads from Pimlico to Victoria Station to Trafalgar Square and then straight up to Camden, before continuing on to  Hampstead Heath. Better yet, arrive via a scenic waterbus ride or canalside bike ride from Little Venice (described on page 81). To escape the crowds, stroll for a while in either direction along the tranquil Regent's Canal; it's possible to walk east from here all the way to Queen Elizabeth Olympic Park in Stratford (about six miles away), or in the opposite direction, to the lovely Little Venice area (2.5 miles).

Leadenhall Market (The City)
One of London's oldest, Leadenhall Market stands on the original Roman center of town. Today, cheese and flower shops nestle between pubs, restaurants, and boutiques, all beneath a beautiful Victorian arcade (Harry Potter fans may recognize it as Diagon Alley). This is not a "street market" in the true sense, but more a hidden gem in the midst of London's financial grind (Mon-Fri 10:00-18:00, +44 20 7332 1523, Tube: Monument or Liverpool; off Gracechurch Street near Leadenhall Street and Fenchurch).

East End Markets
Most of these East End markets are busiest and most interesting on Sundays; the Broadway Market is best on Saturdays. I've listed them from south to north.

📖 For a walk tying together several of these markets, see the East End Walk chapter. For Petticoat Lane, Spitalfields, Truman, and Brick Lane markets, use the Liverpool Street Tube stop.

Petticoat Lane Market: Just a block from Spitalfields Market, this line of stalls sits on the otherwise dull, glass-skyscraper-filled Middlesex Street; adjoining Wentworth Street is grungier and more characteristic. Expect budget clothing, leather, shoes, watches, jewelry, and crowds (Sun 9:00-14:00, sometimes later; smaller market Mon-Fri on Wentworth Street only; no market Sat; Middlesex Street and Wentworth Street).

Spitalfields Market: This huge, mod-feeling market hall combines a shopping mall with old brick buildings and sleek modern ones, all covered by a giant glass roof. The shops, stalls, and a rainbow of restaurant options are open every day, tempting you with a wide variety of eateries, crafts, trendy clothes, bags, and an antique-and-junk market (Sun-Fri 10:00-18:00—but vendors begin shutting down around 17:00, Sat from 11:00; from the Tube stop, take Bishopsgate East exit, turn left, walk to Brushfield Street, and turn right; www.spitalfields.co.uk).

Truman Markets: Housed in the former Truman Brewery on Brick Lane, this cluster of markets is in the heart of the "Banglatown" Bangladeshi community. Of the East End market areas, these are the grittiest and most avant-garde. The markets are in full swing on Sundays, though you'll see some action on Saturdays and possibly other days (see hours below).

From Liverpool Street, head a few blocks east to Brick Lane and turn left. As you work your way north along Brick Lane through the Truman complex, you'll first come to the **Boiler House Food Hall** (on the left, an old warehouse that often hosts food stands and loud music), then the entrance to the **Vintage Market,** which occupies the basement with what claims to be London's largest assortment of vintage vendors (Mon-Sat 11:00-18:00, Sun from 10:00, www.vintage-market.co.uk). Just beyond, on the left, follow the crowds into the **Backyard Market,** with stylish clothing, arts, and crafts (Sat 11:00-18:00, Sun 10:00-17:00). Surrounding shops and eateries, including a fun courtyard of food trucks tucked off Brick Lane, are open all week.

Brick Lane Market: If you leave the Truman Brewery complex and continue north along Brick Lane, the action flows into a more casual assortment of food and arts stands and street performers called the Brick Lane Market (best on Sundays, 9:00-17:00). This spans several short blocks, from about Buxton Street to Bethnal Green Road—a 10-minute walk. Continuing another 10 minutes north, then turning right onto Columbia Road, takes you to the next market.

Columbia Road Flower Market: This colorful shopping street is made even more lively by the Sunday-morning commotion of shouting flower vendors. The prices are good (why not brighten up your hotel room with a bouquet?), and the sales pitches are entertaining (Sun 8:00-14:00, www.columbiaroad.info). Halfway up Columbia Road, be sure to loop left up little Ezra Street, with characteristic eateries, boutiques, and antique vendors.

Broadway Market: Saturdays are best for this festive and sprawling market, aptly named considering the attraction it holds for London's hipsters. A bit farther out, the market can be tricky to reach; it's easiest to take the Overground from Liverpool Street Station three stops to London Fields, then walk through that park to the market. Several blocks are filled with foodie delights, along with a few arts and crafts. The Broadway Schoolyard section is home to popular food trucks—many of them satellites of popular brick-and-mortar restaurants. The lineup changes constantly, but if you happen to see Pockets, Shrimpy, or The Frenchie, you know you've come on a good day (Sat 9:00-17:00, www.broadwaymarket. co.uk). On sunny days, the London Fields park just north of the market is filled with thousands of picnicking and sunbathing locals enjoying their little slice of the city.

West End Markets
Covent Garden Market: Originally the convent garden for Westminster Abbey, the iron-and-glass market hall hosted a produce market until the 1970s (earning it the name "Apple Market"). Now it's a mix of fun shops, eateries, markets, and a more modern-day Apple Store on the corner. Mondays are for antiques, while arts and crafts dominate the rest of the week. Yesteryear's produce stalls are open daily 10:00-18:00, and on Thursdays, a food market brightens up the square (Tube: Covent Garden, +44 20 7395 1350, www.coventgardenlondonuk.com).

☐ For more, see the West End Walk chapter.

Jubilee Hall Market: This market features antiques on Mondays (5:00-17:00); a general market Tuesday through Friday (10:30-19:00); and arts and crafts on Saturdays and Sundays (10:00-18:00). It's located on the south side of Covent Garden (+44 20 7379 4242, www.jubileemarket.co.uk).

South London Markets
This area south of the Thames has several food-focused markets, including the **Borough Market, Southbank Centre,** and **Maltby Street Ropewalk Market** (all described in the Eating in London chapter). For a classic street market, check out **Brixton Market** about three miles south of the river (Tube: Brixton, www. brixtonvillage.com).

FAMOUS AUCTIONS
London's famous auctioneers welcome the curious public for viewing and bidding. You can also preview estate catalogs or browse auction calendars online, and even place bids. To ask questions or set up an appointment, contact **Sotheby's** (opening times vary, +44 20 7293 5000, www.sothebys.com; recommended café on site, 34 New Bond Street, Tube: Oxford Circus) or **Christie's** (Mon-Fri

SHOPPING

9:30-16:30; 8 King Street, Tube: Green Park, +44 20 7839 9060; www.christies.com).

Regent Street Shopping Walk

This mile-long walk—along Regent Street to Piccadilly Circus, then up the street called Piccadilly and down Jermyn Street—takes you by the most typically London stores and shops. While useful for true shoppers, this walk is also a lot of fun for window-shoppers. Only you know how much time—and money—to allow for this walk.

• *Start your walk at the Oxford Circus Tube stop.*

❶ Oxford Street

Today, Oxford Street is a midrange shopping area, lined by less-distinguished chains and department stores, and a bit scruffy. But it was once one of London's great shopping streets, and is still one of the most decorative at Christmastime. The original Selfridges (250 yards west of Oxford Circus), opened in 1910, helped pioneer the modern concept of the department store.

• *From the Oxford Circus Tube stop, head south on Regent Street (heading slightly downhill, away from the steeple in the road). Stay along the left (east) side of Regent Street. As you walk, note the palatial Apple Store on your right at #235. It's popular with tourists who appreciate its free Wi-Fi...and Londoners who are astounded by its customer service. Continue until Regent crosses Great Marlborough Street and turn left to reach...*

❷ Liberty Department Store

The venerable Liberty is a big, stately, local-favorite department store established in 1875. Its distinctive faux-Tudor building was constructed from the timbers of two decommissioned Royal Navy battleships; for more information, see the listing earlier in this chapter.

• *Continue down Great Marlborough Street, and turn right onto...*

❸ Carnaby Street

In the Swinging '60s, when Pete Townshend needed a paisley shirt, John Lennon a Nehru jacket, or Twiggy a miniskirt, they came here—where those mod fashions were invented. If you were a "Dedicated Follower of Fashion" (as a Kinks' song put it), you were one of the trendy "Carnaby-tian army." Today, there's not a hint of hippie. For the

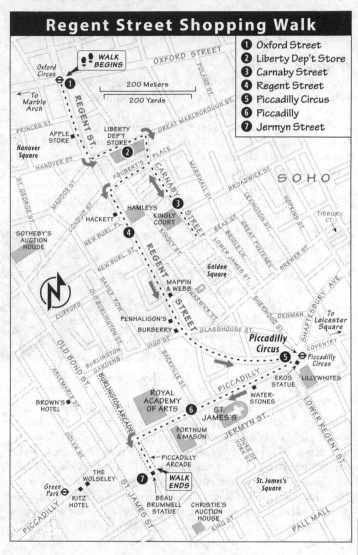

Regent Street Shopping Walk

1. Oxford Street
2. Liberty Dep't Store
3. Carnaby Street
4. Regent Street
5. Piccadilly Circus
6. Piccadilly
7. Jermyn Street

WALK BEGINS

200 Meters
200 Yards

OXFORD STREET

Oxford Circus

To Marble Arch

PRINCES ST.

APPLE STORE

Hanover Square

REGENT ST.

MADDOX ST.

HANOVER ST.

LIBERTY DEP'T STORE

GREAT MARLBOROUGH ST.

FOUBERT'S PLACE

CARNABY STREET

MARSHALL ST.

BROADWICK ST.

S O H O

LEXINGTON ST.

GREAT PULTENEY ST.

HOPKINS ST.

TISBURY CT.

ST. GEORGE'S ST.

CONDUIT ST.

HAMLEYS

HACKETT

KINGLY COURT

NEW BURL. PL.

BEAK ST.

BRIDLE LN.

LOWER JAMES ST.

DREWER ST.

SOTHEBY'S AUCTION HOUSE

NEW BURL. ST.

KINGLY ST.

REGENT STREET

Golden Square

SHERWOOD ST.

SHAFTESBURY AVE.

SAVILE ROW

OLD BURLINGTON ST.

CLIFFORD ST.

MAPPIN & WEBB

WARWICK ST.

DENMAN ST.

To Leicester Square

PENHALIGON'S

BURBERRY

GLASSHOUSE ST.

Piccadilly Circus

COVENTRY

Piccadilly Circus

OLD BOND ST.

BURLINGTON GARDENS

VIGO ST.

SACKVILLE ST.

EROS STATUE

LILLYWHITES

BROWN'S HOTEL

ALBEMARLE ST.

DOVER ST.

BURLINGTON ARCADE

ROYAL ACADEMY OF ARTS

ST. JAMES'S

PICCADILLY

WATER-STONES

LOWER REGENT ST.

FORTNUM & MASON

JERMYN ST.

DUKE OF YORK ST.

PICCADILLY ARCADE

WALK ENDS

THE WOLSELEY

Green Park

RITZ HOTEL

BEAU BRUMMELL STATUE

CHRISTIE'S AUCTION HOUSE

St. James's Square

ST. JAMES'S ST.

KING ST.

PALL MALL

PICCADILLY

most part, Carnaby Street looks like everything else from the '60s does now—sanitized and co-opted by upscale franchises. At least the upper end of the street retains a whiff of funkiness. About a half-block down, on the right, poke into Kingly Court (at #49)—an interior courtyard that's jammed with three floors of eateries, representing virtually every cuisine on earth (for details, see the Eating in London chapter).

• *After exploring Carnaby Street, walk back toward Great Marlborough*

Street, heading left (west) on Foubert's Place (near the Shakespeare's Head pub). Then turn left again to continue strolling downhill along...

❹ Regent Street

You're in the heart of London's shopping neighborhood. By now, you may have noticed a sort of class divide among London shoppers.

Where the area near Oxford Circus was a bit low-rent, you've now entered London's high-class, top-dollar boulevard. This street has wide sidewalks, fine architecture, and royal-family connections. Most of its shops call the Queen their landlord, as she owns much of the land here.

Once on Regent Street, follow the giddy kids to **Hamleys** (just downhill from Foubert's Place, on the left at #188), Britain's

biggest toy store that's been delighting children for more than 250 years. Seven floors buzz with 50,000 toys, managed by a staff of 200. Employees, some dressed in playful costumes, give demos of the latest gadgets. It was here at Hamleys that the world first got to know London's genteel Paddington Bear, and the less-genteel Build-a-Bear Workshop (now a fixture at malls everywhere).

On this stretch of Regent Street, fine bits of old English class dominate. **Hackett** (across from Hamleys at #193) is the place to go for preppy young English menswear. A couple of blocks farther down, **Mappin & Webb** (on the left, at #132) is the Queen's jeweler. **Penhaligon's** (on the right, at #125) is the quintessential English perfumery, where royals shop (note the coat of arms at the door) for classic English scents like lavender and rose (fine sampler gift packs and free sniff samples). **Burberry** (on the corner past Penhaligon's, at #121) is a clothier of the royal family.

• *Regent Street arcs seductively into the ever-vibrant...*

❺ Piccadilly Circus

Piccadilly Circus is where common tastes steamroll the elegance of Regent Street. **Lillywhites** (at the bottom of the square, near the Eros fountain) is a sports store popular as a place to buy the jersey of your favorite football (soccer) team.

• *From Piccadilly Circus, take a sharp right and wander down the busy street called...*

❻ Piccadilly

After a block on your left (at #203), escape from the frenzy of Piccadilly into the quiet of **Waterstones,** Europe's largest bookshop and the flagship store of its widespread chain. Page through seven orderly floors. The fifth floor offers a bar with minimalist furniture and great views (see "London's Best Views" on page 94).

Next you'll pass Christopher Wren's **St. James's Church** (with free lunchtime concerts several days a week—the current schedule is posted on its iron fence out front; for details, see page 478). On Tuesdays and Thursdays, the churchyard is filled with street food carts. One block farther (on the left, at #181) is the **Fortnum & Mason** department store, which eschews the glitz of bigger stores and revels in understated old-school elegance. At the top of the hour, the fancy clock on the facade is the scene of a low-key spectacle, as the venerable store's founders—Fortnum and Mason—come out and bow to each other (best viewed from across the street). This reminds shoppers of the store's humble beginnings 300 years ago, when it was started by these two footmen of Queen Anne; for more information, see the listing earlier in this chapter.

An elegant way to cap your shopping stroll (we'll finish just a block from here) is with a traditional **afternoon tea.** While it's a pricey ritual, many consider it an essential part of any London visit. My two favorite places in town for a traditional afternoon tea are within a block of here: **$$$$ Fortnum & Mason** (with several restaurants and price ranges), and a block farther down Picca-

dilly, **$$$ The Wolseley,** the grand 1920s former showroom of a now-defunct car manufacturer (where couples are allowed to split a tea in sumptuous surroundings; on the left at #160). Nearby **$$$$ Brown's Hotel** serves a fancy afternoon tea in its wood-paneled English Tea Room (33 Albemarle Street). For more details on these and other options, see the "Taking Tea in London" section of the Eating in London chapter. Another fancy spot for tea nearby is the original **Ritz Hotel.**

• *But before we part ways, we'll stroll a block south of big and busy Piccadilly. A half-block beyond Fortnum & Mason, a left at the Piccadilly Arcade leads to quiet...*

❼ Jermyn Street

A statue of **Beau Brummell,** the ultimate dandy, meets you as if to say, "Within a block in either direction are numerous fine gentle-

SHOPPING

men's shirtmakers and many other delightful small shops." It was Brummell (1778-1840) who popularized the understated jacket-trousers-and-tie ensemble that men still wear today. As the quote on his statue reads, "To be truly elegant, one should not be noticed."

Face the statue and survey the landscape of dapper options: To the right, **Bates Hats** (#73, inside Hilditch & Key) still sells bowlers and top hats, as it has for a century. **Turnbull & Asser** (#71) has dressed Winston Churchill, Prince Charles, and James Bond with its "bespoke" (custom-made) shirts and suits. **Tricker's** (#67) has been making shoes for the gentleman since the days of Beau Brummell. Straight ahead, **Taylor of Old Bond Street** (#74), established in the mid-19th century, specializes in gentleman's shaving and botanical products. After sauntering these few blocks, even the weariest traveler will leave Jermyn Street feeling (if not looking) more refined.

• *Our walk is finished. From here, you have several nearby options. If you're ready for teatime, cut back through the block to Piccadilly and the places I mentioned earlier.*

*Or, to head back to Piccadilly Circus (and its handy Tube stop), walk east down Jermyn Street, pausing at the classic perfume shop **Floris** (at #89) and at **Paxton & Whitfield** (#93), which has served exceptional cheese since 1797, with generous tastings. On the little Duke of York Street (behind St. James's Church) is an old-fashioned barbershop called **Geo. F. Trumper** (selling top-quality shaving gear) and the classic **Red Lion pub**. If all of this is just too elegant, dip into any old souvenir shop and buy some Union Jack undies.*

ENTERTAINMENT IN LONDON

London bubbles with top-notch entertainment seven days a week: plays, movies, concerts, exhibitions, walking tours, shopping, and children's activities. For the best list of what's happening and a look at the latest London scene, check www.timeout.com/london. The free monthly *London Planner* covers sights, events, and plays, though generally not as well as the Time Out website.

Choose from classical, jazz, rock, and far-out music, Gilbert and Sullivan, tango lessons, comedy, Baha'i meetings, poetry readings, spectator sports, theater, and the cinema. In Leicester Square, you might be able to catch a film that has yet to be released in the States—if Colin Firth or Keira Knightley (or any other A-list celebrity) is attending an opening-night premiere in London, it will likely be at one of the big movie houses here.

There are plenty of free performances, such as lunch concerts at St. Martin-in-the-Fields (at Trafalgar Square) and summertime events at The Scoop amphitheater near City Hall (see "Summer Evenings Along the South Bank," later).

Theater (a.k.a. "Theatre")

London's theater scene rivals Broadway's in quality and often beats it in price. Choose from 200 offerings—Shakespeare, musicals, comedies, thrillers, sex farces, cutting-edge fringe, revivals starring movie celebs, and more. London does it all well.

Seating Terminology: Just like at home, London's theaters sell seats in a range of levels—but the Brits use different terms: stalls (ground floor), dress circle (first balcony), upper circle (second balcony), balcony (sky-high third balcony), and slips (cheap seats on the fringes). Discounted tickets are called "concessions" (abbreviated as "conc" or "s"). "Restricted view" seats can be a bargain, but you won't be able to see all (or even most) of the stage. For floor plans of the various theaters, see www.theatremonkey.com.

BIG WEST END SHOWS

Nearly all big-name shows are hosted in the theaters of the West End, clustering around Soho (especially along Shaftesbury Avenue) between Piccadilly and Covent Garden. With a centuries-old tradition of pleasing the masses, they present London theater at its grandest.

I prefer big, glitzy—even bombastic—musicals over serious chamber dramas, simply because London can deliver the lights, booming voices, dancers, and multimedia spectacle I rarely get back home. If that's not to your taste—or you already have easy access to similar spectacles—you might prefer some of London's more low-key offerings, or to seek out a big-name actor you'd enjoy seeing in person.

Well-known musicals may draw the biggest crowds, but the West End offers plenty of other crowd-pleasers, from revivals of classics to cutting-edge works by the hottest young playwrights. These productions tend to have shorter runs than famous musicals. Many productions star huge-name celebrities—London is a magnet for movie stars (both British and American) who want to stretch their acting chops.

You'll see the latest offerings advertised all over the city. The *Official London Theatre Guide*, a free booklet that's updated every two weeks, is a handy tool (find it at hotels, box offices, the City of London TI, and online at www.officiallondontheatre.co.uk). You can check reviews at www.timeout.com/london.

Most performances are nightly except Sunday, usually with two or three matinees a week. The few shows that run on Sundays are mostly family fare (such as *The Lion King*).

Buying Tickets for West End Shows

For most visitors, it makes sense to simply buy tickets in London. Most shows have tickets available on short notice—likely at a discount. But if your time in London is limited—and you have your heart set on a particular show that's likely to sell out (usually the newest shows, and especially on weekends)—you can buy peace of mind by booking tickets from home.

Advance Tickets: It's generally cheapest to buy your tickets directly from the theater, either through its website or the theater box office (by phone or in person). In most cases, a theater will reroute you to a third-party ticket vendor such as Ticketmaster (which usually comes with a booking fee of around £3/ticket). You can have your tickets emailed to you or pick them up before show time at Will Call. Note that many third-party websites sell all kinds of London theater tickets, but these generally charge higher prices and fees. It's best to try the theater's website or box office first.

Discount Tickets from the TKTS Booth: This famous outlet at Leicester Square sells discounted tickets (25-50 percent off) for many shows (£3/ticket service charge included, daily 11:30-18:00, possibly longer hours—more like 10:00-19:00—at busy times). TKTS offers a wide variety of shows on any given day, though they may not always have the hottest shows in town.

Buy tickets in person at the kiosk, where staff might be able to creatively help you figure out how to get the best seat or the best price, or on their website (www.tkts.co.uk).

The best deals are **same-day only;** they go on sale online at midnight the night before a performance. (You can't book in person until the kiosk opens the next morning.) Both online and at the kiosk, the list of shows and prices is updated throughout the day. Have a second-choice show in mind, in case your first choice sells out.

TKTS also sells advance tickets for some shows (but not as cheaply) and some regular-price tickets to extremely popular shows—convenient, but no savings. If TKTS runs out of its ticket allotment for a certain show, it doesn't necessarily mean the show is sold out—you can still try the theater's box office.

If you're not committed to a particular show and just want a decent deal, TKTS is a great option. You might snag a top-price seat for a popular-but-not-too-popular show (say, *Wicked*) for about half-price through TKTS. But if you're committed to a particular show—especially a popular one—or if you want the absolutely cheapest seats, it's better to book directly at the theater—read on.

Take note: The real TKTS booth (with its prominent sign) is a freestanding kiosk at the south edge of Leicester Square, behind the Shakespeare statue. Several dishonest outfits nearby advertise "official half-price tickets"—avoid these, where you'll rarely pay anything close to half-price.

Tickets at the Theater Box Office: Even if a show is "sold out," there's usually a way to get a seat. Many theaters offer various discounts or "concessions": same-day tickets, cheap returned tickets, standing-room, matinee, senior or student standby deals, and

What's On in the West End

You're likely to find these perennial favorites among the West End's evening offerings. If spending the time and money for a London play, I like a full-fledged, high-energy production. These long-running shows are fun, and you're likely to find some of them on the discount list at the TKTS booth. For new and popular shows, you'll need to book long in advance and pay top price. Generally, ticket prices range from £20-120, but a few red-hot shows (i.e., *Hamilton*) can shoot up to £250. Shows typically run Monday through Saturday at 19:30, with two or three matinees a week. Matinees are generally cheaper and rarely sell out—though they are more popular for kid-oriented shows. See the map on page 474 for locations.

The Book of Mormon: Who else but the writers of *South Park* could create a snappy, irreverent, and sometimes crude musical about two Mormon missionaries and the nature of faith? (Prince of Wales Theatre, Coventry Street, Tube: Piccadilly Circus or Charing Cross, box office +44 844 482 5115, www.thebookofmormonmusical.com/london).

Dear Evan Hansen: This Tony award-winning musical follows a painfully shy teenage boy as he finds himself fitting in for the first time after telling a lie (Noël Coward Theater, St. Martin's Lane, Tube: Leicester Square, box office +44 844 482 5151, https://dearevanhansen.com).

Hamilton: An American Musical: Lin-Manuel Miranda's tour de force of lyrics and hip-hop/R&B contemporizes early American history; tickets are steeply priced—for a better deal, try your luck via the online lottery (Victoria Palace Theatre, Victoria Street, Tube: Victoria or St. James's Park, www.hamiltonthemusical.co.uk).

Harry Potter and the Cursed Child, Parts One and Two: These plays tell the story of Harry, Hermione, and Ron all grown up, and the exploits of their own children at Hogwarts. The two parts—five

more. Start by checking the show's website, then call the box office or simply drop by (many theaters are right in the tourist zone).

Same-day tickets (called **"day seats"**) can be an excellent deal for those who enjoy being frugal and spontaneous. These tickets (usually £25 or less) often are in the nosebleed rows or have a restricted view—but sometimes they're front-row seats. Some same-day tickets are available *only in person* when the box office opens (typically at 10:00; for popular shows, people start lining up well before then). Increasingly, theaters sell these tickets online, or as "rush tickets" through the TodayTix app. Very popular shows don't bother with "day seats," but a few distribute tickets through a lot-

and a half hours of theater!—are designed to be viewed consecutively (either a matinee and an evening show, or consecutive evenings), but it's time well invested for Potterheads (Palace Theatre, corner of Charing Cross Road and Shaftesbury Avenue, Tube: Leicester Square or Covent Garden, www.harrypottertheplay.com).

Les Misérables: This musical adaptation of Victor Hugo's epic follows the life of Jean Valjean as he struggles with the social and political realities of 19th-century France (Sondheim Theatre, Shaftesbury Avenue, Tube: Piccadilly Circus, box office +44 844 482 5160, www.lesmis.com).

The Lion King: In this Disney extravaganza, Simba the lion learns about the delicately balanced circle of life on the savanna (Lyceum Theatre, Wellington Street, Tube: Charing Cross or Covent Garden, theater info +44 20 7420 8100, box office +44 844 871 3000, www.thelionking.co.uk).

Mamma Mia!: This energetic, spandex-and-platform-boots musical sets a young bride's search for her real dad ahead of her Greek Isle wedding to the tune of a slew of ABBA hits. The production has the audience dancing in their seats (Novello Theatre, Aldwych, Tube: Covent Garden or Charing Cross, box office +44 844 482 5115, www.mamma-mia.com).

Phantom of the Opera: A mysterious masked man falls in love with a singer in this haunting Andrew Lloyd Webber musical about life beneath the stage of the Paris Opera (Her Majesty's Theatre, Haymarket, Tube: Piccadilly Circus or Leicester Square, box office +44 20 7087 7762, www.uk.thephantomoftheopera.com).

Wicked: This lively prequel to *The Wizard of Oz* examines how the Witch of the West met Glinda the Good Witch, and later became so, you know... (Apollo Victoria Theatre, Wilton Road just east of Victoria Station, Tube: Victoria, ATG Tickets +44 844 871 3001, www.wickedthemusical.co.uk).

tery. The more popular the show, the lower your chances are, but it's fun to give it a shot. Look up details on each show's website.

Another strategy is to show up at the box office shortly before show time (best on weekdays) and—before paying full price—ask about cheaper options. Last-minute return tickets are often sold at great prices as curtain time approaches.

For a helpful guide to cheap and last-minute tickets, including "day seats"—with recent user reports on how early you need to show up—consult www.theatremonkey.com/day-seat-finder; also check www.londontheatretickets.org or www.timeout.com/london/theatre.

Booking Through Other Agencies: Although booking

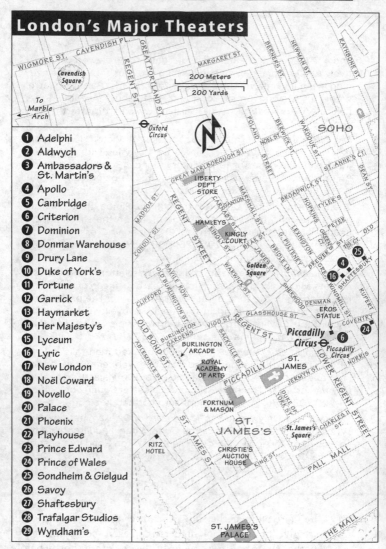

London's Major Theaters

1. Adelphi
2. Aldwych
3. Ambassadors & St. Martin's
4. Apollo
5. Cambridge
6. Criterion
7. Dominion
8. Donmar Warehouse
9. Drury Lane
10. Duke of York's
11. Fortune
12. Garrick
13. Haymarket
14. Her Majesty's
15. Lyceum
16. Lyric
17. New London
18. Noël Coward
19. Novello
20. Palace
21. Phoenix
22. Playhouse
23. Prince Edward
24. Prince of Wales
25. Sondheim & Gielgud
26. Savoy
27. Shaftesbury
28. Trafalgar Studios
29. Wyndham's

through a middleman such as your hotel or a ticket agency is quick and easy (and may be your last resort for a sold-out show), prices are greatly inflated. Ticket agencies and third-party websites are often just scalpers with an address. If you do buy from an agency, choose one who is a member of the Society of Ticket Agents and Retailers (look for the STAR logo—short for "secure tickets from authorized retailers"). These legitimate resellers normally add a maximum 25 percent booking fee to tickets.

Scalpers (or "Touts"): As at any event, you'll find scalpers hawking tickets outside theaters. And, just like at home, those

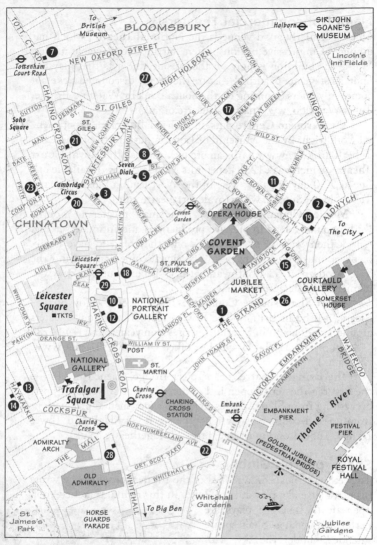

people may either be honest folk whose date just happened to cancel at the last minute...or they may be unscrupulous thieves selling forgeries. London has many of the latter.

THEATER BEYOND THE WEST END

Tickets for lesser-known shows tend to be cheaper (figure £15-30), in part because most of the smaller theaters are government subsidized. Remember that plays don't need a familiar title or famous actor to be a worthwhile experience—read up on the latest offerings online; Time Out's website is a great place to start.

Major Noncommercial Theaters

One particularly good venue is the **National Theatre,** which has a range of impressive options, often starring recognizable names. While the building is ugly on the outside, the acts that play out upon its stage are beautiful—as are the deeply discounted tickets it commonly offers (looming on the South Bank by Waterloo Bridge, Tube: Waterloo, www.nationaltheatre.org.uk).

The **Barbican Centre** puts on high-quality, often experimental work (right by the Museum of London, just north of The City, Tube: Barbican, www.barbican.org.uk), as does the **Royal Court Theatre,** which has £12 tickets for its Monday shows (available online at 9:00 day of show; west of the West End in Sloane Square, Tube: Sloane Square, www.royalcourttheatre.com).

Menier Chocolate Factory is a small theater in Southwark popular for its impressive productions and intimate setting. Check their website to see what's on—they tend to have a mix of plays, musicals, and even an occasional comedian (behind the Tate Modern at 53 Southwark Street, Tube: Southwark, www.menierchocolatefactory.com).

Royal Shakespeare Company: If you'll ever enjoy Shakespeare, it'll be in Britain. The RSC performs at various theaters around London and in Stratford-upon-Avon year-round (+44 1789 748 114 or +44 1789 403 493, box office +44 1789 331 111, www.rsc.org.uk).

The Bridge Theatre, near Tower Bridge, opened in 2017—the first big theater to open in London in about 80 years. It hosts everything from Shakespearean plays to experimental productions from up-and-coming playwrights (between City Hall and Tower Bridge, Tube: London Bridge, https://bridgetheatre.co.uk).

Shakespeare's Globe

To see Shakespeare in a replica of the theater for which he wrote his plays, attend a play at the **Globe.** In this round, thatched-roof, open-air theater, the plays are performed much as Shakespeare intended—under the sky, with no amplification.

The play's the thing from mid-April through mid-October (usually Tue-Sat 14:00 and 19:30, Sun either 13:00 and/or 18:30, tickets can be sold out months in advance). You'll pay £5 to stand and £23-52 to sit, usually on a backless bench (only a few rows and the pricier Gentlemen's Rooms have seats with backs, £2 cushions and £4 add-on backrests a good investment; dress for the weather). Note: While this is a wonderful theater-going experience, the seating is significantly less comfy than most venues—even for the pricier seats.

The £5 "groundling" or "yard" tickets—which are open to rain—are most fun. Scurry in early to stake out a spot on the stage's edge, where the most interaction with the actors occurs. You're a crude peasant. You can lean your elbows on the stage, munch a snack (yes, you can bring in food—but bag size is limited), or walk around. I've never enjoyed Shakespeare as much as here, performed as it was meant to be in the "wooden O." If you can't get a ticket, consider waiting around. Plays can be long, and many groundlings leave before the end. Hang around outside and beg or buy a ticket from someone leaving early (groundlings are allowed to come and go). A few non-Shakespeare plays are also presented each year. If you can't attend a show, you can take a guided tour of the theater and museum by day (see page 96).

In winter—when the outdoor Globe is closed—you can still enjoy plays at the indoor **Sam Wanamaker Playhouse.** This theater—the red-brick structure that runs behind the modern box office building—also feels historic: Its interior is hewn of oak and rich with Jacobean decorative details and a beautiful painted ceiling. Plays are usually performed using only candlelight, with candelabras suspended from the ceiling (which actors set alight and extinguish to adjust the lighting for each scene). It feels intimate (about 350 seats) and is, in its own way, just as impressive as the Globe. And, like the Globe, the seating is on (uncomfortable but historic) wooden benches. The Playhouse season is designed to complement the Globe's summer season—Shakespeare, Shakespearean-era plays, new works by up-and-coming playwrights, and early-music concerts—though a few summer performances may take place here. At the Playhouse, the cheap standing seats are not down below, as in the Globe, but up above, in the upper galleries.

Buying Tickets: To reserve tickets for plays at the Globe or Playhouse, drop by the box office (Mon-Sat 10:00-18:00, Sun until 17:00, open one hour later on performance days, New Globe Walk entrance, box office +44 20 7401 9919; info +44 20 7902 1400). You can also reserve online (www.shakespearesglobe.com, £2.50 booking fee). If tickets are sold out, don't despair: Returns are common, so keep checking online for your preferred dates (especially the day before or day of). Better yet, try calling around noon the day of the performance to see if the box office expects any returned tickets. If so, they'll advise you to show up a little more than an hour before the show, when these tickets are sold (first-come, first-served).

Getting There: The theater is on the South Bank, directly across the Thames over the Millennium Bridge from St. Paul's Cathedral (Tube: Mansion House or London Bridge). The Globe is inconvenient for public transport, but during theater season a regular supply of black cabs waits nearby, or you could try to order an Uber.

Outdoor and Fringe Theater

In summer, enjoy Shakespearean drama and other plays under the stars at the **Open Air Theatre,** in leafy Regent's Park in north London. You can bring your own picnic, order à la carte from the theater menu, or preorder a picnic supper from the theater at least 24 hours in advance (tickets from £25, available beginning in mid-Dec, season runs mid-May–mid-Sept; book at www.openairtheatre. com or—for an extra booking fee—by calling +44 333 400 3562; grounds open 1.5 hours before performances; only one small bag permitted per person; 10-minute walk north of Baker Street Tube, near Queen Mary's Gardens within Regent's Park; detailed directions and more info at www.openairtheatre.com).

London's rougher evening-entertainment scene is thriving. Choose from a wide range of **fringe theater** and comedy acts (find posters in many Tube stations, or search for "fringe theater" on www.timeout.com; tickets start as cheap as £5-10).

Music, Opera, and Dance

CONCERTS AT CHURCHES

For easy, cheap, or free concerts in historic churches, attend a **lunch concert,** especially:

- St. Bride's Church, with free half-hour lunch concerts twice a week at 13:15 (usually Tue and Fri—confirm in advance, church +44 20 7427 0133, www.stbrides.com).
- Temple Church, also in The City, with free organ recitals weekly (Wed at 13:15, www.templechurch.com).
- St. Dunstan-in-the-West, on Fleet Street, hosts free 45-minute concerts; you're welcome to bring a bag lunch (some Wed and Fri at 13:15—confirm at www.stdunstaninthewest.org).
- St. James's at Piccadilly, with 50-minute concerts on Mon, Wed, and Fri at 13:10 (suggested £5 donation, info +44 20 7734 4511, www.sjp.org.uk).
- St. Martin-in-the-Fields offers afternoon concerts on select weekdays; check online for schedule (suggested £5 donation, church +44 20 7766 1100, www.stmartin-in-the-fields.org).

St. Martin-in-the-Fields also hosts fine **evening concerts** by candlelight (£9-35, several nights a week at 19:30) and live folk and jazz in its underground Café in the Crypt (£8-18, Wed at 20:00).

Evensong services are held at several churches, including St. Paul's Cathedral (see details on page 280), Westminster Abbey

Evensong

One of my favorite experiences in Britain is to attend evensong at a great church. Evensong is an evening worship service that is typically sung rather than said (though some parts—including scripture readings, a few prayers, and a homily—are spoken). It follows the traditional Anglican service in the Book of Common Prayer, including prayers, scripture readings, canticles (sung responses), and hymns that are appropriate for the early evening—traditionally the end of the working day and before the evening meal. In major churches with resident choirs, this service is filled with quality, professional musical elements. A singing or chanting priest leads the service, and a choir—usually made up of both men's and boys' voices (to sing the lower and higher parts, respectively)—sings the responses. The choir usually sings a cappella, or is accompanied by an organ. While regular attendees follow the service from memory, visitors—who are welcome—are given an order of service or a prayer book to help them follow along.

You can attend services in many of England's grandest churches—but be aware that evensong typically takes place in the small choir area—which is far more intimate than the main nave. (To see the full church in action, a concert is a better choice.) Evensong generally occurs daily between 17:00 and 18:00 (often two hours earlier on Sun)—check with individual churches for specifics. At smaller churches, evensong is sometimes spoken, not sung.

Note that evensong is not a performance—it's a somewhat somber worship service. If you enjoy worshipping in different churches, attending evensong can be a trip-capping highlight. Most major churches also offer organ or choral concerts—look for posted schedules or ask at the information desk or gift shop.

(see page 145), Southwark Cathedral (see page 99), and St. Bride's Church (Sun at 17:30, +44 20 7427 0133, www.stbrides.com).

Free **organ recitals** are usually held on Sunday at 17:00 in Westminster Abbey (30 minutes, +44 20 7222 5152). Many other churches have free concerts; ask for the *London Organ Concerts Guide* at the TI.

OTHER PERFORMANCES

Prom Concerts: For a fun classical event (mid-July–mid-Sept), attend a Prom Concert (shortened from "Promenade Concert") during the annual festival at the Royal Albert Hall. Nightly concerts are offered at give-a-peasant-some-culture prices (cheap standing-room "Promming" spots sold at the door, nearly-as-cheap restricted-view seats and pricier good ones sold in advance, Tube: South Kensington, www.bbc.co.uk/proms).

Jazz: London's oldest, and by far most famous, jazz venue, **Ronnie Scott's** hosts performances daily. As shows tend to sell out, it's best to book your tickets in advance online (47 Frith Street, Tube: Tottenham Court Road or Leicester Square, +44 20 7439 0747, www.ronniescotts.co.uk). Boisdale also features live jazz, blues, and soul music at their restaurants.

Opera: Some of the world's best opera is belted out at the prestigious **Royal Opera House,** near Covent Garden (www.roh. org.uk), and at the **London Coliseum** (English National Opera, St. Martin's Lane, Tube: Leicester Square, www.eno.org). Or consider taking in an unusual opera at the **King's Head pub** in Islington, home of London's Little Opera House (115 Upper Street, Tube: Angel, www.kingsheadtheatre.com). In the summer, **Holland Park** hosts open-air opera performances (Tube: Holland Park, www.operahollandpark.com).

Dance: The critically acclaimed Royal Ballet—where Margot Fonteyn and Rudolf Nureyev forged their famous partnership—is based at the **Royal Opera House** (www.roh.org.uk). **Sadler's Wells Theatre** features both international and UK-based dance troupes (Rosebery Avenue, Islington, Tube: Angel, www.sadlerswells.com).

More Entertainment Options

EVENING SIGHTSEEING

Museum Visits: Many museums stay open late an evening or two during the week, offering fewer crowds. Museums likely to have

evening hours include the British Library, British Museum, National Gallery, and Tate Modern (check websites for details). On days when Parliament is in session, evenings can be a good time to check out the Houses of Parliament; the legislative action is less exciting than during the day, but it's much quieter and less crowded.

The Shard: The viewpoint from the top of the UK's tallest building is open in the evening; on long summer days, you can enjoy "golden hour" or twilit views over the city well after most London sights have closed (see page 99).

Tours: Guided **walks** are offered several times a day and vary by theme. In the evening, expect a more limited choice: ghosts,

Jack the Ripper, pubs, or literature. See a list of walking-tour companies on page 43.

To see the city illuminated at night, consider an evening **bus tour** (see page 42).

Cruises: In summer, boats sail as late as 19:00 between Westminster Pier (near Big Ben) and the Tower of London. (For details, see page 45.)

A handful of outfits run expensive River Thames evening cruises with four-course meals and dancing. **London Dinner Cruise** offers the best value (nightly at 19:45, 3 hours, departs from Westminster Pier, reservations required, +44 20 7740 0400, www.cityexperiences.com). Dinner cruises are also offered by **Bateaux London** (www.bateauxlondon.com).

SUMMER EVENINGS ALONG THE SOUTH BANK

If you're visiting London in summer, consider hitting the South Bank neighborhood after hours.

Take a trip around the **London Eye** while the sun sets over the city (the wheel spins until late—last ascent at 20:30 or later in summer). Then cap your night with an evening walk along the pedestrian-only **Jubilee Walkway,** which runs east-west along the river. It's where Londoners go to escape the heat. This pleasant stretch of the walkway—lined with pubs and casual eateries—goes from the London Eye past Shakespeare's Globe to Tower Bridge (you can walk in either direction).

If you're in the mood for a movie, take in a flick at the **BFI Southbank,** located just across the river, alongside Waterloo Bridge. Run by the British Film Institute, the state-of-the-art theater shows mostly classic films, as well as art cinema (Tube: Waterloo or Embankment, check www.bfi.org.uk for schedules and prices).

Farther east along the South Bank is **The Scoop**—an outdoor amphitheater next to City Hall. It's a good spot for movies, concerts, dance, and theater productions throughout the summer—with Tower Bridge as a scenic backdrop. These events are free, nearly nightly, and family-friendly. For the latest event schedule, see londonbridgecity.co.uk and click on "What's On" (next to City Hall, Riverside, The Queen's Walkway, Tube: London Bridge).

SPORTING EVENTS

Tennis, cricket, rugby, football (soccer), and horse races all take place within an hour of the city. In summer Wimbledon draws a half-million spectators (www.wimbledon.com), while big-name English Premier League soccer clubs—including Chelsea, Arsenal, Tottenham Hotspur, and West Ham United—take the pitch in London to sell-out crowds (www.premierleague.com). The two

ENTERTAINMENT

biggest horse races of the year take place in June: the Royal Ascot Races (www.ascot.co.uk) near Windsor and the Epsom Derby (www.epsomderby.co.uk) in Surrey are both once-in-a-lifetime experiences.

Securing tickets to anything sporting-related in London can be difficult—and expensive. Check the official team or event website several months in advance; tickets can sell out within minutes of going on sale to the general public. Third-party booking companies such as SportsEvents 365 (www.sportsevents365. com) and Ticketmaster (www. ticketmaster.co.uk) often have tickets to popular events at a premium price—a godsend for

die-hard fans. Many teams also offer affordable, well-run stadium tours—check your favorite side's official website for details. Even if you can't attend a sports event in person, consider cheering on the action in a London pub.

Winter Diversions

London dazzles year-round, so consider visiting in winter, when airfares and hotel rates are generally cheaper and there are fewer tourists. Despite drearier weather and shorter days, London's museums, theaters, concert halls, and pubs offer a warm, cozy welcome.

London at Christmas is especially appealing, with its buildings dressed in their holiday best. Many holiday traditions have their roots in 19th-century Victorian Britain. Beginning in the 1840s, Queen Victoria's German husband, Prince Albert, popularized the decorating of Christmas trees and the sending of Christmas cards. And what could be more traditional than seeing the setting of Charles Dickens' *A Christmas Carol* come to life? God bless us, every one.

NOVEMBER TO JANUARY

Pantomimes, or "pantos," are a British holiday tradition. Though they have nothing to do with silent mimes—and generally don't mention Christmas—these campy fairy-tale plays entertain with outrageous costumes, sets, and dance numbers. The audience is invited to chime in, and it doesn't take long to learn the lines. Adults will laugh at the more risqué jokes; kids will giggle at the slapstick. Two London theaters that often stage pantos are the Hackney Empire (291 Mare Street, northeast London, Tube: Bethnal Green, then 10 minutes on bus #106 or #254, +44 20 8985 2424, www.hackneyempire.co.uk) and the London Palladium (8 Argyll Street, Soho, Tube: Oxford Circus, +44 20 7087 7755, www.lwtheatres.co.uk). For more about the panto tradition, see www.its-behind-you.com.

Get some exercise at the **outdoor ice rinks** at the Somerset House, the Queen's House in Greenwich, and Hampton Court Palace, among other locations (rental skates, generally mid-Nov–mid-Jan, reservations smart).

The **Hyde Park Winter Wonderland** offers kitschy carnival fun with a Ferris wheel, carousel, and other rides, as well as an ice rink and vendors selling silly hats and plenty of food and drink (reservations likely required, admission free or £5-8 depending on date and time, rink and rides extra, late Nov–early Jan, southeast corner of park, Tube: Marble Arch or Hyde Park Corner, www.hydeparkwinterwonderland.com.

Stroll around and enjoy the elaborate **light displays** and store windows on major shopping streets from mid-November to

early January, especially on Oxford Street, Bond Street, Regent Street, and Brompton Road. Post-holiday sales start December 26 for many stores, including the famous Harrods January sale.

The Trafalgar Square **Christmas tree** is given to London every year from the people of Oslo, Norway in appreciation for British help during World War II (lighting ceremony first Thu in Dec, stays up until early Jan, www.london.gov.uk). Free carol concerts are held beneath the tree in December.

The **Museum of the Home**'s 11 historic rooms are decorated for Christmas every year, highlighting holiday customs from the 17th century to today (free, see page 88).

The grand, red-velvet-draped **Royal Albert Hall** hosts seasonal concerts, including sing-along caroling (Tube: South Kensington, box office +44 20 7589 8212, www.royalalberthall.com).

Instead of visiting Santa Claus at the North Pole, British children see **Father Christmas** in his grotto. In London, the poshest Santa is at Harrods, but visits are by invitation only. For alternatives, try the Museum of London (www.museumoflondon.org.uk), London Zoo (www.zsl.org), or St. Pancras rail station (www.stpancras.com). Father Christmas has also been known to visit the Hyde Park Winter Wonderland (described earlier), where you can see him for free.

ENTERTAINMENT

Christmas Travel Strategies

- There is no public transit in London (Tube, train, or bus) at all on Christmas Day, and reduced services on Christmas Eve and Boxing Day (Dec 26). For specifics, see www.tfl.gov.uk. Taxis are scarce, so be prepared for a long wait or try Uber (expect a holiday surcharge, +44 871 871 8710). Better yet, bundle up and walk.
- If arriving at Heathrow Airport on Christmas Day, research transport from the airport to your hotel in advance. Although there is no Tube or train service, buses may run between Heathrow and Hammersmith or Paddington Stations, and between Gatwick Airport and Victoria Station (likely every 15-30 minutes; confirm in advance at www.heathrowexpress.com and www.nationalrail.co.uk, holiday schedules available in Nov). Or you could try a Just Airports private car (book in advance, +44 20 8900 1666, www.justairports.com).
- Pick a central location if staying over December 25, both to save money and avoid transportation difficulties. Stay somewhere with a kitchen (such as an apartment, hostel, or hotel room with kitchenette) so you can prepare some of your own meals. Don't forget to buy groceries before stores close on Christmas Eve. For tips on finding short-term rentals, see the Practicalities chapter.
- If you plan to eat out December 24-26 without reservations, go international: Indian, Chinese, and Middle Eastern restaurants are usually open in Soho, Chinatown, along Edgware Road, or near the East End's Brick Lane.
- Expect closures. Museums are generally closed December 24-26, and smaller shops are usually closed December 26.

Nibble your way through **Borough Market,** where you'll find lots of seasonal and gourmet treats (open daily the week before Christmas, closed Dec 25-26; see market listing in the Eating in London chapter). While at the market, be sure to sample traditional favorites such as mulled wine, mince pie, Christmas cake, and Christmas pudding.

Another popular holiday food event is the **Southbank Centre Winter Market,** on the South Bank between the London Eye and the Royal Festival Hall (daily late Nov-Christmas Eve, Tube: Waterloo, www.southbankcentre.co.uk). The **Christmas by the River** holiday market stretches east from the London Bridge City Pier to near the egg-shaped City Hall (daily mid-Nov-early Jan, www.londonbridgecity.co.uk).

Don't forget to pick up some **Christmas crackers** to give your holiday meals some extra bang. These fun, popping party favors contain a paper crown, a teeny gift, and a corny joke. Buy them at grocery or department stores, find a friend, and pull hard.

CHRISTMAS DAY

Spending December 25 in London? While almost everything is closed, and there is no public transit (not even the Tube), you still have a few options for getting out.

Popular **church services** are held both Christmas Eve and Christmas Day at Westminster Abbey, Westminster Cathedral, St. Paul's, and St. Martin-in-the-Fields, among other places. Warning: These draw large crowds, so ask in advance about when to arrive. (For example, you may need to reserve free tickets in advance—available in Nov—and wait in line several hours for the Abbey's 16:00 service on Christmas Eve; 23:30 service is less crowded; +44 20 7222 5152, www.westminster-abbey.org.)

The Peter Pan Cup **swim race,** held in Hyde Park every Christmas morning since 1864, is named in honor of *Peter Pan* playwright J. M. Barrie, who presented the first cup. Only members of the local swimming club may compete, but spectators are welcome (9:00, south side of The Serpentine—a lake in the center of the park, www.serpentineswimmingclub.com). Break the ice by asking a local where to find the nearby Peter Pan statue.

London Walks offers two guided **walking tours** on December 25, with appropriate themes such as "Christmas Morning 1660" and "Charles Dickens' *A Christmas Carol*" (£15-20, reservations required, meet at Trafalgar Square Christmas tree, +44 20 7624 3978, www.walks.com).

Watch the Queen's annual **Christmas message** on the BBC at 15:00. If you miss it, you can watch it online on Her Majesty's Royal YouTube channel (www.youtube.com/TheRoyalFamilyChannel).

If your visit extends through the **New Year,** here are two events to be aware of: New Year's Eve **fireworks** from the London Eye attract at least 500,000 revelers to the banks of the Thames, with required £10 tickets for good viewing spots sold months in advance (www.london.gov.uk/nye). Public transport is free after the festivities (generally 23:45-04:30). The next day, a **parade** featuring 10,000 performers snakes two miles through central London (free to stand, or pay for grandstand seats, 11:45-15:00, +44 20 3275 0190, www.lnydp.com).

LONDON CONNECTIONS

London is well-connected with the rest of the planet: by train, plane, bus, and cruise ship. This chapter addresses your arrival and departure from the city.

By Plane

London has six airports; I've focused my coverage on the two most widely used—Heathrow and Gatwick—with a few tips for using the others (Stansted, Luton, London City, and Southend).

For accommodations at or near the major airports, see the Sleeping in London chapter. For more on flights within Europe, see the "Transportation" section of the Practicalities chapter.

HEATHROW AIRPORT

Heathrow Airport is one of the world's busiest airports. Consider this: 75 million passengers a year on 500,000 flights from 200 destinations traveling on 80 airlines, like some kind of global maypole dance. For Heathrow's airport, flight, and transfer information, visit the helpful website www.heathrow.com (code: LHR).

Heathrow's terminals are numbered T-2 through T-5. Each terminal is served by different airlines and alliances; for example, T-5 is exclusively for British Air and Iberia Air flights, while T-2 serves mostly Star Alliance flights, such as United and Lufthansa. Screens posted throughout

London's Airports

Luton
✈ Luton
✈ Stansted
#M1 & A1

Reading

ST. PANCRAS
PADDINGTON
LIVERPOOL STREET
Southend
✈ Southend
Windsor #71 & 77
Tube
VICTORIA
D.L.R.
Rail Air Link
✈
To Bath
Heathrow
VICTORIA COACH STN.
London City
Thames
London
Guildford

✈ **Gatwick**
Ashford
To Paris, Amsterdam & Brussels
EUROSTAR
English Channel

↓To Brighton

Not to Scale

- - - - Rail
━━━━ Eurostar Rail
──── Tube & D.L.R.
- — - Bus

ALL BUSES ARE NATIONAL EXPRESS
UNLESS NOTED

the airport identify which terminal each airline uses; this information should also be included on your boarding pass.

You can walk between T-2 and T-3. From this central hub (called "Heathrow Central"), T-4 and T-5 split off in opposite directions (and are not walkable). The easiest way to travel between the T-2/T-3 cluster and either T-4 or T-5 is by Heathrow Express train (train departs every 15-20 minutes). While the train is free, to get through the entry gates you'll need a ticket from one of the ubiquitous machines (or tap your Oyster card—you won't be charged in either case). You can also take a shuttle bus (free, serves all terminals), or the Tube (requires a ticket, serves all terminals).

When flying out of Heathrow, it's critical to confirm which terminal your flight will use (look at your ticket/boarding pass, check online, or call your airline in advance)—if it's T-4 or T-5, allow extra time. Taxi drivers generally know which terminal you'll need based on the airline, but bus drivers may not.

Services: Each terminal has an airport information desk (open long hours daily), car-rental agencies, exchange bureaus, ATMs, a pharmacy, a VAT refund desk (+44 845 872 7627, you must present the VAT claim form from the retailer here to get your tax rebate on purchased items—see page 575 for details), and pay baggage storage (long hours daily, www.left-baggage.co.uk). Heathrow offers both free Wi-Fi and pay internet access points (in each terminal, check map for locations). Each terminal also has a variety of eateries.

Getting Between Heathrow and Downtown London

You have several options for traveling the 14 miles between Heathrow Airport and downtown London: Tube (subway, slow and cheap), bus (even slower and almost as cheap, and handy for Victoria Station area), express train with connecting Tube or taxi (more expensive but efficient), or—most expensive—taxi or car service. The one that works best for you will depend on your arrival terminal, your destination in central London, and your budget.

By Tube: The Tube takes you from any Heathrow terminal to downtown London in 50-60 minutes on the Piccadilly Line (6/hour, buy ticket or Oyster Card at Tube station self-service machine, or use a contactless pay option—see page 31). Depending on your destination in London, you may need to transfer (for example, if headed to the Victoria Station neighborhood, transfer at Hammersmith to the District line and ride six more stops).

If you plan to use the Tube for transport in London, it makes sense to buy a pay-as-you-go Oyster card (possibly adding a 7-Day Travelcard) at the airport's Tube station ticket machines. (For details on these passes, see page 31.) If you add a Travelcard that covers only Zones 1-2, you'll need to pay a small supplement for the initial trip from Heathrow (Zone 6) to downtown.

If you're taking the Tube from downtown London *to* the airport, note that Piccadilly Line trains don't stop at every terminal. Trains either stop at T-4, then T-2/T-3 (also called Heathrow Central), in that order; or T-2/T-3, then T-5. When leaving central London on the Tube, allow extra time if going to T-4 or T-5, and check the reader board in the station to make sure that the train goes to the right terminal before you board.

By Bus: Most buses depart from the outdoor common area called the Central Bus Station, a five-minute walk from the T-2/T-3 complex. To connect between T-4 or T-5 and the Central Bus Station, ride the free Heathrow Express train or the shuttle buses.

National Express has regular service from Heathrow's Central Bus Station to Victoria Coach Station in downtown London, near several of my recommended hotels. While slow, the bus is affordable and convenient for those staying near Victoria Station (£8-10, 1-2/hour, less frequent from Victoria Station to Heathrow, 45-75 minutes depending on time of day, +44 871 781 8181, www.nationalexpress.com). A less-frequent National Express bus goes from T-5 directly to Victoria Coach Station.

By Train: The **Heathrow Express** runs between Heathrow Airport and London's Paddington Station, which is a convenient transit hub for the western parts of London (for example, the Circle and District lines connect to Bayswater, South Kensington, and Victoria Station, and the District line also reaches Earl's Court).

The Heathrow Express is fast but pricey (£25 one-way, £37 round-trip, don't pay more for pointless "business" class, as cheap as £5.50 nonrefundable if purchased online in advance, covered by BritRail pass; 4/hour, daily 5:15-24:00; 15 minutes to downtown from Heathrow Central Station serving T-2/T-3, 21 minutes from T-5, for T-4 take free transfer to Heathrow Central; +44 345 600 1515, www.heathrowexpress.co.uk).

All Heathrow Express stations have ticket barriers, which you can enter only with a ticket (required even for free transfers between terminals). This can be either a paper ticket (you'll see many machines offering these); an Oyster card (the ticket price will be deducted from your balance); or an electronic ticket purchased through the Heathrow Express website or app (at the turnstile, hold the QR code to the scanner below the slot for paper tickets).

A cheaper alternative to the Heathrow Express will be the new **Crossrail Elizabeth line**, which may be operational by the time you visit. It will be faster (and more expensive) than the Tube; see www.tfl.gov.uk for updates.

By Car Service: Just Airports offers a private car service between five London airports and the city center (see website for price quote, +44 20 8900 1666, www.justairports.com).

By Taxi or Uber: Taxis from the airport cost £45-75 to west and central London (one hour). For four people traveling together, this can be a reasonable option. Hotels can often line up a cab back to the airport for about £50. Uber also offers London airport pickup and drop-off.

GATWICK AIRPORT

More and more flights land at Gatwick Airport, which is halfway between London and the south coast (code: LGW, www.gatwickairport.com). Gatwick has two terminals, North and South, which are easily connected by a free monorail (two-minute trip, runs 24 hours). Note that boarding passes say "Gatwick N" or "Gatwick S" to indicate your terminal. British Airways flights generally use Gatwick South. Gatwick Express trains (described next) stop only at Gatwick South. Schedules in each terminal show only arrivals and departures from that terminal.

Getting Between Gatwick and Downtown London: Gatwick is not on a Tube line, making **Gatwick Express trains** the best way into London from this airport. Trains shuttle conveniently between Gatwick South and London's Victoria Station, with many of my recommended hotels close by. As this service has been in flux, check online in advance for the latest schedule and price details (generally £20 one-way, £35 round-trip, at least 10 percent cheaper if purchased online, Oyster cards accepted but no discount offered, 4/hour, 30 minutes, runs 5:00-24:00 daily, a few trains as early as 3:30, +44 845 850 1530, www.gatwickexpress.com). If you buy your tickets at the station before boarding, ask about possible group deals. (If you see others in the ticket line, you could suggest buying your tickets together.) When going *to* the airport, at Victoria Station note that Gatwick Express has its own ticket windows right by the platform (tracks 13 and 14). You'll also find easy-to-use ticket machines nearby.

A train also runs between Gatwick South and **St. Pancras International Station** (£12.40, 3-5/hour, 45-60 minutes, www.nationalrail.co.uk—useful for travelers taking the Eurostar train (to Paris, Amsterdam, or Brussels) or staying in the St. Pancras/King's Cross neighborhood.

While even slower, the **bus** is a cheap and handy option to the Victoria Station neighborhood. National Express runs a bus from Gatwick directly to Victoria Station (£10, at least hourly, 1.5 hours, www.nationalexpress.com); EasyBus has one that stops near the Earl's Court Tube stop (£4-10 depending on how far ahead you book, 2-3/hour, www.easybus.com).

LONDON'S OTHER AIRPORTS

Stansted Airport: From Stansted (code: STN, www.stanstedairport.com), you have several options for getting into or out of London. Two different **buses** connect the airport and London's Victoria Station neighborhood: National Express (£9-14, every 15 minutes, 2 hours, runs 24 hours a day, picks up and stops throughout London, ends at Victoria Coach Station or Liverpool Street Station, www.nationalexpress.com) and Airport Bus Express (£12-14, 2/hour, 1.5-2 hours). Or you can take the faster, pricier Stansted Express **train** (£20, as cheap as £10 if booked online, connects to London's Tube system at Tottenham Hale or Liverpool Street, 2-4/hour, 45 minutes, 4:30-23:00, www.stanstedexpress.com). Stansted is expensive by **cab**; figure £100-120 one-way from central London.

Luton Airport: For Luton (code: LTN, www.london-luton.co.uk), the fastest way to get into London is by **train** to St. Pancras

International Station (£18.40 one-way, 1-6/hour, 30-45 minutes—check schedule to avoid slower trains, +44 0345 712 5678, www.eastmidlandsrailway.co.uk); catch the 10-minute shuttle bus (every 10 minutes) from outside the terminal to the Luton Airport Parkway Station. You can purchase a shuttle bus and train combo-ticket from kiosks or ticket machines inside the airport. When buying your train ticket *to* Luton, make sure you select "Luton Airport" as your destination rather than "Parkway Station" to ensure the shuttle fare is included. A railway extension from Luton Parkway Station to the airport may be open by the time you visit, eliminating the shuttle bus.

National Express **bus** A1 runs from Luton to Victoria Coach Station (£5-12 one-way, 2/hour, 1-1.5 hours, runs 24 hours, www.nationalexpress.com). Green Line express **bus** #757 runs to Buckingham Palace Road, just south of Victoria Station, and stops en route near the Baker Street Tube station—best if you're staying near Paddington Station or in North London (£11.50 one-way, 2-4/hour, 1-1.5 hours, runs 24 hours, +44 344 800 4411, www.greenline.co.uk).

London City and Southend Airports: To get into the city center from London City Airport (code: LCY, www.londoncityairport.com), take the Docklands Light Railway (DLR) to the Bank Tube station, which is one stop east of St. Paul's on the Central Line (less than £6 one-way, covered by Travelcard, a bit cheaper with an Oyster card or contactless, 20 minutes, www.tfl.gov.uk/dlr). Some EasyJet flights land farther out, at Southend Airport (code: SEN, www.southendairport.com). Trains connect this airport to London's Liverpool Street Station (£18.30 one-way, 3-8/hour, 55 minutes, www.abelliogreateranglia.co.uk).

CONNECTING LONDON'S AIRPORTS BY BUS

A handy **National Express bus** runs between Heathrow, Gatwick, Stansted, and Luton airports—easier than cutting through the center of London—although traffic can be bad and can increase travel times (www.nationalexpress.com).

From Heathrow Airport to: Gatwick Airport (£21, 1-6/hour, about 1.25 hours—but allow at least three hours between flights), **Stansted Airport** (£14-16, 4/day direct, 1.5 hours), **Luton Airport** (£16-20, roughly hourly, 1 hour).

By Train

London has a different train station for each region of Britain. There are nine main stations (see the map):

Euston: Serves northwest England, North Wales, and Scotland.

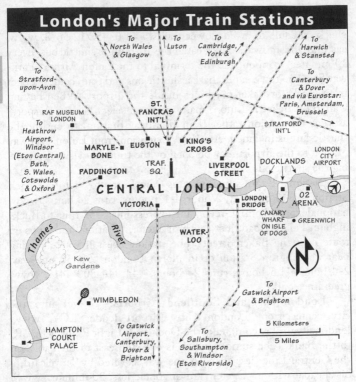

London's Major Train Stations

St. Pancras International: Serves north and south England, plus the Eurostar to Paris, Amsterdam, or Brussels (see "Crossing the Channel," later).

King's Cross: Serves northeast England and Scotland, including York and Edinburgh.

Liverpool Street: Serves east England, including Essex and Harwich.

London Bridge: Serves south England, including Brighton.

Waterloo: Serves south England, including Salisbury and Southampton.

Victoria: Serves Gatwick Airport, Canterbury, Dover, and Brighton.

Paddington: Serves south and southwest England, including Heathrow Airport, Windsor, Bath, Oxford, South Wales, and the Cotswolds.

Marylebone: Serves southwest and central England, including Stratford-upon-Avon.

In addition, London has several smaller train stations that you're less likely to use, such as **Charing Cross** (serves southeast England, including Dover) and **Blackfriars** (serves Brighton).

Any train station has schedule information, can make reservations, and can sell tickets for any destination. Most stations offer a baggage-storage service (£12.50/bag for 24 hours, look for *left luggage* signs); because of long security lines, it can take a while to check or pick up your bag (www.left-baggage.co.uk). For more details on the services available at each station, see www.nationalrail.co.uk/stations. UK train and bus info is available at www.traveline.info. Remember: To access the platforms—both coming and going—you'll need to either insert a paper ticket in the turnstile or scan the QR code from an electronic ticket. For information on tickets and rail passes, see the Practicalities chapter.

TRAIN CONNECTIONS FROM LONDON
To Points West

From Paddington Station to: Windsor (Windsor & Eton Central Station, 2/hour, 35 minutes, easy change at Slough), **Bath** (2/hour, 1.5 hours), **Oxford** (4/hour direct, 1 hour, more with transfer), **Moreton-in-Marsh** (hourly, 1.5 hours), **Penzance** (every 2 hours, 5 hours, more with change in Plymouth), **Cardiff** (2/hour, 2 hours).

To Points North

From King's Cross Station: York (3/hour, 2 hours), **Durham** (hourly, 3 hours), **Edinburgh** (2/hour, 4.5 hours). Trains to **Cambridge** also leave from here (4/hour, 1 hour).

From Euston Station to: Conwy (nearly hourly, 3.5 hours, transfer in Chester), **Liverpool** (hourly, 3 hours, transfer at Liverpool South Parkway), **Blackpool** (hourly, 3 hours, transfer at Preston), **Keswick** (hourly, 4 hours, transfer to bus at Penrith), **Glasgow** (1-2/hour, 4.5 hours).

From London's Other Stations

Trains run between London and **Canterbury:** St. Pancras International Station to Canterbury West (hourly, 1 hour, more with transfer); Victoria Station to Canterbury East (hourly, 2 hours); Charing Cross Station—with stops at Waterloo East and London Bridge—to Canterbury West (hourly, 1.5 hours, more with transfers).

Trains leave for **Stratford-upon-Avon** from Marylebone Station, located near the southwest corner of Regent's Park (2/day direct, 2.5 hours; also 1-2/hour, 2 hours, transfer in Leamington Spa, Dorridge, or Birmingham Moor).

To Other Destinations: Windsor (to Windsor & Eton Riverside Station, 2/hour, 1 hour, from Waterloo Station), **Dover** (hourly, 1 hour, direct from St. Pancras International Station; also 1-2/hour, 2 hours, direct from Victoria Station; or hourly, 2 hours, direct from Charing Cross Station), **Brighton** (2/hour, 1 hour, direct from Victoria Station; 2/hour, 1.5 hours, direct from Blackfriars Station), **Portsmouth** (3/hour, 2 hours, direct from Waterloo Station, a few with change in Clapham Junction from Victoria Station), **Salisbury** (2/hour, 1.5 hours, from Waterloo Station). For more information on trains to **Windsor, Cambridge,** or **Salisbury** (connecting to Stonehenge), see the Day Trips chapter.

By Bus

Buses are slower but considerably cheaper than trains for reaching destinations around Britain and beyond. Most depart from **Victoria Coach Station,** which is one long block south of Victoria Station (near many recommended accommodations, Tube: Victoria). Inside the station, you'll find basic eateries, kiosks, and a helpful information desk stocked with schedules and staff ready to point you to your bus or answer any questions. Watch your bags carefully—thieves thrive at the station.

Ideally you'll buy your tickets online (for tips on buying tickets and taking buses, see page 606). But if you must buy one at the station, try to arrive an hour before the bus departs, or drop by the day before. Ticketing machines are scattered around the station (separate machines for National Express/Eurolines and Megabus; you can buy either for today or for tomorrow); there's also a ticket counter near gate 21. For UK train and bus info, check www.traveline.info.

National Express buses go to: **Bath** (hourly, 3 hours), **Oxford** (2/hour, 2 hours), **Cambridge** (every 60-90 minutes, 2 hours), **Canterbury** (hourly, 2 hours), **Dover** (every 2 hours, 2.5 hours), **Brighton** (hourly, 2.5 hours), **Penzance** (5/day, 9 hours, overnight available), **Cardiff** (hourly, 3.5 hours), **Stratford-upon-Avon** (3/day, 3.5 hours), **Liverpool** (8/day direct, 5.5 hours, overnight available), **Blackpool** (1/day direct, more with transfer, 7 hours, overnight available), **York** (3/day direct, 6 hours), **Durham** (3/day direct, 7 hours, train is better), **Glasgow** (2-4/day direct, 10 hours, train is much better), **Edinburgh** (2/day direct, 10 hours, go by train instead).

To the Continent: Especially in summer, buses run to destinations all over Europe, including Paris, Amsterdam, Brussels, and Germany (sometimes crossing the Channel by ferry, other times through the Chunnel). For any international connection, you need to check in with your passport one hour before departure. For details, visit www.nationalexpress.com. For information on crossing the Channel by bus, see the next section.

Public Transportation near London

Map legend:
- ——— Rail
- – – – Bus
- ········· Boat
- Area covered by Britrail London Plus Pass
- 30 Kilometers / 30 Miles (approx. scale)
- Note: Bus Lines Follow Most Rail Lines

Crossing the Channel

BY EUROSTAR TRAIN

The Eurostar zips you from downtown London to downtown **Paris** (about hourly, 2.5 hours), **Brussels** (6/day, 2 hours), or **Amsterdam** (3/day, 4 hours; more with transfer in Brussels). The train travels at 190 mph, and the tunnel crossing is a 20-minute, silent, 100 mph nonevent. Your ears won't even pop.

Eurostar Tickets and Fares: A one-way ticket between London and Paris, Brussels, or Amsterdam can vary widely in price; for instance, $45-275 (Standard class), $105-375 (Standard Premier), and $350-400 (Business Premier). Fares depend on how far ahead you reserve and whether you're eligible for discounts—available for children (under 12), youths (under 26), and adults booking months ahead or purchasing round-trip. You can book tickets up to 4-6 months in advance. Tickets can be exchanged before the sched-

CONNECTIONS

uled departure for a fee (about $55, may be waived for early exchanges) plus the cost of any price increase, but only Business Premier class allows any refund.

Buy tickets ahead at RickSteves.com/rail or at Eurostar.com (+44 343 218 6186, $14 handling fee if you book via phone).

In Britain, tickets are issued only at the Eurostar office in St. Pancras ($14 fee). In continental Europe, you can buy tickets at any major train station in any country or at any travel agency that handles train tickets (expect a booking fee). If you have a Eurail Global Pass, seat reservations are available at Eurostar departure stations, Eurail.com, or by phone with Eurostar (generally harder to get at other train stations and travel agencies; $35 in Standard, $45 in Standard Premier, can sell out, no benefit with BritRail or other single-country pass).

Taking the Eurostar: Trains depart from and arrive at St. Pancras International Station. Arrive early to go through security and passport control (must be completed at least 30 minutes before departure from London or 45 minutes from the Continent) and locate your departure gate. Times listed on tickets are local; Britain is one hour earlier than continental Europe. The waiting area has shops, newsstands, horrible snack bars and cafés (get food beforehand), free Wi-Fi, and a currency-exchange booth.

CROSSING THE CHANNEL WITHOUT EUROSTAR

For speed and affordability, look into **cheap flights** (see the "Transportation" section of the Practicalities chapter). Or consider the following old-fashioned ways of crossing the Channel (cheaper but more complicated and time-consuming than the Eurostar).

By Train and Boat: To reach **Paris,** take a train from London's St. Pancras International Station, Charing Cross Station, or Victoria Station to Dover's Priory Station (hourly, 1-2 hours), then catch a P&O ferry to Calais, France (hourly, 1.5 hours, www. poferries.com). From Calais, take the TGV train to Paris.

For **Amsterdam,** consider Stena Line's Dutchflyer service, which combines train and ferry tickets. Trains go from London's Liverpool Street Station to the port of Harwich (hourly, 1.5 hours, 1-3 transfers possible). From Harwich, Stena Line ferries sail to Hoek van Holland (6.5 hours), where you can catch a train to Amsterdam (book ahead for best price, 13-14 hours total, www.

Building the Chunnel

The toughest obstacle to building a tunnel under the English Channel was overcome in 1986, when longtime rivals Britain and France reached an agreement to build it together. Britain began in Folkestone, France in Calais, planning a rendezvous in the middle.

By 1988, specially made machines three football fields long were boring 26-foot-wide holes under the ground. The dirt they hauled out became landfill in Britain and a hill in France. Crews crept forward 100 feet a day until June of 1991, when French and English workers broke through and shook hands midway across the Channel. The tunnel was complete. Rail service began in 1994.

The Chunnel is 31 miles long (24 miles of it underwater) and 26 feet wide. It sits 130 feet below the seabed in a chalky layer of sediment. It's segmented into three separate tunnels—two for trains (one in each direction) and one for service and ventilation. The walls are concrete panels and rebar fixed to the rock around it. Sixteen-thousand-horsepower engines pull 850 tons of railcars and passengers at speeds up to 100 mph through the tunnel.

The ambitious project—the world's longest undersea tunnel—helped to show the European community that cooperation between nations could benefit everyone.

stenaline.co.uk, Dutch train info at www.ns.nl). For additional European ferry info, visit www.aferry.to.

By Bus and Boat: Some buses still run to the Continent via ferry or Chunnel (either by day or overnight; entire journey is about 8-12 hours). These depart from London's Victoria Coach Station to **Paris, Brussels,** and **Amsterdam.** For details, see www.eurolines.co.uk.

By Cruise Ship

Many cruises begin, end, or call at one of several English ports offering easy access to London. Cruise lines favor two ports: Southampton, 80 miles southwest of London; and Dover, 80 miles southeast of London. If you don't want to bother with public transportation, most cruise lines offer transit-only excursion packages into London. For more details, see my *Rick Steves Scandinavian & Northern European Cruise Ports* guidebook.

SOUTHAMPTON CRUISE PORT

Within Southampton's sprawling port (www.cruisesouthampton.com), cruises use two separate dock areas, each with two terminals.

To reach London, it's about a 1.5-hour train ride. To get to Southampton Central Station from the cruise port, you can take a taxi or walk 10-15 minutes to the public ferry dock (Town Quay), where you can ride the QuayConnect bus to the train station. From there, trains depart at least every 30 minutes for London's Waterloo Station.

If you have time to kill in port, consider taking the train to Portsmouth (50-60 minutes), best known for its Historic Dockyard and many nautical sights, or stick around Southampton and visit the excellent SeaCity Museum, with a beautifully presented exhibit about the *Titanic,* which set sail from here on April 10, 1912.

DOVER CRUISE PORT

Little Dover has a huge port. Cruises put in at the Western Docks, with two terminals.

Trains go hourly from Dover Priory Station to London. From either cruise terminal, the best way into town (or to the train station) is by taxi or shuttle bus (take it to Market Square, then walk 15 minutes to the train station). From Dover's station, a fast train leaves for London's St. Pancras International Station (hourly, 1 hour); slower, direct trains go to Victoria Station (1-2/hour, 2 hours) and Charing Cross Station (hourly, 2 hours).

If you have extra time in port, Dover Castle, perched upon chalk cliffs, is well worth a visit for its WWII-era Secret Wartime Tunnels. Or take the train to Canterbury (2/hour, less than 30 minutes), notable for its important cathedral and fine historic core.

DAY TRIPS

Windsor • Cambridge •
Stonehenge

Windsor, Cambridge, and Stonehenge are three great day-trip possibilities near London. Any one of these very different but equally enjoyable destinations makes for an entertaining visit from London.

The primary residence of Her Majesty the Queen, **Windsor** hosts a castle that's regally lived-in, yet open to the public. This is simply a charming town to relax in—and its proximity to Heathrow Airport (60 minutes by train west of London) makes Windsor easy to combine with a flight into or out of London. Nearby is an oddball collection of intriguing sights, including Legoland Windsor, Eton College (Britain's most elite high school), Ascot

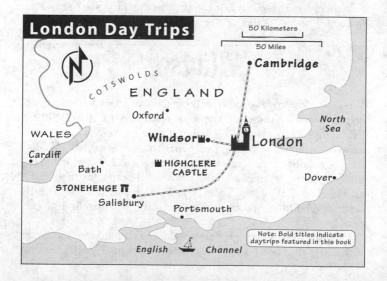

London Day Trips

50 Kilometers

50 Miles

COTSWOLDS

• Cambridge

ENGLAND

Oxford •

North Sea

WALES

Windsor

London

Cardiff •

■ HIGHCLERE
CASTLE

Bath •

Dover •

STONEHENGE

Salisbury

Portsmouth

English Channel

Note: Bold titles indicate
daytrips featured in this book

Racecourse (for horse racing), and Highclere Castle, where the TV series *Downton Abbey* was filmed.

Britain's venerable University of Cambridge is mixed into the delightful town of **Cambridge,** offering a mellow, fun-to-explore townscape with a big-league university.

Stonehenge, the world's most famous rock group, sits lonesome yet adored in a mysterious field 90 miles southwest of London.

Although I only cover these three destinations in this book, London's convenient public transit can easily whisk you to a wealth of other day-trip destinations: Bath (Roman ruins and Georgian townhouses), Canterbury (cathedral), Dover (castle-crowned chalk cliffs), Portsmouth (treasure trove of maritime history), Stratford-upon-Avon (all things Shakespeare), Warwick (fine medieval castle), Oxford (another classic university town), and Brighton (beach and pier). For details, see *Rick Steves England*.

GETTING AROUND

By Train: Take advantage of British Rail's discounts for day-trippers from London. The "off-peak day return" ticket is a round-trip fare that costs virtually the same as one-way, provided you depart London outside rush hour (usually after 9:30 on weekdays and anytime Sat-Sun). Be sure to ask for the "day return" ticket (round-trip within a single day) rather than the more expensive, standard "return" ticket. You can also save a little money if you purchase tickets before 18:00 the day before your trip.

By Train Tour: London Walks offers a variety of "Daytrips from London" tours year-round by train, including a Salisbury and Stonehenge tour, as well as a Cambridge itinerary (see page 43 for more on London Walks).

Windsor

Windsor, a compact and easy walking town of about 30,000 people, originally grew up around the royal residence. In 1070, William the Conqueror continued his habit of kicking Saxons out of their various settlements, taking over what the locals called "Windlesora" (meaning "riverbank with a hoisting winch")—which eventually became "Windsor." William built the first fortified castle on a chalk hill above the Thames; later kings added on to his early designs, rebuilding and expanding the castle and surrounding gardens.

By setting up their primary residence here, modern monarchs increased Windsor's popularity and prosperity—most notably,

Queen Victoria, whose stern statue glares at you as you approach the castle. After her death, Victoria rejoined her beloved husband, Albert, in the Royal Mausoleum at Frogmore House, a mile south of the castle in a private section of the Home Park (house and mausoleum rarely open). Within the grounds of Frogmore House is Frogmore Cottage—the former home of Prince Harry and Meghan Markle).

DAY TRIPS

The current Queen considers Windsor her primary residence, and the one where she feels most at home; she generally hangs her crown here on weekends, using it as an escape from her workaday grind at Buckingham Palace in the city. You can tell if Her Majesty is in residence by which flag is flying above the round tower: If it's the royal standard (a red, yellow, and blue flag) instead of the Union Jack, the Queen is at home.

While 99 percent of visitors just come to tour the castle and go, some enjoy spending the night. Daytime crowds trample Windsor's charm, which is most evident when the tourists are gone. Consider overnighting here—parking and access to Heathrow Airport are easy, and an evening at the horse races (on Mondays) is hoof-pounding, heart-thumping fun.

GETTING TO WINDSOR

By Train: Windsor has two train stations—Windsor & Eton Central and Windsor & Eton Riverside. London's Paddington Station connects with Windsor & Eton Central (2-3/hour, 35 minutes, easy change at Slough—typically just across the platform, www.gwr.com). London's Waterloo Station connects with Windsor & Eton Riverside (2/hour, no changes but slower—55 minutes, www.nationalrail.co.uk). Either trip costs about £11 one-way (a few pounds more for same-day return).

By Bus: Green Line buses #702 and #703 run—very slooooowly—from London's Victoria Colonnades (between the Victoria train and coach stations) to the Parish Church stop on Windsor's High Street, before continuing on to Legoland (1-2/hour, 1.5 hours to Windsor, typically £7-13 one-way, +44 118 959 4000, www.reading-buses.co.uk).

By Car: Windsor is about 20 miles from London. The town (and then the castle and Legoland) is well signposted from the M-4 motorway. It's a convenient first stop if you're arriving at Heathrow and renting a car there.

From Heathrow Airport: The two public transit options are around £13 each. The train requires two changes (first take the Heathrow Express to Hayes & Harlington station, transfer to a train to Slough, then transfer again to Windsor, 50 minutes total). Or take First Bus Company's bus #8 or #9 from Terminal 5 (2/ hour, 1 hour). London black cabs can (and do) charge whatever they like from Heathrow to Windsor; avoid them by calling a local cab company, such as Windsor Cars (£20-27, 25 minutes, +44 1753 677 677, www.windsorcars.com).

Orientation to Windsor

Windsor's pleasant pedestrian shopping zone litters the approach to its famous palace with fun temptations. You'll find most shops and restaurants around the castle on High and Thames streets, and down the pedestrian Peascod Street (PESS-cot), which runs perpendicular to High Street.

TOURIST INFORMATION

The TI is in the Windsor Guildhall, to the right as you face the Queen Victoria statue in front of the castle (Wed-Sun 10:00-16:00 closed Mon-Tue, sells discounted tickets to Legoland; High Street, +44 1753 743 900, www.windsor.gov.uk).

ARRIVAL IN WINDSOR

By Train: Whichever train station you arrive at, you're only a five-minute walk to the castle. From Windsor & Eton Central, walk through the Windsor Royal Shopping Centre and up the hill to the castle. From Windsor & Eton Riverside, you'll see the castle as you exit—just follow the wall up and around to the ticket office.

By Car: Follow signs from the M-4 motorway for pay-and-display parking in the center. River Street Car Park is closest to the castle, but it's pricey and often full. The cheaper, bigger Alexandra Car Park (near the riverside Alexandra Gardens) is farther west, just below the central train station (find the stairs up to the station platform, and exit into the Windsor Royal Shopping Centre). The cheapest parking option is the King Edward VII Avenue car-park-and-ride, northeast of the castle on the B-470 (includes shuttle bus into town).

DAY TRIPS

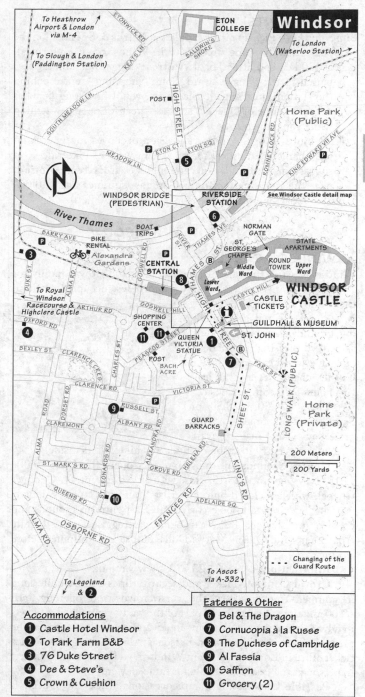

Windsor

To Heathrow Airport & London via M-4

To Slough & London (Paddington Station)

To London (Waterloo Station)

ETON COLLEGE

ETONWICK RD.

BALDWIN'S SHORE

KEATS LN.

SOUTHMEADOW LN.

HIGH STREET

POST

ETON CT.   ETON SQ.

MEADOW LN.

Home Park (Public)

ROMNEY LOCK RD.

KING EDWARD VII AVE.

WINDSOR BRIDGE (PEDESTRIAN)

RIVERSIDE STATION

See Windsor Castle detail map

River Thames

BOAT TRIPS

THAMES AVE.

NORMAN GATE

STATE APARTMENTS

BARRY AVE.

BIKE RENTAL

Alexandra Gardens

DUKE ST.

ALMA RD.

To Royal Windsor Racecourse & Highclere Castle

GOSWELL RD.

CENTRAL STATION

FRIVER ST.

ST. GEORGE'S CHAPEL

Middle Ward

ROUND TOWER

Upper Ward

WINDSOR CASTLE

Lower Ward

CASTLE HILL

CASTLE TICKETS

OXFORD RD.

ARTHUR RD.

GOSWELL HILL

HIGH STREET

GUILDHALL & MUSEUM

BEXLEY ST.

CLARENCE CRES.

CHARLES ST.

SHOPPING CENTER

PEASCOD STREET

POST

BACH-ACRE

QUEEN VICTORIA STATUE

ST. JOHN

PARK ST.

CLARENCE RD.

VICTORIA ST.

SHEET ST.

LONG WALK (PUBLIC)

Home Park (Private)

CLAREMONT

ALMA ROAD

DORSET RD.

RUSSELL ST.

ALBANY RD.

ALEXANDRA RD.

GROVE RD.

HELENA RD.

GUARD BARRACKS

200 Meters

200 Yards

ST. MARK'S RD.

ST. LEONARDS RD.

QUEENS RD.

ADELAIDE SQ.

FRANCES RD.

KING'S RD.

OSBORNE RD.

ALMA RD.

To Legoland & ②

To Ascot via A-332

- - - Changing of the Guard Route

Accommodations

1. Castle Hotel Windsor
2. To Park Farm B&B
3. 76 Duke Street
4. Dee & Steve's
5. Crown & Cushion

Eateries & Other

6. Bel & The Dragon
7. Cornucopia à la Russe
8. The Duchess of Cambridge
9. Al Fassia
10. Saffron
11. Grocery (2)

DAY TRIPS

HELPFUL HINTS

Supermarkets: Pick up picnic supplies at **Marks & Spencer** (on the pedestrian shopping street near the Windsor & Eton Central, at 130 Peascod Street) or at **Waitrose** (bigger but a bit farther, buried in the King Edward Court Shopping Centre behind the station). Just outside the castle, you'll find long benches near the statue of Queen Victoria—great for people-watching while you munch.

Hiking and Biking: Windsor and Eton occupy a lovely area on the Thames that's ideal for a pleasant walk or bike ride—get suggestions at the TI. You can rent bikes at **Extreme Motion,** near the river in Alexandra Gardens (summer daily 10:00-18:00, Sat-Sun only off-season, +44 1753 830 220).

Sights in Windsor

▲▲WINDSOR CASTLE

Windsor Castle, the official home of England's royal family for 900 years, claims to be the largest and oldest occupied castle in the world. Thankfully, touring it is simple. You'll see sprawling grounds, lavish staterooms, a crowd-pleasing dollhouse, and an exquisite Perpendicular Gothic chapel. Allow at least two hours for a complete visit.

Cost: £26.50, £28.50 on Sat, reservations smart but a few same-day tickets may be available, includes entry to castle grounds and all exhibits inside.

Hours: Grounds and most interiors open Thu-Mon 10:00-17:15, Nov-Feb until 16:15, closed Tue-Wed except St. George's Chapel, which is closed Sun to tourists (but open to worshippers; wait at the exit gate to be escorted in). Last entry to grounds and St. George's Chapel is 1.25 hours before closing. Last entry to State Apartments and Queen Mary's Dolls' House is 45 minutes before closing.

Information: +44 303 123 7304, www.rct.uk.

Crowd Control: Ticket and security lines can be quite long in summer. You can expect the worst crowds from opening until 13:00 any time of year. Avoid part of the wait by purchasing tickets in advance at www.rct.uk (print in advance or collect them at the prepaid ticket window), or in person at the Buckingham Palace ticket office in London. (Once in Windsor, you can only buy tickets in person at the castle, and only for same-day entry.)

Possible Closures: On rare occasions when the Queen is

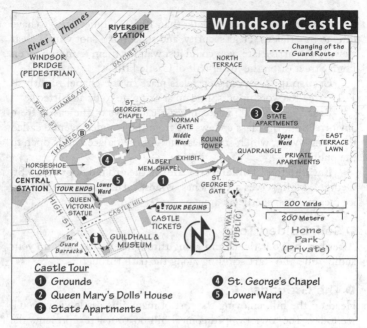

Castle Tour
❶ Grounds
❷ Queen Mary's Dolls' House
❸ State Apartments
❹ St. George's Chapel
❺ Lower Ward

entertaining guests, the State Apartments close (and tickets are slightly reduced). Sometimes the entire castle closes. It's smart to call ahead or check the website (especially in mid-June) to make sure everything is open when you want to go. While you're at it, confirm the Changing of the Guard schedule.

Tours: An included **multimedia guide** covers both the grounds and interiors. Ask about the free 30-minute **guided walk** around the grounds. The official £5 guidebook is full of gorgeous images and makes a fine souvenir but adds no information beyond what is covered in the audioguide and tour.

Changing of the Guard: The Changing of the Guard usually takes place Tue, Thu, and Sat at 11:00 (confirm schedule on website; canceled in very bad weather). The fresh guards, led by a marching band, leave their barracks on Sheet Street and march up High Street, hanging a right at Victoria, then a left into the castle's Lower Ward, arriving at about 11:00. After about a half-

hour, the tired guards march back the way the new ones came. If you want to view the ceremony from inside the castle, it's smart to arrive as early as possible (no later than 10:30 on quiet days) to have time to buy tickets, clear security, and stake out a spot with a clear view. If you arrive late, you could just wait for them to march by on High Street or on the lower half of Castle Hill.

Evensong: An evensong takes place in the chapel nightly at 17:15 (free for worshippers, line up at exit gate to be admitted).

Best View: While you can get great views of the castle from any direction, the classic views are from the wooded avenue called the Long Walk, which stretches south of the palace and is open to the public.

Eating: The **$ Undercroft Café,** on the ground floor below St. George's Hall, serves sandwiches, wraps, salads, teas, sweets, and ice cream under medieval arches.

❷ Self-Guided Tour

After buying your ticket and going through security, pick up your audioguide and start strolling along the path through...

❶ The Grounds

Head up the hill, enjoying the first of many fine castle views you'll see today. The tower-topped conical hill on your left represents the historical core of the castle. William the Conqueror built this motte (artificial mound) and bailey (fortified stockade around it) in 1080—his first castle in England. Among the later monarchs who spiffed up Windsor were Edward III (flush with French war booty, he made it a palace fit for a 14th-century king), Charles II (determined to restore the monarchy properly in the 1660s), and George IV (Britain's "Bling King," who financed many such vanity projects in the 1820s). On your right, the circular bandstand platform has a seal of the Order of the Garter, which has important ties to Windsor (see sidebar). This is where free guided tours depart (look for the posted schedule).

Passing through the small gate, you approach the stately St. George's Gate. Peek through here to the Upper Ward's **Quadrangle,** which is surrounded by the State Apartments (across the field) and the Queen's private apartments (to the right).

Turn left and follow the wall. Step into the long **exhibit** that traces the history of the castle, including models of how the structure evolved over time and illustrations of St. George's Hall in different historical periods.

Back outside, continue up the path. On your right-hand side, you enjoy great views of the **Round Tower** atop that original motte; running around the base of this arti-

DAY TRIPS

The Order of the Garter

In addition to being the royal residence, Windsor is the home of the Most Noble Order of the Garter—Britain's most prestigious chivalrous order. The castle's history is inexorably tied to this order.

Founded in 1348 by King Edward III and his son (the "Black Prince"), the Order of the Garter was designed to honor returning Crusaders. This was a time when the legends of King Arthur and the Knights of the Round Table were sweeping England, and Edward III fantasized that Windsor could be a real-life Camelot. (He even built the Round Tower as an homage to the Round Table.)

The order's seal illustrates the story of the order's founding and unusual name: a cross of St. George encircled with a belt and a French motto loosely translated as "Shame be upon he who thinks evil of it." Supposedly while the king was dancing with a fair maiden, her garter slipped off onto the floor; in an act of great chivalry, he rescued her from embarrassment by picking it up and uttering those words.

The Order of the Garter continues to the present day as the single most prestigious honor in the United Kingdom. There can be only 24 knights at one time (perfect numbers for splitting into two 12-man jousting teams), plus the sitting monarch and the Prince of Wales. Aside from royals and the nobility, past Knights of the Garter have included Winston Churchill, Bernard "Monty" Montgomery, and Ethiopian Emperor Haile Selassie. In 2008, Prince William became only the 1,000th knight in the order's history. Other current members include various ex-military officers, former British Prime Minister John Major, and a member of the Colman's Mustard family.

The patron of the order is St. George—the namesake of the State Apartments' most sumptuous hall and of the castle's own chapel. Both of these spaces—the grandest in Windsor—are designed to celebrate and honor the Order of the Garter.

ficial hill is the delightful, peaceful garden of the castle governor. The unusual design of this castle has not one "bailey" (castle yard), but three, which today make up Windsor's Upper Ward (where the Queen lives, which you just saw), Middle Ward (the ecclesiastical heart of the complex, with St. George's Chapel, which you'll soon pass on the left), and Lower Ward (residences for castle workers).

Continue all the way around this mini moat to the **Norman Gate,** which once held a prison. Walking under the gate, look up to see the bottom of the portcullis that could be dropped to seal off the inner courtyard. Three big holes are strategically situated for dumping boiling goo or worse on whoever was outside the gate. Carry on past the gate for even finer views of the Quadrangle.

Do a 180 and head back toward the Norman Gate, but before

you reach it, go down the staircase on the right. You'll emerge onto the fine **north terrace** overlooking the flat lands all around. It's easy to understand why this was a strategic place to build a castle. That's Eton College across the Thames. Imagine how handy it's been for royals to be able to ship off their teenagers to an elite prep school so close they could easily keep an eye on them...literally. The power-plant cooling towers in the distance mark the workaday burg of Slough (rhymes with "plow," immortalized as the setting for Britain's original version of *The Office*).

• Note that this area may be torn up during your visit, as part of a years-long renovation. Some items mentioned in the next part of the tour may be closed, and you may visit things in a different order than described.

Turn right and wander along the terrace. You'll likely see two lines. The long one leads to Queen Mary's Dolls' House, then to the State Apartments. The short line skips the dollhouse and heads directly to the apartments. Read the following descriptions and decide if the dollhouse is worth the wait (or try again later in the day, when the line sometimes eases up).

❷ Queen Mary's Dolls' House

This palace in miniature (1:12 scale, from 1924) is "the most famous dollhouse in the world." It was a gift for the adult Queen Mary (the wife of King George V, and the current Queen's grandmother), who greatly enjoyed miniatures. It's basically one big, dimly lit room with the large dollhouse in the middle, executed with an astonishing level of detail. Each fork, knife, and spoon on the expertly set banquet table is perfect and made of real silver—and the tiny pipes of its plumbing system actually have running water. But you're kept a few feet away by a glass wall, and constantly jostled by fellow sightseers in this crowded space, making it difficult to fully appreciate. Unless you're a dollhouse devotee, it's not worth waiting half an hour for a five-minute peek, but if the line is short it's worth a look.

❸ State Apartments

Dripping with chandeliers, finely furnished, and strewn with history and the art of a long line of kings and queens, they're the best I've seen in Britain. This is where Henry VIII and Charles I once lived, and where the current Queen wows visiting dignitaries. Remember to take advantage of the talkative docents in each room, who are happy to answer your questions—and can help you find your way in the

likely event that you see the rooms in a different order than described here.

On your way in, you may pass through the **China Museum,** featuring items from the Queen's many exquisite settings for royal shindigs.

You'll climb the Grand Staircase up to the peach-colored **Grand Vestibule,** decorated with exotic items seized by British troops during their missions to colonize various corners of the world. Immediately to the left of the door into the next room, look for the bullet that killed Lord Nelson at Trafalgar.

In the next room, the magnificent wood-ceilinged **Waterloo Chamber** is wallpapered with portraits of figures from the pan-European alliance that defeated Napoleon. Find General Wellington (high on the far wall, in red) who outmaneuvered him at Waterloo, and Pope Pius VII (right wall, in red and white) whom Napoleon befriended...then imprisoned.

A highlight is **St. George's Hall,** decorated with emblems representing the knights of the prestigious Order of the Garter (see sidebar, earlier). This is the site of some of the most elaborate royal banquets—imagine one long table stretching from one end of the hall to the other and seating 160 VIPs. At the end of the hall, you enter the Queen's Guard Chamber, with more weapons and busts of English war heroes, from Nelson to Marlborough to Churchill.

At some point, you'll pass through a **series of living rooms**—bedchambers, dressing rooms, and drawing rooms of the king and queen (who traditionally maintained separate quarters). Many rooms are decorated with canvases by Rubens, Van Dyck, and Holbein. You may also tour some rooms that were restored after a fire in 1992, including the "Semi-State Apartments."

The **Garter Throne Room** is where new members of the Order of the Garter are invested (ceremonially granted their titles).

• *Exiting the State Apartments, you have one more major sight to see. Head back out the way you came in, but bear right/downhill toward (or follow signs to find)...*

❹ St. George's Chapel

This church is known for housing numerous royal tombs, and is an exquisite example of the Perpendicular Gothic style (dating from about 1500). More recently, it's where Prince Harry and Meghan Markle tied the knot in 2018. Enter at the bottom end, pick up a free map, and circle the interior clockwise, finding these highlights:

Stand at the back and look down the **nave,** with its classic fan-vaulting spreading out from each slender pillar and nearly every joint capped with an elaborate and colorful roof boss. Most of these emblems are associated with the Knights of the Garter, who consider St. George's their "mother church." Under the upper stained-glass windows, notice the continuous frieze of 250 angels, lovingly carved with great detail, ringing the church.

In the back-left corner (#4 on your church-issued map), take in the melodramatic monument to **Princess Charlotte of Wales,** the only child of King George IV. Heir to the throne, her death in 1817 (at 21, in childbirth) devastated the nation. Head up the left side of the nave and find the simple chapel (#6, just past the wooden gate) containing the tombs of the current Queen's parents, **King George VI and "Queen Mum" Elizabeth;** the ashes of her younger sister, Princess Margaret, are also kept here (see the marble slab against the wall). It's speculated that the current Queen may choose this chapel for her final resting place. Farther up the aisle is the tomb of **Edward IV** (#8, past the door into the choir), who expanded St. George's Chapel.

Stepping into the **choir area** (#12), you're immediately aware that you are in the inner sanctum of the Order of the Garter. The banners lining the nave represent the knights, as do the fancy helmets and half-drawn swords topping the spire of each wood-carved seat. These symbols honor only living knights; on the seats are some 800 golden panels memorializing departed knights. Under your feet lies the **Royal Vault** (#13), burial spot of Mad King George III (nemesis of American revolutionaries). Strolling farther up the aisle, notice the marker in the floor: You're walking over the burial site of **King Henry VIII** (#14) and Jane Seymour, Henry's favorite wife (perhaps because she was the only one who died before he could behead her). The body of King Charles I, who was beheaded by Oliver Cromwell's forces at the Banqueting House, was also discovered here...with its head sewn back on.

Exiting the choir area at the far end, loop around to the left and head to the back of the church. Leaving the church proper in the far corner, you'll pass the gift shop. On your way out, pause at the door of the sumptuous 13th-century **Albert Memorial Chapel** (#28), redecorated in 1861 after the death of Queen Victoria's husband, Prince Albert, and dedicated to his memory.

• *After exiting the chapel, you come into the castle's...*

DAY TRIPS

❺ Lower Ward

This area is a living town where some 160 people who work for the Queen reside; they include clergy, military, and castle administrators. Just below the chapel, you may be able to enter a tranquil little horseshoe-shaped courtyard ringed with residential doorways—all of them with a spectacular view of the chapel's grand entrance.

Back out in the yard, look for the guard posted at his pillbox. Like those at Buckingham Palace, he's been trained to be a ruthless killing machine...just so he can wind up as somebody's photo op. *Click!*

MORE SIGHTS IN WINDSOR
Legoland Windsor

Paradise for Legomaniacs under age 12, this huge, kid-pleasing park has dozens of tame but fun rides (often with very long lines) scattered throughout its 150 acres. The impressive Miniland has 40 million Lego pieces glued together to create 800 tiny buildings and a mini tour of Europe. Several of the more exciting rides involve getting wet, so dress accordingly or buy a cheap  disposable poncho in the gift shop. While you may be tempted to hop on the Hill Train at the entrance, it's faster and more convenient to walk down into the park. Food is available in the park, but you can save money by bringing a picnic.

Cost: £60 but varies by day, significant savings when booked online a week or more in advance, 10 percent discount at Windsor TI, free for ages 3 and under, optional "Reserve & Ride" app allows you to bypass lines (£25-90 depending on when you go and how much time you want to save).

Hours: Check website for exact schedule; generally Mon-Fri 10:00-17:00, until 18:00 in summer and on Sat-Sun; often closed Tue-Wed outside of summer; closed in winter except for school holidays; +44 1753 626 416, www.legoland.co.uk.

Getting There: A £5 round-trip shuttle bus runs from the Parish Church stop on High Street (3/hour). If day-tripping from London, ask about rail/shuttle/park admission deals from Paddington or Waterloo train stations. For drivers, the park is on the B-3022 Windsor/Ascot road, two miles southwest of Windsor and 25 miles west of London. Legoland is clearly signposted from the M-3, M-4, and M-25 motorways (easy paid parking).

Visiting Highclere Castle

If you're a fan of the TV series *Downton Abbey,* consider a day trip from London to Highclere Castle, the stately house where much of the show was filmed. Though the show is set in Yorkshire, the actual house is located in Hampshire, about an hour's train ride west of London. Highclere has been home to the Earls of Carnarvon since 1679, but the present Jacobean-style house was rebuilt in the 1840s by Sir Charles Barry, who also designed London's Houses of Parliament. Noted landscape architect Capability Brown laid out the traditional gardens in the mid-18th century. The castle's Egyptian exhibit features artifacts collected by Highclere's fifth earl, George Herbert, a keen amateur archaeologist. When Howard Carter discovered King Tut's tomb in 1922, he waited three weeks for his friend and patron Herbert to join him before looking inside. The earl died unexpectedly a few months later, giving birth to the legend of a "mummy's curse."

Cost and Hours: £20.50 for castle and garden, £7.50 more to add Egyptian exhibit. Open in summer Sun-Thu 10:00-17:00, grounds open from 9:30, closed Fri-Sat, last entry one hour before closing. Generally closed mid-Sept-mid-July except around Easter and other special events. Reserve timed-entry tickets well in advance or take your chances; +44 1635 253 204, www.highclerecastle.co.uk.

Getting There: Highclere is 6 miles south of Newbury, about 70 miles west of London, off the A-34.

By Train and Taxi: Great Western trains run from London's Paddington Station to Newbury (about £30 return; 1-2/hour, 40-70 minutes, +44 345 7000 125, www.gwr.com). From Newbury train station, you can take a taxi (about £20 one-way, 15 minutes, taxis wait outside station or call +44 1635 33 333).

By Tour: Brit Movie Tours offers an all-day bus tour of *Downton Abbey* filming locations, including Highclere Castle and the fictional village of Downton (£120, includes transport and castle/garden entry, £5 extra for Egyptian exhibit, 9 hours, depart London from outside Gloucester Road Tube Station, reserve far in advance, +44 20 7118 1007, www.britmovietours.com).

Eton College

Across the bridge from Windsor Castle is the most famous "public" (the equivalent of our "private") high school in Britain. Eton was founded in 1440 by King Henry VI; today it educates about 1,300 boys (ages 13-18), who live on campus. Eton has molded the characters of 19 prime ministers as well as members of the royal family—most recently princes William and Harry. Sparse on actual sights, the college is officially closed to visitors except via guided tour, where you may get a glimpse of the schoolyard, chapel, and cloisters (for tour information visit www.etoncollege.com or call +44 1753 370 100). You can, however, visit the Museum of Eton Life and learn about 600 years of school traditions (free, Sun only 14:30-17:00, access from Baldwin's Shore Road, +44 1753 370 590).

Eton High Street

Even if you're not touring the college, it's worth the few minutes it takes to cross the pedestrian bridge and wander straight up Eton's High Street. A bit more cutesy and authentic-feeling than Windsor (which is given over to shopping malls and chain stores), Eton has a charm that's fun to sample.

Windsor and Royal Borough Museum

Tucked into one room beneath the Guildhall (where Prince Charles remarried), this little museum does its best to give some insight into the history of Windsor and the surrounding area. They also have lots of special activities for kids. Ask at the desk whether tours are running to the Guildhall itself (visits only possible with a guide, leave sporadically, about 20-30 minutes); if not, it's probably not worth the admission—you can see most of the museum with a sweep of your head from the door.

Cost and Hours: £2, Wed-Sun 10:00-16:00, closed Mon-Tue, in the Guildhall on High Street, +44 1628 685 686, www.rbwm. gov.uk.

Boat Trips

Cruise up and down the Thames River for classic views of the castle, the village of Eton, Eton College, and the Royal Windsor Racecourse. Choose from a 40-minute or two-hour tour, then relax onboard and nibble a picnic. Boats leave from the riverside promenade adjacent to Barry Avenue, and run from early spring through late fall.

Cost and Hours: 40-minute tour—£11, 1-2/hour daily 10:00-17:00; 2-hour tour—£18.75, 1-2/day; both cheaper online, +44 1753 851 900, www.frenchbrothers.co.uk.

Horse Racing

The horses race every Monday at the Royal Windsor Racecourse (£27 entry, online discounts, under age 18 free with an adult, April-Oct except no races in Sept, off the A-308 between Windsor and Maidenhead, +44 1753 498 400, www.windsor-racecourse.co.uk). The romantic way to get there from Windsor is by a 10-minute shuttle boat (£7.50 round-trip, www.frenchbrothers.co.uk). The famous Ascot Racecourse (described next) is also nearby.

NEAR WINDSOR
Ascot Racecourse
Located seven miles southwest of Windsor and just north of the town of Ascot, this royally owned track is one of the most famous horse-racing venues in the world. The horses first ran here in 1711, and the course is best known for June's five-day Royal Ascot race meeting, attended by the Queen and 299,999 of her loyal subjects. For many, the outlandish hats worn on Ladies Day (Thu) are more interesting than the horses. Royal Ascot is usually the third week in June. The pricey tickets go on sale the preceding November; while the Friday and Saturday races tend to sell out far ahead, tickets for the other days are often available close to the date (check website). In addition to Royal Ascot, the racecourse runs the ponies year-round—funny hats strictly optional.

Cost: Regular tickets generally start from £27 and go as high as £85—may be available at a discount at TI, dress code enforced in some areas and on certain days, +44 344 346 3000, www.ascot.com.

Sleeping in Windsor

Most visitors stay in London and do Windsor as a day trip. But here are a few suggestions for those staying the night.

$$$$ Castle Hotel Windsor, part of the boutique division of Accor Hotels, offers 108 rooms and elegant public spaces in a central location just down the street from Her Majesty's weekend retreat (air-con, elevator in main building, parking-£25/day, 18 High Street, +44 1753 851 577, www.castlehotelwindsor.com, h6618@accor.com).

$$ Park Farm B&B, bright and cheery, is most convenient for drivers. But even if you're not driving, this beautiful place is such a good value, and the welcome is so warm, that you're unlikely to mind the bus ride into town (no children under 12, free off-street parking, 1 mile from Legoland on St. Leonards Road near Imperial Road, 5-minute bus ride or 1-mile walk to castle, £8 taxi ride from station, +44 1753 866 823 or +44 7909 950 095, www.parkfarm.com, stay@parkfarm.com, Caroline and Drew Youds).

$$ 76 Duke Street has two nice rooms, but only hosts one set of guests at a time. While the bathroom is (just) outside your bedroom, you have it to yourself (15-minute walk from station at—you guessed it—76 Duke Street, +44 1753 620 636 or +44 7884 222 225, www.76dukestreet.co.uk, bedandbreakfast@76dukestreet.co.uk, Julia).

$$ Dee and Steve's is a friendly four-room place that sleeps six, above a window shop on a quiet residential street about a

10-minute walk from the castle and station. The rooms are cozy, Dee and Steve are pleasant hosts, and a fully equipped kitchen makes eating in handy. They also offer a two-bedroom nook, which sleeps three (169 Oxford Road, +44 1753 854 489, www. deeandsteve.com, dee@deeandsteve.com).

$$ Crown and Cushion is a good option on Eton's High Street, just across the pedestrian bridge from Windsor's waterfront (a short uphill walk to the castle). While the pub it's situated over is worn and drab, you're right in the heart of charming Eton, and the eight creaky rooms—with uneven floors and old-beam ceilings—are nicely furnished (free parking, 84 High Street in Eton, +44 1753 861 531, www.thecrownandcushioneton.co.uk, info@ thecrownandcushioneton.co.uk).

Eating in Windsor

Elegant Spots with River Views: Several places flank Windsor Bridge, offering romantic dining after dark. The riverside promenade, with cheap takeaway stands scattered about, is a delightful place for a picnic lunch or dinner with the swans. If you don't see anything that appeals, continue up Eton's High Street, which is also lined with characteristic eateries.

In the Tourist Zone Around the Palace: Strolling the streets and lanes around the palace entrance—especially in the shopping zone near Windsor & Eton Station—you'll find countless inviting eateries. The central area also has a sampling of dependable British chains (including a Wagamama, Honest Burgers, and Thai Square). Residents enjoy a wide selection of unpretentious little eateries just past the end of pedestrian Peascod Street, where it becomes St. Leonards Road. These include Saffron (recommended below) and a fire station turned pub-and-cultural center (The Old Court Artspace, +44 1753 911 333).

$$$ Bel & The Dragon is the place to splurge on high-quality classic British food in a charming half-timbered building with an upscale-rustic dining space (food served Wed-Sat 12:00-15:00 & 17:30-21:30, Sun 12:00-16:00, closed Mon-Tue, bar open longer hours, on Thames Street near the bridge to Eton, +44 1753 866 056).

$$$ Cornucopia à la Russe, with a cozy, woody atmosphere, serves elegant French and international dishes (two- and three-course lunch deals, open Mon 18:00-21:30, Tue-Sat 12:00-14:30 & 18:00-21:30, closed Sun, 6 High Street, +44 1753 833 009).

$$ The Duchess of Cambridge's friendly staff serves up the normal grub in a pub that's right across from the castle walls. It feels big, modern, but tasteful, and with an open fireplace to boot. While the pub predates Kate, it was named in her honor following a recent remodel, and has the photos to prove her endorsement (daily 12:00-22:00 or later, food until 19:45, 3 Thames Street, +44 1753 864 405).

$$ Al Fassia—just beyond the end of the pedestrian zone—has authentic Moroccan cuisine, including tagines served in cone-shaped pottery (Mon-Fri 18:00-22:00, Sat-Sun from 12:00, 27 St. Leonards Road, +44 1753 855 370).

$$ Saffron restaurant, while a fairly long walk from the castle, is the local choice for South Indian cuisine, with a modern interior and tasty dishes. Their vegetable *thali* is a treat (daily 17:00-23:00, 99 St. Leonards Road, +44 1753 855 467).

Cambridge

Cambridge, 60 miles north of London, is world-famous for its prestigious university. William Wordsworth, Isaac Newton, Charles Darwin, Alan Turing, Jane Goodall, and Prince Charles are only a few of its illustrious alumni. The university dominates—and owns—most of Cambridge, a historic town of about 125,000 people. Cambridge is the epitome of a university town, with busy bikers, stately residence halls, plenty of bookshops, and proud locals who can point out where DNA was originally modeled, the atom first split, and electrons discovered.

In medieval Europe, higher education was the domain of the Church and was limited to ecclesiastical schools. Scholars lived in "halls" on campus, which came to be known as "colleges." The first at Cambridge, Peterhouse, was founded in the 1280s. By 1350, Cambridge had eight separate colleges, each one a self-contained world in itself—enclosed behind walls, with a monastic-type courtyard, chapel, library, and lodgings. These colleges allied in a federation known as the University of Cambridge. That same arrangement survives to this day. Today, Cambridge has 31 colleges, totaling about 12,000 undergrads, scattered around the town center.

For travelers, Cambridge offers a pleasant medieval-era town, art-filled churches and museums, and—most of all—a chance to see some of the colleges. Many colleges are open to visitors (some free; others require a ticket at the gate). You can stroll the grounds and pop into a few public areas (mainly chapels and dining halls).

Many of these colleges date back centuries, with ornately decorated facades that try to one-up each other.

The town is easy to sort out. There's a small and youthful commercial center—quiet and traffic free (except for lots of bikes), one important museum (the Fitzwilliam), and lots of minor museums (all generally free). The River Cam has boat tours, three public bridges, and a strip of six colleges whose gardens basically own the river through the center of town and make it feel like an  exclusive park. Trinity College has its famous Wren Library, and King's College has a famous ornate chapel. The city is filled with students year-round—scholars throughout the regular terms and visiting students enjoying summer programs.

DAY TRIPS

PLANNING YOUR TIME

Cambridge can easily be seen as a day trip from London. A good five-hour plan is to follow my self-guided walk, spend an hour on a punt ride, tour the Fitzwilliam Museum (closed Mon), and see the Wren Library at Trinity College (open Mon-Sat for only two hours a day, so plan ahead). For a little extra color, consider joining a walk through town with a local guide (2 hours, repeats much of my self-guided walk but splices in local flavor). Confirm which sights are covered on the guided walk, so you don't duplicate those on your own.

Your visit will be affected somewhat by the university schedule. Cambridge has three terms: Lent term from mid-January to mid-March, Easter term from mid-April to mid-June, and Michaelmas term from early October to early December. During exams (roughly the month of May), the colleges are closed to visitors, which can impede access to some of the town's picturesque little corners. When class is in session, Cambridge is a bustling town of students buzzing to class on bikes. Between terms there's less going on, but the main sights—King's College Chapel and the Wren Library at Trinity College—stay open, and Cambridge is never sleepy. On good-weather weekends, the town overflows with visitors—many of them trying their hand, unsuccessfully, at punting the Cam.

If you're in town for the evening, the evensong service at King's College Chapel (Mon-Sat at 17:30, Sun at 15:30) is a must. And if you like plays and music, events are always happening in this thriving cultural hub.

GETTING TO CAMBRIDGE

By Train: It's an easy 50-minute trip from London's King's Cross Station (hourly express trains; other journeys, also about hourly, take slightly longer). Cheaper direct trains also run from London's Liverpool Street Station, but take longer (2/hour, 1.5 hours). Rail information: +44 845 748 4950, www.nationalrail.co.uk.

By Bus: National Express X90 coaches run from London's Victoria Coach Station to the Parkside stop in Cambridge (every 60-90 minutes, 2 hours, +44 871 781 8181, www.nationalexpress. co.uk).

Orientation to Cambridge

Cambridge has a population of about 125,000, but the area visitors enjoy seeing is compact: Everything is within a pleasant 15-minute walk. The main colleges form a north-south row, bordered on one side by the River Cam and on the other by the town. The town center, brimming with tearooms, has a colorful open-air market square. The train station is about a mile to the southeast.

Tourist Information: Cambridge has no brick-and-mortar TI, but you can find town information at www.visitcambridge.org. The **Cambridge Gift Shop** acts as an unofficial info source and a booking point for tours (Mon-Sat 10:00-17:00, Sun 11:00-16:00, 18 Rose Crescent, at intersection with King's Parade, +44 1223 355 785).

ARRIVAL IN CAMBRIDGE

By Train: Cambridge's train station is about a mile southeast of the center. To get downtown, you can **walk** for about 25 minutes (exit straight ahead on Station Road, bear right at the war memorial onto Hills Road, and follow it into town); pay about £6 for a **taxi;** or take a public **bus.** To find the bus stops, turn left when exiting the station, cross the street, and walk half a block. Bus #1, #3, or #7 are cheapest (referred to as "Citi 1," "Citi 3," and so on in schedules, but buses are marked only with the number; £1, pay driver). The bus labeled U (for "Universal") is pricier at £2.20/ride. Either way, ask the driver which stop is best for the city center.

By Car: To park in the middle of town, follow signs from the M-11 motorway to any of the central (but expensive) short-stay parking lots—including one at the Lion Yard shopping mall. Or leave your car at one of the various park-and-ride lots outside the city, then take the shuttle into town.

HELPFUL HINTS

Live Theater and Entertainment: With all the smart and talented students in town, there is always something going on. Make

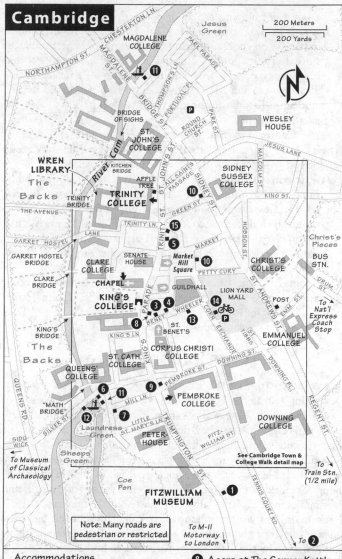

DAY TRIPS

Accommodations
1 Hotel du Vin
2 To Lensfield Hotel

Eateries
3 The Eagle Pub
4 Bread & Meat
5 Michaelhouse Café
6 The Anchor Pub
7 The Mill Pub
8 Agora at The Copper Kettle
9 Fitzbillies

Other
10 Grocery (2)
11 Scudamore's Punts (2)
12 Cambridge Chauffeur Punts
13 Cambridge Live Tickets
14 Bike Rental
15 Cambridge Gift Shop

a point of enjoying a play or concert. The **Cambridge University Amateur Dramatic Club (ADC)** is Britain's oldest university playhouse, offering a steady stream of performances since 1855. It's lots of fun and casual, with easy-to-get and inexpensive tickets. This is your chance to see a future Emma Thompson or Ian McKellen—alumni who performed here as students—before they become stars (+44 1223 300 085, www. adctheatre.com).

    Cambridge Live Tickets is a very helpful service, offering event info and ticket sales in person and online (2 Wheeler Street, +44 1223 357 851, www.cambridgelive.org.uk).

Festivals: The **Cambridge Folk Festival** gets things humming and strumming in late July or early August (tickets go on sale several months ahead and often sell out; www. cambridgefolkfestival.co.uk). From mid-July through August, the town's **Shakespeare Festival** attracts 25,000 visitors for outdoor performances in some of the college's gardens (www. cambridgeshakespeare.com).

Bike Rental: At the Lion Yard shopping mall, **Rutland Cycling** rents bikes (Mon-Fri 8:00-18:00, Sat from 9:00, Sun 10:00-17:00, look for it underground in the Grand Arcade, +44 1223 307 655, www.rutlandcycling.com).

Tours in Cambridge

▲▲Walking Tour of the Colleges

A walking tour is the best way to understand Cambridge's mix of "town and gown." The walks can be more educational (read: dry) than entertaining, but they do provide a good rundown of the historic and scenic highlights of the university, some fun local gossip, and plenty of university trivia. The Society of Cambridge Tour Guides leads tours of various lengths and topics; their 1.5-hour "Cambridge Highlights" tour covers a variety of colleges and landmarks for £25. They also do "ghost walks" after dark (£15, 1 hour, mainly in winter...when it's dark enough). Check out their current offerings and book at www.sctg.org.uk, or, if you're already in town, stop by the Cambridge Gift Shop to book.

Cambridge Town and College Walk

This self-guided walk covers the essential sights. We start in the old market square, visit a couple of typical (if less-visited) colleges, pause at the dreamy River Cam, and finish at the glory of King's College Chapel. Although we won't go as far as the Fitzwilliam Museum, you can easily visit it on your own (covered in "Sights in Cambridge," later).

Cambridge Colleges 101

Cambridge's 31 colleges, where students spend most of their time, are central to the life of the university. Think of them less as schools and more as lodgings and social communities. They house, feed, and parent the students (including a "home professor" who coaches students), while the overall university offers formal teaching and lectures. Over the centuries, each college has developed a reputation: the rich elites, the partiers, the science nerds, the political progressives, and so on.

How to Visit: Some colleges are free to visit and welcoming to the public, some are closed off and very private, and others are famous and make money by charging for visits. Most are open only in the afternoons, and all have a similar design and etiquette. At their historic front gates, you'll find a porter's lodge where the porter delivers mail, monitors who comes and goes, and keeps people off the grass. Only fellows (senior professors) can walk on the grassy courts, which are the centerpiece of each college campus. Other than that, you can relax and roam freely, so long as an area is not locked or blocked with a "for members only" sign. Whether a college is open to visitors or private, you can usually at least pop in through the gate, chat with the porter, and enjoy the view of the court.

What You Will (and Won't) See: The court is ringed by venerable buildings, with a library, dormitories, a dining hall, and a chapel. The dining halls are easy to identify because they have big bay windows that mark the location of a "high table" where VIPs eat. A portrait of the college's founder usually hangs above the high table, and paintings of rectors and important alumni also decorate the walls. Students still eat in these halls, which is why they are rarely open to the public (but you can look in from the main door).

A college's chapel is the building that most often allows visitors (including at evensong services, usually at 17:30 or 18:00). In the chapel, seating is usually arranged in several rows of pews that face each other to allow for antiphonal singing and chanting—where one side starts and the other responds. The chapels often contain memorials to students who died in World Wars I and II. Libraries are treasured and generally not open to the public. There's also a Senior Common Room (like a teachers' lounge but much fancier), where fellows share ideas in an exclusive social hall, creating a fertile intellectual garden. Student rooms are never open to the public during school terms, though some are available as vacation rentals when classes are not in session.

• *Start on Market Hill Square. To find the square from the lively street called King's Parade, go behind Great St. Mary's Church (with the tall tower). Once on the square, stand in front of the Guildhall (the brick building with a big clock up top).*

❶ Market Hill Square

This square has been a center of commerce for more than a thousand years. At a glance, you can see the elements that combined to make Cambridge: church (Great St. Mary's rear end), university (those modern buildings are student lodgings), and trade (the open-air market and Guildhall).

Think of the history this place has seen: Romans first built a bridge over the Cam in AD 43, Anglo-Saxons and Danes established a market here in the Dark Ages, and Normans built a castle here (now gone) in the 11th century. The city's coat of arms (above the Guildhall door) shows medieval boats flocking to trade at the newly built bridge over the River Cam, which established "Cambridge."

But the big year was 1209. After scuffles in Oxford between its scholars and townsfolk, many of Oxford's academics fled here and started their own university. (The Oxford-Cambridge rivalry just seems natural.) Where's "the university"? Everywhere, mixed into the town, with the 31 individual colleges, university halls, and student dorms scattered about.

Cambridge suffered no bomb damage in World War II, so the older buildings you see are original. As you walk, notice how peaceful the town is, with almost no cars, but bikes everywhere. (Be aware: They are silent and pack a punch, and the sidewalks can be very narrow.)

The Guildhall facing this square (the seat of the city council today) overlooks market stalls. The really big market is on Sunday (9:30-16:30) and features produce, arts, and crafts. On other days, you'll find mostly clothes and food stands (Mon-Sat generally 9:30-16:00).

• *Let's get started by exploring a bit of modern Cambridge. Facing the Guildhall, exit the square to your left down **Petty Cury Lane,** a modern pedestrian shopping street. Its international chain stores and student-friendly fast-food places make it clear that Cambridge University invites students and profs from around the globe. At the end of the street, turn right, walking down St. Andrews Street (which connects the town center to the train station).*

*On the left side of the street is our first college: **Christ's College.** Its elaborate 16th-century gatehouse proudly displays the college's coat of arms and colors; look for others around town. Step inside to enjoy the classic court, next to a portrait of alum Charles Darwin (free, open daily 9:00-16:00). Don't linger—we'll see a better one in a minute.*

DAY TRIPS

Cambridge Town & College Walk

ST. JOHN'S COLLEGE

WREN LIBRARY

TRINITY COLLEGE

APPLE TREE

WALK ENDS

TRINITY BRIDGE

GREEN ST.

SIDNEY SUSSEX COLLEGE

KING ST.

MALCOLM ST.

ALL SAINTS PASSAGE

8

TRINITY LN.

CAMBRIDGE GIFT SHOP

200 Meters

200 Yards

N

SENATE HOUSE

GREAT ST. MARY'S

MARKET ST.

SIDNEY ST.

HOBSON ST.

BUS STN.

7

Market Hill Square

WALK BEGINS

CHRIST'S COLLEGE

CLARE COLLEGE

KING'S COLLEGE CHAPEL

CHAPEL TICKETS

1

PETTY CURY

To Nat'l Express Coach Stop

6

RYDER & AMIES

GUILDHALL

ST. EDWARD

LION YARD MALL

POST

EMMANUEL ST.

B

To The Backs

KING'S COLLEGE

THE EAGLE

WHEELER ST.

CORN EXCHANGE

ST. ANDREWS ST.

EMMANUEL COLLEGE

KING'S PARADE

BENET ST.

5

CORPUS CLOCK

ST. BENET'S

P

2

KING'S LN.

ST. CATHARINE'S COLLEGE

CORPUS CHRISTI COLLEGE

FITZBILLIE'S

DOWNING ST.

ST. TIBBS

DOWNING PL.

REGENT ST.

QUEENS' COLLEGE

"MATH BRIDGE"

SILVER ST.

PEMBROKE ST.

3

PEMBROKE COLLEGE

TENNIS COURT RD.

To Train Station (1/2 mile)

ANCHOR PUB

MILL LN.

TRUMPINGTON ST.

DOWNING COLLEGE

4

River Cam

LITTLE ST. MARY'S LN.

PETER-HOUSE

FITZWILLIAM MUSEUM

FITZWILLIAM ST.

Note: Many roads are pedestrian or restricted

DAY TRIPS

1 Market Hill Square
2 Emmanuel College
3 Pembroke College
4 River Cam, Mill Pond & Punting

5 Corpus Clock, Benet Street & The Eagle Pub
6 King's College Chapel
7 Senate House
8 To Trinity College & Wren Library

Continue down St. Andrews Street two long blocks toward the steeple, then pause at the college on the left...

❷ Emmanuel College

This college offers a classic peek at a typical Cambridge college (free, open 9:00-18:00). Emmanuel was founded in 1584 as a Protestant college on land that had once been a Dominican friary. Like many monasteries and convents in the 16th century, the friary had been dissolved by the English king in an epic power struggle that left England with its own version of Christianity and the government with lots of land once owned by the Catholic Church.

Entering the courtyard, take in the layout. On the left is the dining hall, marked by its big bay window. Directly ahead (behind the big clock) is the Senior Common Room, a social hall for college fellows. Below the big clock is the entrance to the chapel. Go inside.

The **chapel** was designed by the famed architect Christopher Wren, who built many churches in the late 1600s, culminating in St. Paul's Cathedral. Wren gave this his typical two-toned treatment: white walls above and carved-wood below, all lit brilliantly. On the ceiling is a typical Wren design (all in white) of circles in squares, adorned with garlands. In the stained glass (left wall) find the portrait of John Harvard—the Emmanuel College student who went to America and founded a prestigious school of his own.

Explore more of the college grounds. (Again, everything is open to the public unless it's locked or marked private.) You can look through the doorway into the dining hall (find it in the near-left corner of the courtyard, from where you came in); enjoy the garden behind the chapel, with its fishpond (dating back to monastic days when this was a source of their food); or chat with the porter.

• *Leaving Emmanuel College, walk straight ahead along Downing Street (which becomes Pembroke Street). You'll pass several museums that are owned by the university to support various fields of study (generally free to enter). Stop when you reach the intersection with King's Parade. Notice the recommended Fitzbillies Café on the right (famous for its local cinnamon roll, the Chelsea Bun), then turn left and walk a few steps to the entrance (on the left) to...*

❸ Pembroke College

Founded in 1347, Pembroke is the third-oldest college in Cambridge. Step into the court, past the porter's lodge—it's polite to say hello and ask whether you can wander around. Survey the court. Ahead of you is the medieval dining hall. The fancy building with the pointed clock

tower is the library (the statue in front is alumnus William Pitt the Younger—a great 18th-century prime minister), with a charming garden beyond.

The highlight here is the chapel, to the right. It dates from about 1660 and is the first building (of any kind, anywhere) Christopher Wren completed. Before stepping inside to enjoy the interior, pause for a moment at the somber WWI and WWII memorial under the arcade. During the Great War, one in four students and faculty was killed.

• *From Pembroke College, cross King's Parade, jog slightly right, and follow Mill Lane directly down to the River Cam and its mill pond.*

❹ River Cam, the Mill Pond, and Punting

From this perch you see the "harbor action" of Cambridge. The city was an important port in medieval times: Trading vessels from

the North Sea (40 miles away) could navigate to here. Today a weir divides the River Cam from one of its tributaries, sometimes called the River Granta (on the left)—which leads through idyllic countryside from the town of Grantchester. Filling the mill pond is a commotion of the iconic Cambridge boats called punts. Students hustle to take visitors on a 45-minute trip with fun commentary (see "Punting on the Cam," later in this chapter). Skilled residents rent boats for themselves, as do not-so-skilled tourists—much to the amusement of locals who sip their beer while watching clumsy visitors fumble with the boats (which are tougher to maneuver than they look). If you'd like a detour from this sometimes-chaotic scene, simply cross the weir and walk along the River Granta into the countryside—it quickly becomes sleepy and idyllic.

But to continue this town walk, turn right and follow the narrow walkway along the harbor past the recommended Anchor Pub, then up the stairs to the Silver Street Bridge. From the bridge, you can watch more punt action and check out the famous "Mathematical Bridge," which links the old and new buildings of Queens' College. This wooden bridge, although curved, is made entirely of straight boards. (It was not designed by Isaac Newton, as a popular fable would have it—Newton died before the bridge was constructed.)

Gazing upstream past the wooden bridge, you see the start of the park known as "the Backs"—the backs of six colleges that line the river, with their fine architecture and most with bridges connecting campus grounds or buildings on both sides of the river.

DAY TRIPS

• *From the Silver Street Bridge, walk up Silver Street, back to King's Parade, and turn left. You'll follow this one very long block (passing the stately Corpus Christi College on your right). At the first corner, find the fancy gilded clock on your right.*

❺ The Corpus Clock, Benet Street, and Eagle Pub

Designed and commissioned by Corpus Christi College alum John Taylor, this **clock** was unveiled by Cambridge physicist Stephen Hawking in a 2008 ceremony. Perched on top is the Chronophage—the "time eater"—a grotesque giant grasshopper that keeps the clock moving and periodically winks at passersby. The message? Time is passing, so live every moment to the fullest. It's a real clock—one blue light marks the hour, the other the minutes. At the top of the hour, it chimes with the sound of rattling chains. The clock cost a million pounds and operates with the same bimetal technology that powers the cordless kettle.

The Eagle Pub, a venerable joint, is just down Benet Street on the left. This is Cambridge's oldest pub and a sight in itself. Poke into the courtyard and atmospheric rooms even if you don't eat or drink here. Before going inside, find the indentation in the base of the wall to the right of the door. This was a common feature on Cambridge doors. You'd stick your foot in there to scrape off mud from the streets. (This example is missing its vital metal scraper, but there's an intact one a few doors to the right.) At the alleyway entrance, find one of the "glancing stones" that protected the corner from careening coaches.

Now enter the pub and find the outdoor tables in a courtyard. Look up at the balcony of second-floor guest rooms that date back to when this was a coachmen's inn as well as a pub. (It's said that in Shakespeare's time, plays were performed from this perch to entertain guests below.) The faded *Bath* sign indicates that this was a posh place—you could even wash. Notice that the window on the right end is open; any local will love to tell you why. Back inside the pub, find the fireplace with a photo and plaque that remember two esteemed regulars—Francis Crick and James Watson—the scientists who first described the structure of DNA. They announced their finding here in 1953, and if you'd like to drink to that, there's a beer on tap for you—a bitter called DNA.

At the back of the Eagle is an annex called the RAF Bar. During World War II, US Army Air Corps pilots famously hung out here before missions over Germany. The fun interior is plastered with stickers of air crews and WWII memorabilia.

St. Benet's Church, across the street from the pub, is the oldest surviving building in Cambridgeshire. The rough stone tower dates from 1020. The Saxons who built the church included circular holes in its bell tower to encourage owls to roost there and keep the mouse population under control.

• *Return to the creepy grasshopper clock and turn right, continuing down King's Parade to the regal front facade of* **King's College.** *We'll stop here to visit...*

❻ King's College Chapel

King's College Chapel, built from 1446 to 1515 by Henrys VI through VIII, is rated ▲▲. It's England's best example of Perpendicular Gothic architecture—and the most impressive building in Cambridge.

Cost and Hours: £11, cheaper online, erratic hours depending on school events—during academic term usually open Tue-Fri 9:45-15:00, Sat until 14:30, closed Sun-Mon—but may stay open later and be open Sun-Mon during busy times; during breaks (see page 517) usually daily 9:45-15:00; +44 1796 340, www.kings.cam. ac.uk. If you didn't buy tickets online, you can get them in person at the King's College visitors center at 13 Kings Parade, across the street from the main entrance gate.

Evensong: When school's in session, you're welcome to enjoy an evensong service in this glorious space, with a famous choir made up of men and boys (free, Mon-Sat at 17:30, Sun at 15:30; for more on evensong, see page 479). It's best to book a seat ahead online; you can reserve starting at 12:00 the day before (www.kings.cam.ac.uk).

Visiting the Chapel: Enter through the grand gateway to the spacious grounds. In the **courtyard,** you're surrounded by buildings from every era of the college's long history. To the right is the famous chapel; straight ahead is the Neoclassical fellows hall; and to the left is the Neo-Gothic dining hall. The statue in the center is Henry VII, the man most responsible for the wonder we'll see next.

Head for the chapel and step **inside.** Stand and look down the nave, with its tunnel-like effect that accentuates both its length (290 feet) and height. It's exactly twice as tall (80 feet) as it is wide. Look up and marvel, as Christopher Wren did, at what was then the largest single span of **vaulted roof** anywhere. Built between 1512 and 1515, its 2,000 tons of incredible fan vaulting—held in place by the force of gravity—are a careful balancing act resting delicately on the buttresses visible outside the building. The round bosses in the center, each weighing nearly two tons, are what hold the structure together.

While Henry VI—who began work on the chapel—wanted it

to be austere, his descendant Henry VII decided it should glorify the House of Tudor. So, lining the cream-colored walls are the personal symbols of Henry VII and

his wife. There's the giant **Tudor coats-of-arms** supported by a dragon (symbolizing Henry's dad) and greyhound (from his mom's side of the family). Find other iconography adorning the nearby pillars: The Tudor double rose (of red and white roses) symbolizes the end of the bitter War of the Roses. The portcullis (the iron grate) honors the family of Henry VII's mother, Lady Margaret Beaufort. And the fleur-de-lis in the coat of arms kept alive the fading hope that someday they might reclaim their place as rulers of France.

The 26 **stained-glass windows** date from the 16th century. It's the most Renaissance stained glass anywhere in one spot. (Most

of the stained glass in English churches dates from Victorian times, but this glass is three centuries older.) The lower panes show scenes from the New Testament, while the upper panes feature corresponding stories from the Old Testament. So (in the first windows to the left), Eve on the top is matched by her New Testament counterpart, Mary.

Considering England's turbulent history, it's miraculous that these windows have survived for half a millennium in such a pristine state. After Henry VIII separated from the Catholic Church in 1534, many such windows and other Catholic features around England were destroyed. (Think of all those ruined abbeys dotting the English countryside.) However, since Henry had just paid for these windows, he couldn't bear to destroy them. A century later, in the days of Oliver Cromwell, another wave of iconoclasm destroyed more windows around England. Though these windows were slated for removal, they stayed put. (Historians speculate that Cromwell's troops, who were garrisoned in this building, didn't want the windows removed in the chilly wintertime.) Finally, during World War II, the windows were taken out and hidden away for safekeeping, then painstakingly replaced after the war ended. The only nonmedieval windows are on the west wall (opposite the altar). These are in the Romantic style from the 1880s; when Nazi bombs threatened the church, all agreed they should be left in place.

The **choir screen** that bisects the church was added by Henry VII's son, King Henry VIII—on the medallions at eye level, see his "H.R." monogram, for Henry Rex. He commissioned the oak screen to commemorate his marriage to Anne Boleyn. By the time it was finished, so was she (beheaded). But it was too late to remove her initials, which were already carved into the screen (look on the far upper left and right for "R.A.," for Regina Anna—"Queen Anne"). Behind the screen is the **choir** area, elaborately carved with the crests of the college and university. This is where the renowned King's College Choir performs. There's a daily evensong (during school terms), with students in the front-row stalls, the choir in the middle, and fellows in back. On Christmas Eve, a special service is held here and broadcast around the world on the BBC—a tradition near and dear to British hearts.

At the far end of the church is Rubens' masterful *Adoration of the Magi* (1634). It's actually a family portrait: The admirer in the front (wearing red) is a self-portrait of Rubens, Mary looks an awful lot like his much-younger wife, and the Baby Jesus resembles their own newborn at the time. In typical Rubens style, there's a diagonal line (running up from the lower left) throwing the focus onto the main figures: Jesus and Mary. Thanks to this painting and the need to conserve it, the chapel got a major renovation in the 1960s to add heaters under the floor.

Inside the chapel to the right (as you face the altar) is a **memorial** to those who died in the two world wars.

Finally, cross the nave to the door on the far side, with a long and fascinating **series of side rooms** that run the length of the nave. Dedicated to the history and art of the church, these are a great little King's College Chapel museum.

• *Return to King's Parade and turn left. Soon you'll see the grand Neoclassical facade of the...*

❼ Senate House

This stately classical building with triangular pediments is the ceremonial heart of the University of Cambridge. It's where the university's governing body meets, and where graduation ceremonies are held. In June, you might notice green boxes lining the front of this house. Traditionally, at the end of the term, students came to these boxes to see whether they had earned their degree; those not listed knew they had flunked. Amazingly, until

2010 this was the only notification students received about their status. (Now they first get an email.)

Looming across the street from the Senate House is **Great St. Mary's Church** (a.k.a. the University Church), with a climbable bell tower (£6, Mon-Sat 10:00-18:00, Sun 12:00-17:00, daily until 16:00 off-season, 123 stairs). On the corner nearby is **Ryder & Amies** (22 King's Parade), which has been the official university outfitter for 150 years. It's a great shop for college gear: sweaters, ties, and so on. Upstairs, if you ask, you can try on an undergraduate gown and mortar board.

• *Carry on along King's Parade to our final stop—less than a five-minute walk from here. The road (and sidewalk) narrows as you squeeze between some old houses. Soon you'll see yet another grand college on your left.*

❽ Trinity College and Wren Library

Of the more than 100 Nobel Prize winners affiliated with Cambridge, about a third come from this richest and biggest of the town's colleges, founded in 1546 by Henry VIII. The college has three sights to see, together worth ▲▲: the entrance gate, the grounds, and the magnificent Wren Library—a grand finale for this walk.

Cost and Hours: Grounds—£3, daily 10:00-16:30, closes earlier off-season; library—free, Mon-Fri 12:00-14:00, during full term also Sat 10:30-12:30, closed Sun year-round; only 20 people allowed in at a time, +44 1223 338 400, www.trin.cam.ac.uk.

Free Entrance to the Library: To see the Wren Library without paying for the grounds, access it from the riverside entrance (a long walk around the college via the Garret Hostel Bridge).

Trinity Gate: You'll notice gates like these adorning facades of colleges around town. Above the door is a statue of **King Henry VIII**, who founded Trinity because he feared that Cambridge's existing colleges were too cozy with the Church. Notice Henry's right hand holding a chair leg instead of the traditional scepter with the crown jewels. This is courtesy of Cambridge's Night Climbers, who first replaced the scepter a century ago. According to campus legend, decades ago some of the world's most talented mountaineers enrolled at Cambridge...in one of the flattest parts of England. (Cambridge was actually a seaport until Dutch engineers drained the surrounding swamps.) Lacking opportunities to practice their skill, they began scaling the frilly facades of Cambridge's college buildings under cover of darkness (if caught, they'd have been expelled). In the 1960s, climbers actually managed to haul an entire automobile onto the roof of the Senate House. The university had to bring in the army to cut it into pieces and remove it. Only 50 years later, at a class reunion, did the guilty parties finally fess up.

In the little park to the right, notice the lone **apple tree.** Supposedly, this tree is a descendant of the very one that once stood in the garden of Sir Isaac Newton (who spent 30 years at Trinity). According to legend, Newton was inspired to investigate gravity when an apple fell from the tree onto his head. This tree stopped bearing fruit long ago; if you do see apples, they've been tied on by mischievous students.

Beyond the gate are the Trinity grounds. Note that there's often a fine and free view of Trinity College courtyard—if the gate is open—from Trinity Lane (along the left side of the college; this leads, under a uniform row of old chimneys, around the school to the Wren Library).

Trinity Grounds: The grounds are enjoyable to explore. Inside the **Great Court,** the clock (on the tower on the right) double-rings at the top of each hour. It's a college tradition to take off running from the clock when the high noon bells begin (it takes 43 seconds to clang 24 times), race around the courtyard, touching each of the four corners without setting foot on the cobbles, and

try to return to the same spot before the ringing ends. Supposedly only one student (a young lord) ever managed the feat—a scene featured in *Chariots of Fire* (but filmed elsewhere).

The **chapel** (entrance to the right of the clock tower)—which pales in comparison to the stunning King's College Chapel—feels like a shrine to thinking, with statues honoring great Trinity minds both familiar (Isaac Newton, Alfred Tennyson, Francis Bacon) and unfamiliar. Who's missing? The poet Lord Byron, who was such a hell-raiser during his time at Trinity that a statue of him was deemed unfit for Church property; his statue stands in the library instead.

Wren Library: Don't miss the 1695 Christopher Wren-designed library, with its wonderful carving and fascinating original manuscripts. Just outside the library entrance, Sir Isaac Newton clapped his hands and timed the echo to measure the speed of sound as it raced down the side of the cloister and back. Inside, admire Wren's design—long, white, and aglow with the bright light of the Enlightenment. Wren designed the whole ensemble, including the bookshelves topped with busts of great thinkers. (The one thing he didn't design is the stained-glass window showing him being honored by George III.) Unlike the other libraries at Cambridge, Wren designed Trinity's on the upper floor, not the damp, dark ground floor. As a result, Wren's library is flooded with light, rather than water (and it's also brimming with students during exam times).

In the library's 12 display cases (covered with cloth that you flip back), you'll see a (rotating) display of medieval manuscripts, first editions, letters, and documents. You might see works by William Shakespeare, John Milton, Samuel Taylor Coleridge, and A. A. Milne's original *Winnie the Pooh* (the real Christopher Robin attended Trinity College). Don't miss the case with Newton's memorabilia—a lock of his hair, notebook, pocket watch, walking stick, a prism he used to see how light bent, and a 1687 edition of his landmark book *Principia Mathematica* that changed forever the way humans viewed the physical world.

• *From here, if you like, you can wander down to the river and walk back past the colleges, from the other side. Or you can head back into the heart of town on King's Parade. Cambridge is yours to explore.*

Sights in Cambridge

My self-guided walk takes you to most of the main sights in Cambridge, but not all. Here are some more sights and activities worth your time.

▲▲Punting on the Cam

For a little levity and probably more exercise than you really want, try renting one of the traditional flat-bottom punts at the river. You'll use a giant pole to push yourself up and down (or around and around, more likely) the lazy Cam. The water's only about six or seven feet deep, so you move by literally pushing off from the river floor (someone in front can use a little paddle to help out). This is one of the best memories the town has to offer, and once you get the hang of it, it's a fine way to enjoy the scenic side of Cambridge. It's less crowded in late afternoon (and less embarrassing).

Better yet, let someone else do the punting while you enjoy the ride. The 45-minute lazy punting trips are a delight—informatively narrated by your punter, who tries to avoid the clueless tourists creating a moving, aquatic obstacle course. Watching amateurs struggle with their massive poles, playing bumper cars in the busy river, you'll be happy someone else is at the helm. On a nice-weather day, there are few more relaxing activities.

Several companies rent punts and also offer tours. Both are open daily from about 9:00 until dusk when the weather's decent (typically March-Nov). **Scudamore's** has two locations: on Mill Lane, just south of the central Silver Street Bridge, and at the less convenient Quayside at Magdalene Bridge, at the north end of town. Prices are extremely slippery—there's a bit of sleight-of-hand as they figure the number of people, offer a variety of discounts, and so on—but typically you'll pay about £40-45 per hour to rent a punt, or around £20-25 per person to join a guided punt. If it's quiet, don't be afraid to bargain (+44 1223 359 750, www.scudamores.com). **Cambridge Chauffeur Punts,** directly across the pond and just under the Silver Street Bridge, is a cheaper outfit (rental-£30/hour, 45-minute tour-£20/person, +44 1223 354 164, www.punting-in-cambridge.co.uk).

If renting a punt in the Silver Street Bridge area, be clear on whether you're punting on the River Cam (the lovely but crowded stream that runs behind the pretty college campuses) or on the other side of the weir, at the River Granta (less crowded and runs through idyllic countryside, but you won't see the famous landmarks). Most prefer the Cam.

▲Fitzwilliam Museum

One of Britain's best museums of antiquities and art outside London is the Fitzwilliam. Housed in a grand Neoclassical building a 10-minute walk south of Market Hill Square, it's a palatial celebration of beauty and humankind's ability to create it.

Cost and Hours: Free, £5 donation suggested; Tue-Sat 10:00-17:00, Sun from 12:00, closed Mon; lockers, Trumpington Street, +44 1223 332 900, www.fitzmuseum.cam.ac.uk.

Visiting the Museum: The Fitzwilliam's broad collection is like a mini-British Museum/National Gallery rolled into one.

Though there aren't any especially famous works, you get a good overview and you're bound to find something you like. Helpful docents—many with degrees or doctorates in art history—are more than willing to answer questions about the collection. The ground floor features an extensive range of antiquities and applied arts—everything from Greek vases, Mesopotamian artifacts, and Egyptian sarcophagi to Roman statues, fine porcelain, and suits of armor.

Upstairs is the painting gallery, with works that span art history: Italian Venetian masters (such as Titian and Canaletto), a worthy English section (featuring Gainsborough, Reynolds, Hogarth, and others), a notable array of French Impressionist art (including Monet, Renoir, Pissarro, Degas, and Sisley), and even a few small Picassos. Rounding out the collection are old manuscripts, including some musical compositions from Handel.

Museum of Classical Archaeology

Although this museum contains no originals, it offers a unique chance to study accurate copies (19th-century casts) of virtually every famous ancient Greek and Roman statue. More than 450 statues are on display. If you've seen the real things in Greece, Istanbul, Rome, and elsewhere, touring this collection is like a high school reunion…"Hey, I know you!" It's a kick in the pants for devotees of classical sculpture…and a bit dull for others.

Cost and Hours: Free; Tue-Fri 10:00-17:00, Sat 14:00-17:00 during term, closed Sun-Mon year-round; Sidgwick Avenue, +44 1223 330 402, www.classics.cam.ac.uk/museum.

Getting There: The museum is a five-minute walk west of Silver Street Bridge (with all the punts); after crossing the bridge, continue straight until you reach a sign reading *Sidgwick Site*.

NEAR CAMBRIDGE
Imperial War Museum Duxford

This former airfield, nine miles south of Cambridge, is popular with aviation fans and WWII history buffs. Wander through seven exhibition halls housing 200 vintage aircraft (including Spitfires, B-17 Flying Fortresses, a Concorde, and a Blackbird, some of which you can enter) as well as military land vehicles and special displays on Normandy and the Battle of Britain. The American Air wing thoughtfully portrays the achievements and controversies of British/US wartime collaboration, including the stories of American airmen based at Duxford. On many weekends, the museum holds special events, such as air shows (extra fee)—check the website for details.

Cost and Hours: £22.70, daily 10:00-18:00, off-season until 16:00, last entry one hour before closing, +44 1223 835 000, www.iwm.org.uk/visits/iwm-duxford.

Getting There: The museum is located off the A-505 in Duxford. If using **public transit,** you'll find helpful details on their website: Mondays through Saturdays, it's best to take the train (from London or Cambridge) to Whittlesford Parkway Station, then catch bus #7A from there (6/day, 10 minutes). On Sundays, Myalls bus #132 runs directly to the museum from Cambridge's train station (5/day, 30 minutes). Or you can take a **taxi** from Cambridge for about £25 one-way.

Sleeping in Cambridge

While Cambridge is an easy side trip from London (and you can enjoy an evening here before catching a late train back), its subtle charms might convince you to spend a night or two. Cambridge has few accommodations in the city center, and none in the tight maze of colleges and shops where you'll spend most of your time. These recommendations are about a 10- to 15-minute walk south of the town center. The city has a few good B&Bs, but they are even farther out.

$$$$ Hotel du Vin is an upscale place that rents 41 spiffy rooms at a high price. It has a crooked-floors, duck-your-head historical character, and a whiff of pretense (air-con, elevator to some rooms, light sleepers ask for quieter room in back, 15 Trumpington Street, +44 1223 928 991, www.hotelduvin.com, reception.cambridge@hotelduvin.com).

$$$ Lensfield Hotel, popular with visiting professors, has 40 comfortable rooms—some old-fashioned, some refurbished (spa and fitness room, 53 Lensfield Road, +44 1223 355 017, www.lensfieldhotel.co.uk, enquiries@lensfieldhotel.co.uk).

Eating in Cambridge

$$ The Eagle, described earlier in my town walk, is the oldest pub in town. While the food is mediocre, the atmosphere is outstanding, and it's a Cambridge institution—with a history so rich that a visit

here practically qualifies as sightseeing (daily 11:00-22:00, 8 Benet Street, +44 1223 505 020).

$ Michaelhouse Café is a heavenly respite from the crowds, tucked into the repurposed St. Michael's Church, just north of Great St. Mary's Church. At lunch, choose from salads, sandwiches, and soups, as well as a few hot dishes. They also have coffee drinks and an enticing array of cakes and cookies (Mon-Sat 9:00-17:00—breakfast until 11:30, Sun 12:00-16:00, occasional free lunchtime concerts, Trinity Street, +44 1223 309 147).

$$ The Anchor Pub has a place in rock-and-roll history as a spot where Pink Floyd band members hung out in their early days. Today it feels modern and fresh, and has some of the best people-watching in town. Choose from its outdoor riverside terrace, inside bar, or more romantic upstairs restaurant (daily 12:00-21:30, on the riverfront at Silver Street, +44 1224 353 554).

$$ The Mill Pub is a livelier, less formal alternative to The Anchor, but enjoys a similar location right on the river. The clientele is a mixture of students and tourists; the tipples are craft brews, local ales, and ciders; and the food is updated pub standards (daily 12:00-22:00, 14 Mill Lane, +44 1223 311 829).

$ Bread & Meat serves simple soups and hearty sandwiches. Grab a signature *porchetta* sandwich to take away or snag a rustic table in the small dining room (Mon-Thu 11:30-20:00, Fri-Sat until 21:00, Sun until 17:00, 4 Benet Street, +44 791 808 3057).

$$ Agora at The Copper Kettle is a popular place for Greek and Turkish *meze*, beautifully situated facing King's College on King's Parade (also fish-and-chips at lunch; open Mon-Wed 8:00-17:00, Thu-Sat 8:00-21:00, Sun 8:00-19:00, possibly longer hours in summer; 4 King's Parade, +44 1223 308 448).

$$ Fitzbillies, long a favorite for cakes (Chelsea Buns) and coffee, offers inviting lunch and afternoon tea menus (daily, 51 Trumpington Street, +44 1223 352 500).

$ Street Food on Market Hill Square: For an interesting lunch on the go, browse the many food carts tucked into the tight aisles of the open-air market that fills the historic old market square (daily 9:00-16:00). There's no real seating, but people squeeze along the wall around the stone fountain in the middle of the square.

Supermarkets/Picnicking: There's a **Marks & Spencer Simply Food** at the train station (long hours daily). Bigger options in the center include a **Marks & Spencer Foodhall** on Market Hill Square and a **Sainsbury's** at 44 Sidney Street (at the corner of Green Street). A good picnic spot is Laundress Green, a grassy park on the river, at the end of Mill Lane near the Silver Street Bridge punts. There are no benches, so bring something to sit on. Remember, the college lawns are private property, so walking or picnicking on the grass is generally not allowed. When in doubt, ask at the college's entrance.

Cambridge Connections

From Cambridge by Train to: London (King's Cross Station: 2/hour express, 50 minutes, additional departures take about 1.25 hours; Liverpool Street Station: 2/hour, 1.5 hours), **York** (hourly, 2.5 hours, transfer in Peterborough). Getting to **Oxford** is complex, requiring a change in London with a Tube transfer between stations (2.5 hours). Train info: +44 345 748 4950, www.nationalrail.co.uk.

　　By Bus to: London (every 60-90 minutes, 2 hours), **Heathrow Airport** (1-2/hour, 3 hours), **Oxford** (2/hour, 4 hours). Bus info: +44 871 781 8181, www.nationalexpress.com.

DAY TRIPS

Stonehenge

As old as the pyramids, and far older than the Acropolis and the Colosseum, this iconic stone circle amazed medieval Europeans, who figured it was built by a race of giants. And it still impresses visitors today. As one of Europe's most famous sights, Stonehenge, worth ▲▲▲, does a valiant job of retaining an air of mystery and majesty (partly because cordons, which keep hordes of  tourists from trampling all over it, foster the illusion that it stands alone in a field). Although cynics manage to be underwhelmed by Stonehenge, most of its almost one million annual visitors agree that it's well worth the trip. At few sights in Europe will you overhear so many awe-filled comments.

GETTING TO STONEHENGE

Stonehenge is about 90 miles southwest of central London. To reach it from London, you can take a bus tour; go on a guided tour that uses public transportation; or do it on your own using public transit, connecting via Salisbury. It's not worth the hassle or expense to rent a car just for a Stonehenge day trip.

　　By Bus Tour from London: Several companies offer big-bus day trips to Stonehenge from London, often with stops in Bath,

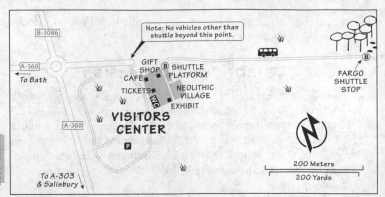

Windsor, Salisbury, and/or Avebury. These generally cost about £50-100 (including Stonehenge admission), last 8-12 hours, and pack a 45-seat bus. Some include hotel pickup, admission fees, and meals; understand what's included before you book. The more destinations listed for a tour, the less time you'll have at any one stop. Well-known companies are **Evan Evans** (their bare-bones Stonehenge Express gets you there and back for £54, +44 20 7950 1777 or +1 800 422 9022, www.evanevanstours.co.uk) and **Golden Tours** (£72, +44 20 7630 2028 or +1 800 509 2507, www.goldentours. com). **International Friends** runs pricier but smaller 16-person tours that include Windsor and Bath (£145, +44 1223 244 555, www.internationalfriends.co.uk).

By Guided Tour on Public Transport: The "Stonehenge and Salisbury Excursion" from **London Walks** travels by train and bus on Tuesdays from mid-May through early October (£98, includes all transportation, Salisbury walking tour, entry fees, and guided tours of Stonehenge and Salisbury Cathedral; pay guide, contactless card or exact cash, Tue at 8:45, meet at Waterloo Station's main ticket office, opposite Platform 16, verify price and schedule online, advance booking required, +44 20 7624 3978, www.walks.com).

On Your Own on Public Transport via Salisbury: From London, you can catch a train to Salisbury, then go by tour bus or taxi to Stonehenge. **Trains** to Salisbury run from London's Waterloo Station (around £42 for same-day return leaving weekdays after 9:30, 2/hour, 1.5 hours, +44 345 600 0650, www.southwesternrailway. com or +44 3457 484 950, www.nationalrail.co.uk).

From Salisbury, take **The Stonehenge Tour bus** to the site. These distinctive double-decker buses leave from the Salisbury train station, stop in Salisbury's center, then make a circuit to Stonehenge and Old Sarum, with lovely scenery and a decent light commentary along the way (£16, £33 includes Stonehenge as well as Old Sarum—whether you want it or not; tickets good all day, order online or pay driver; daily June-Aug 10:00-16:00, hourly;

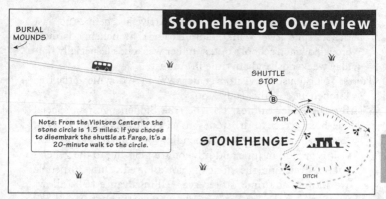

Stonehenge Overview

BURIAL MOUNDS

SHUTTLE STOP

B

PATH

Note: From the Visitors Center to the stone circle is 1.5 miles. If you choose to disembark the shuttle at Fargo, it's a 20-minute walk to the circle.

STONEHENGE

DITCH

DAY TRIPS

may not run June 21 because of solstice crowds, shorter hours and hourly departures off-season; 30 minutes from station to Stonehenge, +44 1202 338 420, timetable at www.thestonehengetour.info).

A **taxi** from Salisbury to Stonehenge can make sense for groups (about £40-60). Try On-Line City Cabs (+44 1722 509 090, onlinecitycabs.co.uk) or Value Cars Taxis (+44 1722 505 050, www.salisbury-valuecars.co.uk).

ORIENTATION TO STONEHENGE

The visitors center, located 1.5 miles west of the circle, is a minimalist steel structure with a subtly curved roofline, evoking the landscape of Salisbury Plain.

Cost: £20-24 depending on day, purchase timed entry ticket in advance online, ticket includes shuttle-bus ride to stone circle, covered by English Heritage Pass (see page 578).

Hours: Daily in summer 9:30-19:00, early Sept-late May until 17:00. Note that the last ticket is sold two hours before closing. Expect shorter hours and possible closures June 20-22 due to huge, raucous solstice crowds.

Information: +44 370 333 1181, www.english-heritage.org.uk/stonehenge.

Advance Tickets Recommended: Up to 9,000 visitors are allowed to enter each day. While Stonehenge rarely sells out completely, you can avoid the long ticket-buying line by prebooking at least 24 hours in advance at www.english-heritage.org.uk/stonehenge. When prebooking, you'll be asked to select a 30-minute entry window; once inside, you can stay as long as you like. You may have to wait in line for the shuttle bus to and from the stones.

Crowd-Beating Tips: For a less crowded, more mystical experience, come early or late. Things are pretty quiet before about 10:30 (head out to the stones first, then circle back to the exhibits); at the end of the day, aim to arrive just before the "last ticket" time (two hours before closing). Stonehenge is most crowded when school's out: summer weekends (especially holiday weekends) and anytime in August.

Tours: You can use the visitors center's Wi-Fi to download the free "Stonehenge Audio Tour" app.

Visiting the Inner Stones: For the true Stonehenge fan, special one-hour access to the stones' inner circle is available early in the morning (times vary depending on sunrise; the earliest visit is at 5:00 in June and July) or after closing to the general public. Touching the stones is not allowed. Only 30 people are allowed at a time, so reserve well in advance (£48, allows you to revisit the site the same day at no extra charge, +44 370 333 0605). For details see the English Heritage website (select "Things to See and Do," then "Stone Circle Experience").

Length of This Tour: Allow at least two hours to see everything.

Services: The visitors center has WCs and a large gift shop. Services at the circle itself are limited to emergency WCs. Even in summer, carry a jacket, as there are no trees to act as a windbreak and there's a reason Salisbury Plain is so green.

Eating: A large **$ café** within the visitors center serves hot drinks, soup, sandwiches, and salads.

❍ SELF-GUIDED TOUR

This commentary is designed to supplement the sight's audio tour app. Start by touring the visitors center, then take a shuttle (or walk) to the stone circle. If you arrive early in the day, do the stones first—before they get crowded—then circle back to the visitors center.

• *As you enter the complex, on the right is the...*

Permanent Exhibit

This excellent, state-of-the-art exhibit uses an artful combination of multimedia displays and actual artifacts to provide context for the stones.

You'll begin by standing in the center of a virtual Stonehenge, watching its evolution through 5,000 years—including simulated solstice sunrises and sunsets.

Then you'll head into the exhibits, where prehistoric bones, tools, and pottery shards tell the story of the people who built Stonehenge, how they lived, and why they might have built the stone circle. Find the forensic reconstruction of a Neolithic man,

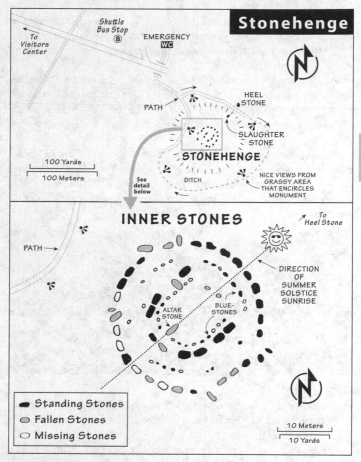

based on a skeleton unearthed in 1863. Small models illustrate how Stonehenge developed from a simple circle of short, stubby stones to the stout ring we know today. And a large screen shows the entire archaeological area surrounding Stonehenge (which is just one of many mysterious prehistoric landmarks near here). In 2010, within sight of Stonehenge, archaeologists discovered another 5,000-year-old henge, which they believe once encircled a wooden "twin" of the famous circle. Recent excavations revealed that people had been living on the site since around 3,000 BC—about five centuries earlier than anyone had realized.

Then step outside and explore a village of reconstructed **Neolithic huts** modeled after the traces of a village discovered just northeast of Stonehenge. Step into the thatched-roof huts to see primitive "wicker" furniture and straw blankets. Docents demonstrate Neolithic tools—made of wood, flint, and antler. You'll also see a huge, life-size replica of the rolling wooden sledge thought to have been used to slooooowly roll the stones across Salisbury Plain. While you can't touch the stones at the site itself, you can touch the one loaded onto this sledge.

• *Shuttle buses to the stone circle depart every 5-10 minutes from just behind the gift shop (there may be a wait). The trip takes six minutes. If you'd prefer, you can walk about 1.5 miles through the fields to the site (use the map you receive with your ticket, or ask a staff member for directions).*

Along the way, you have the option of stopping at **Fargo Plantation**, *where you can see several burial mounds (tell the shuttle attendant when you first get on if you want to disembark here). After wandering through the burial mounds, you'll need to walk the rest of the way to the stone circle (about 20 minutes).*

Stone Circle

As you approach the massive structure, walk right up to the knee-high cordon and let your fellow 21st-century tourists melt away. It's just you and the druids...

England has hundreds of stone circles, but Stonehenge—which literally means "hanging stones"—is unique. It's the only one that has horizontal cross-pieces (called lintels) spanning the vertical monoliths, and the only one with stones that have been made smooth and uniform. What you see here is a bit more than half the original structure—the rest was quarried centuries ago for other buildings.

Now do a slow **clockwise spin** around the monument, and ponder the following points. As you walk, mentally flesh out the missing pieces and re-erect the rubble. Knowledgeable guides posted around the site are happy to answer your questions.

It's now believed that Stonehenge, which was built in phases between 3000 and 1500 BC, was originally used as a cremation cemetery. But that's not the end of the story, as the monument was expanded over the millennia. This was a hugely significant location to prehistoric peoples. There are several hundred burial mounds within a three-mile radius of Stonehenge—some likely belonging

DAY TRIPS

to kings or chieftains. Some of the human remains are of people from far away, and others show signs of injuries—evidence that Stonehenge may have been used as a place of medicine or healing.

Whatever its original purpose, Stonehenge still functions as a celestial calendar. As the sun rises on the summer solstice (June 21), the **"heel stone"**—the one set apart from the rest, near the road—lines up with the sun and the altar at the center of the stone circle. A study of more than 300 similar circles in Britain found that each was designed to calculate the movement of the sun, moon, and stars, and to predict eclipses in order to help early societies know when to plant, harvest, and party. Even in modern times, as the summer solstice sun sets in just the right slot at Stonehenge, pagans boogie.

Some believe that Stonehenge is built at the precise point where six **"ley lines"** intersect. Ley lines are theoretical lines of magnetic or spiritual power that crisscross the globe. Belief in the power of these lines has gone in and out of fashion over time. They are believed to have been very important to prehistoric peoples, but then were largely ignored until the early 20th century, when the English writer Alfred Watkins popularized them (to the scorn of serious scientists). More recently, the concept has been embraced by the New Age movement. Without realizing it, you follow these ley lines all the time: Many of England's modern highways follow prehistoric paths, and most churches are built over prehistoric monuments—placed where ley lines intersect. If you're a skeptic, ask one of the guides at Stonehenge to explain the mystique of this paranormal tradition that continued for centuries; it's creepy...and convincing.

Notice that two of the stones (facing the shuttle bus stop) are blemished. At the base of one monolith, it looks like someone has pulled back the stone to reveal a concrete skeleton. This is a clumsy **repair job** to fix damage done long ago by souvenir seekers, who actually rented hammers and chisels to take home a piece of Stonehenge. Look to the right of the repaired stone: The back of another stone is missing the same thin layer of protective lichen that covers the others. The lichen—and some of the stone itself—was sandblasted off to remove graffiti. (No wonder they've got Stonehenge roped off now.) The repairs were intentionally done in a different color, so as not to appear like the original stone.

Stonehenge's builders used two different types of stone. The tall, stout monoliths and lintels are sandstone blocks called **sarsen stones.** Most of the monoliths weigh about 25 tons (the largest is 45 tons), and the lintels are about 7 tons apiece. These sarsen stones were brought from "only" 20 miles away. Scientists have chemically matched the shorter stones in the middle—called **bluestones**—to outcrops on the south coast of Wales...240 miles away (close if you're taking a train, but far if you're packing a megalith). Imagine the logistical puzzle of floating six-ton stones across Wales' Severn Estuary and up the River Avon, then rolling them on logs about 20 miles to this position...an impressive feat, even in our era of skyscrapers.

Why didn't the builders of Stonehenge use what seem like perfectly adequate stones nearby? This, like many other questions about Stonehenge, remains shrouded in mystery. Think again about the ley lines. Ponder the fact that many experts accept none of the explanations of how these giant stones were transported. Then imagine congregations gathering here 5,000 years ago, raising thought levels, creating a powerful life force transmitted along the ley lines. Maybe a particular kind of stone was essential for maximum energy transmission. Maybe the stones were levitated here. Maybe psychics really do create powerful vibes. Maybe not. It's as unbelievable as electricity used to be.

BRITAIN: PAST & PRESENT

To fully appreciate the many fascinating sights you'll encounter in your travels, learn the basics of the sweeping story of this land and its people. (Generally speaking, the fascinating stories you'll hear from tour guides are not true...and the boring ones are.)

Regardless of the revolution we had more than 240 years ago, many American travelers feel that they "go home" to Britain. This most popular tourist destination has a strange influence and power over us. The more you know of Britain's roots, the better you'll get in touch with your own.

This chapter starts with a once-over of Britain's illustrious history. It's speckled throughout with more in-depth information about current issues and this great country's future.

British History

ORIGINS (2000 BC-AD 500)

When Julius Caesar landed on the misty and mysterious isle of Britain in 55 BC, England entered the history books. He was met by primitive Celtic tribes whose druid priests made human sacrifices and worshipped trees. (Those Celts were themselves immigrants, who had earlier conquered the even more mysterious people who built Stonehenge.) The Romans eventually settled in England (AD 43) and set about building towns and roads and establishing their capital at Londinium (today's London).

But the Celtic natives—consisting of Gaels, Picts, and Scots— were not easily subdued. Around AD 60, Boadicea, a queen of the Isle's indigenous people, defied the Romans and burned Londinium before the revolt was squelched. Some decades later, the Romans built Hadrian's Wall near the Scottish border as protection against their troublesome northern neighbors. Even today, the Celtic language and influence are strongest in these far reaches of Britain.

Londinium became a bustling Roman river-and-sea trading port. The Romans built the original London Bridge and a city wall, encompassing one square mile, which set the city boundaries for 1,500 years. By AD 200, London was a thriving, Latin-speaking capital of Roman-dominated England.

Sights

- Boadicea statue near Westminster Bridge
- Roman Wall near the Tower of London or at the Museum of London

DARK AGES (500-1000)

As Rome fell, so fell Roman Britain—a victim of invaders and internal troubles. Barbarian tribes from Germany, Denmark, and northern Holland, called Angles, Saxons, and Jutes, swept through the southern part of the island, establishing Angle-land. These were the days of the real King Arthur, possibly a Christianized Roman general who fought valiantly—but in vain—against invading barbarians.

In 793, England was hit with the first of two centuries of savage invasions by barbarians from Norway, called the Vikings, or Norsemen. King Alfred the Great (849-899) liberated London from Danish Vikings, reunited England, reestablished Christianity, and fostered learning. Nevertheless, for most of this 500-year period, the island was plunged into a dark age—wars, plagues, and poverty—lit only by the dim candle of a few learned Christian monks and missionaries trying to convert the barbarians. Today, visitors see little from this Anglo-Saxon period.

Sights

- Lindisfarne Gospels, *Beowulf* manuscript (British Library)

WARS WITH FRANCE, WARS OF THE ROSES (1000-1500)

Modern England began with yet another invasion. In 1066, William the Conqueror and his Norman troops crossed the English Channel from France. William crowned himself king in Westminster Abbey (where all subsequent coronations would take place). He began building the Tower of London, as well as Windsor Castle, which would become the residence of many monarchs to come.

Over the succeeding centuries, French-speaking kings would rule England, and English-speaking kings invaded France as the two budding nations defined their modern borders. Richard the Lionheart (1157-1199) ruled as a French-speaking king who spent most of his energy on distant Crusades. This was the time of the legendary (and possibly real) Robin Hood, a bandit who robbed

from the rich and gave to the poor—a populace that felt neglected by its francophone rulers. In 1215, King John (Richard's brother), under pressure from England's barons, was forced to sign the Magna Carta, establishing the principle that even kings must follow the rule of law.

London asserted itself as England's trade center. London Bridge—the famous stone version, topped with houses—was built (1209), and Old St. Paul's Cathedral was finished (1314).

Then followed two centuries of wars, chiefly the Hundred Years' War with France (1337-1443), in which France's Joan of Arc rallied the French to drive English forces back across the Channel. In 1348, the Black Death (bubonic plague) killed half of London's population.

In the 1400s, noble families duked it out for the crown. The York and Lancaster families fought the Wars of the Roses, so called because of the white and red flowers the combatants chose as their symbols. Rife with battles and intrigues, and with kings, nobles, and ladies imprisoned and executed in the Tower, it's a wonder the country survived its rulers.

Sights

- Tower of London
- Westminster Abbey
- Windsor Castle
- Magna Carta, *The Canterbury Tales* (British Library)
- Temple Church

THE TUDOR RENAISSANCE (1500s)

England was finally united by the "third-party" Tudor family. Henry VIII, a Tudor, was England's Renaissance king. Powerful, charismatic, handsome, athletic, highly sexed, a poet, a scholar, and a musician, Henry VIII thrust England onto the world stage. He was also arrogant, cruel, gluttonous, and paranoid. He went

London Almanac

Population: Approximately 9.4 million people

Currency: British pound (GBP)

City Layout: London is divided into the City of London (the main financial district) and 32 administrative boroughs—12 in inner London.

Tallest Building: The Shard stands at 1,020 feet, making it the tallest building in Western Europe—for now.

Tourist Tracks: Each year London hosts 40 million tourists, most of whom stop to take a photo at Trafalgar Square. London's most popular attraction, the British Museum, sees 6 million visitors annually.

Popular Misconception: "Big Ben" refers not to the clock, but instead to its 13-ton bell.

Culture Count: While the Queen's English is still the language of the land, fewer than half the residents of inner London speak English as their first language. Nearly 300 different languages are spoken in London's schools. About 60 percent of Londoners are white (many of them Continental Europeans rather than Brits), but the incredible diversity of the rest of the population makes this city a global melting pot. Some 17 percent of Londoners are Asian (7 percent are Indian and Bangladeshi), and 13 percent are black, including many from African countries (7 percent of Londoners) and the Caribbean (4 percent). Six in 10 Brits call themselves Christian (half of those are Anglican), but in any given week, more Londoners visit a mosque than an Anglican church.

Fun Food Facts: Traditionally, London's most popular takeaway foods were fish-and-chips and minced-meat pie (the pies were originally filled with eels...so minced-meat is an improvement). But it's not all about meat; PETA recently named London the world's most vegan-friendly city. These days you'll find more gourmet sandwich and prepackaged-meal shops than "chippies."

Need a Restroom? Ask for the toilet, loo, lavatory, or bog.

Oldest Pub: The Lamb and Flag in Covent Garden. First licensed in 1623, it was once known as the Bucket of Blood, thanks to rowdy, bare-knuckle fights held there.

Average Londoner: The average Londoner is about 34 years old, has 1.7 children, and will live until age 80. They earn about 25 percent more than people in other parts of Great Britain, but pay more than twice as much for housing. The average Londoner will drink 75,000 cups of tea in a lifetime and consumes less alcohol per week than the average Brit.

through six wives in 40 years, divorcing, imprisoning, or executing them when they no longer suited his needs. (To keep track of each one's fate, British kids learn this rhyme: "Divorced, beheaded, died; divorced, beheaded, survived.")

When the Pope refused to grant Henry a divorce so he could marry his mistress Anne Boleyn, Henry "divorced" England from the Catholic Church. He established the Protestant Church of England (the Anglican Church), thus setting in motion a century of bitter Protestant/Catholic squabbles. Henry's first daughter, "Bloody" Mary, was a staunch Catholic who presided over the burning of hundreds of prominent Protestants. (For more on Henry VIII, see the sidebar on page 190.)

Mary was followed by her half-sister—Queen Elizabeth I— the daughter of Henry and Anne Boleyn. She reigned for 45 years, making England a great trading and naval power (defeating the Spanish Armada) and treading diplomatically over the Protestant/Catholic divide. Elizabeth presided over a cultural renaissance known (not surprisingly) as the "Elizabethan Age." Playwright William Shakespeare moved from Stratford-upon-Avon to London, beginning a remarkable career as the earth's greatest playwright. Sir Francis Drake circumnavigated the globe. Sir Walter Raleigh explored the Americas, and Sir Francis Bacon pioneered the scientific method. London's population swelled.

But Elizabeth—the "Virgin Queen"—never married or produced an heir. So the English Parliament invited Scotland's King James (Elizabeth's first cousin twice removed) to inherit the English throne. The two nations have been tied together ever since, however fitfully.

Sights
- Shakespeare's Globe
- Shakespeare folios (British Library)
- Tower of London execution site
- Chapel of Henry VII and Elizabeth I's tomb in Westminster Abbey
- King's College Chapel in Cambridge

KINGS VS. PARLIAMENT (1600s)
The enduring quarrel between England's kings and Parliament's nobles finally erupted into the Civil War (1642). The war pitted (roughly

speaking) the Protestant Puritan Parliament against the Catholic aristocracy. Parliament forces under Oliver Cromwell defeated—and beheaded—King Charles I. After Cromwell died, Parliament invited Charles' son to take the throne—the "restoration of the monarchy." To emphasize the point, Cromwell's corpse was subsequently exhumed and posthumously beheaded.

This turbulent era was followed by back-to-back disasters—the Great Plague of 1665 (which killed 100,000) and the Great Fire of 1666 (which incinerated London). London was completely rebuilt in stone, centered around New St. Paul's Cathedral, which was built by Christopher Wren. With a population over 200,000, London was now Europe's largest city. At home, Isaac Newton watched an apple fall from a tree, leading him to explain the mysterious force of gravity.

In the war between kings and Parliament, Parliament finally got the last word when it deposed Catholic James II and imported the Dutch monarchs William and Mary in 1688, guaranteeing a Protestant succession.

Sights
- Banqueting House (site of Charles I's beheading)
- Crown jewels (Tower of London)
- City of London
- Fire Monument
- St. Paul's and other Wren churches
- Isaac Newton's apple tree (outside Trinity College Gate, Cambridge)
- Kensington Palace (residence of William, Mary, and Anne)

COLONIAL EXPANSION (1700s)

Britain grew as a naval superpower, colonizing and trading with all parts of the globe. Eventually, Britannia ruled the waves, exploiting the wealth of India, Africa, and Australia. (And America...at least until they lost their most important colony when those ungrateful Yanks revolted in 1776 in the "American War.") Throughout the century, the country was ruled by the German Hanover family, including four kings named George.

The "Georgian Era" was one of great

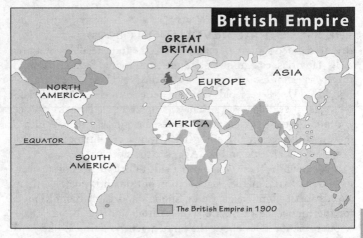

British Empire

GREAT BRITAIN

ASIA

NORTH AMERICA

EUROPE

AFRICA

EQUATOR

SOUTH AMERICA

The British Empire in 1900

wealth. London's population was now half a million, and one in seven Brits lived in London. The nation's first daily newspapers hit the streets. The cultural scene was refined: painters (like William Hogarth, Joshua Reynolds, and Thomas Gainsborough), theater (with actors like David Garrick), music (Handel's *Messiah*), and literature (Samuel Johnson's dictionary). Scientist James Watt's steam engines laid the groundwork for a coming Industrial Revolution.

In 1789, the French Revolution erupted, sparking decades of war between France and Britain. Britain finally prevailed in the early 1800s, when Admiral Horatio Nelson defeated Napoleon's fleet at the Battle of Trafalgar and the Duke of Wellington stomped Napoleon at Waterloo. (Nelson and Wellington are memorialized with many arches, columns, and squares throughout England.)

By war's end, Britain had emerged as Europe's top power.

Sights

- Nelson's Column at Trafalgar Square
- Apsley House (Wellington Museum) and adjacent Wellington Arch
- Portraits by Reynolds and Gainsborough and slices of life by Hogarth (Tate Britain)
- Royal Observatory and National Maritime Museum, Greenwich
- Dr. Johnson's House in The City
- Handel's compositions (British Library)

VICTORIAN GENTILITY AND
THE INDUSTRIAL REVOLUTION (1800s)

Britain reigned supreme, steaming into the Industrial Age with her mills, factories, coal mines, gas lights, and trains. By century's end, there was electricity, telephones, and the first Underground.

In 1837, 18-year-old Victoria became queen. She ruled for 64 years, presiding over an era of unprecedented wealth, peace, and middle-class ("Victorian") values. Britain was at its zenith of power, with a colonial empire that covered one-fifth of the world (for more on Victoria and her Age, see the sidebar).

Meanwhile, there was another side to Britain's era of superiority and industrial might. A generation of Romantic poets (William Wordsworth, John Keats, Percy Shelley, and Lord Byron) longed for the innocence of nature. Jane Austen and the Brontë sisters wrote romantic tales about the landed gentry. Painters like J. M. W. Turner and John Constable immersed themselves in nature to paint moody landscapes.

The gritty modern world was emerging. Popular novelist Charles Dickens brought literature to the masses, educating them about Britain's harsh social and economic realities. Rudyard Kipling critiqued the colonial system. Charles Darwin questioned the very nature of humanity when he articulated the principles of natural selection and evolution. Jack the Ripper, a serial killer of prostitutes, terrorized east London and was never caught. Not even by Sherlock Holmes—a fictional detective living at 221B Baker Street who solved fictional crimes that the real Scotland Yard couldn't.

Sights
- Big Ben and Halls of Parliament
- Buckingham Palace, the Mall, and Hyde Park
- The Tube
- Paintings by Turner and Constable (Tate Britain)
- Writers' manuscripts in the British Library
- Poets' Corner in Westminster Abbey
- Victoria and Albert Museum
- Kensington Palace
- Sherlock Holmes Museum
- London's East End tenements (reminiscent of the Jack the Ripper days)

WORLD WARS AND RECOVERY (20th Century)

The 20th century was not kind to Britain. Two world wars and economic struggles whittled Britain down from a world empire to an island chain struggling to compete in a global economy.

In World War I, Britain joined France and other allies to battle Germany in trench warfare. A million British men died.

Meanwhile, after decades of rebellion, Ireland finally gained its independence—except for the Protestant-leaning Northern Ireland, which remained tied to Britain. This division of the Emerald Isle would result in decades of bitter strife, protests, and terrorist attacks known as "The Troubles."

In the 1920s, London was home to a flourishing literary scene, including T. S. Eliot (American-turned-British), Virginia Woolf, and E. M. Forster. In 1936, the country was rocked and scandalized when King Edward VIII abdicated to marry a divorced American commoner, Wallis Simpson. He was succeeded by his brother, George VI—"Bertie" of *The King's Speech* fame, and father of Queen Elizabeth II.

In World War II, the Nazi Blitz (aerial bombing campaign) reduced much of London to rubble, sending residents into Tube stations for shelter and the government into a fortified bunker (now the Churchill War Rooms). Britain was rallied through its darkest hour by two leaders: Prime Minister Winston Churchill, a remarkable orator, and King George VI, who overcame a persistent stutter. Amid the chaos of war, the colonial empire began to dwindle to almost nothing, and Britain emerged from the war as a shell of its former superpower self.

The postwar recovery began, aided by the United States. Many cheap, concrete (ugly) buildings rose from the rubble.

Culturally, Britain remained world-class. Oxford professor J. R. R. Tolkien wrote *The Lord of the Rings* and his friend C. S. Lewis wrote *The Chronicles of Narnia*. In the 1960s, "Swinging London" became a center for rock music, film, theater, youth culture, and Austin Powers-style joie de vivre. America was conquered by a "British Invasion" of rock bands (The Beatles, The Rolling Stones, and The Who, followed later by Led Zeppelin, Elton John, David Bowie, and others), and James Bond ruled the box office.

Britain joined the European Common Market, an economic precursor to the European Union, in 1973. The decade brought massive unemployment, labor strikes, and recession. A conservative reaction followed in the 1980s and '90s, led by Prime Minister and Eurosceptic Margaret Thatcher—the "Iron Lady." As proponents of traditional Victorian values—community, family, hard work, thrift, and trickle-down economics—the Conservatives took a Reaganesque approach to Britain's serious social and economic problems. They cut government subsidies to old-fashioned heavy

Queen Victoria (1819-1901)

Plump, pleasant, and not quite five feet tall, Queen Victoria, with her regal demeanor and 64-year reign, came to symbolize the global dominance of the British Empire during its greatest era.

Born in Kensington Palace, Victoria was the granddaughter of "Mad" King George III, the tyrant who sparked the American Revolution. Her domineering mother raised her in sheltered seclusion, drilling into her the strict morality that would come to be known as "Victorian." At 18, she was crowned queen. Victoria soon fell deeply in love with Prince Albert, a handsome German nobleman. They married and set up house in Buckingham Palace (the first monarchs to do so) and at Windsor Castle. Over the next 17 years, she and Albert had nine children, whom they married off to Europe's crowned heads. Victoria's descendants include Kaiser Wilhelm II of Germany (who started World War I); the current monarchs of Spain, Norway, Sweden, and Denmark; and England's Queen Elizabeth II, who is Victoria's great-great granddaughter.

Victoria and Albert promoted the arts and sciences, organizing a world's fair in Hyde Park (1851) that showed off London as *the* global capital. Just as important, they were role models for an entire nation; this loving couple influenced several generations with their wholesome middle-class values and devoted parenting. Though Victoria is often depicted as dour and stuffy—she supposedly coined the phrase "We are not amused"—in private she was warm, easy to laugh, plainspoken, thrifty, and modest, with a talent for sketching and journal writing.

In 1861, Victoria's happy domestic life ended. Her mother's death was soon followed by the sudden loss of her beloved Albert to typhoid fever. A devastated Victoria dressed in black for the funeral—and for her remaining 40 years. She hunkered down at Windsor with her family. Critics complained she was an absentee monarch. Rumors swirled that her kilt-wearing servant, John Brown, was not only her close friend but also her lover. For two decades, she rarely appeared in public.

industries (closing many factories, earning working-class ire) as they tried to nudge Britain toward a more modern economy.

In 1981, the world was captivated by the spectacle of Prince Charles marrying Lady Diana in St. Paul's Cathedral. Their children, Princes William and Harry, grew up in the media spotlight, and when Diana died in a car crash (1997), the nation—and the world—mourned.

Over time, Victoria emerged from mourning to assume her role as one of history's first constitutional monarchs. She had inherited a crown with little real power. But beyond her ribbon-cutting ceremonial duties, Victoria influenced events behind the scenes. She studiously learned politics from powerful mentors (especially Prince Albert and two influential prime ministers) and kept well informed on what Parliament was doing. Thanks to Victoria's personal modesty and honesty, the British public never came to disdain the monarchy, as happened in other countries.

Victoria gracefully oversaw the peaceful transfer of power from the nobles to the people. The secret ballot was introduced during her reign, and ordinary workers acquired voting rights (though this applied only to men—Victoria opposed women's suffrage). The traditional Whigs and Tories morphed into today's Liberal and Conservative parties. Victoria personally promoted progressive charities, and even paid for her own crown.

Most of all, Victoria became the symbol of the British Empire, which she saw as a way to protect and civilize poorer peoples. Britain enjoyed peace at home, while its colonial possessions included India, Australia, Canada, and much of Africa. Because it was always daytime someplace under Victoria's rule, it was often said that "the sun never sets on the British Empire."

The Victorian era saw great changes. The Industrial Revolution was in full swing. When Victoria was born, there were no trains. By 1842, when she took her first train trip (with much fanfare), railroads crisscrossed Europe. The telegraph, telephone, and newspapers further laced the world together. The popular arts flourished—it was the era of Dickens novels, Tennyson poems, Sherlock Holmes stories, Gilbert and Sullivan operettas, and Pre-Raphaelite paintings. Economically, Britain saw the rise of the middle class. Middle-class morality dominated—family, hard work, honor, duty, and sexual modesty.

By the end of her reign, Victoria was wildly popular, both for her personality and as a focus for British patriotism. At her Golden Jubilee (1887), she paraded past adoring throngs to Westminster Abbey. For her Diamond Jubilee (1897), she did the same at St. Paul's Cathedral. Cities, lakes, and military medals were named for her. When she passed away in 1901, it was literally the end of an era.

The 1990s saw Britain finally emerging from decades of economic stagnation and social turmoil. An energized nation prepared for the new millennium.

Sights

- Cabinet War Rooms
- Cenotaph

- Imperial War Museum
- National Army Museum
- Blitz photos at St. Paul's
- Beatles memorabilia (British Library)
- Harrods

EARLY 2000s

London celebrated the millennium with a new Ferris wheel (the London Eye), the Millennium Bridge, and an exhibition hall dubbed "The O2." Left-of-center prime minister Tony Blair ruled Britain until his popularity plummeted when he supported the US invasion of Iraq. On "7/7" in 2005, London was rocked by a terrorist attack—a harbinger of others to come.

Britain suffered mightily in the global recession of 2008. Voters turned to the Conservative prime minister David Cameron, who introduced austerity measures, but Britain was slow to recover.

Thankfully, one hot spot—Northern Ireland—was healed. In 2007, ultra-nationalists and ultra-unionists reached an agreement, ending almost 40 years of the Troubles.

In 2011, Prince William married commoner Kate Middleton in a lavish ceremony. And in 2018, William's younger brother Harry married American TV star Meghan Markle. The two couples, along with their children, have stirred renewed enthusiasm for the monarchy (notwithstanding Harry and Meghan's decision to step back from their royal duties).

In 2012, in a one-two punch of festivity, the Brits hosted both the Olympic Games and the Queen's 60th year on the throne. A flurry of renovation turned former urban wastelands into hip, thriving people zones, and the country's future was looking rosy.

Then came Brexit…

Sights
- The London Eye
- Millennium Bridge
- Tate Modern contemporary art exhibits
- West End theaters
- The Docklands skyscraper zone
- Queen Elizabeth Olympic Park
- Parliament Square with its Brexit protesters (pro and con)

Britain Today

Britain is one of the richest, freest, best-educated, and most culturally powerful nations on earth. But it also has its challenges. To understand the British people today, it's helpful to survey the political landscape and global trends that they're dealing with. This includes

---

Get It Right

Americans tend to use "England," "Britain," and the "United Kingdom" (or "UK") interchangeably, but they're not quite the same.

- **England** is the country occupying the center and southeast part of the island.
- **Britain** is the name of the island.
- **Great Britain** is the political union of the island's three countries: England, Scotland, and Wales.
- The **United Kingdom** (UK) adds a fourth country, Northern Ireland.
- The **British Isles** (not a political entity) also includes the independent Republic of Ireland.
- The **British Commonwealth** is a loose association of possessions and former colonies (including Canada, Australia, and India) that profess at least symbolic loyalty to the Crown.

You can call the modern nation either the United Kingdom ("the UK"), "Great Britain," or simply "Britain."

---

the most vexing issue Brits have grappled with since World War II—Brexit. On January 31, 2020, the United Kingdom became the first country to leave the European Union, after 47 years as a member. Today, the consequences continue to ripple out, affecting Brits' relationship with the rest of Europe and with each other.

POLITICAL LANDSCAPE

A constitutional monarchy, Britain is ruled by the House of Commons, with some guidance from the mostly figurehead Queen and House of Lords. The prime minister is the chief executive but is not elected directly by voters; rather, he or she assumes power as the head of the party that wins a majority in parliamentary elections. Elections are held every five years.

Two parties have traditionally dominated Britain's Parliament: left-leaning Labour (currently led by Jeremy Corbyn) and right-leaning Conservative ("Tories," led by Boris Johnson). The dividing lines between them are familiar: Should government nurture the economy through spending on social programs (Labour's platform), or cut programs and taxes to allow businesses to thrive (as Conservatives say)?

In recent elections, third parties have made gains, including the Scottish National Party (SNP, led by Nicola Sturgeon) and the center-left Liberal Democrats. If no single party wins an outright majority, whoever rules must form a coalition. Because Britain does not have a single "constitution" clearly outlining the system of checks and balances, the British body politic relies more on a tradition of civility and mutual respect to make government work.

CHALLENGES

Along with the rest of the world, Britain is dealing with the aftermath of the Covid-19 pandemic.

Britain's other main challenge is Brexit—how to manage the implications of leaving the European Union. It's not just the economic impact: Brexit is inextricably tangled up with other issues that have long divided the nation, from politics to culture to class.

Although the divorce was supposedly final in 2020, the UK and the EU are still figuring out new arrangements on trade, travel, and immigration. Goods have generally continued to flow freely, without major tariffs, and London remains a global financial hub. But there's more red tape, and supply-chain issues crop up (exacerbated by Covid).

Immigration was one of the key reasons many Brits voted for Brexit, with supporters arguing that immigrants were taking jobs and diluting British culture, while receiving overgenerous financial aid. Now migrants must qualify on a points-based system and have the means to support themselves. But the exodus of foreign workers is now causing labor shortages in Britain.

Brexit has also intensified long-standing tensions between the four nations that make up the UK: England, Scotland, Wales, and Northern Ireland. In general, the people of England and Wales voted for Brexit, while Scotland and Northern Ireland opposed it. In Scotland, which voted heavily against leaving the EU, Brexit has stoked the fires of Nicola Sturgeon's Scottish Nationalist Party, which wants independence from the UK. Meanwhile, in Northern Ireland, Brexit has raised the thorny question of how to handle the border between Northern Ireland (part of the UK) and the Republic of Ireland (part of the EU). In a compromise called the "protocol," the UK agreed to enforce EU regulations on goods going into Northern Ireland, while allowing an open border with the Republic of Ireland...but the issue is far from settled.

Brexit has also ratcheted up the class consciousness that has always divided British society. Britain already faced a widening gap of wealth inequality. Brexit exposed the stark political divide between classes: Generally, the poor wanted Brexit, while the rich fought it.

Finally—Brexit or no Brexit—Brits are divided on the eternal question of the royals. Is having a monarch (who's politically irrelevant) and a royal family (who fill the tabloids with their scandals) worth it? Recent polls suggest two in five Brits want to toss the whole lot of them.

NOTABLE BRITS

Only history can judge which British names will stand the test of time, but many Brits stand large on the world stage.

There are well-known politicians, like Theresa May, Boris Johnson, and Jeremy Corbyn.

The list of British actors reads like a roll-call of Oscar and Emmy winners: Helen Mirren, Emma Thompson, Daniel Day-Lewis, Gary Oldman, Helena Bonham Carter, Jude Law, Ricky Gervais, James Corden, Daniel Radcliffe, Kate Winslet, Benedict Cumberbatch, John Oliver, Tilda Swinton, Colin Firth, Eddie Redmayne, etc.

Of course, ever since the "British Invasion" of the '60s, Brits have dominated the pop music scene: Adele, Chris Martin of Coldplay, Jessie J, Ellie Goulding, Ed Sheeran, Sam Smith, Florence Welch of Florence and the Machine, etc.

In the literary field, Britain scoops up major awards, including Britain's own Man Booker Prize. Winners include J. K. Rowling, E. L. James, Hilary Mantel, Tom Stoppard, Nick Hornby, Ian McEwan, and Zadie Smith.

There are well-known visual artists (Damien Hirst, Rachel Whiteread, Tracey Emin, Anish Kapoor), athletes (David Beckham, Bradley Wiggins, Andy Murray), and entrepreneurs (Sir Richard Branson, Lord Alan Sugar, James Dyson).

And, of course, there are Britain's biggest tabloid sensations in years, the new generation of royals: William, Kate, Harry, Meghan, and their cute little kids.

BRITISH TV

For many Americans, their first view of the British lifestyle came through British TV programs beamed into American homes. And no wonder: Although it has its share of lowbrow reality programming, much British television is still so good—and so British—that it deserves a mention as a sightseeing treat. After a hard day of castle climbing, watch the telly over tea in your B&B.

For many years there were only five free channels, but now nearly every British television can receive a couple dozen. BBC television is government-regulated and commercial-free. Broadcasting of its eight channels (and of the five BBC radio stations) is funded by a mandatory £154.50-per-year-per-household television and radio license (hmmm, 50 cents per day to escape commercials and public-broadcasting pledge drives...not bad). Channels 3, 4, and 5 are privately owned, are a little more lowbrow, and have commercials—but those "adverts" are often clever and sophisticated, providing a fun look at British life. About 60 percent of households pay for cable or satellite television.

Whereas California "accents" fill US airwaves 24 hours a day,

Royal Families: Past and Present

Royal Lineage

802-1066	Saxon and Danish kings
1066-1154	William the Conqueror and Norman kings
1154-1399	Plantagenet (kings with French roots)
1399-1461	Lancaster
1462-1485	York
1485-1603	Tudor (Henry VIII, Elizabeth I)
1603-1649	Stuart (civil war and beheading of Charles I)
1649-1653	Commonwealth, no royal head of state
1653-1659	Protectorate, with Cromwell as Lord Protector
1660-1714	Restoration of Stuart dynasty
1714-1901	Hanover (four Georges, William IV, Victoria)
1901-1910	Saxe-Coburg (Edward VII)
1910-present	Windsor (George V to Elizabeth II)

The Royal Family Today

It seems you can't pick up a British newspaper without some mention of the latest event, scandal, or oddity involving the royal family. Here is the cast of characters:

Queen Elizabeth II wears the traditional crown of her great-great grandmother Victoria, who ruled for 63 years, 7 months, and 2 days. In September 2015, Queen Elizabeth officially over-took Victoria as England's longest-reigning monarch, and in April 2016 she became the first UK sovereign to reach 90 years old. Elizabeth's husband, Prince Philip, died in 2021 at age 99.

Their son, Prince Charles (the Prince of Wales), is next in line to become king—and already holds the title as the longest "heir in waiting." For years, Charles' love life was fodder for the British press. There was his fairytale 1981 marriage to Princess Di, then their bitter divorce, Diana's dramatic death in 1997, and the ongoing drama with Charles' longtime girlfriend—and now wife—Camilla Parker Bowles. Camilla will become queen consort when Charles takes the throne.

These days it's Prince Charles' sons who generate the tabloid buzz. The older son, Prince William (b. 1982), is a graduate of Scotland's St. Andrews University and served as a search-and-rescue helicopter pilot with the Royal Air Force. In 2011, when William married Catherine "Kate" Middleton, the TV audience

homogenizing the way our country speaks, Britain protects and promotes its regional accents by its choice of TV and radio announcers. See if you can tell where each is from (or ask a local for help).

Commercial-free British TV, while looser than it used to be, is still careful about what it airs and when. But after the 21:00 "water-

was estimated at one-quarter of the world's population—more than two billion people. Kate—a commoner William met at university—is now the Duchess of Cambridge and will eventually become Britain's queen.

Their son, Prince George Alexander Louis, born in 2013—and later voted the most powerful and influential person in London by a poll in the *Evening Standard*—will ultimately succeed William as sovereign. In 2015, the couple welcomed Princess Charlotte Elizabeth Diana, and in 2018, Prince Louis Arthur Charles.

William's brother, redheaded Prince Harry (b. 1984), managed to shake his earlier reputation as a bad boy by proving his mettle as a career soldier, completing a tour in Afghanistan, doing charity work in Africa, and serving with the Army Air Corps. His 2018 marriage to American actress Meghan Markle, and the births of their children Archie and Lilibet, added sparkle to the once-musty royals—until the pair relinquished their royal titles and moved to California in 2020.

Royal Sightseeing

You can see the trappings of royalty at Buckingham Palace (the Queen's London residence) with its Changing of the Guard; Kens-

ington Palace—with a wing that's home to Will, Kate, and kids; Clarence House, the London home of Prince Charles and Camilla; Althorp Estate (80 miles from London), the childhood home and burial place of Princess Diana; and Windsor Castle, the Queen's royal country home. Don't forget the crown jewels in the Tower of London.

Your best chances to see the Queen are on three public occasions: State Opening of Parliament (on the first day of a new parliamentary session), Remembrance Sunday (early November, at the Cenotaph), or Trooping the Colour (one Saturday in mid-June, parading down Whitehall and at Buckingham Palace). Check www.royal.uk for royal events.

shed" hour, when children are expected to be in bed, some nudity and profanity are allowed, and may cause you to spill your tea.

British comedies have tickled the American funny bone for years, from sketch comedy *(Monty Python's Flying Circus)* to sitcoms (*Fawlty Towers, Blackadder,* and *The Office*). Quiz shows and reality shows are taken very seriously here. Jonathan Ross is the Jimmy Fallon of Britain for sometimes-edgy late-night talk. Other popular late-night "chat show" hosts include Graham Norton and Alan Carr. For a tear-filled, slice-of-life taste of British soaps dealing in all the controversial issues, see the popular and remarkably long-running *Emmerdale, Coronation Street,* or *EastEnders.* The costume drama *Downton Abbey,* the sci-fi serial *Doctor Who,* the small-town dramedy *Doc Martin,* and the modern crime series *Sherlock* have all become hits on both sides of the Atlantic.

WHAT'S SO GREAT ABOUT BRITAIN?

Brexit is the biggest challenge to the British way of life since the days of the Blitz. But it makes Britain no less Great. The Britain you visit today is vibrant and alive. It's smaller, and no longer the superpower it once was, but it's still a cultural and economic powerhouse.

Think of it. At its peak in the mid-1800s, Britain owned one-fifth of the world and accounted for more than half the planet's industrial output. Today, the Empire is down to the Isle of Britain itself and a few token scraps (the Falklands, Gibraltar, Northern Ireland) and a loose association of former colonies (Canada, Australia) called the "British Commonwealth."

Geographically, the Isle of Britain is small—smaller than the state of Oregon—and its highest mountain (Ben Nevis in Scotland at 4,411 feet) is a foothill by US standards. The population is a fifth that of the United States. Despite its size, Britain is the world's fifth-biggest economy, sixth-biggest manufacturer, and largest financial center (London). Twenty-six of the world's 500 largest companies are headquartered here.

The Britain you visit today remains a global superpower of heritage, culture, and tradition. It's a major exporter of actors, movies, and theater; of rock and classical music; and of writers, painters, and sculptors. It's the perfect place for you to visit and make your own history.

Architecture in Britain

From Stonehenge to Big Ben, travelers are storming castle walls, climbing spiral staircases, and snapping the pictures of 5,000 years of architecture. Let's sort it out.

The oldest ruins—mysterious and prehistoric—date from before Roman times back to 3000 BC. The earliest sites, such as Stonehenge and Avebury, were built during the Stone and Bronze ages. The remains from these periods are made of huge stones or mounds of earth, even man-made hills, and were created as celestial calendars and for worship or burial. Britain is crisscrossed with imaginary lines said to connect these mysterious sights (ley lines). Iron Age people (600 BC-AD 50) left desolate stone forts. The

Romans thrived in Britain from AD 50 to 400, building cities, walls, and roads. Evidence of Roman greatness can be seen in lavish villas with ornate mosaic floors, temples uncovered beneath great English churches, and Roman stones in medieval city walls. Roman roads sliced across the island in straight lines. Today, unusually straight rural roads are very likely laid directly on these ancient roads.

As Rome crumbled in the fifth century, so did Roman Britain. Little architecture survives from Dark Ages England, the Saxon period from 500 to 1000. Architecturally, the light was switched on with the Norman Conquest in 1066. As William earned

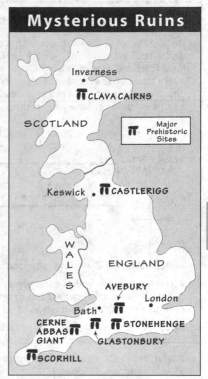

Mysterious Ruins

Inverness
CLAVA CAIRNS
SCOTLAND
Major Prehistoric Sites
Keswick • CASTLERIGG
W A L E S
ENGLAND
AVEBURY
London
Bath•
CERNE ABBAS GIANT
STONEHENGE
GLASTONBURY
SCORHILL

his title "the Conqueror," his French architects built churches and castles in the European Romanesque style.

English Romanesque is called Norman (1066-1200). Norman churches had round arches, thick walls, and small windows; Durham Cathedral and the Chapel of St. John in the Tower of London are prime examples. The Tower of London, with its square keep, small windows, and spiral stone stairways, is a typical Norman castle. You can see plenty of Norman castles around England—all built to secure the conquest of these invaders from Normandy.

Gothic architecture (1200-1600) replaced the heavy Norman style with light, vertical buildings, pointed arches, soaring spires, and bigger windows. English Gothic is divided into three stages. Early English Gothic (1200-1300) features tall, simple spires; beautifully carved capitals; and elaborate chapter houses (such as the Wells Cathedral). Decorated Gothic (1300-1400) gets fancier, with more elaborate tracery, bigger windows, and ornately carved pinnacles, as you see at Westminster Abbey. Finally, the Perpendicular Gothic style (1400-1600, also called "rectilinear") returns to square towers and emphasizes straight, uninterrupted vertical lines from ceiling to floor, with vast windows and exuberant

Typical Church Architecture

History comes to life when you visit a centuries-old church. Even if you wouldn't know your apse from a hole in the ground, learning a few simple terms will enrich your experience. Note that not every church has every feature, and a "cathedral" isn't a type of church architecture, but rather a designation for a church that's a governing center for a local bishop.

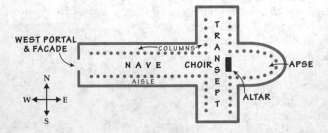

Aisles: Long, generally low-ceilinged arcades that flank the nave

Altar: Raised area with a ceremonial table (often adorned with candles or a crucifix), where the priest prepares and serves the bread and wine for Communion

Apse: Space behind the altar, sometimes bordered with small chapels

Barrel Vault: Continuous round-arched ceiling that resembles an extended upside-down U

Choir ("quire" in British English): Intimate space reserved for clergy and choir, located within the nave near the high altar and often screened off

Cloister: Covered hallways bordering a square or rectangular open-air courtyard, traditionally where monks and nuns got fresh air

Facade: Exterior of the church's main (west) entrance, usually highly decorated

Groin Vault: Arched ceiling formed where two equal barrel vaults meet at right angles

Narthex: Area (portico or foyer) between the main entry and the nave

Nave: Long central section of the church (running west to east, from the entrance to the altar) where the congregation sits or stands during the service

Transept: One of the two parts forming the "arms" of the cross in a traditional cross-shaped floor plan; runs north-south, perpendicularly crossing the east-west nave

West Portal: Main entry to the church (on the west end, opposite the main altar)

Typical Castle Architecture

Castles were fortified residences for medieval nobles. Castles come in all shapes and sizes, but knowing a few general terms will help you understand them.

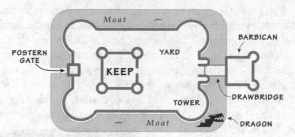

Barbican: Fortifed gatehouse, sometimes a standalone building located outside the main walls

Crenellation: Gap-toothed pattern of stones atop the parapet

Drawbridge: Bridge that could be raised or lowered using counterweights or a chain and winch

Great Hall: Largest room in the castle, serving as throne room, conference center, and dining hall

Hoardings (or Gallery or Brattice): Wooden huts built onto the upper parts of the stone walls; served as watchtowers, living quarters, and fighting platforms

Keep (or Donjon): High, strong stone tower in the center of the complex; the lord's home and refuge of last resort

Loopholes (or Embrasures): Narrow wall slits through which soldiers could shoot arrows

Machicolation: Stone ledge jutting out from the wall, with holes through which soldiers could drop rocks or boiling oil onto wall-scaling enemies below

Moat: Ditch encircling the wall, sometimes filled with water

Motte-and-Bailey: Type of early English castle, with a hilltop fort (motte) and an enclosed, fortified yard (bailey)

Parapet: Outer railing of the wall walk

Portcullis: Iron grille that could be lowered across the entrance

Postern Gate: Small, unfortified side or rear entrance; in wartime, became a sally port used to launch surprise attacks or as an escape route

Towers: Square or round structures with crenellated tops or conical roofs serving as lookouts, chapels, living quarters, or the dungeon

Turret: Small lookout tower rising from the top of the wall

Wall Walk (or Allure): Pathway atop the wall where guards could patrol and where soldiers stood to fire at the enemy

Yard (or Bailey): Open courtyard inside the castle walls

decoration, including fan-vaulted ceilings (King's College Chapel at Cambridge). Through this evolution, the structural ribs (arches meeting at the top of the ceilings) became more and more decorative and fanciful (the most fancy being the star vaulting and fan vaulting of the Perpendicular style).

As you tour the great medieval churches of Britain, remember that almost everything is symbolic. For instance, on the tombs of knights, if the figure has crossed legs, he was a Crusader. If his feet rest on a dog, he died at home; but if his legs rest on a lion, he died in battle. Local guides and books help us modern pilgrims understand at least a little of what we see.

Wales is particularly rich in English castles, which were needed to subdue the stubborn Welsh. Edward I built a ring of powerful castles in North Wales, including Conwy and Caernarfon.

Gothic houses were a simple mix of woven strips of thin wood, rubble, and plaster called wattle and daub. The famous black-and-white Tudor (or "half-timbered") look came simply from filling in heavy oak frames with wattle and daub.

The Tudor period (1485-1560) was a time of relative peace (the Wars of the Roses were finally over), prosperity, and renaissance. But when Henry VIII broke with the Catholic Church and disbanded its monasteries, scores of Britain's greatest churches were left as gutted shells. These hauntingly beautiful abbey ruins (Glastonbury, Tintern, Whitby, Rievaulx, Battle, St. Augustine's in Canterbury, St. Mary's in York, and lots more), surrounded by lush lawns, are now pleasant city parks.

Although few churches were built during the Tudor period, this was a time of house and mansion construction. Heating a home was becoming popular and affordable, and Tudor buildings featured small square windows and many chimneys. In towns, where land was scarce, many Tudor houses grew up and out, getting wider with each overhanging floor.

The Elizabethan and Jacobean periods (1560-1620) were followed by the English Renaissance style (1620-1720). English architects mixed Gothic and classical styles, then Baroque and classical styles. Although the ornate Baroque never really grabbed Britain, the classical style of the Italian architect Andrea Palladio did. Inigo Jones (1573-1652), Christopher Wren (1632-1723), and those they inspired plastered Britain with enough columns, domes, and symmetry to please a Caesar. The Great Fire of London (1666) cleared the way for an ambitious young Wren to put his mark on

London forever with a grand rebuilding scheme, including the great St. Paul's Cathedral and more than 50 other churches.

The celebrants of the Boston Tea Party remember Britain's Georgian period (1720-1840) for its lousy German kings. But in architectural terms, "Georgian" is English for "Neoclassical." Its architecture was rich and showed off by being very classical. Grand ornamental doorways, fine cast-ironwork on balconies and railings, Chippendale furniture, and white-on-blue Wedgwood ceramics graced rich homes everywhere. John Wood Sr. and Jr. led the way, giving the trendsetting city of Bath its crescents and circles of aristocratic Georgian row houses.

The Industrial Revolution shaped the Victorian period (1840-1890) with glass, steel, and iron. Britain had a huge new erector set (so did France's Mr. Eiffel). This was also a Romantic period, reviving the "more Christian" Gothic style. London's Houses of Parliament are Neo-Gothic—they're just 140 years old but look 700, except for the telltale modern precision and craftsmanship. Whereas Gothic was stone or concrete, Neo-Gothic was often red brick. These were Britain's glory days, and there was more building in this period than in all previous ages combined.

The architecture of the mid-20th century obeyed the formula "form follows function"—it worried more about your needs than your eyes. But more recently, the dull "international style" has been nudged aside by a more playful style, thanks to cutting-edge architects such as Lord Norman Foster and Renzo Piano. In the last several years, London has made a point

of adding several creative buildings to its skyline: the City Hall (nicknamed "The Armadillo"), 30 St. Mary Axe ("The Gherkin"), 20 Fenchurch ("The Walkie-Talkie"), and the tallest building in Western Europe, the pointy Shard London Bridge (called simply, "The Shard").

Even as it sets trends for the 21st century, Britain treasures its heritage and takes great pains to build tastefully in historic districts and to preserve its many "listed" (government-protected) buildings. With a booming tourist trade, these quaint reminders of its past—and ours—are becoming a valuable part of the British economy.

For more about British history, consider Europe 101: History and Art for the Traveler *by Rick Steves and Gene Openshaw, available at* RickSteves.com.

PRACTICALITIES

This chapter covers the practical skills of European travel: how to get tourist information, pay for things, sightsee efficiently, find good-value accommodations, eat affordably but well, use technology wisely, and get between destinations smoothly. For more information on these topics, see RickSteves.com/travel-tips.

Travel Tips

Travel Advisories: Before traveling, check updated health and safety conditions, including restrictions for your destination, on the travel pages of the US State Department (www.travel.state. gov) and Centers for Disease Control and Prevention (www.cdc. gov/travel). The US embassy website for Great Britain is another good source of information (see page 569).

Covid Vaccine/Test Requirements: It's possible you'll need to present proof of vaccination against the coronavirus and/or a negative Covid-19 test result to board a plane to Europe or back to the US. Carefully check requirements for each country you'll visit well before you depart, and again a few days before your trip. See the websites listed above for current requirements.

Tourist Information: Before your trip, start with www.visitlondon.com. You can also find information on the official site for the City of London: www.visitthecity.co.uk. The Visit Britain website contains a wealth of knowledge on destinations, activities, accommodations, and transport in Great Britain (www.visitbritain.com). Transportation, sightseeing, and theater tickets can also be purchased (www.visitbritainshop.com/usa).

In Britain, a good first stop is generally the tourist information office (abbreviated **TI** in this book). Unfortunately, many of these have closed around the country, and London has only one official TI, specific to the City of London (near St. Paul's Cathedral—see page 25). The Greenwich Visitors Center is also helpful if you're headed that way (see page 389).

TIs are in business to help you spend money in their town—which can color their advice—but I still swing by to pick up a city map and get info on public transit, walking tours, special events, and nightlife.

Other Helpful Websites: www.timeout.com/london, www.londontown.com.

Emergency and Medical Help: For any emergency service—ambulance, police, or fire—call **112 or 999** from a mobile phone or landline. If you get sick, do as the locals do and go to a pharmacy and see a "chemist" (pharmacist) for advice. Or ask at your hotel for help—they'll know of the nearest medical and emergency services.

Theft or Loss: To replace a passport, you'll need to go in person to an embassy (see next). If your credit and debit cards disappear, cancel and replace them (see "Damage Control for Lost Cards" on page 574). File a police report, either on the spot or within a day or two; you'll need it to submit an insurance claim for lost or stolen items, and it can help with replacing your passport or credit and debit cards. For more information, see RickSteves.com/help.

US Consulate and Embassy: Dial +44 20 7499 9000 (all services), no walk-in passport services; for emergency two-day passport service, schedule an appointment or fill out the online Emergency Passport Contact Form, 24 Grosvenor Square, London, Tube: Bond Street, http://uk.usembassy.gov.

High Commission of Canada in London: Dial +44 20 7004 6000, passport services available Mon-Fri 9:30-12:30, Canada House, Trafalgar Square, London, Tube: Charing Cross, www.unitedkingdom.gc.ca.

Time Zones: Britain is five/eight hours ahead of the East/West Coasts of the US—and one hour earlier than most of continental Europe. The exceptions are the beginning and end of Daylight Saving Time: Europe "springs forward" the last Sunday in March (two weeks after most of North America), and "falls back" the last Sunday in October (one week before North America). For a handy time converter, use the world clock app on your phone or download one (see www.timeanddate.com).

Business Hours: Most stores are open Monday through Saturday (roughly 9:00 or 10:00 until 17:00 or 18:00), with a late night on Wednesday or Thursday (until 19:00 or 20:00). Department stores are usually open later throughout the week (until about 21:00 Mon-Sat). On Sunday, when stores are closed or have shorter hours, many street markets are lively with shoppers.

Watt's Up? Britain's electrical system is 220 volts, instead of North America's 110 volts. Most electronics (laptops, phones, cameras) and appliances (newer hair dryers, CPAP machines) convert automatically, so you won't need a converter, but you will need an adapter plug with three square prongs, sold inexpensively at travel stores in the US.

Rip up this book! Turn chapters into mini guidebooks: Break the book's spine and use a utility knife to slice apart chapters, keeping gummy edges intact. Reinforce the chapter spines with clear wide tape; use a heavy-duty stapler; or make or buy a cheap cover (see the Travel Store at RickSteves.com), swapping out chapters as you travel.

Discounts: Discounts (called "concessions" or "concs" in Britain) for sights are generally not listed in this book. However, seniors (age 65 and over), youths under 18, and students and teachers with proper identification cards (obtain from www.isic.org) can get discounts at many sights—always ask. Some discounts are available only for British citizens.

Going Green: There's plenty you can do to reduce your environmental footprint when traveling. When practical, take a train instead of a flight within Europe, and use public transportation within cities. In hotels, use the "Do Not Disturb" sign to avoid daily linen and towel changes (or hang up your towels to signal you'll reuse them). Bring a reusable shopping tote and refillable water bottle (Europe's tap water is safe to drink). Skip printed brochures, maps, or other materials that you don't plan to keep—get your info online instead. To find out how Rick Steves' Europe is

Exchange Rate

1 British pound (£1) = about $1.30

Britain uses the pound sterling. The British pound (£), also called a "quid," is broken into 100 pence (p). Pence means "cents." You'll find coins ranging from 1p to £2 and bills from £5 to £50.

To convert prices from pounds to dollars, add about 30 percent: £20 = about $26, £50 = about $65. (Check www.oanda.com for the latest exchange rates.) London is so expensive that some travelers try to kid themselves that pounds are dollars. But when they get home, that £1,000 Visa bill isn't asking for $1,000...it wants around $1,400.

offsetting carbon emissions with a self-imposed carbon tax, see RickSteves.com/about-us/climate-smart.

Money

Here's my basic strategy for using money wisely in Europe. I pack the following and keep it all safe in my money belt.

Credit Card: You'll use your credit card for purchases both big (hotels, advance tickets) and small (little shops, food stands). Many European businesses have gone cashless, making a card your only payment option. A "tap-to-pay" or "contactless" card is the most widely accepted and simplest to use.

Debit Card: Use this at ATMs to withdraw a small amount of local cash. Wait until you arrive to get pounds (European airports have plenty of ATMs); if you buy pounds before your trip, you'll pay bad stateside exchange rates. While most transactions are by card these days, cash can help you out of a jam if your card randomly doesn't work, and can be useful to pay for things like tips and local guides. But don't take out too much, or you may find you can't use it all.

Backup Card: Some travelers carry a third card (debit or credit; ideally from a different bank) in case one gets lost or simply doesn't work.

Stash of Cash: I carry $100-200 in US dollars as a cash backup, which comes in handy in an emergency (for example, if your debit card gets eaten by the machine).

BEFORE YOU GO

Know your cards. For credit cards, Visa and MasterCard are universal, while American Express and Discover are less common in Europe. US debit cards with a Visa or MasterCard logo will work in any European ATM.

Go "contactless." Get comfortable using contactless pay options. Check to see if you already have—or can get—a tap-to-pay version of your credit card (look on the card for the tap-to-pay symbol—four curvy lines) and consider setting up your smartphone for contactless payment (see next section for details). Both options are widely used in Europe and are more secure than a physical credit card: Instead of recording your credit card number, a one-time encrypted "token" enables the purchase and expires shortly afterward.

Know your PIN. Make sure you know the numeric, four-digit PIN for each of your cards, both debit and credit. Request it if you don't have one, as it may be required for some purchases (such as to top up your Oyster card at a machine). Allow time to receive the information by mail—it's not always possible to obtain your PIN online.

Report your travel dates. Let your bank know that you'll be using your debit and credit cards in Europe, and when and where you're headed.

Adjust your ATM withdrawal limit. Find out how much you can withdraw daily and ask for a higher daily limit if you want to get more cash at once. Note that European ATMs will withdraw funds only from checking accounts, not savings accounts.

Find out about fees. For any purchase or withdrawal made with a card, you may be charged a currency conversion fee (1-3 percent) and/or a Visa or MasterCard international transaction fee (less than 1 percent). If you're getting a bad deal, consider getting a new card. Reputable no-fee cards include those from Capital One, as well as Charles Schwab debit cards. Most credit unions and some airline loyalty cards have low or no international transaction fees.

IN EUROPE
Using Credit Cards and Payment Apps

Tap-to-Pay or **Contactless Cards:** These cards have the usual chip and/or magnetic stripe, but with the addition of a contactless symbol. Simply tap your card against a contactless reader to complete a transaction—no PIN or signature is required. This is by far the easiest way to pay and has become the standard in much of Europe. Some small businesses (such as market stalls or food stands) accept *only* tap cards, and sometimes don't accept cash.

Payment Apps: Just like at home, you can pay with your smartphone or smartwatch by linking a credit card to an app such as Apple Pay or Google Pay (for instance, at London Underground ticket machines). To pay, hold your phone near a contactless reader; you may need to verify the transaction with a face scan, fingerprint scan, or passcode. If you've arrived in Europe without a tap-to-pay card, you can easily set up your phone to work in this way.

Other Card Types: Chip-and-PIN cards have a visible chip embedded in them; rather than swiping, you insert the card into the payment machine, then enter your PIN on a keypad. In Europe, these cards have largely been supplanted by tap-to-pay cards, but you may be asked to use chip-and-PIN for certain purchases. **Swipe-and-sign** credit cards—with a swipeable magnetic stripe, and a receipt you have to sign—are increasingly rare.

Will My US Card Work? Usually, yes. On rare occasions, at self-service payment machines (such as transit-ticket kiosks, toll-booths, or fuel pumps), some US cards may not work. Usually a tap-to-pay card does the trick in these situations. Just in case, carry cash as a backup and look for a cashier who can process your payment if your card is rejected. Drivers should be prepared to move on to the next gas station if necessary. (In some countries, gas stations sell prepaid gas cards, which you can purchase with any US card). When approaching a toll plaza or ferry ticket line, use the "cash" lane.

Using Cash

Cash Machines: European cash machines work just like they do at home—except they spit out local currency instead of dollars, calculated at the day's standard bank-to-bank rate. In most places, ATMs are easy to locate—in Britain ask for a "cashpoint." When possible, withdraw cash from a bank-run ATM located just outside that bank.

If your debit card doesn't work, try a lower amount—your request may have exceeded your withdrawal limit or the ATM's limit. If you still have a problem, try a different ATM or come back later.

Avoid "independent" ATMs, such as Travelex, Euronet, Moneybox, Your Cash, Cardpoint, and Cashzone. These have high fees, can be less secure, and may try to trick users with "dynamic currency conversion" (see next).

Dynamic Currency Conversion: When withdrawing cash at an ATM or paying with a credit card, you'll often be asked whether you want the transaction processed in dollars or in the local currency. Always refuse the conversion and *choose the local currency*. While DCC offers the illusion of convenience, it comes with a poor exchange rate, and you'll wind up losing money.

Exchanging Cash: Minimize exchanging money in Europe; it's expensive (you'll generally lose 5 to 10 percent). In a pinch you can find exchange desks at major train stations or airports. Banks generally do not exchange money unless you have an account with them.

Security Tips

Even in "Jollie Olde Britain," pickpockets target tourists. Keep your cash, credit cards, and passport secure in your money belt, and carry only a day's spending money in your front pocket or wallet.

Before inserting your card into an ATM, inspect the front. If anything looks crooked, loose, or damaged, it could be a sign of a card-skimming device. When entering your PIN, carefully block other people's view of the keypad.

Avoid using a debit card for purchases. Because a debit card pulls funds directly from your bank account, potential charges incurred by a thief will stay on your account while your bank investigates.

To access your accounts online while traveling, be sure to use a secure connection (see the "Tips on Internet Security" sidebar, later).

Damage Control for Lost Cards

If you lose your credit or debit card, report the loss immediately to the respective global customer-assistance centers. With a mobile phone, call these 24-hour US numbers: Visa (+1 303 967 1096), MasterCard (+1 636 722 7111), and American Express (+1 336 393 1111). From a landline, you can call these US numbers collect by going through a local operator.

You'll need to provide the primary cardholder's identification-verification details (such as birth date, mother's maiden name, or Social Security number). You can generally receive a temporary card within two or three business days in Europe (see RickSteves.com/help for more).

If you report your loss within two days, you typically won't be responsible for unauthorized transactions on your account, although many banks charge a liability fee.

TIPPING

Tipping in Britain isn't as automatic and generous as it is in the US. For special service, tips are appreciated, but not expected. As in the US, the proper amount depends on your resources, tipping philosophy, and the circumstances, but some general guidelines apply.

Restaurants: Virtually all London restaurants with table service automatically tack on a 12.5 percent service charge to your bill. No additional tip is necessary—look for this on your bill before paying to avoid double-tipping.

Taxis: For a typical ride, round up your fare a bit (maximum 10 percent; for instance, if the fare is £7.40, pay £8). If the cabbie hauls your bags and zips you to the airport to help you catch your flight, you might want to toss in a little more.

Services: In general, if someone in the tourism or service industry does a super job for you, a small tip of a pound or two is appropriate...but not required. If you're not sure whether (or how much) to tip, ask a local for advice.

GETTING A VAT REFUND

Wrapped into the purchase price of your British souvenirs is a value-added tax (VAT) of about 20 percent. You're entitled to get most of that tax back if you purchase more than £30 worth of goods at a store that participates in the VAT-refund scheme (although individual stores can require that you spend more—Harrods, for example, won't process a refund unless you spend £50). Typically, you must ring up the minimum at a single retailer—you can't add up your purchases from various shops to reach the required amount. (If the store ships the goods to your US home, VAT is not assessed on your purchase.)

Getting your refund is straightforward...and worthwhile if you spend a significant amount.

At the Merchant: Have the merchant completely fill out the refund document (they'll ask for your passport; a photo of your passport usually works). Keep track of the paperwork and your original sales receipt. Note that you're not supposed to use your purchased goods before you leave Britain. If you show up at customs wearing your new Wellingtons, officials might look the other way—or deny you a refund.

At the Border or Airport: Process your VAT document at your last stop in the European Union (such as at the airport) with the customs agent who deals with VAT refunds (allow plenty of extra time to deal with this process). At some airports, you'll have to go to a customs office to get your documents stamped and then to a separate VAT refund service (such as Global Blue or Planet) to process the refund. At other airports, a single VAT desk handles the whole thing. (Note that refund services typically extract a 4 percent fee, but you're paying for the convenience of receiving your money in cash immediately or as a credit to your card.) Otherwise, you'll need to mail the stamped refund documents to the address given by the merchant.

CUSTOMS FOR AMERICAN SHOPPERS

You can take home $800 worth of items per person duty-free, once every 31 days. Many processed and packaged foods are allowed, including cheeses, dried herbs, jams, baked goods, candy, chocolate, oil, vinegar, condiments, and honey. Fresh fruits and vegetables and most meats are not allowed, with exceptions for some canned items. As for alcohol, you can bring in one liter duty-free (it can be packed securely in your checked luggage, along with any other liquid-containing items).

PRACTICALITIES

Covid Changes:
What to Expect Post-Pandemic

The Covid-19 pandemic caused many disruptions and changes to the way museums and other sights operate—some of which were temporary, others of which may turn out to be permanent. Depending on what's happening during your visit, hours may be modified; reservations may be required (or strongly recommended) to control crowd flow; and paper maps and audioguides may have been replaced by apps.

For any must-see sight on your list, check in advance on its official website (listed throughout this book) to fully understand the current situation. You may learn that it's required to prebook, for example, or you may be able to download an app so you'll have an up-to-date museum map and audioguide on your phone when you arrive.

To bring alcohol (or liquid-packed foods) in your carry-on bag on your flight home, buy it at a duty-free shop at the airport. You'll increase your odds of getting it onto a connecting flight if it's packaged in a "STEB"—a secure, tamper-evident bag. But stay away from liquids in opaque, ceramic, or metallic containers, which usually cannot be successfully screened (STEB or no STEB).

For details on allowable goods, customs rules, and duty rates, visit Help.cbp.gov.

Sightseeing

Sightseeing can be hard work. Use these tips to make your visits to London's finest sights meaningful, fun, efficient, and painless.

MAPS AND NAVIGATION TOOLS

A good map is essential for efficient navigation while sightseeing. The maps in this book are concise and simple, designed to help you locate recommended destinations, sights, hotels, and restaurants. In Europe, simple maps are generally free at TIs and hotels.

The TI sells a good £1 fold-out map that covers central London well, and also includes a Tube map and a diagram of handy bus lines. For something more serious, *Bensons London Street Map* is my favorite for efficient sightseeing and might be the best £4 you'll spend. I also like the *Handy London Map and Guide* version, which shows every little lane and all the sights, and comes with a transit map. The *Rough Guide* map to London is well-designed (£5, sold at London bookstores). The *Rick Steves Britain, Ireland & London City Map* has a good map of London ($9, RickSteves.com). Many Londoners, along with obsessive-compulsive tourists, rely on the highly detailed *London A-Z* map book (generally £5-7, called "A to Zed" by locals, available at newsstands). The color city maps and Tube map at the front of this book are also useful.

You can also use a mapping app on your mobile device, which provides turn-by-turn directions for walking, driving, and taking public transit. Google Maps, Apple Maps, and CityMaps2Go allow you to download maps for offline use; ideally, download the areas you'll need before your trip. For certain features (such as real-time public transit info, and current traffic conditions), you'll need to be online—either using Wi-Fi or an international data plan.

PLAN AHEAD

Set up an itinerary that allows you to fit in all your must-see sights. For a one-stop look at opening hours of the biggest sights, see "London At a Glance" on page 54. Most sights keep stable hours, but you can easily confirm the latest by checking at the TI or on museum websites.

Don't put off visiting a must-see sight—you never know when a place will close unexpectedly for a holiday, strike, or royal audience. Many museums are closed or have reduced hours at least a few days a year, especially on holidays such as Christmas, New Year's, and Bank Holiday Mondays in May and August. A list of holidays is in the appendix; check for possible closures during your trip. In summer, some sights may stay open late. Off-season hours may be shorter.

Plan for rain no matter when you go. Just keep traveling and take full advantage of "bright spells." The weather can change several times a day, but rarely is it extreme. As the locals say, "There's no bad weather, only inappropriate clothing." Bring a jacket, and dress in layers.

Going at the right time helps avoid crowds. This book offers tips on the best times to see specific sights. Try visiting popular sights very early or very late. Evening visits (when possible) are usually more peaceful, with fewer crowds. Late morning is usually the worst time to visit a popular sight.

If you plan to hire a local guide, reserve ahead by email. Popular guides can get booked up.

Study up. To get the most out of the self-guided tours and sight descriptions in this book, read them before you visit. The British Museum rocks if you understand the significance of the Rosetta Stone.

RESERVATIONS AND ADVANCE TICKETS

Given how precious your vacation time is, I recommend getting reservations for any must-see sight that offers them. Many popular sights sell advance tickets that guarantee admission at a certain time of day and allow you to skip ticket-buying lines.

It's worth giving up some spontaneity to book in advance. While other tourists sweat in long lines—or arrive to find the sight sold out—you'll show up at your reserved entry time and be assured of getting in. In some cases (especially for big amusements like the London Eye and Madame Tussauds), you'll save money by prebooking, too.

In some cases, getting a ticket in advance simply means buying your ticket earlier on the same day. But for other sights, you should book as soon as your travel dates are set and tickets are released, often months in advance. As soon as you're ready to commit to a certain date, book it.

SIGHTSEEING PASSES

The following sightseeing passes are sold online and at the City of London Information Centre, near St. Paul's Cathedral; see page 25.

The **London Pass**, while expensive, may save some money for extremely busy sightseers who will be using it on consecutive days. Among the many sights it includes are the Tower of London, Westminster Abbey, St. Paul's Cathedral, and Windsor Castle, plus one day on a hop-on, hop-off bus tour. Think through your sightseeing plans, study their website to see what's covered, and do the math before you buy. Note: Adding an Oyster card to your pass is a needless complication; it's easier to buy them on arrival (£69/1 day, £95/2 days, £109/3 days, £141/4 days, £146/5 days; days are calendar days rather than 24-hour periods; +44 20 7293 0972, www.londonpass.com).

The **English Heritage** society sells passes and memberships that include free entry to its 400 sights (which are exclusive to England); they're worth it only if you'll be thoroughly exploring England, not just London. You can buy passes or memberships at any participating sight. For most travelers, the Overseas Visitor Pass is a better choice than the pricier one-year membership (Visitor Pass: £38/9 days, £45/16 days, discounts for couples and families; membership: £60 for one person, £105 for two, discounts for families, seniors, and students, children under 19 free, www.english-heritage.org.uk/membership; +44 370 333 1181).

AT SIGHTS

Here's what you can typically expect:

Entering: You may not be allowed to enter if you arrive too close to closing time. And guards start ushering people out well before the actual closing time, so don't save the best for last.

Many sights have a security check. Allow extra time for these lines. Some sights require you to check daypacks and coats. (If you'd rather not check your daypack, try carrying it tucked under your arm like a purse as you enter.)

At ticket desks, you may see references to "Gift Aid"—a tax-deduction scheme that benefits museums—but this only concerns UK taxpayers.

Photography: If the museum's photo policy isn't clearly posted, ask a guard. Generally, taking photos without a flash or tripod is allowed. Some sights ban selfie sticks; others ban photos altogether.

Audioguides and Apps: I've produced free, downloadable audio tours for my Westminster Walk, the British Museum, the British Library, St. Paul's Cathedral, and Historic London: The City Walk; look for the ∩ symbol in this book. For more on my audio tours, see page 22.

Some sights offer audioguides with excellent recorded descriptions. In some cases, you'll rent a device to carry around (if you bring your own plug-in earbuds, you'll enjoy better sound). Increasingly, museums and sights instead offer an app you can download with their audioguide (often free; check websites from home and consider downloading in advance as not all sights offer free Wi-Fi).

Tours: Guided tours are most likely to occur during peak season (either for free or a small fee—figure £5-10—and widely ranging in quality). Some sights also run short introductory videos featuring their highlights and history. These are generally well worth your time and a great place to start your visit.

Temporary Exhibits: Museums may show special exhibits in addition to their permanent collection. Some exhibits are included in the entry price, while others come at an extra cost (which you may have to pay even if you don't want to see the exhibit). It's not unusual for a marquee temporary exhibit to sell out well ahead of the permanent collection; if you're an art lover, do your homework a few weeks (or even months) in advance and prebook anything special.

Expect Changes: Artwork can be on tour, on loan, out sick, or shifted at the whim of the curator. (Especially in London, some major museums—including both Tate museums—pride themselves on shuffling around their collections every year or two.) Some museums may hand out (or sell) paper maps, others offer free apps with the latest map; in a pinch, take a photo of a posted map with your phone. Ask museum staff if you can't find a particular item.

Services: Important sights and cathedrals usually have a reasonably priced on-site café or cafeteria (handy and air-conditioned places to rejuvenate during a long visit—try a cheap "cream tea" to pick up your energy in midafternoon, like Brits do). The WCs at sights are free and generally clean.

Before Leaving: At the gift shop, scan the postcard rack or thumb through a guidebook to be sure you haven't overlooked something that you'd like to see. Every sight or museum offers more than what is covered in this book. Use the information I provide as an introduction—not the final word.

Sleeping

Extensive and opinionated listings of good-value rooms are a major feature of this book's Sleeping sections. Rather than list accommodations scattered throughout a town, I choose places in my favorite neighborhoods that are convenient to your sightseeing.

My recommendations run the gamut, from dorm beds to luxurious rooms with all the comforts. I like places that are clean, central, relatively quiet at night, reasonably priced, friendly, small enough to have a hands-on owner or manager, and run with a respect for British traditions. I'm more impressed by a handy location and fun-loving philosophy than oversized TVs and a fancy gym. Most of my recommendations fall short of perfection. But if I can find a place with most of these features, it's a keeper.

Book your accommodations as soon as your itinerary is set, especially if you want to stay at one of my top listings or if you'll be traveling during busy times. See the appendix for a list of major holidays and festivals in Great Britain.

RATES AND DEALS

I've categorized my recommended accommodations based on price, indicated with a dollar-sign rating (see sidebar). Room prices can fluctuate significantly with demand and amenities (size, views, room class, and so on), but relative price categories remain constant. City taxes, which can vary from place to place, are generally insignificant (a few dollars per person, per night). In London, breakfast is often not included in quoted hotel rates; you can opt out of the pricey hotel breakfast and get it on your own for less.

Booking Direct: Once your dates are set, compare prices at several hotels. You can do this by checking hotel websites and booking sites such as Hotels.com or Booking.com. After you've zeroed in on your choice, book directly with the hotel itself. This increases the chances that the hotelier will be able to accommodate special needs or requests (such as shifting your reservation). And when you book on the hotel's website, by email, or by phone, the owner avoids the commission paid to booking sites, giving them

Sleep Code

Hotels in this book are categorized according to the average price of a standard double room with breakfast in high season.

$$$$	**Splurge:** Most rooms over £160
$$$	**Pricier:** £120-160
$$	**Moderate:** £80-120
$	**Budget:** £40-80
¢	**Backpacker:** Under £40
RS%	**Rick Steves discount**

Unless otherwise noted, credit cards are accepted and free Wi-Fi is available. Comparison-shop by checking prices at several hotels (on each hotel's own website, on a booking site, or by email). For the best deal, *book directly with the hotel.* Ask for a discount if paying in cash; if the listing includes **RS%,** request a Rick Steves discount.

wiggle room to offer you a discount, a nicer room, or a free breakfast (if it's not already included).

Getting a Discount: Some hotels extend a discount to those who pay cash or stay longer than three nights. And some accommodations offer a special discount for Rick Steves readers, indicated in this guidebook by the abbreviation **"RS%."** Discounts vary: Ask for details when you reserve. Generally, to qualify for this discount, you must book direct (not through a booking site), mention this book when you reserve, show this book upon arrival, and sometimes pay cash or stay a certain number of nights. In some cases, you may need to enter a discount code (which I've provided in the listing) in the booking form on the hotel's website. Rick Steves discounts apply to readers with either print or digital books. Understandably, discounts do not apply to promotional rates.

TYPES OF ACCOMMODATIONS
Hotels

In London, you'll find big, Old World-elegant hotels with modern amenities, as well as familiar-feeling business-class and boutique hotels no different from what you might experience at home. But you'll also find hotels that are more uniquely European.

Prices are extremely (sometimes shockingly) high in London. A hotel in the £100 range for a double is bare-bones basic; £200 is midrange (decent quality but, most likely, with some quirks and compromises); and for a really "nice" hotel, you may shell out £300-400. If those prices are too steep, consider a chain hotel (see page 414), or less-expensive alternatives (such as Airbnb).

A "twin" room has two single beds; a "double" has one double

Making Hotel Reservations

Reserve your rooms as soon as you've pinned down your travel dates. For busy national holidays, it's wise to reserve far in advance (see the appendix).

Requesting a Reservation: For family-run hotels, it's generally best to book your room directly via email or phone. For business-class and chain hotels, or if you'd rather book online, reserve directly through the hotel's official website (not a booking website).

Here's what the hotelier wants to know:

- Type(s) of room(s) you want and number of guests
- Number of nights you'll stay
- Arrival and departure dates, written European-style as day/month/year (for example, 18/06/23 or 18 June 2023)
- Special requests (en suite bathroom, cheapest room, twin beds vs. double bed, quiet room)
- Applicable discounts (such as a Rick Steves discount, cash discount, or promotional rate)

Confirming a Reservation: Most places will request a credit-card number to hold your room. If the hotel's website doesn't have a secure form where you can enter the number directly, share this info via a phone call.

Canceling a Reservation: If you must cancel, it's courteous—and smart—to do so with as much notice as possible, especially for smaller family-run places. Cancellation policies can be strict; read

bed. Some hotels can add an extra bed (for a small charge) to turn a double into a triple; some offer larger rooms for four or more people (I call these "family rooms" in the listings). If there's space for an extra cot, they'll cram it in for you. In general, a triple room is cheaper than the cost of a double and a single. Three or four people can economize by requesting one big room.

An "en suite" room has a bathroom (toilet and shower/tub) attached to the room; a room with a "private bathroom" can mean that the bathroom is all yours, but it's across the hall. If you want your own bathroom inside the room, request "en suite." If money's tight, ask about a room with a shared bathroom. You'll almost always have a sink in your room, and as more rooms go en suite, the hallway bathroom is shared with fewer guests.

Note that to be called a "hotel," a place technically must have certain amenities, including a 24-hour reception (though this rule is loosely applied).

Arrival and Check-In: Hotels and B&Bs are sometimes located on the higher floors of a multipurpose building with a secured door. In that case, look for your hotel's name on the buttons by the main entrance. When you ring the bell, you'll be buzzed in.

From: rick@ricksteves.com
Sent: Today
To: info@hotelcentral.com
Subject: Reservation request for 19-22 July

Dear Hotel Central,

I would like to stay at your hotel. Please let me know if you have a room available and the price for:
- 2 people
- Double bed and en suite bathroom in a quiet room
- Arriving 19 July, departing 22 July (3 nights)

Thank you!
Rick Steves

the fine print before you book. Many discount deals require pre-payment and can be expensive to change or cancel.

Reconfirming a Reservation: Always call or email to reconfirm your room reservation a few days in advance. For B&Bs or very small hotels, I call again on my arrival day to tell my host what time to expect me (especially important if arriving late—after 17:00).

Phoning: For tips on calling hotels overseas, see page 599.

Hotel elevators are common, though small, and some older buildings still lack them. You may have to climb a flight of stairs to reach the elevator (if so, you can ask the front desk for help carrying your bags up).

At check-in, the receptionist will normally ask for your passport so they can register your details; they may jot the information down immediately, or they may keep your passport for several hours. If you're not comfortable leaving your passport at the desk, bring a copy to give them instead.

If you're arriving in the morning, your room probably won't be ready. Check your bag safely at the hotel and dive right into sightseeing.

In Your Room: Most hotel rooms have a TV and free Wi-Fi, which can vary in strength and quality. Simpler places rarely have a room phone. Air-conditioning isn't a given (I've noted which of my listings have it), but most places have fans. Electrical outlets may have switches that turn the current on or off; if your appliance isn't working, flip the switch at the outlet.

Checking Out: While it's customary to pay for your room

PRACTICALITIES

Using Online Services to Your Advantage

From booking services to user reviews, online businesses play a greater role in travelers' planning than ever before. Take advantage of their pluses—and be wise to their downsides.

Booking Sites

Booking websites such as Booking.com and Hotels.com offer one-stop shopping for hotels. While convenient for travelers, they're both a blessing and a curse for small, independent, family-run hotels. Without a presence on these sites, small hotels become almost invisible. But to be listed, a hotel must pay a sizable commission...and promise that its own website won't undercut the price on the booking-service site.

Here's the work-around: Use the big sites to research what's out there, then book directly with the hotel by email or phone, in which case hotel owners are free to give you whatever price they like. Ask for a room without the commission markup (or ask for a free breakfast if not included, or a free upgrade). If you do book online, be sure to use the hotel's own website. The price will likely be the same as via a booking site, but your money goes to the hotel, not agency commissions.

As a savvy consumer, remember: When you book with an online service, you're adding a middleman who takes a cut. To support small, family-run hotels whose world is more difficult than ever, book direct.

Short-Term Rental Sites

Rental juggernaut Airbnb (along with other short-term rental sites) allows travelers to rent rooms and apartments, often providing more value, space, and amenities than a cookie-cutter hotel. Airbnb fans appreciate feeling part of a real neighborhood and getting into a daily routine as "temporary Europeans." Some places are run by thoughtful hosts, allowing you to get to know a local and keep your money in the community; but beware: others are impersonally managed by large, absentee agencies.

upon departure, it can be a good idea to settle your bill the day before, when you're not in a hurry and while the manager's in.

Hotelier Help: Hoteliers can be a good source of advice. Most know their city well and can assist you with everything from public transit and airport connections to finding a good restaurant, the nearest launderette, or a late-night pharmacy.

Hotel Hassles: Even at the best places, mechanical breakdowns occur: sinks leak, hot water turns cold, toilets may gurgle or smell, the Wi-Fi goes out, or the air-conditioning dies when you need it most. Report your concerns clearly and calmly at the front desk.

Critics of Airbnb see it as a threat to "traditional Europe." Landlords can make more money renting to short-stay travelers, driving rents up—and local residents out. Traditional businesses are replaced by ones that cater to tourists. And the character and charm that made those neighborhoods desirable to tourists in the first place goes too. Some cities have cracked down, requiring owners to obtain a license and to occupy rental properties part of the year (and staging disruptive "inspections" that inconvenience guests).

As a lover of Europe, I share the worry of those who see residents nudged aside by tourists. But as an advocate for travelers, I appreciate the value Airbnb can provide in offering the chance to stay in a local building or neighborhood with potentially fewer tourists.

User Reviews

User-generated review sites and apps such as Yelp and TripAdvisor can give you a consensus of opinions about everything from hotels and restaurants to sights and nightlife. If you scan reviews of a restaurant or hotel and see several complaints about noise or a rotten location, you've gained insight that can help in your decision-making.

As a guidebook writer, my sense is that there is a big difference between the uncurated information on a review site and the vetted listings in a guidebook. A user review is based on the limited experience of one person, who stayed at just one hotel in a given city and ate at a few restaurants there. A guidebook is the work of a trained researcher who forms a well-developed basis for comparison by visiting many restaurants and hotels year after year.

Both types of information have their place, and in many ways, they're complementary. If something is well reviewed in a guidebook and also gets good online reviews, it's likely a winner.

If you find that night noise is a problem (if, for instance, your room is over a noisy pub or facing a busy street), ask for a quieter room in the back or on an upper floor. To guard against theft in your room, keep valuables out of sight. Some rooms come with a safe, and other hotels have safes at the front desk. I've never bothered using one and in a lifetime of travel, I've never had anything stolen from my room.

For more complicated problems, don't expect instant results. Above all, keep a positive attitude. Remember, you're on vacation. If your hotel is disappointment, spend more time out enjoying the place you came to see.

B&Bs and Small Hotels

B&Bs and small hotels are generally family-run places with fewer amenities but more character than a conventional hotel. They range from large inns with 15-20 rooms to small homes renting out a spare bedroom. Places named "guesthouse" or "B&B" typi-

cally have eight or fewer rooms. The philosophy of the management determines the character of a place more than its size and amenities. I avoid places run as a business by absentee owners. My top listings are run by people who enjoy welcoming the world to their breakfast table.

Rules and Etiquette: B&Bs and small hotels come with their own etiquette and quirks. Keep in mind that owners are at the whim of their guests—if you're getting up early, so are they; if you check in late, they'll wait up for you. Most B&Bs have set check-in times (usually in the late afternoon). If arriving outside that time, they will want to know when to expect you (call or email ahead). Most will let you check in earlier if the room is available (or they'll at least let you drop off your bag).

B&Bs and small hotels often come with thin walls and doors, and sometimes creaky floorboards, which can make for a noisy night. If you're a light sleeper, bring earplugs. And please be quiet in the halls and in your rooms at night...those of us getting up early will thank you for it.

In the Room: Most B&Bs offer "tea service" in the room—an electric kettle, cups, tea bags, coffee packets, and a pack of biscuits.

Your bedroom probably won't include a phone, but nearly every B&B has free Wi-Fi. However, the signal may not reach all rooms; you may need to sit in the lounge to access it.

Paying: Most B&Bs take credit cards, but may add the card service fee to your bill (about 3 percent). If you do need to pay cash for your room, plan ahead to have enough on hand when you check out.

Short-Term Rentals

A short-term rental—whether an apartment (or "flat"), a house, or a room in a private residence—is a popular alternative, especially if you plan to settle in one location for several nights. For stays longer than a few days, you can usually find a rental that's comparable to—and cheaper than—a hotel room with similar amenities. Plus, you'll get a behind-the-scenes peek into how locals live.

Many places require a minimum stay and have strict cancellation policies. And you're generally on your own: There's no reception desk, breakfast, or daily cleaning service.

Finding Accommodations: Websites such as Airbnb, FlipKey, Booking.com, and VRBO let you browse a wide range of properties. Alternatively, rental agencies such as InterhomeUSA.com or RentaVilla.com can provide more personalized service (their curated listings are also more expensive). For a list of rental agencies for London, see page 418.

Before you commit, be clear on the location. I like to virtually "explore" the neighborhood using Google Street View. Also consider the proximity to public transportation and how well connected the property is with the rest of the city. Ask about amenities (elevator, air-conditioning, laundry, Wi-Fi, parking, etc.). Reviews from previous guests can help identify trouble spots.

Think about the kind of experience you want: Just a key and an affordable bed...or a chance to get to know a local? Some hosts offer self check-in and minimal contact; others enjoy interacting with you. Read the description and online reviews to help shape your decision.

Confirming and Paying: Many places require payment in full before your trip, usually through the listing site. Be wary of owners who want to take your transaction offline; this gives you no recourse if things go awry. Never agree to wire money (a key indicator of a fraudulent transaction).

Apartments or Houses: If you're staying in one place several nights, it's worth considering an apartment or rental house (shorter stays aren't worth the hassle of arranging key pickup, buying groceries, etc.). Apartment or house rentals can be especially cost-effective for groups and families. European apartments, like hotel rooms, tend to be small by US standards. But they often come with laundry machines and small, equipped kitchens, making it easier and cheaper to dine in.

Rooms in Private Homes: Renting a room in someone's home is a good option for those traveling alone, as you're more likely to find true single rooms—with just one single bed, and a price to match. These can range from air-mattress-in-living-room basic to plush-B&B-suite posh. While you can't expect your host to also be your tour guide—or even to provide you with much info—some are interested in getting to know the travelers who pass through their home.

Other Options: Swapping homes with a local works for people with an appealing place to offer (don't assume where you live is not interesting to Europeans). Good places to start are HomeExchange.com and LoveHomeSwap.com. To sleep for free, Couchsurfing.com is a vagabond's alternative to Airbnb. It lists millions of outgoing members, who host fellow "surfers" in their homes.

Hostels and Dorms

A hostel provides cheap beds in dorms where you sleep alongside strangers for about £20-30 per night. Travelers of any age are welcome if they don't mind dorm-style accommodations and meeting other travelers. Most hostels offer kitchen facilities, guest computers, Wi-Fi, and a self-service laundry. Hostels almost always provide bedding, but the towel's up to you (though you can usually rent one). Family and private rooms are often available.

Independent hostels tend to be easygoing, colorful, and informal (no membership required; www.hostelworld.com). You may pay slightly less by booking directly with the hostel.

Official hostels are part of Hostelling International (HI) and share an online booking site (www.hihostels.com). HI hostels typically require that you be a member or else pay a bit more per night. In Britain, these official hostels are run by the Youth Hostel Association (YHA, www.yha.org.uk).

Many London **colleges** rent out their dorms during school holidays, mainly during July, August, and early September. Types of accommodations vary, but are usually somewhat spartan (no phones or TVs in the rooms) and come with single or twin beds. For listings, see "Dorms" on page 418.

Eating

These days, the stereotype of "bad food in Britain" is woefully dated. Britain has caught up with the foodie revolution—in fact, they're right there, leading the vanguard—and I find it's easy to eat very well here. London, in particular, is one of Europe's best food destinations.

British cooking has embraced international influences and local, seasonal ingredients, making "modern British" food quite delicious. While some dreary pub food still exists, you'll generally find the cuisine scene here innovative and delicious (but expensive). Basic pubs are more likely to dish up homemade, creative dishes than microwaved pies, soggy fries, and mushy peas. Even traditional pub grub has gone upmarket, with gastropubs that serve locally sourced meats and fresh vegetables.

All of Britain is smoke-free. Expect restaurants and pubs to be

Restaurant Code

Eateries in this book are categorized according to the average cost of a typical main course. Drinks, desserts, and splurge items can raise the price considerably.

$$$$	**Splurge:** Most main courses over £20
$$$	**Pricier:** £15-20
$$	**Moderate:** £10-15
$	**Budget:** Under £10

In Great Britain, carryout fish-and-chips and other takeout food is **$**; a basic pub or sit-down eatery is **$$**; a gastropub or casual but more upscale restaurant is **$$$**; and a swanky splurge is **$$$$**.

nonsmoking indoors, with smokers occupying patios and doorways outside. You'll find the Brits eat at about the same time of day as Americans.

For listings in this guidebook, I look for restaurants that are convenient to your hotel and sightseeing. When restaurant-hunting, choose a spot filled with locals, not tourists. Venturing even a block or two off the main drag leads to higher-quality food for a better price.

Tipping: At pubs and places where you order at the counter, you don't have to tip. Regular customers ordering a round sometimes say, "Add one for yourself" as a tip for drinks ordered at the bar—but this isn't expected. Most restaurants and fancy pubs in London add a 12.5 percent tip onto the bill. If it's not included, a tip of generally 10-12 percent is standard, but tip only what you think the service warrants and be careful not to double tip.

RESTAURANT PRICING

I've categorized my recommended eateries based on the average price of a typical main course, indicated with a dollar-sign rating (see sidebar). Obviously, expensive specialties, fine wine, appetizers, and dessert can significantly increase your final bill.

The categories also indicate the personality of a place: **Budget** eateries include street food, takeaway, order-at-the-counter shops, basic cafeterias, and bakeries selling sandwiches. **Moderate** eateries are nice (but not fancy) sit-down restaurants, ideal for a pleasant meal with good-quality food. Most of my listings fall in this category—great for a taste of the local cuisine at a reasonable price.

Pricier eateries are a notch up, with more attention paid to the setting, presentation, and (often inventive) cuisine. **Splurge** eateries are dress-up-for-a-special-occasion-swanky—typically with an elegant setting, polished service, and pricey and refined cuisine.

BREAKFAST (Fry-Up)

The traditional fry-up or full English—generally included in the cost of your room—is famous as a hearty way to start the day. Also known as a "heart attack on a plate," your standard fry-up is a heated plate with eggs, Canadian-style bacon and/or sausage, a grilled tomato, sautéed mushrooms, baked beans, and sometimes potatoes, kippers (herring), or fried bread (sizzled in a greasy skillet). Toast comes in a rack (to cool quickly and crisply)

with butter and marmalade. The meal is typically topped off with tea or coffee. At a B&B or hotel, it may start with juice and cereal or porridge. Many progressive B&B owners offer vegetarian, organic, gluten-free, or other creative variations on the traditional breakfast.

As much as the full breakfast fry-up is a traditional way to start the morning, these days most places serve a healthier continental breakfast as well—with a buffet of yogurt, cereal, fruit, and pastries. At some hotels, the buffet may also include hot items, such as eggs and sausage.

LUNCH AND DINNER ON A BUDGET

Even in pricey cities, plenty of inexpensive choices are available: pub grub, daily lunch and early-bird dinner specials, global cuisine, cafeterias, fast food, picnics, greasy-spoon cafés, cheap chain restaurants, and pizza.

I've found that portions are huge, and **sharing plates** is generally just fine. Ordering two drinks, a soup or side salad, and splitting a £10 meat pie can make a good, filling meal. If you're on a limited budget, share a main course in a more expensive place for a nicer eating experience.

Pub grub is the most atmospheric budget option. You'll usually get hearty lunches and dinners priced reasonably under ancient timbers (see "Pubs," later). Gastropubs, with better food, are more expensive.

Classier restaurants have some affordable deals. Lunch is usually cheaper than dinner; a top-end, £30-for-dinner-type restaurant often serves the same quality two-course lunch deals for about half the price.

Many restaurants have **early-bird** or **pre-theater specials** of two or three courses, often for a significant savings. They are usually available only before 18:30 or 19:00 (and sometimes on weekdays only).

Global cuisine adds spice to Britain's food scene. Eating Indian, Bangladeshi, Chinese, or Thai is cheap (even cheaper if you do takeout). Middle Eastern shops sell gyro sandwiches, falafel, and *shawarmas* (grilled meat in pita bread). An Indian samosa (greasy, flaky meat-and-vegetable turnover) costs about £2 and makes a very cheap, if small, meal. (For more, see "Indian Cuisine," later.) You'll find inexpensive, quick Asian options (often Chinese), such as all-you-can-eat buffets and takeaway places serving up standard dishes in to-go boxes.

Fish-and-chips are a heavy, greasy, but tasty British classic. Every town (and every London neighborhood) has at least one "chippy" selling takeaway fish-and-chips in a cardboard box or (more traditionally) wrapped in paper for about £5-7. You can dip

your fries in ketchup, American-style, or "go British" and drizzle the whole thing with malt vinegar and fresh lemon.

Most large **museums** (and many historic **churches**) have handy, moderately priced cafeterias with forgettably decent food.

Picnicking saves time and money. Fine park benches and polite pigeons abound in most towns and city neighborhoods. You can easily get prepared food to go. The modern chain eateries on nearly every corner often have simple seating but are designed for takeout. Bakeries serve a wonderful array of fresh sandwiches and pasties (savory meat pastries). Street markets, generally parked in pedestrian-friendly zones, are fun and colorful places to stock up for a picnic (see "Street Markets" in the Shopping in London chapter).

Open-air markets and supermarkets sell produce in small quantities. The corner grocery store has fruit, drinks, fresh bread, tasty British cheese, meat, and local specialties. Supermarkets often have good deli sections, even offering Indian dishes, and sometimes salad bars. Decent packaged sandwiches (£3-4) are sold everywhere. Munch a relaxed "meal on wheels" picnic during your open-top bus tour or river cruise to save 30 precious minutes for sightseeing.

PUBS

Pubs are a fundamental part of the British social scene, and whether you're a teetotaler or a beer guzzler, they should be a part of your travel here. "Pub" is short for "public house." Each neighborhood has a "local" where everyone gathers. It's an extended common room where, if you don't mind the stickiness, you can feel the local pulse. Smart travelers use pubs to eat, drink, get out of the rain, watch sporting events, and make new friends.

It's interesting to consider the role pubs filled for Britain's working class in more modest times: For workers with humble domestic quarters and no money for a vacation, a beer at the corner pub was the closest they'd get to a comfortable living room, a place to entertain, and a getaway. And locals could meet people from far away in a pub—today, that's you!

Though hours vary, pubs generally serve beer daily from 11:00 to 23:00, though many are open later, particularly on Friday and Saturday. (Children are served food and soft drinks in pubs, but you must be 18 to order a beer.) As it nears closing time, you'll hear shouts of "last orders." Then comes the 10-minute warning bell. Finally, they'll call "Time!" to pick up your glass, finished or not, when the pub closes.

A cup of darts is free for the asking. People go to a public house to be social. They want to talk. Get vocal with a local. This is easiest at the bar, where people assume you're in the mood to talk (rather than at a table, where you're allowed a bit of privacy). The pub is the next best thing to having relatives in town. Cheers!

Pub Grub: For £8-15, you'll get a basic budget hot lunch or dinner in friendly surroundings. In high-priced London, this is your best indoor eating value. (For something more refined, try a **gastropub,** which serves higher-quality meals for £12-20.) The *Good Pub Guide* is an excellent resource (www.thegoodpubguide.co.uk). Pubs that are attached to restaurants, advertise their food, and are crowded with locals are more likely to have fresh food and a chef—and less likely to sell only lousy microwaved snacks.

Pubs generally serve traditional dishes, such as fish-and-chips, roast beef with Yorkshire pudding (batter-baked in the oven), and assorted meat pies, such as steak-and-kidney pie or shepherd's pie (stewed lamb topped with mashed potatoes) with cooked vegetables. Side dishes include salads, vegetables, and—invariably—"chips" (French fries). "Crisps" are potato chips. A "jacket potato" (baked potato stuffed with fillings of your choice) can almost be a meal in itself. A "ploughman's lunch" is a traditional British meal of bread, cheese, and sweet pickles. These days, you'll likely find more pasta, curried dishes, and quiche on the menu than traditional fare.

Meals are usually served from 12:00 to 14:00 and again from 18:00 to 20:00—with a break in the middle (rather than serving straight through the day). Since they make more money selling beer, many pubs stop food service early in the evening—especially on weekends. There's generally no table service. Order at the bar, and then take a seat. Either they'll bring the food when it's ready or you'll pick it up at the bar. Pay at the bar (sometimes when you order, sometimes after you eat). It's not necessary to tip unless it's a place with full table service. Servings are hearty, and service is quick. A beer, cider, or dram of whisky adds another couple of pounds. Free tap water is always available. For details on ordering beer and other drinks, see the "Beverages" section, later. For a list of recommended historic pubs in London, see page 430.

GOOD CHAIN RESTAURANTS

I know—you're going to Britain to enjoy characteristic little hole-in-the-wall pubs, so mass-produced food is the furthest thing from your mind. But several excellent chains with branches across the UK offer long hours, reasonable prices, reliable quality, and a nice break from pub grub. Expect to see these familiar names wherever you go:

$ Pret (a.k.a. Pret à Manger) is perhaps the most pervasive of these modern convenience eateries. Some are takeout only, and others have seating ranging from simple stools to restaurant-quality tables. The service is fast, the price is great, and the food is healthy and fresh. Their slogan: "Made today. Gone today. No 'sell-by' date, no nightlife."

$$ Côte Brasserie is a contemporary French chain serving good-value French cuisine in pleasant settings (early dinner specials).

Two **$** chains have reliably good coffee and pastries: **Paul** (French-style, with croissants, other pastries, and baguette sandwiches) and **Ole & Steen** (Scandinavian, with generous samples of cinnamon rolls). The coffee at either place is typically better than the ubiquitous British chains Costa and Nero.

$$ Le Pain Quotidien is a Belgian chain serving fresh-baked bread and hearty meals in a thoughtfully designed modern-rustic atmosphere.

$$ Wagamama Noodle Bar, serving pan-Asian cuisine (udon noodles, fried rice, and curry dishes), is a noisy, organic slurpathon. Portions are huge and splittable. There's one in almost every mid-size city in Britain, usually located in sprawling halls filled with long shared tables and busy servers who scrawl your order on the placemat.

$$$ Loch Fyne Restaurant is a Scottish chain that raises its own oysters and mussels. Its branches offer an inviting, lively atmosphere with a fine fishy energy and no pretense (early-bird specials).

$ Marks & Spencer department stores have inviting deli sections with cheery sit-down eating (along with their popular sandwiches-to-go section). M&S food halls are also handy if you're renting a city flat and want to prepare your own meals.

$$ Busaba is a hit in several cities for its snappy (sometimes rushed) service, boisterous ambience, and good, inexpensive Thai cuisine.

$$ Thai Square is a dependable Thai option with a nice atmosphere (salads, noodle dishes, curries, meat dishes, and daily lunch box specials).

$$ Masala Zone is a London chain providing a good, predictable alternative to the many one-off, hole-in-the-wall Indian joints around town. Try a curry-and-rice dish, a *thali* (platter with several small dishes), or their street food specials. Each branch has its own personality.

$$ Franco Manca is a taverna-inspired pizzeria serving Neapolitan-style pies using organic ingredients and boasting typical Italian charm. If you skip the pricey drinks, you can feast cheaply here.

$$ Ask and **Pizza Express** serve quality pasta and pizza in a pleasant, sit-down atmosphere that's family-friendly.

$$ Japanese: Three popular chains serve fresh and inexpensive Japanese food. **Itsu** and **Wasabi** are bright and competitive chains that let you assemble your own plate in a fun and efficient way, while **Yo! Sushi** lets you pick your dish off a conveyor belt and pay according to the color of your plate.

Carry-Out Chains: While the following may have some seating, they're best as places to grab prepackaged food on the run.

Major supermarket chains have smaller offshoot branches that specialize in sandwiches, salads, and other prepared foods to go. These can be a picnicker's dream come true. Some shops are stand-alone, while others are located inside a larger store. The most prevalent—and best—is **M&S Simply Food** (an offshoot of Marks & Spencer; there's one in every major train station). **Sainsbury's Local** grocery stores also offer decent prepared food; **Tesco Express** and **Tesco Metro** run a distant third.

INDIAN CUISINE

Eating Indian food is "going local" in cosmopolitan, multiethnic Britain. You'll find Indian restaurants in most cities, and even in small towns. Take the opportunity to sample food from Britain's former colony. Indian cuisine is as varied as the country itself. In general, it uses more exotic spices than British or American cuisine—some hot, some sweet. Indian food is very vegetarian-friendly, offering many meatless dishes.

For a simple meal that costs about £10-12, order one dish with rice and naan (Indian flatbread). Generally, one order is plenty for two people to share. Many Indian restaurants offer a fixed-price combination that offers more variety, and is simpler and cheaper than ordering à la carte. For about £20, you can make a mix-and-match platter out of several shareable dishes, including dal (simmered lentils) as a starter, one or two meat or vegetable dishes with sauce (for example, chicken curry, chicken *tikka masala* in a creamy tomato sauce, grilled fish tandoori, or chickpea *chana masala*), *raita* (a cooling yogurt that comes on the side—it helps extinguish your mouth if eating spicy dishes), rice, naan, and an Indian beer (wine and Indian food don't really mix) or spiced chai tea (usually served with milk). An easy way to taste a variety of dishes is to order a *thali*—a sampler plate of various specialties.

DESSERTS (SWEETS)

To the British, the traditional word for dessert is "pudding," although it's also referred to as "sweets" these days. Sponge cake, cream, fruitcake, and meringue are key players.

Trifle is the best-known British concoction, consisting of sponge cake soaked in brandy or sherry (or orange juice for children), then covered with jam and/or fruit and custard cream. Whipped cream can sometimes put the final touch on this "light" treat.

The British version of custard is a smooth, yellow liquid. Cream tops most everything that custard does not. There's single cream for coffee. Double cream is really thick. Clotted cream is the consistency of whipped butter.

Fool is a dessert with sweetened pureed fruit (such as rhubarb, gooseberries, or black currants) mixed with cream or custard and chilled. Elderflower is a popular flavoring for sorbet.

Flapjacks here aren't pancakes, but are dense, sweet oatmeal cakes (like a cross between a granola bar and a brownie). They come with toppings such as toffee and chocolate.

Scones are tops, and many inns and restaurants have their secret recipes. Whether made with fruit or topped with clotted cream, scones take the cake.

BEVERAGES

Beer: The British take great pride in their beer. Many locals think that drinking beer cold and carbonated, as Americans do, ruins the taste. Most pubs will have **lagers** (cold, refreshing, American-style

British Chocolate

My chocoholic readers are enthusiastic about British chocolates. As with other dairy products, chocolate seems richer and creamier here than it does in the US, so even standbys such as Mars, Kit Kat, and Twix have a different taste. Some favorites include Cadbury Gold bars (filled with liquid caramel), Cadbury Crunchie bars, Nestlé's Lion bars (layered wafers covered in caramel and chocolate), Cadbury's Boost bars (a shortcake biscuit with caramel in milk chocolate), Cadbury Flake (crumbly folds of melt-in-your-mouth chocolate), Aero bars (with "aerated" chocolate filling), and Galaxy chocolate bars (especially the ones with

hazelnuts). Thornton shops (in larger train stations) sell a box of sweets called the Continental Assortment, which comes with a tasting guide. (The highlight is the mocha white-chocolate truffle.) British M&Ms, called Smarties, are better than American ones. Many Brits feel that the ultimate treat is a box of either Nestlé Quality Street or Cadbury Roses—assortments of filled chocolates in colorful wrappers. (But don't mention the Kraft takeover of Cadbury in 2010—many Brits believe the American company changed the recipe for their beloved Dairy Milk bars, and they're not happy about it). At ice-cream vans, look for the beloved traditional "99p"—a vanilla soft-serve cone with a small Flake bar stuck right into the middle.

beer), **ales** (amber-colored, cellar-temperature beer), **bitters** (hop-flavored ale, perhaps the most typical British beer), and **stouts** (dark and somewhat bitter, like Guinness).

At pubs, long-handled pulls (or taps) are used to draw the traditional, rich-flavored "real ales" up from the cellar. These are the connoisseur's favorites and often come with fun names. Served straight from the brewer's cask at cellar temperature, real ales finish fermenting naturally and are not pasteurized or filtered, so they must be consumed within two or three days after the cask is tapped. Naturally carbonated, real ales have less gassiness and head; they vary from sweet to bitter, often with a hoppy or nutty flavor.

Short-handled pulls mean colder, fizzier, mass-produced, and less interesting keg beers. Mild beers are sweeter, with a creamy malt flavoring. Irish cream ale is a smooth, sweet experience. Try the draft cider (sweet or dry)...carefully.

Order your beer at the bar and pay as you go, with no need to tip. An average beer costs about £4. Part of the experience is standing before a line of hand pulls, and wondering which beer to choose.

As dictated by British law, draft beer and cider are served by the pint (20-ounce imperial size) or the half-pint (9.6 ounces). In 2011, the government sanctioned an in-between serving size—the schooner, or two-thirds pint (it's become a popular size for higher alcohol-content craft beers). A popular summer drink is a **shandy** (half beer and half British "lemonade," similar to 7-Up).

Whisky: While bar-hopping tourists generally think in terms of beer, many pubs are just as enthusiastic about serving whisky. If you are unfamiliar with whisky (what Americans call "Scotch" and the Irish call "whiskey"), it's a great conversation starter. Many pubs list dozens of whiskies and describe their taste profiles (peaty, smoky, woody, and so on).

A glass of basic whisky generally costs around £2.50. Let a local teach you how to drink it "neat," then add a little water. Make a friend, buy a few drams, and learn by drinking. Keep experimenting until you discover the right taste for you.

Other Alcoholic Drinks: Many pubs also have a good selection of wines by the glass and a fully stocked bar for the gentleman's "G and T" (gin and tonic). **Pimm's** is a refreshing and fruity summer liqueur, traditionally popular during Wimbledon. It's an upper-class drink—a rough bloke might insult a pub by claiming it sells more Pimm's than beer.

Non-Alcoholic Drinks: Teetotalers can order from a wide variety of soft drinks—both the predictable American sodas and other more interesting bottled drinks, such as ginger beer (similar to ginger ale but with more bite), root beers, or other flavors (Fentimans brews some unusual options that are stocked in many pubs).

Staying Connected

One of the most common questions I hear from travelers is, "How can I stay connected in Europe?" The short answer? More easily and affordably than you might think.

The simplest solution is to bring your own device—phone, tablet, or laptop—and use it much as you would at home, following the money-saving tips below, such as getting an international plan or connecting to free Wi-Fi whenever possible. Another option is to buy a European SIM card for your mobile phone. Or you can use European landlines and computers to connect. More details are at RickSteves.com/phoning.

USING YOUR PHONE IN EUROPE

Here are some budget tips and options.

Sign up for an international plan. To stay connected at a

The British Accent

In the olden days, a British person's accent indicated his or her social standing. Eliza Doolittle had the right idea—elocution could make or break you. Wealthier families would send their kids to fancy private schools to learn proper pronunciation. But these days, in a sort of reverse snobbery that has gripped the nation, accents are back. Politicians, newscasters, and movie stars are favoring deep accents over the Queen's English. While it's hard for American ears to pick out the variations, most Brits can determine where a person is from based on their accent...not just the region, but often the village, and even the part of town.

---

lower cost, sign up for an international service plan through your carrier. Most providers offer a simple bundle that includes calling, messaging, and data. Your normal plan may already include international coverage (for example, T-Mobile's covers data and text, but not voice calls).

Before your trip, research your provider's international rates. Activate the plan a day or two before you leave, then remember to cancel it when your trip's over.

Use free Wi-Fi whenever possible. Unless you have an unlimited-data plan, save most of your online tasks for Wi-Fi. Most accommodations in Europe offer free Wi-Fi. Many cafés (including Starbucks and McDonald's) offer hotspots for customers; ask for the password when you buy something. You may also find Wi-Fi at TIs, city squares, major museums, public-transit hubs, airports, and aboard trains and buses. In Britain, another option is to sign up for Wi-Fi access through a company such as BT (one hour-£4, one day-£10, www.btwifi.co.uk) or The Cloud (free though sometimes slow, www.skywifi.cloud).

Minimize the use of your cellular network. The best way to make sure you're not accidentally burning through data is to put your device in "airplane" mode (which also disables phone calls and texts) and connect to Wi-Fi as needed. When you need to get online but can't find Wi-Fi, simply turn on your cellular network (or turn off airplane mode) just long enough for the task at hand.

Even with an international data plan, wait until you're on Wi-Fi to Skype or FaceTime, download apps, stream videos, or do other megabyte-greedy tasks. Using a navigation app such as Google Maps over a cellular network can require lots of data, so download maps when you're on Wi-Fi, then use the app offline.

Limit automatic updates. By default, your device constantly checks for a data connection and updates app content. Check your device's settings menu for ways to turn this off, and change your

How to Dial

Here's how to dial from anywhere in the US or Europe, using the phone number of one of my recommended London hotels as an example (020 7730 8191). If a number starts with 0, drop it when dialing internationally (except when calling Italy).

From a US Mobile Phone
Phone numbers in this book are presented exactly as you would dial them from a US mobile phone. For international access, press and hold 0 (zero) to get a + sign, then dial the country code (44 for Britain) and phone number.

▸ To call the London hotel from any location, dial +44 20 7730 8191.

From a US Landline
Replace + with 011 (US/Canada access code), then dial the country code (44 for Britain) and phone number.

▸ To call the London hotel from your home landline, dial 011 44 20 7730 8191.

From a European Landline
Replace + with 00 (Europe access code), then dial the country code (44 for Britain, 1 for the US) and phone number.

▸ To call the London hotel from a French landline, dial 00 44 20 7730 8191.

▸ To call my US office from a British landline, dial 00 1 425 771 8303.

From One British Phone to Another
To place a domestic call (from a British landline or mobile), drop +44 and dial the phone number (including the initial 0).

▸ To call the London hotel from Edinburgh, dial 020 7730 8191.

More Dialing Tips
Local Numbers: European phone numbers and area codes can vary in length and spacing, even within the same country. Mobile phones use separate prefixes (for instance, in Britain, mobile numbers begin with 07).

Toll and Toll-Free Calls: It's generally not possible to dial European toll or toll-free numbers from a US mobile or landline (although you can sometimes get through using Skype). Look for a direct-dial number instead.

Calling the US from a US Mobile Phone, While Abroad: Dial +1, area code, and number.

More Phoning Help: See HowToCallAbroad.com.

email settings from "auto-retrieve" to "manual" (or from "push" to "fetch").

Use Wi-Fi calling and messaging apps. Skype, WhatsApp, FaceTime, and Google Meet are great for making free or low-cost calls or sending texts over Wi-Fi worldwide. Just log on to a Wi-Fi network, then connect with friends, family members, or local contacts who use the same service.

Buy a European SIM card. If you anticipate making a lot of local calls or need a local phone number, or if your provider's in-

PRACTICALITIES

Tips on Internet Security

Make sure that your device is running the latest versions of its operating system, security software, and apps. Next, ensure that your device and key programs (like email) are password-protected. On the road, use only secure, password-protected Wi-Fi. Ask the hotel or café staff for the specific name of their network, and make sure you log on to that exact one.

If you must access your financial info online, use a banking app rather than accessing your account via a browser, and use a cellular connection, not Wi-Fi. Never log on to personal finance sites on a public computer. If you're very concerned, consider subscribing to a VPN (virtual private network).

ternational data rates are expensive, consider buying a SIM card in Europe to replace the one in your (unlocked) US phone or tablet. SIM cards are sold at department-store electronics counters and some newsstands (you may need to show your passport), and vending machines. If you need help setting it up, buy one at a mobile-phone shop.

There are generally no roaming charges when using a European SIM card in other EU countries, but confirm when you buy.

WITHOUT A MOBILE PHONE

It's less convenient but possible to travel in Europe without a mobile device. You can make calls from your hotel and check email or get online using public computers.

Most **hotels** charge a fee for placing calls. You can use a prepaid international phone card (usually available at newsstands, tobacco shops, and train stations) to call out from your hotel.

Some hotels have **public computers** in their lobbies for guests to use; otherwise you may find them at public libraries (ask your hotelier or the TI for the nearest location). On a European keyboard, use the "Alt Gr" key to the right of the space bar to insert the extra symbol that appears on some keys. If you can't locate a special character (such as @), simply copy and paste it from a web page.

MAIL

You can mail one package per day to yourself worth up to $200 duty-free from Europe to the US (mark it "personal purchases"). If you're sending a gift to someone, mark it "unsolicited gift." For details, visit www.cbp.gov, select "Travel," and search for "Know Before You Go." The British postal service works fine, but for quick transatlantic delivery (in either direction), consider services such as DHL (DHL.com). For postcards, get stamps at the neighborhood post office, newsstands within fancy hotels, and some minimarts and card shops.

Transportation

If your trip covers more of Britain than just London, you may need to take a long-distance train or bus, rent a car, or fly. Buses are an alternative to trains (and may be your only option for reaching some small British towns), but they are generally slower and less efficient. Renting a car is great for touring rural areas, such as the Cotswolds, northwest of London. I give some specifics on trains, buses, and flights here. For more detailed information on transportation throughout Europe, see RickSteves.com/transportation.

TRAINS

Regular tickets on Britain's great train system (15,000 departures from 2,400 stations daily) are the most expensive per mile in all of Europe. For the greatest savings, book online in advance and leave after rush hour (after 9:30 weekdays).

Since Britain's railways have been privatized, a single train route can be operated by multiple companies. However, one website covers all train lines (www.nationalrail.co.uk), and another covers all bus and train routes (www.traveline.info for information, not ticket sales). Another good resource, which also has schedules for trains throughout Europe, is German Rail's timetable (www.bahn.com).

As with airline tickets, British train tickets can come at many different prices for the same journey. A clerk at any station can figure out the cheapest fare for your trip.

While generally not required, reservations are free and can normally be made well in advance or up to two hours before train time. They are an especially good idea for long journeys or for travel on weekends or holidays. Make reservations online, at any train station, or by phone. You must reserve in advance for Caledonian Sleeper overnight trains between London and Scotland (www.sleeper.scot).

For information on the high-speed Eurostar train through the "Chunnel" to Paris, Brussels, or Amsterdam, see page 495.

Rail Passes

Since Britain's pay-as-you-go train tickets are some of the most expensive in Europe, BritRail passes can pay for themselves quickly, especially if you ride a long-distance train (for example, between London and Scotland). A rail pass offers hop-on flexibility and no need to lock in reservations, except for overnight sleeper cars and LNER trains.

PRACTICALITIES

Great Britain's Public Transportation

Rail
Eurostar
Bus
(8H) Ferry with crossing time

N

50 Kilometers
50 Miles

Orkney Islands
Stromness
Scrabster   Gill
John O' Groats
Thurso
Lewis
Elgin
Skye   Inverness
Portree
Culloden
Kyle   Loch   Aviemore   Aberdeen
Mallaig   Ness
Fort William   SCOTLAND
Pitlochry
Mull   Perth   Dundee
Oban   Leuchars
Stirling   St. Andrews
Edinburgh
North Sea
Glasgow   Berwick
Holy Island
(2H)   Cairnryan   Hexham
Larne (2-3H)   Carlisle   Newcastle   To Amsterdam (15H)
Stranraer   Durham
Belfast   Keswick   Penrith   Whitby
N. IRE.   Windermere   Danby   Scarborough
Settle
Isle of Man   ENGLAND
Irish Sea   Blackpool   Preston   Leeds   York   Hull
Dublin   (7H)   Liverpool   To Zeebrugge (10H)
(2-3H)   Holyhead   Conwy   Manchester   Grimsby
Bangor   Chester   Lincoln
REP. OF IRE.   Caernarfon   Betws-y-Coed   Stoke   Peter-   King's Lynn
Bed.   Blaenau   Derby   borough   Norwich
Pwllheli   Ffest.   Telford
Harlech   Wolv.   Ely
Aberystwyth   Birmingham   Cambridge
To Rosslare   Ironbridge   Coventry   Harwich
(3.5H)   Gorge   Warwick   To Hoek (6H)
WALES   Stratford
Carmarthen   Chelt.   Moreton   Ebbs-   Canterbury
Fishguard   Stow   Oxford   fleet
Swansea   Newport   London   Dover
Cardiff   Bath   Windsor   Ashford   1.5H
Atlantic Ocean   Bristol   Reading   To Calais
Wells   STONE-   EUROSTAR
Glastonbury   West-   HENGE   Salisbury   (2.5H)
Exeter   bury   Brighton
Dartmoor   Southampton   Portsmouth   Newhaven   (4H)
To Dieppe
Truro   English Channel   To Paris, Brussels & Amsterdam
St. Ives   Plymouth
Penzance   Falmouth   To Roscoff   To St-Malo   To Caen   FRANCE
(6H)   (11H)   (Ouistreham)

The BritRail pass (covering England, Scotland, and Wales) and the BritRail England-only pass come in "consecutive day" and "flexi" versions, with price breaks for youths (under age 26), seniors (60 and up), and groups of three or more. Most allow one child under 16 to travel free with a paying adult or senior. If you're exploring the backcountry with a BritRail pass, second class is a good choice since many of the smaller train lines don't even offer first-class cars.

Other BritRail options include Scotland-only passes, "London Plus" passes (good for travel in most of southeast England but not in London itself), and South West passes (good for the Cotswolds, Bath, Dorset, Devon, Cornwall, plus part of South Wales).

Most rail passes are delivered electronically: It's smart to set this up before you leave home, and make reservations in advance for sleeper trains or LNER departures (required with a Eurail pass, mostly running London-York-Newcastle-Edinburgh, www.lner.co.uk/travel-information/make-a-reservation). You can make optional, free seat reservations (recommended for busy weekends) at staffed train stations.

If your travels are taking you from Britain to the Continent, the Eurail Global Pass covers trains on both sides of the English Channel, and Eurostar trains beneath it (with a paid seat reservation). It's generally cheaper to buy one pass for your whole trip than separate, single-country passes. Global passes also come in "consecutive day" and "flexi" versions, with price breaks for youths (under age 28) and seniors (60 and up). Up to two kids under 12 travel free with you on an adult-rate pass.

For more detailed advice on figuring out the smartest rail-pass options for your train trip, visit RickSteves.com/rail.

Buying Tickets

In Advance: The best fares go to those who book their trips well in advance of their journey. Savings can be significant. For a London-York round-trip (standard class), the peak "anytime" fare is about £245 (usually paid by business travelers) and up to £106 for "off-peak." However, if you book online at least a week ahead, off-peak and advance-purchase discounts can combine for a rate closer to £60. An "advance" fare for the same ticket booked a couple of months out can cost as little as £40. If traveling round-trip on a single line, buy the return ticket at the same time for a big savings over two single (one-way) tickets. If traveling longer distances, such as from Scotland to England, expect higher fares but greater advance discounts.

You'll get the cheapest fare if you lock in a specific time and train operator, with a nonrefundable or nontransferable ticket. On the other hand, full-fare "anytime" rates are valid on any train on

PRACTICALITIES

Rail Pass or Point-to-Point Tickets?

Will you be better off buying a rail pass or point-to-point tickets? It pays to know your options and choose what's best for your itinerary.

Rail Passes

A BritRail Pass lets you travel by train in Scotland, England, and Wales for two to eight days within a one-month period, 15 days within two months, or for continuous periods of up to one month. In addition, BritRail sells England-only and other regional passes. Britain is also covered (along with most of Europe) by the classic Eurail Global Pass. Discounted rates are offered for children, youths, and seniors.

While most rail passes are delivered electronically, it's smart to get your pass sorted before leaving home. For more on rail passes, including current prices and purchasing, visit RickSteves.com/rail.

Point-to-Point Tickets

If you're taking just a couple of train rides, buying individual point-to-point train tickets may save you money over a pass. Use this map to add up approximate pay-as-you-go fares for your itinerary, and compare that to the price of a rail pass. Keep in mind that significant discounts on point-to-point tickets may be available with advance purchase.

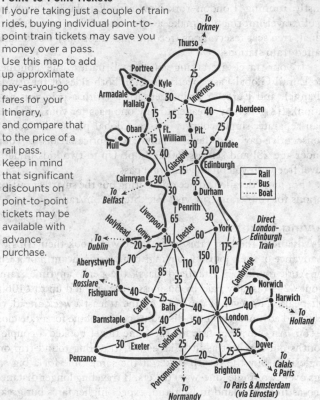

Map shows approximate costs, in US dollars, for one-way, second-class tickets at off-peak rates.

the route within a one- or two-day window (or longer on "open return" tickets). "Off-peak" tickets are similarly flexible outside of rush hours.

To book ahead, you have several options:

Book **online** at NationalRail.co.uk. Once you select a train, you'll be transferred to the website of the company that runs that service, where you can book the ticket. (Choose carefully, as it can be tough to change an online reservation.) Electronic tickets (with a scannable QR code) are increasingly available and the easiest choice; otherwise, you may be able to print out your ticket at home, or you pick it up at the station. (Note that BritRail pass holders cannot make online seat reservations, except on LNER routes.)

Another option is the **Trainline app,** where you can check schedules and book tickets, which are available on your phone instantly (the only downside may be difficulty making exchanges).

You can also **call** +44 345 748 4950 (phone answered 24 hours) to find out the schedule and best fare for your journey; you'll then be referred to the appropriate vendor—depending on the particular rail company—to book your ticket.

If you're already in Britain, and you'd rather have the flexibility of booking tickets as you go, just swing by any train station and talk to a **real person,** who can help you figure out the best option and sell you a ticket straightaway. Plenty of user-friendly **ticket machines** are also standing by. You can save a few pounds by buying before 18:00 the day before you depart; traveling after the morning rush hour (this usually means after 9:30 Mon-Fri); and going standard class instead of first class. Preview your options on NationalRail.co.uk or the Trainline app.

A company called **Megabus** (through their subsidiary Megatrain) sells some discounted train tickets well in advance on a few specific routes, though their focus is mainly on selling bus tickets (www.megatrain.com).

Senior, Youth, Partner, and Family Deals: To get a third off the price of most point-to-point rail tickets in Great Britain for use within a year, seniors can buy a Senior Railcard (ages 60 and up), younger travelers can buy a 16-25 Railcard (ages 16-25, or full-time students 26 and older), and two people traveling together can buy a Two Together Railcard (ages 16 and over). A Family and Friends Railcard gives adults about 33 percent off for most trips and 60 percent off for their kids age 5 to 15 (maximum 4 adults and 4 kids). Each Railcard costs £30; for non-UK citizens, it's best to purchase the card at a staffed rail station in England, Scotland, or Wales as you need a UK delivery address to buy it online (also sold at some London airports, some cards require passport-type photo, passport needed for proof of age; see www.railcard.co.uk).

Using Tickets

Larger British train stations—including in London—have turnstiles for accessing the platforms. You'll need to insert or scan your ticket both to enter the platform and to leave the platform when you arrive at your destination.

There are two general types of tickets. If you buy a ticket in-person at the station, you'll get a **paper ticket** about the size of a credit card. At the turnstile, insert this in the slot, and it'll pop out another slot for you to reclaim. Once a ticket has been used, the turnstile may not give it back. If you purchase a round-trip ticket, you'll get separate tickets for each leg.

An **electronic ticket or rail pass** will appear as a QR code on your smartphone. To open the turnstile, hold this code up to the scanner that sits just below the paper ticket slot.

If you have a **paper rail pass,** simply show it to the attendant at the turnstile, and they will let you through.

BUSES

Most domestic buses are operated by **National Express** (+44 871 781 8181, www.nationalexpress.com); their international departures are called **Eurolines** (www.eurolines.de).

A smaller company called **Megabus** undersells National Express with deeply discounted promotional fares—the further ahead you buy, the less you pay (some trips for just £1.50, toll call +44 871 266 3333, www.megabus.com). While Megabus can be much cheaper than National Express, they tend to be slower than their competitor and their routes mainly connect cities, not smaller towns. They also sell discounted train tickets on selected routes.

Buy tickets early if you are traveling on Friday or Sunday evening, when weekend travelers are more likely to make buses sell out.

To ensure getting a ticket—and to save money with special promotions—book your ticket in advance online or over the phone. The cheapest pre-purchased tickets usually cannot be changed or refunded and must be booked at least two days ahead. Round-trip bus tickets usually cost less than two one-way fares.

TAXIS AND RIDE-BOOKING SERVICES

Most British taxis are reliable and cheap. In many cities, two people can travel short distances by cab for little more than the cost of bus or subway tickets. If you like ride-booking services such as Uber, their apps usually work in Britain just like they do in the US: Request a car on your mobile phone (connected to Wi-Fi or data), and the fare is automatically charged to your credit card.

FLIGHTS

To compare flights, begin with an online travel search engine: Kayak is the top site for flights to and within Europe, easy-to-use Google Flights has price alerts, and Skyscanner includes many inexpensive flights within Europe. To avoid unpleasant surprises, before you book be sure to read the small print about refunds, changes, and the costs for "extras" such as reserving a seat, checking a bag, or printing a boarding pass.

Flights to Europe: Start looking for international flights about four to six months before your trip, especially for peak-season travel. Depending on your itinerary, it can be efficient and no more expensive to fly into one city and out of another. If your flight requires a connection in Europe, see my hints on navigating Europe's top hub airports at RickSteves.com/hub-airports.

Flights Within Europe: Flying between European cities is surprisingly affordable. Before buying a long-distance train or bus ticket, check the cost of a flight on one of Europe's airlines, whether a major carrier or a no-frills outfit like **EasyJet** or **Ryanair.** Other airlines to consider include **TUI Airways** (www.tui.co.uk) and **Brussels Airlines** (with frequent connections from Heathrow to its Brussels hub, www.brusselsairlines.com).

Be aware that flying with a discount airline can have drawbacks, such as minimal customer service, time-consuming treks to secondary airports, and a larger carbon footprint than a train or bus.

Flying to the US and Canada: Because security is extra tight for flights to the US, be sure to give yourself plenty of time at the airport (see www.tsa.gov for the latest rules).

Resources from Rick Steves

Begin Your Trip at RickSteves.com

My mobile-friendly **website** is *the* place to explore Europe in preparation for your trip. You'll find thousands of fun articles, videos, and radio interviews; a wealth of money-saving tips for planning your dream trip; travel news dispatches; a video library of travel talks; my travel blog; our latest guidebook updates (RickSteves.com/update); and the free Rick Steves Audio Europe app. You can also follow me on Facebook, Instagram, and Twitter.

Our **Travel Forum** is a well-groomed collection of message boards, where our travel-savvy community answers questions and shares their personal travel experiences—and our well-traveled staff chimes in when they can be helpful (RickSteves.com/forums).

Our **online Travel Store** offers bags and accessories that I've designed to help you travel smarter and lighter. These include my popular carry-on bags (which I live out of four months a year), money belts, totes, toiletries kits, adapters, guidebooks, and planning maps (RickSteves.com/shop).

Our website can also help you find the perfect **rail pass** for your itinerary and your budget, with easy, one-stop shopping for rail passes, seat reservations, and point-to-point tickets (RickSteves.com/rail).

Rick Steves' Tours, Guidebooks, TV Shows, and More

Small Group Tours: Want to travel with greater efficiency and less stress? We offer more than 40 itineraries reaching the best destinations in this book...and beyond. Each year about 30,000 travelers join us on about 1,000 Rick Steves bus tours. You'll enjoy great guides and a fun bunch of travel partners (with small groups of 24 to 28 travelers). You'll find European adventures to fit every vacation length. For all the details, and to get our tour catalog, visit RickSteves.com/tours or call us at +1 425 608 4217.

Books: This book is just one of many books in my series on European travel, which includes country and city guidebooks, Snapshots (excerpted chapters from bigger guides), Pocket Guides (full-color little books on big cities), "Best Of" guidebooks (condensed, full-color country guides), and my budget-travel skills handbook, *Rick Steves Europe Through the Back Door.* A complete list of my titles—including phrase books, cruising guides, and travelogues on European Art, history, and culture—appears near the end of this book.

TV Shows and Travel Talks: My public television series, *Rick Steves' Europe,* covers Europe from top to bottom with over 100 half-hour episodes—and we're working on new shows every year (watch full episodes at my website for free). My free online video library, Rick Steves Classroom Europe, offers a searchable database of short video clips on European history, culture, and geography (Classroom.RickSteves.com). And to raise your travel I.Q., check out the video versions of our popular classes (covering most European countries as well as travel skills, packing smart, cruising, tech for travelers, European art, and travel as a political act—RickSteves.com/travel-talks.

Audio Tours on My Free App: I've produced dozens of free, self-guided audio tours of the top sights in Europe. For those tours and other audio content, get my free **Rick Steves Audio Europe app,** an extensive online library organized by destination. For more on my app, see page 22.

Radio: My weekly public radio show, *Travel with Rick Steves*, features interviews with travel experts from around the world. It airs on 400 public radio stations across the US. An archive of programs is available at RickSteves.com/radio.

Podcasts: You can enjoy my travel content via several free podcasts. The podcast version of my radio show brings you a weekly, hour-long travel conversation. My other podcasts include a weekly selection of video clips from my public television show, my audio tours of Europe's top sights, and live recordings of my travel classes (RickSteves.com/watch-read-listen/audio/podcasts).

APPENDIX

Holidays and Festivals

This list includes selected festivals in London, major events in Windsor and Cambridge, plus national holidays observed throughout Great Britain. Many sights and banks close on national holidays—keep this in mind when planning your itinerary. Before planning a trip around a festival, verify the dates with the festival website, London TI sites (www.visitlondon.com and www.visitbritain.com), or my "Upcoming Holidays and Festivals in England" web page at RickSteves.com/europe/england/festivals.

In London, hotels get booked up on major holidays—New Year's Day, Easter weekend, Christmas, and Boxing Day—and on Fridays and Saturdays year-round. Some hotels require you to book the full three-day weekend around Bank Holiday Mondays. Sights are also more crowded during holiday periods.

Jan 1	New Year's Day
Mid-late Feb	London Fashion Week (www.londonfashionweek.co.uk)
March/April	Easter Weekend (Good Friday-Easter Monday): April 7-10, 2023; March 29-April 1, 2024
May (first Mon)	Early May Bank Holiday: May 1, 2023; May 6, 2024

May (last Mon)	Spring Bank Holiday: May 29, 2023; May 27, 2024
Late May	Chelsea Flower Show, London (book tickets ahead at www.rhs.org.uk/chelsea)
Early-mid June	Trooping the Colour, London (military bands and pageantry, Queen's birthday parade; www.qbp.army.mod.uk)
Late June	Royal Ascot Horse Race, Ascot (near Windsor; www.ascot.co.uk)
Late June-mid July	Wimbledon Tennis Championship, London (www.wimbledon.com)
Late July-early Aug	Cambridge Folk Festival, Cambridge (buy tickets early at www.cambridgefolkfestival.co.uk)
Late Aug	Notting Hill Carnival, London (costumes, Caribbean music, www.thelondonnottinghillcarnival.com)
Aug (last Mon)	Late summer Bank Holiday: Aug 28, 2023; Aug 26, 2024
Mid-late Sept	London Fashion Week (www.londonfashionweek.co.uk)
Nov 5	Bonfire Night (bonfires, fireworks, effigy burning of 1605 traitor Guy Fawkes)
Nov (second Sun)	Remembrance Sunday (royals lay wreaths at Cenotaph for WWI dead)
Mid-Nov (second Sat)	Lord Mayor's Show, London (huge parade in The City with fireworks, www.lordmayorsshow.london)
Dec 24-26	Christmas holidays (many sights close; limited or no public transport)

Books and Films

To learn more about London past and present, check out a few of these books or films. For kids' recommendations, see the London with Children chapter.

Nonfiction

84, Charing Cross Road (Helene Hanff, 1970). Correspondence between a proper London bookseller and an outspoken New York writer turns into a trans-Atlantic friendship (also a 1987 movie with Anthony Hopkins and Anne Bancroft). In the sequel, *The Duchess of Bloomsbury Street*, the writer travels to London.

Elizabeth's London (Liza Picard, 2005). The author re-creates 16th-century life in the era of England's first great queen.

Fever Pitch (Nick Hornby, 1992). Hornby's memoir illuminates the British obsession with soccer.

A History of London (Stephen Inwood, 1998). Two thousand years of city history is laid out over 1,000 pages.

The Last Lion (William Manchester, final book completed by Paul Reid; 1983, 1988, and 2012). This superb three-volume biography recounts the amazing life of Winston Churchill from 1874 to 1965.

Letters from London (Julian Barnes, 1995). The *New Yorker*'s former London correspondent captures life in the city in the early 1990s.

London: The Biography (Peter Ackroyd, 2001). The author uses an imaginative biographical approach to tell London's story.

Longitude (Dava Sobel, 1995). A London clockmaker solves the problem of keeping time aboard a ship—a timely read for visitors to Greenwich.

Notes from a Small Island (Bill Bryson, 1995). In this irreverent and delightful memoir, US expat Bryson writes about his travels through Britain—his home for two decades.

St Pancras Station (Simon Bradley, 2007). Bradley presents a treasure trove of history about London's iconic gateway to Europe.

A Traveller's History of England (Christopher Daniell, revised 2005). A British archaeologist and historian provides a comprehensive yet succinct overview of English history.

With Wings Like Eagles (Michael Korda, 2009). An English-born writer gives a historical analysis of Britain's pivotal WWII air battles versus the German Luftwaffe.

Fiction

For the classics of British fiction, read anything—and everything—by Charles Dickens, Jane Austen, and the Brontës. Some favorites that feature London include *Persuasion,* the beloved Austen book partially set in Bath, and Charles Dickens' tale of a workhouse urchin, *Oliver Twist.* Here are some other good reads:

Brick Lane (Monica Ali, 2003). A Bangladeshi woman in an arranged marriage to an older man raises her family—and starts an affair with a young radical—in contemporary London (also a 2007 film).

Bridget Jones's Diary (Helen Fielding, 1996). A year in the life of a single 30-something woman in London is humorously chronicled in diary form (also a motion picture).

The Buddha of Suburbia (Hanif Kureishi, 1990). The son of a self-proclaimed suburban guru gets swept up in the fast lane of 1970s London.

Confessions of a Shopaholic (Sophie Kinsella, 2001). A London woman lives beyond her means in this funny tale of modern English life.

The Great Stink (Clare Clark, 2005). A Crimean War veteran seeks refuge working in the London sewer system, but is sucked into a murder mystery.

High Fidelity (Nick Hornby, 1995). This humorous novel traces the romantic misadventures and musical musings of a 30-something record-store owner. Another good read is Hornby's 1998 coming-of-age story, *About a Boy*. (Both books were also made into films.)

In the Presence of the Enemy (Elizabeth George, 1996). London's movers and shakers commit sins and scandals in this detective story.

The Jupiter Myth (Lindsey Davis, 2002). In AD 75, an investigator from Rome probes a murder in what was then known as Londinium.

London (Edward Rutherfurd, 1997). This big and sprawling historical novel begins in ancient times and continues through to the 20th century.

Mapp and Lucia (E. F. Benson, 1931). A rural village in the 1930s becomes a social battlefield. In *Lucia in London* (1927), the protagonist attempts social climbing in the big city.

The Paying Guests (Sarah Waters, 2014). This realistic and suspenseful tale of love, obsession, and murder plays out amid the shifting culture of post-WWII upper-class London.

Pygmalion (George Bernard Shaw, 1913). This stage play, on which the film *My Fair Lady* is based, tells the story of a young Cockney girl groomed for high society.

Rumpole of the Bailey (Sir John Mortimer, 1978). Mortimer's popular detective story about an aging London barrister spawned a series of books and TV shows.

Saturday (Ian McEwan, 2005). The protagonist endures a series of strange events in London during a day of protest over the invasion of Iraq.

SS-GB (Len Deighton, 1979). In Nazi-occupied Great Britain, a Scotland Yard detective finds there's more to a murder than meets the eye.

A Study in Scarlet (Sir Arthur Conan Doyle, 1888). This mystery novel introduced the world to detective Sherlock Holmes and his trusty sidekick, Dr. Watson.

Thank You, Jeeves (P. G. Wodehouse, 1934). The author's first full-length novel is about the competent valet to a wealthy and foolish Londoner (also many short stories and sequels).

White Teeth (Zadie Smith, 2000). The postwar lives of two army buddies, a native Englishman and a Bengali Muslim, are chronicled in this acclaimed novel.

Film and TV

Alfie (1966). In 1960s London, a womanizer (Michael Caine) eventually must face up to his boorish behavior (also a 2004 remake with Jude Law). Other "swinging London" films include *Blow-up* (1966) and *Georgy Girl* (1966).

Battle of Britain (1969). An all-star cast and marvelous aerial combat scenes tell the story of Britain's "finest hour" of World War II.

Blackadder (1983-1989). This wickedly funny BBC sitcom starring Rowan Atkinson skewers various periods of English history over the course of four series (also several TV specials).

Call the Midwife (2012-). London's poor East End comes to gritty, poignant life in this BBC drama tracing the lives of a team of nurse midwives in the late 1950s and early 1960s.

The Crown (2016-). The Netflix biographical drama explores the life of Elizabeth II—England's longest-reigning queen.

The Elephant Man (1980). A severely disfigured man reveals his sensitive soul in this stark portrayal of Victorian London.

GoldenEye (1995). This James Bond film features the first look at the iconic MI6 headquarters, located in the center of London.

A Hard Day's Night (1964). The Beatles star in their debut film, a comedy depicting several days in the life of the band.

Hope and Glory (1987). John Boorman directed this semi-autobiographical story of a boy growing up during World War II and the London Blitz.

The King's Speech (2010). Colin Firth stars as the stuttering King George VI on the eve of World War II.

My Beautiful Laundrette (1985). This gritty, compelling movie tells the story of two gay men in urban London.

My Fair Lady (1964). Audrey Hepburn stars as a poor, Cockney flower seller who is transformed into a lady of high society by an arrogant professor.

Notting Hill (1999). Hugh Grant and Julia Roberts star in this romantic comedy set in the London neighborhood of...you guessed it.

The Queen (2006). Helen Mirren expertly channels Elizabeth II in the days after Princess Diana's death. Its prequel, *The Deal* (2003), probes the relationship between Tony Blair and Gordon Brown.

Sammy and Rosie Get Laid (1987). An unconventional middle-class couple's promiscuous adventures expose racial tensions in multiethnic London.

Shakespeare in Love (1999). Tudor-era London comes to life in this clever, romantic film set in the original Globe Theatre.

Shaun of the Dead (2004): A hapless Londoner and his friends must survive a zombie apocalypse in this action-comedy—the first in Edgar Wright's "Cornetto Trilogy" (along with *Hot Fuzz* and *The World's End*—all starring Simon Pegg and Nick Frost).

Sherlock (2010-). Holmes (Benedict Cumberbatch) and Watson (Martin Freeman) are excellent in this BBC-TV update of the detective's story, set in present-day London.

Ted Lasso (2020-): This fish-out-of-water TV series follows Ted Lasso, a football coach from the American Midwest, as he comes to London to coach a Premier League soccer team. Ted teaches, and learns from, his players far more than just sports.

Tinker, Tailor, Soldier, Spy (2011). There's a Soviet mole inside Britain's MI6 and retired agent George Smiley is summoned to ferret him out in this adaptation of John le Carré's 1974 espionage thriller.

To Sir, with Love (1967). Sidney Poitier grapples with social and racial issues in an East End inner-city school.

Upstairs, Downstairs (1971-1975). This TV series follows an aristocratic family and their servants in their new home at 165 Eaton Place.

Waterloo Bridge (1940). This Academy Award-nominated romantic drama recalls the lost love between a ballerina (Vivien Leigh) and a WWI army officer.

Victoria (2017-). PBS Masterpiece Theatre drama series chronicles the rise and reign of Queen Victoria (Jenna Coleman).

Conversions and Climate

Numbers and Stumblers

- Some British people write a few of their numbers differently than we do: 1 = 1, 4 = 4, 7 = 7.
- In Europe, dates appear as day/month/year, so Christmas 2023 is 25/12/23.
- What Americans call the second floor of a building is the first floor in Britain.
- On escalators and moving sidewalks, Brits keep the left "lane" open for passing. Keep to the right.
- To avoid the British version of giving someone "the finger," don't hold up the first two fingers of your hand with your palm facing you. (It looks like a reversed victory sign.)
- And please...don't call your waist pack a "fanny pack" (see the British-Yankee Vocabulary list at the end of this appendix).

Metric Conversions

Britain uses the metric system for nearly everything. Weight and volume are typically calculated in metric: A kilogram is 2.2 pounds, and one liter is about a quart (almost four to a gallon). Temperatures are generally given in Celsius, although some newspapers also list them in Fahrenheit.

1 foot = 0.3 meter	1 square yard = 0.8 square meter
1 yard = 0.9 meter	1 square mile = 2.6 square kilometers
1 mile = 1.6 kilometers	1 ounce = 28 grams
1 centimeter = 0.4 inch	1 quart = 0.95 liter
1 meter = 39.4 inches	1 kilogram = 2.2 pounds
1 kilometer = 0.62 mile	32°F = 0°C

Imperial Weights and Measures

Britain hasn't completely gone metric. Driving distances and speed limits are measured in miles. Beer is sold as pints (though milk can be measured in pints or liters), and a person's weight is measured in stone (a 168-pound person weighs 12 stone).

1 stone = 14 pounds
1 British pint = 1.2 US pints
1 imperial gallon = 1.2 US gallons or about 4.5 liters

Clothing Sizes

When shopping for clothing, use these US-to-UK comparisons as general guidelines (but note that no conversion is perfect).

Women: For pants and dresses, add 4 (US 10 = UK 14). For blouses and sweaters, add 2. For shoes, subtract 2.5 (US size 8 = UK size 5.5)

Men: For clothing, US and UK sizes are the same. For shoes, subtract about 0.5 (US size 9 = UK size 8.5)

Children: Clothing is sized similarly to the US. UK kids' shoe sizes are about one size smaller (US size 6 = UK size 5).

Climate

First line, average daily high; second line, average daily low; third line, average days without rain. For more detailed weather statistics for destinations in this book (as well as the rest of the world), check Wunderground.com.

J	F	M	A	M	J	J	A	S	O	N	D
43°	44°	50°	56°	62°	69°	71°	71°	65°	58°	50°	45°
36°	36°	38°	42°	47°	53°	56°	56°	52°	46°	42°	38°
16	15	20	18	19	19	19	20	17	18	15	16

Fahrenheit and Celsius Conversion

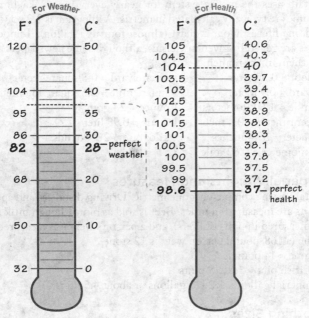

Europe takes its temperature using the Celsius scale, while we opt for Fahrenheit. For a rough conversion from Celsius to Fahrenheit, double the number and add 30. For weather, remember that 28°C is 82°F—perfect. For health, 37°C is just right. At a launderette, 30°C is cold, 40°C is warm (usually the default setting), 60°C is hot, and 95°C is boiling. Your air-conditioner should be set at about 20°C.

APPENDIX

Packing Checklist

Whether you're traveling for five days or five weeks, you won't need more than this. Pack light to enjoy the sweet freedom of true mobility.

Clothing

- ☐ 5 shirts: long- & short-sleeve
- ☐ 2 pairs pants (or skirts/capris)
- ☐ 1 pair shorts
- ☐ 5 pairs underwear & socks
- ☐ 1 pair walking shoes
- ☐ Sweater or warm layer
- ☐ Rainproof jacket with hood
- ☐ Tie, scarf, belt, and/or hat
- ☐ Swimsuit
- ☐ Sleepwear/loungewear

Money

- ☐ Debit card(s)
- ☐ Credit card(s)
- ☐ Hard cash (US $100-200)
- ☐ Money belt

Documents

- ☐ Passport
- ☐ Other required ID: Vaccine card/Covid test, entry visa, etc.
- ☐ Driver's license, student ID, hostel card, etc.
- ☐ Tickets & confirmations: flights, hotels, trains, rail pass, car rental, sight entries
- ☐ Photocopies of important documents
- ☐ Insurance details
- ☐ Guidebooks & maps

Electronics

- ☐ Mobile phone
- ☐ Camera & related gear
- ☐ Tablet/ebook reader/laptop
- ☐ Headphones/earbuds
- ☐ Chargers & batteries
- ☐ Phone car charger & mount (or GPS device)
- ☐ Plug adapters

Toiletries

- ☐ Basics: soap, shampoo, toothbrush, toothpaste, floss, deodorant, sunscreen, brush/comb, etc.
- ☐ Medicines & vitamins
- ☐ First-aid kit
- ☐ Glasses/contacts/sunglasses
- ☐ Face masks & hand sanitizer
- ☐ Sewing kit
- ☐ Packet of tissues (for WC)
- ☐ Earplugs

Miscellaneous

- ☐ Daypack
- ☐ Sealable plastic baggies
- ☐ Laundry supplies: soap, laundry bag, clothesline, spot remover
- ☐ Small umbrella
- ☐ Travel alarm/watch
- ☐ Notepad & pen
- ☐ Journal

Optional Extras

- ☐ Second pair of shoes (flip-flops, sandals, tennis shoes, boots)
- ☐ Travel hairdryer
- ☐ Picnic supplies
- ☐ Disinfecting wipes
- ☐ Water bottle
- ☐ Fold-up tote bag
- ☐ Small flashlight
- ☐ Mini binoculars
- ☐ Small towel or washcloth
- ☐ Inflatable pillow/neck rest
- ☐ Tiny lock
- ☐ Address list (to mail postcards)
- ☐ Extra passport photos

British-Yankee Vocabulary

For a longer list, plus a dry-witted primer on British culture, see *The Septic's Companion* (Chris Rae). Note that instead of asking, "Can I help you?" many Brits offer a more casual, "You alright?" or "You OK there?"

advert: advertisement

afters: dessert

anticlockwise: counterclock-wise

Antipodean: An Australian or New Zealander

aubergine: eggplant

banger: sausage

bangers and mash: sausages and mashed potatoes

Bank Holiday: legal holiday

bap: small roll

bespoke: custom-made

billion: a thousand of our billions (a million million)

biro: ballpoint pen

biscuit: cookie

black pudding: sausage made from dried blood

bloody: damn

blow off: fart

bobby: policeman ("the Bill" is more common)

Bob's your uncle: there you go (with a shrug), naturally

boffin: nerd, geek

bollocks: testicles (used in many colorful expressions)

bolshy: argumentative

bomb: success or failure

bonnet: car hood

booking: reservation

boot: car trunk

braces: suspenders

bridle way: path for walkers, bikers, and horse riders

brilliant: cool

brolly: umbrella

bubble and squeak: cabbage and potatoes fried together

builder: construction worker

bum: butt

candy floss: cotton candy

caravan: trailer

car boot sale: temporary flea market, often for charity

car park: parking lot

cashpoint: ATM

casualty: emergency room

cat's eyes: road reflectors

ceilidh (KAY-lee): informal evening of song and folk fun (Scottish and Irish)

cheap and cheerful: budget but adequate

cheap and nasty: cheap and bad quality

cheers: good-bye or thanks; also a toast

chemist: pharmacist

chicory: endive

chippy: fish-and-chip shop; carpenter (see also "joiner")

chips: French fries

chock-a-block: jam-packed

chuffed: pleased

cider: alcoholic apple cider

clearway: road where you can't stop

coach: long-distance bus

concession: discounted admission

concs (pronounced "conks"): short for "concession"

cos: romaine lettuce

cot: baby crib

cotton buds: Q-tips

council estate: public housing

courgette: zucchini

craic (pronounced "crack"): fun, good conversation (Irish and spreading to England)

crisps: potato chips

cuppa: cup of tea

curry: any Indian meal flavored with curry, popular with Brits

dear: expensive

dicey: iffy, risky

digestives: round graham cookies

dinner: lunch or dinner

diversion: detour

donkey's years: ages, a long time

draughts: checkers

draw: marijuana

dual carriageway: divided highway (four lanes)

dummy: pacifier

elevenses: coffee-and-biscuits break before lunch

elvers: baby eels

engaged tone: busy signal

estate car: station wagon

face flannel: washcloth

faff: bumble (about)

fag: cigarette

fagged: exhausted

faggot: meatball

fairy cake: cupcake

fancy: to like, to be attracted to (a person)

fanny: vagina

fell: hill or high plain (Lake District)

first floor: second floor

fixture: sports schedule

fizzy drink: pop or soda

flat: apartment

flutter: a bet

football: soccer

force: waterfall (Lake District)

fortnight: two weeks

fringe: hair bangs

Frogs: French people

fruit machine: slot machine

full Monty: whole shebang; everything

gallery: balcony

gammon: ham

gangway: aisle

gaol: jail (same pronunciation)

gateau (or gateaux): cake

gear lever: stick shift

geezer: dude (slang for young man)

ginger-haired: redhead

give way: yield

glen: narrow valley (Scotland)

goods wagon: freight truck

green fingers: green thumbs

grizzle: grumble, fuss (especially by a baby)

grotty: unpleasant, lousy

gutted: deeply disappointed

half eight: 8:30 (not 7:30)

hash sign: pound sign, as on a phone

heath: open treeless land

hen night: bachelorette party

High Street: Main Street (in a generic sense)

hire: rent, as in a car or bike

hire car: rental car

hob: stove burner

holiday: vacation

homely: homey or cozy

hoover: vacuum cleaner

ice lolly: popsicle

interval: intermission

ironmonger: hardware store

ish: more or less

jacket potato: baked potato

jelly: Jell-O

Joe Bloggs: John Q. Public

joiner: carpenter (see also "chippy")

jumble sale: rummage sale

jumper: sweater

just a tick: just a second

kipper: smoked herring

knackered: exhausted (Cockney: cream crackered)

knickers: ladies' panties

knocking shop: brothel

knock up: wake up or visit (old-fashioned)

ladybird: ladybug

lady fingers: flat, spongy cookie

lady's finger: okra

lager: light, fizzy beer

left luggage: baggage check

lemon squash: lemonade, not fizzy

lemonade: lemon-lime pop, fizzy

let: rent, as in property

licenced: restaurant authorized to sell alcohol

lie-in, having a: sleeping in late

lift: elevator

listed: protected historic building

loo: toilet or bathroom

lorry: truck

mac: mackintosh raincoat

main: entrée

mains: electrical outlet

mangetout: snow peas

Marmite: yeast paste, spread on sandwiches

marrow: summer squash

mate: buddy (boy or girl)

mean: stingy

mental: wild, memorable

mews: former stables converted to two-story rowhouses (London)

mince: hamburger meat

mobile: cell phone

moggie: cat

M.O.T.: mandatory annual car safety certificate

motorway: freeway

naff: dorky

nappy: diaper

natter: talk on and on

neep: Scottish for turnip

newsagent: corner store

nought: zero

noughts & crosses: tic-tac-toe

O.A.P.: old-age pensioner, retiree

off-licence: liquor store

on offer: for sale

one-off: unique; one-time event

panto, pantomime: fairy-tale play performed at Christmas (silly but fun)

pants: (noun) underwear, briefs; (adj.) terrible, ridiculous

paracetamol: acetaminophen, Tylenol

pasty (PASS-tee): crusted savory (usually meat) pie from Cornwall

pavement: sidewalk

people mover: minivan

pear-shaped: messed up, gone wrong

pensioner: senior citizen, retiree

petrol: gas

pillar box: mailbox

pissed (rude), paralytic, bevvied, wellied, popped up, merry, trollied, ratted, rat-arsed, pissed as a newt: drunk

pitch: playing field

plaster: Band-Aid

pram: baby carriage

publican: pub manager (old-fashioned)

public school: private "prep" school (e.g., Eton)

pudding: dessert in general

pull, to be on the: looking for love

punter: customer, especially in gambling

pushchair: stroller

put a sock in it: shut up

queue: line

queue up: line up

quid: a pound (money)

randy: horny

rasher: slice of bacon

redundant, made: laid off

Remembrance Day: Veterans' Day

return ticket: round-trip

revising; doing revisions: studying for exams

ring up: call (telephone)

rocket: arugula

roundabout: traffic circle

rubber: eraser

rubbish: bad

salad cream: mayo, mustard, and vinegar dressing

Sat Nav: GPS device

sausage roll: sausage wrapped in a flaky pastry

Scotch egg: hard-boiled egg wrapped in sausage meat

scrumpy: type of hard cider

self-catering: accommodation with kitchen

Sellotape: Scotch tape

services: freeway rest area

serviette: napkin

scttee: couch

shag: intercourse (cruder than in the US)

shandy: lager and 7-Up

silencer: car muffler

single ticket: one-way ticket

skip: dumpster

sleeping policeman: speed bumps

smalls: underwear

snogging: kissing, making out

sod: mildly offensive insult

sod it, sod off: screw it, screw off

soda: soda water (not pop)

solicitor: lawyer (a.k.a. barrister)

spanner: wrench

sparkie: electrician

spend a penny: urinate

stag night: bachelor party

starkers: buck naked

starters: appetizers

state school: public school

sticking plaster: Band-Aid

sticky tape: Scotch tape

stone: 14 pounds (measurement of weight)

stroppy: bad-tempered

subway: underground walkway

suet: fat from animal rendering (sometimes used in cooking)

sultanas: golden raisins

surgical spirit: rubbing alcohol

suspenders: garters

suss out: figure out

swede: rutabaga

ta: thank you

take the mickey: tease

tatty: worn out or tacky

taxi rank: taxi stand

telly: TV

tenement: stone apartment house (not necessarily a slum)

tenner: £10 bill

theatre: live stage

tick: a check mark

tight as a fish's bum: cheapskate (watertight)

tights: panty hose

tin: can

tip: public dump

tipper lorry: dump truck

top hole: first rate

top up: refill a drink

torch: flashlight

towel, press-on: panty liner

towpath: path along a river

trainers: sneakers

Tube: subway

twee: quaint, cute

twitcher: bird watcher

Underground: subway

verge: grassy edge of road

verger: church official

way out: exit

wee (adj.): small (Scottish)
wee (verb): urinate
Wellingtons, wellies: rubber
  boots
whacked: exhausted
whinge (rhymes with hinge):
  whine
wind up: tease, irritate
witter on: gab and gab
yob: hooligan
zebra crossing: crosswalk
zed: the letter Z

INDEX

A

Abbey Road: 79

Abbeys: *See* Westminster Abbey

Abstract art, at Tate Modern: 333–336

Accents, British: 598. *See also* Cockneys

Accommodations: Sleeping

Actors' Church (St. Paul's Church): 63, 206

Adams, Douglas: 124

Adoration of the Magi (Rubens): 529

Affordability: London's sights, 58–59. *See also* Money-saving tips

Afternoon tea: *See* Tea

Airbnb: 402–403, 418, 584–585

Airfares (airlines): 19, 607

Airports: 27, 486–491; map, 487; VAT refunds, 456, 575. *See also* specific airports

Albert, Prince: 105, 106–107, 197, 301, 340, 482, 501, 510

Albert Memorial Chapel (Windsor Castle): 510

Allegory with Venus and Cupid (Bronzino): 176–177

Almanac, London: 548

Althorp Estate: 561

Amenhotep III, Head and Arm of: 220

American Memorial Chapel (St. Paul's): 286–287

Amsterdam, transportation: 495–497

Anchor Pub (Cambridge): 525, 536

Anchor Pub (London): 320–321

Anglesea Arms Pub: 434

Anglican Communion: about, 285

Annunciation, with Saint Emidius (Crivelli): 172

Antiques: auctions, 463–464; markets, 460–461

Apartment rentals: 402–403, 418, 445, 584–585, 586–588

Apple Store: 464

Apps: 22, 598–599; maps and navigation, 27–28, 576–577; messaging, 599; sightseeing, 28, 579; transportation, 27–28; Uber, 39, 606; user reviews, 585

Apsley House: 104–105

Aquarium: 452

Archaeological museums: Museum of Classical Archaeology (Cambridge), 534; Museum of London, 84–86, 451; Museum of London Docklands, 115–116. *See also* British Museum

Archaeological sites: *See* Romans, ancient; Stonehenge

Architecture: 562–567. *See also* Castles and palaces; Churches and cathedrals

Ardabil Carpet: 107, 349

Arnolfini Portrait (Van Eyck): 174

Arrival: *See* Traveling

Art: technology of painting, 175. *See also* Archaeological museums; Art museums; *and specific artists, artworks and periods*

Artillery Passage: 380–381

Art museums: daily reminder, 32–33; free, 19, 49, 58; late hours, 480; passes, 578; shopping at, 455; Apsley House, 104–105; Courtauld Gallery, 66–67, 256; Fitzwilliam Museum (Cambridge), 533–534; Guildhall Art Gallery, 83, 272; Museum of Classical Archaeology (Cambridge), 534; Museum of the Home, 88; Queen's Gallery (Buckingham Palace), 68–69; Sir John Soane's Museum, 73–75; Wallace Collection, 76–78. *See also* British Museum; National Gallery; National Portrait Gallery; Tate Britain; Tate Modern; Victoria and Albert Museum

Ascot Racecourse: 482, 514

Ashurnasirpal II: 224–225

Assyrian art, at British Museum: 223–227

ATMs: 571–573

Auctions: 463–464

Auden, W. H.: 154

INDEX

MAP INDEX

MAP INDEX

Explore Europe

At ricksteves.com you can browse through thousands of articles, videos, photos and radio interviews, plus find a wealth of money-saving travel tips for planning your dream trip. And with our mobile-friendly website, you can easily access all this great travel information anywhere you go.

TV Shows

Preview the places you'll visit by watching entire half-hour episodes of *Rick Steves' Europe* (choose from all 100 shows) on-demand, for free.

ricksteves.com

your travel dreams into affordable reality

Radio Interviews

Enjoy ready access to Rick's vast library of radio interviews covering travel tips and cultural insights that relate specifically to your Europe travel plans.

Travel Forums

Learn, ask, share! Our online community of savvy travelers is a great resource for first-time travelers to Europe, as well as seasoned pros.

Travel News

Subscribe to our free Travel News e-newsletter, and get monthly updates from Rick on what's happening in Europe.

Classroom Europe®

Check out our free resource for educators with 500 short video clips from the *Rick Steves' Europe* TV show.

Audio Europe™

Rick's Free Travel App

Experience maximum Europe

Save time and energy

This guidebook is your independent-travel toolkit. But for all it delivers, it's still up to you to devote the time and energy it takes to manage the preparation and logistics that are essential for a happy trip. If that's a hassle, there's a solution.

Rick Steves Tours

A Rick Steves tour takes you to Europe's most interesting places with great

great tours, too!

A Guide for Every Trip

BEST OF GUIDES

Full-color guides in an easy-to-scan format. Focused on top sights and experiences in the most popular European destinations

Best of England
Best of Europe
Best of France
Best of Germany
Best of Ireland
Best of Italy
Best of Scotland
Best of Spain

COMPREHENSIVE GUIDES

City, country, and regional guides printed on Bible-thin paper. Packed with detailed coverage for a multi-week trip exploring iconic sights and venturing off the beaten path

Amsterdam & the Netherlands
Barcelona
Belgium: Bruges, Brussels, Antwerp & Ghent
Berlin
Budapest
Croatia & Slovenia
Eastern Europe
England
Florence & Tuscany
France
Germany
Great Britain
Greece: Athens & the Peloponnese
Iceland
Ireland
Istanbul
Italy
London
Paris
Portugal
Prague & the Czech Republic
Provence & the French Riviera
Rome
Scandinavia
Scotland
Sicily
Spain
Switzerland
Venice
Vienna, Salzburg & Tirol

HE BEST OF ROME

ne, Italy's capital, is studded with
n remnants and floodlit-fountain
es. From the Vatican to the Colos-
, with crazy traffic in between, Rome
derful, huge, and exhausting. The
s, the heat, and the weighty history

of the Eternal City where Caesars walked
can make tourists wilt. Recharge by taking siestas, gelato breaks, and after-dark
walks; strolling from one atmospheric
square to another in the refreshing evening air.

d *Pantheon*—which
t dome until the
y 2,000 years old
y over 1,500).

f Athens in the Vat-
lies the humanistic

ladiators fought
other, entertaining

Rome ristorante.

POCKET GUIDES
Compact color guides for shorter trips

SNAPSHOT GUIDES
Focused single-destination coverage

CRUISE PORTS GUIDES
Reference for cruise ports of call

Complete your library with...

TRAVEL SKILLS & CULTURE
Study up on travel skills and gain insight on history and culture

PHRASE BOOKS & DICTIONARIES

PLANNING MAPS

Credits

RESEARCHER
For help with this edition, Rick and Gene relied on...

Cameron Hewitt

Cameron Hewitt was born in Denver, grew up in Central Ohio, and moved to Seattle in 2000 to work for Rick Steves' Europe. Since then, he has spent about 100 days each year in Europe—researching and writing guidebooks, blogging, tour guiding, and making travel TV (described in his memoir, *The Temporary European*). Cameron married his high school sweetheart, Shawna, and enjoys taking pictures, trying new restaurants, and planning his next trip.

ACKNOWLEDGMENTS
Thank you to Risa Laib for her 25-plus years of dedication to the Rick Steves guidebook series.

PHOTO CREDITS
Front Cover: London Eye and Big Ben © Maurizio Rellini / Sime / eStock Photo

Title Page: Phone Box and Big Ben, London © Dominic Arizona Bonuccelli

Alamy: 101 (top) and 363 (bottom) Chronicle; 156 Steve Vidler; 178 (top) Ian Dagnall Computing; 243 © North Wind Picture Archives; 300 mauritius images GmbH

Dreamstime: 12 (middle left) © Coleong; 12 (middle right) © VVShots; 12 (bottom) © Tonybaggett; 282 © Hel080808; 572 © Areg43

Public Domain via Wikimedia Commons: 106 (bottom), 165, 172 (top), 173 (bottom), 175, 177, 178 (bottom), 179 (top), 179 (bottom), 180 (top), 189, 190, 240, 245, 248 (bottom), 285, 288, 329, 340, 353 (top), 361, 362 (bottom), 363 (top), 364, 368, 369 (top), 369 (bottom), 370, 371, 549, 554

Additional Credits: 242 ©The British Library Board; 367 © Tate, London 2019

Additional Photography: Dominic Arizona Bonuccelli, Orin Dubrow, Cameron Hewitt, David C. Hoerlein, Suzanne Kotz, Cathy Lu, Lauren Mills, Gene Openshaw, Rhonda Pelikan, Carrie Shepherd, Robyn Stencil, Rick Steves, Bruce Van Deventer.
Photos are used by permission and are the property of the original copyright owners.

Avalon Travel
Hachette Book Group
1700 Fourth Street
Berkeley, CA 94710

Printed in Canada by Friesens.
24th Edition. First printing September 2022.

ISBN 978-1-64171-469-3

For the latest on Rick's talks, guidebooks, tours, public television series, and public radio show, contact Rick Steves' Europe, 130 Fourth Avenue North, Edmonds, WA 98020, +1 425 771 8303, RickSteves.com, rick@ricksteves.com.

Rick Steves' Europe
Managing Editor: Jennifer Madison Davis
Assistant Managing Editor: Cathy Lu
Editors: Glenn Eriksen, Suzanne Kotz, Rosie Leutzinger, Teresa Nemeth, Jessica Shaw, Carrie Shepherd
Editorial & Production Assistant: Megan Simms
Researcher: Cameron Hewitt
Graphic Content Director: Sandra Hundacker
Maps & Graphics: Orin Dubrow, David C. Hoerlein, Lauren Mills, Mary Rostad

Avalon Travel
Senior Editor and Series Manager: Madhu Prasher
Associate Managing Editor: Jamie Andrade
Editor: Rachael Sablik
Proofreader: Maggie Ryan
Indexer: Stephen Callahan
Production & Typesetting: Lisi Baldwin, Rue Flaherty, Jane Musser
Cover Design: Kimberly Glyder Design
Maps & Graphics: Kat Bennett

COLOR MAPS

London • West London • East London • The Underground • London & South England

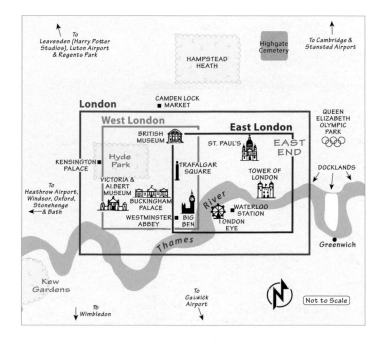

To Leavesden (Harry Potter Studios), Luton Airport & Regents Park

HAMPSTEAD HEATH

Highgate Cemetery

To Cambridge & Stansted Airport

London

CAMDEN LOCK MARKET

West London

East London

QUEEN ELIZABETH OLYMPIC PARK

BRITISH MUSEUM

ST. PAUL'S

EAST END

KENSINGTON PALACE

Hyde Park

TRAFALGAR SQUARE

TOWER OF LONDON

DOCKLANDS

To Heathrow Airport, Windsor, Oxford, Stonehenge & Bath

VICTORIA & ALBERT MUSEUM

BUCKINGHAM PALACE

WESTMINSTER ABBEY

BIG BEN

River

LONDON EYE

WATERLOO STATION

Thames

Greenwich

Kew Gardens

To Wimbledon

To Gatwick Airport

Not to Scale

London

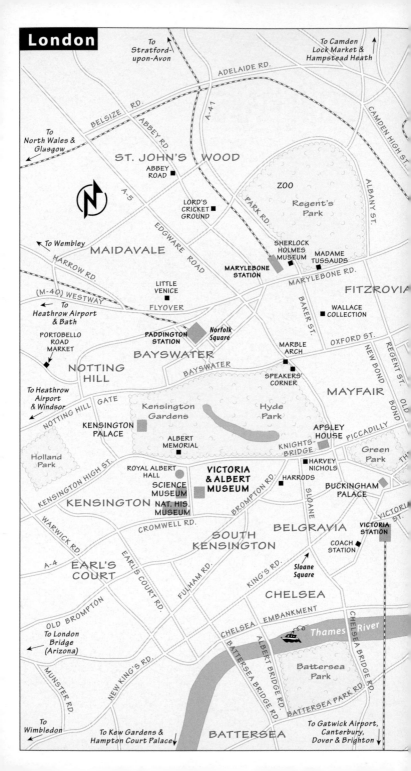

To Stratford-upon-Avon

To Camden Lock Market & Hampstead Heath

ADELAIDE RD.

BELSIZE RD.

ABBEY RD.

A-41

CAMDEN HIGH ST.

To North Wales & Glasgow

ST. JOHN'S WOOD

ABBEY ROAD

LORD'S CRICKET GROUND

A-5

EDGWARE ROAD

PARK RD.

ZOO

Regent's Park

ALBANY ST.

N

MAIDAVALE

HARROW RD.

SHERLOCK HOLMES MUSEUM

MARYLEBONE STATION

MADAME TUSSAUDS

FITZROVIA

(M-40) WESTWAY

To Heathrow Airport & Bath

LITTLE VENICE

FLYOVER

BAKER ST.

MARYLEBONE RD.

WALLACE COLLECTION

PORTOBELLO ROAD MARKET

PADDINGTON STATION

Norfolk Square

MARBLE ARCH

OXFORD ST.

NEW BOND ST.

REGENT ST.

BAYSWATER

BAYSWATER

SPEAKERS' CORNER

MAYFAIR

OLD BOND

NOTTING HILL

To Heathrow Airport & Windsor

NOTTING HILL GATE

Kensington Gardens

Hyde Park

KENSINGTON PALACE

ALBERT MEMORIAL

APSLEY HOUSE

PICCADILLY

Green Park

Holland Park

KENSINGTON HIGH ST.

ROYAL ALBERT HALL

SCIENCE MUSEUM

VICTORIA & ALBERT MUSEUM

KNIGHTS-BRIDGE

HARVEY NICHOLS

HARRODS

BUCKINGHAM PALACE

TH

KENSINGTON

NAT. HIS. MUSEUM

BROMPTON RD.

SLOANE

VICTORI ST.

WARWICK RD.

EARLS COURT RD.

CROMWELL RD.

SOUTH KENSINGTON

BELGRAVIA

VICTORIA STATION

A-4

EARL'S COURT

FULHAM RD.

KING'S RD.

COACH STATION

OLD BROMPTON

Sloane Square

CHELSEA

To London Bridge (Arizona)

NEW KING'S RD.

CHELSEA EMBANKMENT

Thames River

MUNSTER RD.

BATTERSEA BRIDGE RD.

ALBERT BRIDGE RD.

Battersea Park

CHELSEA BRIDGE RD.

To Wimbledon

To Kew Gardens & Hampton Court Palace

BATTERSEA

BATTERSEA PARK RD.

To Gatwick Airport, Canterbury, Dover & Brighton

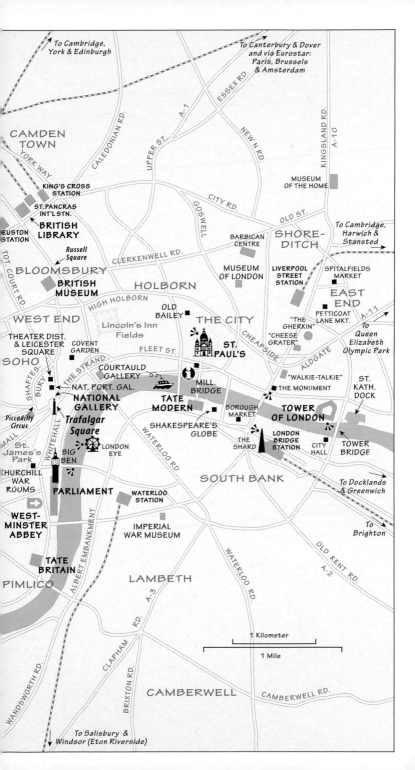

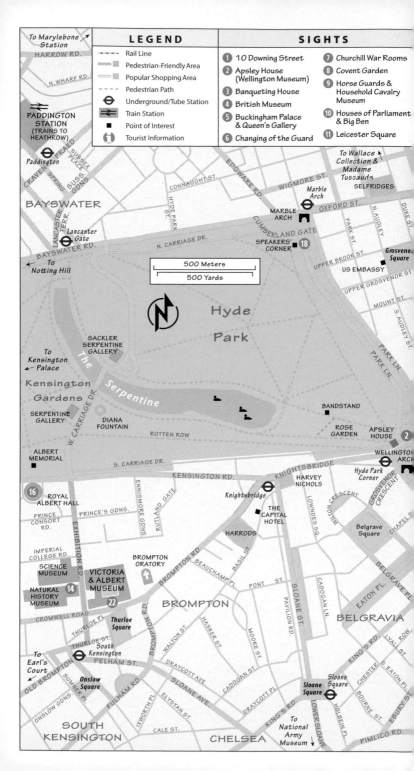

To Marylebone Station
HARROW RD.
N. WHARF RD.
PADDINGTON STATION (TRAINS TO HEATHROW)
Paddington
CRAVEN RD.
PRAED ST.
SUSSEX GDNS.
SPRING ST.
SUSSEX PL.
LANCASTER TERR.
Lancaster Gate
BAYSWATER
BAYSWATER RD.
To Notting Hill
CONNAUGHT ST.
HYDE PARK ST.
EDGWARE RD.
WIGMORE ST.
N. CARRIAGE DR.
To Wallace Collection & Madame Tussauds
SELFRIDGES
Marble Arch
OXFORD ST.
MARBLE ARCH
CUMBERLAND GATE
SPEAKERS' CORNER 18
DUKE ST.
N. AUDLEY ST.
PARK ST.
UPPER BROOK ST.
Grosvenor Square
US EMBASSY
UPPER GROSVENOR ST.
MOUNT ST.
S. AUDLEY ST.

Hyde Park

SACKLER SERPENTINE GALLERY
The Serpentine
To Kensington Palace
Kensington Gardens
SERPENTINE GALLERY
DIANA FOUNTAIN
W. CARRIAGE DR.
ROTTEN ROW
BANDSTAND
ROSE GARDEN
APSLEY HOUSE 2
WELLINGTON ARCH
ALBERT MEMORIAL
S. CARRIAGE DR.
KENSINGTON RD.
KNIGHTSBRIDGE
Hyde Park Corner
PARK LN.
PARK LN.

500 Meters
500 Yards

16 ROYAL ALBERT HALL
PRINCE CONSORT RD.
PRINCE'S GDNS.
EXHIBITION RD.
IMPERIAL COLLEGE RD.
SCIENCE MUSEUM
NATURAL HISTORY MUSEUM 14
CROMWELL ROAD
ENNISMORE GDNS.
RUTLAND GATE
Knightsbridge
HARVEY NICHOLS
THE CAPITAL HOTEL
HARRODS
BROMPTON RD.
BROMPTON ORATORY
VICTORIA & ALBERT MUSEUM 22
BEAUCHAMP PL.
PONT ST.
BASIL ST.
SLOANE ST.
LOWNDES SQ.
WILTON CRESCENT
CRESCENT
Belgrave Square
CHAPEL ST.
BELGRAVIA
BELGRAVE PL.
EATON PL.
LYALL ST.

THURLOE PL.
Thurloe Square
THURLOE ST.
South Kensington
PELHAM ST.
To Earl's Court
OLD BROMPTON RD.
SUMNER PL.
ONSLOW GDNS.
Onslow Square
SOUTH KENSINGTON
WALTON ST.
HASKER ST.
MOORE ST.
DRAYCOTT AVE.
FULHAM RD.
IXWORTH PL.
ELYSTAN ST.
CALE ST.
DRAYCOTT PL.
CADOGAN LN.
PAVILION RD.
SLOANE ST.
CADOGAN PL.
SLOANE AVE.
BROMPTON
To National Army Museum
CHELSEA
KING'S RD.
LOWER SLOANE
Sloane Square
EATON PL.
CHESTER
S. EATON PL.
BOURNE ST.
HOLBEIN PL.
EBURY ST.
PIMLICO RD.
LYALL ROW

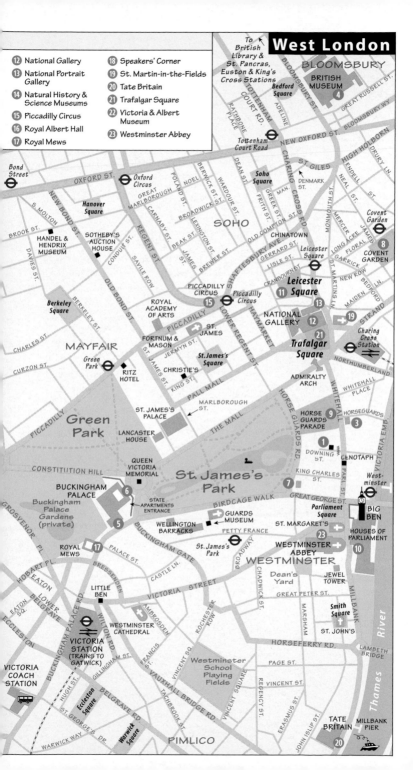

West London

12 National Gallery
13 National Portrait Gallery
14 Natural History & Science Museums
15 Piccadilly Circus
16 Royal Albert Hall
17 Royal Mews
18 Speakers' Corner
19 St. Martin-in-the-Fields
20 Tate Britain
21 Trafalgar Square
22 Victoria & Albert Museum
23 Westminster Abbey

To British Library & St. Pancras, Euston & King's Cross Stations

BLOOMSBURY

BRITISH MUSEUM 4

Bond Street

OXFORD ST.

Oxford Circus

Hanover Square

SOHO

Soho Square

Tottenham Court Road

NEW OXFORD ST.

ST. GILES

HIGH HOLBORN

DENMARK ST.

HANDEL & HENDRIX MUSEUM

SOTHEBY'S AUCTION HOUSE

CHINATOWN

Covent Garden

COVENT GARDEN 8

Berkeley Square

Leicester Square

Leicester Square 11

PICCADILLY CIRCUS

ROYAL ACADEMY OF ARTS

Piccadilly Circus 15

NATIONAL GALLERY 12

13

STRAND

MAYFAIR

FORTNUM & MASON

ST. JAMES

St. James's Square

19

21 Trafalgar Square

Charing Cross Station

Green Park

RITZ HOTEL

CHRISTIE'S

PALL MALL

ADMIRALTY ARCH

NORTHUMBERLAND

ST. JAMES'S PALACE

MARLBOROUGH ST.

THE MALL

HORSE GUARDS PARADE 9

3

LANCASTER HOUSE

1

WHITEHALL

CONSTITUTION HILL

QUEEN VICTORIA MEMORIAL

St. James's Park

DOWNING ST.

CENOTAPH

BUCKINGHAM PALACE 6

Buckingham Palace Gardens (private)

STATE APARTMENTS ENTRANCE

5

BIRDCAGE WALK

GUARDS MUSEUM

WELLINGTON BARRACKS

PETTY FRANCE

KING CHARLES ST.

7

GREAT GEORGE ST.

Parliament Square

Westminster

BIG BEN

ROYAL MEWS 17

PALACE ST.

St. James's Park

BROADWAY

ST. MARGARET'S

WESTMINSTER ABBEY 23

HOUSES OF PARLIAMENT 10

LITTLE BEN

VICTORIA STREET

WESTMINSTER

Dean's Yard

JEWEL TOWER

GREAT PETER ST.

VICTORIA STATION (TRAINS TO GATWICK)

WESTMINSTER CATHEDRAL

Smith Square

ST. JOHN'S

MILLBANK

Thames River

VICTORIA COACH STATION

Westminster School Playing Fields

HORSEFERRY RD.

PAGE ST.

LAMBETH BRIDGE

PIMLICO

TATE BRITAIN 20

MILLBANK PIER

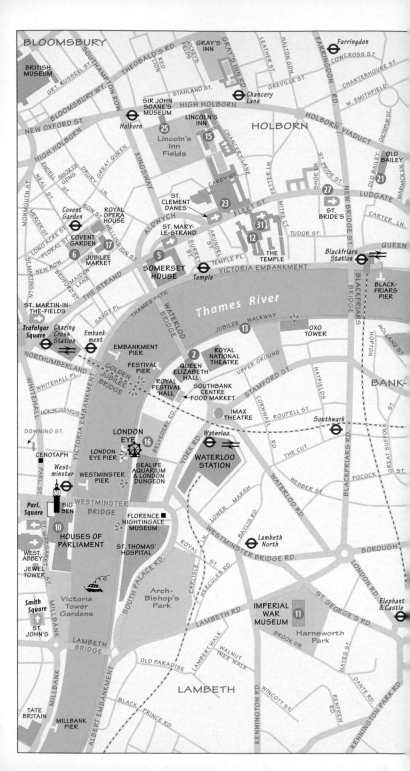

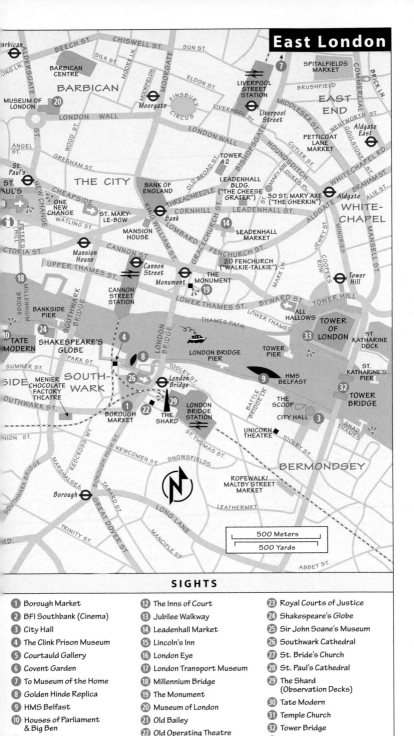

East London

SIGHTS

1. Borough Market
2. BFI Southbank (Cinema)
3. City Hall
4. The Clink Prison Museum
5. Courtauld Gallery
6. Covent Garden
7. To Museum of the Home
8. Golden Hinde Replica
9. HMS Belfast
10. Houses of Parliament & Big Ben
11. Imperial War Museum
12. The Inns of Court
13. Jubilee Walkway
14. Leadenhall Market
15. Lincoln's Inn
16. London Eye
17. London Transport Museum
18. Millennium Bridge
19. The Monument
20. Museum of London
21. Old Bailey
22. Old Operating Theatre Museum & Herb Garret
23. Royal Courts of Justice
24. Shakespeare's Globe
25. Sir John Soane's Museum
26. Southwark Cathedral
27. St. Bride's Church
28. St. Paul's Cathedral
29. The Shard (Observation Decks)
30. Tate Modern
31. Temple Church
32. Tower Bridge
33. Tower of London

MAYOR OF LONDON

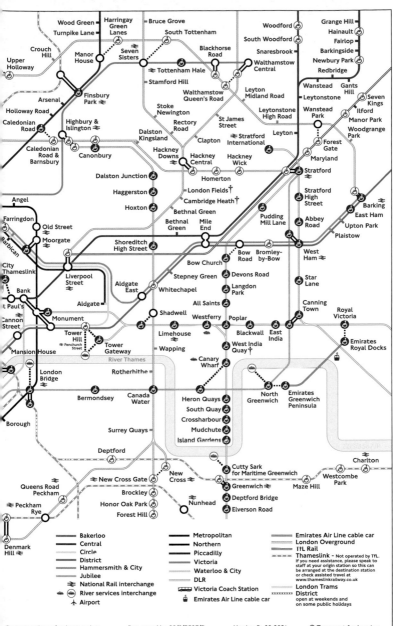

Correct at time of going to print   Reg. user No. 22/S/3587/P   Version B 09.2021   © Transport for London

UNDERGROUND

TRANSPORT
FOR LONDON
EVERY JOURNEY MATTERS

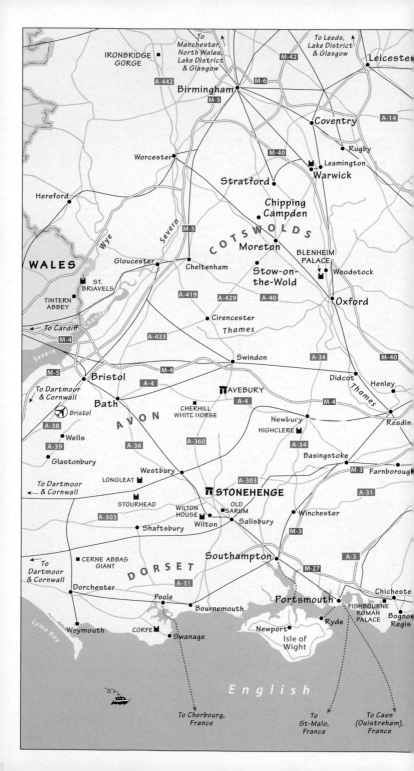

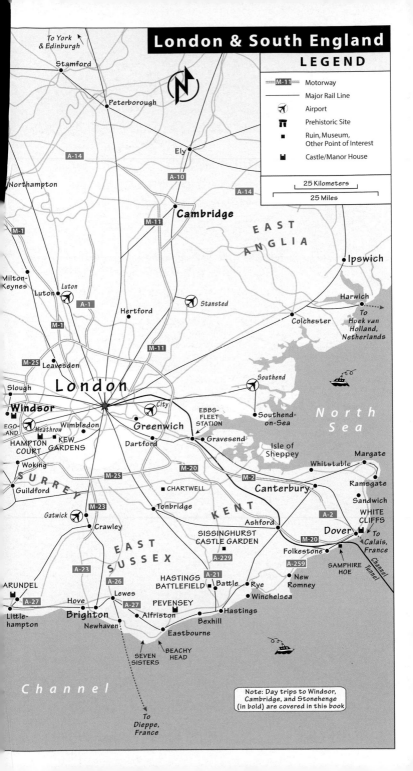

London & South England

LEGEND

M-11	Motorway
	Major Rail Line
✈	Airport
⊓	Prehistoric Site
■	Ruin, Museum, Other Point of Interest
⌷	Castle/Manor House

25 Kilometers
25 Miles

To York & Edinburgh

Stamford

Peterborough

A-14

Northampton

Ely

A-10

A-14

Cambridge

M-11

E A S T A N G L I A

Ipswich

Milton-Keynes

Luton

M-1

Luton

A-1

Hertford

Stansted

Harwich

To Hoek van Holland, Netherlands

Colchester

M-1

M-11

M-25

Leavesden

Slough

LONDON

Southend

North Sea

Windsor

City

EBBS-FLEET STATION

Southend-on-Sea

LEGO-LAND

Heathrow

Wimbledon

Greenwich

Dartford

Gravesend

Isle of Sheppey

HAMPTON COURT

KEW GARDENS

Whitstable

Margate

Woking

S U R R E Y

M-25

CHARTWELL

M-20

M-2

Canterbury

Ramsgate

Sandwich

Guildford

M-23

Tonbridge

K E N T

Ashford

A-2

WHITE CLIFFS

Gatwick

Crawley

Dover

E A S T

SISSINGHURST CASTLE GARDEN

M-20

To Calais, France

Folkestone

SAMPHIRE HOE

A-259

Channel Tunnel

S U S S E X

A-229

A-23

A-26

HASTINGS BATTLEFIELD

A-21

Battle

Rye

New Romney

ARUNDEL

A-27

Hove

Lewes

A-27

PEVENSEY

Winchelsea

Little-hampton

Brighton

Alfriston

Bexhill

Hastings

Newhaven

Eastbourne

SEVEN SISTERS

BEACHY HEAD

C h a n n e l

Note: Day trips to Windsor, Cambridge, and Stonehenge (in bold) are covered in this book

To Dieppe, France

More for your trip!
Maximize the experience with Rick Steves as your guide

Guidebooks
Make side trips smooth and affordable with Rick's Britain and Ireland guides

Planning Maps
Use Rick's pre-trip planning tool for mapping out your itinerary

Rick's TV Shows
Preview your destinations with a variety of shows covering London

Rick's Audio Europe™ App
Get free self-guided audio tours for London's top sights

Small Group Tours
Take a lively, low-stress Rick Steves tour through London

For all the details, visit ricksteves.com